FIFTH EDITION

SOCIAL WORK RESEARCH & EVALUATION

Quantitative and Qualitative Approaches

RICHARD M. GRINNELL, JR.

F.E. Peacock Publishers, Inc.
Itasca, Illinois

Dedicated to the memory of Harry Specht

Contents in Brief

Contents in Detail

Preface

WITH THE INPUT from numerous students and instructors who used the previous four editions of *Social Work Research and Evaluation*, our refinements and modifications of the fifth became so extensive that we decided to retitle it to more accurately reflect its contents. Thus, the subtitle, *Quantitative and Qualitative Approaches*. Nevertheless, the audience of this edition remains the same as the previous ones—advanced undergraduate and beginning graduate social work students who are taking a one-semester (or quarter) research methods course.

THE GOAL OF THE BOOK

As before, our emphasis continues to be on how the goals of social work are furthered by the research process. Our belief is that research endeavors underlie and support our profession. Thus, research in social work is presented as more than just a way to solve human problems, or to add to our knowledge base, or to guide practice—though it is all of these. For the past sixteen years, this book has symbolized tradition and change; it has applied timeless issues of research design and measurement to changing methodologies and social concerns. It has broken some traditions and has taught readers to try new research methods without losing sight of the old.

Many research instructors first cover basic research methodology and then apply this course content to more advanced research courses that specialize in single-system designs or program evaluations. Accordingly, we have designed this book to give students the basic methodological foundation they need in order to obtain the advanced knowledge and skills presented in these two specialized research courses.

STRENGTHS OF THIS EDITION

Particular strengths of this edition are highlighted below.

Expertise of Contributors

Collaborative efforts are certainly not uncommon in academia. In fact, most of the success this book has enjoyed can be attributed to its collaborative nature. We have once again secured an excellent and diverse group of social work research educators. The thirty-one contributors know firsthand, from their own extensive teaching and practice experiences, what social work students need to know in relation to research. They have subjected themselves to a discipline totally uncommon in compendia—that is, writing in terms of what is most needed for an integrated basic research methods book, rather than writing in line with their own predilections. To further our efforts to produce a book that is consistent across chapters, the content has been edited extensively to maintain a common editorial approach and writing style.

Student Learning Features

We have made an extraordinary effort to make this edition less expensive, more esthetically pleasing, and much more useful for students than ever before. In addition, we have incorporated a number of learning features social work students will find useful:

- There is an extensive up-to-date advanced reading list at the end of each chapter, which will be helpful in obtaining more information about a chapter's content.

- Numerous boxes are inserted throughout the book to complement and expand on the chapters; these boxes present interesting research examples, provide additional aids to learning, and offer historical, social, and political contexts of social work research.
- The book's content is explained in terms of social work examples that students can easily understand. In recognition of the need for us to be knowledgeable of their needs and concerns, many of our examples center around women and minorities. Special consideration has been given to the application of research methods concerning these groups.
- Numerous tables and figures have been used to provide visual representations of the concepts presented in the book.
- An integrated *Student Study Guide* (by Yvonne A. Unrau, Judy L. Krysik, and Richard M. Grinnell, Jr.) is available with this edition, from which the "Preface for Students" is reproduced in Box P-1.

A Revised Research Approach

We have made more editorial, style, and content changes in this edition than in the previous four editions combined. With this perspective, and in addition to our new approach to research, we have:

- added six new chapters on qualitative research:
  — Chapter 4: *Qualitative Approaches to the Generation of Knowledge*
  — Chapter 6: *Using Both Research Approaches in a Single Study*
  — Chapter 12: *Case Designs*
  — Chapter 15: *Participant Observation*
  — Chapter 19: *Historical Research*
  — Chapter 22: *Qualitative Data Analysis*
- added three new chapters on data collection strategies:
  — Chapter 15: *Participant Observation*
  — Chapter 17: *Utilizing Existing Statistics*
  — Chapter 19: *Historical Research*
- added two new chapters on data analyses:
  — Chapter 21: *Quantitative Data Analysis*
  — Chapter 22: *Qualitative Data Analysis*
- added three new chapters on evaluation at the case and program level:
  — Chapter 23: *Case-Level Evaluation*
  — Chapter 24: *Program-Level Evaluation*
  — Chapter 25: *Implementing Evaluations*
- added a new appendix:
  — Appendix: *Cultural Factors Related to Research*

In short, a tremendous amount of new content has been added to this edition in an effort to keep current, while retaining material that has stood the test of

BOX P-1

"PREFACE FOR STUDENTS"
FROM
STUDENT STUDY GUIDE

This study guide is to be used as an inexpensive supplement to Grinnell's fifth edition of *Social Work Research and Evaluation: Quantitative and Qualitative Approaches* (F.E. Peacock Publishers, 1997). Like in the Grinnell text, its major goal is to aid your understanding of basic research methodology and its applications to social work problems.

ORGANIZATION

To accomplish this goal, the *Guide* is organized into three basic parts: (1) exercises, (2) sample research studies, and (3) glossary.

Part I: Exercises

Part I contains 25 exercises which correspond directly to the 25 chapters in the Grinnell text. The exercises are intended to provide you with the opportunity to apply the basic concepts presented in the text to actual social work research studies contained in Part II.

To complement a variety of students' learning styles, three types of exercises are provided (i.e, self-study, group, and library). The self-study exercises require an individual, in-depth examination of each chapter. The group exercises facilitate class and group discussion. The library exercises encourage exploration of additional literature in an effort to strengthen your information retrieval skills.

The exercises are presented at varying levels of abstraction and require your creative and thoughtful input. For each set of exercises, you will be required to refer to a sample research study contained in Part II in the *Guide*.

Part II: Sample Research Studies

Part II contains eleven (A–K) real-life social work research studies that provide concrete examples of how the research concepts described in the Grinnell text can be used in actual social work research studies. The sample research studies are:

- A: *An Evaluation of a Group Program for Men who Batter Their Partners*
- B: *Four Studies Toward an Empirical Foundation for Group Therapy*
- C: *Victims of Child Sexual Abuse: A Research Note*
- D: *Social Work Education and Students' Humanistic Attitudes*

- E: *New Directions in Teaching Social Work Methods: A Content Analysis of Course Outlines*
- F: *An Evaluation of the Social Support Component of a Perinatal Program for Adolescents*
- G: *An Evaluation of a Vocational Rehabilitation Program for Ex-Psychiatric Patients*
- H: An Evaluation of the Psychological Component of a Treatment Program for Homeless Alcoholic Men
- I: *How Mothers Support Their Pregnant and Parenting Teenage Daughters*
- J: *What Clients Can Tell Us About the Helping Process*
- K: *Neutrality in Child Protection Mediation*

THE *GUIDE* CAN BE EASILY MODIFIED

In an effort to acknowledge individual preferences of research instructors and students alike, the *Guide* can be modified in three ways:

1. Additional exercises (self-study, group, and library) can be formulated in addition to the ones that are contained in Part I.
2. Additional sample research studies can be used to supplement the ones that are contained in Part II.
3. A different sample research study can be used rather than the one that is presently required for an individual chapter. For example, it may be preferable for you to read Research Study J to correspond with Chapter 1 rather than Research Study F which is now required in the *Guide*.

FIVE-STEP PROCEDURE TO COMPLETE THE EXERCISES

1. Read the exercises that correspond to the specific chapter in the text. As you read the exercises make a mental note of the key terms, concepts, and themes. Highlight these by underlining them in the exercises.
2. Note the sample research study that you will have to read in order to complete the assigned exercises. If a different research study is assigned, make sure to obtain a copy before completing the exercises.
3. Read the assigned chapter in the text, paying particular attention to the terms and concepts you previously identified when you perused the exercises in Step 1.
4. Read the sample research study referred to in the exercises or assigned by your research instructor. Pay special attention to the corresponding terms and concepts contained within the research study.
5. Answer each question by combining your understanding of the material in the chapter and/or its application demonstrated in the research study.

Good luck in your research course!

time. Some research instructors have expressed disappointment that several of the chapters in the earlier editions have been deleted. In general, chapters were dropped because they were not being assigned as required reading in a majority of research courses, and it was necessary to make room for new ideas and development while retaining a manageable and accessible size for this revision. The work of former contributors is still readily available in many copies of the preceding editions, however.

Content Tailored to the CSWE's Research Requirements

We have written this edition to comply strictly with the Council on Social Work Education's (Council) research requirements for accredited schools and departments of social work at the undergraduate and graduate levels.

New Organization

Over the years, we have received hundreds of comments from users of the first four editions. With these comments, and with the Council's research requirements in mind, we determined the specific topics to cover, the depth of the topics covered, and the sequencing of chapters within the book.

As in the preceding editions, this is neither a brief primer in social work research nor a book intended for use as a reference manual. With a tremendous amount of input, this edition has been reorganized into eight parts and 25 chapters. The new organization is an attempt to make the book more functional, practical, and manageable for students and instructors alike. Let us now turn our attention to each part and the chapters it contains.

Part I: The Context of Knowledge Generation

The two chapters in Part I introduce readers to the place of research in social work. More specifically, Chapter 1 presents the five basic ways of obtaining knowledge and provides a definition of social work research. It then presents the motivation and goals of doing social work research and ends with a discussion of the various research roles that social workers can undertake in contemporary practice. Chapter 2 elaborates on Chapter 1 by presenting an in-depth discussion of the various factors that affect social work research studies.

In overview, Chapter 1 presents how research is relevant to social work while Chapter 2 discusses the personal, ethical, political, and social considerations that shape how it is performed.

Part II: Problem Formulation and Research Approaches

The four chapters in Part II provide both the basic content to enable the reader to understand how social work research problems are formulated and the various research approaches we can use to answer them. More specifically, Chapter 3 presents an in-depth discussion of how to formulate research problems and questions, while Chapters 4 and 5 present two different research approaches that could be used to provide data to answer the questions formulated in Chapter 3. The last chapter in Part II, Chapter 6, clearly illustrates the complementarity of the quantitative research approach (Chapter 4) and the qualitative research approach (Chapter 5) by discussing how both approaches can be used in a single research study.

Part III: Measurement in Social Work Research

The three chapters in Part III introduce readers to the measurement process within quantitative research studies. More specifically, Chapter 7 presents the basic content for a student to appreciate and understand how variables are measured. Chapter 8 describes how to select existing standardized and unstandardized measuring instruments, while the final chapter presents how to design one if an existing one is not available.

Part IV: The Logic of Research Design

The three chapters in Part IV are devoted to quantitative and qualitative research designs. Chapter 10 presents a discussion of the role of probability and nonprobability sampling procedures and proceeds to an in-depth discussion of various group research designs (Chapter 11). Chapter 12 presents qualitative case study designs.

Part V: Obtrusive Data Collection Methods

The three chapters in Part V present the three most commonly used obtrusive data collection methods: structured observation (Chapter 13), survey research (Chapter 14), and participant observation (Chapter 15). More specifically, Chapter 13 presents the various direct observational recording methods, while Chapter 14 discusses three approaches to data collection via surveys (i.e., face-to-face interviews, mail surveys, telephone surveys). Chapter 15 presents the main types of participant observation. In a nutshell, these chapters present data collection methods that require us to directly interact (with varying degrees) with our research participants.

Part VI: Unobtrusive Data Collection Methods

The first four chapters in Part VI present the four most commonly used unobtrusive data collection methods: secondary analysis (Chapter 16), utilizing existing statistics (Chapter 17), content analysis (Chapter 18), and historical research (Chapter 19). In contrast to the three obtrusive data collection methods contained in Part V, these chapters within this part do not require us to interact directly with our research participants. The final chapter in this part, Chapter 20, presents a model for selecting a data collection method (obtrusive and unobtrusive) for any given research problem.

Part VII: Data Analysis

The two chapters in Part VII address data analysis. Chapter 21 presents how to analyze quantitative data, while Chapter 22 discusses the analysis of qualitative data.

Part VIII: Evaluation in Action

The three chapters in Part VIII address the concept of evaluation in contemporary social work practice. More specifically, Chapter 23 addresses the concept of evaluation at the case level, while Chapter 24 discusses quantitative and qualitative evaluations at the program level. Chapter 25 presents how case- and program-level evaluations can be integrated to form solid decision making at both levels of practice.

Logical and Flexible Teaching Plan

The book is organized in a way that makes good sense in teaching fundamental research methods. Many other sequences that could be followed would make just as much sense, however. The chapters (and parts) in this book were consciously planned to be independent of one another. They can be read out of the order in which they are presented, or they can be selectively omitted. They will probably make the most sense to students if they are read in the sequence as presented, because each builds upon the preceding one.

Instructor's Manual and Test Bank Is Now Available

A complementary copy of an *Instructor's Manual and Test Bank* is available with this edition. It was written by Christopher B. Aviles, Ph.D., Department of Social Work at Buffalo State College, Buffalo, New York. The 375 page *Instruc-

tor's Manual and Test Bank (including a computer disk) contains over 40 true-false and 40 multiple choice questions for each chapter in the book. It was written on a mastery learning model where each question has a parallel version of it (i.e., parallel forms). Thus, research instructors can test two different research sections of the same course without constructing two different exams.

Research instructors who use this book in the classroom can receive a hard copy and computer disk that contains the *Instructor's Manual and Test Bank* by faxing a request on letterhead stationary to Richard M. Grinnell, Jr. (403) 949-4303, or by calling (403) 949-4303. Please state the platform (e.g., IBM, Mac, ASCII) and the word processing language (e.g., WordPerfect, Word) you desire and allow two weeks for shipping.

A FINAL WORD

The field of research in our profession is continuing to grow and develop. We believe this edition will contribute to that growth. A sixth edition is anticipated, and suggestions for it are more than welcome.

DECEMBER, 1996   RICHARD M. GRINNELL, JR.

Acknowledgments

MANY INDIVIDUALS have contributed to the continual development and preparation of this text. For individual chapters, a number of people, in addition to the contributors, aided in the production by critiquing and reacting to chapter drafts, suggesting text and/or chapter content, and encouraging others to contribute.

These include: Susan Anderson-Ray, David Austin, Mike Austin, Don Beless, Martin Bloom, Floyd Bolitho, Ed Borgatta, Ed Brown, Harry Butler, Harris Chaiklin, Kayla Conrad, Jill Crowell, Rick Dangel, Inger Davis, Liane Davis, Wayne Duehn, Eugene Durman, Paul Ephross, Irwin Epstein, Roland Etcheverry, Michale Fabricant, Phil Fellin, Joel Fischer, Chuck Garvin, Neil Gilbert, Lewayne Gilchrist, Tom Givler, Harvey Gochros, Richard Gorsuch, Don Granvold, Tony Grasso, Ernest Greenwood, Jim Gripton, Charles Grosser, Lynda Hacker, Bud Hansen, Diane Harrison, Joseph Heffernan, George Hoshino, Walt Hudson, Jackie Ismael, Ittleson Foundation, Inc., Sri Jayaratne, Anne Kincaid, Mike Kolevzon, Mike Lauderdale, Alice Lieberman, E.E. LeMasters, Charles Levy, Rona Levy,

Duncan Lindsey, Mary Ann Lynch, Mary Martin Lynch, Tony Maluccio, Rachel Marks, Bob Mayer, John McAdoo, Clyde McDaniel, Grant McDonald, Lynn McDonald, Tom McDonald, Robert Morris, Ed Mullen, Judy Nelson, and Kim Ng.

Others include: Dan O'Brien, Don Pilcher, Norman Polansky, Alan Press, Paul Raffoul, Reyes Ramos, Frank Raymond, Rick Reamer, Bill Reid, Joan Robertson, Peggy Rodway, Sheldon Rose, Mike Rothery, Marti Royer, Mary Russell, Beatrice Saunders, Steve Schinke, Dick Schoeck, John Schuerman, Jim Seaberg, Judith Sears, Fred Seidl, Larry Shulman, Deb Siegel, Max Siporin, Norm Smith, Harry Specht, Dick Stuart, Jim Taylor, Eli Teram, Ed Thomas, Barbara Thomlison, Ray Thomlison, Ron Toseland, Tony Tripodi, John Tropman, Barbara Turman, Lynn Vogal, Tom Watts, Margaret Whelan, Stan Witkin, Sidney Zimbalist, and Lou Zurcher.

Within the limits of time frames and resources, we have tried to follow the suggestions offered by these colleagues. However, they should not be held responsible for our sins of omission or commission. Special thanks go to the contributors for their hard work and individual participation. This book is a product of their experiences and their desire to introduce others to social work research, which they have found so challenging and stimulating.

As usual, the excellent staff at F.E. Peacock Publishers has been more than helpful in seeing this huge project through to completion.

Copyright Acknowledgments

We thank the following publishing houses for providing permission to reprint their material:

Chapter 1: Adapted and modified from Richard M. Grinnell, Jr., Michael A. Rothery, and Ray J. Thomlison, "Research in Social Work," in Richard M. Grinnell, Jr. (Ed.), *Social Work Research and Evaluation* (4th ed.). Copyright © 1993 by F.E. Peacock Publishers. Used with permission; and Richard M. Grinnell, Jr., and Deborah H. Siegel, "The Place of Research in Social Work," in Richard M. Grinnell, Jr. (Ed.), *Social Work Research and Evaluation* (3rd ed.). Copyright © 1988 by F.E. Peacock Publishers. Used with permission.

Boxes 1.1, 3.1, 3.2, 4.1, 4.2, & 4.4: From *Approaches to Social Research*, Second Edition, by Royce A. Singleton, Jr., Bruce C. Straits, and Margaret Miller Straits. Copyright © 1988, 1993 by Oxford University Press, Inc. Reprinted by permission.

Figure 1.1: As cited in Richard M. Grinnell, Jr., Michael A. Rothery, and Ray J. Thomlison, "Research in Social Work," in Richard M. Grinnell, Jr. (Ed.), *Social Work Research and Evaluation* (4th ed.). Originally from: Eva Ferguson, *Calgary Herald*, Calgary, Alberta, Canada, September 6, 1991, Sect. A, p. 1. Used with permission.

Figure 1.2: As cited in Richard M. Grinnell, Jr., Michael A. Rothery, and Ray J. Thomlison, "Research in Social Work," in Richard M. Grinnell, Jr. (Ed.), *Social Work Research and Evaluation* (4th ed.). Originally from: *Calgary Herald*, Calgary, Alberta, Canada, September 6, 1991, Sect. B, p. 6. Used with permission.

Chapters 2, 3, 21, & 23; Figures 3.1, 4.1, 10.1, 10.2, & 15.1: Adapted and modified from Margaret Williams, Leslie M. Tutty, and Richard M. Grinnell, Jr., *Research in Social*

Work: An Introduction (2nd ed.). Copyright © 1995 by F.E. Peacock Publishers. Used with permission.

Boxes 2.1, 2.2, 2.3, 3.3, 4.3 (by Patricia Fisher), & 10.3; Chapter 24: From *Research Methods for Social Work*, 2nd Edition, by Allen Rubin and Earl Babbie. Copyright © 1993 by Brooks/Cole Publishing Co. Reprinted by permission.

Figure 2.2: Source: *Code of Ethics of the National Association of Social Workers*, part 1, sect. E (Silver Spring, MD: National Association of Social Workers, Inc.), p. 4. Used with permission.

Chapter 3; Figure 4.2: Adapted and modified from Michael A. Rothery, "Problems, Questions, and Hypotheses," in Richard M. Grinnell, Jr. (Ed.), *Social Work Research and Evaluation* (4th ed.). Copyright © 1993 by F.E. Peacock Publishers. Used with permission; and Margaret Williams, Leslie M. Tutty, and Richard M. Grinnell, Jr., *Research in Social Work: An Introduction* (2nd ed.). Copyright © 1995 by F.E. Peacock Publishers. Used with permission.

Chapter 4: Adapted and modified from Michael A. Rothery, "The Positivistic Research Approach," in Richard M. Grinnell, Jr. (Ed.), *Social Work Research and Evaluation* (4th ed.). Copyright © 1993 by F.E. Peacock Publishers. Used with permission; Michael A. Rothery, "Problems, Questions, and Hypotheses," in Richard M. Grinnell, Jr. (Ed.), *Social Work Research and Evaluation* (4th ed.). Copyright © 1993 by F.E. Peacock Publishers. Used with permission; Margaret Williams, Leslie M. Tutty, and Richard M. Grinnell, Jr., *Research in Social Work: An Introduction* (2nd ed.). Copyright © 1995 by F.E. Peacock Publishers. Used with permission; and Richard M. Grinnell, Jr., Michael A. Rothery, and Ray J. Thomlison, "Research in Social Work," in Richard M. Grinnell, Jr. (Ed.), *Social Work Research and Evaluation* (4th ed.). Copyright © 1993 by F.E. Peacock Publishers. Used with permission.

Figure 5.1: As cited in James B. Taylor, "The Naturalistic Research Approach," in Richard M. Grinnell, Jr. (Ed.), *Social Work Research and Evaluation* (4th ed., p. 72). Itasca, IL: F.E. Peacock. Originally from John Spradley, *The Ethnographic Interview*. Copyright © 1979 by Holt, Rinehart, and Winston. Used with permission.

Box 5.1: From James B. Taylor, "The Naturalistic Research Approach," in Richard M. Grinnell, Jr. (Ed.), *Social Work Research and Evaluation* (4th ed., pp. 64-65). Itasca, IL: F.E. Peacock. Copyright © 1993 by F.E. Peacock Publishers. Originally from Ellen Finch, *Psychiatric Rehabilitation Outside the Bureaucracy: A Naturalistic Study of the Fountain House Model* (Unpublished Ph.D. dissertation, University of Kansas, 1986).

Figure 5.2: As cited in James B. Taylor, "The Naturalistic Research Approach," in Richard M. Grinnell, Jr. (Ed.), *Social Work Research and Evaluation* (4th ed., p. 68). Itasca, IL: F.E. Peacock. Originally from John Van Maanen, *Tales of the field: On writing ethnography*. Copyright © 1988 by University of Chicago Press. Used with permission.

Boxes 5.2 & 6.1: From Michael A. Rothery, Leslie M. Tutty, and Richard M. Grinnell, Jr., "Introduction," in Leslie M. Tutty, Michael A. Rothery, and Richard M. Grinnell, Jr. (Eds.), *Qualitative Research for Social Workers: Phases, Steps, and Tasks*. Copyright © 1996 by Allyn & Bacon. Used with permission.

Chapter 6: Adapted and modified from John W. Cresswell, *Research Design: Qualitative and Quantitative Approaches.* Copyright © 1994 by Sage Publications, Inc. Reprinted by permission of Sage Publications, Inc.

Figure 8.1: Adapted from Deborah H. Siegel, "Integrating Data-Gathering Techniques and Practice Activities," in Richard M. Grinnell, Jr. (Ed.), *Social Work Research and*

Contributors

EARL R. BABBIE, Ph.D., is a professor within the Department of Social Sciences at Chapman University, Orange, California 92666.

GERALD J. BOSTWICK, Jr., Ph.D., is an associate professor within the School of Social Work at the University of Cincinnati, Cincinnati, Ohio 54221.

ELAINE BOUEY, M.ED., is a Librarian at The University of Calgary, Calgary, Alberta T2N 1N4, Canada.

HEATHER COLEMAN, Ph.D., is an assistant professor within the Faculty of Social Work at The University of Calgary, Calgary, Alberta T2N 1N4, Canada.

DONALD COLLINS, Ph.D., is a professor within the Faculty of Social Work at The University of Calgary, Calgary, Alberta T2N 1N4, Canada.

KEVIN CORCORAN, Ph.D., is a professor within the Graduate School of Social Work at Portland State University, Portland, Oregon 97207.

JOHN W. CRESWELL, Ph.D., is a professor within the Educational Psychology College at the University of Nebraska, Lincoln, Nebraska 68504.

CYNTHIA FRANKLIN, Ph.D., is an associate professor within the School of Social Work at The University of Texas at Austin, Austin, Texas 78712.

PETER A. GABOR, Ph.D., is a professor within the Faculty of Social Work at The University of Calgary, Calgary, Alberta T2N 1N4, Canada.

JANE F. GILGUN, Ph.D., is a professor within the School of Social Work at the University of Minnesota at Minneapolis, Minneapolis, Minnesota 55455.

RICHARD M. GRINNELL, JR., Ph.D., is a professor within the Faculty of Social Work at The University of Calgary, Calgary, Alberta T2N 1N4, Canada.

CAROL ING, MS., is an instructor within the Child and Youth Care Program at Lethbridge Community College, Lethbridge, Alberta P1K 1L6, Canada.

CATHELEEN JORDAN, Ph.D., is a professor within the School of Social Work at The University of Texas at Arlington, Arlington, Texas 76019.

JUDY L. KRYSIK, Ph.D., currently resides in Phoenix Arizona 85287.

NANCY S. KYTE, M.S.W., is a social worker within the Department of Behavioral Medicine at Clermont Mercy Hospital, Batavia, Ohio 54221.

CRAIG W. LECROY, Ph.D., is an associate professor within the School of Social Work at Arizona State University, Tempe, Arizona 85287.

ROBERT W. MCCLELLAND, Ph.D., is an assistant professor within the Faculty of Social Work at The University of Calgary, Calgary, Alberta T2N 1N4, Canada.

STEVEN L. MCMURTRY, Ph.D., is a professor within the School of Social Welfare at the University of Wisconsin at Milwaukee, Milwaukee, Wisconsin 53201.

KEITH MCNEIL, Ph.D., is a professor within the Department of Psychology at New Mexico State University, Las Cruces, New Mexico 88003.

CHARLES H. MINDEL, Ph.D., is a professor within the School of Social Work at The University of Texas at Arlington, Arlington, Texas 76019.

RICHARD A. POLSTER, Ph.D., currently resides in Denver, Colorado 80209.

GAYLA ROGERS, Ph.D., is an associate professor within the Faculty of Social Work at The University of Calgary, Calgary, Alberta T2N 1N4, Canada.

ALLEN RUBIN, Ph.D., is a professor within the School of Social Work at The University of Texas at Austin, Austin, Texas 78712.

JACKIE D. SIEPPERT, Ph.D., is an assistant professor within the Faculty of Social Work at The University of Calgary, Calgary, Alberta T2N 1N4, Canada.

GARY SOLOMON, M.S.W., currently resides in Portland Oregon 97207.

PAUL H. STUART, Ph.D., is a professor within the School of Social Work at The University of Alabama, Tuscaloosa, Alabama 35487.

LESLIE M. TUTTY, D.S.W., is a professor within the Faculty of Social Work at The University of Calgary, Calgary, Alberta T2N 1N4, Canada.

YVONNE A. UNRAU, Ph.D., is an assistant professor within the Faculty of Social Work at The University of Calgary, Calgary, Alberta T2N 1N4, Canada.

WILLIAM K. WILKINSON, Ph.D., Western Health Board, Galway, Ireland.

MARGARET WILLIAMS, Ph.D., is an assistant professor within the Faculty of Social Work at The University of Calgary, Calgary, Alberta T2N 1N4, Canada.

THE CONTEXTS OF KNOWLEDGE GENERATION

$$C \quad h \quad a \quad p \quad t \quad e \quad r \qquad 1$$

The Generation of Knowledge

M ADAME X IS A PSYCHIC card and palm reader. She has practiced in our local community for several years and has gained the highest admiration of many people. She advertises in the newspaper, claiming:

> With my advice and insight, I will guide and help you to a more successful life. I can help you with such things as love, business, health, and marriage. One visit will convince you that I can solve any of your problems—big or small.

A number of questions should immediately come to mind upon reading Madame X's self-proclaimed expertise: Can she really solve human problems? How does she do it? Is she effective in her problem solving? Is she more (or less) effective than others who also claim to solve such problems? A cynical social worker might even ask: What is the future of my social work practice if Madame X were to establish her practice in my community?

While it is doubtful that any of us would be threatened by Madame X's claims, her advertisement does serve to illustrate how the process and objectives of helping people can mistakenly be reduced to simplicity or, in this case, mysticism. A person who is a true believer in psychic card and palm reading would probably ask very few questions of Madame X.

Most of us, however, would want to know much more about her knowledge base. We would want to ascertain why she feels she can take the complex process of human problem solving and claim to "solve any of your problems—big or small" by reading cards or palms.

It is less likely that similar questions would be addressed to social workers. Society generally makes certain assumptions regarding the extent of our knowledge base, the competency of our practice skills, and the effectiveness of our social service programs. Society is more discriminating about Madame X than it is about social workers because it has greater expectations for the way we develop our knowledge base and practice skills. Social workers—like all professionals (e.g., lawyers, physicians, nurses, architects, police officers)—are expected to have a substantial knowledge base to guide and support their interventions.

HOW DO WE OBTAIN OUR KNOWLEDGE BASE?

Each of us already has a great deal of knowledge about various things. Some of the things we know stem from tradition because they are commonly thought of as "true" by everyone in our culture. We now "know" that the Earth is round; although, if we had been born a few centuries earlier, we would have "known" that it was flat. Some things we know because someone in authority told us about them: We may have been told that smoking causes cancer, or that when one spouse batters the other it results in a helpless response rather than flight. Other things we know because we have personally experienced them or believe them to be true: We may have found out through experience that knives are sharp the first time we came into contact with one, or that we intuitively believe that the world would be a better place to live if there were no war.

The previous four example of ways of obtaining knowledge—tradition, authority, experience, and intuition—combined with the research method (the focus of this book)—form five ways of developing our knowledge base. These five ways are highly interactive with one another, but for the sake of simplicity, each one is discussed separately. Let us now turn our attention to the first way of obtaining knowledge—tradition.

Tradition

Most people tend to accept traditional cultural beliefs without much question. They may doubt some of them and test others for themselves, but, for the most part, they behave and believe as tradition demands. Such conformity has its uses, however. Society could not function if each custom and belief were reexamined by each individual in every generation. On the other hand, unquestioning acceptance of traditional dictates can lead to stagnation and to the perpetuation of wrongs. It would be unfortunate if women had never been allowed to vote because "women had never traditionally voted," or if racial segregation were perpetuated because that was the "way things were done."

Authority

The reliance on authority figures is the second way we can "know" something. When Galileo looked through his telescope in the year 1610, for example, he saw four satellites circling the planet Jupiter. His discovery presented a problem, as it was truly believed that there were seven heavenly bodies: the Sun, the Moon, and five planets. Seven was a sacred number proclaimed by previous authority figures, but the addition of Jupiter's satellites brought the number to eleven. And there was nothing mystic about the number eleven! It was partly for this reason that professors of philosophy denounced the telescope and refused to believe in the existence of Jupiter's satellites.

In the twentieth century, we may find it incredible that educated people would behave in this way. After all, the doubting professors in Galileo's time had only to look through the telescope in order to see Jupiter's satellites for themselves. Today's "see for yourself" philosophy is based on the belief that "true" knowledge can best be gained through research, which begins with "objective data" about the real world.

In the seventeenth century, obtaining knowledge through the research method was considered a less valid source of knowledge development than tradition and authority (in addition to experience and intuition, to be discussed shortly). Hence, the professors may not have accepted the "objective data" (in this case, their own personal observations) of their eyes as "*the* truth" if this "new truth" conflicted with traditional beliefs and the established authority of the state or church.

Questioning the Accuracy of Data

The same dilemma exists with authority as with tradition—the question of the accuracy of the data obtained. Students have a right to expect that data, or information, given to them by their teachers are current and accurate. They will not learn very much if they decide it is essential to verify everything the instructor says. In the same way, the general public trusts that statements made by "experts" will be true. This trust is necessary, since lay people usually have neither the time nor the energy to conduct or evaluate the specialized research studies leading to scientific discoveries.

Advertisers both use and misuse this necessary reliance on authority figures. Cat foods are promoted by veterinarians, since veterinarians are assumed to be experts on the nutritional needs of cats and it is expected that cat owners will heed their pronouncements. On the other hand, all kinds of products are promoted by movie stars, rock stars, and athletes, whose authority lies not in their specialized knowledge but only in their personal charisma and status in the public eye.

As might be expected, it is advisable to place most trust in experts speaking within their field of expertise and less trust in those who lack expert knowledge. Even experts can be wrong, however, and the consequences can sometimes be disastrous. A social work treatment intervention that was developed several decades ago provides a good example. The intervention focused on families in which one member suffered from schizophrenia, and primary treatment intervention was an attempt to change the family system. At the time, authority figures in psychoanalysis and family therapy believed that schizophrenia was caused by faulty parenting, so emphasis was placed on such factors as parental discord, excessive familial interdependency, and mothers whose overprotective and domineering behaviors did not allow their children to develop individual identities.

Following this theory, some social workers assumed that all families with a schizophrenic member must be dysfunctional. Because they focused their interventions on changing the family system, they often inadvertently instilled guilt into the parents and increased tensions rather than helping the parents to cope with their child who had been diagnosed as schizophrenic.

Recent research studies have shown that schizophrenia is caused largely by genetic and other biological factors, not by bad parenting. Furthermore, one of the most effective social work interventions is to support the family in providing a nonstressful environment. It is not surprising that, previously, social workers acted on the beliefs of experts in schizophrenia without personally evaluating the research studies that had led to those beliefs. Had they investigated for themselves, and had they been trained in research techniques, they may have found that there was little real objective data to support the bad-parenting theory. Consequently, they may have been more supportive of parents and thus more effective helpers.

While we are in school, our learning is largely structured for us. It is likely that we will spend far more time as practicing social workers than we will in school; and there is an old saying that learning does not really begin until formal education has ended. Out in the field, we will still be required to attend workshops, conferences, and staff training sessions, but most of our learning will come from what we read and from what people tell us. Our reading material is likely to consist mostly of books and journal articles related to our specific field of practice—whether it be senior citizens, children who have been abused, adolescent offenders, or some other special group. Most of the articles that we read will deal with research studies; many of the books we come across will interpret, synthesize, and comment upon research studies. None of them will explain how research studies ought to be conducted, because it is assumed we learned that in school. With this in mind, we now turn our attention to sorting out good advice.

Sorting Out Good Advice

When we first enter a social work agency, as either practicum students or a graduate social workers, our supervisors and colleagues will start to show us how the agencies run. We may be given a manual detailing agency policies and procedures: everything from staff holidays, to locking up client files at night, to standard techniques for interviewing children who have been physically and emotionally abused. Informally, we will be told other things: how much it costs to join the coffee club, whom to ask when we want a favor, whom to phone for certain kinds of information, and what form to complete to be put on the waiting list for a parking space.

In addition to this practical information, we may also receive advice about how to help clients. Colleagues may offer opinions about the most effective treatment intervention strategies. If we work in a child sexual abuse treatment agency, for example, it may be suggested to us that the nonoffending mother of a child who has been sexually abused does not need to address her own history of abuse in therapy in order to empathize with and protect her daughter. Such a view would support the belief that the best interventive approach is a behavioral/learning one, perhaps helping the mother learn better communication skills in her relationship with her daughter. Conversely, the suggestion may be that the mother's personal exploration is essential and that, therefore, the intervention chould be of a psychodynamic nature.

Whatever the suggestion, it is likely that we, as beginning social workers, will accept it, along with the information about the coffee club and the parking space. We will want to fit in, to be a member of the team. If this is the first client for whom we have really been responsible, we may also be privately relieved that the intervention decision has been made for us. We may rightfully believe that colleagues, after all, have more experience than we and they should surely know best.

Perhaps they do know best. At the same time, it is important to remember that they also were once beginning social workers and they formed their opinions in the same way as we are presently forming ours. They too once trusted in their supervisors' knowledge bases and the experiences of their colleagues. In other words, much of what we will initially be told is based upon tradition and authority. Like all knowledge derived from these two sources, the practice recommendations offered by our colleagues allow us to learn from the achievements and mistakes of those who have tried to do our job before us. We do not have to "reinvent the wheel." We are being given a head start.

On the other hand, knowledge derived from tradition and authority has the disadvantage that it can become too comfortable. We know that the traditional approaches to client problems practiced in our agency are effective because everyone says they are; we know that certain intervention strategies work because they have worked for years. And armed with this comfortable and certain knowledge, we may not look for better ways of helping our clients.

In addition, we may not wish to test the intervention methods presently employed to see if they work as well as our colleagues say. We may even be inclined to reject out-of-hand evidence that our present interventions are ineffective or that there is a better way. And if we do happen to seek and find new interventions, we may discover that our colleagues are unreceptive or even hostile. Tradition dies hard, and authority is not so easily relinquished.

In summary, authority is one of the many ways of knowing, and it sometimes gets confused with the use of personal practice experience and intuition as additional ways of knowing. We now turn our attention to how experience and intuition are used in the generation of social work knowledge.

Experience and Intuition

The third and fourth ways of obtaining knowledge are through experience and intuition. Learning from experience is great—no one will ever deny this. Relying solely on intuition, however, is another matter. There are two main reasons why we should not rely solely on practice intuitions when working with clients: (1) professional ethics, and (2) concerns for our profession's survival (Grinnell & Siegel, 1988).

Ethical Concerns

Suppose one day Jane goes to a physician for a medical checkup because she has been feeling tired and depressed. After talking with her for a few minutes, the physician concludes that she has high blood pressure and gives her hypertension medication. Following the physician's advice, Jane takes the medication for a few months and begins to feel better. Since she is now feeling better, she phones the physician and asks if it is all right to stop taking the medication. The physician says yes.

At no time did the physician take her blood pressure, either to confirm the initial diagnostic hunch or to determine the effects of the medication. Hence, it was entirely possible that she was taking a drug for which she had no need, or a drug that could actually harm her, or that she stopped taking the medication that was helping her. The point here is that the physician made crucial decisions to begin and end intervention (treatment) without gathering all the necessary data.

Ethical social workers do *not* do what the physician did in the preceding two paragraphs. Just as the wrong medication has the potential to harm, so does the wrong social work intervention. In the past, some studies have shown that the recipients of social work services fare worse, or no better, than people who do not receive our services. Thus, we have a responsibility always to evaluate the impact of our interventions.

We must fully realize that we have no business intervening in other peoples' lives simply on the assumption that our *good* intentions lead to *good* client outcomes. Although we may mean well, our good intentions alone do not ensure that we really "help" our clients. Research and evaluation must be integrated within our practice so we can measure the effects of our helping efforts. We have a moral obligation to do this—even more so when clients have not asked for our services. Truly professional social workers never rely solely on their good intentions, intuitions, subjective judgments, and practice wisdoms. They use the research process to *guide* their interventions and assess their effectiveness.

Despite the compelling ethical reason for using research and evaluation in social work practice, a few social workers still continue to rely only on their intuitions, informed judgments, and practice wisdoms to assess, monitor, and "evaluate" their practice activities. These workers usually argue that they simply lack the expertise, time, money, and inclination to gather the data needed to determine whether their clients have improved at all. These workers believe that trying to measure the effects of their practices is like trying to catch a sunbeam. They maintain that what social workers do is an art that cannot be measured and guided by the research method. Additionally, they *feel* that important changes in their clients' lives are not measurable in the first place.

These social workers are making a serious mistake. They are ignoring four important problems inherent in their sole reliance on intuition: (1) intuition and reality do not always mesh, (2) intuitive judgments may lead to superstitious behavior and complacency, (3) intuitive judgments vary dramatically from person to person, and (4) intuition is susceptible to bias.

Intuition and Reality Do Not Always Mesh　　The first problem that is inherent when we use *only* intuition in assessing, monitoring, and evaluating our practices is that intuition and reality do not always mesh. It is deceptively easy to underestimate the impact of our practice efforts on our clients. For example, if we fail to recognize our clients' growth and change when growth and change have in fact occurred, several unfortunate consequences are possible. The clients may be deprived of the reinforcement that strengthens their future efforts and encourages further movement.

In addition, we may suffer unnecessary feelings of defeat and impotence. Such feelings may contribute to burnout or simply diminish our effectiveness, since effective helpers must have faith in their own abilities as change agents and belief in their clients' ability to self-actualize. Further, our profession is deprived of knowledge about the effectiveness of a particular intervention with a particular client system.

On the other hand, we may overestimate the extent of our client's growth and change. Such overestimation may result in loss of opportunity for the client to progress in further problem resolution; reinforcement of the client's ineffective coping efforts; misapplication by the worker of similarly ineffective interventions in future cases; and wasted time and money for the client, the worker, and the agency.

Intuitive Judgments May Lead to Superstitious Behaviors　　A second limitation of intuition is that an erroneous intuited judgment may lead to a superstitious behavior and complacency. A social worker may, for example, use certain interventions assuming that they are effective when they are in fact useless. This is akin to the people who wear a rabbit's foot around their necks in order to keep vampires away. They are certain that the charm works because vampires have never appeared. A knowledge-based social worker knows that this same fallacious kind of logic can lead to equally superstitious behaviors in our profession.

Intuitive Judgments Vary Dramatically   A third limitation of intuition is that intuitive, subjective judgments vary dramatically from person to person. Obviously, one social worker's intuition is not necessarily the same as another's. Two people who observe the same phenomenon can easily come to very different conclusions about what was seen. So, for example, in the absence of valid and reliable data documenting client change over the course of an intervention, there is no basis to support the assertions of either the worker who maintains that "little change" has occurred or the worker who asserts that "much change" has occurred.

Intuition Is Susceptible to Bias   Finally, intuition is notoriously susceptible to bias. Workers who believe it is important to uncover early childhood experiences in order to unleash pent-up rage and grief, for example, may consider the client's newfound tears as indicators of forward "movement." The client, on the other hand, may be horrified at falling apart. Is the client growing or decompensating? This is a question that intuition alone cannot answer.

Or, consider a director of residential institutions for juveniles who have committed violent crimes. The director may view a child whose only offense is truancy to be less in need of help than other children because he or she compares the child with the other youths at the institution. Health planners who come from a mental health background may see mental illness as the most compelling community health problem to be addressed simply because, in their own work, they are confronted by it daily, even when other public health issues may in fact be more widespread or intense. In short, our individual biases color our intuitions and thus our intuitions are not necessarily valid indicators of reality.

Survival Concerns

There are economic as well as ethical reasons for our profession's commitment to research and evaluation. It was once believed that perhaps throwing money at social problems would solve them. Today, funding sources demand evidence that social service agencies are accomplishing their intended goals and objectives. Anecdotal case studies alone are lame when unaccompanied by valid and reliable data of the agency's effectiveness. In the competitive scramble of social service agencies for limited funds, the agencies that can demonstrate their effectiveness and efficiency will prevail. Hence, learning how to integrate practice activities with the research process is a matter of survival in our profession.

Expanding our research/practice base is also a way of enabling our profession to assert its place in the community of human service professionals. It is a way of carving out a niche of respectability, of challenging the insidious stereotype that, although social workers have their hearts in the right place, they are uninformed and ineffective.

Any profession (and especially ours) that bases its credibility on faith or ideology alone will have a hard time surviving. Although a research base to our profession will not guarantee us public acceptance, the absence of such a base and the lack of vigorous research efforts to expand it will—in the long run—undoubtedly erode our credibility.

The Research Method

This fifth method of obtaining knowledge is sometimes called the problem-solving method and contains two complementary research approaches to generating knowledge in our profession—the quantitative approach (Chapter 4) and the qualitative approach (Chapter 5).

We will highlight these throughout this book, as they are today's primary two approaches to obtaining knowledge in contemporary social work research. However, we emphasize that the other four forms of knowledge development are also of some importance in the knowledge-building enterprise.

On a very general level, and in the simplest of terms, the two research approaches utilize four generic highly interrelated steps:

1. Observing (or measuring) a person, an object, or an event
2. Making an assumption on the basis of the observation (or measurement)
3. Testing the assumption to see to what extent it is true
4. Revising the assumption on the basis of the test

Suppose, for example, we observe that the hairy males of our acquaintance seem more intelligent than males endowed with a lesser amount of body hair. It has, in fact, been suggested—though by no means "proven"—that body hair is related to intelligence, since the skin and brain develop from the same embryonic tissues. Therefore, we might make the assumption that, if males in general are placed on a continuum from the most hairy to the least hairy, those on the hairy end will be significantly more intelligent than those on the other end.

We might test this assumption by selecting a number of males, measuring their intelligence, and devising a means of measuring their body hair that is both accurate and socially acceptable. If we find that pronounced hairiness is positively associated with high intelligence in a significant number of cases, we can be reasonably certain that our original assumption was correct. If we find no such association, our assumption was probably wrong.

Whatever we find, our conclusions will be suspect until someone else has undertaken a similar study and confirmed our results. Utilizing the research method to obtain knowledge is a *public method of knowing*. It relies not on private avenues to knowledge—such as inspiration or visions—but rather on a careful sequence of activities that can be duplicated (as much as possible) by other people. We will be more certain of the relationship between hairiness and intelligence if someone else has found the same relationship. The more people who find it, the more certain we will become.

Nevertheless, we cannot be *certain* that a thing exists, no matter how many people have found it. We cannot be certain that there is a relationship between two or more things no matter how many people have found one. Nothing is certain; nothing is absolute. It is a matter of slowly acquiring knowledge by making observations, via qualitative and quantitative research approaches, deriving theories from those observations, and testing the theories by making further observations. Even the best-tested theory is held to be true only until something comes along to disprove it. Nothing is forever.

Besides the comfortable certainty of tradition and authority, the research method of obtaining knowledge is a prickly bedfellow. But, of all the possible ways of knowing, we have discovered that it has brought us farthest in terms of food, clothing, shelter, and freedom from diseases. Mystic numbers have not successfully predicted the end of the world; authoritative statements have often proved to be inaccurate; and ill-conceptualized efforts at helpfulness, no matter how well intended, may not provide assistance to some of our clients. Social workers must know *how* to help—for our own sakes, and for the sake of our profession and the clients we serve.

Approaches to the Research Method

As we have established, the research method of knowing contains two complementary research approaches, the quantitative approach and the qualitative approach. Quantitative research studies rely on quantification in collecting and analyzing data and sometimes use statistics to test hypotheses established at the outset of the study. On the other hand, qualitative studies rely on qualitative and descriptive methods of data collection and generate hypotheses and generalizations as a part of the research process.

Their unique characteristics and contributions to the knowledge base of social work are examined in Chapters 4 and 5, respectively. Which approach is to be taken is determined by the research question or hypothesis, or by the philosophical inclination of the researcher. The quantitative and qualitative research approaches complement each other and are equally important in the generation and testing of social work knowledge.

The development of knowledge through the use of the research method (e.g., quantitative or qualitative) is not always as rational as we may predict, as illustrated in Box 1.1.

BOX 1.1

THE SERENDIPITY PATTERN IN SCIENCE

Scientific inquiry, for the most part, works within the framework of a theory. Hypotheses are derived, research studies are planned, and observations are made and interpreted in order to test and elaborate theories. Occasionally, however, unanticipated findings occur that cannot be interpreted meaningfully in terms of prevailing theories as the *serendipity pattern*. In the history of science, there are many cases of scientific discoveries in which chance, or serendipity, played a part. One of these is Pasteur's discovery of immunization.

> Pasteur's researches on fowl cholera were interrupted by the vacation, and when he resumed he encountered an unexpected obstacle. Nearly all the cultures had become sterile. He attempted to revive them by sub-inoculation into broth and injection into fowls. Most of the sub-cultures failed to grow and the birds were not affected, so he was about to discard everything and start afresh when he had the inspiration of re-inoculating the same fowls with a fresh culture. His colleague Duclaux relates: "To the surprise of all, and perhaps even of Pasteur, who was not expecting such success, nearly all these fowls withstood the inoculation, although fresh fowls succumbed after the usual incubation period." This resulted in the recognition of the principle of immunization with attenuated pathogens. (Beveridge, 1957:27)

Social science has had its share of serendipitous findings also. The well-known "Hawthorne effect," which refers to the effect that a worker's awareness of being under study has on his or her performance, was an unanticipated finding of a series of studies carried out between 1927 and 1932 at the Western Electric Hawthorne plant in Chicago (Roethlisberger & Dickson, 1939). In one of the studies six women with the task of assembling telephone relays were placed in a special test room for observation. The idea of the study was to determine the effects of various changes in working conditions (e.g., method of payment, number and length of rest pauses, length of working day) on productivity, as measured by the number of relays completed. Over an extended period of time, numerous changes, each lasting several weeks, were introduced while the women's output was recorded. To the researchers' surprise, however, the changes were not related systematically to output. Instead, the women's output rate rose slowly and steadily throughout the study, even when working conditions introduced early in the study were reintroduced later. As the women were questioned it became evident that their increased productivity was a response to the special attention given to them as participants in what was considered an important experiment.

The fun of the test room and the interest of management simply had made it easier to produce at a higher rate. This was an important finding in the history of social research, for it indicated that subjects' awareness of being under study could affect the very actions that an investigator wishes to observe. Experiments, in particular, must take into account such effects, as presented in Chapter 11.

The Quantitative Approach   A quantitative research study follows the general steps of the generic research process in a more-or-less straightforward manner. First, a problem area is chosen and a relevant researchable question (or specific hypothesis) is specified. Second, relevant variables within the research question (or hypothesis) are delineated. Third, a plan is developed for measuring the variables within the research question (or hypothesis). Fourth, relevant data are gathered for each variable and then analyzed to determine what they mean. Fifth, on the basis of the data generated, conclusions are drawn regarding the research question (or hypothesis). Finally, a report is written giving the study's findings, conclusions, and recommendations.

The study may then be evaluated by others and perhaps replicated (or repeated) to support or repudiate the application of the study's findings. Chapter 4 presents in more detail how to do a quantitative research study.

The Qualitative Approach   Qualitative research studies are also driven by meaningful problem areas. However, their direct relationship to the research process is somewhat different. In a quantitative study, conceptual clarity about the research question (or hypothesis) usually precedes the collection and analysis of data. In contrast to the quantitative approach, researchers doing qualitative studies do not use the data collection and analysis process simply to answer questions (or to test hypotheses). It is used first to discover what the most important questions are, and then to refine and answer questions (or test hypotheses) that are increasingly more specific. The process is one of moving back and forth between facts and their interpretation, between answers to questions and the development of social work theory. We will discuss in more detail of how to do a qualitative research study in Chapter 5.

Now that we know that the *purpose* of social work research is to generate knowledge that is as value free and objective as possible, via the research method, let us turn to a brief *definition* of social work research.

DEFINITION OF RESEARCH

So far, we have discussed the five ways of obtaining knowledge and looked at the characteristics of the research method. Armed with this knowledge, we now need a definition of *research*, which is composed of two syllables, *re* and *search*. Dictionaries define the former syllable as a prefix meaning again, anew, or over again, and the latter as a verb meaning to examine closely and carefully, to test and try, or to probe. Together, these syllables form a noun describing a careful and systematic study in some field of knowledge, undertaken to establish facts or principles. Social work research therefore can be defined as a structured inquiry that utilizes acceptable methodology (i.e., quantitative and qualitative) to solve human problems and creates new knowledge that is generally applicable. While we obtain much of our knowledge base from the findings derived from research studies, all research studies have built-in biases and limitations that create errors and keep us from being absolutely certain about the studies' outcomes.

This text helps us to understand these limitations and to take them into account in the interpretation of our research findings, and it helps us avoid making errors or obtaining wrong answers. One of the principal products of a research study is obtaining "objective" data—via the research method—about reality as it is, "unbiased" and "error-free."

MOTIVATION AND GOALS OF SOCIAL WORK RESEARCH

To examine how social work research studies are motivated and what the goals of such studies are, two articles from Canadian newspapers will be used as examples (Rothery, 1993). The article reproduced in Figure 1.1 is concerned with the attempted abduction of a child in an elementary school at Innisfail, Alberta, and the article in Figure 1.2 remarks on the unusual lack of stereotyping of Native Indians in a Canadian television program. These articles can be applied equally to the problems of child abuse and racism throughout the world. These two figures will also be referenced in Chapter 4.

Factors Motivating Research Studies

What motivates social workers to do research studies? One way to answer this question is by examining possible reactions to the articles reproduced in Figures 1.1 and 1.2.

Readers will have different reactions to the story about the kidnapped child. Parents of young children, for example, may feel fear and anxiety about the safety of their children because they may be reminded that in their communities there are those who could harm them. They and others may experience anger toward those who victimize children and a desire to see them caught, restrained, or punished. They may feel concern for the abducted seven-year-old, mixed with feelings of relief that she was returned to her family.

An adult who was victimized as a child may be likely to have more complex and strong emotional reactions than a person who was not victimized as a child. Teachers, social workers, and police officers whose jobs entail responsibility for such situations may experience professional curiosity.

With the second article, a reader may react with admiration for Marianne Jones, who has overcome the barriers imposed by racism to establish herself in a difficult career. Those of you who are members of a minority group may well applaud more enthusiastically than those of you who are not; you may even share her success in some way.

An administrator in a school system that serves minority students may sense an opportunity—a chance to do a meaningful research study into what images of minorities are perpetuated through the educational system and what impact

---

ANOTHER KIDNAP BID HAS PARENTS NERVOUS

INNISFAIL—Anxious parents are uniting to protect their kids after the fifth child abduction incident since June in this normally peaceful town.

And teachers are on red alert for strangers.

The drastic precautions have been forced on them by the latest kidnap bid—the attempted abduction last Friday of a seven-year-old girl inside the town's only elementary school.

As John Wilson Elementary School ended its day Tuesday, the parking lot was jammed with parents, big brothers, big sisters, friends and neighbors.

"Now, everybody's coming to the school to pick up their kids—or other people's kids. Even parents that never used to come and get their kids are walking them to school every day now," said Jeanette Clark, waiting for her daughter.

"We have to make sure every child gets home safely now.

"This last abduction was really serious because the guy went right into the school," she said.

The culprit, described as a 50-year-old white male with brown hair and a moustache, walked into the school, grabbed the girl, who was just coming out of the bathroom, and demanded: "Come with me."

But the girl bit his arm and ran for help.

Laurie Moore, mother of a Grade 3 girl, said she and her friends with children are emphasizing "stay away from strangers" warnings.

"I tell my daughter not to talk to anyone, and if anyone comes near her she has to scream and run. It really is sad that we all have to go through this," she said.

School Principal Bill Hoppins has created a volunteer program where parents can help each other by supervising kids on the play-ground during the morning.

Tim Belbin, whose daughter attends Grade 2, said he's willing to offer his time to watch his and other children.

"I find this all really disturbing . . . really scary."

The abduction attempt has also prompted teachers to supervise all the students in their classes as they leave the school grounds and make sure they can identify all adults in the area.

"If we don't know them, we have to go up and ask them, even if they don't like it," said Hoppins.

And Hoppins said that when students are absent without a parental notification, their homes are called immediately. "There have been a number of precautions taken here since the last abduction attempt. And we are working together with the parents."

FIGURE 1.1   NEWSPAPER ARTICLE ON CHILD MOLESTER

this has on the students. Some readers may have little or no reaction, however. If nothing in their past history or current involvements is linked to the issues of child abuse or racism, they may merely glance at the articles and pass them over quickly (Grinnell, Thomlison, & Rothery, 1993).

A great variety of responses to these two news items is possible, each shaped by the reader's history and circumstances. It is in reactions such as these that research projects are born. We may be drawn into projects simply because they are there—support is available to conduct a particular study, or our careers will benefit from seizing the opportunities. Nevertheless, a research project would not be initiated without someone, somewhere, sometime, confronting a situation or

---

SHOW IGNORES NATIVE STEREOTYPE

GIBSONS, B.C. (CP)—Native actress Marianne Jones had to fight to keep from laughing when a script once called for her to utter the line: "Him shot six times."

"It was really a difficult thing to say," recalls Jones, who now plays Laurel on CBC's Beachcombers.

That, she says, is typical of the way natives are portrayed on TV and films.

And that, she says, is what's different about Beachcombers.

"It's one of the only shows that portray native people on a day-to-day basis," says Jones.

"No other series has that sort of exposure. When you think of how many native people there are in the country, it's amazing that there isn't more."

Television's portrayal of natives touches a nerve in Jones.

The striking actress with shoulder-length raven hair cherishes her Haida heritage. She identifies her birthplace as "Haida Gwaii—that's the Queen Charlotte Islands, the real name."

The four natives in Beachcombers are depicted as people rather than stereotypes.

"I've done a lot of other shows and they sort of want to put you in a slot: You're a noble savage, you know, the Hollywood stereotypes that have been perpetuated forever."

She admits that natives are struggling with their identity these days; wrestling with tradition and the attractions of the 20th century.

"We're all weighing the traditional life, the spirituality, against being human . . . . We're living today."

"Everybody has a fridge, so to speak," she adds with a raspy laugh.

Jones is doing her part by venturing into video production, starting with a documentary on a Haida artist.

"For a long time, native people have not been allowed or able to define their own images."

"We need to take control to get rid of those Hollywood stereotypes, and to change native people on television to real people."

FIGURE 1.2   NEWSPAPER ARTICLE ON RACISM

event and finding it relevant. Potential researchers begin with the sense (often vaguely formulated) that there is more to be known about a problem area; a question exists that is important enough to justify investing time and other resources in the search for an answer.

The most important thing to know before doing any research study is what implications the study's findings might produce that will advance the knowledge base of social work practice, education, and policy.

The Goals of Research Studies

The goals of social work research studies differ according to whether the study can be described as pure or applied. The goal of pure research studies is to develop theory and expand the social work knowledge base. The goal of applied studies is to develop solutions for problems and applications in practice. The distinction between theoretical results and practical results marks the principal difference between pure and applied research studies.

Pure Research Studies

Pure research studies are motivated primarily by a researcher's curiosity. The questions they address are considered important because they can produce results that improve our ability to describe or explain phenomena. Successfully answering a pure research question advances theory.

Social workers with a sociological background may be interested, for example, in the organizational patterns that evolve in a social system such as the John Wilson Elementary School when an intruder threatens children (Figure 1.1). What are the specific processes whereby the teachers formulate a coherent response to the threat? How are parents, often relatively marginal members of the school community, drawn into more central positions and made effective partners in the effort to maintain a defense? What differentiates this school, where the children reportedly cope with danger while maintaining good morale, from other schools where similar stress would have more debilitating effects?

Social workers with a psychological background also would be interested in responses to stress, but from a different perspective. If their focus is on the development of personality, they may attempt to identify traits that allow some children to cope more effectively with danger than others. If they focus on the perpetrators, they may try to learn what it is about such people that could explain why they behave in ways that are repellent to most other people.

All of these potential research questions are motivated by a desire to increase or improve the knowledge base of our profession. The questions have a theoretical relevance, and the purpose in seeking to answer them is to advance basic knowledge about how social systems organize themselves or how personality develops (Grinnell, Thomlison, & Rothery, 1993).

Applied Research Studies

The advantage of applied research over pure research is pointed up in a defense of "useful" rather than "useless" facts presented by Sherlock Holmes to his companion, Dr. Watson, in Conan Doyle's story titled, *A Study in Scarlet*:

> "You see," he explained, "I consider that a man's brain originally is like a little empty attic, and you have to stock it with such furniture as you choose. ... It is a mistake to think that the little room has elastic walls and can distend to any extent. ... There comes a time when for every addition of knowledge you forget something that you knew before. It is of the highest importance, therefore, not to have useless facts elbowing out the useful ones."
>
> "But the Solar System!" I protested.
>
> "What the deuce is it to me?" he interrupted impatiently: "You say that we go around the sun. If we went around the moon it would not make a pennyworth of difference to me or to my work." (Doyle, 1901/1955, p. 11)

A worker with professional responsibilities for knowing how to be helpful in circumstances like those at Innisfail's Elementary School may have some sympathy for Holmes's position. Theory about the dynamics of social organizations or the development of personality is fine for those who have time to invest in such issues. For an applied researcher, there is reason to be interested in the young girl who bit her assailant and ran for help, for example. How did she know so clearly what to do that she could handle the attack against herself with such competence? Can anything be learned from her history that would help parents or teachers prepare other children to be equally effective should the need arise?

A researcher could also be interested in how the principal of the school handled the situation. Are there generalizable guidelines that can be extracted from the principal's approach to mobilizing teachers and parents? Should other professionals be informed about what the principal did to enable the children to keep their spirits up, while at the same time alerting them to the danger?

Many practicing social workers would be interested in the long-term effects of this kind of experience on the children. Some children will certainly be more deeply affected than others, and it is important to know how they are affected and what kinds of attention to their emotional needs will help them cope adaptively with the experience and its aftermath.

These questions are motivated in part by curiosity, as pure research questions are, but there is another need operating as well, and that is mastery. In a nutshell, the goal of an applied research study is more practical than theoretical.

Pure Versus Applied Research Studies

The distinction between pure and applied research studies is emphasized in many research texts, and academics and funding bodies often use this distinction as one of several criteria for assessing the "value" of a research study. There is some merit to this. If a research project is intended to accomplish nothing more than to determine whether a particular social work intervention has a given effect, its use is limited. It is fair to suggest that this type of study is less important in the long run than a research study that adds permanently to the body of theoretical knowledge that would help us understand why our interventions and their outcomes are related.

In practice, however, the goals of pure and applied research studies overlap to some degree. This is why the research questions asked in both cases are not totally dissimilar. Many supposedly pure research findings (especially in the area of human relations) have practical implications. Conversely, most applied research findings have implications for knowledge development.

Like quantitative and qualitative studies, pure and applied research studies also complement each other. They both have a place in the generation of our knowledge base. With a little forethought, we could easily design a single research study that could include a "pure" component and an "applied" component in addition to a "quantitative" component and a "qualitative" component.

THE SOCIAL WORKER'S ROLES IN RESEARCH

Now that we know the goals of social work research, let us explore how we can perform three complementary research-related roles: (1) the research consumer, (2) the creator and disseminator of knowledge, and (3) the contributing partner.

The Research Consumer

As we have said, social workers deal with people's lives. We have a responsibility to evaluate the effectiveness of our interventions before we use them with clients; and we must also ensure that the interventions we select are the best possible ones, given the limits of social work knowledge. In other words, we must keep up with advances in our field, as doctors, lawyers, and other professionals do. We must acquaint ourselves with the findings from the latest research studies (i.e., quantitative *and* qualitative) and decide which findings are important, which might possibly be useful, and which should be ignored.

Sometimes, social workers want to conduct their own research studies, particularly when they have read about findings that come into the "possibly useful" category. Nevertheless, every new intervention must be tried once for the first time, and a social worker who wants to build a repertoire of interventions will experience a number of "first times." It is particularly important to understand how others have implemented the intervention—if others have—and to monitor the client's progress carefully.

Social workers contemplating larger research studies will obviously need to be well acquainted with previous studies. However, it is a mistake to believe that only those who "do research" read research studies. The purpose of a research study is to collect data, which is combined with other data to generate knowledge. The purpose of generating knowledge, in social work, is to pass the knowledge to social workers, who will accomplish the primary purpose of the profession—helping clients to help themselves.

Consuming research findings—reading with understanding in order to utilize the findings—is the most important research role a social worker can play.

Knowledge Creator and Disseminator

Social workers who conduct their own research studies are helping to create knowledge, provided that they inform others about their findings. Many social workers try something new from time to time. However, comparatively few social workers use the research method of testing their new interventions in an effort to gather evidence about how well these interventions work with different clients in various situations. Even fewer share their findings—or even their interventions—with their colleagues; and fewer still disseminate the information to the profession as a whole by writing manuscripts to submit to professional journals for possible publication.

The consequence, as previously mentioned, is that most of the best work accomplished by social work professionals is never recorded and never used by anyone but its creator. Clients who could be helped derive no benefit, because a social worker in Chicago does not know that the problem has already been solved by a colleague in Boston.

Contributing Partner

The third research role that social workers undertake is that of contributing partner. We have said that researchers conducting a large study are often dependent on agency staff for help and advice, and many studies can succeed only if staff and researchers form a team. Different staff members can contribute their own various talents to the team effort. One member may be particularly acute and accurate when it comes to observing client behavior; another may have practical and innovative ideas about how to solve a problem; a third may act as a liaison between researcher and client, or between one agency and another. All may be asked to help in testing and designing measuring instruments and gathering or providing data.

It is a rare social worker who is not involved in one research study or another. Some social workers are cooperative, some less so, depending on their attitudes toward research. The ones who know most about research methods tend to be the most cooperative, and also the most useful. Hence, the greater the number of social workers who understand research principles, the more likely it is that relevant studies will be successfully completed and social work knowledge will be increased.

Integrating the Three Research Roles

The three research roles are not independent of one another. They must be integrated if research is to accomplish its goals of increasing our profession's knowledge base and improving the effectiveness of our interventions with clients.

The issue is not whether social workers should consume research findings, produce and disseminate research results, or become contributing partners in research studies. Rather it is whether they can engage the full spectrum of available knowledge and skills in the continual improvement of their practices. Social workers who adopt only one or two research roles are shortchanging themselves and their clients. As William J. Reid and Audrey D. Smith (1989) note:

> ... If research is to be used to full advantage to advance the goals of social work, the profession needs to develop a climate in which both doing and consuming research are normal professional activities. By this we do not mean that all social workers should necessarily do research or that all practice should be based on the results of research, but rather that an ability to carry out studies at some level and the facility in using scientifically based knowledge should be an integral part of the skills that social workers have and use. (p. ix)

SUMMARY

Knowledge is essential to human survival. Over the course of history, there have been many ways of knowing, from divine revelation to tradition and the authority of elders. By the beginning of the seventeenth century, people began to rely on a different way of knowing—the research method, more commonly referred to as the problem-solving method.

Social workers derive their knowledge from tradition, authority, experience, and intuition, as well as from findings derived from research studies—which differ in important ways from the other four methods.

There are two basic complementary research approaches—quantitative and qualitative. They obtain and use data differently, and each approach has utility in the generation of relevant social work knowledge.

There are two main goals of social work research—pure and applied. The purpose of a pure research study is to develop theory and expand the social work knowledge base. The purpose of an applied study is to develop solutions for problems and relevant applications for social work practice. Both goals complement each other.

Social workers engage in three research roles. They can consume research findings by using the findings of others in their day-to-day practices, they can produce and disseminate research results for others to use, and they can participate in research studies in a variety of ways.

Now that we have explored the place of research in social work, in the following chapter we will turn to the contexts in which it takes place.

REFERENCES AND FURTHER READINGS

BABBIE, E.R. (1995). *The practice of social research* (7th ed., pp. 17-62). Belmont, CA: Wadsworth.

BAILEY, K.D. (1994). *Methods of social research* (4th ed., pp. 2-19, 474-485). New York: Free Press.

BALASSONE, M.L. (1994). Does emphasizing accountability and evidence dilute service delivery and the helping role? No! In W.W. Hudson & P.S. Nurius (Eds.), *Controversial issues in social work research* (pp. 15-19). Needham Heights, MA: Allyn & Bacon.

BEVERIDGE, W.I.B. (1957). *The art of scientific investigation* (3rd ed.). London: Heinemann.

BRONSON, D.E. (1994). Is a scientist-practitioner model appropriate for direct social work practice? No! In W.W. Hudson & P.S. Nurius (Eds.), *Controversial issues in social work research* (pp. 81-86). Needham Heights, MA: Allyn & Bacon.

CALGARY HERALD: "Another kidnap bid has parents nervous," September 6, 1991, p. 1.

CALGARY HERALD: "Show ignores Native stereotype," September 6, 1991, Section B, p. 6.

CHANDLER, S.M. (1994). Is there an ethical responsibility to use practice methods with the best empirical evidence of effectiveness? No! In W.W. Hudson & P.S. Nurius (Eds.), *Controversial issues in social work research* (pp. 106-111). Needham Heights, MA: Allyn & Bacon.

CHEETHAM, J. (1992). Evaluating social work effectiveness. *Research on Social Work Practice, 2,* 265-287.

DANGEL, R.F. (1994). Is a scientist-practitioner model appropriate for direct social work practice? Yes! In W.W. Hudson & P.S. Nurius (Eds.), *Controversial issues in social work research* (pp. 75-79). Needham Heights, MA: Allyn & Bacon.

DEPOY, E., & GITLIN, L.N. (1994). *Introduction to research: Multiple strategies for health and human services* (pp. 3-14, 28-39). St. Louis: Mosby.

DOYLE, C. (1901/1955). *A treasury of Sherlock Holmes.* Garden City, NY: Hanover House.

DUEHN, W.D. (1985). Practice and research. In R.M. Grinnell, Jr. (Ed.), *Social work research and evaluation* (2nd ed., pp. 19-48). Itasca, IL: F.E. Peacock.

GABOR, P.A., & GRINNELL, R.M., JR. (1994). *Evaluation and quality improvement in the human services* (pp. 3-17). Needham Heights, MA: Allyn & Bacon.

GARVIN, C.D. (1981). Research-related roles for social workers. In R.M. Grinnell, Jr. (Ed.), *Social work research and evaluation* (pp. 547-552). Itasca, IL: F.E. Peacock.

GRINNELL, R.M., JR. (1985). Becoming a practitioner/researcher. In R.M. Grinnell, Jr. (Ed.), *Social work research and evaluation* (2nd ed., pp. 1-15). Itasca, IL: F.E. Peacock.

GRINNELL, R.M., JR., ROTHERY, M., & THOMLISON, R.J. (1993). Research in social work. In R.M. Grinnell, Jr. (Ed.), *Social work research and evaluation* (4th ed., pp. 2-16). Itasca, IL: F.E. Peacock.

GRINNELL, R.M., JR., & SIEGEL, D.H. (1988). The place of research in social work. In R.M. Grinnell, Jr. (Ed.), *Social work research and evaluation* (3rd ed., pp. 9-24). Itasca, IL: F.E. Peacock.

GRINNELL, R.M., JR., & WILLIAMS, M. (1990). *Research in social work: A primer* (pp. 28-57). Itasca, IL: F.E. Peacock.

KRYSIK, J., HOFFART, I., & GRINNELL, R.M., JR. (1993). *Student study guide for the fourth edition of social work research and evaluation* (pp. 1-2). Itasca, IL: F.E. Peacock.

REID, W.J., & SMITH, A.D. (1989). *Research in social work* (2nd ed.). New York: Columbia University Press.

ROETHLISBERGER, F.J., & DICKSON, W.J. (1939). *Management and the worker: An account of a research program conducted by the Western Electric Co. Hawthorne Works, Chicago.* Cambridge, MA: Harvard University Press.

ROTHERY, M.A. (1993). Problems, questions, and hypotheses. In R.M. Grinnell, Jr. (Ed.), *Social work research and evaluation* (4th ed., pp. 17-37). Itasca, IL: F.E. Peacock.

RUBIN, A., & BABBIE, E. (1993). *Research methods for social work* (2nd ed., pp. 2-55). Pacific Grove, CA: Wadsworth.

RUCKDESCHEL, R. (1994). Does emphasizing accountability and evidence dilute service delivery and the helping role? Yes! In W.W. Hudson & P.S. Nurius (Eds.), *Controversial issues in social work research* (pp. 9-14). Needham Heights, MA: Allyn & Bacon.

SINGLETON, R.A., JR., STRAITS, B.C., & MILLER STRAITS, M. (1993). *Approaches to social research* (2nd ed., pp. 3-60, 94-96). New York: Oxford.

ROTHERY, M.A., TUTTY, L.M., GRINNELL, R.M., JR. (1996). Introduction. In L.M. Tutty, M.A. Rothery, & R.M. Grinnell, Jr. (Eds.), *Qualitative research for social workers: Phases, steps, and tasks* (pp. 2-22). Needham Heights, MA: Allyn & Bacon.

WEINBACH, R.W., & GRINNELL, R.M., JR. (1996). *Applying research knowledge: A workbook for social work students* (2nd ed., pp. 1-8). Needham Heights, MA: Allyn & Bacon.

WILLIAMS, M., TUTTY, L.M., & GRINNELL, R.M., JR. (1995). *Research in social work: An introduction* (2nd ed., pp. 3-30). Itasca, IL: F.E. Peacock.

Margaret Williams
Richard M. Grinnell, Jr.
Leslie M. Tutty

C h a p t e r **2**

Research Contexts

I N THE PREVIOUS CHAPTER we presented the place of research in our profession and five ways of obtaining knowledge. We highlighted the research method as the most useful approach to knowledge development within our profession, as this approach has the capability of producing objective, unbiased data (with various degrees of uncertainty) through the means of research studies. In this chapter, we will continue our discussion of social work research by presenting the contexts in which the studies take place.

No social work research study (quantitative or qualitative) is conducted in a vacuum. People engaged in studies work with colleagues and research participants (who are often clients), frequently in a social work agency whose operation is affected by social and political factors. In addition, and most importantly, we must follow strict ethical procedures when carrying out our studies. The concept of ethics is stressed throughout this text and overrides all aspects of the research process, from selecting an initial research problem and research participants to report writing.

FACTORS AFFECTING RESEARCH STUDIES

Essentially, there are six factors that have a major impact on the way research studies are conducted. For the sake of clarity, they are presented separately, although in reality they always act in combination. These factors are: (1) the social work profession, (2) the social work agency, (3) the researcher, (4) the social work practitioner, (5) professional ethics, and (6) political and social considerations.

The Social Work Profession

Doing a research study in a social work practice setting is enormously different from doing one in a scientific laboratory or in an artificial setting. Research participants (who many times are clients) have special needs that must be taken into consideration, beyond the ethical concerns to be discussed later in this chapter. As we have established, if we are to remain involved in the well-being of our clients, we must become more active in assessing the effectiveness and efficiency of our interventions and social service programs.

Identifying a body of social work knowledge, as distinct from sociological or psychological knowledge, is often a difficult task. Our profession has always been something of a poor relation among the social sciences, borrowing bits of information from psychology, anthropology, and sociology, pieces from political science and economics, and never finding much that can be classed as distinctly and uniquely social work.

However, we are hardly in a position to complain about this. The knowledge garnered from psychology is obtained largely from research studies undertaken by psychologists. Similarly, the knowledge borrowed from anthropology, sociology, political science, and economics is gathered by people in these fields. It seems only reasonable that the knowledge specific to our field should be obtained by social workers conducting their own research studies in their particular areas of expertise.

There are other reasons for the growing importance of research studies in social work. One has to do with economic restraint as well as a simultaneous loss of faith in the idea that throwing money at social problems will solve them in the end. The social problem of domestic violence, for example, will not be solved by indiscriminate funding of emergency shelters for women who have been battered, by treatment for men who have been abusive toward their partners, by services for children who have been victimized, or by higher education for all and sundry. Careful research studies are needed both to determine the most effective ways of helping people and to evaluate the usefulness of the social service programs currently being funded.

Evaluation of existing social service programs is no longer the rather lackadaisical affair that it once was. As recently as the 1970s, it would have been enough for a program's director to convince a funding body that the program it was funding was meeting its goal, keeping within its budget and generally providing a useful service to the community, without having to produce detailed documentation to that effect. Today, funders want "objective data," via research studies, that goals are being met at the least possible cost. They want the results of evaluative studies, performed according to accepted research methods. They simply want proof.

The demand for evaluation is so pervasive that if we do not evaluate our own programs, the evaluations will often be conducted for us by professional evaluators, hired by funding bodies. Until recently, all evaluations of social work programs were carried out by non–social workers who were skilled in such techniques as planning, programing, and budget systems (PPBS) but who knew very little about social work values and practices.

Few of our programs are cost efficient in the way that businesses must be in order to survive. The purpose of a business is to make a profit; the purpose of a social work program is to salvage human lives. Because of this distinction, social work administrators objected to the use of business cost efficiency criteria to measure the worth of human services. They questioned the meaning of the word "efficient" in the human context: Did it mean efficient in terms of time, money, labor, suffering, human rights, or something else?

Eventually, we began to conduct evaluative studies and tried to reach a compromise between PPBS efficiency and client needs. The prestige of our profession has benefitted from the fact that we are now empowered to evaluate our own programs in light of our own value systems. Clients have also benefitted, since their needs are not now sacrificed arbitrarily to costs. These gains are lost, however, if agency staff ignore evaluation until it is imposed upon them from outside the agency.

In sum, it would be to the benefit of both social workers and their clients if we were to take more responsibility for conducting research studies on our own programs. This would provide us with the authority to advocate for clients, to be heard by other professionals with regard to clients, to maintain control over programs serving clients, and to bring about needed change. In this present age of accountability, there is no doubt that a profession that strives for status must be accountable.

To some degree it is a question of "the more accountability the more status," because accountability *is* status. It symbolizes power. It is apparent, therefore, that if our profession wishes to make its way up the status ladder, its driving force must be accountability. The way to achieve accountability is through well-designed research studies.

However, we must never forget that accountability is not all a facade. The research method—as one of the many ways of knowing—is not just a path to authority and status. It also allows us to determine how best to serve our clients, how to determine the effectiveness of our services, and how to improve the services we offer.

Knowing that our profession is the first factor that affects research projects, we now turn our attention to the second, the social work agency.

The Social Work Agency

The second factor affecting research studies is the social work agency. Most of us are employed by a social work program housed within an agency. A child protection agency, for example, may run an investigation program whose purpose is to investigate alleged cases of child abuse and neglect. The same agency may provide in-home support services to families who have abused or neglected their children—a second program. The agency may run a survivor-witness program for children and nonoffending parents who have to appear in court—a third program.

Research studies are usually conducted within the confines of a program. The word "confines" is used advisedly since no study can be undertaken without the support, or at least the toleration, of the program's director. Some program directors are supportive of research studies, while others shiver at the merest mention, but there are some things that all of them have in common. The first of these is that they all worry about money.

Program directors of social work agencies have very little money. They worry that in the coming year they may have even less money; that their funding will be cut or even terminated, their clients will suffer, and their staff will be unemployed. They worry that all these disasters will follow in the wake of an evaluative research study. People doing research studies often have access to client files and to clients. We sometimes talk to staff and examine agency procedures. We are in an excellent position to embarrass everyone by breaching client confidentiality, making inappropriate statements at the wrong times to the wrong people, and writing reports that comment on the program's weaknesses but disregard its strengths.

All programs, like all people, have flaws. Few are efficient in the business sense and most are open to doubt concerning their effectiveness. Program directors know this. They work to improve programs, serving their clients as best they can with limited resources and knowledge that is patchy at best—because the knowledge has not been gained and the research studies necessary to gain it have not been undertaken.

It is not surprising, then, that program directors find themselves torn with regard to the place of research in our profession. They understand that increased knowledge is necessary in order to serve clients better but sometimes they wish that the knowledge could be gathered somewhere else: not through their program, not with their client files, not using their scarce resources, and not taking up the time of their staff. They argue that resources given to research studies are resources taken away from client service. They may think, privately, that research reports are useful only to those engaged in the study.

There is an upside to all of this gloom, however. It is possible that the research report might reflect the program in a good light, delighting its funders and improving its standing in the public eye. In addition, the study might reveal a genuinely practical way in which the program could improve its services to clients or do what it does more efficiently. Many program directors will therefore give permission for research studies to be conducted, provided that the person(s) doing the study is of good standing in the social work community, the proposed study meets with approval, and agreements are entered into concerning confidentiality and the use of staff and financial resources. Larger agencies often have a special committee to evaluate research requests.

Few, if any, of our programs are designed with the notion that someday the program will be engaged in the research process. In some programs, client files have become more ordered with the advent of the computer, but frequently data are difficult both to find and to interpret. The entries in client files may be made by different workers at different times, in writing ranging from copperplate to scrawl, with different viewpoints on the people and events involved, and sometimes with vital data missing. Policies and procedures manuals, long outdated, may bear little relationship to the policies presently in place and the procedures actually undertaken. When this occurs, we must often become dependent upon the goodwill of staff to provide guidance and explanations, even when the original plan was just a quiet session with client files. A researcher's positive relationships with program staff cannot be overemphasized.

The Researcher

The third factor affecting social work research is the person doing the study—the researcher. At every stage in the research process, there are decisions to be made based on the knowledge and value systems of the person conducting the research study. If we are investigating poverty, for example, and believe that poverty results from character flaws in the poor, we might study treatment interventions designed to overcome those flaws. On the other hand, if we believe that ghettos are a factor, we might prefer to focus on environmental causes. The research questions we finally select are determined by our own value systems as well as by the social and political realities of the hour.

Another factor in our study of poverty is how we define "poor." What annual income should a person earn in order to be categorized as poor? We may decide that "poor," in the context of our study, means an annual income of less than $5,000, and that we do not need to talk to anyone who earns more than that. If we decide that the upper limit should be $20,000, we are automatically including many more people as potential participants for our study. Thus, the data collected about "the poor" will depend largely on whom is defined as "poor."

Our final report will probably include recommendations for change based on our study's findings. These recommendations, too, will depend on our personal value systems, modified by social, political, and economic realities. It may be our private opinion that welfare recipients should be given only the absolute minimum of resources necessary to sustain life in order to motivate them to find work. On the other hand, we may believe that a decent standard of living is every human being's birthright. Whatever our opinion, it is likely that we will clothe it in suitable phraseology and incorporate it somehow into our recommendations.

Personal value systems are particularly evident in program evaluation. Our programs are often labeled as ineffective, not as a result of poor goal achievement, but because there is disagreement about the goal itself. Is a drug prevention program "successful" if it *reduces* drug use among its clients, or must clients *abstain* altogether before success can be claimed? Then there is the question of how much success constitutes "success." Is a job placement program worth funding if it finds jobs for *only* 50 percent of its clients? Should an in-home support program be continued if the child is removed from the home in 30 percent of the cases? Next, there is the matter of what types of clients are the most deserving. Should limited resources be used to counsel people dying of cancer, or would the money be better spent on those who are newly diagnosed? Is it worthwhile to provide long-term treatment for one family whose potential for change is small, while other families with more potential linger on the waiting list?

The Social Work Practitioner

Social workers' beliefs and attitudes also affect the place of research in agency settings. Some social workers, for example, refuse to have an observer present at an interview with a client on the grounds that the client will be unable to speak freely and the social worker–client relationship will be disrupted. This difficulty can be resolved in facilities with one-way mirrors; but, if no such mirror exists, a person wishing to evaluate a treatment intervention may not be able to watch the intervention in a practical, clinical setting.

An alternative to the physical presence of the person doing the study is a video recorder. A few social workers—whose belief in disruption leads them to be disrupted—also object to video recorders, although experience has shown that most clients ignore video recorders after the first few curious glances. Indeed, some social workers seem to believe that there is a sort of an aura surrounding practice relationships that is shattered by such devices.

To the extent that video recorders, paper-and-pencil questionnaires, and computer question-and-answer programs are shunned out of hand, the effectiveness of the intervention can never be objectively established. To a degree, it is true that the act of measuring alters what it measures, but often the change is neither great nor long-lasting.

The opinions and attitudes of social workers in regard to research practices thus play a vital part in the outcome of the study. It is not just our attitude that makes a difference; it is the attitudes of *everyone* involved in the study.

Ethical Considerations

The fifth important factor affecting social work research directly is ethics. Physical scientists are by no means exempt from ethical considerations. Consider

Robert Oppenheimer and other atomic scientists, who learned too late that their scientific findings about splitting the atom were used to create an atomic bomb—a purpose the scientists themselves opposed. A physical scientist who wishes to run tests on water samples, however, does not have to consider the feelings of the water samples or worry about harming them. No large dilemma is presented if one of the water samples must be sacrificed to the cause of knowledge building.

For people engaged in social work research studies, the ethical issues are far more pervasive and complex. A fundamental principle of social work research is that increased knowledge, while much to be desired, must never be obtained at the expense of human beings. Since much of our research activities revolve directly around human beings, safeguards must be put in place to ensure that our research participants are never harmed, either physically or psychologically.

An American committee known as the National Commission for the Protection of Human Subjects of Biomedical and Behavioral Research is only one of several professional organizations and lay groups that focus on protecting the rights of research participants. (Most research participants have never heard of any of them.) Clients participating in studies do not put their trust in committees; they trust the individual practitioners who involve them in the studies. It is therefore incumbent upon all of us to be familiar with ethical principles so that our client's trust will never be betrayed.

Essentially, there are three precautionary ethical measures that must be taken before beginning any research study. These are: (1) obtaining the participant's informed consent, (2) designing the study in an ethical manner, and (3) ensuring that others will be properly told about the study's findings.

Obtaining Informed Consent

The most important consideration in any research study is to obtain the participants' *informed* consent. The word "informed" means that each participant fully understands what is going to happen in the course of the study, why it is going to happen, and what its effect will be on him or her. If the participant is psychiatrically challenged, mentally delayed, or in any other way incapable of full understanding, our study must be fully and adequately explained to someone else—perhaps a parent, guardian, social worker, or spouse, or someone to whom the participant's welfare is important.

It is clear that no research participant may be bribed, threatened, deceived, or in any way coerced into participating. Questions must be encouraged, both initially and throughout the course of the study. People who believe they understand may have misinterpreted our explanation or understood it only in part. They may say they understand, when they do not, in an effort to avoid appearing foolish. They may even sign documents they do not understand to confirm their supposed understanding, and it is our responsibility to ensure that their understanding is real and complete.

It is particularly important for participants to know that they are not signing away their rights when they sign a consent form. They can decide at any time to withdraw from the study *without penalty*, without so much as a reproachful glance. The results of the study will be made available to them as soon as the study has been completed. No promise will be made to them that cannot be fulfilled. Figure 2.1 contains an example of a simple consent form that was used by a research department within a child welfare agency. The purpose of the study was to obtain the line-level practitioners' views on burnout.

A promise that is of particular concern to many research participants is that of anonymity. A drug offender, for example, may be very afraid of being identified; a person on welfare may be concerned whether anyone else might learn that he or she is on welfare. Also, there is often some confusion between the terms "anonymity" and "confidentiality." Some studies are designed so that no one, not even the person doing the study, knows which research participant gave what response. An example is a mailed survey form, bearing no identifying mark and asking the respondent not to give a name. In a study like this, the respondent is *anonymous*. It is more often the case, however, that we do know how a particular participant responded and have agreed not to divulge the information to anyone else. In such cases, the information is *confidential*. Part of our explanation to a potential research participant must include a clear statement of what information will be shared with whom.

All this seems reasonable in theory, but ethical obligations are often difficult to fulfill in practice. There are times when it is very difficult to remove coercive influences because these influences are inherent in the situation. A woman awaiting an abortion may agree to provide private information about herself and her partner because she believes that, if she does not, she will be denied the abortion. It is of no use to tell her that this is not true: She feels she is not in a position to take any chances.

There are captive populations of people in prisons, schools, or institutions who may agree out of sheer boredom to take part in a research study. Or, they may participate in return for certain privileges, or because they fear some penalty or reprisal. There may be people who agree because they are pressured into it by family members, or they want to please the social worker, or they need some service or payment that they believe depends on their cooperation. Often, situations like this cannot be changed, but at least we can be aware of them and try to deal with them in an ethical manner.

A written consent form should be only part of the process of informing research participants of their roles in the study and their rights as volunteers. It should give participants a basic description of the purpose of the study, the study's procedures, and their rights as voluntary participants. All information should be provided in plain and simple language, without jargon.

A consent form should be no longer than two pages of single-spaced copy, and it should be given to all research participants. Survey questionnaires may have a simple introductory letter containing the required information, with the written statement that the completion of the questionnaire is the person's agreement to participate. In telephone surveys, the information will need to be given

[AGENCY LETTERHEAD]

Ms. Blackburn, MSW
Intake Worker II
City Social Services
Dallas, Texas 75712

Dear Ms. Blackburn:

As discussed on the phone, burnout among child protection workers is an issue of concern not only to child protection workers like yourself but to management alike. Research Services is asking you to voluntarily participate in our study. We will need this signed informed consent form before our interview can begin. We are deeply appreciative of your willingness to voluntarily participate in the department's research project.

Our interview will be held in your office and should last no more than one hour. Our objective is to elicit your views on the nature of the stresses (if any) that you face on a day-to-day basis. We may be discussing politically sensitive issues from time to time, and you have our assurance that we will maintain absolute confidentiality with respect to views expressed by you.

We will be asking you to complete a standardized measuring instrument that assesses a worker's degree of burnout before our interview begins. This task should take no more than ten minutes. All research materials will be kept in a locked file, and the identity of all workers interviewed for this study will be safeguarded by assigning each a number, so that names do not appear on any written materials.

With respect to any research or academic publications resulting from this study, specific views and/or opinions will not be ascribed either to you or to your organization without your prior written consent.

Your signature below indicates that you have understood to your satisfaction the information regarding your participation in our research project. Should you decide not to participate for whatever reason, or should you wish to withdraw at a later date, this will in no way affect your position in the agency. If you have any further questions about our study, please contact Research Services and we will address them as quickly as possible.

Sincerely,

Beulah Wright, MSW
Director, Research Services

YES: I AM WILLING TO PARTICIPATE IN THE RESEARCH PROJECT

Signature_____ Today's Date:_____

FIGURE 2.1   EXAMPLE OF A SIMPLE CONSENT FORM

verbally and must be standardized across all calls. A written consent form should contain the following items, recognizing that the relevancy of this information and the amount required will vary with each research project:

1. A brief description of the purpose of the research study, as well as the value of the study to the general/scientific social work community (probability and nature of direct and indirect benefits) and to the participants and/or others.
2. An explanation as to how and/or why participants were selected and a statement that participation is completely voluntary.
3. A description of experimental conditions and/or procedures. Some points that should be covered are:
   a. The frequency with which the participants will be contacted.
   b. The time commitment required by the participants.
   c. The physical effort required and/or protection from overexertion.
   d. Emotionally sensitive issues that might be exposed and/or follow-up resources that are available if required.
   e. Location of participation (e.g., need for travel/commuting).
   f. Information that will be recorded and how it will be recorded (e.g., on paper, by photographs, by videotape, by audiotape).
4. Description of the likelihood of any discomforts and inconveniences associated with participation, and of known or suspected short- and long-term risks.
5. Explanation of who will have access to the collected data and to the identity of the participants (i.e., level of anonymity or confidentiality of each person's participation and information) and how long the data will be stored.
6. Description of how the data will be made public (e.g., scholarly presentation, printed publication). An additional consent is required for publication of photographs, audiotapes, and/or videotapes.
7. Description of other projects or other people who may use the data.
8. Explanation of the participants' rights:
   a. That they may terminate or withdraw from the study at any point.
   b. That they may ask for clarification or more information throughout the study.
   c. That they may contact the appropriate administrative body if they have any questions about the conduct of the people doing the study or the study's procedures.

Designing an Ethical Study

A second necessary precaution before beginning a research study is to ensure that the study is designed in an ethical manner. One of the more useful research designs, presented in Chapter 11, involves separating participants into control and experimental groups, and providing a treatment to the experimental group but not to the control group. The essential dilemma here is whether or not it is ethical to withhold a treatment, assumed to be beneficial, from participants in the control group. Even if control group participants are on a waiting list and will receive the treatment at a later date, is it right to delay service in order to conduct the study?

Proponents of this research design argue that people on a waiting list will not receive treatment any faster whether they are involved in the research study or not. Furthermore, it is only *assumed* that the treatment is beneficial; if its effects were known for sure, there would be no need to do the study. Surely, we have an ethical responsibility to test such assumptions through research studies before we continue with treatments that may be ineffective or even harmful.

The same kind of controversy arises around a research design in which clients are randomly assigned to two different groups whereby each group receives a different treatment intervention. Proponents of this research design argue that no one is sure which treatment is better—that is what the research study is trying to discover—and so it is absurd to assert that a client in one group is being harmed by being denied the treatment offered to the other group.

Social workers, however, tend to have their own ideas about which treatment is better. Ms. Gomez's worker may believe that she will derive more benefit from behavioral than from existential therapy, for example, and that it will be harmful to her if random assignment happens to put her in the existential group.

Controversy also exists around the ethics of deception when the study's results will not be valid without the deception. We may wish to study the prevalence of abuse and neglect of adolescents who are psychiatrically challenged and live in residential institutions, for example. Staff in institutions are unlikely to abuse or neglect residents while being directly watched, but a person who poses as a new staff member may be able to document mistreatment (if any). Some of us may consider that such a deception is justified in order to protect the adolescents. Others may argue that it is unethical to spy on people, no matter how noble the cause. Consider the ethical implications of Stanley Milgram's 1963 study, presented in Box 2.1.

The study cited in Box 2.1 may be judged to be unethical for a number of reasons, but Milgram did not consider it unethical or he would not have performed it. Ethics, like politics, hinges on points of view, values, ideologies, cultural beliefs, and perspectives. People disagree about the political aspects of research studies just as they do about ethics.

Informing Others About Findings

A third important ethical consideration in a research study is the manner in which the findings are reported. It may be tempting, for example, to give great weight to positive findings while playing down or ignoring altogether negative

BOX 2.1

OBSERVING HUMAN OBEDIENCE

One of the more unsettling cliches to come out of World War II was the German soldier's common excuse for atrocities: "I was only following orders." From the point of view that gave rise to this comment, any behavior—no matter how reprehensible—could be justified if someone else could be assigned responsibility for it. If a superior officer ordered a soldier to kill a baby, the fact of the *order* was said to exempt the soldier from personal responsibility for the action.

Although the military tribunals that tried the war crime cases did not accept the excuse, social scientists and others have recognized the extent to which this point of view pervades social life. Very often people seem willing to do things they know would be considered wrong by others, *if* they can cite some higher authority as ordering them to do it. Such was the pattern of justification in the My Lai tragedy of Vietnam, and it appears less dramatically in day-to-day civilian life. Few would disagree that this reliance on authority exists, yet Stanley Milgram's study (1963, 1974) of the topic provoked considerable controversy.

To observe people's willingness to harm others when following orders, Milgram brought 40 adult men—from many different walks of life—into a laboratory setting designed to create the phenomenon under study. If you had been a subject in the experiment, you would have had something like the following experience.

You would have been informed that you and another subject were about to participate in a learning experiment. Through a draw of lots, you would have been assigned the job of "teacher" and your fellow subject the job of "pupil." He would have then been led into another room, strapped into a chair, and had an electrode attached to his wrist. As the teacher, you would have been seated in front of an impressive electrical control panel covered with dials, gauges, and switches. You would have noticed that each switch had a label giving a different number of volts, ranging from 15 to 315. The switches would have had other labels, too, some with the ominous phrases "Extreme-Intensity Shock," "Danger—Severe Shock," and "XXX."

The experiment would run like this. You would read a list of word pairs to the learner and then test his ability to match them up. Since you couldn't see him, a light on your control panel would indicate his answer. Whenever the learner made a mistake, you would be instructed by the experimenter to throw one of the switches—beginning with the mildest—and administer a shock to your pupil. Through an open door between the two rooms, you'd hear your pupil's response to the shock. Then you'd read another list of word pairs and test him again.

As the experiment progressed, you'd be administering ever more intense shocks, until your pupil was screaming for mercy and begging for the experiment to end. You'd be instructed to administer the next shock anyway. After a while, your pupil would begin kicking the wall between the two rooms and screaming. You'd be told to give the next shock. Finally, you'd read a list and ask for the pupil's answer—and there would be no reply whatever, only silence from the other room. The experimenter would inform you that no answer was considered an error and instruct you to administer the next higher shock. This would continue up to the "XXX" shock at the end of the series.

What do you suppose you would have done when the pupil first began screaming? Or when he became totally silent and gave no indication of life? You'd refuse to continue giving shocks, right? Of the first 40 adult men Milgram tested, nobody refused to administer the shocks until the pupil began kicking the wall between the two rooms. Of the 40, 5 did so then. Two-thirds of the subjects, 26 of the 40, continued doing as they were told through the entire series—up to and including the administration of the highest shock.

As you've probably guessed the shocks were phoney, and the "pupil" was another experimenter. Only the "teacher" was a real subject in the experiment. You wouldn't have been hurting another person, even though you would have been led to think you were. The experiment was designed to test your *willingness* to follow orders, to the point of presumably killing someone.

Milgram's experiments have been criticized both methodologically and ethically. On the ethical side, critics particularly cited the effects of the experiment on the subjects. Many seem to have personally experienced about as much pain as they thought they were administering to someone else. They pleaded with the experimenter to let them stop giving the shocks. They became extremely upset and nervous. Some had uncontrollable seizures.

How do you feel about this research study? Do you think the topic was important enough to justify such measures? Can you think of other ways in which the researcher might have examined obedience?

---

or disappointing findings. There is no doubt that positive findings tend to be more enthusiastically received, often by journal editors who should know better; but it is obviously just as important to know that two things are not related as to know that they are. Consider the ethical implications of William Epstein's study contained in Box 2.2.

All studies have limitations, because practical considerations make it difficult to use the costly and complex research designs that yield the most certain results. Since studies with more limitations yield less trustworthy findings, it is important to be honest about our study's limitations and for other social workers to be able to understand what the limitations imply.

Finally, there are issues concerned with giving proper credit to colleagues and ensuring that results are shared in an appropriate manner. With the exception of single-case designs, presented in Chapters 12 and 23, where one social worker may do all the work, research studies are normally conducted by teams. The principal person, whose name is usually listed first on the report, must be sure that all team members are given recognition and all research participants are apprised of the results.

Sometimes, the sharing of results will be a delicate matter. Staff may be reluctant to hear that the program is less effective than they thought. It will also

---

BOX 2.2

SOCIAL WORKER SUBMITS BOGUS ARTICLE TO TEST JOURNAL BIAS

This illustration of an ethical controversy is the first well-publicized ethical controversy involving a social worker's research. Several articles reported it in national news media, including two stories on it in the *New York Times* (September 27, 1988, pp. 21, 25 and April 4, 1989, p. 21) and one in the *Chronicle of Higher Education* (November 2, 1988, p. A7). The information for this illustration was drawn primarily from those three news articles.

The social worker, William Epstein, hypothesized that journal editors were biased in favor of publishing research articles whose findings confirmed the effectiveness of evaluated social work interventions and biased against publishing research articles whose findings failed to support the effectiveness of tested interventions. To test his hypothesis, Epstein fabricated a fictitious study that pretended to evaluate the effectiveness of a social work intervention designed to alleviate the symptoms of asthmatic children. (Asthma is often thought to be a psychosomatic illness.)

Epstein concocted two versions of the bogus study. In one version, he fabricated findings that supported the effectiveness of the intervention; in the other version, he fabricated data that found the intervention to be ineffective.

Epstein submitted the fictitious article to 146 journals, including 33 social work journals and 113 journals in allied fields. Half of the journals received the version supporting the effectiveness of the intervention, and half received the other version. Epstein did not enter his own name as author of his fabricated article; instead, he used a pair of fictitious names.

In his real study, Epstein interpreted his findings as providing some support for his hypothesis that journal editors were biased in favor of publishing the version of the bogus article with positive findings and against publishing the version with negative findings. Among the social work journals, for example, 8 accepted the positive version and only 4 accepted the negative version. Nine journals rejected the positive version, and 12 rejected the negative version. Among the journals in allied fields, 53 percent accepted the positive version, compared to only 14 percent that accepted the negative version. A statistical analysis indicated that the degree of support these data provided for Epstein's hypothesis was "tentative" and not statistically significant.

After being notified of the acceptance or rejection of his fictitious article, Epstein informed each journal of the real nature of his study. Later, he submitted a true article, under his own name, reporting his real study, to the *Social Service Review*, a prestigious social work journal. That journal rejected publication of his real study, and its editor, John Schuerman, led a small group of editors who filed a formal complaint against Epstein with the National Association of Social Workers. The complaint charged Epstein with unethical conduct on two counts: (1) deceiving the journal editors who reviewed the bogus article, and (2) failing to obtain their informed consent to participate voluntarily in the study. Schuerman, a social work professor at the University of Chicago and an author of some highly regarded research articles, recognized that sometimes the benefits of a study may warrant deceiving subjects and not obtaining their informed consent to participate. But he argued that in Epstein's (reai) study, the benefits did not outweigh the time and money costs associated with many editors and reviewers who had to read and critique the bogus article and staff members who had to process it.

When an article is submitted for publication in a professional social work journal, it is usually assigned to several volunteer reviewers, usually social work faculty members who are not reimbursed for their review work. The reviewers do not know who the author is, so that the review will be fair and unbiased. Each reviewer is expected to read each article carefully, perhaps two or three times, recommend to the journal editor whether the article should be published, and develop specific suggestions to the author for improving the article.

The journal editor, too, is usually a faculty member volunteering his or her own time as part of one's professional duties as an academician. Schuerman noted that in addition to the time and money costs mentioned, there is an emotional cost: "the chagrin and embarrassment of those editors who accepted the [bogus] article" (*New York Times*, September 27, 1988, p. 25).

Epstein countered that journal editors are not the ones to judge whether the benefits of his (real) study justified its costs. In his view, the editors are predisposed to value their own costs very dearly and unlikely to judge any study that would deceive them as being worth those costs. Epstein argued that the journals are public entities with public responsibilities, and that testing whether they are biased in deciding what to publish warrants both the deception and lack of informed consent to participate that were necessary to test for that bias.

One might argue that if journal editors and reviewers are biased against publishing studies that fail to confirm the effectiveness of tested interventions, then the field may not learn that certain worthless interventions in vogue are not helping clients. Moreover, if several studies disagree about the effectiveness of an intervention, and only those confirming its effectiveness get published, then an imbalanced and selective set of replications conceivably might be disseminated to the field, misleading the field into believing that an intervention is yielding consistently favorable outcomes when in fact it is not. This could hinder the efforts of social workers to provide the most effective services to their clients, and therefore ultimately reduce the degree to which we enhance the well-being of clients.

One could argue that Epstein's study could have been done ethically if he had forewarned editors that they might be receiving a bogus paper within a year and obtained their consent to participate in the study without knowing the specifics of the paper. An opposing viewpoint is that such a warning might affect the phenomenon being studied, tipping off the reviewers in a manner that predisposes them to be on guard not to reveal a real bias that actually does influence their publication decisions.

Some scholars who have expressed views somewhat in sympathy with those of Epstein have argued that journal editors and reviewers exert great influence on our scientific and professional knowledge base and therefore their policies and procedures should be investigated. Schuerman, who filed the charges against Epstein, agreed with this view, but argued that Epstein's study was not an ethical way to conduct such an investigation.

In an editorial in the March 1989 issue of the *Social Service Review*,

Schuerman elaborated his position. He noted that journals have low budgets and small staffs and depend heavily on volunteer reviewers "who see their efforts as a professional responsibility" and receive few personal or professional benefits for their work (p. 3). He also portrayed Epstein's research as "badly conducted," citing several design flaws that he deemed to be so serious that they render the anticipated benefits of the Epstein study as minimal, and not worth its aforementioned costs. Schuerman also cited Epstein as admitting to serious statistical limitations in his study and to characterizing his research as only exploratory. "It is at this point that issues of research design and research ethics come together," Schuerman argued (p. 3). In other words, Schuerman's point is that the methodological quality of a study's research design can bear on its justification for violating ethical principles. If the study is so poorly designed that its findings have little value, then it becomes more difficult to justify the ethical violations of the study on the grounds that its findings are so beneficial.

The initial ruling of the ethics board of the National Association of Social workers was that Epstein had indeed violated research rules associated with deception and failure to get informed consent. It could have invoked serious sanctions against Epstein, including permanent revocation of his membership in the professional association and referral of the case to a state licensing board for additional sanctions. But Epstein was permitted to appeal the decision before any disciplinary action was taken. His appeal was upheld by the executive committee of the Association, which concluded that his research did not violate its ethical rules. The committee exonerated Epstein, ruling that the case was a "disagreement about proper research methodology," not a breach of ethics. It did not publicize additional details of its rationale for upholding Epstein's appeal and reversing the initial ruling. Epstein speculated that the reversal may have been influenced by the publicity the case received in the press.

If Epstein's speculation is valid, one might wonder whether the reversal was prompted by the executive committee's sincere judgment that the research really did not violate ethical rules or by expediency considerations, perhaps connected to concerns regarding potential future publicity or other costs. What do *you* think? What ideas do you have about the two rulings and about the ethical justification for Epstein's study? Which ruling do you agree with? Do you agree with Schuerman's contention that methodological flaws in the research design can bear on research ethics? Is it possible to agree with Schuerman on that issue and still agree with the executive committee that this case was a disagreement about methodology and not a breach of ethics? If, just for the sake of discussion, you assume that Epstein's study had very serious design flaws that prevented the possibility of obtaining conclusive findings, how would that assumption affect your position on the ethical justification for Epstein's study?

be difficult, and often inadvisable, for us to share with research participants results that show them in an unfavorable light. It may be honest to tell Mr. Yen, for example, that he scored high on an anxiety scale of some kind, but it may also be extremely damaging to him. Practitioners wrestle every day with the problems of whom to tell, as well as how, when, and how much. The same difficulties arise in social work research.

To summarize, the National Association of Social Workers (1980) has published a code of ethics in which scholarship and research are addressed in six ethical guidelines. These guidelines are presented in Figure 2.2.

Political and Social Considerations

The last factor that affects social work research is political and social considerations. Ethics and politics are interrelated, but a useful distinction exists in that ethics has to do with the methods employed in the research study, whereas politics is concerned with the practical costs and uses of the study's findings.

Consider, for example, the area of race relations. Most social researchers in the 1960s supported the cause of African American equality in America. In 1969, Arthur Jensen, a Harvard psychologist, examined data on racial differences in IQ test results and concluded that genetic differences between African Americans and Caucasians accounted for the lower IQ scores of African Americans. Jensen was labeled a racist, and such was the furor surrounding his study that other

---

GUIDELINES FOR SOCIAL WORK RESEARCH

E. SCHOLARSHIP AND RESEARCH. The social worker engaged in study and research should be guided by the conventions of scholarly inquiry.

1. The social worker engaged in research should consider carefully its possible consequences for human beings.
2. The social worker engaged in research should ascertain that the consent of participants is voluntary and informed, without any implied deprivation or penalty for refusal to participate, and with due regard for participants' privacy and dignity.
3. The social worker engaged in research should protect participants from unwarranted physical or mental discomfort, distress, harm, danger, or deprivation.
4. The social worker who engages in the evaluation of services or cases should discuss them only for professional purposes and only with persons directly and professionally concerned with them.
5. Information obtained about participants in research should be treated as confidential.
6. The social worker should take credit only for work actually done in connection with scholarly and research endeavors and should credit contributions made by others.

FIGURE 2.2   SCHOLARSHIP AND RESEARCH GUIDELINES

BOX 2.3

BIAS AND INSENSITIVITY REGARDING GENDER AND CULTURE

In this book you will encounter examples of how gender and cultural bias and insensitivity can hinder the methodological quality of a study and therefore the validity of its findings. Much has been written about these problems in recent years, and some have suggested that when researchers conduct studies in a sexist manner or in a culturally insensitive manner, they are not only committing methodological errors, but they are also going awry ethically.

The question of ethics arises because some studies are perceived to perpetuate harm to women and minorities. Feminist and minority scholars have suggested a number of ways that such harm can be done. Interviewers who are culturally insensitive can offend minority respondents. If they conduct their studies in culturally insensitive ways, their findings may yield implications for action that ignore the needs and realities of minorities, may incorrectly (and perhaps stereotypically) portray minorities, or may inappropriately generalize in an unhelpful way. By the same token, studies with gender bias or insensitivity may be seen as perpetuating a male-dominated world or failing to consider the potentially different implications for men and women in one's research.

Various authors have recommended ways to try to avoid cultural and gender bias and insensitivity in one's research. We will cover some of these recommendations in greater depth in later chapters on methodology, but we will mention them here as well, in light of their potential ethical relevance. Among the more commonly recommended guidelines regarding research on minorities are the following:

- Spend some time immersing yourself directly in the culture of the minority group(s) that will be included in your study (for example, using participant observation methods described in Chapter 15) before finalizing your research design.
- Engage minority scholars and community representatives in the formulation of the research problem and in all the stages of the research to ensure that the research is responsive to the needs and perspectives of minorities.
- Involve representatives of minority groups who will be studied in the development of the research design and measurement instruments.
- Do not automatically assume that instruments successfully used in prior studies of whites can yield valid information when applied to minorities.
- Use culturally sensitive language in your measures, perhaps including a non-English translation.
- Use in-depth pretesting of your measures to correct problematic language and flaws in translation.
- Use bilingual interviewers when necessary.
- Be attuned to the potential need to use minority interviewers instead of non-minorities to interview minority respondents.
- In analyzing your data, look for ways in which the findings may differ among different categories of ethnicity.
- Avoid an unwarranted focus exclusively on the deficits of minorities; perhaps focus primarily on their strengths.

Margrit Eichler (1988) recommends the following feminist guidelines to avoid gender bias and insensitivity in one's research:

- If a study is done on only one sex, make that clear in the title and the narrative and do not generalize the finding to the other sex.
- Do not use sexist language or concepts (i.e., males referred to as head of household, while females referred to as spouses).
- Do not use a double standard in framing the research question (such as looking at the work-parenthood conflict for mothers but not for fathers).
- Do not overemphasize male-dominated activities in research instruments (such as by assessing social functioning primarily in terms of career activities and neglecting activities in homemaking and child rearing).
- In analyzing your data, look for ways in which the findings may differ for men and women.
- Do not assume that measurement instruments that have been used successfully with males are automatically valid for women.
- Be sure to report the proportion of males and females in your study sample.

people were reluctant to pursue any line of inquiry involving comparisons between Caucasians and African Americans.

Consequently, a needed investigation into the higher rate of mortality seen in African-American women with breast cancer as compared to similarly afflicted Caucasian women was not conducted. The study may have revealed racial differences in genetic predispositions to breast tumors, and the National Cancer Institute, at that time, was understandably reluctant to use the word "genetic" in connection with African Americans. It is not infrequently the case that sensitivity about vulnerable populations leads to avoidance of research studies that might benefit those groups. Consider Box 2.3, which presents a useful discussion on bias and insensitivity regarding gender and culture.

Politics plays an important role not only in what research studies are funded or conducted but in what findings are published. Contrary opinions or unpopular opinions are no longer punished, as they were in Galileo's day, by the Inquisitional Tribunal or the rack, but they are still punished. Punishment may be delivered in the form of articles and books that are never published, invitations to present research papers that are never offered, academic appointments that are never given—and research proposals that are never funded.

A research study can be an extremely expensive endeavor. If a funding body cannot be found to support the research proposal, the study may never be conducted. Funding bodies tend either to be governments or to be influenced by government policies; and a person doing a research study is as interested as anyone else in money, recognition, and professional advancement. It is therefore often the case that funded studies follow directions consistent with the prevailing political climate.

Studies under one government may inquire into ways of improving social services and better designs for public housing. Under another government, attention may shift to the efficiency of existing programs, as measured through program evaluations.

It is important to remember, though, that not all research studies are expensive and many can be conducted without the aid of government money. No extra funding is needed to integrate evaluation into the normal routine of clinical practice. Program evaluations do not cost large amounts of money when conducted by program staff themselves.

In sum, social work research projects are affected not only by the personal biases of the person conducting the study, but also by prevailing beliefs on such sensitive issues as race, gender, poverty, disability, sexual orientation, violence, and so forth. Government positions both shape and are shaped by these beliefs, leading to support of some research directions but not of others.

Legitimate inquiry is sometimes restricted by fear that data uncovered on one of these sensitive issues will be misinterpreted or misused, thereby bringing harm to vulnerable client groups.

SUMMARY

In this text we deal with widely accepted standardized procedures used to conduct social work research studies. Underlying these procedures, however, are the research contexts in which our studies must take place. Some of these factors are the profession, the social work agency, the researcher, the practitioners, professional ethics, and political and social factors.

From an ethical perspective, before beginning any research study, there are three precautionary measures that must be taken: obtaining the participant's informed written consent, designing the study in an ethical manner, and ensuring that others will be properly told about the findings.

This chapter presented the basic contexts that underlie social work research studies and the social and political contexts in which they are conducted. Now that we know the six factors that shape all research studies, we will turn our attention to how we go about selecting *what* to study—the topic of Chapter 3.

REFERENCES AND FURTHER READINGS

AMERICAN PSYCHOLOGICAL ASSOCIATION. (1973). *Ethical principles in the conduct of research with human participants.* Washington, DC: Author.

ANASTAS, J.W., & MACDONALD, M.L. (1994). *Research design for social work and the human services* (pp. 233-257). New York: Lexington Books.

BABBIE, E.R. (1995). *The practice of social research* (7th ed., pp. 447-466). Belmont, CA: Wadsworth.

BISNO, H., & BOROWSKI, A. (1985). The social and psychological contexts of research. In R.M. Grinnell, Jr. (Ed.), *Social work research and evaluation* (2nd ed., pp. 83-100). Itasca, IL: F.E. Peacock.

BOROWSKI, A. (1988). Social dimensions of research. In R.M. Grinnell, Jr. (Ed.), *Social work research and evaluation* (3rd ed., pp. 42-64). Itasca, IL: F.E. Peacock.

CHRONICLE OF HIGHER EDUCATION: "Scholar who submitted bogus article to journals may be disciplined," November 2, 1988, pp. A1, A7.

EICHLER, M. (1988). *Nonsexist research methods.* Boston, MA: Allen & Unwin.

FRANKFORT-NACHMIAS, C., & NACHMIAS, D. (1992). *Research methods in the social sciences* (4th ed., pp. 73-94). New York: St. Martin's Press.

GABOR, P.A., & GRINNELL, R.M., JR. (1994). *Evaluation and quality improvement in the human services* (pp. 301-316). Needham Heights, MA: Allyn & Bacon.

GRINNELL, R.M., JR., & WILLIAMS, M. (1990). *Research in social work: A primer* (pp. 2-26). Itasca, IL: F.E. Peacock.

JUDD, C.M., SMITH, E.R., & KIDDER, I.H. (1991). *Research methods in social relations* (6th ed., pp. 477-528). Fort Worth, TX: Harcourt Brace.

KRYSIK, J., HOFFART, I., & GRINNELL, R.M., JR. (1993). *Student study guide for the fourth edition of social work research and evaluation* (pp. 5-6). Itasca, IL: F.E. Peacock.

LEEDY, P.D. (1993). *Practical research: Planning and design* (3rd ed., pp. 128-131). New York: Macmillan.

MARLOW, C. (1993). *Research methods for generalist social work practice* (pp. 13-14, 40, 58-59, 94-95, 117-120). Pacific Grove, CA: Wadsworth.

MILGRAM, S. (1974). *Obedience to authority: An experimental view.* New York: Harper & Row.

MILGRAM, S. (1963). Behavioral study of obedience. *Journal of Abnormal and Applied Social Psychology, 67,* 371-378.

NATIONAL ASSOCIATION OF SOCIAL WORKERS. (1980). *National association of social workers code of ethics.* Silver Spring, MD: Author.

NEUMAN, W.L. (1994). *Social research methods* (2nd ed., pp. 427-459). Needham Heights, MA: Allyn & Bacon.

NEW YORK TIMES: "Charges dropped on bogus work," April 4, 1989, p. 21.

NEW YORK TIMES: "Test of journals is criticized as unethical," September 27, 1988, pp. 21, 25.

ROYSE, D.D. (1995). *Research methods in social work* (2nd ed., pp. 99-100, 301-317). Chicago: Nelson-Hall.

RUBIN, A., & BABBIE, E.R. (1993). *Research methods for social work* (2nd ed., pp. 56-87). Pacific Grove, CA: Wadsworth.

SCHINKE, S.P., & GILCHRIST, L.D. (1993). Ethics in research. In R.M. Grinnell, Jr. (Ed.), *Social work research and evaluation* (4th ed., pp.79-90). Itasca, IL: F.E. Peacock.

SCHUERMAN, J. (1989). Editorial. *Social Service Review, 63,* 1,3.

WEINBACH, R.W. (1985). The agency and professional contexts of research. In R.M. Grinnell, Jr. (Ed.), *Social work research and evaluation* (2nd ed., pp. 66-82). Itasca, IL: F.E. Peacock.

WEINBACH, R.W. (1988). Agency and professional contexts in research. In R.M. Grinnell, Jr. (Ed.), *Social work research and evaluation* (3rd ed., pp. 25-41). Itasca, IL: F.E. Peacock.

WEINBACH, R.W., & GRINNELL, R.M., JR. (1996). *Applying research knowledge: A workbook for social work students* (2nd ed., pp. 9-16). Needham Heights, MA: Allyn & Bacon.

WILLIAMS, M., TUTTY, L.M., & GRINNELL, R.M., JR. (1995). *Research in social work: An introduction* (2nd ed., pp. 30-46). Itasca, IL: F.E. Peacock.

PART II

PROBLEM FORMULATION AND RESEARCH APPROACHES

Leslie M. Tutty
Richard M. Grinnell, Jr.
Margaret Williams

C h a p t e r **3**

Research Problems and Questions

A FTER CONSIDERING the various "research" contexts in doing a quantitative or qualitative research study, we now discuss the factors that influence how research ideas, more commonly referred to as research problems, are selected. We then determine how general and vague research problems are converted into more specific exploratory, descriptive, or explanatory research questions. Let us begin by examining research problems more closely.

RESEARCH PROBLEMS

In social work practice, the client's problem, or at least the general problem area, is determined largely by the client (with the help of the worker). Researchers, however, have the freedom to select research problems at their leisure, and this freedom, in itself, may sometimes be a problem. It is a little like walking through a shopping mall, looking for a gift to give a friend, surrounded by tantalizing possibilities, and wondering what to buy. In general, the selection of the gift will be influenced by four main factors. It will be something that the giver likes and can afford, something the recipient will like, something that is socially acceptable (perhaps not a book on social work research), and, very probably, something that just happens to catch the giver's eye.

Selecting Research Problems

The selection of a social work research problem is influenced by the same four factors that were faced by the gift-giver. First, the problem must attract the researcher and must not be too difficult to solve, given the researcher's own capabilities and resources. Second, the problem must be important to those who will receive, consume, or facilitate the research study such as agency staff, administrators, and the professional community. Third, the problem should take into account the current social and cultural values. And, fourth, there will probably be an element of opportunity or luck.

The Researcher

Personal interest on the part of the researcher is usually the main motivating factor in the selection of a research problem. A research study may continue for a lengthy period, sometimes years; it may involve dull and seemingly endless stretches in which the work is mechanical and boring. Therefore, it is important for the initial interest to be deep and abiding, not just a passing fancy.

The interest will often arise from personal or work experience. The person doing a study may be interested in bereavement counseling because of a personal loss, or in parent-support groups because of family problems with a child. Perhaps a client's past experience in court provoked an interest in the criminal justice system, or an interest in single mothers stemmed from work with high school adolescents who were pregnant.

Interest on the part of the researcher forms the foundation of a successful study. Interest can also prejudice the study's results, however, since people tend to hold the firmest opinions on topics they feel most strongly about. A research study must therefore be designed in such a way that our biases have the least possible chance of influencing our study's results.

The selection of the research problem will be influenced not only by our personal interests but also by our particular abilities. A person who has a great deal of skill and experience in interviewing children, for example, may choose a problem area in which data must be collected through interviews with children. The problem selected may be to discover if there is a relationship between the success of foster care placements and foster children's attitudes toward their biological parents. Some of the data on both "success" and "attitudes" will need to be collected through interviews with children.

The selection of the problem will also depend on our personal resources. If there is no money for travel, for example, the problem cannot be one that involves interviewing children across the country. Money for travel might be acquired through a research grant, but then we must have the skills and contacts necessary to acquire the grant. Similarly, we will need to have the professional status required to gain permission to interview the children. It is not only the desire to solve a problem that is important: Personal skills, professional status, and access to resources also play a part.

Professional and Agency Considerations

Sometimes, our own interest is directed or shaped by outside sources. Career aspirations may necessitate some research experience, even for people whose talents and interests lie in other areas. A student in a graduate program may be offered a position as a research assistant that involves various research tasks. Similarly, staff members working in an agency may be asked to take on a research study for their organization. Perhaps the board of directors may decide that a program evaluation should be undertaken and a senior staff member will be asked to oversee the task. Or a problem may arise within the agency that a particular departmental supervisor is expected to resolve.

There may be a concern, for example, that child protection staff are spending too much time investigating child abuse allegations that turn out to be unfounded. The director may want to know if this is so and, if it is so, why. Perhaps there really has been an increase in the number of unfounded child abuse complaints, possibly due to increased pressure on local teachers to report the slightest suspicion of child abuse. Perhaps less experienced staff are failing to verify actual abuse, or new regulations have led to confusion about how "unfounded" is defined.

Research studies related to agencies are frequently required of senior staff, even those who have little interest in research and only rudimentary skills in research methods. Often line-level workers will be involved, sometimes gathering data as directed and sometimes participating more fully in the development of problem-solving strategies. Occasionally, line-level workers will themselves identify problems and initiate smaller studies, either alone or together with other staff. It is, therefore, very important that we all know at least enough about research methods to be able to competently tackle problems arising within the normal course of day-to-day agency operations.

Not only are research endeavors useful in terms of solving problems: They can improve the agency's image in the eyes of its funders and community groups. The image-building aspect is particularly important if the agency serves a client group that has caught the public's attention. Public attention, for example, may focus on the mentally delayed following a decision to integrate these children into the "regular" school system. Concern about the decision will be averted more readily if research results can show that integration is beneficial to these children, has no adverse effect upon the "regular" school population, and serves, in addition, to increase public acceptance of these children in general.

The danger here is that the decision to integrate may precede the research studies necessary to determine the advantages and limitations of the integration. If this is the case, there will inevitably be pressure upon researchers, first to select integration as a topic for study and, second, to produce the "right" results: that is, results that support a decision already made. Even the least biased researcher using the best possible research design will find it difficult to maintain total objectivity under such conditions.

Nevertheless, it is not uncommon for policy decisions to be made without the support of objective data, or evidence, often because the relevant data are not available when the decision has to be made. Instead, decisions may be based upon such factors as political expediency, personal beliefs, and the social and cultural values accepted at the time.

Applied and Pure Research Studies   As we saw in Chapter 1, there is no doubt that research results can be immediately useful to agencies in terms of satisfying funding bodies, promoting good public relations, or improving the agency's own service delivery. Research that is useful in this way is known as *applied research*. Often, the problem selected by the applied researcher is concerned with evaluating the effectiveness or efficiency of agency practice. How well is the agency serving its clients? How well is it meeting the needs of the local community? Does it wastefully duplicate services provided by some other local social service agency? These kinds of applied research questions are the province of *program evaluation*.

We can use applied research techniques to evaluate the effectiveness of a particular intervention with a particular type of client or client system. Is one intervention more effective than another in solving a particular social problem? Such questions are addressed through *single-case designs*, which are discussed in Chapters 11 and 23.

Applied research studies involve problems that need to be solved in order to aid decision making at line levels, managerial levels, or policy levels. Such studies are designed to directly benefit a specific client system, whether it be a national organization, a single agency, or an individual worker helping a client. Some research studies, however, are not intended to be immediately and practically useful. Instead, their purpose is to increase theoretical knowledge in the belief that such knowledge will provide indirect benefit to all agencies and clients later on. These studies are known as *pure research studies* and involve problems that are unrelated to the immediate needs of the agencies in which the studies are conducted.

A pure research problem, for example, might concern the relationship between divorce and loneliness, or between family cohesion and delinquency. A study of delinquent youths in less and more cohesive families will require cooperation from one or several agencies in order to locate the families and collect the data. Since the study will not directly benefit the agency, the staff will inevitably have to give time to the project, and some reluctance on the part of the agency is to be expected.

Cooperation will likely be given only if the research study is designed to use the least possible amount of the agency's resources, and to intrude only minimally on the agency's normal operations and its current or former clients. The research problem will have to be selected with these limitations in mind, and perhaps its scope will have to be reduced to meet the agency's requirements.

In summary, applied research directly benefits agencies, administrators, social workers, and clients in that it facilitates immediate decision making. Conversely, the purpose of pure research is to increase knowledge for the indirect benefit of social workers and clients at a later time.

Personal, Social, and Cultural Values

The previous chapter indicated the importance of how current value systems shape research studies. Values also shape how research problems are selected. Research studies in sensitive areas may not be undertaken and, even if they are undertaken, their results may not be used. For example, as president of the United States, Richard Nixon appointed a national commission to inquire into the consequences of pornography. One of the results of the commission was that no connection could be found between exposure to pornography and an increased likelihood of committing sex crimes. Since this finding ran contrary to the prevalent belief that viewing pornography leads to sex crimes, the research results were disregarded.

The probability that results will be used is usually taken into account when selecting a research problem. It will not be useful to explore the possible effectiveness of sex education in the local school, for example, if members of the school board believe that sex education is sinful. On the other hand, we may not be interested in the reactions of the board. We may prefer to adopt a pure research perspective, aiming to increase knowledge about the consequences of sex education in general, without reference to the needs of any particular school.

Social value systems are inextricably linked to the issue of social change. Few of us would be comfortable investigating poverty without some hope that the results from our studies would be used to alleviate the conditions of the poor. Similarly, most researchers who study women's issues would like their studies to contribute to the improved status of women. The danger here is that the search for truth may be compromised by the desire to effect political reform.

A researcher with a feminist orientation, for example, may not wish to publish a finding suggesting that some women invite sexual harassment, because such a finding may hinder political action or offend feminist colleagues. The result of attention to social-change issues may thus be that unpalatable results are deliberately not found, or are not published if they are found: In other words, that truth is compromised.

From the opposite perspective, of course, the result of attention to truth may be that legitimate social-change goals remain unmet. It is a matter for the individual researcher to decide: whether a particular research study should be *about* the problem or *for* the problem; *about* poverty or *for* the poor; *about* women or *for* women. The nature of the research problem selected will be greatly influenced by this decision.

Opportunity or Luck

Very often, the final decision about which research problem will be studied depends on chance. We may encounter an old acquaintance who suggests cooperating in a certain study; an agency serving a particular client group may offer facilities; data about a particular problem may be found to be available; a research proposal made long ago may suddenly be accepted; or funding may be offered for a research study into a specific problem area. None of these eventualities alone will determine the problem to be studied, but there is no doubt that the balance is often tipped by an unforeseen opportunity, an element of luck. Consider the origins of research ideas presented in Boxes 3.1 and 3.2.

BOX 3.1

ON THE ORIGINS OF RESEARCH IDEAS

In this chapter, we outline some of the sources of ideas for social work research. As discussed, some research studies are derived from existing theory. This is especially true of the hypothesis-testing research that characterizes experiments to be discussed in Chapters 4 and 11. More often than not, however, we get our research ideas from everyday observations and experiences.

According to John Darley, his and Bibb Latane's research study (1968) on bystander interventions stemmed from a widely publicized incident in New York City. A young woman named Kitty Genovese was brutally murdered while thirty-eight of her neighbors watched from their windows—without so much as calling the police—until her assailant had departed. Shocked by this incident, Darley and Latane:

> met over dinner and began to analyze the bystanders' reactions. Because we were social psychologists, we thought not about how people are different nor about the personality flaws of the "apathetic" individuals who failed to act that night, but rather about how people are the same and how anyone in that situation might react as did these people. By the time we finished our dinner, we formulated several factors that together could lead to the surprising result: no one helping. Then we set about conducting experiments that isolated each factor and demonstrated its importance in an emergency situation. (Reported in Myers, 1983:394)

BOX 3.2

MORE ON THE ORIGINS OF RESEARCH IDEAS

Robert Cialdini (1980:27-28), whose research involves social influence processes, tells how a personal experience led him to investigate a highly effective fund-raising tactic.

> ... I answered the door early one evening to find a young woman who was canvassing my neighborhood for the United Way. She identified herself and asked if I would give a monetary donation. It so happened that my home university has an active United Way organization and I had given in-house a few days earlier. It was also the end of the month and my finances were low. Besides, if I gave to all the solicitors for charity who came to my door, I would quickly require such service for myself. As she spoke, I had already decided against a donation and was preparing my reply to incorporate the above reasons. Then it happened. After asking for a contribution, she added five magic words. I know they were *the* magic words because my negative reply to the donation request itself literally caught in my throat when I heard them. "Even a penny will help" she said. And with that, she demolished my anticipated response. All the excuses I had prepared for failing to comply were based on financial considerations. They stated that I could not afford to give to her now or to her, too. But she said, "Even a penny will help" and rendered each of them impotent. How could I claim an inability to help when she claimed that "even a penny" was a legitimate form of aid? I had been neatly finessed into compliance. And there was another interesting feature of our exchange as well. When I stopped coughing (I really had choked on my attempted rejection), I gave her *not* the penny she mentioned but the amount I usually allot to charity solicitors. At that, she thanked me, smiled innocently, and moved on.

Together with his then-graduate student Dave Schroeder, Cialdini analyzed the situation and concluded that two sources of social influence had been activated by the addendum "Even a penny will help." First, it removed any excuses for not offering at least some aid. Second, it made it more difficult to maintain one's altruistic self-image without contributing. Cialdini and Schroeder then went out to find a naturalistic fund-raising context for testing their ideas.

Criteria for Research Problems

No final decision can be made about the problem to be studied until we have determined that the prospective problem meets four criteria. These criteria are that the research problem must be: (1) relevant, (2) researchable, (3) feasible, and (4) ethically acceptable.

All four factors interact with one another and it is extremely difficult to discuss each one in insolation. However, for the sake of simplicity, each factor is discussed separately.

Relevancy

Every conceivable research problem is relevant to someone in some context. Relevancy here will therefore be taken to mean relevant to social workers in a social work context. Since the person undertaking the study will be a social worker, the first questions to be asked with regard to relevancy are: Would persons in other disciplines be more qualified than social workers to study the problem? and, Will they study it if social workers do not?

Consider a study to explore the relationship between family stress and children dropping out of school, for example. Such a study would be of interest to educational psychologists and sociologists as well as to social workers, and might properly be undertaken by people within any of these three disciplines. One of the purposes of the study, for example, may be to assess whether hiring a social worker to combat family stress would assist a certain school board in its efforts to reduce its student dropout rate. If this is the case, it could be argued that the problem is particularly a social work problem since it is specifically relevant to us.

Naturally, of most importance is that the study be conducted, no matter by whom. Disciplines in the social sciences—social work, sociology, psychology, anthropology, political science, education, economics—overlap to such a degree that it is often difficult to distinguish *social work* research from *social* research. In general, the problem must be relevant to some aspect of social welfare: It must be important to us whether or not it is important to others as well.

Another question to be asked with regard to relevancy has to do with priorities. In an ideal world, any problem of concern to people or society would be worthy of study, but in the real word of limited resources, the relative importance of the problem has to be addressed. Some social problems have already been studied to such an extent that, while not everything is known, further studies would be difficult to justify. The effects of poverty on social functioning, for example, are widely understood, and additional data may only confirm what is already known.

"Known" of course, is a relative word in itself since nothing in science is known for certain, and all confirmatory studies are useful in that they increase the likelihood of the known being true. Nevertheless, research efforts are best focused on gaps in knowledge: what do we *not* know and, most important, how badly do we want to know it?

The relative importance of various areas of study is a sensitive topic since the majority of us would argue that our own field of endeavor is at least as important as any other, and more important than most. Probably the best way to ascertain what gaps in knowledge most need to be filled is to turn to the professional literature. Journal articles and books often indicate that more work needs to be done in such and such a specific area. When several authors agree that a knowledge gap exists, the reader can be fairly sure that it does exist and that others are interested in seeing it filled.

If there are several knowledge gaps, all of potential interest to the researcher, an additional criterion might be the practical use to which the results of the study can be put. Some pure research problems are highly abstract and, while they are of interest, have little foreseeable practical application. Other problems, of more immediate practical concern, might have a higher priority in these times of budget restraint.

Researchability

When a problem has been tentatively selected for study, the next question to ask is: Is it researchable? As previously mentioned, some problems by their very nature do not lend themselves to scientific study. One such problem is the difficulty that so absorbed medieval theologians concerning how many angels could sit on the head of a pin. Problems relating to ethical controversies, phrased in terms of "should" or "ought," are another example.

It is not possible to use the research method to determine whether abortion is "right " and should be legalized. Neither is it possible to solve the problem of whether fathers ought to have the same rights as mothers to decide to abort an unborn child. These are questions of ethics and opinion, and research studies cannot determine a "correct" answer to either.

Feasibility

If the problem can be solved using the research method (the quantitative approach or the qualitative approach), the next question is: How readily can it be solved? or How feasible is it? This is a question that relates both to available resources and to ethical concerns. Some social problems, for example, are just too large to be tackled without an army of researchers and a multimillion-dollar budget. Sexism in the workplace is a problem falling into this category, whereas the smaller problem of discriminatory hiring by employers in a particular profession might be a feasible project for study.

All research studies involve the collection of data. Sometimes data are collected from clients or people involved with clients, sometimes from client files or other agency records. Data are often very hard to obtain. Records may be incomplete; clients may disappear or refuse to be interviewed; court records may be sealed; permission may not be granted by agencies to access various files.

Sometimes, the difficulty of obtaining the necessary data can be resolved without abandoning or altering the problem. A problem concerning the effect of community action on street gangs, for example, requires data about street gangs. It may not be possible or safe to interview street gang members, but data collected through interviews with police and probation officers and community leaders may be sufficient, depending on the precise nature of the research question.

Sometimes, the difficulty of obtaining data cannot be satisfactorily resolved.

If the problem concerns the attitudes of the terminally ill toward social work counseling, for example, and permission is not granted by a hospital to interview its patients who are terminally ill, the study cannot be conducted. A different problem will have to be formulated: perhaps the attitudes of relatives of the terminally ill toward social work counseling. Be that as it may, possible difficulties associated with collecting the data must always be considered before we decide to explore a particular problem.

It is not only the data collection process that is sometimes difficult: The data must also be analyzed. Our own skills, previously mentioned as an important factor, play a large part here. If we do not have the expertise to perform the required data analysis and cannot afford to hire a consultant, the solution of the problem is not feasible.

Issues of time and cost may also mean that a study is not feasible for a particular researcher. Costs can be easily underestimated. There may be travel costs incurred in the collection of data, long-distance telephone charges, printing and copying expenses, costs for data processing and analysis, postage costs for mailing out questionnaires, and perhaps remuneration if research assistants are to be hired for interviewing or data entry. Nonresponse to questionnaires may mean multiple mailings; canceled interviews may involve additional travel costs.

In sum, a problem is researchable if it lends itself to solution by the research method (quantitative or qualitative) of obtaining knowledge. The solution of the problem is feasible if all the necessary data can be collected and analyzed by the particular researcher, given the availability of resources.

Ethical Acceptability

Ethical acceptability is a primary issue in any research study. Most universities have ethics committees to which proposed studies by faculty or students must be submitted for approval before the studies commence. Many social service agencies have similar committees, whose responsibility it is to see that ethical standards are not violated by any research study conducted within the agency.

Usually, the ethical standards in question have to do with service to clients. Client confidentiality is always a concern since many researchers request access to clients and/or client files. A second concern is that service to clients may be interrupted or compromised by research requirements. We may be understandably reluctant to have clients who are in crises bothered by people whose primary interest lies with the research study and not with our client. The completion of questionnaires takes time—time that we may well feel could be better spent in direct work with clients.

In addition, there is the ever-controversial matter of random assignment of clients to two or more groups. The ethical dilemmas associated with randomly assigning clients to control and experimental groups were discussed in Chapter 2, as were dilemmas to do with deceiving research participants. It is sufficient here to stress again the fundamental principle of social work research: Increased knowledge must never be obtained at the expense of human beings. Consider the ethical implications presented in Box 3.3.

RESEARCH QUESTIONS

The research problems previously considered covered a wide area and were intentionally vague: for example, the attitudes of people toward counseling the terminally ill, or the relationship between family stress and high school dropout rates. These general and vague problem areas cannot be studied until they have been defined more precisely. What exactly do we want to know about the terminally ill and social work counseling? Why are these data needed? What precisely is the problem? What is the question, or more precisely, what is the specific *research* question that is contained within the general problem area?

All research ideas, or research problems, must be further developed and refined into specific research questions. In general, research questions fall into three broad categories: exploration, description, and explanation. If little is known about the general problem area and we want to simply explore and gather facts, an *exploratory* study will be in order. Such a study will not provide data that can be relied upon with any certainty nor can its results be generalized to other individuals with similar experiences who were not included in the study. The purpose of exploratory studies is largely to prepare the ground for later, more intensive work.

When some knowledge has been obtained through exploratory studies, the next task may be to describe a specific aspect of the problem area in greater detail, in either words or numbers. This will entail a *descriptive* study.

After descriptive studies have provided a substantial knowledge base in the problem area, we will be in a position to ask very specific and complex questions that hopefully will explain the facts that were previously gathered. These *explanatory* studies are needed in order to confirm or reject the possible explanations that were proposed in the descriptive study.

As shown in Figure 3.1, the three types of studies—exploratory, descriptive, and explanatory—lie on a knowledge continuum.

Exploratory studies, at the left end of the continuum, begin with very little knowledge in the problem area and produce knowledge at only a low level of certainty. Descriptive studies, at the center of the continuum, begin with more knowledge and produce knowledge at a higher level of certainty. Explanatory studies, at the right end of the continuum, begin with quite a lot of knowledge and produce the most certain results.

It should be stressed that the knowledge-building continuum is just that—it is a *continuum*. Neither the level of knowledge possessed prior to the study nor the level of knowledge attained by the study can be assigned to discrete sections labeled exploratory, descriptive, and explanatory. Such a distinction is totally arbitrary. Despite the arbitrary nature of the labels, exploratory, descriptive, and

BOX 3.3

WELFARE STUDY WITHHOLDS BENEFITS FROM 800 TEXANS

The preceding front-page headline greeted readers of the Sunday, February 11, 1990, edition of the *Dallas Morning News*. On the next line they read:

> Thousands of poor people in Texas and several other states are unwitting subjects in a federal experiment that denies some government help to a portion of them to see how well they live without it.

This was pretty strong stuff, and soon the story was covered on one of the national TV networks. Let's examine it further for another illustration of research ethics:

The Texas Department of Human Services received federal money to test the effectiveness of a pilot program designed to wean people from the welfare rolls. The program was targeted to welfare recipients who found jobs or job training. *Before* the new program was implemented, these recipients received four months of free medical care and some child care after they left the welfare rolls. The new program extended these benefits to one year of Medicaid coverage and subsidized child care. The theory was that extending the duration of the benefits would encourage recipients to accept and keep entry-level jobs that were unlikely to offer immediate medical insurance or child care.

The federal agency granting the money attached an important condition. States receiving grants were required to conduct a scientifically rigorous experiment to measure the program's effectiveness in attaining its goal of weaning people from welfare. Some federal officials insisted that this requirement entailed randomly assigning some people to a control group that would be denied the new (extended) program and instead kept on the old program of only four months of benefits. The point of this was to maximize the likelihood that the recipient group (the experimental group) and the nonrecipient (control) group were equivalent in all relevant ways except for the receipt of the new program. If they were, and if the recipient group was weaned from welfare to a greater extent that the nonrecipient group, then it could be safely inferred that the new program, and not something else, caused the successful outcome. (We will examine this logic further in Chapter 11.)

If you have read many journal articles reporting on experimental studies, you are probably aware that many of them randomly assign about one-half of their subjects to the experimental group and the other half to the control group. Thus, this routine procedure denies the experimental condition to about one-half of the subjects. The Texas experiment was designed to include all eligible welfare recipients statewide, assigning 90 percent of them to the experimental group and 10 percent to the control group. Thus, only 10 percent of the subjects, which in this study amounted to 800 people, would be denied the new benefits if they found jobs. Although this seems more humane than denying benefits to 50 percent of the subjects, the newspaper account characterized the 800 people in the control group as "unlucky Texans" who seemed to be unfairly left out of a program that was extending benefits to all those who were eligible state-wide, who numbered in the many thousands. Moreover, the newspaper report noted that the 800 control subjects would be denied the new program for two years in order to provide ample time to compare outcomes between the two groups. To boot, these 800 "unlucky Texans" were not to be informed of the new program or of the experiment. They were to be told of only the normal four-month coverage.

Advocates of the experiment defended this design, arguing that the control group would not be denied benefits. They would receive routine benefits, and the new benefits would not have been available for anyone in the first place unless a small group was randomly assigned to the routine policy. In other words, the whole point of the new benefits was to test a new welfare policy, not merely to implement one. They further argued that the design was justified by the need to test for unintended negative effects of the new program, such as the possibility that some businesses might drop their child care or insurance coverage for employees, knowing that the new program was extending these benefits. That, in turn, they argued, could impel low-paid employees in those businesses to quit their jobs and go on welfare. By going on welfare and then getting new jobs, they would become eligible for the government's extended benefits, and this would make the welfare program more expensive.

Critics of the study, on the other hand, argued that it violated federal ethics standards such as voluntary participation and informed consent. Anyone in the study must be informed about it and all its consequences and must have the option to refuse to participate. One national think tank expert on ethics likened the experiment to the Tuskegee syphilis study, saying, "It's really not that different." He further asserted, "People ought not to be treated like things, even if what you get is good information."

In the aftermath of such criticism, Texas state officials decided to try to convince the federal government to rescind the control group requirement so that they could extend the new benefits to the 800 people in the control group. Instead of using a control group design, they wanted to extend benefits to everyone and find statistical procedures that would help ferret out program defects (a design that might have value, but which would be less conclusive as to what really causes what, as we will see in later chapters). They also decided to send a letter to the control group members explaining their special status.

Two days after the *Dallas Morning News* broke this story, it published a follow-up article reporting that the secretary of the U.S. Department of Health and Human Services, in response to the first news accounts, instructed his staff to cooperate with Texas welfare officials so that the project design would no longer deny the new program to the 800 control group members. Do you agree with his decision? Did the potential benefits of this experiment justify its controversial ethical practices?

It probably would not have been possible to form a control group had recipients been given the right to refuse to participate. Who would want to be denied extended free medical and child care benefits? Assuming it were possible, however, would that influence your opinion of the justification for denying them the new program? Do you agree with the expert who claimed that this study, in its original design, was not that different from the Tuskegee syphilis study? What if, instead of assigning 90 percent of the subjects to the experimental group, the study assigned only 10 percent to it? That way, the 800 assigned to the experimental group may have been deemed "lucky Texans," and the rest might not have been perceived as a small group of unlucky souls being discriminated against. In other words, perhaps there would have been fewer objections if the state had merely a small amount of funds to test out a new program on a lucky few. Do you think that would have changed the reaction? Would that influence your perception of the ethical justification for the experiment?

explanatory studies do differ considerably with respect to the way a research study is designed and the nature of the research question asked.

Exploratory Research Questions

Exploratory studies are most useful when the problem area is relatively new. In the United States during the 1970s, for example, the development of new drugs to control the symptoms of mental illness, together with new federal funding for small community-based mental health centers, resulted in a massive discharge of people from large state-based mental health institutions.

Some of us applauded this move as restoring the civil liberties of these people; others were concerned that inadequate community facilities would result in harm to them and community members alike. Social workers active in the 1970s were anxious to explore the results of the new movement, some with an eye to influencing local, state, and federal social policy. Others were interested in developing social service programs to serve these people and their families.

The general problem area here is very broad: What are the consequences of a massive discharge of people who were psychiatrically challenged and who were once institutionalized? Many widely different research questions pertaining to this situation can be asked. Where are these recently discharged people living? Alone? In halfway houses? With their families? On the streets? Are they receiving proper medication and nutrition? What are their financial situations? What stresses are they imposing on family members and the communities in which they now reside? Do neighbors ridicule or help them? How do they spend their time? What work and leisure activities are appropriate for them? How do local authorities respond to them?

These kinds of questions are exploratory and attempt to gather facts in a hitherto unmapped general problem area. No single research study can answer all of them. We must decide what specific aspect of the general research problem the study will address, always in light of the use that will be made of the data derived from the study.

For example, we may consider setting up community support groups for the families of these discharged people. In this case, a relevant research question

KNOWLEDGE-LEVEL CONTINUUM:

    Exploratory → Descriptive → Explanatory

KNOWLEDGE PRIOR TO THE STUDY:

    Very Little → More → Substantial

KNOWLEDGE RESULTING FROM THE STUDY:

    Uncertain → More Certain → Highly Certain

FIGURE 3.1   THE KNOWLEDGE-GENERATION ENTERPRISE

might be: What types of community support (if any) would most benefit families trying to care for them? Alternatively, we may try to determine their needs in order to develop various sorts of community-based social support facilities such as halfway houses. Relevant research questions here might be: What type of previously institutionalized person would benefit the most from a halfway house?

These two different, but related, questions will involve attention to different factors. In the first case, our study would focus on the needs of the families with respect to the provision of community services. In the second case, our focus would be on the discharged people in relation to the services provided by halfway houses.

In each situation, the underlying purpose of our study would be to explore the problem of a massive discharge of people who were psychiatrically challenged and were once institutionalized, by asking more specific questions related to the problem area. The broad, vague, general problem area is gradually being refined until it is small enough and specific enough to be the subject of a feasible research study.

So, for example, at an exploratory level, we might interview these previously institutionalized people in an attempt to identify meaningful themes or issues that may characterize them. These themes may raise further, more specific questions about the initial broad problem area. In response to the current question of what happens to these people after discharge, interviews with them may reveal a central theme, or issue: Because of difficulty finding housing, many return home to live with their parents. This situation then leads to emotional turmoil for some, but support for others. Having identified this trend to move home, we might then decide to pursue further inquiry focused on a descriptive question such as, "How many families are supportive to them and how many are not?"

The process of sifting a feasible research question from the broad mass of a problem area is like putting the problem through a series of successively finer sieves. Much of the larger problem will be temporarily set aside as topics for other studies. Only the small, definitive question surviving the final sieve will be addressed in the present study.

Descriptive Research Questions

The same sifting process applies to all three types of research studies. A descriptive study can describe one factor within a problem area, or it may describe the ways in which one factor is related to a second factor. Taking the previous example, we may decide to investigate not only how many of these previously institutionalized people return home to live with their families, but also how many of the families are supportive and how many are not. We could hypothesize that those families who are not supportive tend to have negative views about their offspring and to communicate these nonverbally, through exasperated sighs and angry confrontations.

Such negative reactions in response to family members diagnosed with a mental illness have been labeled "expressed emotion." We may decide to do a research study to determine which families appear supportive to see whether, in fact, they show high levels of expressed emotion. The purpose of doing a descriptive research study is to gather facts. No attempts are made to explain *why* some families are more supportive than others, or *why* some families have high expressed emotion while others do not. The *why* belongs to an explanatory study. A descriptive study only determines the *what*.

Explanatory Research Questions

Suppose a descriptive study has determined that the families who are perceived as supportive to their previously institutionalized children show low levels of expressed emotion, while those perceived as nonsupportive show high levels. An explanatory study may be undertaken to determine why this is so, or to identify appropriate interventions that might lower their expressed emotions.

If we hypothesize that high levels of expressed emotion are found when families do not know how to communicate clearly, we may wonder whether a psycho-educational group treatment intervention aimed at improving communication in families would resolve the amount of support perceived by their children.

We may also look at the problem from many different angles. We might want to know whether involving these previously institutionalized people in a supportive network of peers could improve their self-independence so that they have less need of support from their parents. Again, these different questions will involve attention to different factors. One study may be concerned with family interaction and another with peer support. The research question finally selected determines the basic concepts around which the study will be designed.

SUMMARY

The selection of a research problem is influenced by four main factors: the researcher's personal history, professional and agency considerations, social and cultural values, and opportunity (or luck). A particular problem area is considered to be appropriate for a social work research study only if it meets four criteria: relevancy, researchability, feasibility, and ethical acceptability.

Reading and discussion around the general problem area will enable us to continually narrow our focus of interest until specific research questions related to the problem can be developed. We will usually ask different kinds of questions, depending on the purpose for which the answers are required.

The possible reasons for conducting a research study can be categorized broadly as exploration, description, and explanation. These three categories fall on a knowledge-level continuum. At one end of the continuum, exploratory studies yield only uncertain knowledge and are conducted when there is little prior knowledge in the problem area. Further along the continuum, when some knowledge has been obtained, descriptive studies are undertaken to yield additional descriptive information. At the far end of the continuum, when substantial knowledge is available, explanatory studies attempt to explain the facts already gathered.

Now that we know the place of research in social work, the various contexts in which it takes place, and how to formulate research problems and questions, we will turn our attention to the quantitative research approach to knowledge development—the topic of the following chapter.

REFERENCES AND FURTHER READINGS

BABBIE, E.R. (1995). *The practice of social research* (7th ed., pp. 55-60). Belmont, CA: Wadsworth.

CIALDINI, R.B. (1980). Full-cycle social psychology. In L. Bickman (Ed.), *Applied social psychology annual* (vol 1, pp. 21-47). Beverly Hills, CA: Sage.

DALLAS MORNING NEWS: "Welfare study withholds benefits from 800 Texans," February 11, 1990, p. 1.

DARLEY, J.M., & LATANE, B. (1968). Bystander intervention in emergencies: Diffusion of responsibility. *Journal of Personality and Social Psychology, 8,* 377-383.

GABOR, P.A., & GRINNELL, R.M., JR. (1994). *Evaluation and quality improvement in the human services* (pp. 72-97). Needham Heights, MA: Allyn & Bacon.

GRINNELL, R.M., JR., & WILLIAMS, M. (1990). *Research in social work: A primer* (pp. 49-63). Itasca, IL: F.E. Peacock.

JUDD, C.M., SMITH, E.R., & KIDDER, I.H. (1991). *Research methods in social relations* (6th ed., pp. 20-27). Fort Worth, TX: Harcourt Brace.

KRYSIK, J., HOFFART, I., & GRINNELL, R.M., JR. (1993). *Student study guide for the fourth edition of social work research and evaluation* (pp. 2-3). Itasca, IL: F.E. Peacock.

MONETTE, D.R., SULLIVAN, T.J., & DEJONG, C.R. (1994). *Applied social research* (3rd ed., pp. 68-76). Fort Worth, TX: Harcourt Brace.

MYERS, D.G. (1983). *Social psychology.* New York: McGraw-Hill.

NEUMAN, W.L. (1994). *Social research methods* (2nd ed., pp. 55-78, 108-112). Needham Heights, MA: Allyn & Bacon.

ROTHERY, M.A. (1993). Problems, questions, and hypotheses. In R.M. Grinnell, Jr. (Ed.), *Social work research and evaluation* (4th ed., pp. 17-37). Itasca, IL: F.E. Peacock.

RUBIN, A., & BABBIE, E.R. (1993). *Research methods for social work* (2nd ed., pp. 88-104). Pacific Grove, CA: Wadsworth.

SINGLETON, R.A., JR., STRAITS, B.C., & MILLER STRAITS, M. (1993). *Approaches to social research* (2nd ed., 67-69, 87-88). New York: Oxford.

WEINBACH, R.W., & GRINNELL, R.M., JR. (1996). *Applying research knowledge: A workbook for social work students* (2nd ed., pp. 17-24). Needham Heights, MA: Allyn & Bacon.

WILLIAMS, M., TUTTY, L.M., & GRINNELL, R.M., JR. (1995). *Research in social work: An introduction* (2nd ed., pp. 47-80). Itasca, IL: F.E. Peacock.

Judy Krysik
Richard M. Grinnell, Jr.

C h a p t e r **4**

Quantitative Approaches to the Generation of Knowledge

A S PRESENTED in Chapters 2 and 3, the two research approaches we use to develop knowledge for our profession are categorized as quantitative and qualitative. What distinguishes the main differences between these research approaches? In a general sense, and in a nutshell, the qualitative approach to research acquisition is *expansive* in its inquiry to social work problems, whereas, the quantitative approach is intentionally *limiting*.

There is an unnecessary controversy in our profession over which of these two research approaches is more useful in the development of our knowledge base. As in the previous four editions of this text, we continue to take the position that both approaches compliment each other. That is, each approach serves an important and distinct function in reflecting reality, contributing to our knowledge base, and guiding our practice activities. Thus, we should never subscribe to any *one* research approach, but should be methodologically pluralistic, guided by the type of knowledge required for our research problem and the contexts in which our study takes place (Tutty, Rothery, & Grinnell, 1996).

THE QUANTITATIVE TRADITION

The French philosopher Auguste Comte is credited with pioneering the application of the quantitative research approach to the study of social phenomena. In the 1820s, Comte attempted to apply the principles of "scientific" inquiry to practical social purposes. The history of our profession is rich with examples of how knowledge generated from quantitative research approaches have been instrumental in influencing social problems and social change. In 1870, for example, Marion Talbot used the quantitative research approach to knowledge acquisition when she challenged the unsubstantiated theory that intellectual work was damaging to women's reproductive capacities (Reinharz, 1992). At that time, this theory was being used as a rationale for denying women access to higher education.

The Hypothetico-Deductive Method of Obtaining Knowledge

The quantitative approach embraces the hypothetico-deductive method of knowledge building, as presented in Box 4.1. It is often inappropriately defined too narrowly by equating it with this method. In this narrow definition, the quantitative research approach to knowledge building follows four basic premisses (Rothery, 1993a).

1. We draw upon theories of human behavior or social work practice to develop a hypothesis. The hypothesis takes the form of a testable prediction derived from a theory (or model of practice).
2. The hypothesis is subsequently tested using an appropriate research design.
3. If the results of the research study are consistent with those predicted by the hypothesis, the hypothesis is thereby supported or corroborated. If the results differ from this prediction, the hypothesis is rejected (or not confirmed).
4. When a sufficient number of research studies that corroborate hypotheses derived from a specific theory (or model) of practice have been conducted, there is confidence in that theory (or model). When a number of studies fail to corroborate hypotheses derived from a given theory (or model), the hypothesis is judged to be invalid and should be discarded.

An example from the history of medicine, presented in Box 4.1, illustrates the steps of the hypothetico-deductive method in action. This example is a testimony to the value of applying the quantitative research approach to the study of social problems. In the case of Semmelweis, the results were life saving.

In our opinion, the idea that quantitative research studies are primarily a matter of testing propositions or hypotheses derived from established theory, however, is much too restrictive for our profession. Thus, we believe a more

---

BOX 4.1

THE HYPOTHETICO-DEDUCTIVE METHOD:
AN EXAMPLE FROM THE HISTORY OF MEDICINE

Carl Hempel (1966), noted philosopher of science, provides an excellent example of the application of the hypothetico-deductive method in his story of Ignaz Semmelweis's work on a fatal illness known as puerperal fever, or child-bed fever. The physician Semmelweis worked from 1844 to 1848 at the Vienna General Hospital. As a medical staff member of the First Maternity Division, he was distressed by the division's high incidence of childbed fever, especially compared with the incidence in the Second Maternity Division of the same hospital.

According to Hempel's account, Semmelweis entertained numerous explanations. "Some of these he rejected out of hand as incompatible with well-established facts; others he subjected to specific tests." For example, one view held that overcrowding was the cause; however, Semmelweis noted that overcrowding was in fact heavier in the Second Division than in the First. Two other conjectures were similarly rejected "by noting that there were no differences between the two Divisions in regard to diet or general care of the patients." Among several other ideas suggested to Semmelweis was the position of the women during delivery: in the First Division, women delivered lying on their backs, while in the Second, they delivered on their sides. But when the lateral position was introduced in the First Division, mortality remained unchanged.

In a similar fashion, Semmelweis rejected idea after idea until finally, in 1847, an accident gave him the critical clue for solving the puzzle. While performing an autopsy, a colleague of his, Kolletschka, received a puncture wound from a scalpel and "died after an agonizing illness during which he displayed the same symptoms that Semmelweis had observed in the victims of childbed fever." Semmelweis reasoned that "cadaveric matter" introduced into Kolletschka's bloodstream from the scalpel "had caused his colleague's fatal illness."

> And the similarities between the course of Kolletschka's disease and that of the women in his clinic led Semmelweis to the conclusion that his patients had died of the same kind of blood poisoning; he, his colleagues, and the medical students had been the carriers of the infectious material, for he and his associates used to come to the wards directly from performing dissections in the autopsy room, and examine the women in labor after only superficially washing their hands, which often retained a characteristic foul order. (p. 5)

Semmelweis tested this idea by having all medical personnel who attended the women carefully disinfect their hands before making an examination. The mortality from childbed fever promptly decreased.

In seeking to explain childbed fever, Semmelweis repeated the hypothetico-deductive method. First, he formulated a hypothesis: that the illness was due to overcrowding, delivery position, or blood poisoning from cadaveric matter.

Second, he deduced testable consequences from this hypothesis. That is, he reasoned that if his hypothesis were true, then certain facts or observations should follow: overcrowdedness will be greater in the First Division than the Second; adoption of the lateral position in the First Division will reduce the mortality; or having attendants disinfect their hands will reduce fatalities.

Third, Semmelweis checked the observable consequences of the hypothesis against reality. In the case of the delivery position and blood poisoning hypotheses, this meant first establishing certain conditions for making his observations—changing the delivery procedure or requiring disinfection.

Finally, having found the observable consequences to be true or false, Semmelweis drew conclusions about his hypotheses. When the consequences were disconfirmed (e.g., when it was shown that the lateral position did *not* decrease fatalities), he rejected the hypothesis. When the consequences were confirmed (e.g., when disinfection lowered fatalities), he tentatively accepted the hypothesis as true.

flexible view of the quantitative approach to knowledge generation should be as follows (Rothery, 1993a):

1. There are two realities. The first reality consists of people's subjective beliefs, assumptions, and experiences of the world. Beliefs can range from relatively vague, undifferentiated hunches or intuitions to well-organized, logically developed formal theories. The second reality is objective and independent of subjective beliefs held about it.
2. The objective world is knowable.
3. The objective world is worth knowing. While subjective reality is obviously of value to researchers, they must test how well it conforms to the objective world. Documenting this goodness of fit is a central purpose of many quantitative research studies.
4. When credible research studies establish that the objective world is somehow different from subjective beliefs about it, the professionally responsible reaction is to influence change in these beliefs accordingly.
5. The most reliable way to know the objective world is through examination of data, collected and assessed according to certain rules of logic. If these rules are followed carefully and the data produced meet the standards for validity and reliability (see Chapter 7), the conclusions reached should have solid logical support.

The importance of testing the fit between subjective beliefs and objective observations is illustrated by the quantitative research efforts of Marion Talbot, where her purpose was to study the relationship between women's participation in formal education and their reproductive capacities. Without the collection of standardized, valid, reliable, and objective data, via the quantitative research approach, subjective beliefs that bar women from institutes of higher learning might still prevail today (Rothery, 1993a; Williams, Tutty, & Grinnell, 1995).

Example of "Two Realities"

According to Rothery (1993a, pp. 40-42), contemporary social workers have had to acknowledge that violence and coercion play a significant factor in the day-to-day functioning of families, as elsewhere in modern society. Traditionally, however, the lack of attention we have given to this problem is dismaying. For years, our awareness of the effects of family violence was limited, and we failed to address this critical issue—even while we were providing marital counseling, family therapy, and other services to families in which women or children were being victimized. As a consequence, domestic assaults undoubtedly continued in situations where something could have been done to stop them.

How could we have failed to recognize this widespread and often devastating problem? The explanation can be considered in terms of the first quantitative principle mentioned earlier in that there are two realities—one objective and the other subjective. Thus, many of us would work for years with families in which violence was present without recognizing it, because our shared subjective beliefs about the family and female-male relations prevented us from "seeing" the problem (Rothery, 1993a,b).

The family was traditionally viewed in American culture as a benign patriarchy in which the husband/father is firmly in charge and exercises power fairly and with good intentions. The idea of husbands brutalizing their wives or sexually exploiting their children would have been regarded as a direct contradiction of a widely held cherished fantasy about the family.

At the same time there was another cultural belief stating that it is acceptable and even admirable for men to exert their authority toward their partners through physical force. A simple extension of this belief was that men could use violence against their marital partners as a valid and necessary means of exerting authority. Thus, culturally prescribed norms or standards of conduct that would condemn physical assault in most other contexts actually sanctioned it in the family. Repulsive behavior that would be treated as criminal in other situations was excused, minimized, or even tacitly applauded within the family context.

Not only were we influenced by such cultural beliefs, but our subjective beliefs referred to as "clinical wisdom," on which practice theory was largely based, compounded the problem. On the basis of clinical studies, for example, it was widely believed that serious or harmful forms of domestic violence were in reality quite rare. Consider the case of sexual assaults against girls by family members. Imagined incest was seen as common; real sexual exploitation was considered to be extremely rare. This position was supported as late as the 1970s by clinical studies in which the conclusion was that the true yearly incidence of incest was between one and five cases per million families, a rate low enough to render the "incest problem" a nonissue (Russell, 1984).

It should not be hard to see how our collective beliefs about reality, in both cultural assumptions and practice theory, contributed to our erroneous beliefs, which in turn had serious consequences for women and children. Efforts are now being made to remedy this situation, and quantitative research studies should receive much of the credit for bringing into question past misconceptions about family violence.

Quantitative research studies that have been done on family violence have since become milestones (Badgley, 1984; Finkelhor, 1984; Russell, 1984; Walker, 1979). After identifying a possible discrepancy between people's widely held subjective beliefs and objective reality, these studies gathered data, via the quantitative research approach, about the occurrence of various forms of family violence. The studies followed certain rules that ultimately allowed them to state whether earlier beliefs about family violence should logically be considered true (consistent with objective reality).

The data accumulated by these and other quantitative studies have forced us to change our beliefs and to recognize that the various forms of family violence are not rare. Rather, the incidence of violence in families is so high that responsible social work practice requires us to be constantly alert to the possibility that our clients may be (or may have been) victims.

CLASSIFICATION BY FUNCTION

Quantitative research studies can be classified in as many ways as there are people willing to classify them. Criteria such as data collection method (Chapters 13–19) or type of research design (Chapters 11–12), perhaps ordered hierarchically according to the level of experimental rigor required, may be used. We will classify them according to the functions they serve when it comes to building upon our knowledge base. These functions can be classified as: (1) description of variables and relationships, (2) prediction and comparison of outcomes, (3) analysis of components of interventions, and (4) causal analyses (Rothery, 1993a, pp. 43-44).

Description of Variables and Relationships

As we know from the last chapter, the primary goal of many research projects is to simply describe variables and determine the relationships between and among them. One purpose of a quantitative research study on sexual exploitation by Diana Russell (1984) was to simply document the frequency of the various forms of this type of abuse. Frequency data on such social problems, and their relationship to other variables (e.g., relationship to the perpetrator, as well as to cultural and socioeconomic factors), is of great value not only to policy makers but also to line-level practitioners.

Prediction and Comparison of Outcomes

Many quantitative research studies that predict client outcomes look at policies or prevention and treatment programs to determine their impact on our clients and profession. There is evidence, for example, that regulations under which police officers are encouraged to press charges for domestic assault against women can reduce the prevalence of this crime. Studies that document such impacts (or lack of impact) are clearly useful in their effects on our everyday practice decisions. They do not always advance our knowledge base as to *why* certain interventions have (or have not) had particular effects, however.

Comparative studies of client outcomes by different social service programs are a logical successor to simple inquiries into client outcomes. Put simply, comparative studies are conducted by directly comparing the findings of two or more different outcome studies. In the treatment of men who commit domestic violence against women, for example, we have a considerable interest in whether voluntary treatment is more (or less) desirable than treatment mandated by the courts.

Analysis of Components of Interventions

Quantitative research studies that analyze the various components of treatment interventions aim to determine what elements in a given intervention are producing particular client outcomes. Assume, for example, that we are supported in our belief that male perpetrators of domestic assaults against females can be treated most effectively through group therapy. A subsequent set of questions could concern the desired impacts being produced by specific components of the group therapy experience. Is confrontation by peers really the key component in reducing the perpetrator's reliance on denial? Does exploration of a male perpetrator's own victimization in his family of origin help him learn to empathize with his victim(s) and the pain he has inflicted?

Answers to such questions help us to plan clearly specified treatment interventions that are effective, efficient, and economical (Chapters 23–25). Knowledge is acquired about which components within a treatment package most reliably serve particular objectives or can be safely discarded, and which objectives are not being met and therefore will require modifications in the treatment process.

Causal Analyses

From a knowledge-building point of view, quantitative studies that try to establish cause-effect relationships are comparatively more advanced. Assuming that it is known that certain treatment interventions have specific impacts on male perpetrators of domestic assaults on females, for example, the next questions would be related to how and why these interventions have the effects they do. With this type of causal question, quantitative studies are linking the phenomena they observe with the theories about their causes.

Findings that physical or chemical castration of male sexual abusers is effective in preventing them from offending again, for example, would provide evidence for biological theories as to why certain men have been abusers. Similarly, if systematic efforts at changing male perpetrators' attitudes toward females are effective, support is provided for certain social learning theories of causation.

The argument for causation becomes stronger as we are able to rule out competing explanations as to why a certain event has the impact it does. As seen later in this chapter, these competing explanations are also referred to as rival or alternative hypotheses. The example contained in Box 4.2 illustrates the complexity of research studies that attempt to determine causation.

CHARACTERISTICS

The quantitative research approach of gaining knowledge differs in a number of important ways from the methods of tradition, authority, intuition, and practice wisdom as outlined in Chapter 1. These differences stem from the five essential characteristics that quantitative research efforts strive for: (1) measurability, (2) objectivity, (3) reducing uncertainty, (4) duplication, and (5) standardized procedures (Williams, Tutty, & Grinnell, 1995, pp.13-17).

Striving Toward Measurability

The quantitative research approach tries to study only those variables that can be objectively measured. That is, knowledge gained through this research approach is based on "objective measurements" of the real world, not on someone's opinions, beliefs, or past experiences. Conversely, knowledge gained through tradition or authority *depends* on people's opinions and beliefs. Entities that cannot be measured, or even seen, such as id, ego, or superego, are not amenable to a quantitative study but rather rely on tradition and authority.

In short, the phenomena we believe to exist must be measurable. However, at this point in our discussion, it is useful to remember that quantitative researchers believe that practically everything in life is measurable.

Striving Toward Objectivity

The second characteristic of the quantitative research approach is that it strives to be as *objective* as possible. The direct measurements of the real world that comprise *empirical data* must not be affected in any way by the person doing the observing, or measuring. Physical scientists have observed inanimate matter

BOX 4.2

PROBLEMS IN CAUSAL INTERPRETATION:
THE CASE OF EXERCISE AND HEART ATTACKS

Of the three criteria needed to establish a causal relationship, the most difficult to assess is nonspuriousness. One can never be sure that a causal connection exists between correlated variables. Indeed, mistaken impressions of causality may remain undetected for years. An interesting example of this problem in social science research is related by psychologists Schuyler Huck and Howard Sandler (1979:151, 152, 227).

In recent years there has been much interest in the relative benefits of regular exercise. One controversial claim is that exercise can reduce the risk of heart attacks. An early study by Dr. J.N. Morris of London shows, however, just how difficult this is to establish. Examining drivers and conductors of London's double-decker buses, Morris found that the drivers were far more likely to suffer from heart disease and to die from coronaries than the conductors. Since the drivers sat in their seats all day while the conductors ran up and down stairs to collect fares, he concluded that it was the differential amount of exercise inherent in the two jobs that brought about the observed differences in health. Before reading further, you might try to think of variables other than exercise that could have produced the difference in heart problems between the drivers and conductors. Morris uncovered one variable in a follow-up study, and Huck and Sandler mention two others.

Some time after the publication of the above results, Morris examined the records maintained on the uniforms issued to drivers and conductors and discovered that drivers tended to be given larger uniforms than conductors. Therefore, he concluded, differences in weight rather than exercise might be the causal factor. That is, heavier men, who were more coronary-prone to begin with, may have chosen the sedentary job of driver, whereas thinner men chose the more physically active job of conductor.

Another explanation is related to the amount of tension associated with the two jobs. As Huck and Sandler (1979:227) point out.

> The conductors probably experienced very little tension as they went up and down the bus collecting fares from the passengers; the worst thing that they probably had to deal with in their jobs was a passenger who attempted to ride free by sneaking around from one seat to another. Normally, however, we suspect that the conductors actually enjoyed their interaction with other people while on the job.
>
> But on the other hand, each driver had the safety of everyone on the bus as his responsibility. And as anyone who lives in or visits a city knows, driving in rush-hour traffic is anything but restful. Having to dodge pedestrians, being cut off by other vehicles, watching for signal changes—these activities can bring about temporary outbursts of anger and chronic nervousness. Imagine how it would affect your heart to be in the driver's seat of a bus for eight hours each working day!

Finally, a third variable that could account for the different rate of heart problems is age. If mobility or seniority or some other function of age were related to job assignment, then employees assigned to the driver jobs may have been older and those assigned to the conductor jobs younger. And since we would expect more heart attacks among older persons, age rather than the nature of the job could be the causal variable.

In this example it is difficult if not impossible to tell which cause—exercise, weight, job stress, or age—may have produced the observed differences in health between drivers and conductors. Since both weight and age are antecedent to job type and heart disease, either of these uncontrolled extraneous variables could have created a spurious relationship. However, if exercise or job stress were the correct interpretation, then the original relationship would not be spurious, since exercise and job stress specify intervening variables through which the job itself can make a person more or less susceptible to heart problems. The diagram below shows the difference in those two outcomes.

Of course, it is possible that two or more of these variables are operating jointly to produce the health differential between the two groups. The only safe conclusion is that we really do not know which interpretation is correct.

In general, correlation does not imply causation. All correlations must be interpreted; like any fact, they do not speak for themselves. To infer a causal relationship from a correlation, an investigator must detect and control for extraneous variables that are possible and plausible causes of the variable to be explained. The fatal flaw in Morris's study is that relevant extraneous variables were not controlled; without directly assessing the effects of such "hidden" causes, we cannot tell which interpretation is valid.

for centuries, confident in the belief that objects do not change as a result of being observed. In the subworld of the atom, however, physicists are beginning to learn what social workers have always known. Things *do* change when they are observed. People think, feel, and behave very differently as a result of being observed. Not only do they change, they change in different ways depending on who is doing the observing. A quick review of the last section of Box 1.1 provides a clear example of how people change their behaviors when they are being watched.

There is yet another problem. Observed behavior is open to interpretation by the observer. To illustrate this point, let us take a simple example of a client we are seeing, named Ron, who is severely withdrawn. He may behave in one way in our office in individual treatment sessions, and in quite another way when his mother joins the interviews. We may think that Ron is unduly silent, while his mother remarks on how much he is talking. If his mother *wants* him to talk, perhaps as a sign that he is emerging from his withdrawal, she may perceive him to be talking more than he really is.

Researchers go to great lengths to ensure that their own hopes, fears, beliefs, and biases do not affect their research results, and that the biases of others do not affect them either. Nevertheless, as discussed in later chapters, complete objectivity is rarely possible in social work despite the many strategies we have developed in our efforts to achieve it. Suppose, for example, that a social worker is trying to help a mother interact more positively with her child. The worker, together with a colleague, may first observe the child and mother in a playroom setting, recording how many times the mother makes eye contact with the child, hugs the child, criticizes the child, makes encouraging comments, and so forth on a three-point scale (i.e., -1 = discouraging, 0 = neutral, 1 = encouraging). The social worker may perceive a remark that the mother has made to the child as "neutral," while the colleague thinks it was "encouraging."

In such a situation, it is impossible to resolve the disagreement. If there were six objective observers, however, five opting for "neutral" and only one for "encouraging," the one observer is more likely to be wrong than the five, and it is very likely that the mother's remark was "neutral." As more people agree on what they have observed, the less likely it becomes that the observation was distorted by bias; and the more likely it is that the agreement reached is "objectively true."

As should be obvious by now, objectivity is largely a matter of agreement. There are some things—usually physical phenomena—about which most people agree. Most people agree, for example, that objects fall when dropped, water turns to steam at a certain temperature, sea water contains salt, and so forth. However, there are other things—mostly to do with values, attitudes, and feelings—about which agreement is far more rare.

An argument about whether Beethoven is a better composer than Bach, for example, cannot be "objectively" resolved. Neither can a dispute about the rightness of capital punishment, euthanasia, or abortion. It is not surprising, therefore, that physical researchers, who work with physical phenomena, are able to be more "objective" than social work researchers, who work with human beings.

Striving Toward Reducing Uncertainty

The quantitative research approach tries to rule out uncertainty. Since all observations in both the physical and social sciences are made by human beings, personal bias cannot be entirely eliminated, and there is always the possibility that an observation is in error, no matter how many people agree about what they saw. There is also the possibility that the conclusions drawn from even an accurate observation will be wrong. A number of people may agree that an object in the sky is a UFO when in fact it is a meteor. Even if they agree that it is a meteor, they may come to the conclusion—probably erroneously—that the meteor is a warning from an angry extraterrestrial person.

In the twentieth century, most people do not believe that natural phenomena have anything to do with extraterrestrial people. They prefer the explanations that modern researchers have proposed. Nevertheless, no researcher would say—or at least be quoted as saying—that meteors and extraterrestrial beings are not related for certain. When utilizing the research method of knowledge development, nothing is certain. Even the best-tested theory is only tentative, accepted as true until newly discovered evidence shows it to be untrue or only partly true. All knowledge gained through the research method (whether quantitative or qualitative) is thus provisional. Everything presently accepted as true is true only with varying degrees of probability.

Let us suppose we have lived all alone in the middle of a large forest. We have never ventured as much as a hundred yards from our cabin and have had no access to the outside world. We have observed for our entire life that all of the ducks that flew over our land were white. We have never seen a different-colored duck. Thus, we theorize, and rightfully so, that all ducks are white. We would only have to see one nonwhite duck fly over our land to disprove our theory: Nothing is certain no matter how long we "objectively observed" it.

Striving Toward Duplication

The quantitative research approach tries to do research studies in such a way that they can be duplicated. Unlike qualitative studies, if quantitative studies cannot be duplicated, they are not really quantitative endeavors. As we have said before, the quantitative research approach, and to some extent, the qualitative approach as well, is a public method of knowing.

Evidence for the relationship between students' grade point average and their future abilities as good social workers must be open to public inspection if it is to be believed. Furthermore, belief is more likely if a second researcher can produce the same findings by using the same research methods.

Duplication Versus Replication

In scientific laboratories, the word "replication" refers to the same experiment conducted more than once in the same way, at approximately the same time, by the same person. A person testing a city's water supply for pollutants, for example, will take several samples of the water and test them simultaneously under identical conditions, expecting to obtain close to identical results. If the water needs to be retested for some reason, further samples will be taken and the same procedures followed, but now another person may do the work and the test conditions may be very slightly different: A recent downpour of rain may have flushed some of the pollutants out of the reservoir, for example. The second set of tests are then said to be *duplicates* of the first. Social workers are not able to replicate research studies, because no person, situation, or event is identical to any other. Therefore, despite the fact that most texts use the word "replicate" in reference to repeating studies, we will use the word "duplicate" instead.

Example of Duplication   Suppose we are running a 12-week intervention program to help fathers who have abused their children to manage their anger without resorting to physical violence. We have put a great deal of effort into designing this program, and believe that our intervention (the program) is more effective than other interventions currently used in other anger-management programs. We develop a method of measuring the degree to which the fathers in our group have learned to dissipate their anger in nondamaging ways and we find that, indeed, the group shows marked improvement.

Improvement shown by one group of fathers is not convincing evidence for the effectiveness of our program. Perhaps our measurements were in error and the improvement was not as great as we hoped for. Perhaps the improvement was a coincidence, and the fathers' behavior changed because they had joined a health club and each had vented his fury on a punching bag. In order to be more certain, we duplicate our program and measuring procedures with a second group of fathers: In other words, we duplicate our study.

After we have used the same procedures with a number of groups and obtained similar results each time, we might expect that other social workers will eagerly adopt our methods. As presented in Chapter 1, tradition dies hard. Other social workers have a vested interest in *their* interventions, and they may suggest that we found the results we did only because we *wanted* to find them.

In order to counter any suggestion of bias, we ask another, independent social worker to use the same anger-management program and measuring methods with other groups of fathers. If the results are the same as before, our colleagues in the field of anger management may choose to adopt our intervention method (the program). Tradition does not merely die hard, however. It dies with enormous difficulty, and we should not be surprised if our colleagues choose, instead, to continue using the familiar interventions they have always used.

Whatever our colleagues decide, we are excited about our newfound program. We wonder if our methods would work as well with women as they do with men, with adolescents as well as with adults, with Native Americans, Asians, or African Americans as well as with Caucasians, with mixed groups, larger groups, or groups in different settings. In fact, we have identified a lifetime project, since we will have to apply our program and measuring procedures repeatedly to all these different groups.

Striving Toward the Use of Standardized Procedures

Finally, the quantitative research approach tries to use well-accepted standardized procedures. For quantitative research studies to be creditable, and before others can accept our results, they must be satisfied that our study was conducted according to accepted scientific standardized procedures. The allegation that our work lacks "objectivity" is only one of the criticisms they might bring. In addition, they might suggest that the group of fathers we worked with was not typical of abusive fathers in general, and that our results are not therefore applicable to other groups of abusive fathers. It might be alleged that we did not make proper measurements, or we measured the wrong thing, or we did not take enough measurements, or we did not analyze our data correctly, and so on.

In order to negate these kinds of criticisms, social work researchers have agreed on a set of standard procedures and techniques that are thought most likely to produce "true and unbiased" knowledge—which is what this book is all about. Certain steps must be performed in a certain order. Foreseeable errors must be guarded against. Ethical behavior with research participants and colleagues must be maintained. These procedures must be followed if our study is both to generate usable results and to be accepted as useful by other social workers.

STEPS IN THE QUANTITATIVE RESEARCH PROCESS

Most, but not all, quantitative research studies, regardless of function, follow nine highly interrelated steps: (1) selecting a problem area, (2) conceptualizing variables, (3) operationalizing variables, (4) identifying constants and labeling variables, (5) formulating a research hypothesis, (6) developing a sampling plan, (7) selecting a data collection method, (8) analyzing the data, and (9) writing the report.

Step 1: Selecting a Problem Area

As we have seen in the previous three chapters, selecting the problem area to be studied involves a decision by the researcher to invest time, energy, and personal resources in the study of a specific problem. Russell (1984), for example, decided that the need for objective data about sexual exploitation of American females was so great that she should devote several years of her life to investigating this problem area. Her choice was fortuitous, because her work in this field has been recognized as extremely important. As we know from Chapter 3, she could have chosen other relevant social problems requiring disciplined study from a virtually limitless supply (Rothery, 1993a).

Step 2: Conceptualizing Variables

The process of selecting the concepts to include in a research study is known as *conceptualization*. In short, it is the process whereby fuzzy and imprecise concepts are made more specific and precise by selecting variables, sometimes called indicators, that will be used to describe the concepts under investigation (Williams, Tutty & Grinnell, 1995, pp. 68-71). But what are concepts?

Concepts

Concepts are nothing more than ideas. The research questions mentioned previously all involve *concepts*. Take a female university professor, for example. She is a woman, and also a teacher. If she is married, she is a wife. If she has children, she is a mother. She may be a home owner, a committee member, an Asian, or a Catholic. She may be demanding or compassionate. All these characteristics of the university professor are concepts: They are ideas that are shared among members of a society to a greater or lesser degree.

Some ideas are perceived by all members of the same society in much the same way, while other ideas give rise to disagreement. The concept of being a mother, for example, involves the concept of children and, specifically, the concept of having given birth to a child. Today, most people would agree that giving birth to a child is only one way of defining a mother. The idea of motherhood in Western society involves more than that, however.

Also involved are the concepts of loving, of caring for the child's physical needs, of offering the child emotional support, of advocating for the child with others, of accepting legal and financial responsibility for the child, and of being there for the child in all circumstances and at all times. Some would argue that a woman who does all these things is a mother, whether she has given birth or not. Further, however we feel about it, others would say that the biological mother is the only real mother even if she abandoned the child at birth.

Like many other qualities of interest to social workers, compassion is a highly complex, abstract concept with many possible dimensions. Intelligence is another such complex concept, as are alienation, morale, conformity, cohesion, motivation, delinquency, prejudice, social status, and a host of others.

Concepts Exist Only in the Mind

None of the concepts just named exist in the sense that they can be touched, seen, heard, or in any way directly observed. They do not exist at all, in fact, except as abstractions in the human mind. Let us return to the example we used in Chapter 3, and ask the descriptive research question: Where do people who were once psychiatrically challenged and institutionalized live after they are discharged? There are two related concepts here, "previously institutionalized people who were psychiatrically challenged" and "discharged." Both concepts must be further clarified as they mean different things to different people. Should these individuals be conceptualized as people who have previously received treatment for a mental disorder but are not presently receiving treatment? If this definition is accepted, what about some of those who suffer frequent relapses and are "in treatment" and "not in treatment" alternately over long periods?

Similarly, a discharged person could be conceptualized as a person who was once institutionalized and no longer is. But what about individuals who were released from an institution on the understanding that they continue to receive treatment on an out-patient basis? Can they be said to have been "discharged" for the purposes of the study?

We could conceptualize "discharged people" as people who were "psychiatrically challenged and received institutional care but are not receiving it at the time of our study, whether or not they are still receiving outpatient care, and whether or not they are expected to need institutional care in the future."

We could also conceptualize a discharged person simply as a person who is no longer obliged to live in an institution. So far, the "discharged people," no matter how well defined, still includes all similar individuals everywhere, even those who were discharged a very long time ago. If our study is to be feasible, we need to define "previously institutionalized people who were psychiatrically challenged" in such a way that a research study can feasibly take place.

If our study is being conducted in the Oak Lawn community, for example, we may decide that only those previously institutionalized people who were psychiatrically challenged in Oak Lawn will be included; or, if Oak Lawn happens to be a large community with several institutions that once served people with psychiatric diagnoses, only those from one of the institutions may be included. If the purpose of our study is to explore a recent massive discharge, only those recently discharged—say, within the last six months—may be of interest.

Step 3: Operationalizing Variables

After the variables have been conceptualized, they need to be operationalized, or measured. Operationalization goes one step beyond conceptualization in that it is the process of developing operational definitions of the variables contained within the concepts included in the study. Operationalization of variables is highly interrelated with identifying constants and labeling variables (Step 4).

Using our previous example, one of the many research questions Russell chose to address was an obvious one: What is the incidence of rape experienced by American women? The specification process requires a considerable amount of work, even on such a straightforward descriptive research question as this. Russell (1984) began by utilizing the state of California's legal definition for rape:

> Forced intercourse (i.e., penile-vaginal penetration) or intercourse obtained by threat of force, or intercourse completed while the woman was drugged, unconscious, asleep, or otherwise totally helpless and hence unable to consent.

The above is a nominal definition which establishes what the variable—

rape—means conceptually. The next step, operationalizaton, establishes specifically how the nominally described variable is to be measured. In Russell's study, interview questions were developed. The following were asked with reference to strangers as well as to friends, husbands, and others (Rothery, 1993a, pp. 46-47):

1. At any time in your life, have you ever been the victim of rape or attempted rape?
2. Did a stranger (etc.) ever physically force you, or try to force you, to have any kind of sexual intercourse...?
3. Have you ever had any kind of unwanted sexual experience, including kissing, petting, or intercourse with a stranger (etc.)... because you felt physically threatened? IF YES: Did he (any of them) either try or succeed in having any kind of sexual intercourse with you?
4. Have you ever had any kind of unwanted sexual experience with a stranger (etc.) because you were asleep, unconscious, drugged, or in some other way helpless ...? IF YES: Did he (any of them) either try or succeed in having any kind of sexual intercourse with you?

Referring back to the nominal definition of rape, it is clear that the responses of women to these four questions could be used to determine whether or not they were reporting experiences that could be considered incidences of rape. Russell's operational definition was that a woman could be said to have experienced rape when, in response to these interview questions, she described experiences that conformed to the very specific four predetermined criteria.

The importance of operationalization in a quantitative research study can be appreciated by reflecting on the principles of the quantitative research approach identified at the beginning of this chapter. Ideas such as the concept of rape exist in the world of theory and belief. To operationalize a concept like rape is to say what rape is in the objective world of fact: How will we know it when we see it (or hear about it)?

Operationalizing variables, in effect, is building bridges between the subjective world of ideas and the world of objective reality. As we know, quantitative research studies seek to determine how well people's subjective ideas conform to objective reality, and these bridges must be constructed with considerable care. Thus, operational definitions are the concrete and specific ways the variables, or indicators, contained within a quantitative research study are measured. The unambiguous clarity of variables will never be sufficient to permit the measurement of them (Rothery, 1993a; Williams, Tutty, & Grinnell, 1995).

Let us proceed further with our discussion of operationalization by going back to our example of previously institutionalized people who were psychiatrically challenged. From the above discussion, we are now in a position to define, operationally, "previously institutionalized people who were psychiatrically challenged," as:

A person who received residential care for a minimum of one year at Pine Brook Homes but is not receiving it at the time of the study, whether or not he or she is still receiving outpatient care, and whether or not he or she is expected to need institutional care in the future.

The above operational definition is sufficiently narrow and precise to enable us to list all the people who fit the definition. We can then ask them where they are presently living and where they have lived since their discharge.

In sum, operational definitions are precise definitions that help us to measure all the variables involved in a research study. Other people may not agree with our operational definitions (or variables for that matter), but at least they will be in no doubt as to what our definitions are. Another person who believes that a different result would be obtained if, for example, "previously institutionalized people who were psychiatrically challenged" were operationally defined differently, may choose to repeat the study, using another operational definition and making whatever measurements the definition demands. A concept usually contains a number of potential variables that can be used to measure it.

As we saw in Step 2, the more abstract the concept, the greater is the potential for disagreement. Consider compassion, for example. A single individual may know what he or she means when describing another person as compassionate. However, it is unlikely that others will totally agree with his or her definition. The dictionary may not agree with anyone and may define compassion as "pity for suffering, with desire to help or to spare." Additionally, everyone may agree that this is, indeed, what is meant by compassion.

Difficulties still arise, however, because the quality of compassion, no matter how well defined, cannot be directly observed. "Pity for suffering" must be inferred from words or actions, and so must "desire to help." In other words, compassion can only be recognized by measuring the variables, or indicators, it contains. Thus, a variable is something that is associated with a concept and is measurable (Rothery, 1993a; Williams, Tutty, & Grinnell, 1995).

Often, it is not the concept about which people disagree; it is the variables that we believe make up the concept. Such disagreements about what variables make up concepts have profound implications for research studies. It will not be possible, for example, to undertake a study to find out whether women are more compassionate than men if no agreement can be reached about what words, feelings, or behaviors (variables) indicate compassion.

The example in Box 4.3 illustrates the many options to be considered in moving from a nominal to an operational definition of a concept. In addition, consider Box 4.4 in reference to how hard it is to operationalize variables for quantitative research studies within the "hard" and "soft" sciences.

Step 4: Identifying Constants and Labeling Variables

After the research question has been selected (Step 1), narrowed down to a researchable level by conceptualizing the variables it contains (Step 2), and operationalized to the extent that the concepts can be measured (Step 3), we need to identify the constants and label the variables that the research question contains. Steps 3 and 4 are highly interrelated, and more often than not, are usually done at the same time within quantitative research studies. In short, it

BOX 4.3

THE IMPORTANCE OF VARIABLE NAMES

Operationalization is one of those things that are easier said than done. It is quite simple to explain to someone the purpose and importance of operational definitions for variables, and even to describe how operationalization typically takes place. However, until you've tried to operationalize a rather complex variable, you may not appreciate some of the subtle difficulties involved. Of considerable importance to the operationalization effort is the particular name that you have chosen for a variable. Let's consider an example from the field of Urban Planning.

A variable of interest to planners is citizen participation. Planners are convinced that participation in the planning process by citizens is important to the success of plan implementation. Citizen participation is an aid to planners' understanding of the real and perceived needs of a community, and such involvement by citizens tends to enhance their cooperation with and support for planning efforts. Although many different conceptual definitions might be offered by different planners, there would be little misunderstanding over what is *meant* by citizen participation. The name of the variable seems adequate.

However, if we asked different planners to provide very simple operational measures for citizen participation, we are likely to find a variety among their responses that does generate confusion. One planner might keep a tally of attendance by private citizens at city commission and other local government meetings; another might maintain a record of the different topics addressed by private citizens at similar meetings; while a third might record the number of local government meeting attendees, as well as letters and phone calls received by the mayor and other pubic officials during a particular time period.

As skilled researchers, we can readily see that each planner would be measuring (in a very simplistic fashion) a different *dimension* of citizen participation: extent of citizen participation, issues prompting citizen participation, and form of citizen participation. Therefore, the original *naming* of our variable, citizen participation, which was quite satisfactory from a conceptual point of view, proved inadequate for purposes of operationalization.

The precise and exact naming of variables is important in research. It is both essential to and a result of good operationalization. Variable names quite often evolve from an iterative process of forming a conceptual definition, then an operational definition, then renaming the concept to better match what can or will be measured.

This looping process continues (our example above illustrates only one iteration), resulting in a gradual refinement of the variable name and its measurement until a reasonable fit is obtained. Sometimes the concept of the variable that you end up with is a bit different from the original one that you started with, but at least you are measuring what you are talking about, if only because you are talking about what you are measuring!

BOX 4.4

OPERATIONALIZATION ACROSS THE SCIENCES

One aspect of the stereotype of science shared by many educated persons is that it invariably involves precise measurements with instruments that are accurate to several decimal places. Indeed, this is seen as a crucial difference between the so-called hard sciences, such as chemistry and physics (more accurately called the natural or physical sciences), and the soft sciences, such as psychology, sociology, and anthropology (most of which are social sciences).

Of course, the hard–soft distinction is not meant to be flattering to that which is considered soft; and many natural scientists, who misunderstand the nature of social measurement, believe that the social sciences do not constitute science at all. According to biologist Jared Diamond (1987), however, this criticism misses two crucial points. First, all scientists, natural or social, face the step of operationalizing concepts. As Diamond says," To compare evidence with theory requires that you measure the ingredients of your theory." Second, the "step of operationalizing is inevitably more difficult and less exact in the [social] sciences, because there are so many uncontrolled variables."

Diamond illustrates operationalization with examples drawn from both the natural and social sciences. Learning how various scientists go about this should help your understanding and appreciation of the measurement process. The first example comes from mathematics. As Diamond says,

> I'd guess that mathematics arose long ago when two cave women couldn't operationalize their intuitive concept of "many." One cave woman said, "Let's pick this tree over here, because it has many bananas." The other cave woman argued, "No, let's pick that tree over there, because it has more bananas." Without a number system to operationalize the concept of "many," the two cave women could never prove to each other which tree offered better pickings. (p. 38)

Diamond's second example comes from another "hard" science, analytical chemistry, which generally seeks to measure the properties of substances.

> When my colleagues and I were studying the physiology of hummingbirds, we knew that the little guys liked to drink sweet nectar, but we would have argued indefinitely about how sweet it was if we hadn't operationalized the concept by measuring sugar concentrations. The method we used was to treat a glucose solution with an enzyme that liberates hydrogen peroxide, which reacts (with the help of another enzyme) with another substance called dianisidine to make it turn brown, whereupon we measured the brown color's intensity with an instrument called a spectrophotometer. A pointer's deflection on the spectrophotometer dial let us read off a number that provided an operational definition of sweet. (p. 38)

One of Diamond's "soft" science examples is taken from the field of clinical psychology, specifically his wife Marie Cohen's work with cancer patients and their families. Marie was interested in how doctors reveal the diagnosis of cancer. What determines how frank they are and how much information they withhold? She guessed that this

> might be related to differences in doctors' attitudes toward things like death, cancer, and medical treatment. But how on earth was she to operationalize and measure such . . . ? . . . Part of Marie's solution was to use a questionnaire that other scientists had developed by extracting statements from sources like tape-recorded doctors' meetings and then asking other doctors to express their degree of agreement with each statement. It turned out that each doctor's responses tended to cluster in several groups, in such a way that his [or her] responses to one statement in a cluster were correlated with his [or her] responses to other statements in the same cluster.
>
> One cluster proved to consist of expressions of attitudes toward death, a second cluster consisted of expressions of attitudes toward treatment and diagnosis, and a third cluster consisted of statements about patients' ability to cope with cancer. The responses were then employed to define attitude scales, which were further validated in other ways, like testing the scales on doctors at different stages in their careers (hence likely to have different attitudes). By thus operationalizing doctors' attitudes, Marie discovered (among other things) that doctors most convinced about the value of early diagnosis and aggressive treatment of cancer are the ones most likely to be frank with their patients. (p. 39)

Notice how the problem (finding and creating ways of operationalizing one's intuitive concepts) is the same in each case. Notice also how operationalization can be very indirect, as in both the chemistry and clinical psychology examples, irrespective of the accuracy of the measurement. Finally, these examples might suggest, as Diamond (p. 39) concludes, that the "ingrained labels 'soft science' and 'hard science' could be replaced by hard (i.e., difficult) science and easy science, respectively" For the social sciences "are much more difficult and [to some] intellectually challenging than mathematics and chemistry."

is difficult to operationalize variables without knowing what variables are going to be independent variables, dependent variables, and which concepts are constants. Let us turn our attention first to constants.

Step 4a: Defining Constants

As mentioned, most research studies involve concepts that vary and thus are called variables. Concepts that do not vary are called *constants*. We might want to compare the social adjustment of previously institutionalized people who were psychiatrically challenged, for example, to the social adjustment of people in the general population. In this situation, whether the person is, or is not, a previously institutionalized person who was psychiatrically challenged will fluctuate and, so, is a variable. If, however, it is not feasible to include a group of "normal" individuals in our study, then our research participants will all be previously institutionalized people who were psychiatrically challenged. In this research design, these people would be a constant. It is important to note that, depending on how a study is conceptualized, a concept can be a constant in one study and a variable in another (Rothery, 1993b; Williams, Tutty, & Grinnell, 1995).

Step 4b: Refining the Research Question So It Is Researchable

Unlike a constant, a variable must be capable of varying from one value to another. Suppose we have posed the question: Do job training programs help participants find jobs? This study is concerned with two variables—job training programs (Variable 1), and whether or not the participants who attended the programs found jobs (Variable 2)—and these will be the two variables under investigation. From the way the question is presently phrased, the first variable, job training programs, refers to *all* job training programs everywhere in the world. Similarly, the second variable, jobs found by program participants, involves all jobs found by all participants in every job training program the world over.

Unless the person doing the research study has unlimited money and time, such a study will not be feasible, and the research question needs to be more narrowly phrased. It may be more sensible to ask: Does a job training program, Program *X*, help participants find jobs? Now, the first variable refers only to a single job training program—Program *X*—and the second variable involves only jobs found by participants in Program *X*.

If the program has been running for a long time, all the jobs found by all the participants may still add up to a larger number than we wish to handle. Perhaps the research question should be rephrased yet again, as: Did Program *X* help participants to find jobs within six months after leaving the program? The point here is that the two variables that are going to be studied are directly derived from the research question, which is derived from the general problem area (unemployment). If they do not seem sensible it is time to go back and look again at the research question.

Let us take another example. Suppose that a study is being conducted to determine whether the establishment of a small community mental health center, a form of a social work intervention, increases the social adjustment of previously institutionalized people who were psychiatrically challenged in the Oak Lawn community. At first glance, it may appear that there are four variables involved in our study: the community mental health center (the intervention), social adjustment, previously institutionalized people who were psychiatrically challenged, and the Oak Lawn community.

It is not just social adjustment that our study will explore. It is the social adjustment of previously institutionalized people who were psychiatrically challenged. Similarly, our study is not concerned with *all* previously institutionalized people who were psychiatrically challenged—only those in the Oak Lawn community (Rothery, 1993b; Williams, Tutty, & Grinnell, 1995).

On closer examination, therefore, it becomes apparent that there are really only two variables: the community mental health center, and the social adjustment of previously institutionalized people who were psychiatrically challenged in the Oak Lawn community. These two variables can be classified into two types: independent variables and dependent variables.

Step 4c: Defining Independent and Dependent Variables

Many research studies, such as the one concerning the community mental health center above, focus on the relationship between two variables, called a *bivariate relationship*, from the prefix *bi-*, meaning *two*. It asks, in general terms: Does Variable *X* affect Variable *Y*? Or, how does Variable *X* affect Variable *Y*? If one variable affects the other, the variable that does the affecting is known as the *independent variable*, symbolized by *X*; and the variable that is affected is known as the *dependent variable*, symbolized by *Y*. If enough is known about the topic, and we have a good idea of what the effect will be, the question may be phrased: If *X* occurs, will *Y* result? If Variable *X* affects Variable *Y*, whatever happens to *Y* will depend on *X* (Williams, Tutty, & Grinnell, 1995).

In both of the examples given above, the purpose of the study is to determine whether one variable affects another. In the first example, the study sought to determine whether a job training program affected the jobs found by participants within six months after they finished the program. The job training program is not dependent on anything; at least, it is not dependent on anything made evident in the research question, and it is certainly not dependent on the jobs found by its graduates.

So, the number of jobs found by participants is the dependent variable and will hopefully be affected by the job training program, which is the independent variable. In the second example, the purpose is to discover whether the community mental center affects the social adjustment of previously institutionalized people who were psychiatrically challenged. Similarly, the social adjustment of these people is the dependent variable, while the independent variable is the community mental health center.

Some studies toward the exploratory end of the knowledge-building continuum are not concerned with the effect that one variable might have on another. Perhaps it is not yet known whether the two variables are even associated, and it is far too soon to postulate what the relationship between them might be. A descriptive study, for example, might ask: Is there a relationship between the attitudes of social workers toward transracial adoptions and the proportion of successful transracial adoptions in the Bowness community? Here, there are two variables, the attitudes of social workers toward transracial adoptions in the Bowness community and the proportion of successful transracial adoptions in the community. There is no suggestion that one affects the other, however. There is no independent variable; neither is there a dependent variable. They are just two variables (Williams, Tutty, & Grinnell, 1995).

Step 4d: Defining Extraneous Variables

We are rarely in a position to control all the factors that might influence the results of a particular quantitative research study. Thus, we must identify (if at all possible) other important variables that we need to control for. Suppose, for example, a study is conducted to determine the effectiveness of a particular treatment intervention in reducing drug use among adolescents. The research question could be: To what degree does a social work intervention, say a small community-based educational prevention program, reduce drug use in adolescents who attend the program? As we know by now, the independent variable is the prevention program, and the dependent variable is adolescent drug use.

In theory, the question may be answered by measuring the adolescents' drug use before and after they attend the program and calculate the difference. However, all sorts of factors may contribute to reduced drug use, quite apart from the prevention program. Perhaps a new drug abuse awareness program was offered in all the high schools in the community and made an impression on a number of the adolescents who attended the community-based program.

Suppose, further, that one of the adolescents who had dropped out of the community-based program died of an overdose—an upsetting experience for everyone. If we were unaware of all these other influences we could well conclude that the program was responsible for the observed reduction in drug use. In fact, however, the other factors, the high school awareness programs and the death of the friend, were really responsible for the decrease in drug use among the adolescents. In visual terms, Figure 4.1 may explain what actually happened.

In other words, a number of other extraneous (or other independent) variables may have been introduced into the study without our knowledge. Extraneous variables such as these can invalidate the relationship between the independent and dependent variables that we imagine has been found.

Let us take another example. Suppose a previous research study has determined that the proportion of reported AIDS cases is higher in one ethnic group

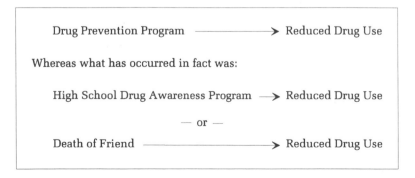

FIGURE 4.1   Relationship Between and
Among Variables

than in another. Erroneous conclusions may easily be drawn from such results: that one ethnic group is genetically more susceptible to AIDS than the other; or that homosexuality or drug use is more prevalent in one group than in the other. In fact, a variety of socioeconomic factors may be at work. Perhaps the group with a higher proportion of AIDS cases is also the group with higher rates of poverty, school dropout, substance abuse, and related social problems. Perhaps the higher AIDS rate has more to do with greater intravenous drug use and less awareness of AIDS prevention than it does with genetic susceptibility or homosexuality.

Step 5: Formulating a Research Hypothesis

In our example of Russell's study, once she had chosen the general problem area of sexual exploitation of females, she needed to specify exactly what research questions her study would be designed to answer and what hypotheses would be tested. The research questions she chose to examine were related to the three principal concepts of her study: rape, child sexual abuse, and workplace harassment (Rothery, 1993a,b).

A descriptive research study may begin with the idea that *X*, the independent variable, may be related to *Y*, the dependent variable. Perhaps in an explanatory study, we can go so far as to speculate that if *X* occurs, then *Y* will result. Our speculation can be written in the form of an explanatory statement—"X affects *Y*." The explanatory statement form is known as a *hypothesis*. In short, a hypothesis is an answer to a specific research question *before* a research study has been conducted to test whether the answer is true or not.

A hypothesis is not just any statement: It is a statement that can be proved or disproved by comparison with "objective facts." "Twenty-four angels can sit on the head of a pin" is not a hypothesis because it is not possible to count the number of angels who may (or may not) be sitting on a pin. "Moral values are declining" is not a good hypothesis because it is difficult to define "moral values" precisely in order to determine whether they are declining or not. Besides, the word "declining" begs the question, declining from what?

It *is* possible to define and measure the concept "moral values," via the variables (or indicators) that it contains. Moral values might be conceptualized in terms of such variables as divorce rates, rights for homosexuals, or a host of other variables depending on the personal values of the researcher. "Declining" can also be conceptualized as the difference in moral values now as opposed to 50 years ago. "Moral values are declining" is not an impossible statement to be used as a hypothesis, but it is certainly not a sensible one.

Step 5a: Evaluating the Research Hypotheses

As we know by now, a hypothesis is derived from the research question which is derived from the research problem area. There are four criteria that can used to differentiate a good, useful hypothesis from one that is not so good or useful. They are: (1) relevance, (2) completeness, (3) specificity, and (4) potential for testing (Rothery, 1993a,b; Williams, Tutty, & Grinnell, 1995).

Relevance   It is hardly necessary to stress that a useful hypothesis is one that contributes to our knowledge base. Nevertheless, some social work problem areas are enormously complex, and it is common for people to get so sidetracked in reading the professional literature that they develop very interesting hypotheses totally unrelated to the original problem area they wanted to investigate in the first place. The relevancy criterion is a reminder that, to repeat, the research hypothesis must be directly related to the research question, which in turn must be directly related to the general research problem area.

Completeness   A hypothesis should be a complete statement that expresses our intended meaning in its entirety. The reader should not be left with the impression that some word or phrase is missing. "Moral values are declining" is one example of an incomplete hypothesis. Other examples include a whole range of comparative statements without a reference point. The statement, "Males are more aggressive," for example, may be assumed to mean "Men are more aggressive than women," but someone investigating the social life of animals may have meant, "Male humans are more aggressive than male gorillas."

Specificity   A hypothesis must be unambiguous. The reader should be able to understand what each variable contained in the hypothesis means and what relationship, if any, is hypothesized to exist between them. Consider, for example, the hypothesis, "Badly timed family therapy affects success." Badly timed family therapy may refer to therapy offered too soon or too late for the family to benefit; or to the social worker or family being late for therapy sessions; or to sessions that are too long or too short to be effective. Similarly, "success" may mean resolution of the family's problems as determined by objective measurement, or it may mean the family's—or the social worker's—degree of satisfaction with therapy, or any combination of these.

With regard to the relationship between the two variables, the reader may assume that we are hypothesizing a negative correlation: That is, the more badly timed the therapy, the less success will be achieved. On the other hand, perhaps we are only hypothesizing an association: Bad timing will invariably co-exist with lack of success.

Be that as it may, the reader should not be left to guess at what we mean by a hypothesis. If we are trying to be both complete and specific, we may hypothesize, for example:

Family therapy that is undertaken *after* the male perpetrator has accepted responsibility for the sexual abuse of his child is more likely to succeed in reuniting the family than family therapy undertaken *before* the male perpetrator has accepted responsibility for the sexual abuse.

The above hypothesis is complete and specific. It leaves the reader in no doubt as to what we mean, but it is also somewhat wordy and clumsy. One of the difficulties in writing a good hypothesis is that complete, specific statements tend to need more words than incomplete, ambiguous statements.

Potential for Testing   The last criterion for judging whether a hypothesis is good and useful is the ease with which the truth of the hypothesis can be verified. Some statements cannot be verified at all with presently available measurement techniques. "Telepathic communication exists between identical twins," is one such statement. Moreover, much of Emile Durkheim's work on suicide was formulated in such a way that it was not testable by the data-gathering techniques available in the 1960s.

A hypothesis of sufficient importance will often generate new data-gathering techniques, which will enable it to be eventually tested. Nevertheless, as a general rule, it is best to limit hypotheses to statements that can be tested immediately by available measurement methods in current use.

Step 5b: Formulating One- and Two-Tailed Research Hypotheses

In light of the preceding four criteria, a research hypothesis can be defined as a complete, specific, testable statement which, when verified, will generate knowledge relevant to the problem area being investigated. Arriving at such a statement is often a difficult and time-consuming step that involves a detailed review of the professional literature, extensive dialogue with colleagues, repeated revisions of the research question, and several unsuccessful attempts at formulating the actual hypothesis.

Suppose, for example, that we are interested in why some social workers seem to develop negative attitudes toward our profession and others do not. As a result of reading, conversation, and personal experience, we may come to believe that social workers' attitudes toward our profession are influenced mainly by their own value systems. Accordingly, a research hypothesis may be developed, as follows (Williams, Tutty, & Grinnell, 1995):

Research Hypothesis:
Social workers who value a social institutional change model of practice will evidence more negative attitudes toward the social work profession than social workers who value an individual client change model.

As we know, the above research hypothesis is a statement that we propose to test and hope to verify by undertaking a quantitative research study. It is the entire focus of our study, as it guides the study's research design, the data-collection methods, measuring instruments used, the selection of the research participants studied, and the type of data analysis.

There are two types of research hypotheses—one-tailed research hypotheses and two-tailed research hypotheses.

One-Tailed Research Hypotheses   A one-tailed research hypothesis simply predicts a specific relationship between the independent variable and the dependent variable. The following hypothesis is an example of a one-tailed research hypothesis: The more positive support statements that social workers provide clients during individual therapy sessions, the better the chances of positive client outcomes. This statement is predicting a direct and specific relationship between an independent variable (number of positive support statements) and a dependent variable (client outcome). One-tailed research hypotheses are used mainly in explanatory research studies where there is a large amount of previous literature available.

Two-Tailed Research Hypotheses   Unlike the one-tailed research hypothesis, which predicts a specific relationship between two variables, the two-tailed hypothesis does not. The following hypothesis is an example of a two-tailed research hypothesis: There is a relationship between the gender of social workers and their effectiveness with their clients. This statement does not say whether male social workers will be more effective with their clients than will female workers, or vice versa. All it says is that it predicts a relationship between the two variables—gender of workers and their effectiveness with their clients. These types of hypotheses are used primarily in descriptive research studies.

Step 5c: Formulating Rival Hypotheses

A hypothesis that competes with one- and two-tailed research hypotheses is known as a *rival hypothesis*. Rival hypotheses use other extraneous independent variables that may affect the dependent variable (Step 4d). In some cases, the best way to show that a research hypothesis is true is to show that other, or rival hypotheses, are *not* true. If it can be shown, for example, that social workers' attitudes toward our profession (dependent variable) are *not* affected by their socioeconomic background (independent variable) it becomes more likely that their attitudes toward our profession are determined solely by whether they value a social institutional change model or individual client change model of practice (Williams, Tutty, & Grinnell, 1995).

If we wished to verify the above research hypothesis, we could hypothesize that the social workers' socioeconomic backgrounds were also related to their attitudes, in the hope that this rival hypothesis would be untrue.

In order to test our initial research hypothesis, we need to: (1) select a sample of social workers, (2) measure their attitudes toward the social work profession, (3) determine which model of practice each values most, and (4) perform a statistical analysis to discover whether the workers who value a social institutional change model have more negative attitudes toward our profession than do social workers who value an individual client change model. The possibility that socioeconomic background might be an extraneous variable can be controlled by making it an independent variable in the following:

Rival Hypothesis:
Social workers who have high socioeconomic backgrounds (a second potential independent variable) will evidence more negative attitudes toward the social work profession (the same dependent variable) than social workers who have low socioeconomic backgrounds.

Obviously there are other extraneous variables that could invalidate the results, such as gender, age, personality, type of job, educational level, parents' occupations, or length of work experience. We could formulate further rival hypotheses to deal with these, a potentially confusing procedure. An alternative is to declare that these extraneous variables might have affected our study's results but were not addressed in the current study. Others interested in the area may choose to address these extraneous variables in future studies.

Step 6: Developing a Sampling Plan

Sample selection is an essential part of a quantitative research study. In this step, representatives from a total population are chosen to constitute a sample. In Russell's study, for example, her population was American women. From this population, she selected a sample of these women. Her intention in collecting data from the sample was to be able to generalize her findings to the population of American women as a whole. Since selecting the sample involves an element of chance as to who is chosen, statistical techniques are used to determine the probability that the sample accurately represents the population from which it was drawn (Rothery, 1993a; Williams, Tutty, & Grinnell, 1995).

The sampling plan is integrally related to the other steps in the research process. Russell wanted to know the frequency of reported and unreported rapes committed against women representing a cross-section of American society—women from different age groups, different racial and cultural backgrounds, and different social and economic circumstances. This goal demanded certain methodological decisions.

Because Russell wanted to know about unreported as well as reported rapes, she opted to gather self-report data directly from women themselves, rather than relying on secondary sources such as police reports. Because she wanted to be able to estimate the frequency of rape in the general population of American women, she elected to do what no researcher before her had done in investigating this question: She studied a sample of women she had randomly selected from a larger population.

And because she wanted to learn about the experiences of women from diverse subgroups comprising the larger population, she had to utilize a large sample (930 women). A random sample of this size offers reasonable assurance that different racial, cultural, and socioeconomic groups are represented.

Step 7: Selecting a Data Collection Method

The decisions as to what problem area to study, how the variables are going to be conceptualized, how the variables are to be operationalized and labeled, what type of research hypothesis is going to be tested, and what sample is to be used in the study affect the decisions as to what data collection strategy is to be used (Step 7). In Russell's study, since operationalization of the variable, rape, required a self-report from the women interviewed regarding their experiences, her decision to develop questions for use in a personal interview logically followed (Rothery, 1993a).

If she had taken the lead of other researchers, she might have chosen instead to document the occurrence of rape from existing statistics such as police records. In this case, her operationalization of rape would have been very different. An event could be considered as a rape when police officers decided to record it as such.

Having decided that women's self-reports of their own experiences were what she wanted to measure, Russell then had to consider various measurement options. If standardized measuring instruments had been available to gather data about the criteria she had identified as critical, she could have used one of these (Chapter 8). After she had determined that the data being sought required the development of specific questions for her study, she could have decided to use a mailed questionnaire instead of interviewing (Chapter 14).

Each choice makes a difference in the kind of data collected and the kinds of findings they generate. The principal standardized measurement options available to us are discussed in Part III (Chapters 7–9) of this text. The various obtrusive data collection methods that we can use in research studies are discussed Part V (Chapters 13–15), and the unobtrusive ones are presented in Part VI (Chapters 16–19).

Step 7a: Collecting the Data

Data collection, in which plans developed in the earlier steps of the research process are implemented, is a critical stage in most research projects. Mistakes, poor responses, unforeseen problems with measuring instruments, and bad luck at this stage can seriously affect the quality of the data that are subsequently available for analysis.

The need for meticulous planning, groundwork, and clear contracts with those who can affect our access to the data is obvious. The considerable effort invested in the research project before this point can be wasted if the data collection is flawed or unsuccessful (Rothery, 1993a; Williams, Tutty, & Grinnell, 1995).

Step 8: Analyzing the Data

Raw data seldom provide a direct answer to a research question or a direct test of a hypothesis. Such answers emerge only when the data are organized, the patterns that exist within them are identified, and the meaningfulness and significance of those patterns are assessed.

It is likely that the data for Russell's study consisted of 930 rows of numbers stored in a computer, which would produce a printout that would make decidedly uninteresting reading. The numbers are useful only when the data are analyzed to reveal the patterns in them. How many women reported having had experiences that fit the researcher's established operational definition of rape? Are women of a particular age more vulnerable or more at risk than others? Is rape more commonly experienced by poor rather than rich women? Are the perpetrators more often strangers, or are they likely to be known to their victims?

The purpose of the analytical stage of a quantitative research study is to answer such questions by examining patterns within the data, primarily through the use of statistical techniques. A knowledge of statistics provides us with logically sound procedures we can use to state both the patterns that exist within our data set and the probability that such patterns are statistically significant rather than random events appearing in the data by chance.

This knowledge can best be obtained from a statistics course that examines statistical techniques for describing and making inferences about data in social work research. A brief explanation of the procedures used in testing hypotheses and correlating data can be found in Chapter 21.

Step 9: Writing the Report

In the final stage of a quantitative research study, our study's findings are written up and made available to the appropriate professional and scientific audience. There is no point in accumulating social work knowledge if it is not disseminated to social workers who can use it. Our findings must be made public also so that other researchers can evaluate them in light of the research design and perhaps subject them to further tests.

It is in this step that our study's potential for adding to our knowledge base can be realized. Evaluation of the findings determines the worth of our research effort in relation to social work theory and practice.

Figure 4.2 on the following page presents a detailed diagram of how research hypotheses are constructed using all the steps presented in this chapter.

THE QUANTITATIVE RESEARCH APPROACH AND PRACTICE

The beliefs that social work interventions should be modeled on quantitative principles and that practice theory should be anchored in the pursuit of quantita-

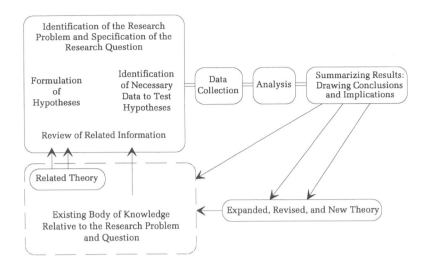

FIGURE 4.2   HYPOTHESIS CONSTRUCTION AND
THE RESEARCH PROCESS

tive data have been dominant in our profession for decades. Not all of us, however, have embraced quantitative principles with a great deal of zeal. There are those of us who are fearful of the effects of such a commitment by our profession (Rothery, 1980). One concern is that in striving for "scientific and objective" ways to deal with people and their problems, we may subordinate our human values and social commitment.

Another argument is that the helping relationship is a unique and creative exchange that inevitably will be distorted by ill-conceptualized quantitative investigations in which the overall goal is to reduce this relationship to common measurable terms. The position we take here is that the art of caring and creative exchange, and the use of quantitative research approach, can and should coexist. In fact, their coexistence is necessary if we are to be effective in creating social change by drawing attention to social problems, evaluating our practices, and testing hypotheses (Rothery, 1993a,b; Williams, Tutty, & Grinnell, 1995).

Ethical Considerations

It is precisely because of our humane concern for people and our desire to help that the findings from quantitative studies must be incorporated into our practices. If large-scale quantitative studies have the potential to raise public consciousness about issues such as family violence, serving as a catalyst for positive social change, for instance, then it would be inhumane not to study such an issue. If data are already available, or can be gathered, that will indicate the most effective methods of dealing with client problems, it would be irresponsible not to utilize them. In any discipline, creative people work within constraints, and social work practice will not become less of an art by becoming more disciplined. In recent years, respect for the contributions that scientific inquiry can make through the quantitative research approach has become a firmly established value in our profession (Rothery, 1993a,b; Williams, Tutty, & Grinnell, 1995).

LIMITATIONS

Both the quantitative and qualitative research approaches have limitations. In quantitative studies the principal limitations have to do with the: (1) principle of reactivity, (2) principle of reductionism, (3) principle of scientific determinism, and (4) need for logical consistency (Rothery, 1993a).

Principle of Reactivity

Criticisms of the ideal of objectivity often invoke the reactivity principle, which states that things observed or measured are affected by the fact that they are being observed or measured (see Box 1.1). As interviewers or observers, researchers are an active influence on the phenomena being studied. It is difficult for them to be truly neutral, objective, outside observers. Because we normally study other people, there is some degree of interaction between us and the research participants we are studying. Even contacting people via a mailed questionnaire entails a relationship of some sort. When a questionnaire is used, the respondent is influenced directly by the questions (items) on the questionnaire itself and indirectly by the person who developed it.

In the past, we have attempted to avoid this problem by adopting a kind of pseudoneutrality, making everything we said or did in relation to our research participants as impersonal and standardized as possible. In retrospect, we went to great lengths that may seem silly, and our efforts were often futile. It is impossible for two people to not communicate, and rigid formality on our part undoubtedly would affect the kinds of data provided by the research participants (i.e., the respondents).

Nevertheless, while this limitation has to be accepted, steps can be taken to minimize its effects. Russell, for example, used only women as interviewers in her study on rape. She may have risked serious distortions to her data if she had men interviewing the women about their experiences of victimization by other men. It is also possible, however, that being interviewed by women could have induced the respondents to exaggerate their experiences.

Russell minimized such a potential risk by giving attention to the selection and training of her interviewers, as well as taking great care in the development of her interview schedule and the questions it contained. There are no logical grounds for absolute certainty that interviewer biases did not affect what the research participants said in some systematic way, however. Most quantitative research studies suffer from this problem to some extent. The only solution is that we must take vigilant efforts to take account of it and minimize its impact whenever possible.

Principle of Reductionism

Measurement imposes boundaries. As we know from Step 3, the operationalization of concepts is a matter of reducing them to measurable variables. Because the quantitative research approach has conceptual demands that require the placement of boundaries around concepts, or ideas, Russell had to reduce the meaning of the concept of rape to certain specified types of events, excluding all others. Some respondents, for example, reported feeling forced rather than being forced, or having intercourse because of a threat that was not a threat of physical force or bodily harm. For Russell's purposes, such experiences were not classified as rapes. Other researchers might opt for a broader definition that would include them, but the concept of rape would still require boundaries. Without them, measurement is impossible.

The primary danger of reductionism is that it may distort or oversimplify the concept being studied to the point that the concept is trivialized or rendered unrecognizable. In order to meet such demands, highly complex and subtle concepts such as the "therapeutic relationship" may be described as nothing but a few selected measurable variables—eye contact in seconds per minute (Variable 1), forward trunk lean measured in degrees from the vertical (Variable 2), or the number of affective words employed per minute of interviewing time (Variable 3). Such definitions can produce reliable measures (see Chapter 7), but line-level workers will know that the concept of "therapeutic relationship" is somehow being missed and may find the variables that it contains simplistic, unrealistic, and meaningless.

While reductionism cannot be avoided in quantitative research studies, the problems associated with it can be minimized. Simple awareness of the risk of such problems on the part of researchers and research consumers is helpful. As we know from Chapter 1, practicing social workers can become actively involved in research studies as producers, as well as consumers or contributing partners. The more firmly we are rooted in practice research, the less likely we are to overlook the possibility that reductionism is creating distortions in the concepts under study.

Principle of Scientific Determinism

Quantitative research studies have their roots in the positivistic research tradition. The foundation of the positivist doctrine is based on the idea that there is only one true "scientific method" and from this method comes certain knowledge. The principle of scientific determinism suggests that facts are generalizable and must be independent of our subjective feelings, beliefs, and values. In other words, the "data speak for themselves." The failure to acknowledge the influence of individual, situational, and contextual factors, however, has been a major shortcoming of the quantitative paradigm (Chapter 2). This criticism is especially valid when it comes to research studies on gender and race. Family violence research studies that were based on the Conflict Tactics Scale, a highly standardized measuring instrument that counts individual acts of violence by husbands and wives, for instance, has resulted in reports that women are about as violent within the family as men (Straus, Gelles, & Steinmetz, 1980; Straus & Gelles, 1986).

Despite the limited relationship between these findings and the reports from those of us who work with women who are victims of family violence, these studies have been considered "truth" and were used to justify the withdrawal of financial support from women's shelters and domestic violence treatment programs. The Conflict Tactics Scale, however, ignores both the fact that many women resort to violence in self-defense and the gender difference that occurs in severity of injury.

Equally harmful has been the operationalization of intelligence by the IQ (intelligence quotient) test. On the basis of IQ testing, some studies have made claims that Caucasians are more intelligent than African Americans. Such claims have resulted in differential treatment and privilege, ignoring the fact that IQ scores are a function of training in the white-oriented educational system. These examples of family violence and race studies argue against scientific determinism. Any study that does not account for the interactive effects of the person, environment, and context can only serve to distort reality.

Need for Logical Consistency

All the steps within a quantitative research study must be logically related to the research problem, which is related to the research question, which is related to the research hypothesis. They also must be specified in enough detail that others would be able to duplicate the study.

Russell elected to use a cross-sectional, one-time survey to measure the incidence of rape inflicted on American women. A person with a different research question, such as establishing the efficacy of a particular treatment for rape victims or comparing the relative value of court-mandated versus voluntary treatment for perpetrators, would likely be drawn to group and explanatory designs (see Chapter 11). These research designs are more logically powerful in their ability to address such questions.

The formulation of the research design is an important factor in determining whether Russell's findings are logically worthy of belief. If her operationalization of variables, development of her sampling plan, and selection of her data collection method are logically consistent with her research question, her data on the incidence of rape experienced by American women, based on the answers of the survey respondents in her sample, are likely to be accurate. They should take precedence over earlier lower estimates, which were based on personal impressions or research studies that utilized less-rigorous research designs.

1. EXAMPLES OF GENERAL PROBLEM AREAS

    a. Threats of abduction and sexual abuse of schoolchildren.
    b. Racism and its effects on the cultural identities of Native Americans.

2. EXAMPLES OF PROBLEMS AFTER BEGINNING SPECIFICATION

    a. Families react in different ways to threats like the danger facing the children at the school in Innisfail. How might other possible familial reactions affect the emotional responses of the children to this threat?
    b. Can we identify different stereotypes presented to Native American children that are particularly important in their effect on cultural identity?

3. EXAMPLES OF RESEARCH QUESTIONS DERIVED FROM PROBLEMS

    a. What do different families say when their children are threatened with abuse by a stranger? How are the children affected by these reactions with respect to their anxiety levels?
    b. How does the portrayal of Native Americans in standard school textbooks affect the cultural identity of students?

4. EXAMPLES OF RESEARCH QUESTIONS AFTER SPECIFICATION (OPERATIONALIZATION) OF THE CONCEPTS

    a. How do children at John Wilson Elementary School from egalitarian families differ from children from patriarchal families in the amount of anxiety they experience respecting the threat posed by the abductor?
    b. Who do latency-age (6–11) Native American boys choose as heroes to identify with, and how does this relate to their expressed pride in their native culture?

5. EXAMPLES OF RESEARCH HYPOTHESES

    a. Girls from patriarchal families will be more anxious than girls from egalitarian families when confronted with the threat of adult male violence.
    b. Latency-age (6–11 years old) Native American children who name nonnatives as their heroes will have lower self-esteem than those who name natives as their heroes.

FIGURE 4.3   EXAMPLES OF PROBLEMS, QUESTIONS, AND HYPOTHESES

Departures from the Ideal Study

While the research design attempts to create an ideal study, capable of generating data that are logically consistent with the research questions and hypotheses, and that will provide accurate measurements of the variables, the ideal is rarely accomplished. One reason is that seldom are enough resources available to conduct a perfect study, and compromises are always necessary.

To document the incidence of rape experienced by American women, Russell ideally should have studied a nationwide sample. As a concession to limited resources, she selected a sample of women from only one large city. It is statistically possible to examine the sample she obtained and assess how similar the women in it were to the entire population of American women, but the true representativeness of the sample cannot be assured (Rothery, 1993a).

Aside from practicality, fate also affects how close a research study can come to meeting the quantitative ideal. The social world that is the object for study is complex and untidy, and unpredictable factors invariably impinge on any research study. What can be anticipated can be planned for, but unanticipated elements or effects can only be dealt with creatively when they are encountered and then reported faithfully in the published findings.

In sum, while the steps of quantitative research studies have been discussed in a logical order, the true sequencing of events in this process is considerably less tidy. Work on the steps associated with one step lays the groundwork for those in subsequent steps, but there is a good deal of moving back and forth between and among steps in most quantitative research projects.

Thus, the formulation of research questions and hypotheses is undertaken before variables are operationalized, for example, but the step of developing operational definitions usually has a retroactive influence on how the research questions or hypotheses are stated. Similarly, consideration of sampling plans and data collection options may result in changes to operational definitions of variables, which can in turn modify the way key variables are conceptualized. The situation is analogous to the life cycle, which consists of a series of developmental steps. Some steps lay the groundwork for others, but no accomplished step is ever finally set aside (Rothery, 1993a).

FROM RESEARCH PROBLEMS TO RESEARCH HYPOTHESES

Two contemporary examples presented in Chapter 1 will be used to illustrate how we can go from a general problem area to formulating research questions from the problem area to formulating hypotheses utilizing the quantitative research approach. As presented in Chapter 1, Figures 1.1 and 1.2 contain two newspaper articles that appeared in Canada. As can be easily seen, however, they could have appeared anywhere in the world. Figure 1.1 focuses upon a child molester in an elementary school and Figure 1.2 focuses on racism (Rothery, 1993b).

Figure 4.3 on the previous page clearly illustrates how the two general problem areas depicted in the two articles have been refined to research questions and hypotheses. It must be kept in mind that there are many other research questions and hypotheses that could have been formulated from the same two general problem areas (Rothery, 1993a,b; Williams, Tutty, & Grinnell, 1995).

SUMMARY

The quantitative research approach roughly follows the highly interrelated steps outlined in this chapter. In a spirit of challenge and inquiry, quantitative studies seek to reveal the objective world by constantly checking to see if subjectively held assumptions, beliefs, and theories are independently valid. This spirit motivates a disciplined approach to investigating problem areas and research questions and testing hypotheses with quantitative data. In addition to testing ideas through the use of the hypothetico-deductive method, quantitative studies describe variables and their relationships, predict and compare outcomes, analyze components of an intervention, or seek to establish cause-effect relationships.

The quantitative research approach is currently used in the great majority of social work research studies. It is not a panacea for every difficulty social workers face and it is not value-free, but it is effective in providing critically important knowledge respecting issues about which much is still to be learned. This approach has made, and will continue to make, vital contributions to the social work knowledge base and a demonstrable difference in the methods we use to help our clients. The usefulness of the quantitative research approach has been tempered by its misuse. Criticisms of the quantitative approach, especially where race and gender are concerned, are undoubtedly justified. The criticisms of the quantitative research approach, however, have less to do with quantification and much to do with its application. Quantitative researchers are ultimately responsible for the knowledge they generate. This implies a concern for: the problems we choose to study, choices made in the operationalization of concepts, and decisions on where results are presented and published. These concerns are technical in nature and can be addressed without questioning the merit of the quantitative research approach.

The quantitative research approach is not the only method for pursuing knowledge for our profession. The qualitative approach produces a distinctively different type of knowledge and is examined in detail in the following chapter.

REFERENCES AND FURTHER READINGS

BADGLEY, R. (Chairman). (1984). *Sexual offenses against children. Volume 1: Report of the committee on sexual offenses against children and youths.* Ottawa, Canada: Ministry of Supply and Services.

CALGARY HERALD: "Show ignores Native stereotype," September 6, 1991, Section B, p. 6.

CALGARY HERALD: "Another kidnap bid has parents nervous," September 6, 1991, p. 1.

DIAMOND, J. (1987). Soft sciences are harder than hard sciences. *Discover, 8* (August), 34-39.

FINKELHOR, D. (1984). *Child sexual abuse: New theory and research.* New York: Free Press.

GRINNELL, R.M., JR., & WILLIAMS, M. (1990). *Research in social work: A primer* (pp. 58-85). Itasca, IL: F.E. Peacock.

HEMPEL, C.G. (1966). *Philosophy of natural science.* Englewood Cliffs, NJ: Prentice-Hall.

HUCK, S.W., & SANDLER, H.M. (1979). *Rival hypotheses: Alternative interpretations of data-based conclusions.* New York: Harper & Row.

MYERS, D.G. (1983). *Social psychology.* New York: McGraw-Hill.

NATIONAL ASSOCIATION OF SOCIAL WORKERS (1980). *National Association of Social Workers code of ethics.* Silver Spring, MD: Author.

REINHARZ, S. (1992). Feminist survey research and other statistical research formats. In S. Reinharz (Ed.), *Feminist methods in social research* (pp. 76-94). New York: Oxford University Press.

ROTHERY, M. (1980). *The contribution of science to social work practice theory and education: Implications for the development of an empirically grounded knowledge base.* Toronto: University of Toronto Faculty of Social Work.

ROTHERY, M.A. (1993a). The positivistic research approach. In R.M. Grinnell, Jr. (Ed.), *Social work research and evaluation* (4th ed., pp. 38-52). Itasca, IL: F.E. Peacock.

ROTHERY, M.A. (1993b). Problems, questions, and hypotheses. In R.M. Grinnell, Jr. (Ed.), *Social work research and evaluation* (4th ed., pp. 17-37). Itasca, IL: F.E. Peacock.

RUSSELL, D. (1984). *Sexual exploitation: Rape, child sexual abuse, and workplace harassment.* Newbury Park, CA: Sage.

SINGLETON, R.A., JR., STRAITS, B.C., & MILLER STRAITS, M. (1993). *Approaches to social research* (2nd ed., pp. 88-93). New York: Oxford.

SMITH, N.J. (1988). Formulating research goals and problems. In R.M. Grinnell, Jr. (Ed.), *Social work research and evaluation* (3rd ed., pp. 89-110). Itasca, IL: F.E. Peacock.

STRAUS, M. A., & GELLES, R. (1986). Societal change and change in family violence from 1975 to 1985 as revealed by two national surveys. *Journal of Marriage and the Family, 48*, 465-479.

STRAUSS, M., GELLES, R., & STEINMETZ, S. (1980). *Behind closed doors: Violence in the American family.* Garden City, NY: Anchor Books.

TUTTY, L.M., ROTHERY, M., & GRINNELL, R.M., JR. (1996). *Qualitative research for social workers: Phases, steps, and tasks.* Needham Heights, MA: Allyn and Bacon.

WALKER, L. (1979). *The battered woman.* New York: Harper & Row.

WEINBACH, R.W., & GRINNELL, R.M., JR. (1996). *Applying research knowledge: A workbook for social work students* (2nd ed., pp. 33-40). Needham Heights, MA: Allyn & Bacon.

WILLIAMS, M., TUTTY, L.M., & GRINNELL, R.M., JR. (1995). *Research in social work: An introduction* (2nd ed.). Itasca, IL: F.E. Peacock.

YLLO, K. (1988). Political and methodological debates in wife abuse research. In K. Yllo & M. Bograd (Eds.), *Feminist perspectives on wife abuse* (pp. 28-49). Newbury Park, CA: Sage.

Cynthia Franklin
Catheleen Jordan

Chapter 5

Qualitative Approaches to the Generation of Knowledge

I N THIS CHAPTER WE present the steps of the qualitative research approach and parallel the format of the previous chapter on quantitative research to enable the reader to see how the steps contained within each approach are similar (and dissimilar) to each other. The qualitative research approach, also referred to as naturalistic research, interpretive research, and field research, is a generic umbrella concept that represents a myriad of nonquantitative research approaches. On a general level, qualitative studies involve the careful collection and use of a variety of empirical data sources such as: (1) data gathered from case studies, (2) personal experiences of people, (3) interviews with people, (4) introspections, (5) life stories, (6) observations, and (7) historical interactional and visual texts.

As described throughout this chapter, the qualitative research approach to knowledge building is relatively interpretive and diverse when directly contrasted with the quantitative research approach. In this spirit, qualitative researchers study concepts in natural or field settings, such as homes, schools, and communities, in an attempt to make sense of the meanings that people bring to their personal experiences.

A qualitative research study is multi-method in its focus. It also involves an interpretive, naturalistic approach, to answering research questions. Thus, it uses no single methodology at the expense of another. That is, it has no distinct theory, or perspective. There are many traditions of the qualitative research approach that vary across the social science disciplines such as sociology, psychology, anthropology, and ethnology, each having its own guiding theory, assumptions, and methods. Rather than comparing and contrasting the numerous qualitative approaches to knowledge building, however, we will only focus on the most common generic steps that are contained within most qualitative research studies. First, we need to describe qualitative research studies.

WHAT DO QUALITATIVE RESEARCH STUDIES LOOK LIKE?

With the previous comments in mind, let us take a look at how Leslie M. Tutty, Michael A. Rothery, and Richard M. Grinnell, Jr. (1996) describe qualitative research studies:

- Research studies that are conducted primarily in the natural settings where the research participants carry out their daily business in a "non-research" atmosphere
- Research studies where variables cannot be controlled and experimentally manipulated (though changes in variables and their effect on other variables can certainly be observed)
- Research studies in which the questions to be asked are not always completely conceptualized and operationally defined at the outset (though they can be)
- Research studies in which the data collected are heavily influenced by the experiences and priorities of the research participants, rather than being collected by predetermined and/or highly structured and/or standardized measurement instruments
- Research studies in which meanings are drawn from the data (and presented to others) using processes that are more natural and familiar than those used in the quantitative method. The data need not be reduced to numbers and statistically analyzed (though counting and statistics can be employed if they are thought useful) (p. v)

As can be expected, and like the quantitative research approach, there are as many definitions of the qualitative research approach as there are people willing to define it. We have adapted and modified Robert Emerson's (1983) definition of *field research* to offer the following definition of the qualitative research process:

Qualitative research is the study of people in their natural environments as they go about their daily lives. It tries to understand how people live, how they talk and behave, and what captivates and distresses them.... More importantly, it strives to understand the *meaning* people's words and behaviors have for them.

WHAT DO QUALITATIVE RESEARCHERS DO?

With the above definition in mind, we can now describe what some of our roles and responsibilities would be if we actually carried out a qualitative research study. W. Lawrence Neuman (1994) has provided a helpful summary of what would be required to do a qualitative investigation. The qualitative researcher:

- Observes ordinary events and everyday activities as they happen in natural settings, in addition to any unusual occurrences.
- Is directly involved with the people being studied and personally experiences the process of daily social life in the field setting.
- Acquires an insider's point of view while maintaining the analytic perspective or distance of an outsider.
- Uses a variety of techniques and social skills in a flexible manner as the situation demands.
- Produces data in the form of extensive written notes, as well as diagrams, maps, or pictures to provide very detailed descriptions.
- Sees events holistically (e.g., as a whole unit, not in pieces) and individually in their social context.
- Understands and develops empathy for members in a field setting, and does not just record "cold" objective facts.
- Notices both explicit (recognized, conscious, spoken) and tacit (less recognized, implicit, unspoken) aspects of culture.
- Observes ongoing social processes without upsetting, disrupting, or imposing an outside point of view.
- Is capable of coping with high levels of personal stress, uncertainty, ethical dilemmas, and ambiguity. (p. 73)

Many of the above roles and activities are not only carried out in qualitative research studies but are required for good social work practice as well. We will now turn to the steps in a qualitative research study. (This is a good time to review the previous chapter on the quantitative research approach so comparisons of the two approaches can be made as you read along.)

STEPS IN THE QUALITATIVE RESEARCH PROCESS

Like quantitative research studies, qualitative studies share a common set of interrelated steps. Norman K. Denzin (1989) and Buford H. Junker (1960) have provided us with a composite summary of them:

- Prepare yourself, read the literature, and defocus.
- Select a field site and gain access to it.
- Adopt a social role, learn the ropes, and get along with members.
- Watch, listen, and collect quality data.
- Begin to analyze data, generate and evaluate working hypotheses.

- Focus on specific aspects of the setting and use theoretical sampling.
- Conduct field interviews with member informants.
- Physically leave the field setting, complete the analysis, and write a research report.

We have rearranged the above steps to form 12 highly interrelated steps. It should be noted that the process of actually doing a qualitative research study, via following its steps as outlined in this chapter, is never as tidy as it appears; instead of moving through the steps in an orderly linear fashion, we will inevitably be moving back and forth between and among them. You will recall that this is also true of the quantitative research process.

The 12 steps of a qualitative research study are: (1) selecting a research topic and hypothesis, (2) selecting research participants, (3) selecting a site or setting, (4) getting permission and gaining access to the field, (5) entering the field, (6) identifying key informants and gaining understanding, (7) selecting a research design, (8) selecting a data collection method, (9) recording and logging data, (10) analyzing data, (11) leaving the field, and (12) writing the report.

This chapter uses an example of a qualitative research study conducted by a social work researcher, Jane Gilgun (1995). Her study presented the moral discourses of ten men and one woman (her research participants) who were incest perpetrators. People often have difficulty understanding how conventional morality would allow parents to perpetrate sex acts against their own children, and Gilgun's study provides some interesting insights concerning this perplexing situation. Of course, to get the "whole story," we need to read the entire study, but the brief examples included here provide snapshot glimpses into the processes of the qualitative research approach.

Step 1: Selecting a Research Topic and Hypothesis

What do we, as qualitative researchers, want to know? In short, what will we want to be able to say or report by the end of our study? Like those of quantitative researchers, the questions formulated by qualitative researchers are often guided by findings from prior research studies, in addition to unanswered meaningful questions. Topics are often selected based on the researcher's: (1) personal interests, (2) life experiences, (3) desire to inductively explore possible constructs for a theory, (4) desire to solve a social problem, and (5) desire to empower individuals or groups.

Like quantitative studies, research questions guiding qualitative studies may be exploratory, descriptive, or explanatory. Descriptive questions usually elucidate the what, when, and how of a situation at a descriptive level. They describe phenomena but do not go much further in their inquiry or analysis. Explanatory questions, on the other hand, may ask how and what, but they also want to know why and seek to demonstrate relationships between or among variables. These types of questions are often used in qualitative studies seeking to test hypotheses or inductively discover hypotheses, concepts, or theories. The topic from Gilgun's study was chosen based on a guiding theory, as well as her past experiences with studying sexual abuse (Gilgun & Connor, 1989). According to her:

> The hypotheses of this study were derived from the literature on justice and care (two dominant concepts in the moral reasoning literature), and were shaped by my assumptions about incest. (p. 268)
>
> I used the concepts of justice and care to analyze the narrative accounts of incest perpetrators. These concepts are fundamental ideas in moral philosophy and theories of moral development and were brought to widespread attention by the work of Carol Gilligan and her colleagues. (pp. 265-266)

Gilgun did a literature review on the moral domains of care and justice and discussed the relationships between these concepts and incest (i.e., moral dimensions of incest). Two hypotheses were derived from her guiding theory.

1. Incest perpetrators have special regard for themselves and do not have regard for the impact of incest on their victims.
2. Incest perpetrators are not morally integrated, and if they have a moral focus, it will be on justice. (p. 268)

Gilgun's study was at the explanatory level of knowledge building since it tested two hypotheses. It hypothesized that incest perpetrators were not morally integrated (Number 1 above), and if they had a moral focus, it would be on justice (Number 2 above). In short, her study sought to understand the relationship between moral reasoning and incestuous behavior.

Social work theory can be developed by asking explanatory questions such as these. The questions then can be answered using grounded theory or analytical induction (which are two systematic approaches to data analysis). These two approaches attempt to discover hypotheses and build theories that are completely grounded in the data collected. On a case-by-case basis, they help us to discover new ideas and test relationships concerning those ideas. Grounded theory and analytical induction are described in detail latter in this chapter.

Many social work researchers like being able to choose research questions based on their personal interests, practice experiences, and perceived human needs. There are thousands of case examples that could be used to illustrate how qualitative researchers become interested in research topics. We will use the following case example because it provides an example of how to formulate exploratory, descriptive, and explanatory research questions.

An Example of Problem Selection

A clinical social worker, named Wilma, experienced the sudden death of one of her clients. This impacted her emotionally because she had been seeing her client for a long time. In addition, her client's family members wanted to talk to her about the death and even invited her to the funeral. Wilma wondered how this type of experience may have affected other social workers as well. She also wondered how they had handled similar situations. She sought advice from the professional literature—but to no avail.

Consequently, Wilma decided to conduct her own exploratory qualitative research study. She identified various colleagues who had a client die and proceeded to interview them about their experiences. At this point in time her research questions remained at an exploratory and descriptive levels. How did the client's death affect each worker? What did they do to handle this situation with family members and themselves? When Wilma entered a doctoral program (because of her experience) she remained interested in this topic.

At this time, Wilma began to ask more explanatory research questions about how this type of loss affects social workers. She wanted to explain the importance of the grief experienced in relationship to the loss. She also wanted to explore her hypothesis that the type of grief experienced by social workers is unique to the expression of grief. When she completes her study it might be possible for Wilma to move her research question to an evaluative level by suggesting a treatment intervention to help other social workers, and then exploring the effectiveness of the intervention.

Step 2: Selecting Research Participants

When compared to quantitative studies, qualitative studies usually have fewer research participants. Copeland and White (1991), for example, describe qualitative researchers who studied families as:

> using research designs that collect data from small samples who are interviewed and observed, or more accurately, are visited in the natural environment (e.g., their own homes)... Family researchers using qualitative designs are "involved intensely with participants throughout a time period, watching change unfold before them... (p. 11).

In contrast to quantitative researchers, who sometime focus on obtaining random or probability samples, qualitative researchers focus on finding a few of the best research participants who match the characteristics they want to study. Instead of increasing the size of their sample in order to attend to issues such as statistical power and the generalizability of their findings, qualitative researchers are more concerned about the personal qualities of the research participants and their suitability to provide useful and reliable data on the concepts being studied. As stated in Chapter 10, sampling techniques used in qualitative studies include:

- *Purposive sampling* — selecting participants based on certain characteristics and viability
- *Snowball sampling* — finding one or more research participants with the desirable characteristics, and then letting those participants and the field setting lead the researcher to other participants

• *Negative case sampling* — purposefully selecting participants based on the fact that they have different characteristics than previous cases

Research participants are usually experts based on their personal experiences or life situations. They become the means to gain an "insiders' perspective" and a guide for us to understand the private meanings associated with different cultures.

Let us now go back to Gilgun's study. The selection of her research participants was guided by her problem area and the availability of potential research participants. Her participants were eleven incest perpetrators, ten men and one woman, recruited on a voluntary basis from maximum- and medium-security prison sex offender treatment programs and from snowball sampling from among persons in community treatment and self-help groups. They ranged in age from 32 to 54, and they were predominantly working- and middle-class whites.

Nine were married at the time of the interview, and two were divorced. They had abused both boy and girl children. Several had abused brothers and sisters and other relatives such as cousins and nieces during adolescence. As adults, they primarily victimized their biological children, with two cases of stepfather-stepchild incest and one case of abuse of a niece.

It should be strongly noted that Step 2, selecting research participants, is heavily interrelated to Step 3, selecting a site or setting. That is, we cannot select a potential site without keeping in mind the potential research participants who would be available within a site or setting, and vica versa. In reality, then, Steps 2 and 3 are carried out at the same time. They are broken down into discrete steps only for illustrative purposes.

Step 3: Selecting a Site or Setting

As should be evident by now, qualitative research studies take place in natural or field settings. We usually gain entry into and attach ourselves to one or more field settings. As mentioned, relatively few sites are chosen for study. The study of one specific neighborhood or two or three schools may be all that is needed to answer a research question, for example.

Substantial preparatory work is needed when considering a site and getting permission to enter the field. The proper selection of a site (Step 3) and obtaining permission (Step 4) are highly interrelated steps. In reality, they are only one step; they go hand-in hand and are carried out at the same time. They are broken down into discrete steps only for illustrative purposes.

Step 4: Getting Permission and Gaining Access to the Field

Getting permission to conduct any sort of research study can, at times, be very difficult. Our research proposal has to pass through the scrutiny of at least one ethics review committee, sometimes known as a Human Subjects Review Committee, or an Internal Review Board (IRB). Sometimes research proposals must go through several ethics committees, depending on the situation. This process usually takes a good amount of time and can range from one month, if everything goes well, to six. During the ethical review process, the committees will critique our proposed study for ethical considerations and informed consent, as discussed in Chapter 2.

It may be difficult to get couples who are experiencing domestic violence to agree to fill out a short questionnaire that is a survey about their behavior patterns. It may even be more difficult to get these individuals to consent to being interviewed. This, however, is exactly what Hyden (1994) did in her study on woman battering. She found it especially difficult to persuade men to participate in her study. However, by understanding and identifying with their fears, she was successful in getting them to participate.

Beyond informed consent, however, we need to persuade potential research participants, and those people involved in the field setting, that it is a good idea for us to be in that setting and that our study is important not only to us but to them as well. This usually requires several prearranged meetings and associations with individuals long before our study actually begins. Relationships have to be formed and mutual trust and benefits have to be negotiated.

Social work researchers sometimes work within ideal field settings that make it easier to gain access to clients (research participants). Relationships with clients, agency administrators, and boards may have already been established, for example. This task is much more difficult when we have no prior knowledge of, or contact with, the setting in which our study is to take place. Even more preparation has to be completed because it is imperative that we become well acquainted with the culture and organizational dynamics of the field setting before entering the field.

Five methods that may be used for learning about field settings and forming beginning relationships include:

1. Reading everything we can about the field setting.
2. Talking at length with informed individuals about their experiences.
3. Spending time and observing in a setting.
4. Volunteering, if practical.
5. Making sure we have established rapport with insiders to the point that we have obtained informed consent, and that at least one insider we know will support our study in a "team effort."

Step 5: Entering the Field

Immersion in the field requires that we set aside an elongated period of time for the study. Getting to know the people and the field setting is the most critical aspect. We generally enter the field very deliberately, slowly increasing the hours we spend over a few weeks or months. We start out by being a kind of a "fly on the wall" in our observations and interactions and eventually increase our participation as we get to know key people and begin to feel more accepted.

Step 6: Identifying Key Informants and Gaining Understanding

Key informants are a subpopulation of the research participants who seem to know more about "the situation" than others." Hopefully, we will have identified at least one key informant in our potential research participant population (Step 2) before entering the field (Step 5). But once in the field, it may be important to identify other key informants. Good interpersonal and communication skills are a must, as they build relationships. One way to find other key informants is to be social (liked) and to ask to be introduced to other persons by people we know. Purposefully identifying, and building relationships with, internal leaders is also a good idea.

In short, research participants and key informants become partners with us. As we will see, data are recorded in a detailed and meticulous fashion, and are often passed back for review by the person who provided the information in order to make sure we recorded the data accurately. Our notes or answers from an interview, for example, should be given back to the interviewee for checking. Data may also be given to all key informants who may add their insights or ideas about the meaning of the data obtained. This promotes our understanding, and helps to prevent misinterpretations of the data as a result of our lack of knowledge of the field setting or issues.

Step 7: Selecting a Research Design

Prolonged or intense engagements in a field setting are preferred and necessary to conduct a rigorous qualitative research study. On the other hand, some researchers have collected qualitative data for very brief periods of time. There are numerous examples of qualitative studies that collected data using varying time frames. However, in order for a study to provide the depth of understanding and analysis traditionally associated with qualitative research studies, we usually need to arrange to have either long or intense periods of contact with our research participants and key informants. Qualitative studies, for example, may range from several months to many years.

New research questions may be asked during the course of collecting data. In this manner, qualitative research designs differ from experimental designs in their flexibility, in that they use a circular process of data gathering and analysis. In contrast to quantitative researchers, who usually prefer to preset the parameters of a study and stick to their original research questions and data collection methods, qualitative researchers are open for change and may welcome it as being a natural part of the process of discovery.

Qualitative researchers start out with a question, a guiding purpose, a design, and a set of techniques for gathering data but go with the flow after they enter the field. This does not mean that they completely abandon their original research questions or data collection methods; rather, they may refine them or add to them as they gain more and more data. After Gilgun had collected some data, for example, both of her major hypothesis were reformulated based on what she found. Her study started out with two hypotheses but they were modified after she collected and analyzed some of her data from her first few participants. As she puts it:

> The first hypothesis, as originally formulated, was that incest perpetrators have a special regard for themselves and do not have regard for the impact of incest on their victims. As a result of the analysis, I reformulated the hypothesis as follows:
>
> - Perpetrators have special regard for the pleasure that they define in incest.
> - Concepts of romantic love and mutuality are prominent in many but not all incestuous relationships.
> - Many perpetrators interpret their behaviors as promoting children's welfare and not hurting them.
> - The sense of love and caring that many perpetrators express for the children are contraindicated by behaviors which are sometimes unresponsive and cruel." (p. 270)

> My second original hypothesis was that incest perpetrators are not morally integrated, and if they have a moral focus, it will be on justice. I found this hypothesis inadequate. It was based on Gilligan's thesis that men tend to focus on justice and women on care and my assumptions that incest perpetrators are unlikely to integrate justice and care. Because all but one of the perpetrators were men, I assumed that they would emphasize justice aspects of their moral understanding of incest. (p. 274).

Based on her beginning data, Gilgun reformulated the justice hypotheses (Hypothesis 2) as follows:

> I formulated three statements related to justice:
>
> - Incest perpetrators are aware that incest is wrong.
> - Incest perpetrators take advantage of children's vulnerability, but many do not see their behavior this way.
> - Some incest perpetrators try and diffuse their authority and responsibility by making children the pseudo-gatekeepers of the incest.

Qualitative designs are particularly beneficial for studying hidden or obscured phenomenon. Qualitative research methods, for example, are believed to be especially relevant to studying families because there are many aspects of family processes and interactions (e.g., incest) that are not transparent, or may be too personal or complicated to be easily ascertained with quantitative methods such as structured questionnaires or standardized measures. As explained by LaRossa and Wolf (1985):

Family research owes much of its heritage to qualitative research methods. Family researchers are "outsiders" to family life but qualitative research methods provide an approach whereby they may get a glimpse of the inside through the process of intense and prolonged observations or interviews in a field setting.

Step 8: Selecting a Data Collection Method

Qualitative researchers are the principal instruments of data collection. They use a reflexive stance and do their best to minimize their biases, beliefs, and life experiences associated with the research topic. Guiding theories are also acknowledged. Reflexivity comprises critical introspection and analysis of the self as researcher, as well as deliberate, critical dialogue within research communities about assumptions and practices (Gilbert & Schmid, 1994). Actually, reflexivity is similar to the type of personal analysis therapists go through in analyzing both their personal reactions and countertransferences toward clients. The difference is that qualitative researchers do these personal analyses in relationship to their data.

Using this reflexive process, for example, a researcher who had worked for several years in women's advocacy reported that she became aware that her feminist belief system did not match with the interview data she collected from women rape victims concerning their personal experiences with having to take polygraph tests. She found it a personal struggle to accept what the women said about their experiences versus trying to force the data into her own personal conceptualizations about how women who have been raped are victimized when they have to take the polygraph.

She realized for the first time in her life that some of her ideas about the societal oppression of women may not apply in this situation. Thus, reflexivity requires critical thinking and a testing of ones own assumptions. As Gilgun notes:

> I conducted all interviews. Although, a general topical interview guide was used, the timing and wording of each question was individualized in order to capture the perspectives of my informants in their own words. The interview was primarily a dialogue, during which I frequently checked my understandings, and interpretations of the information, words, and meanings. I introduced my interpretations by saying, "I want you to know how I'm thinking about what you're saying. Let me know if I'm not understanding what you are saying." (p. 270)

Gilgun also underscores the importance of reflexivity in her study:

> Dealing with incest perpetrators in long interviews was emotionally challenging to me, and at times the informants. An important next step may be for researchers to write about reflexive processes in their research studies, closely tying accounts of Reflexivity with sections of the narratives that were evocative. (p. 279)

It should be obvious by now that the method finally used must provide good data to answer the research question. There are many ways to collect data, and we will briefly discuss three: (1) interviewing, (2) participant observation, and (3) analyzing documents.

Interviewing

Interviewing, which can be defined as a conversation with a purpose, is by far the most commonly used method of gathering data for qualitative studies. We can simply interview individuals and/or groups (focus groups). Focus groups are group interviews that rely on the interactions within groups to add to the information solicited by the interviewer. Interviewing techniques range from structured questionnaires to open-ended conversations. Depth of interviews may also vary from brief informational sets of questions to in-depth life interviews aimed at elucidating the experiences and meanings contributed to life events by individuals or groups (Berg, 1994).

Rapport is a necessary and important condition for conducting interviews and should enhance the quality of data gathered from the interviewing method. Also, we can use interview guides to gather the data. They can vary in their structure, format, length, and composition. Some interview guides are very structured, while others are totally open-ended and flexible, allowing for a broad range of responses (Berg, 1994). John Spradley (1979) has identified four types of interview questions that can be asked, and James B. Taylor (1993) has summarized them as illustrated in Figure 5.1.

Data gathering instruments are important aspects of qualitative studies in the same manner that they are important in quantitative ones. Qualitative studies can contain: (1) structured and semistructured interview schedules, (2) tape recorders, (3) video recorders, (4) cameras, (5) field notes/ journals, (6) transcription machines, and (7) computers and associated software programs.

Obtaining good equipment is a must. Using high-quality tape recorders, microphones, and cassette tapes can get expensive, but in the long run, we can save much time and money later on in the research process because it is difficult to transcribe low-quality recordings. Also, purchasing a laptop computer and appropriate software that can record the interviews on the computer may ease the burden of transcribing data.

On a general level, interviews can be: (1) structured, (2) semistructured, (3) unstructured/conversational, (4) in-depth, and (5) ethnographic. Let us now turn our attention to the five interview formats.

Structured Interviews   A formally structured interview schedule contains specific questions and directs each research participant to respond to each question in a structured predetermined fashion. This type of interview schedule is very much like a formal questionnaire. In order to develop structured interview schedules, however, we need to have information on the possible domains

> ### FOUR TYPES OF INTERVIEW QUESTIONS
>
> GRAND TOUR QUESTIONS   The informant is asked to provide wide-ranging background information. Examples: Could you describe a typical day on the substance abuse ward? Could you tell me all the things that happened when you got arrested, from the moment you saw the police to the time you got out of jail?
>
> EXAMPLE QUESTIONS   The informant is asked to provide an example of some single act, event, or category. Example: You have talked about the catch-22s in the mental health system. Could you give me an example?
>
> STRUCTURAL QUESTIONS   The informant is asked to list items in a set or category. Examples: What are the different kinds of street drugs? What are all the ways people can become members? Where are all the places you can get a flop when you first come to Kansas City?
>
> CONTRAST QUESTIONS   The informant is asked about similarities and differences in symbols or is asked to sort symbols into categories. Example: Here are three kinds of tramps, a bindle stiff, an Airedale, and a home guard. Which two of these are alike? How is the other one different?

FIGURE 5.1   TYPES OF INTERVIEW QUESTIONS IN QUALITATIVE RESEARCH STUDIES

of knowledge that may be covered within the research question. Specific questions are developed from these domains and asked of each research participant in an exact manner. The assumption is that all participants will understand each question in the same way. Thus, each question must use language that is common to every research participant in the study.

Semistructured Interviews   Unlike structured interviews, semistructured interviews allow for optional follow-up questions that may vary from participant to participant. We can develop a list of possible follow-up probes that can be used. Or, we can allow the probes to develop from the content of the interview, whereby we can use different probes in an open-ended manner. In a nutshell, semistructured interviews lie between structured and unstructured.

Unstructured/Conversational Interviews   Open-ended interviews allow for maximum variation in responses. No list of questions is used. These types of interviews are often used with the participant observation method of data gathering (to be described below). We simply direct a specific question to participants and allow other questions and probes to flow from the interview interactions. This type of interviewing is more like a friendly chat, but with specific purposes in mind.

In-Depth Interviews These interviews can be structured, semistructured, or open-ended. This form of interviewing gathers in-depth data from research participants about their lives. Personal accounts, oral histories, biographies, and life histories are commonly gathered using in-depth interviews. They usually occur over time and may be scheduled for intervals of approximately 90 minutes, every three to seven days, or on a continuing basis as the study goes along. Gilgun (1995) used open-ended life history interviews for obtaining the narrative accounts of the eleven incest perpetrators that she interviewed.

Ethnographic Interviews Ethnographic interviews are nonstructured forms of interviewing that encourage us to join with the subjective meanings (or narratives) of the research participants being interviewed. In ethnographic interviewing, our goal is to use "a conversation" as a means to form a dialogue with the person and to understand the situation from his or her viewpoint. During face-to-face speaking and mutual observation, we treat our interviewee (research participant) like "the expert" and assume a position of "not knowing" or "one down equality" (Fetterman, 1989; Jorgensen, 1989; Taylor & Bogdan, 1984).

This type of interviewing is often conducted by qualitative researchers who collect data from the perspectives of anthropological traditions. To someone watching an ethnographic interview, the interviewer appears empathic, nondirective, and conversational. The tone of the interviewer is tentative, curious, spontaneous, and caring. Conversations are structured to match the language and belief systems of the research participants.

Ethnographic interviews are similar to some other forms of clinical interviewing such as approaches stemming from client-centered or humanistic practice models. These interviewing methods encourage us to verbally follow client responses, reflect responses and feelings, and probe for deeper and more specific meanings.

In short, ethnographic methods help us gain entrance into a person's world in such a way that makes it possible to become aware of our own unique perspectives (Franklin & Jordan, 1995). Chapters 14 and 15 discuss interviewing in more detail.

Participant Observation

Participant observation is the second way we can collect data for a qualitative study. It is a nonstructured method of collecting data as we purposefully observe our research participants in their everyday life situations in the most non-intrusive manner possible. This methodology, of course, requires us to get permission from our participants and assumes a prolonged period of observation during which the processes and relationships among people are studied (Jorgensen, 1989).

Participant observation emphasizes the understanding of how the activities of groups, and interactions of settings, give meaning to certain behaviors or beliefs. It is especially useful in the following four situations (Crabtree & Miller, 1992; Jorgensen, 1989):

1. When little is known about our research participants
2. When there are important differences between outsider and insider views as in the case of diverse cultures
3. When the phenomenon is usually obscured from outsiders such as in the case of family life
4. When the phenomenon is intentionally hidden from public view such as in the case of illegal behaviors

Chapter 15 discusses in much more detail how participant observation can be used as a data collection method for qualitative studies.

Analyzing Documents

The third way to collect data for a qualitative study is through the use of existing documents. Like quantitative research studies, qualitative studies can also collect data by gathering and analyzing existing documents. In studying an organization, for example, a qualitative researcher might collect the organization's mission statement, organizational chart, and minutes from meetings. These documents become additional data, and may be used along with other data gathering methods such as interviews and observations. This means, however that we will need to develop methods for analyzing these data as complimentary to the other data obtained. Chapters 16–19 explain in depth how we can use existing documents as one form of data collection.

It is not unusual for a qualitative study to use interviews, participant observation, and documents to collect data.

Step 9: Recording and Logging Data

Laborious and meticulous writings, sometimes referred to as "thick descriptions," must be kept in the form of notes, logs, and transcripts. Thick descriptions require us to write down and record data such as meanings, intentions, and histories, within the contexts of our observations. As has been discussed previously, we write field notes and memos, transcribe audio recordings, and may synchronize and code data from videotapes, pictures, and documents. In addition to these data sources, we routinely keep personal journals and logs or calendars that detail our private personal experiences, appointments, and daily routines.

The personal journal is like a personal diary and it records our private thoughts and feelings about research participants and their lives. This information records our private interpretations and beliefs and is used to aid the reflexive process of the qualitative research enterprise. Other researchers and peer debriefers may read our journal in order to help us understand our interpretations and how our personal feelings may be influencing our data interpretations.

Two types of logs and calendars are especially important to keep. In one the date and time of every appointment is kept. This information should be coordinated with notes and transcripts in such a way that we can look at our notes and immediately look back at the log and track by date and hour who the interviewed participant was and where we were when we collected the data.

A second type of log details decision points about our data collection, interpretation, and analysis. This type of log, for example, is sequential and lets us know exactly when we decided to change our hypothesis, go in a different direction in the data collection, or interpret the data in a certain manner.

The log further explains the type of thinking and logic that went into this decision making, and may present evidence or arguments for why the data were handled in this manner. Such a log makes it easier for us to leave what is sometimes called an "audit trail." Audit trails make it possible for others to reconstruct our thinking and test our assumptions concerning our data collection, interpretations, and analyses.

Step 10: Analyzing Data

As we will see in Chapter 22, data analysis of narrative data is especially complex (Coleman & Unrau, 1996). Quantitative researchers usually rely on statistical methods such as correlation analyses, significance tests, statistical power analyses, and effect sizes to decide if the relationships between and among variables hold a meaning worth considering.

But how does a qualitative researcher build evidence from the complexities of interview transcripts, field notes, recorded observations, memos (notes about notes or speculative insights about observations), and document sources from which to draw conclusions? The answer is simple: We usually rely on conceptual schemes and narrative analyses. In order to do this, however, we need to immerse ourselves in the data.

Step 10a: Immersion in the Data

Once some data are collected in the field, we need to begin to read and interpret them right away. This means that almost every day, or at least several times a week while still in the field, we must read our field notes and transcribe our audio or video field recordings. We must set aside many hours to read the data and begin to formulate ideas about what we are observing. Ideas or questions that we may have in relationship to the data are also written and attached to the data. This is usually done in the margins of our field notes or transcribed data. Our notes, or intuitive reflections about our data, are called memos (notes about the notes). Memos are important and may be used in our data analysis. In fact, as we will see latter, qualitative data analysis programs provide mechanisms for including the memos as a part of the data analysis process.

Feedback from colleagues, preferably members of our research team (if one exists) who are also working with the data, are sought constantly concerning the data and their interpretations. We can use "peer debriefers"—outsiders to our research study—who read the data and serve as confidants and sounding boards concerning issues and interpretations that may be made from the data (Erlandson, Harris, Skipper, & Allen, 1993).

As we (and others) read the data, interesting ideas and patterns should begin to emerge and more questions may be asked. More data may be collected to fill in gaps from the prior data. We can also seek out a new case and/or return to one or more prior research participants with new questions that arose from the previously collected data.

Step 10b: Developing and Using Codebooks

Codebooks are used to organize data by applying labels and descriptions that draw distinctions between different parts of the data that have been collected. They allow us to sort and organize the data into meaningful categories that aid in the analysis. Quantitative researches use codebooks to organize data so that they can enter them into a data base or statistical analysis program. A codebook often serves the same sort of function as a table of contents in a book. By looking at the table of contents, we can easily know where certain information is and how to tell the computer to access that information. All this is accomplished by assigning code names (or values) to different pieces of data so that every data element has its own descriptor and identification number.

Qualitative researchers use codebooks to sort and organize the data, but also as a means of developing useful schemes for understanding them. Data are sorted into meaningful codes (descriptive narrative labels) and categories (conceptual narrative labels) so that we can begin to make sense of the data. This process serves a function similar to the statistical technique known as cluster analysis in quantitative research studies. In short, data are simply grouped together into coherent but distinct categories of meaning. A code is usually one word that is applied to describe a meaning associated with a string of other words or narrative dialogue (e.g., sentences, paragraphs).

In literature classes, for example, we may recall being asked to pick out the main theme in a paragraph and label it. Analyzing qualitative data is very much a similar process. It is usually not necessary to code every paragraph in the data set with a different theme or code. All we need to do is to discover re-occurring themes, and code each theme with the same code. Some data logically fit together as in a library, for example. In the library there is usually a section called "social sciences," which houses all the books about that subject. In qualitative research studies, we sort the data that fit together under that code in a similar manner as a librarian would.

Codes help discover themes in the data in addition to serving as the basis of a descriptive analysis (or first level of analysis) before developing higher order explanations, or theories. Codes describe meaning and serve as a label or source-tag that provides an index to all the data with that meaning.

Step 10c: Developing Categories

Data may also be attached to a descriptor known as a category. A category is a conceptually based code depicting a concept that we are drawing from the data, and it may have further propositions and dimensions. Categories impose further meaning on the data and are a basis for constructing them into conceptual schemes. Categories may serve as an umbrella idea, for example, with more than one theme. A category may ultimately be comprised of several codes. During the data analysis, we simply code all the data into a codebook that represents all the codes (descriptions) and categories (meanings) that have been attached to the data in a coding process.

During further analysis, these codes and categories may be collapsed or expanded. Box 5.1 presents an example of how codes were derived in an effort to build a conceptual framework for a study intended to find out why there was no burnout among staff members who worked at a halfway house for people who were previously mentally challenged.

Types of Codebooks   Two types of codebooks are generally used in qualitative studies: (1) priori codebooks, and (2) apriori codebooks (Crabtree & Miller, 1992). Priori codebooks are the most structured approach to qualitative data analysis because they are developed before data are collected. Using this type of codebook means that we developed codes and categories for the data before entering the field. These codes are usually generated from previous research studies. Gilgun developed a coding scheme before she went into the field to collect data from the incest perpetrators. She based these codes on the concepts of caring and justice.

Using priori codebooks, the data are matched to the codes and categories on the codebook. In other words, we read through the data and apply the labels and meanings from the priori codebook to the data. The codes, however, are only applied if the data match them. If there is not a good match, however, we will know that our previous assumptions are not supported by the data. Of course, this is exactly what Gilgun found in her study. At this point, we may change our

BOX 5.1

BUILDING A CONCEPTUAL FRAMEWORK
FOR THE FOUNTAIN HOUSE STUDY

In the Fountain House study, Ellen Finch wanted to find out why staff members there had not experienced the burnout that had been reported for other such helping professionals. She began by spending a week at Independence Center, Missouri, a setting closer to home but modeled on Fountain House, a New York facility for former mental patients. After this preliminary study, she had a much better idea of what to look for, what to expect, and how to approach people at Fountain House, which was four times as large and nine times as old. Once at Fountain House, she reviewed agency documents, attended unit meetings, spoke with members and staff, went to the social programs, and instituted formal staff interviews.

Finch's study was guided by a linked set of concepts which formed a conceptual framework. The concepts were drawn primarily from role theory and provided the terms, ideas, cues, categories, and assumptions that determined how the study was to be conducted. She therefore structured the interviews to cover at least the following conceptual categories:

- Individual background
- Recruitment/selection into the Fountain House staff
- Fountain House model and ideology
- Initial and ongoing socialization
- Role expectations
- Organizational processes, such as leadership, supervision, evaluation, communication, decision making, recognition, rewards
- Occupational stress
- Role adaptations and negotiation
- Organizational changes
- Growth in recent years

By thinking through in advance what the interviews should cover, Finch was well on her way to a preliminary list of categories and codes. Her field notes from the first site visit filled a large notebook.

They were organized into five types of notes: interview, observational, theoretical, methodological, and personal. She explains her procedures as follows:

> Every few days I would carefully review these notes and write descriptive code words developed prior to the fieldwork in the left margin.... These code words were derived from the interview questions and common categories of response.... The brief analytic reviews during the data collection period were used to increase awareness of patterns and recurrent themes, speculate on apparent processes, redirect interview questions and strategies, point out gaps in information, and develop explanatory paradigms.

After her first two-week visit Finch went through her notes again, seeking to clarify and refine concepts and to think through issues to be covered on a second site visit. She used the cut-and-paste method to organize field notes into coded categories, which helped make evident the patterns in the responses and observed processes. Codes were checked and revised if necessary; the original categories were modified to incorporate emergent themes. The answer to questionnaires administered to measure burnout were scored.

From this immersion in the data, new ideas and insights become evident. In this conceptualization, Finch observes, "Some patterns which emerged were consistent with initial thinking; some did not support earlier assumptions; and some were altogether new pieces of the organizational puzzle." To explain the new concepts and patterns, she had to review a large, diverse body of literature.

Finch then made plans for the second site visit. She determined that she needed to follow certain conceptual threads and drop others. More verbatim information derived from audiotaped interviews was needed to tap the information available from members. More material was needed on unit activities and what people actually did.

This evaluation led to a much revised set of categories and codes. The number of categories was reduced from 37 to 24, and the descriptors were more finely focused. The final version included such codes and categories as:

Code	Category
Stress/soc	Stressor related to socialization
Stress/wrk	Stressor related to work overload
Stress/mem	Stressor related to member behavior
R exp	Role expectations
Refram	Reframing stressors (adaptation)
Sur skil	Survival skills (adaptation)
Recruit	Recruitment and selection of staff
Soc sup	Social support
Ideo	Ideology
C lead	Charismatic leadership

Interviews during the second visit covered less material but were more in-depth, lasted longer, and seemed more relaxed. Finch was feeling more at home with the staff, and the staff was more at ease with her. After this visit came a second round of conceptualization and analysis which included ongoing revision of concepts and evaluation of patterns. The initial data analysis was supplemented with theoretical notes and summaries made in the field. The field notes and transcribed interviews were reviewed and coded, and additional demographic information was combined with the earlier data.

Without the processes of categorizing, coding, and conceptualization, Finch's strenuous work in building relationships, framing the sample, and collecting and logging the data would have yielded only so many pages of text.

analytical strategy and explore the data using an apriori codebook to see what the data are "saying." A combination of these approaches may also be used.

Unlike priori codebooks, apriori codebooks are developed after we have collected the data. These codebooks emerge from the data analysis itself. Some authors have referred to apriori codebooks as a template (Crabtree & Miller, 1992). When using an apriori codebook, we simply read through the data and ask, "what do the data mean?" We then apply a code to chunks of the data (i.e., paragraphs, sentences) and begin to develop our categories of meaning. An apriori codebook has been developed once the data have been finally read and coded. Next we read through the data again, in a reiterative fashion, to make sure if each piece of datum matches the code and category that was previously chosen. If there is not a good fit, we may expand the code and category, and make modifications to the coding process as needed.

Coding is usually started while in the field. As more data are collected in the field, if the new data do not match the existing codebook, the codes may be expanded further. This process continues until the research study ends or the data begin to be repetitive in a manner that does not require any new codes or categories of meaning. We may also begin to collapse codes and develop higher-order codes and categories of meaning as we proceed in our analysis of the data. Final analysis is usually completed after leaving the field.

Step 10d: Using Analytical Approaches

An analytical approach is a set of methods that we use to make sense of the data collected. Analytical approaches to qualitative data analysis range from structured methods at one end of the continuum to intuitive methods at the other. We briefly highlight two approaches to data analysis—grounded theory and analytic induction.

Grounded Theory   The grounded theory method provides a data analysis approach that is helpful for understanding the essence of structured qualitative data (Glaser & Straus, 1967; Straus & Corbin, 1990). It emphasizes discovering theories, concepts, propositions, and new hypotheses from the data collected in the field instead of relying on already existing theories. Gilgun (1992) descriptively lists 21 steps of analyzing qualitative data using the grounded theory approach to data analysis:

1. Develop a general area of inquiry based on previous knowledge, such as personal experiences as members of families, observations in clinical practice, or ideas generated through knowledge of research and theory, or a combination of these types of experience.
2. Brainstorm possible research questions.
3. Think about, write down, or discuss your own theoretical perspective, ideologies, and biases.
4. Review the literature based on what you think is relevant to your area of inquiry.

5. Formulate questions based on Numbers 2–4. Symbolic interactionists call these questions "sensitizing." Allow them to change as you collect and analyze data.

6. Develop an idea of the parameters of your study, such as the time you will devote to it, range of informants, and settings. Some people set few parameters and others set more. Many of these decisions are guided by emerging findings.

7. Enter the field as open-mindedly as possible, attempting to be aware of your personal styles, ideologies, and theoretical perspectives and the way in which they may influence how you ask questions, how you present yourself to research participants and informants, and how you interpret the data.

8. Observe the first case, literally through observation, or through combinations of observations and interview questions.

9. Write field notes. Include observer comments in the field notes. (Observer comments are subjective reactions we record in our field notes, but label as observer comments and set them off from the descriptive portions of the notes.)

10. Write memos in the field notes. (Memos are speculative and wide-ranging comments, including comparisons of findings with and across cases, speculations about the theoretical sense of the data, and ideas about the relevance of emerging findings to existing bodies of research and theories.)

11. Develop initial definitions of emerging concepts and speculate on the connections among the concepts. These processes are steps toward developing hypotheses.

12. Observe the second case, and as you do, many of your questions will be based on emerging findings.

13. Write field notes, including observer comments and memos, as with the first case. Continue to develop definitions of concepts and the connections among them.

14. Compare patterns (hypotheses) within the second case and with patterns in the first case.

15. Change hypotheses to fit both cases.

16. Continue this process, choosing cases through theoretical sampling—meaning you have a rationale for the selection of the next case—to explore themes further, either with similar cases or with cases that vary slightly from the cases you have observed so far.

17. When you have confidence that you have developed some hypotheses, even if they are tentative, review the literature you think might be relevant to your emerging findings.

18. Link relevant literature to the empirically grounded hypotheses. You could guide your efforts with the question: How do these findings fit with other theories and research in this or related areas? What you develop in this process can be considered theoretical formulations.

19. Test the theoretical formulations on a subsequent case or cases.

20. Change the theoretical formulation to fit the empirical patterns of this subsequent case.

21. Continue this process until you have developed findings that are linked both to phenomena of interest and to theoretical formulations.

Analytic Induction   Analytic induction is a data analysis method similar to grounded theory, but it allows us to enter the study with some predetermined type of hypothesis that may be modified in relationship to the data collected. In grounded theory, we usually enter the study without a guiding theory. Both data analysis approaches have many similarities with one another (Gilgun, 1995). Recall that modified analytic induction is the analytical approach that Gilgun used to analyze her data from her incest study.

Step 10e: Assessing the Trustworthiness of Our Results

Although developing interpretations and theory can be an exciting step in qualitative analysis, throughout the research process we must act responsibly to ensure the trustworthiness of the conclusions that we finally draw. Qualitative researchers have identified a number of issues for consideration to enhance the believability of our research findings. Approaches and emphases vary (as does the depth of detail in discussions of techniques that can be employed). At this point, we will discuss the challenges that are important to address during the analysis.

Step 11: Leaving the Field

Qualitative researchers plan for leaving the field in a manner similar to the way social work practitioners plan terminations with their clients. First of all, research participants should have prior knowledge that we are only in the field for a certain time parameter (e.g., one year). As the time draws nearer for our research study to come to a close, we should prepare our research participants by talking to them about leaving, saying good-bye, and making arrangements for additional contacts, if any, in the future. We often make arrangements for participants to give input into our final report (Step 12), for example, and make sure they get copies of our findings.

We may diminish our involvement in the field setting and start to establish a new routine and lifestyle for ourselves. In this manner we will have less and less contacts with the field setting and more contacts with our new routine. If we had moved into a neighborhood to conduct a study, for example, we might move out and only visit the field setting periodically. This helps us to disengage from the setting and gain a sense of distance. It also helps our research participants prepare for our final departure.

Step 12: Writing the Report

This step is identical to Step 9 in the quantitative study as discussed in Chapter 4. John Van Maanen (1988) has classified qualitative research reports into three types, as illustrated in Figure 5.2. Robert McClelland and Carol D. Austin (1996) have a few words to say about writing up and disseminating qualitative research reports:

Writing up and disseminating our research findings is a critical phase of the qualitative research process. Without an adequate plan and strategy for the dissemination of our findings, they will not reach practitioners who may find them useful. As far as we are concerned, too many research reports gather dust on shelves because the researchers have overlooked the significance of disseminating their findings. A commitment to adding to our knowledge base requires a carefully conceived and implemented publishing method for informing our practice community. It is extremely important to know that qualitative research findings can result either in improved social scientific understanding or in meaningless gibberish, as is so aptly pointed out by Bruce L. Berg (1994):

My children, Alex and Kate, were eating alphabet soup for lunch one Sunday afternoon. Kate, then about four years old, was stirring her soup with great care and deliberation. She managed to capture several of the letters on her spoon, carefully spill off the liquid, and spell out her name.
"Look daddy, I wrote my name with my noodles!" She held her spoon up for my inspection. She had arranged the letters to spell "KATIE." Alex, seeing the attention his sister had received, pulled his dripping spoon from his soup, and spilling much of it onto the floor exclaimed, "Me too!" Unfortunately, his letters spelled out "XCYU," a unique spelling of "Alex," or simply failure to "sort the noodles from the soup" in a fashion that made his noodles mean something to others.

With the above quote in mind, it must be noted, however, that our research findings may not merit dissemination. This is true regardless of the type of research undertaken—quantitative or qualitative. All researchers must assess the utility and practical significance of their findings before they decide whether a report should be written for possible publication. Several assessment criteria can be applied to qualitative research studies:

- Do our research findings extend current theory?
- Has our research study added anything to the theoretical base of social work practice?
- How well does our research study meet the test of trustworthiness? How credible is our research study?
- To what extent could our study's findings inform day-to-day social work practice activities?

Each of the above criteria must be evaluated keeping in mind the audience we want to reach. Effective distribution requires a clear idea of who should know about our study. Such clarity will greatly assist in selecting and implementing a strategy for its dissemination. There can be little doubt that the written word has dominated publication activities over time. In addition to journals and books, improved access to the literature is now available through on-line bibliographic searches. Nevertheless, publication methods have diversified and the presentation of qualitative research findings through non-print outlets is growing. Social work practitioners who are developing agency-specific models of intervention may find the non-print approach useful as a supplement to staff training.

Video- and audiotapes are particularly effective ways to disperse information that involves practice skills. Unfortunately, most of us do not have access to the means of creating non-print media products, so these approaches may prove difficult to develop. (pp. 121-122)

VAN MAANEN'S TAXONOMY OF TALES

John Van Maanen has classified qualitative research reports into three types, which he describes as different categories of tales. Each uses a distinctive type of literary exposition.

REALIST TALES   A single author narrates the outcome of the study in a dispassionate, third-person voice. According to Van Maanen, "Perhaps the most striking characteristic of ethnographic realism is the almost complete absence of the author from most segments of the finished text. Only what members of the studied culture say and do and, presumably, think are visible."

CONFESSIONAL TALES   The author attempts to demystify field-work or participant observation by showing how the technique is practiced in the field. Such accounts are in the first person, seldom are dispassionate, and unfold over time. Fieldwork is narrated as a series of events leading to certain conclusions or results. The narrator-hero is typically beset along the way by troubles, uncertainty, and doubt.

IMPRESSIONIST TALES   The author provides vivid, memorable stories, reconstructing in dramatic detail the "facts" of an episode or life. Such yarns are often incorporated into "realist" writing.

FIGURE 5.2   TYPES OF QUALITATIVE REPORTS

CORE ELEMENTS IN QUALITATIVE RESEARCH STUDIES

With the foregoing in mind, all approaches to qualitative research share in common an emphasis on the use of nonstructured and naturalistic observations, interviews, narrative dialogues (or stories), and existing documents. We may be interested in the living experiences of children who have been removed from their homes, for example, and are living in substitute care facilities. To investigate this research question, we could observe and participate in the daily interactions of a residential treatment facility for children who have been placed in substitute care due to child abuse or neglect.

Within this context, we could write down, or observe verbatim, dialogues and interactions between the youths and the staff. We also could collect the daily logs kept by staff, and some documents in the form of personal diaries and letters kept by the youths.

Qualitative researchers often prefer words, or narrative symbols, and other empirical data in the form of lived experiences over numbers or operationalized constructs. Therefore, when we use the word "data" we are most often referring not to statistics or other numbers, but to words, pictures, dialogue, and conceptual interpretations we made in relation to our observations.

In our example concerning the adolescents in substitute care, data may refer to the audiotaped dialogue between adolescents and staff, to a picture taken of a youth's room, to a diagram of the facility, and to documents such as a diary or letter. In addition, we may be referring to our written notes and intuitive reflections about our observations.

We often choose not to reduce our data to numbers or statistical significance because these techniques remove us too far away from the actual context and detailed descriptions that give "meaning" to our data. Since we are usually interested in meanings and processes, we want these data to stand out, and be unmistakably evident from our data.

Qualitative researchers take the attitude that meaningful differences must be found in the data set instead of statistically significant differences. That is, the findings should "hit you between the eyes" and be obvious from the data that have been analyzed.

The qualitative research approach shares many commonalties with clinical methods used in social work practice, just as the quantitative research approach does. Some social work practitioners, for example, use quantitative methods such as scales and standardized assessment instruments in their practices (see Chapters 7–9). However, Carol Meyer (1993) recently defined "assessment" as a search for the meaning of a problem: the cognitive process whereby the social worker comes to understand cases in their full complexity.

This simple definition of assessment is consistent with the philosophy of the qualitative research approach. Like clinical assessment methods, qualitative research methods are designed to provide access to difficult-to-obtain phenomena such as life experiences, meaning systems, frame of reference, personal beliefs, cognitive schemes, values, cultural realities, and personal motivations.

IS QUALITATIVE RESEARCH GOOD RESEARCH?

There are a few general criticisms leveled against the qualitative research approach when it is directly compared to the quantitative approach. Some people claim that it is too subjective, its procedures are so vague they cannot be replicated, sweeping conclusions are made on the basis of too few cases, and often there is no way to tell if the conclusions are really supported by the data. As James B. Taylor so aptly points out (1993):

> There is also confusion between the terms empiricist and empirical. Empiricist refers to the teaching of the twentieth-century philosophy of science known as logical empiricism or logical positivism (see Chapter 4). The qualitative research approach does not follow this school, so qualitative research is nonempiricist. Empirical, on

the other hand, refers to data or knowledge derived from observation, experience, or experiment. All science therefore is empirical, and qualitative research is about as empirical as anything can be.

Confusion also arises because some qualitative research studies are not intended to be "science." The aim of science is to produce robust generalizations (capable of standing up to further research) about the real world. Some qualitative studies aim instead to broaden awareness of the human condition and perhaps to move the reader to empathy, indignation, or action. Such studies, which are not much different from good journalism or investigative reporting, are usually described as ideographic. Their aims are worthy, but they are not the aims of science.

What should be asked of any research approach that claims to be "objective"? Four requirements apply:

1. If someone else examines the data a researcher has collected and applies the same analytic procedures, the same results should be obtained.
2. If a second researcher collects data from the same kinds of sources, under similar circumstances, and using comparable methods of data elicitation and coding, then similar results should be obtained. If the second researcher's findings differ, the data were probably not much good in the first place.
3. The conclusions drawn from the data should be clearly supported by those data. Data that seem contradictory to the conclusions should be fully reported, and it must be demonstrated that the data do not negate the conclusions.
4. If researchers generalize their findings and claim that the results they have obtained from X_1 will also hold for X_2, X_3 ... X_n, their claims should be clearly supported by the data, and the rationale for the conclusions should be clear and compelling.

These four requirements are no more than common sense. They are also the general standards of science. In traditional research terms, the first requirement speaks to the reliability of measurement methods, the second to the replicability of findings, the third to the internal validity of conclusions, and the fourth to the external validity of results. These concepts are discussed later on in this text. There is no inherent reason why qualitative studies cannot meet all four requirements, although practical realities sometimes stand in the way.

Simple checks on the reliability of coding procedures take care of the first requirement, but the second requirement is not so cut and dried. Many qualitative studies cannot be replicated even in part: the cost is too high, the interest too low, or the setting too difficult. Cultures and groups change; today's observations are tomorrow's history. However, a researcher can often test the replicability of findings using several methods. In Hanson's (1989) study of families with chronic mental patients, for example, he used his interview findings as the basis for a brief mailback questionnaire and obtained comparable results from this larger sample (see Box 5.1).

The third requirement—that any conclusion should be in accord with the empirical findings—has to do with the care with which the analysis has been done. Has the researcher systematically examined all relevant data to support the conclusions, or simply picked some convenient piece of text to illustrate them, without searching for counterexamples? Are counterexamples adequately explained? Does any other evidence bear on the conclusions? And beyond the data is the argument itself; useful data can be nullified by shoddy thinking. Does the researcher make a good case for the conclusions? Are the concepts clear and well enough defined so that another person could judge their fit to the data, or are "weasel words" used which sound profound but have unclear referents? Is the reasoning straightforward?

The fourth requirement, concerning generalization to other groups, places, or times, also primarily rests on logic. Hanson, for example, found that the families all described similar issues, whether they were old or young, in a rural or urban community, poor or rich. Nor did the findings vary for different institutions and centers. He had chosen his informants by purposive sampling in order to maximize diversity. Since nevertheless the informants agreed, then other informants probably would also. By this logic, the conclusions could be generalized. (pp. 76-77)

ETHICAL CONSIDERATIONS

Qualitative studies can contribute powerfully to an understanding of the real world. But they also can pose ethical dilemmas, especially when, as is sometimes necessary, the purpose of the study must be concealed from the research participants. From the ethical guidelines for social work research adopted by the National Association of Social Workers (listed in Figure 2.2), three ideas are particularly relevant to qualitative studies:

1. Researchers should not lie about their research study or misrepresent it in any way, or accept wrong understandings without challenge.
2. Participants have a right to know what the project is about, what its results may be, and any possible problems that could result from their participation.
3. Participants' consent to take part in a study cannot be coerced.

Once again, as James B. Taylor notes (1993):

These ideas are to some extent ambiguous, and living up to them can create problems for researchers. Some qualitative experiments, in fact, require deception. Rosenhan's study of mental hospitals would have been impossible if the pseudo patients had said to the admitting interviewer, "As part of my research study, I will pretend that I have a symptom. Let me explain the study to you to see if you will participate. . . ." Insofar as ethical guidelines require informed consent, they may be read as prohibiting most qualitative experiments. Yet Rosenhan's work and similar studies can contribute much to social understanding and reform. Which "good thing" should take priority: informed consent or social knowledge? There is no easy answer.

Ethical dilemmas also arise when the researcher must choose between two evils. A situation in which it was necessary either to break confidentiality or to go along with abusive behavior is described in Taylor and Bogdan (1984). In an institutional study which focused on how attendants defined and accounted for abuse, one of the coauthors regularly observed acts of beating, brutality, and abuse of residents by attendants.

The decision not to do anything about the situation at the time reflected the researcher's own uncertainty about how to deal with it and his judgment that whis

BOX 5.2

GOOD RESEARCH IS GOOD RESEARH

Fundamental to knowledge acquisition through quantitative and qualitative research studies is the idea that what we think should be rooted in and tested against good evidence, and that sound articulated methods—systematic, disciplined inquiry—are necessary to bring this about. A good research study respects these essentials, regardless of the tradition within which it is conducted—quantitative or qualitative.

Bad research can also be found in both approaches. Qualitative case studies that pathologized women, and lower-income people as well, are abundant in the literature into the 1970s and beyond. Often, quantitative methods are now being used to repair the damage. Quantitative studies that evaluated social work interventions without recognizing their complexity or that dismissed the perceptions of the practitioners and their clients as subjective, and therefore irrelevant, did harm that qualitative researchers are working to correct.

Neither research approach can claim that its adherents have never done harm, and neither can deny that the other has made a genuine contribution. Neither deserves blind faith in its inherent virtues, and neither is innately perverse. As we discussed, however, differences do in fact exist. We now will turn to a brief discussion of the implications of those differences as they relate to: (1) our profession's knowledge base, (2) the social work practitioner, (3) gender, and (4) culture.

Research and the Profession's Knowledge Base

All approaches to research must generate and test the knowledge we need to be effective with our clients. Quantitative and qualitative approaches alike can contribute significantly in both ways. The main difference between the two is the kinds of knowledge they generate, which overlap but still tend to have different advantages and uses.

The cumulative effect of well-conducted quantitative research methods can be tremendously powerful in establishing client needs and documenting the effectiveness of our interventions. As examples, the steady accumulation in recent decades of evidence about the incidence of child abuse, sexual abuse, and AIDS, as well as violence against women, has both changed the awareness of the public and professionals and had a wide-ranging impact on services to those populations. Indifference and skepticism about these issues have retreated as increasingly well-designed research has reinforced the message of earlier studies. Quantitative studies have an enviable ability to say, "This is true whether you want to believe it or not."

On the other hand, we need to know more than just the frequencies of the different forms of victimization, or how often a particular social work program produces particular outcomes for traumatized clients. When we want to understand the impacts of trauma in more depth and detail, when we want rich data about the experience of social workers and survivors working to ameliorate the effects of abuse, when we need to describe healing processes in ways that capture this human experience as something highly individual and sensitive to context—when these are our goals, the qualitative research approach is useful.

The two approaches can contribute differently at different stages in the knowledge-building enterprise. When not much is known about a problem—in the early days of designing social service programs for women who have been physically abused by their partners, for example—qualitative methods are well suited to providing exploratory data about possible needs and interventions. Once a reasonable understanding of such variables has been accumulated, quantitative methods can be efficiently used to provide more precise and generalizable data about the impacts that specific interventions have on needs. Qualitative researchers continue to contribute, however, by persisting in exploring issues, adding depth and texture to quantitative findings.

Considerations such as these lead us to believe that our profession would be foolish to reject the contribution to our knowledge base of either research approach. Irwin Epstein (1988) had a few strong words to say about the complementarity of the two research approaches over a decade ago:

- Thus far we have maintained that quantitative and qualitative methods each have their special uses—it is only the uneducated person who states that one method is unequivocally better than the other. As a result, rather than asking which is best, it makes more sense for us to ask under what conditions each method is better than the other as a research strategy.
- To imply that we, as professional social workers, must make a choice between one or the other research method is senseless, idiotic, and simple-minded, to say the least. Both methods make meaningful contributions to our understanding of the social world and, when used together, can obviously augment it.

Research and the Practitioner

In recent years, some educators have suggested that front-line social workers should integrate quantitative research techniques into their practices. This was to be accomplished by educating students to become practitioner/researchers— that is, practitioners who regularly employ quantitative research methods to evaluate the effectiveness and efficiency of their practices.

Arguably, there is little evidence that the researcher/practitioner model has succeeded in winning significant numbers of adherents. One of the many reasons for this is that the quantitative research methods that were offered to practitioners for their consideration were too foreign to practice to be easily integrated with day-to-day activities. The tasks of administering standardized measuring instruments and collating, coding, and statistically analyzing client data are unnatural and intrusive when they are introduced into a practice setting. Additionally, and probably more importantly, they were too time consuming to use on a regular basis.

It has been hinted within the literature that qualitative research methods may be more promising than quantitative methods when it comes to evaluating the effectiveness of our treatment interventions. Unfortunately, it does not seem to us that this is likely, for reasons of feasibility: Qualitative research remains a highly demanding exercise, and the time involved in preparing transcripts and subjecting them to a systematic qualitative analysis is no less formidable than the demands of quantitative research. A somewhat different issue is that of research utilization: Will practitioners find the data generated by either approach more accessible and relevant to their work? Only time will tell.

Research and Gender

There have been rumblings throughout the literature that there are gender issues associated with the quantitative and qualitative research approaches. The suggestion, in brief, is that since the quantitative approach strives for objectivity (read "distance") at all costs, dispassionate logic, and well-engineered and thought-out research designs, it is rooted in male values.

A more extreme extension of this argument is that quantitative researchers, subjecting the people in their studies to procedures imposed with no consultation or agreement and reducing peoples' experience to numbers, are acting in patriarchal ways. Therefore, some believe that the quantitative research approach is inherently oppressive and morally inferior to the qualitative options. We know of women researchers with clear feminist commitments, however, who have had difficulty getting their work published because its quantitative approach was ideologically unpalatable.

The qualitative research approach, on the other hand, has been said to employ research methods that value relationships, egalitarianism, and empowerment of all research participants, sometimes called co-researchers. With their respect for individual experience, subjectivity, and subtlety, qualitative methods have been said to be more compatible with women's ways of knowing and experiencing the world.

Whatever the general validity of this position, it can easily be seriously overstated. While there appears to be current evidence that women and men are cognitively different, or have "different ways of knowing," the evidence also suggests that these differences are not particularly strong. Differences within the sexes are much greater than differences between them—men and women may experience life somewhat differently, but they do not inhabit separate cognitive worlds. Thus, it is easy to identify male qualitative researchers (as well as females) who do good research studies—regardless of research approach used.

As well, quantitative research studies and qualitative ones alike have been oppressively used. Practitioners who dismissed women's reports of sexual abuse as wish-fulfilling fantasy, for example, had solid support for their position in an extensive body of qualitative research findings beginning with the case studies of Sigmund Freud. To a large extent, quantitative studies have exposed this falsehood—an example of how this research approach had a liberating and empowering effect of considerable importance.

Research and Culture

Considerable concern has been expressed in recent years about research studies that involve people from diverse cultures. The concerns have indicated difficulties with both quantitative and qualitative approaches. Quantitative researchers have used standardized instruments developed in studies of one culture when studying others, without recognizing the problems this can create. A measure of social support employed with women who have been abused by their partners in a Haitian community in Florida, for example, might be quite inappropriate if it were developed with white college students in New York.

Language, assumptions, and values implicit in an instrument's questions—and the way they are interpreted—could be foreign to research participants, making the process confusing or difficult and rendering the study's findings invalid. It is also possible that the lack of any meaningful relationship between the researcher and the research participant can be experienced as strange or even intimidating by someone from another culture. Many research studies conducted with diverse cultures have been qualitative in nature (the studies of cultural anthropologists, for example), and these have also been subject to criticism.

To the extent that qualitative researchers carry their own cultural assumptions into the field, they risk imposing a foreign frame of reference in interpreting the experience and meanings of the people they study. The problem is severe enough in the eyes of some critics that they have suggested that the only people who should study a culture should be members of that culture.

There are no easy answers to these complex problems. Quantitative researchers are working to develop methods and measures that are sensitive to cultural diversity. At the same time, some qualitative researchers are hopeful that their efforts to develop research approaches that are sensitive to social contexts and different ways of interpreting human experience will help them answer the concerns that have been raised. In part, the issue will be less of a problem to the extent that members of different cultural groups develop ways of using both research approaches in the service of their own communities' agendas.

As we have noted more than once, research in either tradition can be used oppressively. There is truth, however, in the cliché that knowledge is power, and there are certainly examples of culturally disadvantaged groups who are doing good research studies to further their legitimate aims.

tle-blowing would have done no good. There was reason to hold back; a parent had in fact complained to the state police, and they had investigated and arrested 24 attendants, none of whom had been observed by the author. Eventually these attendants were cleared of abuse charges on the basis of insufficient evidence and reinstated in their jobs.

Similar issues arose for researchers who observed police brutality (Van Maanen, Dabbs, & Faulkner, 1982) and for others who observed numerous illegal acts committed by social workers in social service agencies (Johnson, 1975). In these instances, too, the researchers did nothing.

The NASW Code of Ethics provides no help, since both horns of the dilemma are represented. The code stipulates that "Information obtained about participants in research should be treated as confidential." It also says that "The social worker engaged in research should protect participants from unwarranted physical or mental discomfort, distress, harm, danger, or deprivation."

Conscience transcends professional codes, and social workers may have no choice in such a situation. The authors believe that to stand by and do nothing would be unethical; and in some states, it would be illegal. The belief that whistle-blowing would be ineffective (as in Taylor's study) is irrelevant. Professionals with a commitment to helping cannot allow themselves such easy, self-serving excuses as the following:

1. In the long run, the research study will prove more important than the abuse.
2. If I speak up I will not be able to finish my master's thesis or doctoral dissertation.
3. The problem has been going on a long time and will not change.
4. Nobody will thank me if I make trouble.
5. To really be effective I would have to change the system.

SUMMARY

This chapter defined qualitative research and briefly discussed the generic steps and processes involved in conducting a qualitative research study. Box 5.2, written by Tutty, Williams, and Grinnell (1996), summarizes how quantitative and qualitative research studies differ in relation to: (1) our profession's knowledge base, (2) the social work practitioner, (3) our client's gender, and (4) our client's culture.

Three of the more common data collection methods were described along with two methods of data analyses. Finally, ways to increase the validity and reliability of qualitative research data were briefly highlighted. In the following chapter we will show how to combine quantitative and qualitative research approaches within a single research study.

REFERENCES AND FURTHER READINGS

BERG, B.L. (1994). *Qualitative research methods for the social sciences* (2nd ed.). Needham Heights, MA: Allyn & Bacon.

BORDEN, W. (1992). Narrative perspectives in psychosocial intervention following adverse life events. *Social Work, 37,* 135-141.

COLEMAN, H., & UNRAU, Y. (1996). Phase three: Analyzing your data. In L.M. Tutty, M.A. Rothery, & R.M. Grinnell, Jr. (Eds.), *Qualitative research for social workers: Phases, steps, and tasks* (pp. 88-119). Needham Heights, MA: Allyn & Bacon.

COPELAND, A.P., & WHITE, K.M. (1991). *Studying families.* Newbury Park, CA: Sage.

CRABTREE, B.F., & MILLER, W.L. (Eds.). (1992). *Doing qualitative research.* Newbury Park, CA: Sage.

DENZIN, N.K. (1989). *The research act: A theoretical introduction to sociological methods* (3rd ed.). Englewood Cliffs, NJ: Prentice-Hall.

DENZIN, N.K., & LINCOLN, Y.S. (1994). *Handbook of qualitative research.* Newbury Park, CA: Sage.

EMERSON, R.M. (1983). Introduction. In R.M. Emerson (Ed.), *Contemporary field research* (pp. 1-16). Boston: Little Brown.

EPSTEIN, I. (1988). Quantitative and Qualitative methods. In R.M. Grinnell, Jr. (Ed.), *Social work research and evaluation* (3rd ed., pp. 185-198). Itasca, IL: F.E. Peacock.

ERLANDSON, D.A., HARRIS, E.L., SKIPPER, B.L., & ALLEN, S.D. (1993). *Doing naturalistic inquiry: A guide to methods.* Newbury Park, CA: Sage.

FETTERMAN, D.M. (1989). *Ethnography: Step by step.* Newbury Park CA: Sage.

FIELDING, R., & LEE, R. (Eds.). (1991). *Using computers in qualitative analysis.* Newbury Park, CA: Sage.

FRANKLIN, C., & JORDAN, C. (1995). Qualitative assessment: A methodological review. *Families in Society, 76*, 281-295.

GILBERT, K.R., & SCHMID, K. (1994). Bringing our emotions out of the closet: Acknowledging the place of emotion in qualitative research. *Qualitative Family Research, 8*, 1-3.

GILGUN, J.F. (1992). Definitions, methodologies, and methods in qualitative family research. In J.F. Gilgun, K. Daly, & G. Handel (Eds.), (1992). *Qualitative methods in family research* (pp. 22-40). Newbury Park, CA: Sage.

GILGUN, J.F. (1995). The moral discourse of incest perpetrators. *Journal of Marriage and the Family, 57*, 265-282.

GILGUN, J.F., & CONNOR, T.M. (1989). How perpetrators view child sexual abuse. *Social Work, 34*, 349-351.

GILGUN, J. F., DALY, K., & HANDEL, G. (Eds.). (1992). *Qualitative methods in family research.* Newbury Park, CA: Sage.

GLASER, B.G., & STRAUS, A.L. (1967). *The discovery of grounded theory: Strategies for qualitative research.* Chicago: Aldine.

GUBA, E.G. (1990). *The paradigm dialog.* Newbury Park, CA: Sage.

HANSON, J. (1989). *The experience of families of people with a severe mental illness: An ethnographic view.* Unpublished doctoral dissertation, University of Kansas.

HYDEN, M. (1994). Woman battering as a marital act: Interviewing and analysis in context. In C.K. Reissman (Ed.), *Qualitative studies in social work research* (pp. 95-112). Newbury Park, CA: Sage.

JACOB, E. (1987). Qualitative research traditions: A review. *Review of Educational Research, 57*, 150.

JOHNSON, J.M. (1975). *Doing field research.* New York: Free Press.

JORDAN, C., & FRANKLIN, C. (1995). *Clinical assessment for social workers: Quantitative and qualitative methods.* Chicago: Lyceum.

JORGENSEN, D.L. (1989). *Participant observation: A methodology for human studies.* Newbury Park, CA: Sage.

JUNKER, B.H. (1960). *Field work.* Chicago: University of Chicago Press.

LANCY, D.F. (1993). *Qualitative research in education: An introduction to the major traditions.* White Plains, NY: Longman.

LAROSSA R., & WOLF, J.H. (1985). On qualitative family research. *Journal of Marriage and the Family, 47*, 531-541.

MCCLELLAND, R., & AUSTIN, C.D. (1996). Phase four: Writing your report. In L.M. Tutty, M.A. Rothery, & R.M. Grinnell, Jr. (Eds.), *Qualitative research for social workers: Phases, steps, and tasks* (pp. 120-150). Needham Heights, MA: Allyn & Bacon.

MEYER, C.H. (1993). *Assessment in social work.* New York: Columbia University Press.

MILES, M., & HUBERMAN, M. (1994). *Qualitative data analysis: A sourcebook of new methods.* Newbury Park, CA: Sage.

MILES, M., & WEITZMAN, E. (1995). *Computer programs for qualitative data analysis.* Newbury Park, CA: Sage.

MOON, S.M., DILLON, D.R., & SPRENKLE, D.H. (1990). Family therapy and qualitative research. *Journal of Marital and Family Therapy, 16,* 357-373.

NATIONAL ASSOCIATION OF SOCIAL WORKERS (1978). *NASW standards for social work services in schools: Professional standards.* Washington, DC: Author.

NATIONAL ASSOCIATION OF SOCIAL WORKERS (1980). *National Association of Social Workers code of ethics.* Silver Spring, MD: Author.

NEIMEYER, R.A. (1993). An appraisal of constructivist psychotherapies. *Journal of Consulting and Clinical Psychology, 61,* 221-234.

NEUMAN, W.L. (1994). *Social research methods: Qualitative & quantitative approaches* (2nd ed.). Needham Heights, MA: Allyn & Bacon.

POLKINGHORNE, D.E. (1991). Two conflicting calls for methodological reform. *The Counseling Psychologist, 19,* 103-114.

RIESSMAN, C.K. (1994). *Qualitative studies in social work research.* Newbury Park: CA: Sage.

ROGERS, G., & BOUEY, E. (1996). Phase two: Collecting your data. In L.M. Tutty, M.A. Rothery, & R.M. Grinnell, Jr. (Eds.), *Qualitative research for social workers: Phases, steps, and tasks* (pp. 50-87). Needham Heights, MA: Allyn & Bacon.

ROSENHAN, D. (1973). On being sane in insane places. *Science, 179,* 250-258.

ROTHERY, M.A., TUTTY, L.M., GRINNELL, R.M., JR. (1996). Introduction. In L.M. Tutty, M.A. Rothery, & R.M. Grinnell, Jr. (Eds.), *Qualitative research for social workers: Phases, steps, and tasks* (pp. 2-22). Needham Heights, MA: Allyn & Bacon.

SEIDMAN, I.E. (1991). *Interviewing as qualitative research.* New York: Teachers College Press.

SELLS, S.P., SMITH, T. E., COE, M.J., YOSHIOKA, M., & ROBBINS, J. (1994). An ethnography of couple and therapist experiences in reflecting team practice. *Journal of Marital and Family Therapy, 20,* 247-266.

SPRADLEY, J.P. (1979). *The ethnographic interview.* New York: Holt, Rinehart, and Winston.

STRAUS, A., & CORBIN, J. (1990). *Basics of qualitative research: Grounded theory procedures and techniques.* Newbury Park, CA: Sage.

TAYLOR, J.B. (1993). The naturalistic research approach. In R.M. Grinnell, Jr. (Ed.), *Social work research and evaluation* (4th ed., pp. 53-78). Itasca, IL: F.E. Peacock.

TAYLOR, S.J., & BOGDAN, R. (1984). *Introduction to qualitative research: The search for meanings.* New York: Wiley.

TESCH, R. (1990). *Qualitative research: Analysis types and software tools.* New York: Falmer.

TODD, T.A., JOANNING, H., ENDERS, L., MUTCHLER, L., & THOMAS, F. N. (1990). Using ethnographic interviews to create a more cooperative client-therapist relationship. *Journal of Family Psychotherapy, 1,* 51-63.

VAN MAANEN, J. (1988). *Tales of the field: On writing ethnography.* Chicago: University of Chicago Press.

VAN MAANEN, J., DABBS, J.M., JR., & FAULKNER, R.R. (Eds.). (1982). *Varieties of qualitative research.* Newbury Park, CA: Sage.

John W. Creswell

C h a p t e r **6**

Using Both Research Approaches in a Single Study

THE PREVIOUS TWO CHAPTERS presented the quantitative and qualitative research approaches to the generation of knowledge. More often than not, a research study uses only one approach—either quantitative or qualitative. The reasons for following only one research approach to knowledge generation are generally pragmatic, such as the extensive time required to use both approaches adequately, the extensive expertise needed by the researcher(s), and the desire to limit a study's scope.

Assuming, for a moment, that the above factors do not pose any significant barriers, how could we design a single research study that combines both research approaches? Before we answer this question, however, it may be a good time to review the previous two chapters—Chapter 4 on quantitative research and Chapter 5 on qualitative research. In addition, Box 6.1, written by Tutty, Rothery, & Grinnell (1996), provides a summary of how the two research approaches differentially contribute to our knowledge base in six research-related areas.

BOX 6.1

A BRIEF COMPARISON OF THE QUANTITATIVE AND QUALITATIVE RESEARCH APPROACH USING ONE EXAMPLE

As mentioned throughout this book, both quantitative and qualitative research approaches contribute to our knowledge base, in different but complementary ways. They are like two good wines, one red, the other white (white wine may go better with fish and red wine with lamb, for example). In short, one may be more appropriate than the other depending on the circumstances—and personal preference.

Let us now compare the two research approaches in relation to one social work example. They could be directly compared with each other on many criteria, but for the sake of simplicity we will discuss only six: (1) the objectivity of their findings, (2) the generalizability of their findings, (3) their reductionistic properties, (4) their differential use of theory, (5) the numbers or words they use, and (6) the flexibility of their research techniques.

All of these characteristics are interrelated, but, again, for the sake of simplicity we will discuss each separately.

Objectivity

Both research approaches strive for objectivity in that they provide ways of helping us assess whether what we believe is actually true. Anyone studying why some women return to abusive relationships after they leave the safety of a women's emergency shelter, for example, will have a few prior ideas and beliefs regarding that issue. It is possible that some believe such a decision suggests a psychological compulsion for the woman to place herself at risk—a variation on the discredited "female masochism" premise. Both qualitative and quantitative researchers would agree that it is important to assess the objective truth of such an idea, and their findings could influence the treatment social workers provide to large numbers of female clients.

The quantitative research approach accepts that there is a reality independent of what we believe, and its goal is to determine how congruent our beliefs are with the reality as it exists "out there." By contrast, some qualitative theorists have suggested that objectivity is a myth, or is at least unattainable. Some even believe that nothing objectively exists outside of our beliefs about it. We argue against this, as we believe that testing our beliefs for their objectivity is not only possible, but is an ethical requirement for all responsible professionals. Our willingness to do so is the reason we now know that many men who are violent toward women will victimize women no matter what those women do: The "female masochism" hypothesis has been challenged and found not to be generally, objectively true.

Quantitative researchers studying women who return to abusive partners after leaving shelters will attempt to improve objectivity by using research methods that limit their personal involvement with the women, in an effort not to "contaminate" the study in any way. As Mary E. Swigonski (1994) puts it:

Logical positivism builds on the epistemological assumption of the possibility of separation of the observer from the observed, the knower from the known (Lincoln & Guba, cited in Wood, 1990). This thinking requires that the subject and object of research activities be treated as separate, noninteracting entities. The scientist is viewed as an independent observer who minimizes any relationship between the self and the subject of study. The actions of the researcher are constructed so that they do not infect or alter objective truth.

In contrast to the above, the qualitative research approach expects that a close relationship between the researchers and the women will develop and that they will have a reciprocal influence on each other. Qualitative researchers do not remain indifferent to the lives of the people they talk with, and such personal involvement is welcomed rather than distrusted. The experience of the researchers may also be included as important data for analysis.

Another difference between the two research approaches is that quantitative researchers will often seek objectivity by gravitating to research questions employing variables that can be measured using well-established, standardized measuring instruments. Sometimes, they have to reword the initial research question to fit their strict quantitative methodological expectations. Quantitative researchers exploring why women do or do not return to abusive partners, for example, may look to variables such as the extent of their social support network, their economic circumstances, or their levels of self-esteem—variables that can be easily measured.

Qualitative studies, by contrast, favor more open and subjective data collection and analysis approaches, setting out to understand the personal experiences of the women as they wrestle with their options. Some people may argue that the use of standardized measuring instruments presupposes too much, and may prefer to hear about self-esteem issues (if these emerge at all) as they are experienced and expressed by each woman. In our qualitative research example, the quest for objectivity means:

> We want to understand the experience of women who have decided not to return to abusive partners as they really live it, independent of what we or others think is involved in their choice.

Generalization

One of the main objectives of quantitative research studies is to discover facts or principles that are generally true. Though ideals are always compromised when any research study is conducted in the field, quantitative researchers studying women who do not return to abusive partners will want what they learn from the women in their study to be generally true for a larger group. Thus, they want their study's findings (derived from relatively few women) to be relevant to other similar women who did not participate in the study.

In the pursuit of this ideal, quantitative researchers have developed an extensive knowledge of sampling and statistical procedures for determining how confidently they can believe that what they discovered in a study sample of abused women is true for a larger population of women with similar histories. On the other hand, qualitative researchers place much less importance on the generalizability of a study's findings. They correctly assert that the pressure to select a representative sample and then measure the same variable in each member of the sample limits the research inquiry in important ways. More often than not, a quantitative study would collect data that would sacrifice depth and detail, and the unique experiences of the women would be left aside. Qualitative researchers, however, may well talk with a smaller number of women about their decisions concerning their relationship to a violent former partner, aiming to learn about their experience in a more profound and personal way.

The goal of a qualitative study would be to understand each woman's unique experience in depth and with a richness of detail that a quantitative study can seldom achieve. The extent to which the results may be relevant to other women is important in many qualitative studies, but it is clear that the priorities between the two research approaches differ in regard to generalizability. This is appropriate as long as we know the goal of each research approach when it comes to the generalizability of its findings. To apply the issue of generalizability to our qualitative example:

> We will be doing a qualitative research study in order to understand each woman's unique experiences related to her decision not to return to her partner after leaving a women's emergency shelter. The women we will be talking with will not be randomly sampled, but selected on the basis of their interest and availability. What we learn from them will probably be relevant to some extent to others in similar situations (other women and the people who work with them will judge), but this is not a primary concern in planning the study.

Reductionism

The matter of reductionism has some parallels to the issue of generalizability described above. As we know from Chapter 4, reductionism is the measurement of a complex concept by reducing it to a number of measurable variables. Studying women who do not return to an abusive former partner, quantitative researchers will reduce this complex problem to a set of questions or hypotheses containing variables that can be easily measured, for example: What is the relationship between available social support and economic resources and the decision to forge an independent life or to resume living with a perpetrator?

No research approach can come close to understanding "the interrelationships between all the elements of reality." When qualitative researchers say their approach generates a more holistic understanding of issues, however, their claim is indeed valid. The qualitative researcher would talk in an open-ended frame of mind with the women who are living the process of deciding to stay separated from their violent ex-partners. They would not ask the women to respond to a set of standardized questions, but simply to describe their situations, their experiences, and what it all means to them. This approach will very likely yield data that are richer and more attuned to the complexities of context and individual differences than the quantitative approach could ever produce. To apply the concept of reductionism to our qualitative example:

> In a qualitative study, we do not need to restrict ourselves to the measurement of variables that can be measured in the same way for all participants, rendering standardized information. Instead, we will invite each woman to share her unique

experience, what that experience means to her, and the context within which these experiences and meanings unfold. This information will be used to try to understand what it is like to be her in her unique situation as a woman forging a new life, independent of the partner who has victimized her.

Use of Theory

The two research approaches also use theory in different ways. Based on existing theory, quantitative researchers could, for example, at an early point in their work, easily advance a series of simple hypotheses containing variables that can be measured:

- On leaving a women's shelter, women victims of domestic abuse are more likely to live independently rather than return to their abusive former partner *if they have adequate economic means.*
- On leaving a women's shelter, women victims of domestic abuse are more likely to live independently rather than return to their abusive former partner *if they enjoy adequate social support networks as opposed to being socially isolated.*
- On leaving a women's shelter, women victims of domestic abuse are more likely to live independently rather than return to their abusive former partner *if their self-esteem is high rather than low.*

Each hypothesis above could easily be tested via the quantitative research approach. These hypotheses are not a product of the researcher's unfettered imagination, but are derived from existing knowledge and theory, which the researcher will have delved into as part of planning the study. Quantitative researchers often (not always) work *deductively*; beliefs are identified, stated formally (as illustrated above), and put to the test.

Qualitative researchers, by contrast, do not require rigorously defined questions and hypotheses before they can get to work; in fact, they may argue that the exercise of developing them is counterproductive. It may be enough to pursue the general goal of understanding how women leaving the shelter experience their relationship to the men who victimized them. Clarity about important concepts and variables then emerges in response to what the women have to say, not in response to preordained theory and beliefs. Qualitative researchers thus work primarily (though not exclusively) *inductively*, "from the facts up," rather than deductively, "from theory down." Referring to the use of theory in our example:

The goal of our qualitative study is to gather information from each woman about her own unique experience, what that experience means to her, and the context within which these experiences and meanings unfold. This goal is not pursued in ignorance of what is already known, but care is taken to assure that preexisting knowledge and theory do not interfere with our ability to hear each woman's account afresh, minimizing interference from our biases and preconceptions.

What we learn may be informed by theory in various ways, but it is driven by what our participants have to tell us. Theory may tell us that self-esteem influences a woman's ability to separate from an abusive spouse. While that theory may sensitize us to self-esteem issues, we will nevertheless be careful to let each woman we interview tell us how much weight her self-esteem deserves as a consideration. Rather than letting previous research findings dictate how self-esteem must be defined and measured, we will let each woman tell us what that concept means to her in the context of her experience.

The Use of Numbers and Words

On a general level, quantitative studies use numbers to describe their findings and qualitative studies use words (or other "natural" means of communication, like images). Quantitative researchers who are interested in women victims' decision making, for example, would gather data that can be expressed in numbers. Whether or not a woman returns to her abusive partner, the adequacy of her financial resources, how much social support she enjoys, and her level of self-esteem—all these variables can be measured, reduced to numbers, and manipulated statistically in order to discover any meaningful patterns. Is there in fact a relationship between levels of social support and the likelihood that an abused woman will return to live with her abuser? Can such a pattern be detected statistically, and is it strong enough to be considered statistically significant?

Qualitative researchers would often prefer to represent their data in non-numerical forms, such as texts (words) or images. These kinds of statements are better suited to capturing and communicating the complexities and subtleties of human experiences. Instead of analyzing such data statistically, qualitative researchers may study a text for meaningful elements, look for similarities and differences between them, and establish how elements can fit into categories and how these categories can form more general themes.

When women are interviewed regarding their decision making about the future of their relationship to their abusive partners, a range of experiences and meanings will emerge: remembrances of past abuse that led to earlier decisions to leave, concerns about their children, hopes and fears regarding a future as a single person, weighing of the reactions and advice of friends and extended family members, the practical difficulties associated with establishing an independent household, and so on. With reference to our qualitative example:

> If our goal were to know clearly how success at leaving an abusive partner relates to self-esteem as measured by a standard instrument, we would certainly consider a quantitative study, where these variables could be expressed in numbers and our findings analyzed statistically. Since our goal is to gain a complex understanding of our participants' experience, and to retain as much of that complexity and subtlety in our eventual presentation of findings, we will leave the information in the form in which the women give it to us—in words.
>
> We will still be looking for meaningful patterns and relationships, making sense out of a formidable amount of information, teasing out themes that will have relevance to other women in similar circumstances and to their social workers, but we will not reduce information to numbers and use statistics to assist us in our search.

Flexibility

There is no question that the qualitative research approach is more flexible than the quantitative one. Quantitative researchers, for example, design studies that utilize strict rules regarding sampling, research design, measurement, and the analysis of data. These rules indicate what they need to do to be reasonably sure of the validity, reliability, and generalizability of their studies' findings. When rules must be compromised for one reason or another, the quantitative researcher generally acknowledges this as a limitation of the study and provides an assessment of the degree to which this compromise undermines the overall soundness of the study's findings.

In a way, quantitative researchers place more faith in their research methods than in themselves. Someone conducting a quantitative study needs knowledge of and skills in research methods to employ them properly, but beyond that it does not matter who he or she is. In theory, once the details of the research design are established, anyone with the requisite training could implement the study and the findings should theoretically be the same.

In fact, quantitative researchers hope that others will replicate their work. A single study may find a statistically significant relationship between two variables: the more social support a women has upon leaving the shelter (Variable 1), the better are her chances of terminating an abusive relationship (Variable 2). While this finding alone is certainly useful, if the same research design is implemented with a similar sample of women and generates the same results on subsequent occasions, the believability of those results is vastly improved.

Qualitative researchers also have accomplished much over the years in spelling out guidelines for increasing the rigor of their methods. However, it is still the case that the credibility we assign to qualitative findings depends on our trust in the intelligence and discipline of the researcher as much as on our faith in qualitative methods. Further, a qualitative researcher who interviews women who leave the shelter, then studies the transcripts of those interviews and determines the categories of meaning and the themes that they contain, is conducting a unique study. No matter how closely subsequent researchers follow his or her approach, there is no expectation that the results will be exactly the same.

A different person with a different mind-set, research experience, knowledge base, and interviewing skills will have a different kind of relationship with the research participants, and thus will inevitably produce a somewhat different set of understandings. Replication is not the major goal in qualitative studies that it is with quantitative ones. With respect to our qualitative study:

> While we will approach our study with a conceptual map in mind, this framework will be facilitative rather than constraining. Flexibility is never absolute, but in our interviews, we will be able to take whatever direction is appropriate, within the general goal of the study. In our analysis, we will not be directed by predetermined hypotheses, but will follow concepts and themes as they emerge from our examination of our interview transcripts. With this kind of flexibility, eventual outcomes cannot be predicted. Also, while future researchers will, hopefully, learn from and build on our work, there is no expectation that our study will ever be replicated by someone else.

COMBINING RESEARCH APPROACHES IN A SINGLE STUDY

The idea of combining quantitative and qualitative research approaches in a single study owes much to past discussions about mixing approaches, linking specific paradigms to specific approaches, and combining research designs (Chapters 11 and 12) in all the steps associated within a single research study. Denzin (1978) uses a term called *triangulation* and argues for the combination of the two research approaches in the study of a phenomena. The concept of triangulation is based on the assumption that any bias inherent in any particular data source (Chapter 20), in any particular researcher, and in any research approach would be neutralized when used in conjunction with other data sources, other researchers, and other research approaches.

These techniques contain "within methods" approaches, such as different types of "typical" quantitatively oriented data collection methods, such as experiments (Chapter 11), structured observations (Chapter 13), surveys (Chapter 14), secondary analyses (Chapter 16), existing statistics (Chapter 17), and content analyses (Chapter 18). Alternatively it might involve "between data collection methods," drawing on "typical" quantitative and "typical" qualitative data collection methods—such as opinion surveys (quantitative) and in-depth interviews (qualitative). Thus, triangulation, in its most common form:

- Seeks convergence of a study's results,
- Is complimentary, in that overlapping and different facets of a phenomenon may emerge (e.g., peeling the layers of an onion),
- Can be used developmentally, wherein the first research approach is used sequentially to help inform the second approach,
- May provide contradictions of the results between the two research approaches and may provide a fresh perspective, and
- Adds breadth and depth to a single research study.

Regardless of the purpose for combining the two research approaches, the concept of mixing them raises an additional issue: Should specific inductive and deductive paradigms be linked with specific approaches? For example, if we used an inductive, emerging qualitative stance in a research study, does this mean that we must also use qualitative data collection procedures usually associated with qualitative research studies such as observations and interviews? Alternatively, should a deductive, quantitative theory-driven study always be linked with quantitative data collection procedures such as surveys and experiments?

The answers to these questions are not simple. The "purists" claim that the two research approaches should never be mixed; the "situationalists" assert that certain research approaches are appropriate for specific situations; and the "pragmatists" integrate both approaches in a single study. We take the position of the pragmatists and believe a false dichotomy exists between the quantitative and qualitative approach.

MODELS OF COMBINING BOTH RESEARCH APPROACHES

By now, it should be obvious that it is advantageous for a researcher to combine both research approaches in a single study to better understand the study's problem area. This can be done by using one of three models: (1) the two-phase model, (2) the dominant–less dominant model, or (3) the mixed-model.

Two-Phase Model

The first model of combining both research approaches is the two-phase model, in which we conduct a quantitative phase (Phase 1, or Chapter 4) within a research study and a separate, or second, qualitative phase (Phase 2, or Chapter 5) within the same study. The advantage of this model is that the two research approaches (Phase 1 and 2) are clearly separate; it also enables us to present thoroughly the assumptions behind each of the two distinct approaches, or phases.

Example

Kushman (1992) studied two types of teacher workplace commitment—organizational commitment and commitment to student learning—in 63 urban elementary and middle schools. He used a two-phase model as presented below:

> The central premise of this study was that organizational commitment and commitment to student learning addressed distinct but equally important teacher attitudes for an organizationally effective school, an idea that had some support in the published literature but required further empirical validation.... Phase 1 was a quantitative study that looked at statistical relationships between teacher commitment and organizational antecedents and outcomes in elementary and middle schools. Following this macrolevel analysis, Phase 2 looked within specific schools, using qualitative/case study methods to better understand the dynamics of teacher commitment. (p. 13)

The introduction to his study, however, was not presented in two distinct phases: It examined the problem leading to the study and focused on the purpose of the study—to examine organizational commitment and commitment to student learning. The introduction was followed by sections defining organizational commitment and commitment to student learning (operational definitions). Extensive literature was used to document these two concepts. A conceptual framework then followed (complete with a visual model), and research questions were proposed to explore relationships between and among variables. Kushman then presented the two phases of his study—first the quantitative phase, and next the qualitative phase.

Study results also were presented in terms of the two phases. The quantitative results contained correlations, regressions, and two-way ANOVAs. The case study results were then presented next in terms of themes and subthemes supported by quotes taken from the research participants. The final discussion highlighted the quantitative results (Phase 1) and the complexities that surfaced within the study's findings from the qualitative results (Phase 2). In the final analysis, his study demonstrated a two-phase model as it had all the advantages of an extensive use of each research approach.

Dominant–Less Dominant Model

The second model of combining both research approaches is the dominant–less dominant model. In this model, a study has a single dominant research approach with another smaller component (dominant–less dominant approach) of the overall study drawn from the alternative approach. A classic example of this model is a quantitative study based on testing a theory using an experiment with a small qualitative interview component in the data collection phase. Alternatively, we might engage in qualitative observations with a limited number of research participants, or informants, followed by a quantitative survey of a sample of research participants drawn from a larger population.

The advantage of this model is that it presents a consistent research approach (dominant) within the study and still gathers limited data in reference to another approach (dominant-less) within the same study. The chief disadvantage of this model is that qualitative purists may see it as misusing the qualitative approach because the central assumptions of the study would not link or match "typical qualitative data collection methods and procedure." Quantitative purists also would be concerned about the match.

Example

Hofstede, Neuijen, Ohayv, and Sanders (1990) studied organizational cultures in 20 units from 10 different organizations in Denmark and The Netherlands. Their study consisted of three phases, with one phase based on in-depth interviews in order, "to get a qualitative feel for the gestalt of the unit's culture and to collect issues to be included in the questionnaire" (p. 290). The second and third phases consisted of typical surveys. After presenting descriptions from interviews for two units from two organizations, the authors analyzed extensively the survey data, which included extensive statistical hypothesis testing.

This study represents a dominant quantitative approach with a less-dominant qualitative approach. In a quantitatively oriented introduction, the authors reviewed the literature on organizational cultures and summarized past research studies on national cultures. From this introduction they moved directly into the methods and identified the three phases. They next presented two mini-case studies of two organizations and followed these cases with detailed information about the survey questionnaire and data analysis. From this point on, the results were presented quantitatively, with statistical tests about the differences in the cultures of the organizations. In summary, the qualitative aspect of this study was limited to two mini-case studies; other components of the study's design were quantitative, leading the reader to conclude that the overall design of the study was dominated by the quantitative research approach.

Mixed-Model

The third model of combining both research approaches is the mixed-model and represents the highest degree of mixing both research approaches. We simply mix aspects of the quantitative and qualitative approaches within all (or many) the methodological steps contained within a single research study. The approaches might be mixed in the study's introduction, in the study's literature review and theory use, in the study's purpose statement, and in the study's research question/hypothesis. This model adds complexity to the study's design and uses the advantages of both the quantitative and qualitative research approaches. Moreover, the overall model perhaps best mirrors the research process of working back and forth between inductive and deductive ways of thinking. On the negative side, this model requires a sophisticated knowledge of both research approaches, conveys the linking of paradigms that may be unacceptable to some people, and requires that the writer convey a combination of research approaches that may be unfamiliar to many readers.

Example

Gogolin and Swartz (1992) used a combination of the quantitative and qualitative research approaches throughout a single study. They studied the attitudes toward science of 102 nonscience and 81 science majors in a college. They posed three questions: How attitudes toward science of nonscience college students compared with attitudes of science majors; whether attitudes toward science change with instruction; and the students' attitude development as it relates to science. Gogolin and Swartz measured six attitudinal variables by using the *Attitudes Toward Science Inventory (ATSI)*. They collected interview data by means of an interview questionnaire containing closed-ended and open-ended items.

After taking a science course, the science and nonscience students were compared in terms of the *ATSI* at the beginning (pretest) and at end of the study (posttest). A statistically significant difference was found in these two scores for the nonscience students. The study's results indicated a favorable change in students' attitudes toward science. As a second aspect of their study, they interviewed 25 randomly selected nonscience students. Four themes about attitudes toward science emerged from these interviews: home environment, school environment, peer relationship, and self-concept. Implications of these quantitative and qualitative results were discussed by the authors.

Gogolin and Swartz presented a concept map of the flow of quantitative and qualitative ideas. They began with an introduction, moved on to related research studies, advanced the research approaches from both the quantitative and qualitative data collection phase, discussed quantitative results followed by qualitative results, presented a discussion summarizing the quantitative and qualitative results separately, and then ended the article with an implication section wherein they also discussed the quantitative and qualitative implications separately.

The flow of ideas in this study showed how both quantitative and qualitative approaches were used throughout the several stages within the study. Their introduction section advanced objectives related to description (qualitative), as well as comparison and relationships (quantitative). Their methods section involved comparing groups in terms of experimental effects (quantitative), as well as interviews (qualitative). Their results section interpreted quantitative data (statistical tests) and qualitative data (themes). Their discussion section summarized both quantitative and qualitative results, and implications were drawn from both results. In summary, in almost all of the steps within their research study, the authors included elements of the quantitative and qualitative approaches to the same research problem.

THE MODELS AND DESIGNING A RESEARCH STUDY

The most efficient use of both research approaches suggests another step toward combining them: Can aspects of a study's research design other than the research approach—such as a study's introduction, a study's literature review and use of theory, a study's purpose statement, and a study's research question/hypothesis—also be drawn from different paradigms in a single social work research study?

To further illustrate each one of the three models (i.e., two-phase, dominant–less dominant, and mixed-model), we will relate each one to selected steps in designing a research study as presented in the previous chapters in this book. Our discussion will specifically address: (1) writing an introduction to a research study, (2) using the published literature and theory, (3) writing a purpose statement and research questions/hypotheses, and (4) describing the study's methodology and findings.

Writing an Introduction

As mentioned in the previous two chapters, subtle differences exist between the introductions of quantitative and qualitative research studies. In a qualitative study, minimal literature is used—enough to discuss the study's problem area;

language to suggest an emerging research design, and words to convey that we hope to understand, to discover, or to develop a theory; and perhaps the use of the personal voice through pronouns in the writing. Alternatively, in quantitative introductions to research studies, we usually find the study's problem area firmly grounded in the published literature, a hypothesis is usually advanced that is to be tested, and the impersonal voice of writing is used. Below are some guidelines to follow when writing an introduction section for a research study, broken down by each of the three models.

- *In the two-phase model*, we simply introduce a quantitative phase and a qualitative phase. Typically this presentation takes the form of introducing a two-phase project. An alternative is to present two introductions, spaced apart in the presentation, with each introduction introducing a separate phase within the same research study.
- *In the dominant–less dominant model*, the introduction is presented from the framework of the dominant research approach of the study. For instance, in a quantitative-dominant study, we might advance an *apriori* theory to be tested and use the impersonal voice.
- *In the mixed-model*, the introduction might be presented in the research approach consistent with either paradigm, but we would suggest explicitly that the study will be based on both paradigms. We should always keep our assumptions explicit.

Using the Existing Literature and Theory

The use of the literature and theory within a research study must be consistent with the study's research approach. Usually, the literature and theory are used inductively in qualitative studies, are introduced in the study's emerging research design toward the end of a study, and are positioned in a limited sense at the beginning of the study to "frame" the problem area. In quantitative studies, however, theory and literature are used deductively, are advanced to help guide the study and the development of research questions, and are discussed at some length in the beginning of a study. Below are some guidelines to follow on how to use the published literature and theory within a research study, broken down by each of the three models.

- *In the two-phase model*, the literature and theory are used inductively in a qualitative phase of the study and deductively in the quantitative phase. An exception, of course, are qualitative approaches with strong theory orientations, such as critical ethnography.
- *In the dominant–less dominant model*, the literature and theory would be used within the research approach consistent with the dominant approach (inductive in qualitative; deductive in quantitative). In short, a project is theoretically driven by a qualitative research approach that incorporates

a complementary quantitative component, or theoretically driven by a quantitative research approach that incorporates a complementary qualitative component (Morse, 1991).

- *In the mixed-model*, it is difficult, if not impossible, to mix the two research approaches in the use of the literature and theory. However, it is possible to use them in modes unassociated with accepted research approaches. The following brief examples illustrate some of these forms.

— Write the theory into the beginning of the study in a qualitative project. This would challenge the inductive approach in a qualitative study but would combine a quantitative use of theory in the study. Moreover, the theory would be introduced, not as a series of propositions to be tested, but as a series of propositions to be modified. An example of this model can be found in Murguia et al. (1991). They presented a published model in the introduction of the study but stated they thought the model was "incompletely conceptualized" and sought, through their qualitative study, to improve and modify the model.

— In a quantitative project, present the theory at the beginning as a tentative model or conceptualization to be developed and to be refined during data collection (Miles & Huberman, 1984). This is contrary to the deductive model in most quantitative research designs. It advances an emerging theoretical orientation within a quantitative project.

— Write a substantial literature review, even a separate "review of the literature" section, into the introduction section of a qualitative study. This model suggests a quantitative orientation to the literature in a qualitative study. This approach appears frequently in qualitative studies reported in journals aimed toward more quantitatively oriented audiences. For example, in Mandell's (1984) symbolic interaction study of children's negotiation of meaning, she provided an extensive review of the literature at the outset of the study. Her literature review on research on childhood socialization and role-taking was presented within a symbolic interaction qualitative research design.

— Design a literature review for a qualitative study that organizes the subtopics around the literature published on the grand tour questions and subquestions in the study. This approach uses a quantitative model for organizing the literature. Use the grand tour questions and subquestions as a framework for deciding on the appropriate sections for the review of the literature.

— Review both quantitative and qualitative studies in a review of the literature in quantitative and qualitative studies. We can make explicit the understanding of the assumptions of both research approaches by grouping qualitative studies together and quantitative studies together (and labeling them accordingly). Alternatively we can identify the paradigm assumptions associated with each study.

Writing a Purpose Statement and Research Questions/Hypotheses

The purpose statement and general research questions in a qualitative study, as discussed in Chapter 5, are usually designed to be open-ended, descriptive, and nondirectional. As presented in Chapter 4, in a quantitative study they may be directional and state a relationship or comparison of variables, specify a multivariate relationship between the independent and dependent variables, and relate to a theoretical perspective. Below are some guidelines to follow on how to write purpose statements and research questions/hypotheses within a research study, broken down by each of the three models.

- *In the two-phase model,* two sets of purpose statements and research questions are presented, each in the phase to which they apply. Their form represents the characteristics of the research approach used in each phase. For instance, the qualitative characteristics are written into the qualitative phase of the study.
- *In the dominant–less dominant model,* a purpose statement and research question/hypothesis are written in the language of the dominant research approach. The secondary purpose (and questions/hypotheses) is described in the language of the less dominant approach. This implies a sequence, as well as a weighting, of the two approaches. Morse (1991) illustrates the use of shorthand labels for quantitative and qualitative research questions and a sequence for ordering the two research approaches. She contends that the two approaches cannot be weighted equally in a single study and assigns capital and small letters (e.g., *QUAN or quan*) to signify the weight given to an approach in any given study. She further suggests that "methodological triangulation" can occur between quantitative and qualitative approaches in two ways: (1) by simultaneous triangulation, and (2) by sequential triangulation.

Simultaneous Triangulation

In simultaneous triangulation, the quantitative and qualitative research questions are answered at the same time. Results to the qualitative research questions, for example, are reported separately and do not necessarily relate to, or confirm, the results from the quantitative phase. Let us take two illustrations from the literature to see how simultaneous triangulation can be used.

(QUAL + quan) What is it like to be a relative of a patient in an Intensive Care Unit (ICU)? This is clearly a qualitative research question, and the methods of ethnography or grounded theory can easily be used to describe the experience of anxious waiting relatives *(QUAL)*. From the inception of the project, we can quite safely assume that relatives will be anxious. But how anxious? Clearly, it would strengthen our description of the study's sample if we administered a standardized anxiety scale and included a description of the degree of anxiety that the relatives are experiencing *(quan)*.

(QUAN + qual) The conceptual framework of the above study can predict that the sicker the child, the greater the spatial distance between the parents and the child; and the greater the spatial distance between the parents and the child, the greater the child's anxiety. How do we measure spatial distance in this situation? One way would be to do participant observation at randomly selected intervals *(qual):* another way would be to use video cameras to observe the distance between the parents and their children *(QUAN)*.

Sequential Triangulation

In sequential triangulation, two distinct and separate phases of the research project are conducted, with the results of the first phase essential for planning the second. Thus, the research questions in Phase 1 are answered before the questions of Phase 2 are formulated. Let us take two illustrations from the literature to see how sequential triangulation can be used.

(QUAL – quan) A research study on the responses of adolescents to menarche provided many insights into adolescent behavior and their affective response to menstruation. But what were the normative attitudes of adolescent girls toward menarche? The domains from a content analysis *(QUAL)* were used to construct a Likert-type scale, and the items were derived directly from the qualitative data. Quantitative methods of ensuring reliability and validity were used, and the Likert-type scale was administered to a randomly selected sample *(quan)*.

(QUAN – qual) A large infant-feeding survey of a Third World country produced the unexpected findings that there was no difference in the incidence of infantile diarrhea in infants from homes with or without refrigeration *(QUAN)*. Qualitative interviews with a sample of residents from homes with refrigerators revealed that infant formula bottles were not kept in the refrigerator. Refrigerators were used for making and storing ice, which was sold to supplement the family income *(qual)*.

- *In the mixed-model*, two purposes for the study are presented—one quali- tative and one quantitative—presented in the language characteristic of both approaches. Moreover, the research questions could be advanced by first presenting descriptive questions (grand tour questions and sub- questions) for the qualitative component of the study and multivariate questions (comparing groups or relating variables) for the quantitative component. In fact, a variation on this is presented in Chapter 4, for writing quantitative research questions. The distinction would be that in the mixed-model, the descriptive questions follow more closely the character- istics of good qualitative research questions rather than on quantitative descriptive questions focused on independent and dependent variables.

Describing the Methodology and Findings

In Chapters 10 to 14, we discuss commonly used experimental designs and surveys. The data they produce are sometimes analyzed statistically to generalize the study's results to a larger population. In qualitative research approaches, there are generally four common types of ways to collect data: participant observations (Chapter 14), interviews (Chapters 14 and 15), and existing docu- ments and visual materials (Chapters 17–19). The analyses of these data sources provide a method for deriving themes or categories and help us to develop a qualitative narrative that presents a pattern (or a larger picture) through multiple levels of analyses. Below are some guidelines to follow on how to describe methods and findings within a research study, broken down by each of the three models.

- *In the two-phase model*, the methods and results sections of the study's qualitative phase are reported separately from the methods and results section of the qualitative phase. Separate headings in the study are used to separate both phases. The intent of a two-phase project is, in all probabil- ity, to triangulate or converge the study's findings, and a separate section of a report could easily address this issue after both phases are discussed.
- *In the dominant–less dominant model*, the methods and results sections relate to the dominant research approach, with a smaller segment for methods and results section for the less-dominant approach. In the illustra- tion in which a major quantitative study is undertaken, supplemented by a few qualitative interviews, we can elaborate, enhance, or illustrate, the results from one approach by using another approach.
- *In the mixed-model*, a "mixed approach section" is used to present the use and collection of both quantitative and qualitative data. Both themes (qualitative) and statistical analysis (quantitative) are presented at the same time. This model has several purposes: triangulating or converging a study's findings, elaborating on a study's results, using one method to inform the other, discovering paradox or contradiction in a study's find-

ings, and extending the breadth and depth of the inquiry (Greene et al., 1989).

SUMMARY

This chapter presented a brief introduction on how to mix quantitative and qualitative research approaches within a single study. It advanced three models of doing this with an emphasis on how a single study is enhanced when both approaches are utilized.

REFERENCES AND FURTHER READINGS

CRESWELL, J.W. (1994). *Research design: Qualitative & quantitative approaches.* Newbury Park, CA: Sage.

DENZIN, N.K. (1978). *The research act: A theoretical introduction to sociological methods* (2nd ed.). New York: McGraw-Hill.

GOGOLIN, L, & SWARTZ, F. (1992). A quantitative and qualitative inquiry into the attitudes toward science of nonscience college students. *Journal of Research in Science Teaching, 29,* 487-504.

GREENE, J.C., CARACELLI, V.J., & GRAHAM, W.E. (1989). Toward a conceptual framework for mixed-method evaluation designs. *Educational Evaluation and Policy Analysis, 11,* 255-274.

HOFSTEDE, G., NEUIJEN, B., OHAYV, D.D., & SANDERS, G. (1990). Measuring organizational cultures: A qualitative and quantitative study across twenty cases. *Administrative Science Quarterly, 35,* 286-316.

JICK, T. D. (1979). Mixing qualitative and quantitative methods: Triangulation in action. *Administrative Science Quarterly, 24,* 602-611.

KUSHMAN, J.W. (1992). The organizational dynamics of teacher workplace. *Educational Administration Quarterly, 28,* 5-42.

MANDELL, N. (1984). Children's negotiation of meaning. *Symbolic Interaction, 7,* 191-211.

MATHISON, S. (1988). Why triangulate? *Educational Researcher, 17,* 13-17.

MILES, M.B., & HUBERMAN, A.M. (1984). *Qualitative data analysis: A sourcebook of new methods.* Newbury Park, CA: Sage.

MORSE, J.M. (1991). Approaches to qualitative-quantitative methodological triangulation. *Nursing Research, 40,* 120-123.

MURGUIA, E., PADILLA, R.V., & PAVEL, M. (1991). Ethnicity and the concept of social integration in Tinto's model of institutional departure. *Journal of College Student Development, 32,* 433-439.

SWIGONSKI, M.E. (1994). The logic of feminist standpoint theory for social work research. *Social Work, 39,* 737-741.

TUTTY, L.M., ROTHERY, M., & GRINNELL, R.M., JR. (1996). Introduction. In L.M. Tutty, M. Rothery, & R.M. Grinnell, Jr. (Eds.), *Qualitative research for social workers: Phases, steps, and tasks* (pp. 1-17). Needham Heights, MA: Allyn and Bacon.

MEASUREMENT IN SOCIAL WORK RESEARCH

Nancy S. Kyte
Gerald J. Bostwick, Jr.

C h a p t e r 7

Measuring Variables

T HIS IS THE FIRST chapter in Part III of this text that deals with the measurement of variables. At this point, it is assumed the reader will have read the previous six chapters and has an appreciation of how both research approaches can be used to develop knowledge for our profession. As we have seen, both research approaches require measuring something or another, usually referred to as variables. Thus, this chapter will provide a brief discussion of how variables can be measured, in addition to discussing the validity and reliability of the measurements used.

Measurement is a pervasive part of daily living. Our morning routine, for example, may include stepping on a scale, adjusting the water for a shower, and making breakfast. Not much thought needs to be given to these activities, but measurements are being taken of weight, water temperature, and food portions. The scale, a heat-sensitive finger, and a measuring cup or spoon are all measuring instruments.

What distinguishes this type of measurement from that engaged in by social workers is the nature of the measuring procedures used. For us, measurement is a systematic process involving the assignment of symbols to properties of objects, according to specified rules. As we have seen in Chapter 4, these rules are designed to increase the probability that the world of concepts corresponds accurately to the world of reality.

The development of measurement procedures is an intricate process in the physical sciences, but it is even more complex in the social sciences (see Boxes 4.3 and 4.4). In physics, for example, measurement is concerned largely with such fundamental variables as weight, length, time, density, volume, and velocity. In social work, our interest is primarily in psychosocial variables such as racial conflict, social status, aggression, and group cohesion. We focus on the properties of individuals, families, groups, communities, and institutions, for which accurate measurement is always problematic.

DEFINITIONS AND FUNCTIONS OF MEASUREMENT

This chapter adopts a broad definition of measurement as the assignment of numerals to the properties or attributes of objects or events, according to rules. Another way to understand measurement is in terms of the functions it serves.

Because the assignment of numerals carries a quantitative meaning, the terms *measurement* and *quantification* have often been used as if they were interchangeable. Recent efforts to develop a less restrictive view of measurement have produced broader definitions with less emphasis on quantification. These definitions have included the assignment of symbols to observations, the assignment of quantitative or qualitative values to attributes, and the assignment of numerals to either quantitative or qualitative response categories.

Common Characteristics of Measurement Definitions

Whether or not qualitative as well as quantitative components are included in these definitions, they all have in common three interrelated characteristics. First is the assignment of numerals (e.g., 1, 2, 3) or symbols (e.g., A, B, C), which are basically synonymous. When a numeral is used to identify something it has no intrinsic quantitative meaning and is nothing more than a label. Thus the numeral 1 is simply a symbol of a special kind, like a + is used to refer to addition or a $ used to refer to money. The letter A could be used just as easily. Measurement, however, has traditionally used numerals, which become numbers after they are assigned a quantitative meaning.

The second common characteristic of measurement definitions is that numerals or symbols are assigned to properties of objects rather than to the objects themselves. Put another way, objects are not measured *per se*; rather, their properties or characteristics are measured. To be even more precise, indicants of these properties are measured. This is important when measuring a complex concept where direct observation is impossible. Hostility, depression, and intelligence, for example, are concepts that cannot be directly observed. These properties must always be inferred from observations of their presumed variables (or indicants), such as fighting, crying, or responses on an achievement test.

The third characteristic is that numerals or symbols are assigned to (indicants of) properties of objects according to specified rules. The importance of these rules, often referred to as rules of correspondence or assignment, cannot be overemphasized (Kaplan, 1964). Measurement is a game played with objects and numerals. Games have rules, and rules can be good or bad. Other things being equal, good rules lead to good measurement, and bad rules lead to bad measurement. At its most basic level, then, a rule is a guide, method, or command that says what to do (Kerlinger, 1986).

Suppose a client is asked to identify five possible solutions to a problem and then rank-order them according to some criterion, such as probable effectiveness. A rule may be formulated that states that the range of numerals (1–5) should be assigned in such a manner that the highest (5) represents the solution the client judges to be the most effective and the lowest (1) represents the least effective solution. This rule clearly tells how to assign the range of numerals to the domain of problem-solving options that the client has identified.

While a definition of measurement stipulates the formulation of and adherence to rules, it does not restrict the kind of rules that can be used. Rules may be developed deductively, be based on previous experience, stem from common sense, or be pure hunches. Whatever the origin of the rules, the utility of any measure is contingent on its ability to explain adequately the variable being studied. Therefore, no measurement procedure is any better than its rules.

In summary, any endeavor attempting to assign numerals or symbols to (indicants of) properties of objects according to specified rules qualifies as measurement, and measurement of anything is theoretically possible if rules can be set up on some rational or empirical basis. Whether that measurement is good or bad will depend on the formulation of clear, unambiguous rules of correspondence that can themselves be empirically tested.

Functions of Measurement

Measurement is not an end in itself. We can appreciate its usefulness only if we know what it is intended to do and what role and function it has in our profession. Its functions include correspondence, objectivity and standardization, quantification on different levels, and replication and communication.

Correspondence

Measurement theory calls for the application of rules and procedures to increase the correspondence between the real world and the world of concepts.

The real world provides us with empirical evidence; the world of concepts provides us with a theoretical model for making sense out of that segment of the real world that we are trying to explain or predict. It is through measurement's rules of correspondence that this theoretical model can be connected with the world of reality.

Objectivity and Standardization

Measurement helps take some of the guesswork out of scientific observation; the observations are considerably more objective than, for example, personal judgments. The scientific principle that any statement of fact made by one person should be independently verifiable by another is violated if there is room for disagreement about observations of empirical events.

In the absence of a standardized measurement of narcissism, for instance, two social workers may disagree strongly about how narcissistic a particular client is. Obviously, then, we would find it impossible to make any empirical test of hypotheses derived from theories of narcissism. This, unfortunately, is frequently the case. We have a myriad of theories at our disposal, but because these theories often involve variables that cannot be adequately measured, the hypotheses they generate must remain untested. Thus, additions to our knowledge base depend on the extent to which it becomes possible to measure certain variables and theoretical constructs accurately.

Quantification

By allowing for the quantification of data, measurement increases not only the objectivity of our observations but also the ability for us to describe them precisely. Different types or levels of measurement result in different types of data. Classification, for example, makes it possible to categorize variables such as gender and religion into subclasses such as male-female and Protestant-Catholic-Jewish.

A second, higher level of measurement makes it possible not only to define differences between and among variable subclasses but also to determine greater-than and less-than relationships. Thus, a particular variable might be classified not only as occurring or not occurring but also as never, rarely, sometimes, often, or always occurring.

An even higher level makes it possible to rank-order certain variable characteristics and specify the exact distances between the variable subclasses. This makes it possible to say that a family with an income of $13,000 has $5,000 more than a family with an income of $8,000, or a social service agency employing 20 social workers has a professional staff that is twice as large as that of an agency employing 10 social workers.

Each type of measurement provides important data which enable us to describe physical, psychological, or social phenomena empirically. The precision of the measurement increases as it moves from the lower (less sophisticated and refined) to the higher levels.

A related advantage of measurement is that it permits the use of powerful methods of statistical analysis. Once numbers are assigned, information can be analyzed with statistical techniques (Weinbach & Grinnell, 1995). Suppose we are conducting a study to determine what characteristics differentiate clients who continue in family therapy from those who drop out. We collect data from a variety of sources, such as clients, social workers, and independent judges, using questionnaires, in-person interviews, case records, and tape recordings of family therapy sessions. We must then be able to make some sense out of all these data, in order to explain what is going on and why. The variables studied must be quantified, or reduced to numerical form, so that our data can be analyzed with statistical techniques and the formulated hypotheses can be tested.

As seen throughout this text, when a hypothesis is supported in social work practice or research, the theory or theories from which it was derived are also supported, at least tentatively. Supporting a theory is tantamount to endorsing the explanations it provides for why certain events occur as they do. Measurement, therefore, facilitates the ability to discover and establish relationships among variables. When numbers are properly applied, the full range of mathematics can be used in constructing and testing theories aimed at explaining or predicting the phenomena of the real world.

Replication and Communication

The research process is concerned not only with conducting tests of theories but also with replicating and communicating the results. The more objective and precise the measurement procedures used in a particular study, the easier it will be for others to replicate the study and thereby to confirm or refute the results obtained. And the more rigorously measurement procedures have been specified, the greater will be the potential for increasing the effective communication of the study's findings.

MEASUREMENT VALIDITY AND RELIABILITY

The two most important considerations in choosing a measuring instrument are the validity and reliability of the instrument and, as a consequence, the validity and reliability of the data it generates. Where these two concepts have been referred to in preceding chapters, they have been identified only briefly and in simple terms. Validity has been described as the degree to which an instrument measures what it is supposed to, and reliability has been described as the degree of accuracy or precision of a measuring instrument.

The next three sections explore the meanings of validity and reliability in measurement more precisely. If we do not know how valid and reliable our measures are, we can put little faith in the results they obtain or the conclusions that are drawn from those results. In short, we cannot be sure of what we have measured.

VALIDITY OF MEASURING INSTRUMENTS

A measuring instrument is valid when it does what it is intended to do (Cronbach, 1970). To put it another way, valid measuring instruments measure what they are supposed to measure and yield scores whose differences reflect the true differences of the variable they are measuring.

An instrument such as a self-administered questionnaire, achievement test, personality inventory, or problem checklist is valid to the extent that it actually measures what it is meant to measure. An instrument that measures a variable such as dominance is valid only to the degree that it truly measures this trait—dominance. If the instrument actually measures some other variable, such as sociability, it is not a valid measure of dominance, but it may be a valid measure of sociability.

The definition of measurement validity has two parts: the extent to which an instrument actually measures the variable in question, and the extent to which it measures that variable accurately. While it is possible to have the first without the second, the second cannot exist without the first. That is, a variable cannot be measured accurately if some other variable is being measured instead.

To establish the validity of a measuring instrument, therefore, we must think in terms not of its validity but rather of its validities. Validity refers broadly to the degree to which an instrument is doing what it is intended to do—and an instrument may have several purposes that vary in number, kind, and scope.

The various kinds of validity—content, criterion, and construct—relate to the different purposes of measurement. Each type has a specific purpose that dictates the type of evidence (logical or statistical) that is needed to demonstrate that the instrument is valid. The three types of validity (and face validity, a subtype) are listed in Table 7.1, along with the questions of validity each one can address.

Content Validity

Content validity is concerned with the representativeness or sampling adequacy of the content of the measuring instrument, such as the items or questions it contains. The instrument must provide an adequate sample of items (or questions) that represent the variables of interest, and it must measure the variable it is assumed to be measuring.

All variables being measured, therefore, must produce operational definitions (Nunnally, 1975). Moreover, the data gathered to measure the variables must be directly relevant and meaningful to these variables. If the properties of

TABLE 7.1   TYPES OF MEASUREMENT VALIDITY
AND QUESTIONS ADDRESSED BY EACH

Type	Question Addressed
CONTENT VALIDITY	Does the measuring instrument adequately measure the major dimensions of the variable under consideration?
(*Face Validity*)	Does the measuring instrument appear to measure the subject matter under consideration?
CRITERION VALIDITY	Does the individual's measuring instrument score predict the probable behavior on a second variable (criterion-related measure)?
CONSTRUCT VALIDITY	Does the measuring instrument appear to measure the general construct (element) it purports to measure?

the measured variables are not all equally represented in the measuring instrument, a biased sample of responses will result, and the data will be meaningless and therefore useless.

Suppose, for example, we want to construct an instrument to measure students' general social work knowledge. The variable of general social work knowledge is operationally defined as including the following properties: knowledge about social welfare policy, social work research, casework, group work, and community organization. Before administering the instrument, several colleagues who are experts in these fields are asked to evaluate the instrument's contents—that is, to determine its content validity.

The community organization expert points out that no mention is made of several important functions of community organization, and the group work expert advises that there are no questions dealing with group cohesion and the normal phases of group development. Does the instrument have content validity? No, because its intended purpose—to measure general social work knowledge—will not be achieved.

Assuming that the other areas of the instrument are judged to be adequate, could the obtained data be used to validly determine a student's knowledge about casework, social work research, and social welfare policy? Here the answer is yes. Although there would be no justification for using the instrument to determine general social work knowledge, it could be used to assess knowledge about these three areas. Thus the instrument is content valid for one purpose but not for another.

Content validation is, by and large, a judgmental process; the colleagues asked to assess the instrument were also being asked to use their judgments to establish content validity. It may be assessed in the same instrument as high by one person but low by another. But if we had not asked for the judgments of colleagues or consulted with experts in each of the major areas of social work, the questions on the instrument might not have been representative of general social work knowledge. The resultant interpretations would have been open to question, to say the least.

Content validity also requires (at least in principle) specification of the universe of questions from which the instrument's questions are to be drawn. That is, the instrument must contain a logical sampling of questions from the entire universe of questions that are presumed to reflect the variable being measured. Further, the sampling of questions must correspond with the universe of questions in some consistent fashion. This is no easy task. There may be no consensus about the definition of the variable to be measured, and it may be difficult to identify the universe of questions. The potential number of representative questions to be included in the measuring instrument could approach infinity, particularly in measuring variables that are complex and multidimensional in nature.

The personal judgment of the person constructing the instrument determines how a variable is to be defined, how the universe of questions is to be identified, and how the sample of representative questions from that universe is to be drawn. Thus the general content validity of any instrument rests to a large extent on the skill and judgment of the person who constructs it. If poor judgment has been used—and this is always a possibility—the instrument is likely to have little, or no, content validity.

Face Validity

The terms *face validity* and *content validity* are often used interchangeably in the professional literature, but they are incorrectly thought of as synonymous. Technically, face validity is not a form of validation because it refers to what an instrument "appears to" measure rather than what it "actually" measures (that is, it appears relevant to those who will complete or administer it). Nevertheless, face validity is a desirable characteristic for a measuring instrument. Without it, there may be resistance on the part of respondents, and this can adversely affect the results obtained. Consequently, it is important to structure an instrument so that it not only accurately measures the variables under consideration (content validity) but also appears to be a relevant measure of those variables (face validity).

To assess the effects of a communication skills training course offered at a school of social work, for example, an assessment form is to be administered to each student at the beginning and end of the course. A search of the literature locates a standardized instrument that measures the types of skills the course is designed to teach.

This instrument, however, was originally developed for use with upper- and middle-management personnel. If our students were presented with items reflecting the business world, they might well question how their responses could tell anything about how they work with clients. The items should be rephrased to reflect social work situations in order to increase the face validity of the instrument.

Criterion Validity

Criterion validity, which involves multiple measurement, is established by comparing scores of the measuring instrument with an external criterion known (or believed) to measure the variable being measured. Thus there must be one or more external, or independent, criteria with which to compare the scores of the instrument.

In order to validate an instrument that has been constructed to predict our students' success in a BSW program, for example, the measuring instrument is administered to students entering their first semester. These test scores are then compared with their subsequent grade point averages. Here, the external criterion (or dependent variable) is grade point average. Other potential external criteria might be individual or combined ratings of academic and practicum performance and graduation from the program.

The external criterion used, of course, should itself be reasonably valid and reliable. If a criterion that is inaccurate or undependable is chosen, the instrument itself will not be validated adequately. Unfortunately, valid and reliable criteria may not exist or may not have been thoroughly tested. In such a case, the one that seems most adequate (keeping in mind its limitations) should be chosen, supplemented, if possible, with other relevant criteria. The nature of the predictions and the techniques available for checking out criteria generally determine which ones are relevant.

Concurrent and Predictive Validity

Criterion validity may be classified as concurrent or predictive. Concurrent validity refers to the ability of a measuring instrument to predict accurately an individual's current status. An example of an instrument with concurrent validity is a psychopathology scale that is capable of distinguishing between adolescents who are *currently* in need of psychiatric treatment and those who are not.

Predictive validity denotes an instrument's ability to predict future performance or status from present performance or status. An instrument has predictive validity if it can distinguish between individuals who will *differ at some point in the future*. A psychopathology scale with predictive validity would be capable of differentiating not only those adolescents who need psychiatric treatment but those who will need it one year from now.

Both concurrent and predictive validity are concerned with prediction, and both make use of some external criterion that is purportedly a valid and reliable measure of the variable being studied. What differentiates the two is time. Concurrent validity predicts current performance or status, while predictive validity predicts future performance or status. Moreover, concurrent validity involves administering an instrument and comparing its scores with an external criterion at approximately the same time, or concurrently. In contrast, predictive validity entails comparative measurement at two different (present and future) points in time.

The major concern of criterion validity, however, is not whether an instrument is valid for concurrent or future discriminations. Rather, the concern is with the use of a second measure as an independent criterion to check the validity of the first measure.

Construct Validity

What sets construct validity apart from content and criterion validity is its preoccupation with theory, explanatory constructs, and the testing of hypothesized relationships between and among variables. Construct validity is difficult to understand because it involves determining the degree to which an instrument successfully measures a theoretical concept. The difficulty derives in part from the abstract nature of concepts.

A concept is a characteristic or trait that does not exist as an isolated, observable dimension of behavior. It cannot be seen, felt, or heard, and it cannot be measured directly—its existence must be inferred from the evidence at hand. Thus the concept, hostility, may be inferred from observations of presumably hostile or aggressive acts; the concept, anxiety, may be inferred from test scores, galvanic skin responses, observations of anxious behaviors, and so on. Other typical concepts of concern to us are motivation, social class, delinquency, prejudice, and organizational conflict.

Construct validity is evaluated by determining the degree to which certain explanatory concepts account for variance, or individual differences, in the scores of an instrument. Put another way, it is concerned with the meaning of the instrument—that is, what it is measuring and how and why it operates the way it does. To assess the construct validity of the Rorschach inkblot test, for example, we would try to determine the factors, or concepts, that account for differences in responses on the test. Attempts might be made to determine if the test measures emotional stability, sociability, or self-control and whether it also measures aggressiveness. The question would be: What proportion of the total test variance is accounted for by the concepts of emotional stability, sociability, self-control, and aggressiveness?

With construct validity, there is usually more interest in the property, or concept, being measured than in the instrument itself. Thus it involves validation not only of the instrument but also of the theory underlying it. To establish construct validity, the meaning of the concept must be understood, and the propositions the theory makes about the relationships between this and other concepts must be identified. We try to discover what predictions can be made on the basis of these propositions and whether the measurements obtained from the instrument will be consistent with those predictions. If the predictions are not supported, there is no clear-cut guide as to whether the shortcoming is in the instrument or in the theory.

Suppose a study is conducted to test the hypothesis that self-referred clients are more likely to have favorable attitudes toward treatment than those who come to the agency on some other basis. If the findings do not support the predicted relationship between self-referral and attitude toward treatment, should it be concluded that the measure is not valid or that the hypothesis is incorrect? In such a situation the concept of attitude toward treatment and the network of propositions that led to this prediction should be reexamined. Then the concept might be refined with more detailed hypotheses about its relationship to other concepts, and changes might be made in the instrument.

Construct validation makes use of data from a variety of sources. It is a painstaking building process much like theory construction—an attempt to ferret out the dimensions that an instrument is tapping and thereby to validate the theory underlying the instrument. This can be accomplished through a three-step process: (1) suggesting what concepts might account for performance on an instrument, (2) deriving hypotheses from the theory surrounding the concepts, and (3) testing these hypotheses empirically (Cronbach, 1970). The testing of the hypotheses can involve many procedures, including convergent-discriminant validation and factor analysis.

Convergent-Discriminant Validation

Convergent validity means that different measures of a concept yield similar results (i.e., they converge). Put another way, evidence gathered from different sources and in different ways leads to the same (or a similar) measure of the concept. If two different instruments, each alleging to measure the same concept, are administered to a group of people, similar responses or scores should be found on both instruments. And if one instrument is administered to groups of people in two different states, it should yield similar results in both groups. If it does not, the theory underlying the concept being measured should be able to explain why.

Discriminant validity means that a concept can be empirically differentiated (i.e., discriminated) from other concepts. The test is to see if an instrument is (or is not) related to other concepts from which, according to theory, it should differ. If it can be shown that an instrument measures a concept in the same way other instruments measure it, and that it is not related to any other concepts from which it should theoretically differ, it has both convergent and discriminant validity.

Factor Analysis

Another powerful method for determining construct validity is factor analysis, a statistical procedure in which a large number of questions or instruments (called factors) is reduced to a smaller number. The procedure is used to discover which factors go together (i.e., measure the same or similar things) and to determine what relationships exist between these clusters of factors.

Suppose we develop a measuring instrument and administer it, along with seven other different instruments, to a group of clients. Factor analysis would allow us to identify the concepts that are being measured by these eight instruments and to determine which instruments, if any, are essentially measuring the same concepts. The relationships of the new instrument to the other seven could be examined to determine which concept(s) it actually measures. Our understanding of that concept is improved by knowledge of the degree to which the other concepts are or are not related to the one measured in the new instrument.

Choosing the Best Approach

Content, criterion, and construct validity are three interrelated approaches to instrument validation. They are all relevant to any research situation. Because each type of validation functions in a different capacity, it is difficult to make any blanket generalizations about which is the best approach.

Three questions can be asked to discover how valid an instrument is (Thorndike & Hagen, 1969). They are:

1. How well does this instrument measure what it should measure?
2. How well does this instrument compare with one or more external criteria purporting to measure the same thing?
3. What does this instrument mean—what is it in fact measuring, and how and why does it operate the way it does?

The questions we choose to answer dictate which types of validation are of primary concern. The first would require content validity, the second criterion validity, and the third, construct validity. Our objectives and planned use of the instrument determine what kind of validity evidence is needed the most. When an instrument is employed for different purposes, it should be validated in different ways. If it is used for any purpose other than that for which it was intended—or if it is used with a different client population or in a different setting—we have the responsibility to revalidate it accordingly.

RELIABILITY OF MEASURING INSTRUMENTS

The degree of accuracy, or precision, in the measurements an instrument provides is called reliability. Dependability, stability, consistency, predictability, reproducibility, and generalizability are all synonyms for reliability. A measuring instrument is reliable to the extent that independent administrations of the same instrument (or a comparable instrument) consistently yield similar results.

In its broadest sense, an instrument's reliability indicates the degree to which individual differences in scores are attributable to "true" differences in the property being measured or to errors of measurement. As will be discussed in a later section of this chapter, errors of measurement involving reliability are random, rather than constant. They are the product of causes and conditions, such as fatigue and fluctuations of memory or mood, which are essentially irrelevant to the purpose of the instrument. Scores on an instrument therefore tend to lean now this way, now that.

Since random errors are present in all measurement, no instrument is 100 percent reliable. The data yielded by an instrument will be dependable only to the extent that the instrument is relatively free from errors of measurement. Consequently, every instrument should be tested for reliability before it is formally administered, rather than after.

The term *reliability* is frequently used to refer to three different but interrelated concepts: (1) stability, (2) equivalence, and (3) homogeneity. Underlying each of these is the notion of consistency.

- Stability, also called temporal stability, refers to an individual's responses from one administration of an instrument to another. It is determined by the test-retest method, which compares the results of repeated measurements.
- Equivalence concerns an individual's responses on different instruments intended to measure the same thing. It can be established using alternate, or parallel, forms.
- Homogeneity focuses on the internal consistency of an instrument and can be determined with the split-half method.

All three concepts and procedures essentially involve establishing the degree of consistency or agreement between two or more independently derived sets of scores. The three general methods for establishing the reliability of a measuring instrument are listed in Table 7.2, along with the measurement reliability question addressed in each.

The Test-Retest Method

A common approach to establishing reliability is through repeated measurement. The same instrument is administered to the same group of individuals on two or more separate occasions. Then the results are compared by correlating the sets of scores and calculating what is known as a reliability coefficient, which indicates the extent of the relationship between the scores. If this coefficient is high, it can be concluded that the instrument has good test-retest reliability.

TABLE 7.2   Types of Measurement Reliability and Questions Addressed by Each

Type	Question Addressed
Test-Retest Method	Does an individual respond to a measuring instrument in the same general way when the instrument is administered twice?
Alternate-Forms Method	When two forms of an instrument that are equivalent in their degree of validity are given to the same individual, is there a strong convergence in how that person responds?
Split-Half Method	Are the scores on one half of the measuring instrument similar to those obtained on the other half?

Test-retest reliability thus estimates the stability of an instrument by permitting it to be compared with itself and by showing the extent to which its scores are consistent over time. The higher the reliability, the less susceptible the scores are to random daily changes in the condition of the individual (e.g., fatigue, emotional strain, worry) or the testing environment (e.g., noise, room temperature). And the less susceptible the instrument is to such extraneous influences, the more reliable it is.

Effects of Retesting

To determine if a difference between measurements of the same measuring instrument is due to extraneous factors or to a genuine change in the variable being measured, the first consideration is the possibility that the first testing has influenced the second. The very process of remeasuring may have increased the influence of extraneous factors. Individuals may be less interested, less motivated, and less anxious during the second testing because they are already familiar with the instrument, for example. If the time interval between retests is fairly short, they may remember their answers and simply repeat many of the responses they provided the first time.

Another possibility is that the first testing has actually changed the variable being measured. For instance, a self-administered questionnaire assessing attitudes toward the elderly may raise questions people have never thought about before, so their interest in the issue is heightened and they form definite opinions. Thus a "do not know" response on the first testing may be replaced by a "definitely agree" or "definitely disagree" response on the second. It is also possible that a genuine change due to influences unrelated to the testing has occurred.

Because test-retest reliability is subject to a number of biases due to the effects of recall, practice, or repetition, measuring instruments that are appreciably affected by memory or repetition do not lend themselves to this method. If the measures obtained on an instrument will not be appreciably affected by a repeat testing, the test-retest method can be used, but careful consideration must be given to the time interval between tests. The shorter this interval, the more likely it is that the first testing will have an effect on the second one; the longer the interval, the more likely it is that real change will have occurred. A shorter interval increases the likelihood of erring in the direction of overestimating reliability, and a longer interval may result in underestimating reliability.

There are no hard and fast rules for judging the optimal time interval between tests. A two- or four-week interval is generally considered suitable for most psychological measures, and the waiting period should rarely exceed six months. On a general level, wait long enough for the effects of the first testing to wear off, but not long enough for a significant amount of real change to occur. If an IQ test is administered to a group of children on two separate occasions, approximately one month apart, for example, changes in scores would not be anticipated, but an interval of five years could be expected to produce significant changes.

An example of the use of the test-retest method in social work practice involves a series of instruments to assess the extent of clients' problems and to obtain evaluative feedback on therapeutic progress (Nurius & Hudson, 1993). Clients complete them every week or two weeks, and we can use their scores to monitor and guide the course of our treatment. The test-retest reliability of these scales was established by asking a group of clients to complete them at one sitting, wait a minimum of two hours and a maximum of 24 hours, and complete them again. The resultant reliability coefficients were high. In clinical applications, the reliability of these measures has not appeared to change markedly as a result of repeated administrations.

The Alternate-Forms Method

One way to avoid some of the problems encountered with test-retest reliability is to use alternate (or parallel) forms. The alternate-forms method involves administering, in either immediate or delayed succession, supposedly equivalent forms of the same instrument to the same group of individuals. The reliability coefficient obtained indicates the strength of the relationship between the two alternate forms.

Alternate forms can be thought of as instruments with equivalent content that are constructed according to the same specifications. The forms contain questions that are different (thus eliminating exact recall) but are intended to measure the same variable equally. Form A and Form B of a reading comprehension test, for example, should contain passages of equal difficulty and should ask similar types of questions. If Form A uses a passage from a novel and Form B uses an excerpt from a research text, the levels of difficulty can be expected to be quite different. Any observed differences, then, could be explained as a result of the test's content, not differing levels of reading comprehension.

Use of the alternate-forms method requires both appropriate time intervals and equivalent sets of questions. Each alternate form must contain a sampling of questions that is truly representative. Questions must be randomly drawn from the universal pool of potential questions in such a way that if the same procedure were followed a second or even a third time, essentially equivalent sets of questions would result each time. Each set would then qualify as an alternate form of the instrument. In addition to content-equivalent questions, alternate forms should contain the same number of questions, questions expressed in a similar form, and questions of equal difficulty, and they should have comparable instructions, formats, illustrative examples, and time limits.

Considerable time and effort are needed to develop and administer truly equivalent forms. All the problems of measuring social and psychological phenomena are compounded by the need to construct two instruments.

The Split-Half Method

The split-half method of establishing reliability involves administering an instrument to a group of people, with the questions divided into comparable halves and the scores on the two parts compared to determine the extent to which they are equivalent. This is in many ways analogous to alternate-forms reliability because each half is treated as if it were a parallel form of the same instrument.

If the two halves are not equivalent, the instrument may not have a representative sampling of questions, and an individual's score may be influenced more by the questions than by the variable being measured. If the scores obtained from the two halves are similar, it can be assumed that the individual's performance is not appreciably affected by the sampling of questions in either half of the instrument.

One of the main problems with split-half reliability is how to divide the instrument into equivalent halves. The first thought might be to divide the instrument in half by counting the total number of questions and dividing by two; a 30-question instrument would be split so that Questions 1 through 15 would make up the first half and Questions 16 through 30 the second half. But what happens if the nature or level of difficulty of the questions is different at the beginning and end of the instrument? And how can such extraneous factors as fatigue and boredom, which may influence responses at the beginning and end of the instrument differently, be controlled for?

One answer is the odd-even procedure, whereby all the even-numbered questions are assigned to one group and all the odd-numbered questions to the other group. Then the scores from the two groups are compared.

THE VALIDITY-RELIABILITY RELATIONSHIP

Although validity and reliability have been treated as separate properties of a measuring instrument, they are clearly related. There cannot be validity without reliability, but there can be reliability without validity. Put simply, high reliability does not guarantee validity. Reliability can only show that something is being measured consistently, but that "something" may or may not be the variable that is to be measured. Thus an instrument that is reliable may not be valid. However, it is not possible to have an instrument that is valid but not reliable. If an instrument measures what it says it measures, then by definition it must be reliable.

The relationship between validity and reliability can be illustrated with an analogy. Suppose a new rifle is used in a sharpshooter contest, but first the new sight and overall accuracy of the weapon must be checked out. A target is set up and five rounds are fired. As Figure 7.1*a* shows, the shots are scattered all over; not one has hit the target, let alone the bull's-eye.

Luckily, another shooter notices that the rifle is jerked when fired, which could account for the scattering of shots. The rifle is then put on a stand to minimize this effect, and on the next try five rounds are fired. As Figure 7.1*b* illustrates, all five shots are grouped together in a pattern, which seems to indicate that the inconsistency on the first attempt was due to the jerking of the rifle and not to a problem with the rifle itself. However, the shots are still off target.

The problem must be the new rifle sight; the target is not being hit where the rifle is aimed. After realigning the sight, another five rounds are fired, and this time they hit the bull's-eye every time (Figure 7.1*c*). This analogy shows that it is possible to have an instrument that is both unreliable and invalid (Figure 7.1*a*), that has high reliability and no validity (Figure 7.1*b*), or that has high reliability and high validity (Figure 7.1*c*).

SOURCES OF MEASUREMENT ERROR

Measurement error is any variation in responses on a measuring instrument— such as answers on a questionnaire or ratings made by an independent observer—that cannot be attributed to the variable being measured. Thus measurement error is inversely related to the validity and reliability of an instrument. The greater the variation due to extraneous factors, the lower will be the validity and reliability of the measurements taken.

Our goal, therefore, is to develop or locate a measuring instrument that is as free as possible from outside, unwanted influences. However, most measurement occurs in more-or-less complex situations in which numerous factors may affect both the variable being measured and the process of measurement. As a result, it is virtually impossible to construct a perfectly valid and reliable instrument.

Because measurements are never totally free of error, we must identify

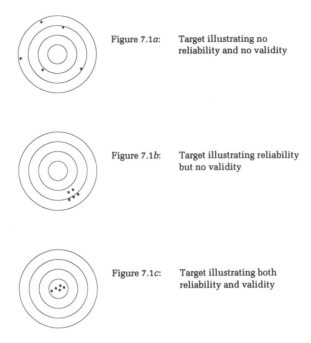

Figure 7.1a: Target illustrating no reliability and no validity

Figure 7.1b: Target illustrating reliability but no validity

Figure 7.1c: Target illustrating both reliability and validity

FIGURE 7.1   VALIDITY AND RELIABILITY
                        RELATIONSHIP

potential sources of error and then control or lessen their impact. Put simply, the aim is to minimize error and maximize accuracy. Of the myriad of extraneous influences that could be operating in any measurement situation as sources of error, only the most common will be reviewed in this section. There are basically two categories of the factors that may have unwanted influence on a measurement so that they obscure the "true" differences in the variable being measured—either constant (systematic) or random (variable) sources of error.

Constant Error

Constant, or systematic, error refers to those factors that consistently or systematically affect the variable being measured. By their nature, these factors are concerned with relatively stable qualities of the respondents to the measuring instruments. Demographic characteristics and personal style are the two most common sources of constant error.

Demographic variables that could influence an individual's responses include intelligence, education, socioeconomic status, race, culture, and religion.

Suppose an assessment is to be made of the job satisfaction of a group of young people who dropped out of high school and enrolled in a job training program. The measuring instrument (a self-administered job satisfaction questionnaire) requires an ability to read at the eighth-grade level.

If the measuring instrument is administered to the trainees without determining their reading levels in advance, it is likely to produce a set of confounded scores. That is, the scores will reflect not their job satisfaction, either before or after completing the program, but rather their ability to read and understand the questions. It cannot be assumed that the respondents represent a homogeneous group with respect to demographic characteristics or that these characteristics exert little influence on the measurements. In this example, there would be no justification for assuming that since all of the trainees had dropped out of high school, they can all read at the eighth-grade level.

Personal Styles or Response Sets

Test constructors and research methodologists have devoted most attention to the personal styles of the respondents as a source of error. This is partly because different personal styles, or response sets, have come to be viewed as indicants of personality traits. Some of the common personal styles that can consistently affect the responses of individuals or the reactions of observers are listed in Figure 7.2.

There is some controversy about the actual biasing or error effects of response sets. Some maintain that they explain only a small portion of the variance in measurement and do not apply to all types of instruments. Ideally, however, every measurement situation would be examined for such sources of error and appropriate steps would be taken to reduce their confounding effects. Control procedures for errors due to personal styles of respondents include development of subtle or socially neutral questions and items, incorporation of various response-set or "faking" indicators, and concealment of the instrument's true purpose. Control efforts to minimize observers' reactions include careful training of observers and use of multiple observers.

Random Error

Random error (or variable error), refers to unknown or uncontrolled factors that affect the variable being measured and the process of measurement in an inconsistent (variable) fashion. Unlike constant error, random error effects have no uniform trend or direction. Measurements are affected in such a way that both overestimates and underestimates of the "true" differences in the variable being measured may result.

These errors therefore are self-compensating; that is, they tend to cancel each other out, especially where there is a relatively large sample of respondents.

RESPONSE-SET SOURCES OF ERROR

ERRORS DUE TO PERSONAL STYLES OF RESPONDENTS:

- *Social Desirability*   A tendency to try to give a favorable impression of oneself in one's responses.
- *Acquiescence*   A tendency to agree with statements regardless of their content.
- *Deviation*   A tendency to give unusual or uncommon responses.

ERRORS DUE TO REACTIONS OF OBSERVERS:

- *Contrast Error*   A tendency to rate others as opposite to oneself in regard to a particular trait or characteristic.
- *Halo Effect*   A tendency to be unduly influenced by a single favorable trait or to let one's general impression affect one's ratings of a single trait or characteristic.
- *Error of Leniency*   A tendency to rate too high or to always give favorable reports.
- *Error of Severity*   A tendency to rate too low or to always give unfavorable reports.
- *Error of Central Tendency*   A tendency to rate in the middle, thus avoiding any extreme positions.

FIGURE 7.2   CONSTANT ERRORS IN MEASUREMENT ATTRIBUTABLE TO RESPONDENTS' PERSONAL STYLE OR OBSERVERS' REACTIONS

Nevertheless, it is advisable to try to minimize their potential effects. The ideal situation is one in which the respondent's physical or emotional state, the testing environment, and the procedures used to administer the instrument all exert little or no influence on the measurement process.

The types of random errors reflect three criteria: (1) the transient qualities of the respondent, (2) situational factors in the measurement, and (3) factors related to the administration of the instrument. The transient qualities of respondents to a measuring instrument are those that can vary from day to day—indeed, from moment to moment. These include physical or mental health, mood, motivation, and degree of alertness, boredom, or fatigue. We must consider each quality separately and make a judgment as to how germane or influential it may be in a particular measurement situation.

External, or situational, factors also can introduce unwanted sources of variation into the measures. These include factors in the physical setting, such as seating arrangements, work space, noise, lighting, or the presence of a tape recorder, as well as factors in the social setting, such as the degree of anonymity afforded respondents and the presence or absence of peers. It would not be surprising, for example, to find that adolescents provide different responses to questions about gang behavior when interviewed on the street or at a police station, as a group or individually, or in the presence or absence of family members.

Random error attributable to the administration of the measuring instrument often stems from a lack of uniformity in applications. For instance, interviewers without adequate training might add or omit material or change the wording of questions; group administrators might improvise their own instructions; observers might use different criteria or types of information to classify behaviors. Standardization helps minimize the amount of subjectivity influencing the measurement process and maximize the comparability and objectivity of measurements.

The administrator of the instrument also can be a source of error. It has been found, for example, that an administrator's demeanor and physical appearance, as well as such characteristics as race, gender, age, and socioeconomic status, can affect how an individual will respond. Administrators of measuring instruments must be aware of the image they present and try to minimize the effects of demographic dissimilarities between themselves and respondents.

Administrative factors have a good deal to do with controlling or reducing all three types of random errors. One way is for the administrator to foster rapport with the respondents by arousing interest in the instrument, eliciting cooperation, spending time getting acquainted, increasing motivation, reducing anxiety, and making sure the respondents are capable of completing the tasks required. Another is to select a setting that is conducive to the types of responses needed, such as separate interviews for husbands and wives to determine their attitudes toward their marriages. The use of clear, standardized instructions and the advance preparation of interviewers, observers, and administrators with rehearsals or trial runs will further reduce administrative errors.

SUMMARY

Measurement is a necessary part of social work research that facilitates the correspondence between the world of concepts and the world of observations. It has a meaningful role not only in the selection of appropriate methods of data collection but also in the operationalization of variables and the testing of hypotheses. Through its rules of correspondence, measurement serves to increase the objectivity of observations, the potential replicability of research studies, and the effective communication of findings.

Validity and reliability are the most important characteristics to be considered in selecting a measuring instrument. Validity refers to the degree to which an instrument measures what it is supposed to measure. An instrument may have several purposes that vary in number, kind, and scope, for each of which validity must be established. There are three types of validity: content, criterion, and construct. Measurement reliability refers to the accuracy or precision of an instrument. There are three general methods for establishing reliability: the test-retest, alternate-forms, and split-half methods. Reliability and validity are highly interrelated.

Measurement error refers to variations in instrument scores that cannot be attributed to changes in the variable being measured. Basically, all measurement errors can be categorized as constant (systematic) error or random (variable) error. While measurement errors can never be completely eliminated, all possible steps must be taken to minimize their impact, since the validity and reliability of the instrument decrease as the measurement error increases.

The next two chapters deal with the basic types of measuring instruments. A thorough treatment of standardized instruments, describing how they are constructed and used, is given in Chapter 8, and instruments designed by a social worker for a specific purpose are discussed in Chapter 9. The choice between these two types is usually moot; if a standardized measuring instrument is available that will provide valid and reliable measures of the variables under consideration, it is almost always used.

REFERENCES AND FURTHER READINGS

ADAMS, G.R., & SCHVANEVELDT, J.D. (1991). *Understanding research methods* (2nd ed., pp. 75-98, 149-158). White Plains, NY: Longman.

ANASTAS, J.W., & MACDONALD, M.L. (1994). *Research design for social work and the human services* (pp. 283-314, 432-439). New York: Lexington.

BABBIE, E.R. (1992). *The practice of social research* (6th ed., pp. 115-144). Pacific Grove, CA: Wadsworth.

BAILEY, K.D. (1994). *Methods of social research* (4th ed., pp. 62-77). New York: Free Press.

BOSTWICK, G.J., JR., & KYTE, N.S. (1993). Measurement in research. In R.M. Grinnell, Jr. (Ed.), *Social work research and evaluation* (4th ed., pp. 174-197). Itasca, IL: F.E. Peacock.

COLEMAN, H., & UNRAU, Y. (1996). Phase three: Analyzing your data. In L.M. Tutty, M.A. Rothery, & R.M. Grinnell, Jr. (Eds.), *Qualitative research for social workers: Phases, steps, and tasks* (pp. 88-119). Needham Heights, MA: Allyn & Bacon.

CRONBACH, L.J. (1970). *Essentials of psychological testing* (3rd ed.). New York: Harper & Row.

DEPOY, E., & GITLIN, L.N. (1994). *Introduction to research* (pp. 194-209). St. Louis: Mosby.

GABOR, P.A., & GRINNELL, R.M., JR. (1994). *Evaluation and quality improvement in the human services* (pp. 98-120). Needham Heights, MA: Allyn & Bacon.

GRINNELL, R.M., JR., & WILLIAMS, M. (1990). *Research in social work: A primer* (pp. 86-114). Itasca, IL: F.E. Peacock.

JORDAN, C., FRANKLIN, C., & CORCORAN, K.J. (1993). Standardized measuring instruments. In R.M. Grinnell, Jr. (Ed.), *Social work research and evaluation* (4th ed., pp. 198-220). Itasca, IL: F.E. Peacock.

KAPLAN, A. (1964). *The conduct of inquiry: Methodology for behavioral science.* New York: Harper & Row.

KERLINGER, F. (1986). *Foundations of behavioral research* (3rd ed.). New York: Holt.

KRYSIK, J., HOFFART, I., & GRINNELL, R.M., JR. (1993). *Student study guide for the fourth edition of social work research and evaluation* (pp. 10-11). Itasca, IL: F.E. Peacock.

LEEDY, P.D. (1993). *Practical research: Planning and design* (5th ed., pp. 31-42, 213-215). New York: Macmillan.

MARLOW, C. (1993). *Research methods for generalist social work* (pp. 47-63). Pacific Grove, CA: Brooks/Cole.

MONETTE, D.R., SULLIVAN, T.J., & DeJONG, C.R. (1994). *Applied social research* (3rd ed., pp. 93-118). Fort Worth, TX: Harcourt Brace.

NEUMAN,W.L. (1994). *Social research methods* (2nd ed., pp. 120-144). Needham Heights, MA: Allyn & Bacon.

NUNNALLY, J.C. (1975). *Introduction to statistics for psychology and education.* New York: McGraw-Hill.

NUNNALLY, J.C. (1978). *Psychometric theory* (2nd ed.). New York: McGraw-Hill.

NURIUS, P.S., & HUDSON, W.W. (1993). *Human services: Practice, evaluation, and computers.* Pacific Grove, CA: Brooks/Cole.

ROYSE, D.D. (1995). *Research methods in social work* (2nd ed., pp. 106-112, 241-243). Chicago: Nelson-Hall.

RUBIN, A., & BABBIE, E. (1993). *Research methods for social work* (2nd ed., pp. 119-181). Pacific Grove, CA: Wadsworth.

SINGLETON, R.A., JR., STRAITS, B.C., & MILLER STRAITS, M. (1993). *Approaches to social research* (2nd ed., pp. 100-130). New York: Oxford.

THORNDIKE, R.L., & HAGEN, E. (1969). *Measurement and evaluation in psychology and education* (3rd ed.). New York: Wiley.

WEINBACH, R.W., & GRINNELL, R.M., JR. (1995). *Statistics for social workers* (3rd ed.). White Plains, NY: Longman.

WEINBACH, R.W., & GRINNELL, R.M., JR. (1996). *Applying research knowledge: A workbook for social work students* (2nd ed., pp. 33-40). Needham Heights, MA: Allyn & Bacon.

WILLIAMS, M., TUTTY, L.M., & GRINNELL, R.M., JR. (1995). *Research in social work: An introduction* (2nd ed., pp. 99-114). Itasca, IL: F.E. Peacock.

YEGIDIS, B.L., & WEINBACH, R.W. (1996). *Research methods for social workers* (2nd ed., pp. 125-136). Needham Heights, MA: Allyn & Bacon.

Catheleen Jordan
Cynthia Franklin
Kevin Corcoran

C h a p t e r **8**

Measuring Instruments

A GREAT VARIETY of standardized measuring instruments is available to cover most of our research needs. The selection of an appropriate instrument(s) for a specific measurement purpose requires a thorough understanding of how standardized instruments are constructed and used. Only with this knowledge can we evaluate competing instruments and choose the one(s) that will provide the most valid and reliable data for a particular purpose. A measuring instrument is standardized through rigorous research procedures aimed at empirically verifying its characteristics, results, and applicability. The level of their development varies from minimal to extensive.

ADVANTAGES OF STANDARDIZED MEASURING INSTRUMENTS

Every person to whom a particular standardized measuring instrument is administered should be treated in exactly the same way. In theory, the only reason individuals should score differently on the instrument is because they differ on the variable that is being measured. By providing uniform administration and scoring procedures and normative data that can be used as a basis for comparison, standardized measuring instruments help ensure that the data collected will be valid and reliable measures.

Uniform Administration and Scoring

In standardized measuring instruments, measurement conditions and outcomes are clearly specified to assure comparability across respondents and across research situations. Detailed instructions about how the instrument is to be administered, to whom it is to be administered, and the exact meaning of the results usually are included in a technical manual that accompanies the instrument. Specifications include the materials to be used, the oral instructions to be given while administering the instrument, preliminary demonstrations, scoring methods, and the meaning of the scores produced.

These directions must be followed explicitly in order to reduce the sources of measurement error. With any instrument, care must be taken that constant errors, such as personal style and demographic characteristics, and random errors, such as changeable qualities of the respondents and situational and administrative factors, do not affect the measurements taken (see Chapter 7).

Generation of Normative Data

Normalization, or the establishment of normative data (norms), is essential to the scoring and interpretation of a standardized instrument. Norms are group standards, usually based on a group's average or mean score on a measuring instrument. By giving information on the typical (or average) performance of a particular group, norms provide a point of comparison that can be used to interpret individual scores (Sattler, 1988; Graham & Lilly, 1984). Norms also empirically define the limits and applicability of the measuring instrument by establishing data such as the means and standard deviations of the measures and identifying types of groups for which the instrument is appropriate.

Norms are developed by administering the instrument to a large representative sample (the normalization or norm group) whose demographic characteristics are known. Descriptive statistics are computed for the sample, and an individual's score on an instrument can then be compared to the norms established by the representative sample group.

The raw score of a respondent also can be converted into a derived score, which can be directly compared to the average score achieved by the sample to determine the respondent's standing in relation to the normalization group. Examples of derived scores used in normative measurement include clinical cutting points (such as "A score of 30 or above is considered clinically significant") and age-grade equivalents. Statistical concepts such as standard scores (for example, a *T*-score with a mean of 50 and a standard deviation of 10) and percentile ranks are also derived scores.

Jerome Sattler (1988) provides three guidelines for evaluating the norms of a standardized instrument:

1. The norm group (the sample) should have the same characteristics as the potential respondents. For example, if Asian students are to be assessed to determine why they consistently score high in academic programs, an instrument for which few or no Asians had been included in the sample should not be used.
2. The larger and more representative the norm group, the better. As a general rule, the sample should consist of at least 100 individuals with similar characteristics.
3. The relevance of a particular norm group to the population to be studied must be determined. Many standardized measuring instruments provide several different norm groups ranked by characteristics, from which the group that best characterizes the one to be measured can be chosen.

VALIDITY OF STANDARDIZED INSTRUMENTS

It is through standardization that the validity of the measuring instrument is established. This concept has been defined as the extent to which the instrument actually measures what it is intended to measure. The scores on a measuring instrument should reflect the true differences of the variable they are measuring. The definition therefore includes not only the extent to which an instrument actually measures the variable in question, but also the extent to which it measures that variable accurately.

Three types of validity for measuring instruments were identified in the previous chapter: content, criterion, and construct. Some guidelines for establishing each of these validities in evaluating standardized instruments are briefly discussed in this section. Each type of validity is related to a different purpose of measurement, and no one type is appropriate for every measurement situation. Validity, therefore, must be verified with reference to the intended use of a particular standardized instrument. In other words, potential users of an instrument must ask what it is valid for and for whom it is valid. Let us now turn to the three types of validity.

Content Validity

To ensure content validity, a measuring instrument must include an adequate sample of the universe of questions or items that represent the variable under consideration. This type of validity represents the extent to which the content of a measuring instrument reflects the variable that is being measured and in fact measures that variable and not another.

Eight general guidelines have been proposed for the establishment of content validity in a standardized measuring instrument. Many of these points are discussed further in Chapter 11 in relation to the design and construction of a measuring instrument for specific purposes. We need to consider the following points when it comes to adopting a standardized measuring instrument:

1. Each question or item must represent an aspect of the variable being measured. (*Question* is the term used to designate the item to be rated or responded to, although it could be in the form of a statement)
2. Questions should be empirically related to the construct being measured.
3. Questions must differentiate among individuals at different points in the dimension being measured. In other words, the instrument should discriminate between individuals at low and high extremes and in the middle.
4. Double-barreled questions or otherwise ambiguous interpretations should be avoided (see Chapter 9).
5. Some questions should be worded positively and others negatively so the variable being measured can be indicated by a yes or agree response approximately half the time and by a no or disagree response half the time. Alternating positive and negative wording for questions breaks up the social desirability response set (see Chapter 9).
6. Short questions should be used when possible.
7. Negative questions should be avoided.
8. Biased questions should be avoided, including derogatory statements, slang terms, and prejudicial or leading questions.

The two principal methods used in selecting questions for a measuring instrument so as to ensure content validity—the rational-intutitive and empirical methods—are discussed later in this chapter.

Criterion Validity

Criterion validity has been defined as a process of comparing scores on a measuring instrument with an external criterion. Some criteria that can be used to establish criterion validity for standardized measuring instruments are described in this section (Anastasi, 1988).

One criterion is performance in school or training programs. Independent criteria against which instrument scores can be compared include grades, commendations, and credits earned. This method is used for all types of achievement and diagnostic measuring instruments.

Another criterion involves contrast groups. The scores of one group may be compared with those of another that is assumed to be different, such as the scores of salespersons and accountants, or the scores of an individual may be compared with those of a group. This method is used in the development of personality, interest, and aptitude inventories.

Psychiatric diagnoses also can be used as an external criterion. This involves comparing an individual's performance on a measuring instrument with the psychiatric diagnosis of the person. As a basis of test validity, a psychiatric diagnosis is often used to validate personality instruments and other diagnostic measuring instruments. The validity of a psychiatric diagnosis should be checked before it is used as an indicator or predictor in this way, however.

Other measuring instruments for which criterion validity has been established are often used to establish an instrument's validity. Comparing scores on these instruments with those of the instrument under consideration is a validation method that can be used with all types of measuring instruments.

Other criteria are provided through ratings by observers. Ratings of children's behavior by teachers, parents, or peers and ratings of employees' attitudes by supervisors, co-workers, or others are frequently used in the development of personality measuring instruments.

Construct Validity

Construct validity has been defined as the degree to which an instrument successfully measures a theoretical construct, or an unobservable characteristic or trait. There is more interest in the construct being measured than in the measuring instrument or the scores it generates. The ability to predict developmental changes in children, for example, is a traditional criterion for the construct of IQ scores, which should increase as children get older (Anastasi, 1988). Developmental changes reflected in test scores may be taken as evidence of the measuring instrument's construct validity.

Another way to establish construct validity suggested by Anastasi is to use other measuring instruments with proven construct validity to validate new instruments for measuring related constructs. Scores on the new instrument should correlate highly with those on the other one, but not too highly. There might not be a good reason for developing the new measuring instrument if it does not improve on already available instruments in some way.

Statistical techniques and hypothesis testing procedures such as factor analysis and the establishment of convergent-discriminant validation (see Chapter 7) also can be used to establish construct validity. Factor analysis is particularly relevant because it identifies underlying dimensions of traits or behaviors, as well as the common factors existing in or between measuring instruments. Convergent-discriminant validation concerns the extent to which measures of a construct from different instruments yield similar results, or converge, and the extent to which constructs tested can be empirically discriminated, or differentiated, from other constructs.

The constructs of a measuring instrument also can be validated with experimental interventions, as in the one-group pretest-posttest research design described in Chapter 11. For example, we might be given a pretest in the form of an anxiety-measuring instrument, be subjected to some type of anxiety-raising stimulus such as having to meet higher productivity levels, and then be retested to see if our anxiety scores had risen. In this case, a rise in scores could be taken as evidence of the measuring instrument's ability to reflect our current anxiety levels.

CONSTRUCTION OF STANDARDIZED INSTRUMENTS

A standardized measuring instrument that lacks both validity and reliability would not be a good candidate for selection. Constructors of standardized instruments, therefore, seek to develop instruments that are as valid and reliable as possible. After questions have been selected to maximize content validity, the principal concerns are with the response categories for each question and the length of the instrument.

Question Selection

Two basic methods of selecting questions so as to enhance the content validity of a measuring instrument are the rational-intuitive and empirical methods (Fairweather & Tornatsky, 1977).

The rational-intuitive method involves choosing questions in a logical manner. A group of experts such as clinical social workers, for example, might be asked to suggest questions for determining the presence of a high-risk suicidal behavior. Similar questions suggested might be included, while dissimilar questions would be excluded. Questions selected would then be arranged in groups that logically appear to measure the same variable. Questions related to level of impulse control, such as drug usage and temper tantrums, might be grouped together, and questions related to the immediate danger of suicidal action, such as having a clear plan of doing the act and the means to do it, might form another group.

In the empirical method of establishing content validity, statistical techniques are used to select questions. In the development of a service- satisfaction measuring instrument for a social work agency, for example, we might conduct a simple exploratory study and sample the agency's records to determine all the different services offered by the agency. The various types of services offered would then guide the types of questions to be included on the satisfaction questionnaire.

A combination of the rational-intuitive and the empirical methods is often used in the development of measuring instruments. Questions are generated utilizing experts (rational-intuitive method) and later tested using factor analysis techniques (empirical method).

Response Category Selection

Once the questions have been developed for a standardized instrument, the possible responses for each question are assigned. This provides some notion of the magnitude of the variable being measured for an individual respondent. One logical way is to assign a value for each response, with a low value indicating a low level of the variable being measured and a larger value indicating a higher level.

Values can be thought of as being situated on a continuum of degree, intensity, or magnitude. An example of a question with five responses (i.e., never, rarely, occasionally, frequently, very frequently) and their respective values (i.e., 1, 2, 3, 4, 5) is:

I often get angry at my spouse. (Circle one number below.)

1. Never
2. Rarely
3. Occasionally
4. Frequently
5. Very frequently

Number of Categories

The next decision concerns the number of response categories for a particular variable. Should five responses be included, as in the example above, or should as many as 10 or 20 be used?

As a general rule, the number of response categories should be large enough to allow for some variance in responses but small enough so that appropriate discriminations can be made between the levels. If there are too many response categories, the difference between one level and the next may not be clear. The Subjective Units of Disturbance Scale has 100 possible deviations, and respondents rate their anxiety along a 100-point continuum (Barlow, Hayes, & Nelson, 1984). The problem is to determine the meaningfulness of a score of, say, 85, compared to a score of 90. The opposite is true if an instrument uses only three or four response categories; not enough latitude is allowed to determine the true differences in responding. Including between five and nine response categories is generally the most appropriate and reliable method for standardized instruments (Bloom, Fischer, & Orme, 1995).

A choice also must be made between using an odd or an even number of categories. If an odd number is chosen, respondents may choose the middle-of-the-road responses to avoid revealing their true feelings. An example of a question with an odd number of response categories is:

The bus service in this city is adequate. (Circle one number below.)

1. Strongly disagree

2. Disagree
3. Neither agree nor disagree
4. Agree
5. Strongly agree

If an even number of categories is chosen, however, there is no middle road, so respondents are forced to respond one way or the other. Then the problem is that they may develop a response set favoring one side or the other, or refuse to answer questions at all. An example of a question with an even number of response categories is:

The bus service in this city is adequate. (Circle one number below.)

1. Strongly disagree
2. Disagree
3. Agree
4. Strongly agree

Unfortunately, there are no guidelines for determining the ideal number of response categories or the advantages of an odd or an even number of categories. The choice is left to the discretion of the instrument's developer.

The Response-Value Continuum

Defining the response-value continuum involves decisions about how respondents should be rated—according to frequencies or to agree-disagree, true-false, or yes-no dichotomies. Hudson (1981) suggests that in rating human or social problems, an appropriate approach is to first write questions so that a yes-no or true-false answer indicates that the problem is either present or absent and then scale the responses to get some idea of their magnitude.

Determination of Instrument Length

Ordinarily, the longer the measuring instrument, the greater its reliability. However, lengthy instruments are cumbersome to use and difficult to administer and score. The general rule is that the instrument should include as many questions as necessary to establish its content validity. A minimum of five questions is usually needed.

TYPES OF STANDARDIZED INSTRUMENTS

There are three basic types of standardized measuring instruments: (1) rating scales, (2) questionnaire-type scales, and (3) modified scales. All three aim to measure variables; the difference lies in the scaling techniques they use. Rating scales use judgments by self or others to assign an individual a single score (or value) in relation to the variable being measured. Questionnaire-type scales combine the responses of all the questions within an instrument to form a single overall score for the variable being measured. Modified scales do not fit into either of these classifications.

Rating Scales

The common feature in the various types of rating scales is the rating of individuals, objects, or events on various traits or characteristics at a point on a continuum or a position in an ordered set of response categories. In order to rate the person or thing, numerical values are assigned to each category.

Rating scales for individuals may be completed by the person being evaluated (self-rating) or by some significant other, such as a parent, supervisor, spouse, or social worker. Sometimes a client and a significant other are asked to complete the same rating scale in order to provide us with two different views. A wife and her husband might each rate the latter's openness to communication and other characteristics, for example. Self-ratings are helpful because individuals can evaluate their own thoughts, feelings, and behaviors accurately, provided they are self-aware and willing to be truthful.

Four types of rating scales—graphic rating, itemized rating, comparative rating, and self-anchored scales—are discussed in this section.

Graphic Rating Scales

In graphic rating scales, a variable is described on a continuum from one extreme to the other, such as low to high or most to least. The points of the continuum are ordered in equal intervals and are assigned numbers. Most points have descriptions to help respondents locate their correct positions on the scale. The example below is a "feeling thermometer" on which children are asked to rate, via a check mark, their level of anxiety from very anxious to very calm:

```
___ 100   Very anxious
___  90
___  80
___  70
___  60
___  50   Neither anxious nor calm
___  40
___  30
___  20
___  10
___   0   Very calm
```

Another example is a scale on which clients are asked to rate their individual therapy sessions from not productive to very productive:

> Please circle the number that comes closest to describing your feelings about the session you just completed.

1	2	3	4	5
Not productive		Moderately productive		Very productive

The major advantage of graphic rating scales is that they are easy to use, though care should be taken in the development of appropriate descriptive statements. End statements that are excessive, such as "extremely hot" or "extremely cold," should not be used.

Itemized Rating Scales

Itemized rating scales offer a series of statements designed to rank different positions on the variable being measured. Respondents may be asked to check all the statements with which they agree, or only the one statement that is closest to their own position. On the itemized rating scale below, for example, clients are asked to prioritize questions related to self-image (Warwick & Lininger, 1975):

> If someone asked you to describe yourself, and you could tell only one thing about yourself, which of the following answers would you be most likely to give? (Put a 1 in the space to the left of that question.)
>
> ___ I come from (home state)
> ___ I work for (employer)
> ___ I am a (my occupation or type of work)
> ___ I am a (my church membership or preference)
> ___ I am a graduate of (my school)

Itemized rating scales vary according to the number of statements given and the specificity of the descriptive statements. Higher scale reliability is associated with clear definitions of categories. Even the use of precise categories, however, cannot obviate the fact that clients respond differentially, due to their individual frames of reference. The less homogeneous the group of respondents, the less suitable is an itemized rating scale.

Comparative Rating Scales

In comparative rating scales, respondents are asked to compare an individual (or object) being rated with others. An often-cited example is the ratings that professors are asked to give for students applying to enter graduate school. They may be asked to compare a student with others they have known and then to rate the individual in the top 10 or 20 percent of students.

A variation of the comparative rating scale is the rank-order scale, in which the rater is asked to rank individuals (or objects or events) in relation to one another on some characteristic. Below is an example of a rank-order scale on which a social work supervisor is asked to rank-order four workers who have been recommended for promotion:

> Below are the four individuals that your department has recommended for promotion. Please rank-order these individuals from highest to lowest.
>
> ___ Mary Smith
> ___ Mike Jones
> ___ Jane Johnson
> ___ Jim Jackson

The assumption underlying comparative rating scales is that the rater has some knowledge of the comparison groups. If a small, select group such as the one above is being ranked, the scale would have little usefulness in other settings or with other groups.

Self-Anchored Rating Scales

Self-anchored rating scales are similar to others in that respondents are asked to rate themselves on a continuum, usually a seven- or nine-point scale from low to high. However, the specific referents for each point on the continuum are defined by the respondent. This type of scale is often used to measure such attributes as intensity of feeling or pain. Clients who have difficulty in being honest in group therapy sessions, for example, could complete the following question, which is intended to measure their own perceptions of their honesty. The advantage is that they do not have to attempt to compare themselves with any external group.

> Extent to which you feel you can be honest in the group:
>
>   1   2   3   4   5   6   7   8   9
>
> Can never   Can sometimes   Can always be
> be honest   be honest   completely honest

Questionnaire-Type Scales

Whereas rating scales require judgments on the part of a respondent who is asked to make a single judgment about the topic of interest, questionnaire-type scales include multiple questions that the respondent is asked to answer. Then a total composite score of all the questions is obtained to indicate the individual's position on the variable of interest. The most useful questionnaire-type scale is the summated scale.

Summated Scales

Summated scales are widely used in assessing individual or family problems, for needs assessment, and for other types of program evaluation. In the summated scale, respondents indicate the degree of their agreement or disagreement with each question. Response categories may include strongly agree, agree, neutral, disagree, or strongly disagree.

Modified Scales

Modified scales such as the semantic differential scale and the Goal Attainment Scale have been developed to elicit responses that are not ordinarily included in a rating scale or questionnaire-type scale.

Semantic Differential Scales

The semantic differential scale rates the respondent's perception of three dimensions of the concept under study: evaluation (bad-good), potency (weak-strong), and activity (slow-fast). Each dimension includes several questions scored on a 7- or 11-point continuum on which only the extreme positions are identified. Below are a few questions taken from a scale designed to measure patients' feelings toward the nursing home in which they live (Atherton & Klemmack, 1982):

Below are 29 pairs of words that can be used to describe nursing homes in general. For each pair of words, we would like you to circle the number that comes closest to your feelings about nursing homes. For example, if you feel that nursing homes are more good than bad, circle a number closer to good. The closer the number you circle is to good, the more good and less bad you feel nursing homes in general to be. Continue with each pair.

Good	1	2	3	4	5	6	7	Bad
Beautiful	1	2	3	4	5	6	7	Ugly
Rigid	1	2	3	4	5	6	7	Flexible
Dirty	1	2	3	4	5	6	7	Clean
Happy	1	2	3	4	5	6	7	Sad

The semantic differential scale correlates well with, and appears more direct than, some other scales. However, the scale is not completely comparable across variables. Much depends on the variable being measured and whether or not the three dimensions—evaluation, potency, and activity—are the best ways to measure a particular variable.

Goal Attainment Scales

Goal Attainment Scaling (GAS) is used widely to evaluate client or program outcomes. Specific areas of change are described and the range of possible outcomes, which usually consists of most unfavorable to best anticipated or most favorable outcomes, is identified. These scales can be completed by clients, independent judges, social workers, or other interested persons. Figure 8.1 is an example of a GAS for a nine-year-old boy with three problem areas: being over-weight, spending too much time alone, and behavior problems in school (Siegel, 1988).

SELECTION OF A STANDARDIZED INSTRUMENT

The selection of a standardized measuring instrument for a particular social work research study is dependent on how the research question has been concep-tualized and operationalized. It is through operational definitions of the variables being measured that the independent and dependent variables in a research hypothesis are quantified. If it is asserted in a single-system research design, for example, that a particular intervention (independent variable) causes a particular change in a client's target problem (dependent variable), both the intervention and the client's problem must be operationalized in such a way that they can be objectively measured. The operational definitions of the variables determine the field of available standardized measuring instruments that are capable of measur-ing them.

There are three general considerations in the selection of a measuring instru-ment: determining measurement need (why, what, who, which type, where, and when), locating measuring instruments capable of measuring the variables, and evaluating the alternatives among the instruments that are available.

Determining Measurement Need

The first consideration in selecting an appropriate standardized measuring instrument is to determine measurement need as specifically as possible. In order to do this, we need to know precisely why we want to measure a particular variable, who would complete the instrument, which type of measurement

Outcomes	Scale 1 Overweight	Scale 2 Spending Time Alone	Scale 3 Behavior Problems in School
Most unfavorable outcome thought likely (Score −2)	Gain of 3 lbs.	Spends 12 hours or more in own room	School contract indicates fighting and time in isolation
Less favorable outcome (Score −1)	Loss of 1 lb.	Spends 10 hours in own room	School contract indicates fighting
Expected outcome (Score 0)	Loss of 5 lbs.	Goes to activity room on staff suggestion	School contract shows point loss for behavior modification
More favorable outcome (Score +1)	Loss of 7 lbs.	Spends time in activity room on own initiative	School contract shows no point loss
Most favorable outcome thought likely (Score +2)	Loss of 10 lbs.	Participates in some activities	School contract gives points for cooperation

FIGURE 8.1   EXAMPLE OF A GOAL ATTAINMENT SCALE

format is acceptable, which type should be used in a specific setting or environment, and how often the instrument is to be administered. The six critical questions listed below are guides that can be used to determine measurement need:

1. Why will the measurement occur?
   a. Research
   b. Assessment/diagnosis
   c. Evaluation
2. What will be measured?
   Specify_____
3. Who is appropriate for making the most direct observations?
   a. Research participant/client
   b. Practitioner or researcher
   c. Relevant other

4. Which type of format is acceptable?
   a. Inventories and surveys
   b. Indexes
   c. Scales
   d. Checklists and rating systems
5. Where will the measurement occur?
   a. General setting
   b. Situation-specific environment
6. When will the measurement occur?
   a. Random
   b. Posttest only
   c. Repeated over time

Why Is the Measurement Needed?

Standardized measuring instruments are used for three general purposes, each with different measurement requirements. Some measuring instruments are more appropriate than others, depending on the purpose of the research study: applied research, assessment and diagnosis, or evaluation of practice effectiveness (Sunberg, 1977). In an applied research study where participation is involuntary, for example, participants may have little investment in completing an instrument, so shorter instruments are preferable. In single-system research designs, both the social worker and the client often are more interested in treating feelings, behaviors, or cognitions than in measuring them, so short instruments that can measure specific presenting problems or treatment goals are needed (Barlow & Hersen, 1984).

The purpose of a research study also has an influence on how stringent the psychometric properties (mental measurement techniques) of the instrument must be. Requirements for validity and reliability may be less rigid if the purpose is applied or theoretical research, where the resulting theory will be tentative. These requirements are more rigid in testing a hypothesis or if the results will impact on a person's life. The most rigid requirements apply to measuring instruments used for assessment and diagnostic purposes and to those used in single-system studies where the results can affect termination, referral, or third-party reimbursement.

What Is to Be Measured?

The second question is what is to be measured. Many measuring instruments are used to collect data about a variable such as thoughts, feelings, or behaviors. The variable may be covert and known only to the research participants, or it may be overt and observable.

The guiding principle in determining what to measure is the degree of specificity required, which is less when there is an interest in a broad trait or characteristic and greater when an explicitly defined variable is being measured. Measurement instruments for global, or broad, variables, which are called wideband instruments, assess variables in a general sense but lack specificity. Measures for more narrowly focused variables, which are called narrowband instruments, provide more precision in measuring the variable but little meaningful overall data.

Who Could Make Direct Observations?

Measurement need also depends on who could make the most reliable direct observations to complete the instrument. Chapter 13 on structured observations differentiates between three sources of observers: outside observers, usually professionals; indigenous observers, including relevant others (such as family members or peers) and collaterals (such as staff members); and self-observers, the research participants themselves. The instrument chosen must allow use of the type of observer that we consider most effective.

A school social worker, for example, may want to evaluate how an interpersonal skills training program affects the quality of the social relationships among students and teachers. An instrument that can be used for self-reports by students or teachers or one that calls for students and teachers to rate one another might be selected. Since both of these sources may be biased, however, the observations could be made by some other relevant person such as a school principal or a research assistant (Hops & Greenwood, 1981).

The decision about which source to use must always be made on the basis of who will provide the most accurate and objective assessment. If at all possible, more than one source of observations should be used in order to increase the reliability of the observations.

Which Type of Format Is Most Acceptable?

The fourth question concerns the format of the measuring instrument to be used. The choice among inventories, surveys, indexes, scales, checklists, or rating systems is based on consideration of the variable being measured and who is to complete the instrument.

In general, inventories and surveys are multidimensional, wideband instruments. The questions may take on a variety of formats, such as true-false or ratings of intensity or frequency. Traditionally, inventories and surveys have been fairly lengthy; an example is the Minnesota Multiphasic Personality Inventory. Scales and indexes generally are unidimensional and fairly short, with no more than 50 questions. Scales and indexes can be defined as narrowband measuring instruments that assess a particular variable at an interval or ratio level of measurement (Weinbach & Grinnell, 1995).

These distinctions among formats are fairly arbitrary. Inventories, surveys, indexes, and scales are similar in that they can be used when the variable is observable only to the respondent. When a relevant other can observe the variable, an option is to use a rating system or checklist. These instruments also have a variety of formats; in fact, some self-report types may be checklists, such as the Symptom Checklist (Derogates, Rickles, & Rock, 1976). Examples of rating systems include the Discharge Readiness Inventory, which is multidimensional (Hogerty & Ulrich, 1972), and the Behavior Rating Scale, which is unidimensional (Cowen et al., 1970).

Where Will the Measurement Be Done?

Measurement can be done in various settings and can reflect behaviors or feelings that are specific to an environment (Wicker, 1981). Moreover, observations in one situation may not necessarily generalize to others (Bellack & Hersen, 1977; Mischel, 1968). Determination of measurement need therefore depends on the setting where the measuring instrument is to be completed and the environment the observations represent.

Many variables of interest to us are situation-specific; that is, the variable may be observable only in certain environments and under certain circumstances or with particular people. When a measuring instrument is needed for a situation-specific variable, it is best to choose one that can be completed in that environment (Nelson & Barlow, 1981). It is more valuable to have a parent complete a checklist of a child's problems at home where the trouble occurs than in a social worker's office, for example (Goldman, Stein, & Guerry, 1983). If the variable is not situation-specific (that is, it is assumed to be a trait manifested in a variety of settings), an instrument can be chosen that can be completed in any environment that does not influence the respondent's observations (Anastasi, 1988).

When Will the Measurements Be Taken?

The final question to be considered in determining measurement need is the time frame for administering the instrument. Ideally, the instrument chosen would allow the measurement to be made after the independent variable has been introduced, so the change to be measured (the dependent variable) has occurred. In many single-system research designs, for example, target problems are measured both before and after the intervention has been introduced. The instrument should also allow for the instrument to be administered as closely as possible to the occurrence of a change in behavior or feeling. Observing these two principals increases the accuracy and reliability of the observations.

An additional consideration is how often the measurement will be taken. A single-case design such as the *ABAB* design requires two administrations of the instrument over a period of time, whereas group designs such as the one-group posttest-only design require only one administration. When a measuring instrument is to be administered more than once, the internal validity of the results may be threatened by the effects of retesting (see Chapter 11). Respondents' answers on a posttest may be affected by their ability to recall questions or responses on a pretest, or they may be less interested, less motivated, or less anxious during the second testing.

Locating Standardized Instruments

Once the measurement need has been established, the next consideration is locating appropriate standardized measuring instruments from which to choose. The two general sources for locating such instruments are commercial or professional publishers and the professional literature.

Publishers

Numerous commercial and professional publishing companies specialize in the production and sale of standardized measuring instruments for use in social work research and practice. The cost of instruments purchased from a publisher varies considerably, depending on the instrument, the number of copies needed, and the publisher. The instruments generally are well developed and their psychometric properties are supported by the results of several research studies. Often they are accompanied by manuals that include the normative data.

Publishers are expected to comply with professional standards such as those established by the American Psychological Association. These standards address the claims made about the instrument's rationale, development, psychometric properties, administration, and interpretation of results.

Standards for the use of some instruments have been developed to protect the integrity of research participants, clients, respondents, and the social work profession. Consequently, purchasers of instruments may be required to have certain qualifications, such as a college course in testing and measurement or an advanced degree in a relevant field. A few publishers require membership in particular professional organizations. Most publishers will accept an order from a student if it is cosigned by a qualified person, such as an instructor, who will supervise the use of the instrument. A selected list of publishers of standardized measuring instruments can be found in Jordan, Franklin, and Corcoran (1993).

Journals and Books

Standardized measuring instruments are most commonly reproduced in professional research journals; in fact, most commercially marketed instruments appear first in one of these publications. The instruments usually are supported by evidence of their validity and reliability, although they often require cross-validation and normative data from more representative samples and subsamples.

Locating instruments in journals or books is not easy. Of the two methods used most often, computer searches of data banks and manual searches of the literature, the former is faster, unbelievably more thorough, and easier to use. This is especially true when the research question combines several important variables, such as the effects of poverty on the self-esteem of minority youth from rural and urban areas. Moreover, the data banks used in computer searches are updated regularly.

Financial support for the development of comprehensive data banks has been limited and intermittent, however. Another disadvantage is that many articles on instruments are not referenced with the appropriate indicators for computer retrieval. These limitations are being overcome by the changing technology of computers and information retrieval systems. Several services allow for a complex breakdown of measurement need. Data banks that include references from over 1300 journals, updated monthly, are now available from a division of Psychological Abstracts Information Services, and Bibliographic Retrieval Services offers the entire eighth edition of O. K. Buros's Mental Measurements Yearbook (1978).

Nevertheless, in the absence of means for making thorough and inexpensive computer searches for measuring instruments, most social workers will probably rely on manual searches of references such as Psychological Abstracts. While the reference indices will be the same as those in the data banks accessible by computer, the literature search can be supplemented with appropriate seminal (original) reference volumes.

A selected lists of books and journals that publish standardized measuring instruments can be found in Jordan, Franklin, and Corcoran (1993).

Evaluating Standardized Instruments

A literature search should produce several standardized instruments that would be suitable for use in measuring a particular variable. The choice of one instrument over others depends on the strength of the quantitative data the instrument provides and its practicality in application. These two dimensions can be evaluated by finding answers to a number of questions that focus on the population or sample to be used, the validity and reliability of the instrument, and the practicality of administering the instrument:

1. *The Sample from Which Data Were Drawn:*
   a. Are the samples representative of pertinent populations?
   b. Are the sample sizes sufficiently large?
   c. Are the samples homogeneous?

    d. Are the subsamples pertinent to respondents' demographics?

    e. Are the data obtained from the samples up to date?

2. *The Validity of the Instrument:*

    a. Is the content domain clearly and specifically defined?

    b. Was there a logical procedure for including the items?

    c. Is the criterion measure relevant to the instrument?

    d. Was the criterion measure reliable and valid?

    e. Is the theoretical construct clearly and correctly stated?

    f. Do the scores converge with other relevant measures?

    g. Do the scores discriminate from irrelevant variables?

    h. Are there cross-validation studies that conform to the above concerns?

3. *The Reliability of the Instrument:*

    a. Is there sufficient evidence of internal consistency?

    b. Is there equivalence between various forms?

    c. Is there stability over a relevant time interval?

4. *The Practicality of Application:*

    a. Is the instrument an appropriate length?

    b. Is the content socially acceptable to respondents?

    c. Is the instrument feasible to complete?

    d. Is the instrument relatively direct?

    e. Does the instrument have utility?

    f. Is the instrument relatively nonreactive?

    g. Is the instrument sensitive to measuring change?

    h. Is the instrument feasible to score?

The questions related to the validity and reliability of both the instrument and the data collected with it are concerned with issues discussed in Chapter 7. These issues are the most crucial concerns in evaluating any standardized measuring instrument.

Representativeness of the Sample

Another major concern in the evaluation of standardized instruments is the extent to which the data collected in setting the norms for the instrument represent the population from which the sample is to be drawn for the proposed study (see Chapter 10). If the instrument being considered, for example, was formulated and tested on a sample drawn from a population of white Anglo-Saxon males, it might give perfectly valid results when administered to white Anglo-Saxons males but not if it is to be administered to Native Americans, African Americans, or females.

In general terms, the samples used in setting the norms for an instrument must reflect a population that is pertinent to the respondents who will complete the instrument. Subsamples of demographic characteristics such as age, gender, race, and socioeconomic status must be considered. Thus if the sample on which the norms were established consisted of middle-class African Americans, its applicability to a sample of inner-city African Americans would be suspect.

Another consideration is the size of the sample, which affects sampling error. As pointed out in Chapter 10, sampling error is reduced to the extent that the sample is sufficiently large and homogeneous. The larger the sample, and the less variance there is in the population from which the sample has been drawn, the smaller the standard error will be.

When the data were collected from the sample is another concern. Data based on samples gathered 20 years ago may not be an adequate basis for accepting the instrument as psychometrically sound for today's use. One popular measure of social desirability developed over 30 years ago, for example, includes questions pertaining to the social status derived from owning an automobile (Crowne & Marlowe, 1960). Predicted responses would be substantially different today.

Practicality of Application

Consideration of the practicality of application in social work research and practice involves implementation of the instrument and analysis of the data it generates. The first three practicality questions (i.e., 4a–c) concern the likelihood that research participants will complete the instrument. Even the most valid and reliable instrument has no practical utility if it is left unanswered because it is too long, it is not socially acceptable to the respondent, or the respondent does not understand the instructions or questions.

While a longer instrument is usually more reliable than a shorter one (Allen & Yen, 1979), it is also more time-consuming and may not be completed. This is especially important in single-case research designs where multiple measures are needed and in survey research where the response rate is critical.

The social acceptability of a measuring instrument concerns the respondent's evaluation of the appropriateness of the content (Haynes, 1983). The perceived appropriateness of the content as a measure of the variable of interest—not what the instrument measures but what it appears to measure—is referred to as *face validity* (see Chapter 7). An instrument that is offensive or insulting to respondents will not be completed. Instruments also should be easy for respondents to complete, with content and instructions that are neither above nor below their typical functioning level and questions that can be answered easily.

The other five practicality questions (i.e., 4d–h) concern the meaning or interpretation of the results provided by the instrument. Interpretation is easiest and most practical when the instrument provides direct measurements, has utility, is nonreactive, is sensitive to small changes, and is easy to score.

Variables that can be measured directly include physical ones such as height, weight, and age. Other variables, such as self-esteem or depression, can only be measured indirectly. The advantages in selecting direct measures rather than indirect ones are described in Chapter 13.

An instrument is considered to have utility if the results provide some practical advantage or useful data. The results of an instrument are influenced by whether the instrument is obtrusive, or reactive, or it is unobtrusive. An instrument is said to be reactive if administration of it can affect the respondent or alter the variable being measured. The self-monitoring of cigarette smoking, for example, actually influences this behavior. The degree of internal and external validity depends on minimizing the reactive effects that completing an instrument can have by selecting instruments that are unobtrusive, or nonreactive.

The instrument also has to be sensitive enough to pick up small changes in the variable being measured. If the research purpose is assessing client change, for example, the instrument must be sensitive to changes in the dependent variable that could occur from one administration to the next.

What is done with the instrument after it has been completed is also a practicality consideration. It may seem self-evident that if an instrument is to provide meaningful information it must be possible to score it. However, many instruments have scoring procedures that are too complicated and time-consuming to be practical in social work research and practice situations. Even though they are psychometrically sound, they should be eliminated in favor of others that can be scored more easily.

NONSTANDARDIZED MEASURING INSTRUMENTS

Wherever possible, we should select a standardized measuring instrument, not only because it has been developed and tested by someone else—which saves us an inestimable amount of time and trouble—but also because of the advantages it has with regard to uniformity of content, administration, and scoring. There will be occasions, however, when no standardized instrument seems to be right for our particular purpose. Some standardized instruments are excessively long, complicated, and difficult to score and interpret: That is, they do not meet the criteria for practicality previously mentioned.

Let us take an example from a practice perspective on how to use nonstandardized instruments. No standardized instrument may enable us to discover how Ms. Yen feels about her daughter's marriage. The only way to get this information is to ask Ms. Yen; and if we want to keep on asking Ms. Yen—if the object of our intervention, say, is to help her accept her daughter's marriage—it will be best to ask the questions in the same way every time, so that we can compare the answers and assess her progress with some degree of certainty.

In other words, we will have to develop our own measuring instrument. Perhaps we might begin by asking Ms. Yen to list the things that bother her about her daughter's marriage; that is, we might ask her to develop an inventory. Or, if we do not think Ms. Yen is up to making a list, we might develop our own checklist of possibly relevant factors and ask her to check off all that apply.

Once we know what the factors are, we might be interested in knowing to what degree each one bothers Ms. Yen. Perhaps her daughter's marriage will involve moving to a distant town with her new husband, and it is this that is most important to Ms. Yen. Or perhaps her daughter's prospective husband has characteristics that Ms. Yen perceives as undesirable: He may be non-Asian, while Ms. Yen is Asian, or he may hold unacceptable religious or political views, or come from the "wrong" social or occupational class, and so on.

With Ms. Yen's help, we might develop a simple scale, running from "very bothersome" to "not at all bothersome." Perhaps, we might settle on something like the following:

> Here are a number of statements about your daughter's marriage. Please show how bothersome you find each statement to be by writing the appropriate number in the space to the left of each statement.
>
> **1** = Not at all bothersome
> **2** = A little bothersome
> **3** = Quite bothersome
> **4** = Very bothersome
>
> _____ My daughter will move away after her marriage.
> _____ My daughter's husband is non-Asian.
> _____ My daughter's husband has been married before.
> _____ I don't like my daughter's husband's family.
> _____ My daughter's husband is unemployed.
> _____ ...

We then assess Ms. Yen's total botherment by adding up her scores on the individual items.

Sometimes we will stumble across an existing instrument that has not been standardized. Figure 8.2 presents a checklist of some questions to ask when trying to determine if a specific nonstandardized instrument should be used.

Advantages

The major advantage of a nonstandardized instrument is that it is customized: That is, it is totally pertinent and appropriate to a particular client because it was designed with the client in view; possibly it was even designed *by* the client or at least with the client's help. We are not worried, as we would be with a standardized instrument, that the instrument was developed with a population different from the client's, or that the sample used for development and testing was not representative of the population from which it was drawn.

This advantage is more likely to apply if we have developed our own instrument than if we have borrowed one from a colleague who happened to have a similar client in a similar situation. Our colleague's client is not our client, and so we do not really know how appropriate the instrument will be. Neither can we be sure that we are administering or scoring the instrument in the same way as

	YES	NO
1. Will the responses to the questionnaire provide the data needed to answer the research question?	____	____
2. Does the questionnaire address the same types of variables that are to be studied (i.e., value, attitude, personality traits, behavior, knowledge, skill, perception, judgment)?	____	____
3. Is the level of measurement appropriate for the intended statistical analyses?	____	____
4. Is the format of the items appropriate to the level of inquiry?	____	____
5. Does the questionnaire have known reliability? Are the circumstances in which reliability was established known?	____	____
6. Does the questionnaire have known validity?	____	____
7. Have there been other applications of the instrument? Or has the instrument been reviewed by other professionals in journals, books, or other publications?	____	____
8. Is the language of the questionnaire appropriate for the sample or population?	____	____
9. Are the instructions clear and easy to follow?	____	____
10. Do the items meet standards for item construction (i.e., clear, precise, not double-barreled, or biased)?	____	____
11. Is the flow of the questionnaire logical and easy to follow?	____	____
12. Is the questionnaire the appropriate length for the time available for data collection, the attention span of intended respondents, and other circumstances related to the design?	____	____

FIGURE 8.2   CHECKLIST FOR ASSESSING EXISTING NONSTANDARDIZED MEASURING INSTRUMENTS

did our colleague, since the administration and scoring instructions are unlikely to be written down.

If we develop our own instrument, it will probably be simple to administer and score because we knew when we designed it that we would personally have to administer and score it. Most of the previous questions about an instrument's practicality will have been answered in the affirmative. We know that the instrument provides useful information, and that it is relatively direct, of an appropriate length, feasible to complete, and acceptable to the client. We do not know, however, whether it is sensitive to real, small changes and to what degree it is nonreactive.

The main advantage, then, of using nonstandardized measures is that they can be constructed for an individual measurement purpose. We could use an instrument like the one displayed in Figure 8.3, however. Here, we are interested in ascertaining the perceptions of people who live in a specific community.

Disadvantages

Because the instrument is nonstandardized, we do not know to what degree it is valid and reliable. With respect to reliability, we do not know whether a difference in score from one administration to the next means that Ms. Yen's attitudes toward her daughter's marriage have really changed, or whether the difference is due to the instrument's instability over time or measurement error. With respect to validity, we do not know to what degree the instrument is content valid: that is, to what degree the items on our instrument include every aspect of Ms. Yen's feelings about the marriage. Perhaps what is really bothering her is that she believes her daughter suffers from an emotional disorder and is in no fit state to marry anyone. She has not mentioned this, there is no item on the instrument that would reveal it, and so we will never be able to discuss the matter with her.

In other words, we are not sure to what degree our instrument is providing a reliable and valid measure of Ms. Yen's attitudes toward her daughter's marriage. Perhaps the instrument focuses too much on the prospective husband, and it is really Ms. Yen's attitudes toward the husband that we are measuring, not her attitudes toward the marriage.

Unless we have a real interest in the development of measuring instruments, however, we are unlikely to run validity and reliability checks on instruments we have developed ourselves. Our nonstandardized instruments may therefore be somewhat lacking with respect to validity and reliability. We will not be able to use them to evaluate our own practice, nor to compare our client's scores with the scores of other similar people in similar situations. We will, however, be able to use them both to help determine the problem and to assess the client's progress in solving the problem. And a nonstandardized instrument is sometimes better than no instrument at all.

SUMMARY

Standardized measuring instruments are designed to quantify the variables being measured. They have the advantages of uniform administration and scoring and the generation of normative data.

Constructors of standardized measures seek to develop instruments that are

This part of the survey is to learn more about your perceptions of these problems in the community. Listed below are a number of problems some residents of Northside have reported having.

Please place a number from 1 to 3 on the line to the right of the question which represents how much of a problem they have been to you within the last year:

1. No problem (or not applicable to you)
2. Moderate problem
3. Severe problem

	Questions	*Responses*			
1.	Finding the product I need	1	2	3	_____
2.	Impolite salespeople	1	2	3	_____
3.	Finding clean stores	1	2	3	_____
4.	Prices that are too high	1	2	3	_____
5.	Not enough Spanish-speaking salespeople	1	2	3	_____
6.	Public transportation	1	3	3	_____
7.	Getting credit	1	2	3	_____
8.	Lack of certain types of stores in Northside	1	2	3	_____
9.	Lack of an employment assistance program	1	2	3	_____
10.	Finding a city park that is secure	1	2	3	_____
11.	Finding a good house	1	2	3	_____

FIGURE 8.3   EXAMPLE OF A NONSTANDARDIZED SURVEY MEASURING INSTRUMENT

as valid and reliable as possible. The major considerations are the selection of questions that will maximize content validity, the number of response categories, and the length of the instrument.

The difference between the three major types of measuring instruments (i.e., rating scales, questionnaire-type scales, and modified scales), is the scaling techniques used. Rating scales use judgments by self or others to assign an individual a single score (or value) in relation to the variable being measured. Questionnaire-type scales combine the responses on several questions to form a single overall score on the variable of interest for each respondent. Modified scales do not fit either of these classifications.

The selection of a standardized measuring instrument for a particular research study depends on how the research question has been conceptualized and the variables represented in it have been operationally defined. The three general considerations are determination of measurement need, locating a number of measuring instruments capable of measuring the variables, and evaluating the alternatives among the instruments available. Measurement need is related to our purpose, the research question, and the circumstances in which the instrument is to be administered.

Instruments that satisfy these needs can be selected from the two principal sources: publishing houses and the professional literature. They can be evaluated by considering questions that focus on the sample used in developing each instrument, the instrument's validity and reliability, and practicality issues such as the likelihood that respondents will complete the instrument and interpretation of the results.

The following chapter completes the discussion of measurement by describing how we can design and construct a measuring instrument to fit a particular research need in the event that a suitable standardized instrument cannot be located.

REFERENCES AND FURTHER READINGS

ALLEN, M. J., & YEN, W. M. (1979). *Introduction to measurement theory*. Monterey, CA: Brooks/Cole.

ANASTASI, A. (1988). *Psychological testing* (6th ed.). New York: Macmillan.

ATHERTON, C., & KLEMMACK, D. (1982). *Research methods in social work*. Lexington, MA: Heath.

BABBIE, E.R. (1995). *The practice of social research* (7th ed., pp. 110-139). Belmont, CA: Wadsworth.

BARLOW, D.H., HAYES, S.C., & NELSON, R.O. (1984). *The scientist-practitioner: Research and accountability in applied settings*. Elmsford, NY: Pergamon.

BARLOW, D.H., & HERSEN, M. (1984). *Single-case experimental designs: Strategies for studying behavior change* (2nd ed.). Elmsford, NY: Pergamon.

BELLACK, A.S., & HERSEN, M. (1977). Self-report inventories in behavioral assessment. In J.D. Cone & R. P. Hawkins (Eds.), *Behavioral assessment: New directions in clinical psychology* (pp. 52-76). New York: Brunner/Mazel.

BLOOM, M., & FISCHER, J., & ORME, J. (1995). *Evaluating practice: Guidelines for the accountable professional* (2nd ed.). Needham Heights, MA: Allyn & Bacon.

BUROS, O.K. (Ed.). (1978). *The eighth mental measurements yearbook* (2 vols.). Highland Park, NJ: Gryphon Press.

COWEN, E.L., HAUSER, J., BEACH, D.R., & RAPPAPORT, J. (1970). Parental perception of young children and their relation to indexes of adjustment. *Journal of Consulting and Clinical Psychology, 34*, 97-103.

CROWNE, D.P., & MARLOWE, D. (1960). A new scale of social desirability independent of psychopathology. *Journal of Consulting Psychology, 24*, 349-354.

DEROGATES, L.R., RICKLES, K., & ROCK, A.F. (1976). The SCL-90 and the MMPI: A step in the validation of a new self-report scale. *British Journal of Psychiatry, 128*, 280-289.

FAIRWEATHER, G., & TORNATSKY, L. (1977). *Experimental methods for social policy research*. Elmsford, NY: Pergamon.

GABOR, P.A., & GRINNELL, R.M., JR. (1994). *Evaluation and quality improvement in the human services* (pp. 98-120). Needham Heights, MA: Allyn & Bacon.

GOLDMAN, J., STEIN, C.L., & GUERRY, S. (1983). *Psychological methods of clinical assessment*. New York: Brunner.

GRAHAM, J.R., & LILLY, R.S. (1984). *Psychological testing*. Englewood Cliffs, NJ: Prentice-Hall.

HAYNES, S.N. (1983). Behavioral assessment. In M. Hersen, A.E. Kazdin, & A.S. Bellack (Eds.), *The clinical psychology handbook* (pp. 397-425). Elmsford, NY: Pergamon.

HOGERTY, G.F., & ULRICH, R. (1972). The discharge readiness inventory. *Archives of General Psychiatry, 26*, 419-426.

HOPS, H., & GREENWOOD, C.R. (1981). Social skills deficits. In E.J. Mash & L.G. Terdal (Eds.), *Behavioral assessment of childhood disorders* (pp. 347-394). New York: Guilford.

HUDSON, W.W. (1981). Development and use of indexes and scales. In R.M. Grinnell, Jr. (Ed.), *Social work research and evaluation* (pp. 130-155). Itasca, IL: F.E. Peacock.

JORDAN, C., FRANKLIN, C., & CORCORAN, K. (1993). Standardized measuring instruments. In R.M. Grinnell, Jr. (Ed.), *Social work research and evaluation* (4th ed., pp. 198-220). Itasca, IL: F.E. Peacock.

MISCHEL, W. (1968). *Personality and assessment*. New York: Wiley.

NELSON, R., & BARLOW, D.H. (1981). Behavioral assessment: Basic strategies and initial procedures. In D. Barlow (Ed.), *Behavior assessment of adult disorders* (pp. 13-43). New York: Guilford.

SATTLER, J.M. (Ed.). (1988). *Assessment of children* (3rd ed.). San Diego, CA: Jerome M. Sattler Publications.

SIEGEL, D.H. (1988). Integrating data-gathering techniques and practice activities. In R.M. Grinnell, Jr. (Ed.), *Social work research and evaluation* (3rd ed., pp. 465-482). Itasca, IL: F.E. Peacock.

SUNBERG, N.D. (1977). *Assessment of persons*. Englewood Cliffs, NJ: Prentice-Hall.

WARWICK, D., & LININGER, C. (1975). *The sample survey: Theory and practice*. New York: McGraw-Hill.

WEINBACH, R.W., & GRINNELL, R.M., JR. (1995). *Statistics for social workers* (3rd ed.). White Plains, NY: Longman.

WICKER, A.W. (1981). Nature and assessment of behavior settings: Recent contributions from the ecological perspective. In P. McReynolds (Ed.), *Advances in psychological assessment* (Vol. 5, pp. 22-61). San Francisco: Jossey-Bass.

ZOOK, A., JR., & SIPPS, G.J. (1985). Cross-validation of a short form of the Marlowe-Crowne social desirability scale. *Journal of Clinical Psychology, 41*, 236-238.

Charles H. Mindel

C h a p t e r **9**

Designing Measuring Instruments

I
F AN APPROPRIATE standardized measuring instrument is not available for a particular research purpose, we need to know how to design and construct one. While, as noted in Chapter 8, a standardized measuring instrument is rarely unavailable, knowledge of how valid and reliable instruments are designed not only is useful in certain research situations, it also improves understanding of measurement principles.

The type of measuring instrument used as an example in this chapter is primarily applicable to survey research (Chapter 14), one of the data collection methods discussed in Parts V and VI of this text. The principles of design and construction described here, therefore, are most appropriate to survey instruments, but they generally also apply to most other types of measuring instruments as well.

In our discussion of how we can design and construct measuring instruments, our two guiding principles are based on sampling procedures (described in Chapter 10) and measurement validity and reliability (described in Chapters

7 and 8). First, the design and construction of our instrument should attempt to maximize the response rate of individuals in our sample or population. Second, our instrument should minimize the amount of measurement error in the responses of individuals. An instrument that embodies these two principles is well constructed.

The product of the research process, particularly in quantitative research studies, is data that have been gathered with some type of measuring instrument so they can be quantified and analyzed. In survey research, the instrument utilized to collect data is called a *self-administered questionnaire*. When data are collected by means of face-to-face interviews or telephone surveys, the data collection instrument is referred to as an *interview schedule*. In this text, a measuring instrument is considered to be any type of data collection device or procedure designed to gather data in any research study.

SOCIAL WORKERS' USE OF SURVEY RESEARCH

The survey is a popular form of data collection because it provides a useful and convenient way to acquire large amounts of data about individuals, organizations, or communities. It can be used to determine what people know, believe, or expect about a research question. It also can provide data on how they feel, what they want, what they intend to do, what they have done, and why.

One of the most important uses of survey research is to determine certain kinds of facts about individuals or other units of analysis. Social service agencies, for example, undertake surveys to collect facts about people in order to gather such data as the number and characteristics of individuals who request our services.

Survey research also is useful for gathering reports about people's behavior, both past and present. These kinds of data are often needed in our profession, particularly in service utilization studies. Clients might be asked how many times they had visited a physician in the past year or the past month, for example. The potential problem with these types of data is their accuracy. The instrument must not require individuals to reconstruct events from so far in the past that they cannot remember them accurately. It is much better to ask specific questions about events within a reasonable time frame than to ask global, general questions ranging over a long period.

Determining Beliefs, Feelings, and Ethical Standards

Surveys are particularly useful in helping to investigate unobservable variables such as attitudes, beliefs, feelings, and ethical standards. The distinction between what the facts are and what people believe them to be is often important. A social service agency, for example, might want to investigate why it is having difficulty recruiting staff or serving an intended population. A study might show that the beliefs of individuals in the community about that agency (whether or not they are based on fact) are quite negative.

In program planning, the existence of a certain social problem may or may not coincide with the attitudes in the community toward the existence of that problem. At one time, for example, African-American families were considered dysfunctional by outside observers, but many African Americans disputed this evaluation and maintained that their family form worked well for them. Difficulties are inevitable if an agency attempts to organize a program to address a social problem that the community does not recognize. An important part of a community needs assessment therefore is to determine the beliefs of individuals and constituencies about it.

Measuring instruments also explore individuals' feelings and desires. We often need to measure our clients on a variety of feelings or states, such as anxiety or marital satisfaction. Many well-established, standardized instruments which explore feelings are available. Instruments also can probe individuals' ethical standards, or their attitudes toward what should be done or what can feasibly be done with respect to certain social policies. Many instruments have examined attitudes toward abortion, women's rights, and education, for example. Ethical standards are also represented in questions that explore what individuals would do in certain situations. Questions that explore what people should or would do do not necessarily indicate what they actually do, however. Attitudes are not the same as behavior (LaPiere, 1934).

We can also use survey research to try to ascertain why people behave, believe, or feel the way they do. Instruments often contain questions exploring this. In a research study on elderly parents who live with their adult children, for example, one question asked why and under what circumstances this family arrangement had been formed. The history of the event, the types of reactions individuals felt at the time this event occurred, and the process at work were all relevant.

VALIDITY FACTORS IN INSTRUMENT DESIGN

The most crucial considerations in the construction of a measuring instrument by a social worker are the same as those in the development of a standardized instrument—validity and reliability. Applications of these concepts to measurement and the evaluation of standardized measuring instruments were examined in the two preceding chapters. Chapter 7 defines reliability as the accuracy or precision of the results the instrument produces, and validity in terms of content, criterion, and construct validities.

This chapter adopts the external and internal validity terms used in Chapter 11 on group research designs. Internal validity refers to the degree to which the instrument actually measures the concept being studied and, moreover, measures that concept accurately. External validity goes a step further to consider the degree to which the answers to the questions given by the individuals in the sample can be generalized to a larger population or a different research setting. Some methods we can use to improve the external and internal validities of the instruments we construct are reviewed in the following sections.

Maximizing External Validity

There are several reasons why an instrument will fail to achieve an adequate response rate, thus affecting the degree to which responses to the questions can be generalized to a larger population or a different population or setting. Following the suggestions below for design and construction of the instrument, including the choice and wording of questions and their format and layout, can help to achieve external validity and ensure generalizability. The external validity of an instrument we construct may be compromised, however, by the fact that there are no normative data to compare scores against and uniform administration procedures are not specified, as in standardized instruments.

Clearly State the Purpose of the Study

One way to assure an adequate response rate is to be explicit in explaining to potential respondents why a study is being undertaken. If they feel it is being used for purposes other than those stated, or if they have other misgivings about the study or the person conducting the study, their responses may be inhibited or inaccurate. One way to offer this explanation is with a cover letter to respondents or research participants describing the study, written under the official letterhead of the sponsoring organization (see Figure 9.1). Public knowledge that the study is to take place also helps.

Feelings of being exploited by research studies are most common among minority group members. One way to counter this attitude is to demonstrate that there is something of value to the group or individuals that justifies their participation. This might involve meetings with community members to discuss the purposes of the study and its value to them or hiring minority group members as staff.

Keep Sensitive Questions to a Minimum

Some individuals may feel that a particular research study would invade their privacy. The instrument may include personal questions in sensitive areas, and respondents often believe that participants can be identified. These fears can be alleviated by omitting or reducing personal or sensitive questions and by assuring anonymity or confidentiality. On many mailed questionnaires, however, some form of identification of participants is necessary so a follow-up can be sent in order to ensure an adequate response.

[Agency Letterhead]

Dear _____:

Our agency recognizes research as a basic method for evaluating old ways and developing new ways of providing more effective services for couples adopting children. The State Division of Child Welfare, in cooperation with this and other Twin City adoption agencies, is currently conducting a study of the supervisory period in adoption.

Because you have recently adopted a child through this agency, your experiences and opinions would be of much value. We are therefore asking your cooperation in this study. Your participation will involve an interview between each of you and a researcher from the State Division of Child Welfare.

We wish to emphatically assure you that the information requested in your interview will be treated confidentially by the researcher. Your observations and comments will in no way be identified with your name to this agency. Your information will be known only to the researcher who is conducting this study and will be incorporated anonymously, with that of many other adoptive parents, into the final research report.

Within the next few weeks you will be called by Mr. Smith to arrange an appointment with you. We hope you will be able to participate in this most important study. Thank you for your anticipated cooperation.

Sincerely,

Executive Director

FIGURE 9.1   EXAMPLE OF A SIMPLE COVER LETTER

Sensitive questions will also be disregarded if their content or wording causes them to be perceived by respondents as insulting or offensive. As pointed out in Chapter 7, the face validity of an instrument (not what it does but what it appears to do) often determines whether or not it will be completed.

Avoid Socially Desirable Responses

The tendency of respondents to adopt the social desirability response set and answer in a way they think will make them look good is another threat to achieving a valid and reliable response. With direct-service questionnaires, particularly, respondents are apt to be unsophisticated and unfamiliar with the types or format of questions used. University students may be used to taking tests and filling out answer sheets, but others will be at a loss as to how to complete an instrument. If they answer as they think they should, the possibility of measurement error is increased and the generalizability of the results is reduced. The constructor of the instrument therefore must word questions sensitively and assure respondents that there are no right or wrong answers.

Ask Only Relevant Questions

The relevancy of questions is particularly important in social work policy studies, where the population being studied often consists of professionals facing time constraints who may not feel justified in responding to numerous or lengthy questions. The importance of the research question under study and of their responses should be emphasized, and the instrument must not be too long or vague. No item should be included that is not relevant to the study's research question. Sending professionals a questionnaire that is too long or too general would demonstrate that the person doing the study is unsophisticated in using the research process, and potential respondents would be apt to ignore the instrument.

Maximizing Internal Validity

Internal validity is basically concerned with reducing or eliminating measurement error in the content of the instrument. The paragraphs that follow comprise a checklist of procedures to be used in selecting and presenting effective questions. As in the preceding chapter, question is the general term used to refer to the items, statements, or questions that, together with the accompanying response categories, comprise the instrument.

Make Questions Clear

Aside from the fact that all questions on an instrument must be relevant to the research question being investigated, the most important factor in wording questions to avoid measurement error is clarity. The words used must not mean different things to different individuals; this applies to ambiguous or vague words as well as to slang terms or colloquial expressions that may be familiar to certain groups but not to others. Meanings can vary across age levels, ethnic groups, social classes, and regions. We can become so close to the studies we are doing that questions that are perfectly clear to us are not clear at all to others. Consider the following example:

What is your marital status? (Circle one number below.)

1. Married
2. Divorced
3. Separated
4. Widowed
5. Never Married

It is not clear whether "marital status" refers to present status or whether the respondents are being asked if they were ever married, divorced, separated, or widowed. The way the question is stated, a person might in fact fit into the first four of the five categories. This question is more accurately stated: What is your present marital status?

Other problems with ambiguity are apt to occur when we are not familiar with the population being studied, such as elderly people, a racial or ethnic minority group, or professionals. Questions with little or no meaning to respondents can result.

Use Simple Language

The language used in questions may also be much too complicated for a respondent. The wording must be simple enough for the least educated person, while at the same time it must not insult the intelligence of anyone who could be presented with the instrument. If we were interested in the types of health care services utilized by individuals, for example, we might provide a checklist that would include such medical specialties as ophthalmology, otolaryngology, and dermatology. A list more likely to be understood by all respondents would call these specialists eye doctors, ear, nose, and throat doctors, and doctors for skin diseases.

Ask Questions That Respondents Are Qualified to Answer

Some measuring instruments ask individuals to respond to questions to which they have not given much thought or which they may not be competent to answer. In a public opinion poll, for example, an unknowledgeable research sample might be asked to provide opinions about psychotherapeutic techniques or needs tests in social welfare. We run the risk of being misled by the responses if the respondents are not qualified to answer such a question.

Avoid Double-Barreled and Negative Questions

Double-barreled questions contain two questions in one. A simple example of such a question is:

Do you feel that the federal government should make abortion or birth control available to women in households that receive welfare?

The problem with this question is that some respondents might agree to tax support for birth control but not for abortion, or for abortion but not birth control. The way the question is worded, we would never know which position the respondents are taking. The solution, of course, is to present the two questions separately. A clue to double-barreled questions is the presence of an *and* or an *or*. Such questions should be reexamined to see whether they include two questions.

Another type of question to be avoided is negative questions, such as asking whether respondents agree or disagree with a negative statement. An example is:

Federal funds should not be used to pay for abortions for women receiving welfare benefits.

The word *not* is often overlooked in these kinds of questions, and the error that is therefore introduced can be considerable. This question should be re-phrased in one of these two ways:

The federal government should pay for abortions for women receiving welfare benefits.

— or —

Abortions for women receiving welfare benefits should only be paid for by nongovernmental sources.

Keep Questions Short

Questions that are kept short get to the point quickly, so respondents will be more likely to read them and complete them. Keeping questions short and to the point helps maintain the relevance, clarity, and precision of the instrument.

Pretest the Instrument

The traditional way in which the clarity of questions (and consequent internal validity) is examined is by pretesting the instrument on a sample of individuals who will not take part in our final study. Our pretest is not concerned with the answers to the questions *per se* but rather with the difficulties respondents may have in answering the questions. Are the questions clear and unambiguous, and do respondents understand what our instrument is trying to accomplish?

The pretest should be followed by a debriefing to uncover any difficulties. Pretesting is discussed further in the last section of this chapter.

OPEN- AND CLOSED-ENDED QUESTIONS

When constructing a measuring instrument, we must take into account differences not only in the wording of questions but in the kinds of responses asked for. There are two general categories: open-ended questions, in which the response categories are not specified in detail and are left unstructured, and closed-ended or fixed-alternative questions, in which respondents are asked to select one (or more) of several response categories provided in the instrument. Each of these methods for responding has particular purposes, as well as certain strengths and disadvantages.

Open-Ended Questions

Open-ended questions are designed to permit free responses; they do not incorporate any particular structure for replies. An example is:

We would like to know some of your feelings about your job as an employee of the Department of Social Services.

1. What types of duties are most satisfying to you?
2. What types of duties are most dissatisfying to you?

The above open-ended questions ask for much information and considerable thought, since they deal with a complex issue that could involve several dimensions of feeling.

If we are unaware of the various sources of satisfaction and dissatisfaction in the department, answers to the two open-ended questions will produce some clues. Open-ended questions are often used when all of the possible issues (and responses) involved in a question are not known or when we are interested in exploring basic issues and processes in a situation. Such questions are usually used in a preliminary phase of the study. Responses to open-ended questions, however, may be used in constructing questions for use in a later phase. An important function of open-ended questions, in fact, is their use in the development of closed-ended questions.

An additional advantage of open-ended questions is that they put few constraints on individuals' statements of their feelings. A closed-ended question might list various sources of satisfaction and ask individuals to check how they feel about them. Open-ended questions allow respondents to go into detail and to express greater depth in their answers. They are not forced to choose among alternatives we developed but can express their feelings on a matter more precisely. If an interviewer administers the instrument, it is possible to probe responses and elicit them by using appropriate attending behaviors. These techniques encourage respondents to provide fuller, more thoughtful answers.

There are also some distinct disadvantages; open-ended questions may lead to a lower response rate and decrease external validity. A measuring instrument with many open-ended questions takes considerable time to complete, and a long questionnaire can discourage potential respondents. Some people may be discouraged from replying to an instrument composed of open-ended questions because they are not articulate enough to provide their own responses, particularly if they must express themselves in writing. Only those with high levels of education may respond to such questions. In a study with a population that is homogeneous with respect to education, this is less of a problem. With a well-educated population, it may even be advisable to take advantage of the respondents' expertise by using open-ended questions.

Internal validity can also be a consideration with respect to open-ended questions, which introduce an element of subjectivity to the responses. Suppose 100 social workers on the staff of a department of social services complete a measuring instrument that asks for a paragraph describing why they are satisfied with the agency. In order to analyze the data, we need to code these individual replies into meaningful categories.

From answers to the question, "Are you satisfied working in the department?" a list of different sources of satisfaction could be deduced. The problem is that different individuals may state the same kind of satisfaction in different ways. One respondent, for example, may say: "I like the personal autonomy that is provided by this agency," and another might say, "They leave me alone here, and the supervisor does not bother me very much." It is our responsibility to decide whether or not such answers fall in the same category. The potential for error is the miscoding of responses, or lack of interrater reliability.

Interrater reliability can be achieved by having more than one person (usually called a rater) code the responses. When several raters code the same responses and develop their own sets of categories, a measure of interrater reliability, such as the percentage of responses for which the raters agree on an appropriate code, can be calculated. When low interrater reliability is found for the response to a particular question, we should try to ascertain the reasons why. If it is impossible to solve this problem, serious consideration should be given to eliminating the question, because it is useless to include a question that different respondents will interpret in different ways.

Closed-Ended Questions

In closed-ended questions, responses can be selected from a number of specified choices: expressing a simple yes or no, selecting degrees of agreement, or choosing one or more of a list of response categories. Two examples of closed-ended questions are:

1. If the abused child is out of the home, which situation best describes your current plan of action? (Circle one number below.)

    1. Return child to intact family
    2. Return child if abuser remains out of home

    3. Continue foster care
    4. Seek adoptive placement
    5. None of the above
    8. Not applicable
    9. Do not know

2. Did the mother deny having knowledge of sexual abuse? (Circle one number below.)

    1. Yes
    2. No
    8. Not applicable
    9. Do not know

The advantages of fixed-alternative questions are fairly obvious. These kinds of questions can be presented in such a way as to attract and maintain reliable responses from individuals. Answers are easily compared from person to person, and there is no need for time-consuming coding procedures such as those involved with open-ended questions. Because choices are provided, respondents are less apt to leave certain questions blank or to choose a "do not know" response. Missing data can be a serious problem when analyzing the data collected for a study, particularly if the response rate is low.

Closed-ended questions can elicit data on topics that would be difficult to obtain by other methods. It is difficult to get responses to an open-ended question on sexual behavior, for example. A series of short, closed-ended questions inquiring whether respondents agree or disagree with a statement or whether they participate in a certain behavior to a greater or lesser extent is much more likely to be answered. Moreover, a variable such as income level, for example, can be difficult to measure when asked as an open-ended question, such as:

- What is your present income?
- How much money did you make last year?

It is much more effective to ask individuals to place themselves in a set of categories containing a range of income levels, such as $10,000–$20,000.

Respondents may also be reluctant to answer questions about their age; this may or may not be a sensitive topic, depending on the study's population. As a rule, however, data on variables such as age, which are primarily measured at the interval or ratio level (such as years of education, income level, number of children in the home, or number of years married), should be gathered with open-ended questions. Thus, a more precise answer will be provided by an open-ended question on age that uses the following form:

What was your age at your last birthday? (Place number of years on line below.)

_____

Less usable data will be provided by a closed-ended question with a range of responses, such as:

What is your age? (Circle one number below.)

1. 1 to 5 years
2. 6 to 10 years
3. 11 to 15 years
4. 16 to 20 years
5. More than 20 years

Only when questions about these kinds of variables are sensitive and there is reason to believe there will be a low or mistaken response to them should the responses be grouped into categories. By grouping, we are throwing away important data; putting a child who is 10 years old into the same category as one who is 6 years old, for example, is needlessly inexact.

There are other problems with closed-ended questions. Respondents may not feel that the alternatives provided are appropriate to their answers. They also may be tempted to give an opinion on something they have never thought about before; the tendency to simply circle a fixed alternative is much greater than to answer an open-ended question where it is necessary to write something down. In respect to closed-ended questions used in interview situations, respondents who do not want to appear ignorant or who want to give socially desirable answers may say they do not know.

Comparison of the Two Types of Questions

As the preceding sections have shown, both open- and closed-ended questions have advantages and disadvantages, and each serves purposes that make it most appropriate for certain usages. One type of question therefore cannot be said to be better than the other. Open-ended questions are appropriate in exploratory studies with complex research questions, especially when all the alternative choices are not known. Closed-ended questions are preferable when the choices are all known or limited in number or when respondents have clear opinions on specific issues and feelings.

An important consideration in the choice of open- or closed-ended questions is the time and cost required to measure the responses. Open-ended questions are time-consuming to code, introduce error, and require more personnel for data processing. Closed-ended questions can be designed so they do not require extensive coding and can be moved to the data processing stage quickly.

The type of question to be used is not necessarily an either/or choice; a measuring instrument can easily include both open- and closed-ended questions. It is possible to analyze the responses to open-ended questions individually and to have the responses to a series of closed-ended questions processed and analyzed by a computer.

INSTRUMENT CONSTRUCTION AND APPEARANCE

A list of questions is not a measuring instrument. How an instrument is constructed and what it looks or sounds like also determine whether or not those to whom it is sent or administered will respond. Those who receive a measuring instrument in the mail or in person or who interact with an interviewer face-to-face or on the telephone must be given the impression that completing the questionnaire or being interviewed is worthwhile and will not be too difficult or time-consuming. This is particularly the case with a mailed instrument, which can easily be discarded.

To assure an adequate response rate, a written instrument should be designed to provide immediate positive impressions about its importance, difficulty, and length. Each of these factors can be manipulated by careful attention to detail. To some extent it is possible to indicate the importance of an instrument by a professional appearance, and the difficulty can be indicated by how the questions are ordered. The length can be controlled by structuring the questions to save space or by including only those questions that are absolutely necessary for studying the research question.

Somewhat different methods are necessary when the instrument is to be used in interviewing respondents face-to-face or on the telephone. Procedures for developing an interview schedule for use in these cases are described in Chapter 14.

General Impression

Appearance, or how the instrument looks to potential respondents, often is affected by cost constraints. If these considerations can be overlooked, we can think in terms of the best way to present the instrument to make a good appearance.

The brief description of the design of a printed measuring instrument in this section is based on Donald Dillman's (1978) total design method for survey instruments. This is an expensive design to execute, but it illustrates the preferred method. The instrument is printed as a booklet. It consists of 8¼" by 12¼" sheets of paper folded in the middle and, if more than one sheet is used, stapled to form a booklet with the dimensions of 8¼" by 6⅛".

No questions are included on the front or back pages, which should stimulate the interest of recipients of the instrument. Pages are typed on a word processor using 12-point (Elite) type in a 7" by 9½" space on regular 8½" by 11" paper. To fit the booklet format, the pages are photographically reduced to 70 percent of the original size. They are reproduced on white or off-white paper by a printing method that produces quality work.

This format has several advantages. Photographically reducing the size of the page makes the questionnaire appear shorter and uses less paper; it also lowers postage costs if a mailed questionnaire is used. The booklet format and the use of a cover page give the appearance of a professionally produced document, which lends the impression that considerable thought has gone into the process.

In contrast, instruments that are typed, photocopied, and held together with a single staple in the upper-left corner present an uneven and unprofessional appearance. Particularly to be avoided is a form that consists of several 8½" by 14" sheets of legal-size paper, folded several times to fit into a business envelope. Though this design probably saves money, the larger size and unattractive appearance are likely to discourage respondents.

Page Layout

In addition to how the questions in an instrument are presented in type, the design format determines how they are laid out on the page. This is an important consideration in producing a professional-appearing instrument that will encourage a high response rate. The instrument must be constructed so that respondents decide to complete it and do not overlook any question or section.

To keep sections of questions together and separated from other sections, various levels of spacing are used. If possible, questions and response categories should not start on one page and continue on another. Questions in a series, particularly, should be kept together or clearly follow one another. Confusion and mistakes often result when parts of questions or questions and responses become separated. Nevertheless, large blank spaces should be avoided when possible, for economy as well as appearance.

Typographical considerations in the layout of the instrument also can facilitate data processing by making answers easier to locate and to score. Careful design and planning with respect to how the instrument is to be processed once the questions have been answered can save much time, energy, and money.

Question Order

The ordering of questions in measuring instruments has been a topic of debate, but there appears to be some consensus on certain aspects. It is generally agreed, for example, that instruments should begin with questions that are interesting to the respondent and relevant to the purpose of the study, as stated in either the cover letter accompanying the mailed instrument or the introductory statement delivered by an interviewer.

To begin by asking for demographic data such as gender, age, or educational level can irritate respondents, who may regard the instrument as an application or evaluation form of some kind. Questions should be ordered along a descending gradient of social usefulness or importance. That is, questions that are judged to be the most important to the research question should be stated first. Demographic data should appear at the end of the instrument.

Potentially sensitive or objectionable questions also should be positioned later. It would not be wise, for example, to begin by asking how many times respondents had engaged in sexual intercourse in the previous week.

Another principle of ordering is that questions should be arranged by content area. Respondents should not be forced to constantly switch their train of thought by having to consider a question on one topic, followed by another on a totally different topic. Some of us maintain that forcing respondents to switch from one topic to another reduces their tendency to try to structure answers so they appear consistent. In fact, however, respondents are apt to give more thought to their answers if the instrument presents consecutive questions on a single general topic. Much less mental effort is required in responding to an instrument if the questions are organized by topic or content area.

Within the content areas, questions should be grouped by type of question (closed- versus open-ended). This means that questions requiring a simple yes or no answer or those in which responses are asked on a range of agreement to disagreement should appear together. Not only does this ease the mental effort required in responding to the questions, but it makes the instrument appear more logically constructed.

At times, of course, compromises must be made in question ordering; it is not always possible to follow all these principles. For example, we may not be able to sort the questions by content area and then sort them again by type of question in such a way as to give the appearance of a well-thought-out instrument. The goal always is to try to strike a satisfactory balance.

Presentation of Questions and Responses

One of the most common reasons for mistakes in constructing questionnaires is the mistaken assumption that the average person will know how to complete the instrument. Procedures that we take for granted can be mysteries to respondents, and detailed directions on how to answer the questions often are needed. In face-to-face or telephone interviews, explanations can be given verbally. But in a mailed questionnaire, or one that respondents are to complete on their own, questions that are not understood can be a source of serious error.

Figure 9.2 shows both unacceptable and acceptable ways of asking five typical questions in a survey instrument. In a question where the appropriate answer is to be circled, for example, unless this is explicitly stated in the instructions, respondents may circle more than one. For each question, directions such as "Circle one number below" must be given (see Questions 1–5 in Section B).

Response categories should not appear on the same line as the question but should be placed on the line below, and questions should not be squeezed onto a page with little room between items or between a question and its response categories. This not only produces a very cluttered and unsightly appearance, it increases the likelihood that respondents will overlook questions or make mistakes in answering.

A. UNACCEPTABLE QUESTION FORMS

    1. Sex: M _____   F _____

    2. Number of children at home
        0–1 _____   2–3 _____   4–5 _____   6 or more _____

    3. Do you own your own home? Y _____   N _____

    4. Religious preference:
        Protestant _____
        Catholic _____
        Jewish _____

    5. Health: Good _____   Fair _____   Poor _____

B. ACCEPTABLE QUESTION FORMS

    1. What is your gender? (Circle one number below.)
        0. Male
        1. Female

    2. How many of your children live at home with you? (Place number on line below.)

        _____

    3. Do you own your own home? (Circle one number below.)
        0. No
        1. Yes
        8. Not applicable
        9. Do not know

    4. What is your religious preference? (Circle one number below.)
        1. Protestant
        2. Catholic
        3. Jewish
        4. None
        5. Other (please specify) _____

    5. How would you describe your physical health? (Circle one number below.)
        1. Poor
        2. Fair
        3. Good
        9. Do not know

FIGURE 9.2   UNACCEPTABLE AND ACCEPTABLE SURVEY QUESTIONS

Precoding Responses

There are several ways to provide for questions to be answered, such as blank lines to be filled in or boxes to be checked. A better technique is precoding, or numbering the categories on the left and asking respondents to circle the appropriate number. This technique aids in data analysis because a number is preassigned to each alternative or response, as in Section B of Figure 9.2. Having respondents circle the number when they answer the question eliminates an additional step in data processing and another potential source of error. The number for each response should be placed at the left of the answer rather than at the right or anywhere else because responses could have different lengths (see Question 4 in Section B in Figure 9.2).

As an aid to both respondents and coders, it is helpful if certain numerical values are always used for the same types of responses. If there are numerous questions asking for yes or no responses, for example, the same value should be used for all the yes answers and another value for all the no answers. Thus, a value of 0 might be used for "no" and a value or 1 for "yes," throughout the instrument. A single value can also be used for the "missing data" category, so that all "Do not know," "No opinion," or "Not applicable" answers would have the same value. Thus, in Section B, 9 is the value for the "Do not know" answers in Questions 3 and 5, and 8 is the value for the "Not applicable" response in Question 3.

Precoded questions should be arranged one below the other, and response categories also should be in vertical order rather than side by side. If there are several choices of response categories on the same line, respondents may circle the wrong number or overlook some responses.

Edge-Coding Responses

In edge coding, another technique that aids in data processing, a series of blanks is added at the right side of the instrument (see Figures 8.3 and 9.3). Respondents are instructed not to write on these lines; they are utilized by us to transfer the response number circled by the respondent over to the blank line allocated for each question. This simple procedure eliminates the preparation of coding sheets, onto which responses otherwise are transferred after being converted into numbers. The inclusion of edge-coding lines may be distracting on the page, but the lines need not be obtrusive. Considering the savings of time and effort they provide, the possible disadvantages are minimal.

Organization of Content

In the two principal ways of organizing the contents of a questionnaire, respondents are asked to respond to a series of questions or to rank order their responses. With a series of questions, respondents may be asked, for example, to choose whether they strongly agree, disagree, or strongly disagree on several questions. If the guidelines given above for question and response presentation were all followed, this type of scale would likely take up a large amount of space, as well as being needlessly repetitive. There are special ways to handle a series of questions in a small amount of space so the instrument appears less cluttered and easier to follow.

Figure 8.3, for example, is an example of a needs assessment in a specific community. Rather than asking 11 separate questions regarding the severity of problems in the community, the questions have been set up in a multiquestion format. First there is an opening statement briefly describing the purpose of the questionnaire and providing directions for answering the series of questions. Respondents are requested to circle the number that represents how they feel, and the three choices are given with their appropriate values (e.g., 1, 2, 3). The questions are listed consecutively on the left side of the page. The values appear in columns at the right of the 11 statements, and at the far right are the edge-coding lines.

Other techniques can be used when the same data are needed about a number of different people, such as collapsing questions into a single matrix. In the example presented in Figure 9.3, respondents are requested to state the occupational categories of their fathers and mothers. Rather than presenting the list of occupational categories twice, it is given once, and the same series of values is repeated for father and for mother in separate columns. The values must appear in both columns, and clear instructions must be given to circle only one number in each column.

An alternative way of presenting questions is the use of rank-ordering. Respondents might be asked to consider the 11 problems listed in Figure 8.3, for example, and rank them in terms of the severity each problem represents for them.

This form of question is not recommended, for several reasons. It is very difficult to consider more than three or four different concepts at once for rank-ordering purposes. If the list consists of 11 or more problems (as in Figure 8.3), it would be virtually impossible to give adequate thought to the severity of each problem. In addition, rank-ordering usually takes more time than if each question is considered on an individual basis. And, for data analysis purposes, rank-ordering restricts the type of analyses that can be carried out with the question.

If a series of questions is used, we can rank-order the responses and carry out other analyses as well. By calculating the mean score for each of the 11 questions listed in Figure 8.3 and then rank-ordering these means, for example, the same result can be achieved as if we had been asked to rank-order the questions themselves. In addition, using a series of questions makes it possible to create an index or scale and calculate its reliability, which could not be done if rank-orders were used.

Into which occupational category do your father
and mother presently fall? (Circle one number in
each column below.)

Occupational Category	Relationship		
	Father	Mother	
Professional	1	1	_____
Manager	2	2	_____
Sales worker	3	3	_____
Clerical worker	4	4	_____
Craftsperson	5	5	_____
Equipment operator	6	6	_____
Laborer	7	7	_____
Farmer	8	8	_____
Service	9	9	_____
Unemployed	10	10	_____
Do not know	88	88	_____
Deceased (not applicable)	99	99	_____
Other (specify)	13	13	_____

FIGURE 9.3   SINGLE QUESTIONNAIRE FORMAT
FOR DUAL RESPONSES

Transition Statements

Transition statements are used for several purposes. One is that by speaking directly to the respondents, they lend informality to the instrument and reduce monotony. This type of statement helps respondents answer the questions and become involved in the task. An example is:

In this section of our survey we would like to develop a sort of thumbnail sketch of your everyday life, the things you do, the things that worry or concern you, and the things that make you happy.

Transition statements are also used when the instrument introduces a new line of questioning. These statements in a sense tell people that they will be changing directions and forewarn them not to be surprised when they get to the next section. An example is:

Now I would like to ask you a few questions concerning recreational activities.

A third type of transition statement occurs toward the end of the questionnaire. The section asking for demographic data should be introduced with a statement such as the following:

Finally, we would like to ask you a few questions about yourself for statistical purposes.

This kind of statement indicates the approaching end of the instrument. Transition statements are important, but they can be overdone. Overly long statements and those that may inadvertently bias the response by pressuring the respondent toward a certain kind of answer should be avoided. Moreover, the approach should not be so didactic that it alienates respondents or makes them appear ignorant or foolish.

EVALUATING AND PRETESTING THE INSTRUMENT

A measuring instrument should be evaluated before it is administered. This can be done by providing answers to the questions presented in Chapter 8. The instrument also should be pretested to determine whether individuals responding understand the questions and have a favorable impression of the appearance and utility of the instrument. Beginning researchers often conduct pretests as an afterthought, as something that must be done as part of the research process. This does not fulfill the real purposes of a pretest, which, according to Dillman (1978), should provide answers to eight specific questions about the measuring instrument:

1. Is each question measuring what it is intended to measure?
2. Are all the words understood?
3. Are questions interpreted similarly by all individuals?
4. Does each closed-ended question have a response category that applies to each person?
5. Does the questionnaire create a positive impression, one that motivates people to answer it?
6. Can the questions be answered correctly?
7. Are some questions missed? Do some questions elicit uninterpretable answers?
8. Does any aspect of the instrument suggest bias on the part of the investigator?

Answers can be found for some of these questions by mailing out the questionnaire to a sample of individuals who are similar to the study's sample or population. What we are really concerned with, however, is feedback from these individuals, and this can best be gathered by direct interaction with them.

Essentially, a sample of respondents from three types of groups is preferable for use in a pretest of a measuring instrument: colleagues, the potential users of the data, or individuals drawn from the population to be surveyed. Each of these groups can provide a different type of feedback to the instrument designer. Colleagues may be fellow students, instructors, or associates. All should have specialized experience and understand the study's purpose. Potential users of the data—agency personnel, policy makers, clients, professionals—can indicate whether any of the questions are irrelevant to their purposes or reveal a lack of knowledge on our part. People who might be the focus of the study can provide information as to the clarity and difficulty of the questions, the appropriateness of the response categories, and so on.

To gather this feedback, perhaps the best method is to administer the instrument to representatives of one of these types of groups, individually or together, and follow with a debriefing session. This gives the pretest respondents an opportunity to discuss with us what they did and did not like about the instrument, what kinds of problems they had with it, and how they felt about the experience.

SUMMARY

We can construct measuring instruments when standardized instruments are simply not available. We can use them to determine and quantify facts about people and their behaviors, beliefs, feelings, and ethical standards.

The validity and reliability of the instrument are the most crucial concerns in the design and construction of a measuring instrument. External validity can be maximized by assuring an adequate response rate. This can be done by clearly stating the purpose of the study, avoiding sensitive questions and socially desirable answers, and asking only relevant questions. Internal validity can be maximized by reducing or eliminating measurement error in the content of the instrument. The principal concern in achieving internal validity is to make the questions clear and understandable.

The constructor of an instrument must take into account not only the content of the questions but the kinds of responses asked for. The two principal types of questions and response categories are open-ended questions, for which respondents supply their own responses, and closed-ended questions, for which they can select responses from a number of specified choices.

A measuring instrument should give an immediate positive impression to potential respondents. This can be achieved by attention to the appearance of the instrument, the order of questions, the manner of presenting questions and responses, the organization of questions in a series or rank-ordering format, and the use of transition statements.

The principles of measurement set forth in Chapter 7, the help given in Chapter 8 for understanding and evaluating measuring instruments, and the concrete suggestions for constructing instruments given in this chapter have laid a solid foundation for the next phase of the research process—selecting an appropriate sample and a corresponding research design.

REFERENCES AND FURTHER READINGS

ATHERTON, C., & KLEMMACK, D. (1982). *Research methods in social work*. Lexington, MA: Heath.

AUSTIN, M.J., & CROWELL, J. (1985). Survey research. In R.M. Grinnell, Jr. (Ed.), *Social work research and evaluation* (2nd ed., pp. 275-305). Itasca, IL: F.E. Peacock.

BABBIE, E.R. (1995). *The practice of social research* (7th ed., pp. 139-182). Belmont, CA: Wadsworth.

BAILEY, K.D. (1994). *Methods of social research* (4th ed., pp. 106-146, 350-375). New York: Free Press.

BLOOM, M., FISCHER, J., & ORME, J. (1994). *Evaluating practice: Guidelines for the accountable professional* (2nd ed.). Englewood Cliffs, NJ: Prentice-Hall.

DILLMAN, D.A. (1978). *Mail and telephone surveys: The total design method*. New York: Wiley.

FISCHER, J., & CORCORAN, K. (1994). *Measures for clinical practice: A sourcebook* (2nd ed., 2 vols.). New York: Free Press.

FRANKFORT-NACHMIAS, C., & NACHMIAS, D. (1992). *Research methods in the social sciences* (4th ed., pp., 239-269, 427-446). New York: St. Martin's Press.

GABOR, P.A., & GRINNELL, R.M., JR. (1994). *Evaluation and quality improvement in the human services* (pp. 98-120). Needham Heights, MA: Allyn & Bacon.

GRINNELL, R.M., JR., & WILLIAMS, M. (1990). *Research in social work: A primer* (pp. 86-114). Itasca, IL: F.E. Peacock.

JORDAN, C., FRANKLIN, C., & CORCORAN, K.J. (1993). Standardized measuring instruments. In R.M. Grinnell, Jr. (Ed.), *Social work research and evaluation* (4th ed., pp. 198-220). Itasca, IL: F.E. Peacock.

JUDD, C.M., SMITH E.R., & KIDDER, I.H. (1991). *Research methods in social relations* (6th ed., pp. 145-170, 228-253). Fort Worth, TX: Harcourt Brace.

KRYSIK, J., HOFFART, I., & GRINNELL, R.M., JR. (1993). *Student study guide for the fourth edition of social work research and evaluation,* (pp. 11-12). Itasca, IL: F.E. Peacock.

LAPIERE, R. (1934). Attitudes and actions. *Social Forces, 13*, 230-237.

MINDEL, C. (1985). Instrument design. In R.M. Grinnell, Jr. (Ed.), *Social work research and evaluation* (2nd ed., pp. 206-230). Itasca, IL: F.E. Peacock.

RUBIN, A., & BABBIE, E. (1993). *Research methods for social work* (2nd ed., pp. 182-216). Pacific Grove, CA: Wadsworth.

WEINBACH, R.W., & GRINNELL, R.M., JR. (1996). *Applying research knowledge: A workbook for social work students* (2nd ed., pp. 105-112). Needham Heights, MA: Allyn & Bacon.

WILLIAMS, M., TUTTY, L.M., & GRINNELL, R.M., JR. (1995). *Research in social work: An introduction* (2nd ed., pp. 115-132, 277-282). Itasca, IL: F.E. Peacock.

PART IV

THE LOGIC OF RESEARCH DESIGN

Peter A. Gabor
Carol Ing

C h a p t e r **10**

Sampling

AFTER WE HAVE CHOSEN AN INSTRUMENT to measure the dependent variable(s) in our quantitative research study—or after we have chosen our research question for a qualitative study—we need to start thinking about how we are going to select a sample of research participants (or events or objects) that will provide data to answer our research question or test our hypothesis. Ideally, we should collect data from or about each and every person (or event or object) in a given population, or set. The resulting data would then be descriptive of the entire set. In practice, however, it is rarely possible (or feasible) to obtain data about every single unit in a population; such a process would be way too time-consuming and costly.

The common practice therefore is to gather data from some units and use these data to describe the entire set from which they came. Thus, sampling is defined as the selection of some units to represent the entire population (or set) from which the units were drawn. If the selection is carried out in accordance with the requirements of sampling theory, the data obtained from the sample should quite accurately pertain to the entire population from which the sample was taken.

SAMPLING THEORY

To illustrate the logic of sampling theory, consider the example of a research project in Kansas City that seeks to assess the extent of drug dependence among people who are elderly and chronically ill. As we know, the total set of people is referred to as a population—in this case, the entire group of people who have the following three characteristics: (1) they are chronically ill, (2) they are older, and (3) they live in Kansas City. Because it would not feasible to study the drug dependence of each and every individual in this specific population, some of these people are selected for a sample. Data are then collected about the sample's drug dependency.

The findings from the sample are then generalized to the population from which the sample was drawn. This procedure can only be justified if our sample is representative of the population—that is, if the relevant characteristics of the sample are similar to the characteristics of the population from which the sample was drawn. To ensure that a sample and population will be similar in all relevant characteristics, the sample must be chosen with a procedure that provides each member of the population with the same probability of being selected. If we study drug dependency of an appropriately drawn sample of people—who are chronically ill, who are older, and who live in Kansas City—we are in a position to describe drug dependency for the entire group of these people.

The use of sampling techniques is not limited to the study of people, however. Any population can be described with considerable accuracy through the selection of an appropriate sample. A population, for example, can be composed of objects such as client files. Through the selection of a sample of files, questions relating to all the files in the agency could be answered. Similarly, events and processes such as decision making about foster home placement in a particular county can be the objective of a research study. An appropriately selected sample would yield data about placement decision making in that county.

There are two major categories of sampling procedures, probability and nonprobability. In probability sampling, every member within a population has a known probability of being selected for the sample, so it can be established that the sample is representative of the population from which it was drawn. In nonprobability sampling, the probability of selection cannot be estimated, and it is difficult to determine the representativeness of the sample.

The Sampling Frame

In selecting a probability sample, our first step is to compile a sampling frame. The sampling frame is that collection of units (e.g., people, objects, or events) having a possibility of being selected. In short, it is simply the list from which our sample is actually selected. Ideally, it would be best to use the entire population as the sampling frame; however, this is seldom feasible because complete lists of populations rarely exist.

An example could be a research project that tries to ascertain the experiences social workers in Phoenix have had with their supervision. The population of interest in this study is defined as all social workers in Phoenix on January 1, 1997. Ideally, the procedure would begin with drawing a sample from this population. There is no definitive list containing the names of all social workers in Phoenix, however, so our first task is to create a list of social workers from which the sample can be drawn. This list is known as a sampling frame.

A number of strategies can be employed in compiling a sampling frame in our example. One strategy is to obtain lists of social workers from all social service agencies and organizations that are known to employ them. Social workers in private practice who are listed in the telephone book could then be added to this list. If the task is executed with care, a reasonably complete list of social workers in Phoenix would result.

For a number of reasons, however, it is not likely that our sampling frame would be identical to the population. The lists of workers provided by agencies and organizations may not be up to date; some workers may have been hired since the agency lists were compiled, others might have resigned or found positions in other agencies. Social workers who have recently entered private practice may not be listed in the telephone book, while others who are listed may have left private practice. Some organizations that employ social workers may have been missed entirely.

In short, the sampling frame and the population are not identical, although it is desirable that the sampling frame approximate the population as closely as possible. Because in practice it is from our sampling frame that our sample is actually drawn, the representativeness of our sample is limited by how closely our sampling frame approximates the population of interest.

PROBABILITY SAMPLING

In probability sampling, because every member of a designated population has a known probability of being selected for a sample, it is possible to calculate the degree to which the sample is representative of the population from which it was drawn. Probability sampling strategies may have one or several stages.

One-Stage Probability Sampling

In one-stage probability sampling, the strategies or procedures can be classified as simple, systematic, or stratified random sampling. In each case, the selection of the sample is completed in one process or one stage.

Simple Random Sampling

In simple random sampling, members of a population are selected, one at a time, until the desired sample size is obtained. Once an individual unit (e.g., person, object, event) has been selected, it is removed from the population and has no chance of being selected again. This procedure is often used in selecting winning lottery numbers.

The objective of a particular lottery, for example, may be to guess 6 of 50 numbers. The winning numbers are selected by placing 50 balls, numbered 01–50, in a bowl and asking a blindfolded person to select, one at a time, six balls from the bowl. Each time a ball is selected, it is set aside and becomes one of the winning numbers; the end result is that six different numbers are selected by chance.

In practice, it is necessary to assign a unique number to each member within the population. As an example, consider a situation where our population consists of 500 full-time students in a school of social work. We decide that a sample of 100 (a sampling fraction of 1/5, or 20 percent, of the population) is required. First, each student is assigned a number from 001 to 500. Next, 100 numbers in the range 001–500 are randomly selected. The students who had been assigned the 100 selected numbers constitute our sample. The selection of numbers can be carried out with the assistance of a computer or by using a published table of random numbers.

A variety of computer programs that generate random numbers is available. Typically, all that is required is entering into the computer the range from within which selections are to be made, as well as the quantity of random numbers required. The computer then generates a list of the required quantity of numbers.

Alternatively, a published table of random numbers can be used to select the sample manually. Part of such a table is shown in Table 10.1. The selection process begins with the random selection of a single number anywhere in the table. Suppose the numeral zero in the number 63028 (third column from left, eighth row) is selected in this manner. Actually, three-digit numbers are required for our example, because the possible range of selection is from 001 to 500. Accordingly, the two digits to the right of the selected number (in this case 2 and 8) will also be used, making the first entry 028. (We also could have decided to use the two digits to the left, in which case the first entry would be 630—too large to fit the 001–500 range.)

The student who had been assigned the number 028 is the first person selected for our sample. Because we have planned to move down the table, immediately under 028 the next three-digit number would be 846. This number is out of range, so it is skipped. The next number is 441; the student who had been assigned that number is selected.

Our selection then continues with student number 334, and so on. At the bottom of the column we move either right or left to the next column, according to a preset plan. When all 100 numbers have been selected, our random sample is complete.

TABLE 10.1   PARTIAL TABLE OF
RANDOM NUMBERS

68184	44863	98829	87654	98712	08417
90103	90103	61257	56521	74090	09650
90103	89378	11410	45871	80932	15798
39883	87129	51877	25803	12597	35799
59342	89532	92446	68743	69876	12120
91041	76320	90940	12987	23099	43787
15685	56009	14001	35988	11435	56545
90159	76010	**63028**	56279	43450	09714
40814	09125	31846	09213	53074	27651
09299	09135	13441	98723	09123	76500
16920	78327	38334	38945	12345	89743
70083	90438	26713	23854	09457	67412
95826	67409	70856	76321	32198	69829
95791	81209	65385	45097	38764	90543
30403	40981	39854	76093	76328	40999
16036	76109	04720	76512	21232	09816
21652	89613	71900	50091	98541	89036
06990	90231	17209	78451	57690	90846

Systematic Random Sampling

Conceptually, the selection of a simple random sample is a relatively simple and straightforward process. In practice, however, such a procedure is rarely used, particularly when the population from which a sample is to be selected is fairly large and the random numbers are to be selected one-by-one, by hand. The procedure can be quite tedious and time-consuming. A more practical alternative is systematic random sampling.

In this procedure, we determine the total number of units in the sampling frame and decide on the size of the sample. Assume that our sampling frame is again comprised of 500 students and the desired size of our sample is 100. Dividing the former by the latter (500/100 = 5) provides the size of the sampling interval, which in this case is five.

Thus, every fifth student on the list will be selected to constitute the sample. The selection process begins by randomly selecting a number from 1 to 5. The number selected designates the first student, and every fifth student is subsequently chosen. Suppose the number selected is 2. In such a case, students who had been assigned 002, 007, 012, 017, 022, and so forth will be chosen; student number 497 will complete the sample.

In most cases, a systematic random sample is equivalent to a simple random sample. However, it is possible that the sampling frame on which the selection is based has a recurring pattern that can bias the sample. For example, professional staff members in a social service agency may be listed on a unit-by-unit basis, with each unit having nine line-level social workers and one supervisor. The supervisor is listed as the tenth person in the unit. A systematic sample drawn from such a listing would almost certainly contain a bias.

In a sampling plan that calls for names to be selected at intervals of five, the first number chosen would determine if supervisors would be either over-represented or under-represented in the sample. If the first number selected were 1, 2, 3, or 4, no supervisors at all would be included in the sample, even though they comprise 10 percent of the population. If the first number selected is 5, every second person selected for the sample would be a supervisor, and supervisors would be grossly overrepresented.

With systematic random sampling, it is essential to closely study the sampling frame from which the selections are to be made to ensure that no underlying patterns that could bias the sample are present. If it can be confirmed that the list is free of recurring patterns, systematic random sampling is an efficient and effective way of selecting a sample from a population.

Stratified Random Sampling

Stratified random sampling is a procedure that can help reduce chance variation between a sample and the population it represents. This procedure may be used when a population can be divided into two or more distinct groups, called strata. The strata are then sampled separately, using simple random-sampling or systematic random-sampling techniques.

In our example above, the population of professional staff members in the social service agency is constituted of 90 percent social workers and 10 percent supervisors. Of the professional staff complement of 500, therefore, 450 are social workers and 50 hold supervisory positions. Theoretically, a 20 percent simple random sample of the professional staff should yield 90 social workers and 10 supervisors. However, this will not always happen because although a random sample may be representative of the population, it is not necessarily identical to it. Chance (or normal sampling error) may result in a sample that is composed of 92 social workers and 8 supervisors, or 87 social workers and 13 supervisors, or some other combination.

But this population of agency professionals is composed of two groups, or strata: line-level social workers and supervisors. A separate sample therefore can be drawn from each group, using simple random-sampling or systematic random-sampling techniques. A 20 percent sample can be drawn from each group, resulting in a total sample of 100 people, 90 social workers and 10 supervisors.

Because the same sampling fraction is used for each stratum, the approach is known as proportional stratified sampling. One of the advantages of such a sample is that it perfectly represents the characteristics of the population from which it was drawn in regard to the variable, or variables, on which the stratification was based. Some sampling error would normally be expected if either simple random sampling or systematic random sampling had been used. Using stratified random sampling can eliminate this source of sampling error.

It is also possible to draw a disproportional sample from the strata. In this procedure, different sampling fractions are used for some or all of the strata. We might use a 1/5 sampling fraction (a 20 percent sample), for example, when selecting line-level social workers but a 3/5 sampling fraction (a 60 percent sample) in the selection of supervisors. This procedure would yield 90 line-level social workers and 30 supervisors.

It would make sense to proceed in this manner if one of the objectives of the study were to examine closely some characteristic of the supervisors. Using proportional sampling, only ten supervisors would be available for study. If the subsequent analysis required further division of this group (for example, according to educational level, age, or gender), only a small number of supervisors would be left in each group, making such analysis difficult. By sampling dis proportionally, the total number of supervisors in the sample is increased, which makes it possible to conduct further detailed analyses.

When strata that have been disproportionately sampled are combined in order to make estimates about the total population, it is necessary to weight each stratum that was sampled at a higher rate to compensate for the higher rate of selection. If supervisors were selected at three times the rate of line-level social workers, an adjustment factor of 1/3 (the inverse of 3 to 1) is used to adjust for the disproportional selection of supervisors. The numbers and percentages of line-level workers and supervisors in the sample then would accurately represent those in the population. Table 10.2 provides a brief summary of disproportional sampling and the adjustment process in relation to our hypothetical example in this section.

Multistage Probability Sampling

The single-stage probability sampling procedures described above depend on the availability of a sampling frame from which the sample is to be selected. It is not always possible to compile a sampling frame for the population of interest, however; this is likely to be the case when a population from a city, county, or state is to be sampled. Multistage-sampling procedures provide a strategy through which a population can be sampled when a comprehensive list does not exist and it is not possible to construct one. The most commonly used procedure is cluster sampling.

Cluster Sampling

Cluster sampling is more complicated than the single-stage sampling strategies; essentially, each stage of multistage sampling is in itself a simple random

TABLE 10.2   DATA FOR DISPROPORTIONAL STRATIFIED SAMPLING FOR A POPULATION OF LINE-LEVEL WORKERS AND SUPERVISORS

	Line-Level Workers	Supervisors
Number in population	450	50
Percent of population	90	10
Sampling fraction	1/5	3/5
Number in sample	90	30
Percent of unweighted sample	75	25
Weighting factor	1	1/3
Number in weighted sample	90	10
Percent of weighted sample	90	10

sample or a systematic random sample. The stages are combined to build on one another and arrive at a final sample.

Suppose we are conducting a community needs assessment, for example, and want to determine the types of community support that single parents need. Many of the agencies and social workers providing help to single parents undoubtedly have opinions about this, but suppose very little is known about what single parents themselves perceive their needs to be. In fact, it is not even known how many single parents there are in the community. Since no comprehensive list of single parents can be compiled, it is not possible to proceed with a one-stage probability sampling strategy.

A form of cluster sampling, known as area probability sampling, provides the means to carry out such a study. Stage 1 of this strategy involves listing all the residential blocks, known as clusters, within the community and then drawing a sample from these clusters. Suppose there are 300 residential blocks and we decide that a sample of 50 (a sampling fraction of about 1/6) will constitute an adequate sample.

Fifty blocks are selected, using simple random sampling. In the next stage, the residential units located on those blocks are to be sampled.

We then decide that in Stage 2, 20 percent of the residential units located on the blocks selected in Stage 1 will provide an appropriate sample. All 2000 units on the 50 blocks are listed, and 20 percent are randomly selected. Interviewers are assigned to contact the residents in these 400 units to determine if any resident is a single parent.

When the number of single parents in the sample has been determined, the incidence of single parenthood in the community can be estimated. Moreover, we now have a list of single parents, which is required for Stage 3.

In Stage 3, a sample is drawn of the single parents listed. We may decide, for example, that about 25 percent of the single parents should be interviewed. A random list of the names of the 100 single parents who were located in Stage 2 is compiled, and, using a systematic random sample strategy, every fourth name is selected for the final sample. A final sample of 25 single parents is thus obtained. In-depth interviews are then conducted with the single parents in the sample to determine the types of community support that single parents generally would like. Box 10.1 illustrates how the multistage probability sampling procedure works in a nationwide survey.

NONPROBABILITY SAMPLING

With nonprobability sampling, the probability of selection cannot be estimated, so there is little or no support for the claim that the sample is representative of the population from which it was drawn. Nevertheless, there are many situations where it is unfeasible or impossible to draw a probability sample, and nonprobability sampling is the only alternative. Four types of nonprobability sampling—convenience, purposive, quota, and snowball sampling—are described in this section. Box 10.2 presents a graphic summary of these sampling strategies.

Convenience Sampling

Convenience sampling, sometimes called availability sampling, relies on the closest and most available subjects to constitute the sample. This procedure is used extensively in social work research.

Let us say, for example, we are interested in the various therapeutic techniques social workers use with clients who are depressed. We could use this specific group of people being treated at a specific social service agency within the past six months as our sample. Our findings could yield data on the various techniques social workers use with this group of people in general.

It would be very difficult, however, to determine to what degree the clients in our sample are representative of all people who are depressed and receiving treatment in other geographical locations. It is possible that clients receiving services from our particular agency are different, in important ways, from people who are depressed and receiving services elsewhere. These differences may well affect the nature of the services provided. For this reason, the opportunity to generalize the findings from our study is limited.

Purposive Sampling

In purposive sampling, also known as judgmental or theoretical sampling, we use our own judgment in selecting a sample. The basis for selecting such a sample is that it can yield considerable data particularly when used within qualitative research studies, as pointed out in Chapter 5.

Let us say, for example, the objective of our exploratory research study is to examine the workings of new legislation regarding young offenders. It might make sense to interview a small number of social workers, probation officers, lawyers, judges, and directors of detention facilities who have worked extensively under this legislation. The people in this sample could be used as key informants in an attempt to construct a picture of how the legislation has been implemented.

BOX 10.1

SAMPLING DESIGN FOR A NATIONWIDE SURVEY

Survey organizations such as the Survey Research Center (SRC) at the University of Michigan use multistage cluster sampling to conduct nationwide surveys. The steps involved in selecting the SRC's national sample in the 1970s are roughly diagramed in the accompanying figure. The steps are numbered and labeled according to the type of unit selected.

STEP 1: The United States is divided into *primary areas* consisting of counties, groups of counties, or metropolitan areas. These areas are stratified by region and a proportionate stratified sample of seventy-four areas is selected.

STEP 2: The seventy-four areas are divided into *locations* such as towns, cities, and residual areas. After these have been identified and stratified by population size, a proportionate stratified sample of locations is drawn within each area.

STEP 3: All sample locations are divided into *chunks*. A chunk is a geographic area with identifiable boundaries such as city streets, roads, streams, and county lines. After division into chunks, a random sample of chunks is drawn.

STEP 4: Interviewers scout each sample chunk and record addresses and estimates of the number of housing units at each address. They then divide the chunks into smaller units called *segments*, and a random sample of segments is selected.

STEP 5: Within each sample segment either all or a sample of the housing units, usually about four, are chosen for a given study. Finally, for every housing unit in the sample, interviewers randomly choose one respondent from among those eligible, which ordinarily consists of all U.S. citizens 18 years of age or older.

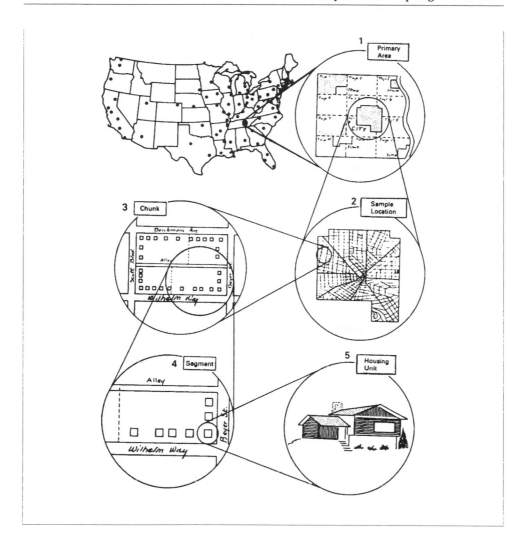

The selection might also be made with a view of choosing information-rich cases. One approach to studying the reasons for breakdown in foster care placement for preschool children, for example, would be to select a sample of cases where five or more placement changes have taken place. While these cases would (it is hoped) not be representative of foster care cases generally, they could provide clues to the factors involved in placement breakdown.

Quota Sampling

Quota sampling is somewhat analogous to stratified random sampling. Essentially, the strategy consists of identifying variables or characteristics of the sample that are relevant to the study, determining the proportion (quota) of these characteristics in the population, and then selecting participants in each category until the quota is achieved.

Let us take an example of a research study that examines the skills social workers use to establish working relationships with their clients. We have a hunch that there are differences in the various approaches taken by female and male social workers (Variable 1) and by older and younger social workers (Variable 2). These two variables are displayed in Table 10.3 (i.e., gender and age) and are combined into four discrete groups: younger female social workers, younger male social workers, older female social workers, and older male social workers.

Then the percentage of workers in each of the four categories within the population of interest is determined. Suppose we determine that the percentages

---

BOX 10.2

NONPROBABILITY SAMPLING STRATEGIES

CONVENIENCE SAMPLING:
   Sample is composed of nearest and most available participants.

PURPOSIVE SAMPLING:
   Research participants who are known or judged to be good sources of information are specifically sought out and selected for the sample.

QUOTA SAMPLING:
   1. Variables relevant to the study are identified (e.g., gender and age).
   2. Variables are combined into discrete categories (e.g., younger female, younger male, older female, older male).
   3. The percentage of each of these categories in the population is determined (e.g., 35% younger female, 25% younger male, 30% older female, 10% older male).
   4. The total sample size is established (e.g., $N = 200$).
   5. Quotas are calculated (younger females = 35% of 200 = 70; younger males = 25% of 200 = 50; older females = 30% of 200 = 60; older males = 10% of 200 = 20).
   6. The first available participants possessing the required characteristics are selected to fill the quotas.

SNOWBALL SAMPLING:
   1. A small number of participants are located in the population of interest.
   2. Data are obtained from these participants and they are also asked to identify others in the population.
   3. The newly identified participants are contacted, data are obtained, and this group is also asked to identify others in the population.
   4. The process continues until the desired sample size is obtained.

TABLE 10.3   Quota Sampling Matrix: Percentages and Quotas of Gender and Age among Social Workers

| | Age | | | | | |
| | Younger (n = 120) | | Older (n = 80) | | Total (N = 200) | |
Gender	Number	Percent	Number	Percent	Number	Percent
Female	70	35	60	30	130	65
Male	50	25	20	10	70	35
Totals ...	120	60	80	40	200	100

are 35, 25, 30, and 10 percent, respectively, as indicated in Table 10.3. If a total sample of 200 is required, 70 younger females (35 percent of 200), 50 younger males, 60 older females, and 20 older males will constitute the sample. The final step in selecting a quota sample is to find a sufficient number of social workers to fit each of these characteristics.

The main limitation of quota sampling is that considerable discretion is exercised in selecting individuals to fill each quota. In our example, we might go to two large agencies and find sufficient numbers of social workers to draw the entire sample. While this would be convenient, the representativeness of such a sample would be questionable. It could be argued, for example, that social workers in smaller agencies relate to clients differently than those in larger agencies.

A second problem with quota sampling is that to establish the quotas, reasonable knowledge of the characteristics of the population under study is required. Where precise data about the variables relevant to quota setting are not available, the quotas may not accurately represent the characteristics of the population.

Snowball Sampling

Snowball sampling is particularly useful when members of a population are difficult to identify and locate. This is often the case when studying people whose behavior is regarded as deviant or illegal or is otherwise received with social disapproval. It is often difficult to identify members of such populations as teenage prostitutes, homeless people, or intravenous drug users, for example.

The strategy of snowball sampling is to locate a few individuals in the population of interest and ask them to identify other people in the same group. These people, in turn, are asked to identify still other respondents. The cycle continues until an adequate sample size has been achieved. Although this strategy may be the only one through which a sample can be drawn from certain populations, it has the evident drawback that the sample depends entirely on the individuals who are first contacted. If the sampling were initiated with a different set of individuals, the entire sample might be differently constituted. Consequently, the degree to which a snowball sample is representative of any population cannot be determined.

Snowball sampling may also be used to locate people with divergent views on a topic to ensure that the sample represents all segments of a population. This is important in a population where minority opinions might otherwise be disregarded. It is particularly useful in qualitative research studies.

SAMPLE SIZE

To illustrate the concept of sample size, let us take the case of Antonia, a school social worker at Wilson Elementary School, who wants to teach second-grade students how to protect themselves from being physically abused by their parents. In a nutshell, she wants to institute a school-based program that will teach these children how to defend themselves from being abused. Before Antonia institutes the program, however, she wants to make sure the parents approve of their children learning such material.

Let us say that Antonia wants to conduct a very simple study with mothers who have at least one child attending her school. She wants to ascertain their opinions of her idea—that is, teaching their children about the prevention of child abuse. In order to gather data—the parents' opinions, that is—to help her decide if the content should be taught to second-grade children, Antonia wants to survey the mothers of 100 children in grade two.

Before her sample can be selected, it is obviously necessary to decide how large the sample needs to be. The correct sample size for any particular study depends on how confident we need to be about the results. If Antonia wants to be completely (100 percent) confident about the mothers' opinions on child abuse prevention education being taught to second-grade children, she needs to survey every mother: That is, she must not draw a sample at all. Generally speaking, the more mothers she surveys, the more confident she can be that the results of her survey reflect the opinions of the population of mothers at Wilson.

The sample size also depends on how homogeneous, or how alike, the population is. If Antonia's population of mothers were all identical robots, she would need only to survey one to be completely confident of the opinions of the rest. If they were all middle-aged, middle-income Caucasian Catholics, she would need to survey fewer than if they comprised a wide range of ethnic and religious groups of varying ages and incomes.

Sample size must also be considered in relation to the number of categories required. If Antonia had wanted to look at mothers of 5 to 9 year old children and mothers of 10 to 14 year old children, she would have needed two mothers—one from each category—even if all the mothers are identical robots. The more dissimilar the mothers are, the more she will need to survey in each of the categories she wants to consider. In addition, if there are very few mothers in one category, she may need to survey all the mothers in that category, or at least a large proportion of them, while surveying smaller proportions of parents in the other categories.

Generally speaking, the larger the sample the better, taking into account restrictions of time and cost. With respect to the minimum sample size required, experts differ. Some say that a sample of 30 is large enough to perform basic statistical procedures, while others advise a minimum sample size of 100. There are formulas available for calculating sample size but they are somewhat complicated. Usually, a sample size of one-tenth of the population (with a minimum of 30) is considered sufficient to provide reasonable control over sampling error. The same one-tenth convention also applies to categories of the population: One-tenth of each category can be included in the sample.

ERRORS

Errors in research findings may result either from the sampling procedure, in which case they are called sampling errors, or from other errors arising in the study, called nonsampling errors.

Sampling Errors

Sampling errors have to do with the fact that a representative sample—a sample that exactly represents the population from which it was drawn—almost never exists in reality. When Antonia surveys a random sample of mothers, she will not obtain exactly the same results from the sample as she would have obtained had she surveyed the entire population of mothers. The difference between the results she did obtain (actuality) and the results she would have obtained (theoretical) comprises the sampling error.

In order to better understand the concept of representativeness, suppose that two variables are particularly important in determining whether mothers (parents) will approve of child abuse prevention education taught to their second-grade children: the mothers' degree of belief that their own children are at risk of abuse (Figure 10.1); and the mothers' degree of fear that child abuse prevention education may somehow psychologically harm their children (Figure 10.2).

Suppose further that these two variables can be measured, both for a random sample of 100 mothers and for the entire population 1000 mothers. All the mothers in the school may be asked to rate the degree to which they feel their own children are at risk of abuse, on a scale of 1 to 10, from "no risk at all" to "very high risk." A graph may then be drawn of the number of mothers on the vertical axis against rating of risk on the horizontal axis, as illustrated in Figure 10.1 on the following page.

As Figure 10.1*a* shows, a few of the mothers in the population feel that their children are at high risk (rating the risk as 10 on the scale), a few feel that there is very little risk (a rating of 1), and most believe that there is moderate risk. If a random sample of mothers is then selected from the population of mothers and the same procedure is carried out, almost identical results may be obtained, as shown in Figure 10.1*b*. The degree of similarity between graphs 10.1*a* and 10.1*b* is the degree to which the sample is representative of the population, with respect to the belief that their children are at risk.

Now suppose that the population of mothers and the sample of mothers are separately asked to rate the degree to which they fear that child abuse prevention education may somehow harm their children. The results for the population and the sample are shown in Figure 10.2.

As Figure 10.2*a* shows, the majority of the population of mothers have very little fear that their children will be harmed by child abuse prevention being taught in schools. A few have extreme fear, a few have moderate fear, and a few have no fear at all. Conversely, the majority of the sample display moderate fear that their children will be harmed; the hump of the graph, which is skewed to the left in Figure 10.2*a* is essentially centered in Figure 10.2*b*. If these graphs were placed one on top of another, they would not coincide. Thus, the sample does not very adequately represent the population of mothers, with respect to fear that their children will be harmed.

In sum, while no sample will perfectly represent the population from which

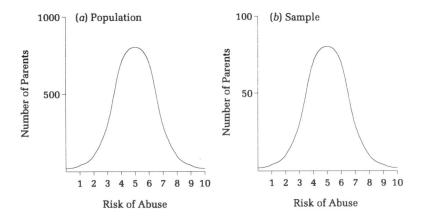

FIGURE 10.1   THEORETICAL DISTRIBUTIONS OF
MOTHERS' RISK OF ABUSE RATINGS
FROM A POPULATION OF 1000 (*A*) AND
A RANDOM SAMPLE OF 100 (*B*)

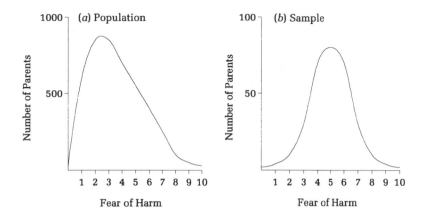

FIGURE 10.2   THEORETICAL DISTRIBUTIONS OF
MOTHERS' FEAR OF HARM RATINGS
FROM A POPULATION OF 1000 (*A*) AND
A RANDOM SAMPLE OF 100 (*B*)

it was drawn, it is quite probable that a randomly drawn sample will represent the population adequately with respect to one variable. It is less probable that the sample will represent the population adequately with respect to two variables, and, the more variables there are, the less probable adequate representation becomes. A member of congress, for example, may represent his or her constituents' views on state-funded abortions exactly, but it is unlikely that their views on Medicare will also be reflected, as well as their views on capital punishment and their views on national health care.

Nonsampling Errors

In addition to reducing sampling error to a minimum, efforts must also be made to reduce nonsampling sources of error. One source of nonsampling error is an inadequate sampling frame, which has already been mentioned. Because the sample is drawn from the sampling frame, if the list does not correspond well to the population of interest, it will be difficult to infer anything about the population from the sample.

Other nonsampling errors include nonresponse from research participants, field errors, response errors, and coding and data entry errors. While these are not sampling errors, they also affect our ability to estimate the precision of the sample. Box 10.3 provides an interesting discussion on sampling and sex bias.

BOX 10.3

SAMPLING AND SEX BIAS

In recent years feminists have been sensitizing social researchers to the relationship of women's issues to research. All aspects of the research process can be affected by sex bias, and sampling is one area where such bias can be particularly problematic. Even probability sampling can be affected by sex bias, for example, when we inappropriately decide to exclude a particular gender from our sampling frame.

Perhaps the most commonly encountered sex bias problem in sampling is the unwarranted generalization of research findings to the population as a whole when one gender is not adequately represented in the research sample. (The same type of problem, by the way, is encountered when certain minority groups are inadequately represented in the sample but generalizations are made to the entire population.)

Campbell (1983) reviewed the occurrence of sex biases in the sex-role research literature and identified a number of illustrations of this problem. For example, she cited studies on achievement motivation and on management and careers whose samples included only white, middle-class male subjects but whose conclusions did not specify that their generalizations were limited to individuals with those attributes. She was particularly critical of life-cycle research, as follows (p. 206):

> Nowhere is the effect of bias on sampling more evident than in the popular and growing field of the life cycle or stages. Beginning with Erikson's...work on the "Eight Stages of Man" to Levinson's *Seasons of a Man's Life*...the study of life cycles has focused on male subjects. When women are examined, it is in terms of how they fit or don't fit the male model. Without empirical verification, women are said to go through the same cycles as men...or are said to go through cycles that are antithetical to men's...Based on a survey of the literature on life cycles, Sangiuliano...concluded that "Mostly we (researchers) persist in seeing her (woman) in the reflected light of men"...

The inadequate representation of a particular gender in a sample can be much subtler than just excluding them entirely or including an insufficient proportion of them. It could also occur due to biased data-collection procedures, even when the number of individuals of a particular sex is not the issue. For example, Campbell notes that the Gallup poll interviews male subjects beginning at 6:00 PM, while conducting most interviews with females between 4:00 and 6:00 PM. Thus, Campbell argues that most professional women would not be home before 6:00 PM and are not adequately represented in the sample. If she is correct, then even if the overall proportion of women in the Gallup poll seems to be sufficient, the views expressed by the women in the sample are not adequately representative of the views of the population of women.

As another example, if we wanted to generalize about gender-related differences in job satisfaction, we would not want to select our sample only from those work settings where professional or managerial positions go predominately to men and where semi-professional jobs go predominately to women.

There may be instances, however, when the exclusion of a particular gender from a study's sample is warranted or inescapable—instances where only one gender is relevant and where generalizations will be restricted to that gender. Thus, only one gender would be included in the sample of a survey of client satisfaction in a program whose clientele all happen to be of the same gender. For example, perhaps it is a group support program for battered women.

But we must be on guard not to let any sex-role biases improperly influence us to deem a particular gender irrelevant for a given study. For example, we should not be predisposed to restrict our samples to men when we study research topics like aggression, management, unemployment, or criminal behavior and to women when we study topics like parenting, nurturing, or housekeeping.

Effects of Nonresponse

In making estimates from probability samples, it is assumed that we have collected data from every unit designated for our sample. In this sense, however, a sample is only a theoretical entity, for seldom can a complete set of data be collected. The sample always includes some individuals who cannot be reached or refuse to respond. A high rate of nonresponse offers a distinct possibility that the sample obtained will be biased, since those who do respond may be in some way different from those who do not. Nonresponse is particularly a problem when data are collected by mail surveys.

In a study to examine the frequency of evaluation activities in children's group-care programs in a large state, for example, data are collected by mailing questionnaires to the executive directors of a sample of agencies offering such programs. Completed questionnaires are returned by 55 percent of the directors sampled. Does the 45 percent nonresponse rate result in a biased sample?

There is no simple answer to such a question, and, unless further data are collected from nonrespondents, it is not possible to answer it with any degree of certainty. Suppose (as is likely the case) that the directors who respond are more interested in evaluation because there is a high level of such activities in their agencies. Under such circumstances, the sample would be biased, resulting in an overestimation of evaluation activities. The sample would not be biased if the reasons for the lack of response are not related to the variables under study. Clearly, every effort should be made to incorporate into the research design strategies that will ensure a high response rate.

Field Errors and Response Errors

Other nonsampling errors occur in the field or in participants' responses to interviews or questionnaires. Ideally, the research design would not allow the field staff much discretion in selecting the sample. If given latitude they might select for the sample only those files that are well organized and neatly written, those individuals who are easily accessible and nonthreatening, or those housing units that are well maintained and easy to reach.

Interviewers can almost always exercise some discretion in conducting complex interviews, providing prompts, or recording the data. When the data collection method is observation (Chapter 13), observers can decide what to observe and how to record it. Field errors resulting from such circumstances can be minimized by ensuring that field staff are well trained and supervised and that the procedures they are to follow have been explicitly stated in detail.

Skillfully designed questionnaires and well-trained interviewers also can minimize the impact of response errors. The quality of the data collected will suffer if large numbers of respondents misunderstand questions or are not qualified to answer but provide answers nevertheless. Respondents also may attempt to present themselves (or their opinions) in a socially desirable manner. They may profess views they do not actually hold or deny behaviors or feelings that they believe might be met with disapproval.

Coding and Data Entry Errors

In the final analysis, the best sampling design and the most meticulous data collection will be to no avail if the resulting data are inaccurately coded or entered. Training and supervision of the clerical staff responsible for these functions and judicious use of double-coding and double-entry procedures lessen the possibility of coding and data entry errors.

SUMMARY

Because it is usually not feasible to obtain data from an entire population (of people, things, or events) in which we are interested, sampling procedures are used to select some individuals (or other units) as representative of the entire population. The two main types of sampling procedures are probability and nonprobability sampling.

The first step in probability sampling is to construct a sampling frame, a list of units from which the sample is to be selected. The sample is then drawn, using either one-stage sampling (with simple random, systematic random, or stratified random sample strategies) or multistage (cluster) sampling. In all forms of probability sampling, random selection procedures are used, all units in the sampling frame have the same known probability of selection, and it is possible to make an estimate of the precision of the sample.

In some situations where probability sampling is not possible, a nonprobability sample may be drawn. The four kinds of nonprobability samples described in this chapter are convenience, purposive, quota, and snowball sampling. Such samples may provide data that would otherwise be inaccessible, but these approaches are less powerful than probability sampling because various selection biases in them cannot be ruled out. In addition, it is not possible to estimate the precision of the sample.

If probability sampling is used, sampling errors can be estimated. Such errors can be controlled by using a sample of sufficient size or by employing a sampling design that incorporates stratification. Nonsampling errors also contribute to the overall possibility of error in the research project. Care should be taken in the design to minimize nonresponse, an inadequate sampling frame, field and response errors, and coding and data entry errors.

Now that we know something about how to obtain a sample for a research study, let us turn our attention to the selection of an appropriate research design that will help us obtain the most "objective" data possible that will help us answer our research question or test our research hypothesis.

REFERENCES AND FURTHER READINGS

ANASTAS, J.W., & MACDONALD, M.L. (1994). *Research design for social work and the human services* (pp. 258-282). New York: Lexington.

BABBIE, E.R. (1995). *The practice of social research* (7th ed., pp. 187-226, 310-311). Belmont, CA: Wadsworth.

BAILEY, K.D. (1994). *Methods of social research* (4th ed., pp. 82-104). New York: Free Press.

CAMPBELL, P.B. (1983). The impact of societal biases on research methods. In B.L. Richardson, & J. Wirtenberg (Eds.), *Sex role research* (pp. 197-213). New York: Praeger Publishers.

COMMITTEE ON THE STATUS OF WOMEN IN SOCIOLOGY (1985-86). *The status of women is sociology.* New York: American Sociological Association.

DEPOY, E., & GITLIN, L.N. (1994). *Introduction to research* (pp. 163-183). St. Louis: Mosby.

FRANKFORT-NACHMIAS, C., & NACHMIAS, D. (1992). *Research methods in the social sciences* (4th ed., pp. 169-193). New York: St. Martin's Press.

GABOR, P.A. (1993). Sampling. In R.M. Grinnell, Jr. (Ed.), *Social work research and evaluation* (4th ed., pp. 154-170). Itasca, IL: F.E. Peacock.

GABOR, P.A., & GRINNELL, R.M., JR. (1994). *Evaluation and quality improvement in the human services* (pp. 190-207). Needham Heights, MA: Allyn & Bacon.

GRINNELL, R.M., JR., & WILLIAMS, M. (1990). *Research in social work: A primer* (pp. 116-136). Itasca, IL: F.E. Peacock.

JUDD, C.M., SMITH, E.R., & KIDDER, L.H. (1991). *Research methods in social relations* (6th ed., pp. 128-142, 201-212). Fort Worth, TX: Harcourt Brace.

KRYSIK, J., HOFFART, I., & GRINNELL, R.M., JR. (1993). *Student study guide for the fourth edition of social work research and evaluation* (pp. 9-10). Itasca, IL: F.E. Peacock.

MARLOW, C. (1993). *Research methods for generalist social work practice* (pp. 103-123). Pacific Grove, CA: Wadsworth.

MONETTE, D.R., SULLIVAN, T.J., & DEJONG, C.R. (1994). *Applied social research* (3rd ed., pp. 119-152). Fort Worth, TX: Harcourt Brace.

ROTHERY, M.A., TUTTY, L.M., & GRINNELL, R.M., JR. (1996). Introduction. In L.M. Tutty, M.A. Rothery, & R.M. Grinnell, Jr. (Eds), *Qualitative research for social workers: Phases, steps, and tasks* (pp. 3-22). Needham Heights, MA: Allyn & Bacon.

RUBIN, A., & BABBIE, E. (1993). *Research methods for social work* (2nd ed., pp. 217-260). Pacific Grove, CA: Wadsworth.

SEABERG, J.R. (1988). Utilizing sampling procedures. In R.M. Grinnell, Jr. (Ed.), *Social work research and evaluation* (3rd ed., pp. 240-257). Itasca, IL: F.E. Peacock.

SURVEY RESEARCH CENTER (1976). *Interviewer's manual* (revised edition). Survey Research Center, Institute of Social Research, University of Michigan.

WEINBACH, R.W., & GRINNELL, R.M., JR. (1996). *Applying research knowledge: A workbook for social work students* (2nd ed., pp. 89-96). Needham Heights, MA: Allyn & Bacon.

WILLIAMS, M., TUTTY, L.M., & GRINNELL, R.M., JR. (1995). *Research in social work: An introduction* (2nd ed., pp. 223-238). Itasca, IL: F.E. Peacock.

YEGIDIS, B.L., & WEINBACH, R.W. (1996). *Research methods for social workers* (2nd ed., pp. 113-125). Needham Heights, MA: Allyn & Bacon.

Richard M. Grinnell, Jr.
Yvonne A. Unrau

Chapter **11**

Group Designs

NOW THAT WE KNOW how to draw samples for qualitative and quantitative research studies, we turn our attention to the various designs that research studies can take. The two most important factors in determining what design to use in a specific study are: (1) what the research question is, and (2) how much knowledge about the problem area is available. If there is already a substantial knowledge base in the area, we will be in a position to address very specific research questions, the answers to which could add to the explanation of previously gathered data. If less is known about the problem area, our research questions will have to be of a more general, descriptive nature. If very little is known about the problem area, our questions will have to be even more general, at an exploratory level.

It is difficult to fit a research question to a specific knowledge level, however. Rather than existing as separate categories, therefore, research knowledge levels are arrayed along a continuum, from exploratory at the lowest end to explanatory at the highest, as illustrated in Figure 3.1.

Because research knowledge levels are viewed this way, the assignment of the level of knowledge accumulated in a problem area prior to a research study, as well as the level that might be attained by the research study, is totally arbitrary. There are, however, specific research designs that can be used to provide us with knowledge at a certain level.

At the highest level are the explanatory designs, also called experimental designs or "ideal" experiments. These designs have the largest number of requirements (examined in the following section). They are best used in confirmatory research studies where the area under study is well developed, theories abound, and testable hypotheses can be formulated on the basis of previous work or existing theory. These designs seek to establish causal relationships between the independent and dependent variables.

In the middle range are the descriptive designs, sometimes referred to as quasi-experimental. A quasi-experiment resembles an "ideal" experiment in some aspects but lacks at least one of the necessary requirements.

At the lowest level are the exploratory designs, also called preexperimental or nonexperimental, which explore only the research question or problem area. These designs do not produce statistically sound data or conclusive results; they do not intend to. Their purpose is to build a foundation of general ideas and tentative theories, which can be explored later with more precise and hence more complex research designs, and their corresponding data-gathering techniques.

The research designs that allow us to acquire knowledge at each of the three levels are described in a later section of this chapter. Before doing so, however, it is necessary to establish the characteristics that differentiate an "ideal" experiment, which leads to explanatory knowledge, from other studies that lead to lower levels of knowledge.

CHARACTERISTICS OF "IDEAL" EXPERIMENTS

An "ideal" experiment is one in which a research study most closely approaches certainty about the relationship between the independent and dependent variables. The purpose of doing an "ideal" experiment is to ascertain whether it can be concluded from the study's findings that the independent variable is, or is not, the only cause of change in the dependent variable. As pointed out in previous chapters, some social work research studies have no independent variable—for example, those studies that just want to find out how many people in a certain community wish to establish a community-based halfway house for people who are addicted to drugs.

The concept of an "ideal" experiment is introduced with the word "ideal" in quotes because such an experiment is rarely achieved in social work research situations. On a general level, in order to achieve this high degree of certainty and qualify as an "ideal" experiment, an explanatory research design must meet six conditions:

1. The time order of the independent variable must be established.
2. The independent variable must be manipulated.
3. The relationship between the independent and dependent variables must be established.
4. The research design must control for rival hypotheses.
5. At least one control group should be used.
6. Random assignment procedures (and if possible, random sampling from a population) must be employed in assigning research participants (or objects) to groups.

Controlling the Time Order of Variables

In an "ideal" experiment, the independent variable must precede the dependent variable in time. Time order is crucial if our research study is to show that one variable causes another, because something that occurs later cannot be the cause of something that occurred earlier. Suppose we want to study the relationship between adolescent substance abuse and gang-related behavior. The following hypothesis is formulated after some thought:

Adolescent substance abuse causes gang-related behavior.

In the hypothesis, the independent variable is adolescent drug use, and the dependent variable is gang-related behavior. The substance abuse must come *before* gang-related behavior because the hypothesis states that adolescent drug use causes gang-related behavior. We could also come up with the following hypothesis, however:

Adolescent gang-related behavior causes substance abuse.

In this hypothesis, adolescent gang-related behavior is the independent variable, and substance abuse is the dependent variable. According to this hypothesis, gang-related behavior must come *before* the substance abuse.

Manipulating the Independent Variable

Manipulation of the independent variable means that we must do something with the independent variable in terms of at least one of the research participants in the study. In the general form of the hypothesis, if X occurs then Y will result, the independent variable (X) must be manipulated in order to effect a variation in the dependent variable (Y). There are essentially three ways in which independent variables can be manipulated:

1. *X present versus X absent.* If the effectiveness of a specific treatment

intervention is being evaluated, an experimental group and a control group could be used. The experimental group would be given the intervention, the control group would not (see Box 3.3).

2. *A small amount of X versus a larger amount of X.* If the effect of treatment time on client's outcomes is being studied, two experimental groups could be used, one of which would be treated for a longer period of time.

3. *X versus something else.* If the effectiveness of two different treatment interventions is being studied, Intervention X_1 could be used with Experimental Group 1 and Intervention X_2 with Experimental Group 2.

There are certain variables, such as the gender or race of our research participants, that obviously cannot be manipulated because they are fixed. They do not vary, so they are called constants, not variables, as was pointed out in Chapter 4. Other constants, such as socioeconomic status or IQ, may vary for research participants over their life spans, but they are fixed quantities at the beginning of the study, probably will not change during the study, and are not subject to alteration by the one doing the study.

Any variable we can alter (e.g., treatment time) can be considered an independent variable. At least one independent variable must be manipulated in a research study if it is to be considered an "ideal" experiment.

Establishing Relationships Between Variables

The relationship between the independent and dependent variables must be established in order to infer a cause-effect relationship at the explanatory knowledge level. If the independent variable is considered to be the cause of the dependent variable, there must be some pattern in the relationship between these two variables. An example is the hypothesis: The more time clients spend in treatment (independent variable), the better their progress (dependent variable). See Box 4.1 for an interesting example of how hard it is to establish relationships between and among variables.

Controlling Rival Hypotheses

Rival hypotheses, or alternative hypotheses as described in Chapter 4, must be identified and eliminated in an "ideal" experiment. The logic of this requirement is extremely important, because this is what makes a cause-effect statement possible.

The prime question to ask when trying to identify a rival hypothesis is, "What other extraneous variables might affect the dependent variable?" (What else might affect the client's outcome besides treatment time?) At the risk of sounding redundant, "What else besides *X* might affect *Y*?" Perhaps the client's motivation for treatment, in addition to the time spent in treatment, might affect the client's outcome. If so, motivation for treatment is an extraneous variable that could be used as the independent variable in the rival hypothesis, "The higher the clients' motivation for treatment, the better their progress."

Perhaps the social worker's attitude toward the client might have an effect on the client's outcome, or the client might win the state lottery and ascend abruptly from depression to ecstasy. These extraneous variables could potentially be independent variables in other rival hypotheses. They must all be considered and eliminated before it can be said with reasonable certainty that a client's outcome resulted from the length of treatment time and not from any other extraneous variables.

Control over rival hypotheses refers to efforts on our part to identify and, if at all possible, to eliminate the extraneous variables in these alternative hypotheses. Of the many ways to deal with rival hypotheses, three of the most frequently used are to keep the extraneous variables constant, use correlated variation, or use analysis of covariance.

Keeping Extraneous Variables Constant

The most direct way to deal with rival hypotheses is to keep constant the critical extraneous variables that might affect the dependent variable. As we know, a constant cannot affect or be affected by any other variable. If an extraneous variable can be made into a constant, then it cannot affect either the study's real independent variable or the dependent variable.

Let us take an example to illustrate the above point. Suppose, for example, that a social worker who is providing counseling to anxious clients wants to relate client outcome to length of treatment time, but most of the clients are also being treated by a consulting psychiatrist with antidepressant medication. Because medication may also affect the clients' outcomes, it is a potential independent variable that could be used in a rival hypothesis. However, if the study included only clients who have been taking medication for some time before the treatment intervention began, and who continue to take the same medicine in the same way throughout treatment, then medication can be considered a constant (in this study, anyway).

Any change in the clients' anxiety levels after the intervention will, therefore, be due to the intervention with the help of the medication. The extraneous variable of medication, which might form a rival hypothesis, has been eliminated by holding it constant. In short, this study started out with one independent variable, the intervention, then added the variable of medication to it, so the final independent variable is the intervention plus the medication.

This is all very well in theory. In reality, however, a client's drug regime is usually controlled by the psychiatrist and may well be altered at any time. Even if the regime is not altered, the effects of the drugs might not become apparent until the study is under way. In addition, the client's level of anxiety might be affected by a host of other extraneous variables over which the social worker has no control at all: for example, living arrangements, relationships with other people, the condition of the stock market, or an unexpected visit from an IRS agent. These kinds of pragmatic difficulties tend to occur frequently in social work practice and research. It is often impossible to identify all rival hypotheses, let alone eliminate them by keeping them constant.

Using Correlated Variation

Rival hypotheses can also be controlled with correlated variation of the independent variables. Suppose, for example, that we are concerned that income has an effect on a client's compulsive behavior. The client's income, which in this case is subject to variation due to seasonal employment, is identified as an independent variable. The client's living conditions—in a hotel room rented by the week—are then identified as the second independent variable that might well affect the client's level of compulsive behavior. These two variables, however, are correlated since living conditions are highly dependent on income.

Correlated variation exists if one potential independent variable can be correlated with another. Then only one of them has to be dealt with in the research study.

Using Analysis of Covariance

In conducting an "ideal" experiment, we must always aim to use two or more groups that are as equivalent as possible on all important variables. Sometimes this goal is not feasible, however. Perhaps we are obliged to use existing groups that are not as equivalent as we would like. Or, perhaps during the course of the study we discover inequivalencies between the groups that were not apparent at the beginning.

A statistical method called *analysis of covariance* can be used to compensate for these differences. The mathematics of the method is far beyond the scope of this text, but an explanation can be found in most advanced statistics texts.

Using a Control Group

An "ideal" experiment should use at least one control group in addition to the experimental group. The experimental group may receive an intervention that is withheld from the control group, or equivalent groups may receive different interventions or no interventions at all.

A social worker who initiates a treatment intervention is often interested in knowing what would have happened if the intervention had not been used or had some different intervention been substituted. Would members of a support group for alcoholics have recovered anyway, without the social worker's efforts?

Would they have recovered faster or more completely had family counseling been used instead of the support group approach?

The answer to these questions will never be known if only the support group is studied. But, what if another group of alcoholics is included in the research design? In a typical design with a control group, two equivalent groups, 1 and 2, would be formed, and both would be administered the same pretest to determine the initial level of the dependent variable (e.g., degree of alcoholism). Then an intervention would be initiated with Group 1 but not with Group 2. The group treated—Group 1 or the experimental group—would receive the independent variable (the intervention). The group not treated—Group 2 or the control group—would not receive it.

At the conclusion of the intervention, both groups would be given a posttest (the same measure as the pretest). The pretest and posttest consist of the use of some sort of data-gathering procedure, such as a survey or self-report measure, to measure the dependent variable before and after the introduction of the independent variable. Group designs can be written in symbols as follows:

$$\text{Experimental Group: } R \quad O_1 \quad X \quad O_2$$
$$\text{Control Group: } R \quad O_1 \qquad O_2$$

Where:

R = Random assignment to group
O_1 = First measurement of the dependent variable
X = Independent variable
O_2 = Second measurement of the dependent variable

The two *R*s in this design indicate that the research participants were randomly assigned to each group. The symbol X, which, as usual, stands for the independent variable, indicates that an intervention is to be given to the experimental group after the pretest (O_1) and before the posttest (O_2). The absence of X for the control group indicates that the intervention is not to be given to the control group. This design is called a classical experimental design because it comes closest to having all the characteristics necessary for an "ideal" experiment.

Table 11.1 displays results from a research study of this type. If the experimental group is equivalent to the control group, the pretest results should be approximately the same for both groups. Within an acceptable margin of error, 24 is approximately the same as 26. Since the control group has not received the intervention, the posttest results for this group would not be expected to differ appreciably from the pretest results.

TABLE 11.1   CLIENTS' OUTCOMES
                   BY GROUP

Group	Pretest	Posttest	Difference
Experimental	24	68	– 44
Control	26	27	– 1

In fact, the posttest score, 27, differs little from the pretest score, 26, for the control group. Because the experimental and control groups may be considered equivalent, any rival hypotheses that affected the experimental group would have affected the control group in the same way. No rival hypothesis affected the control group, as indicated by the fact that without the intervention, the pretest and posttest scores did not differ. Therefore, it can be assumed that no rival hypothesis affected the experimental group, either, and the difference (–44) between pretest and posttest scores for the experimental group was probably due to the intervention and not to any other factor.

Randomly Assigning Research Participants to Groups

Once a sample has been selected (see previous chapter), the individuals (or objects or events) in it are randomly assigned to either an experimental or a control group in such a way that the two groups are equivalent. This procedure is known as random assignment or randomization. In random assignment, the word *equivalent* means equal in terms of the variables that are important to the study, such as the clients' motivation for treatment, or problem severity.

If the effect of treatment time on clients' outcomes is being studied, for example, the research design might use one experimental group that is treated for a comparatively longer time, a second experimental group that is treated for a shorter time, and a control group that is not treated at all. If we are concerned that the clients' motivation for treatment might also affect their outcomes, the research participants can be assigned so that all the groups are equivalent (on the average) in terms of their motivation for treatment.

The process of random sampling from a population followed by random assignment of the sample to groups is illustrated in Figure 11.1. Let us say that the research design calls for a sample size of one-tenth of the population. From a population of 10,000, therefore, a random sampling procedure is used to select a sample of 1,000 individuals.

Then random assignment procedures are used to place the sample of 1,000 into two equivalent groups of 500 individuals each. In theory, Group A will be equivalent to Group B, which will be equivalent to the random sample, which will be equivalent to the population in respect to all important variables contained within the research study.

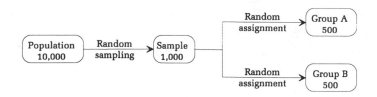

FIGURE 11.1   RANDOM SAMPLING AND
RANDOM ASSIGNMENT
PROCEDURES

Matched Pairs

Besides randomization, another, more deliberate method of assigning people or other units to groups involves matching. The matched pairs method is suitable when the composition of each group consists of variables with a range of characteristics. One of the disadvantages of matching is that some individuals cannot be matched and so cannot participate in the study.

Suppose a new training program for teaching parenting skills to foster mothers is being evaluated, and it is important that the experimental and control groups have an equal number of highly skilled and less skilled foster parents before the training program is introduced. The women chosen for the sample would be matched in pairs according to their parenting skill level; the two most skilled foster mothers are matched, then the next two, and so on. One person in each pair of approximately equally skilled foster parents is then randomly assigned to the experimental group and the other is placed in the control group.

Let us suppose that in order to compare the foster mothers exposed to the new training program with women who were not, a standardized measuring instrument that measures parenting skill level (the dependent variable) is administered to a sample of ten women. The scores can range from 100 (excellent parenting skills) to zero (poor parenting skills).

Then their scores are rank-ordered from the highest to the lowest, and out of the foster mothers with the two highest scores, one is selected to be assigned to either the experimental group or the control group. It does not make any difference which group our first research participant is randomly assigned to, as long as there is an equal chance that she will go to either the control group or the experimental group. In this example the first person is randomly chosen to go to the experimental group, as illustrated below and on the following page:

Rank Order of Parenting Skills Scores (in parentheses)

First Pair:
(99) Randomly assigned to the experimental group
(98) Assigned to the control group

Second Pair:
(97) Assigned to the control group
(96) Assigned to the experimental group

Third Pair:
(95) Assigned to the experimental group
(94) Assigned to the control group

Fourth Pair:
(93) Assigned to the control group
(92) Assigned to the experimental group

Fifth Pair:
(91) Assigned to the experimental group
(90) Assigned to the control group

The foster parent with the highest score (99) is randomly assigned to the experimental group, and this person's "match," with a score of 98, is assigned to the control group. This process is reversed with the next matched pair, where the first person is assigned to the control group and the match is assigned to the experimental group. If the assignment of research participants according to scores is not reversed for every other pair, one group will be higher than the other on the variable being matched.

To illustrate this point, suppose the first participant (highest score) in each match is always assigned to the experimental group. The experimental group's average score would be 95 (99 + 97 + 95 + 93 + 91 = 475/5 = 95), and the control group's average score would be 94 (98 + 96 + 94 + 92 + 90 = 470/5 = 94). If every other matched pair is reversed, however, as in the example, the average scores of the two groups are closer together; 94.6 for the experimental group (99 + 96 + 95 + 92 + 91 = 473/5 = 94.6) and 94.4 for the control group (98 + 97 + 94 + 93 + 90 = 472/5 = 94.4). In short, 94.6 and 94.4 (difference of 0.2) are closer together than 95 and 94 (difference of 1).

INTERNAL AND EXTERNAL VALIDITY

We must remember that the research design we finally select should always be evaluated on how close it comes to an "ideal" experiment in reference to the six characteristics presented at the beginning of this chapter. As stressed through out this book, most research designs used in social work do not closely resemble an "ideal" experiment. The research design finally selected needs to be evaluated on how well it meets its primary objective—to adequately answer a research question or to test a hypothesis. In short, a research design will be evaluated on how well it controls for internal and external validity factors.

Internal validity has to do with the ways in which the research design ensures that the introduction of the independent variable (if any) can be identi-fied as the sole cause of change in the dependent variable. In contrast, external validity has to do with the extent to which the research design allows for general-ization of the findings of the study to other groups and other situations.

Both internal and external validity are achieved in a research design by taking into account various threats that are inherent in all research efforts. A design for a study with both types of validity will recognize and attempt to control for potential factors that could affect our study's outcome or findings. An "ideal" experiment tries to control as many threats to internal and external validity as possible.

Threats to Internal Validity

In any explanatory research study, we should be able to conclude from our findings that the independent variable is, or is not, the only cause of change in the dependent variable. If our study does not have internal validity, such a conclusion is not possible, and the study's findings can be misleading.

Internal validity is concerned with one of the requirements for an "ideal" experiment—the control of rival hypotheses, or alternative explanations for what might bring about a change in the dependent variable. The higher the internal validity of any research study, the greater the extent to which rival hypotheses can be controlled; the lower the internal validity, the less they can be controlled. Thus, we must be prepared to rule out the effects of factors other than the inde-pendent variable that could influence the dependent variable.

History

The first threat to internal validity, history, refers to any outside event, either public or private, that may affect the dependent variable and was not taken into account in our research design. Many times, it refers to events occurring between the first and second measurement of the dependent variable (the pretest and the posttest). If events occur that have the potential to alter the second measurement, there would be no way of knowing how much (if any) of the observed change in the dependent variable is a function of the independent variable and how much is attributable to these events.

Suppose, for example, we are investigating the effects of an educational program on racial tolerance. We may decide to measure the dependent variable, racial tolerance in the community, before introducing the independent variable, the educational program.

The educational program is then implemented. Since it is the independent variable, it is represented by X. Finally, racial tolerance is measured again, after the program has run its course. This final measurement yields a posttest score, represented by O_2. The one-group pretest-posttest study design can be written as:

$$O_1 \quad X \quad O_2$$

Where:

O_1 = First measurement, or pretest score, of racial tolerance
X = Educational program (independent variable) (see Box 11.1)
O_2 = Second measurement, or posttest score, of racial tolerance

The difference between the values O_2 and O_1 represent the difference in racial tolerance in the community before and after the educational program. If the study is internally valid, $O_2 - O_1$ will be a crude measure of the effect of the educational program on racial tolerance; and this is what we were trying to discover. Suppose before the posttest could be administered, an outbreak of racial violence, such as the type that occurred in Los Angeles in the summer of 1992, occurred in the community. Violence can be expected to have a negative effect on racial tolerance, and the posttest scores may, therefore, show a lower level of tolerance than if the violence had not occurred. The effect, $O_2 - O_1$, will now be the combined effects of the educational program *and* the violence, not the effect of the program alone, as we intended.

Racial violence is an extraneous variable that we could not have anticipated and did not control for when designing the study. Other examples might include an earthquake, an election, illness, divorce, or marriage—any event, public or private that could affect the dependent variable. Any such variable that is unanticipated and uncontrolled for is an example of history.

BOX 11.1

TREATMENT: A VARIABLE OR A CONSTANT?

For instructional purposes, group designs are displayed using symbols where X is the independent variable (treatment) and O is the measure of the dependent variable. This presentation is accurate when studies are designed with two or more groups. When one-group designs are used, however, this interpretation does not hold. In one-group designs, the treatment, or program, cannot truly vary because all research participants have experienced the same event; that is, they all have experienced the program. Without a comparison or control group, treatment is considered a constant because it is a quality shared by all members in the research study. In short, *time* is the independent variable.

Maturation

Maturation, the second threat to internal validity, refers to changes, both physical and psychological, that take place in our research participants over time and can affect the dependent variable. Suppose that we are evaluating an interventive strategy designed to improve the behavior of adolescents who engage in delinquent behavior. Since the behavior of adolescents changes naturally as they mature, the observed changed behavior may have been due as much to their natural development as it was to the intervention strategy.

Maturation refers not only to physical or mental growth, however. Over time, people grow older, more or less anxious, more or less bored, and more or less motivated to take part in a research study. All these factors and many more can affect the way in which people respond when the dependent variable is measured a second or third time.

Testing

The third threat to internal validity, testing, is sometimes referred to as the initial measurement effect. Thus, the pretests that are the starting point for many research designs are another potential threat to internal validity. One of the most utilized research designs involves three steps: measuring some dependent variable, such as learning behavior in school or attitudes toward work; initiating a program to change that variable (the independent variable); then measuring the dependent variable again at the conclusion of the program.

This simple one-group pretest-posttest design can be written as follows:

$$O_1 \quad X \quad O_2$$

Where:

O_1 = First measurement of the dependent variable, or pretest score
X = Independent variable (see Box 11.1)
O_2 = Second measurement of the dependent variable, or posttest score

The testing effect is the effect that taking a pretest might have on posttest scores. Suppose that Roberto, a research participant, takes a pretest to measure his initial level of racial tolerance before being exposed to a racial tolerance educational program. He might remember some of the questions on the pretest, think about them later, and change his views on racial issues before taking part in the educational program. After the program, his posttest score will reveal his changed opinions, and we may incorrectly assume that the program was responsible, whereas the true cause was his experience with the pretest.

Sometimes, a pretest induces anxiety in a research participant, so that Roberto receives a worse score on the posttest than he should have; or boredom with the same questions repeated again may be a factor. In order to avoid the testing effect, we may wish to use a design that does not require a pretest. If a pretest is essential, we then must consider the length of time that elapses between the pretest and posttest measurements. A pretest is far more likely to affect the posttest when the time between the two is short. The nature of the pretest is another factor. Questions dealing with factual matters, such as knowledge levels, may have a larger testing effect because they tend to be more easily recalled.

Instrumentation Error

The fourth threat to internal validity is instrumentation error, which refers to all the troubles that can afflict the measurement process. The instrument may be unreliable or invalid, as presented in Chapter 7. It may be a mechanical instrument, such as an electroencephalogram (EEG), that has malfunctioned. Occasionally, the term *instrumentation error* is used to refer to an observer whose observations are inconsistent; or to measuring instruments, such as the ones presented in Chapter 8, that are reliable in themselves, but not administered properly.

"Administration," with respect to a measuring instrument, means the circumstances under which the measurement is made: where, when, how, and by whom. A mother being asked about her attitudes toward her children, for example, may respond in one way in the social worker's office and in a different way at home when her children are screaming around her feet.

A mother's verbal response may differ from her written response; or she may respond differently in the morning than she would in the evening, or differently alone than she would in a group. These variations in situational responses do not indicate a true change in the feelings, attitudes, or behaviors being measured, but are only examples of instrumentation error.

Statistical Regression

The fifth threat to internal validity, statistical regression, refers to the tendency of extremely low and extremely high scores to regress, or move toward the average score for everyone in the research study. Suppose that a student, named Maryanna, has to take a multiple-choice exam on a subject she knows nothing about. There are many questions, and each question has five possible answers. Since, for each question, Maryanna has a 20 percent (one in five) chance of guessing correctly, she might expect to score 20 percent on the exam just by guessing. If she guesses badly, she will score a lot lower; if well, a lot higher. The other members of the class take the same exam and, since they are all equally uninformed, the average score for the class is 20 percent.

Now suppose that the instructor separates the low scorers from the high scorers and tries to even out the level of the class by giving the low scorers special instruction. In order to determine if the special instruction has been effective, the entire class then takes another multiple-choice exam. The result of the exam is that the low scorers (as a group) do better than they did the first time, and the high scorers (as a group) worse. The instructor believes that this has occurred because the low scorers received special instruction and the high scorers did not.

According to the logic of statistical regression, however, both the average score of the low scorers (as a group) and the average score of the high scorers (as a group) would move toward the total average score for both groups (i.e., high and low). Even without any special instruction and still in their state of ignorance, the low scorers (as a group) would be expected to have a higher average score than they did before. Likewise, the high scorers (as a group) would be expected to have a lower average score than they did before.

It would be easy for the research instructor to assume that the low scores had increased because of the special instruction and the high scores had decreased because of the lack of it. Not necessarily so, however; the instruction may have had nothing to do with it. It may all be due to statistical regression.

Differential Selection of Research Participants

The sixth threat to internal validity is differential selection of research participants. To some extent, the participants selected for a research study are different from one another to begin with. "Ideal" experiments, however, require random sampling from a population (if at all possible) and random assignment to groups. This assures that the results of a study will be generalizable to a larger population, thus addressing threats to external validity. In respect to differential selection as a threat to internal validity, "ideal" experiments control for this since equivalency among the groups at pretest is assumed through the randomization process.

This threat is, however, present when we are working with preformed groups or groups that already exist, such as classes of students, self-help groups, or community groups. In terms of the external validity of such designs, because there is no way of knowing whether the preformed groups are representative of any larger population, it is not possible to generalize the study's results beyond the people (or objects or events) that were actually studied. The use of preformed groups also affects the internal validity of a study, though. It is probable that different preformed groups will not be equivalent with respect to relevant variables, and that these initial differences will invalidate the results of the posttest.

A child abuse prevention educational program for children in schools might be evaluated by comparing the prevention skills of one group of children who have experienced the educational program with the skills of a second group who have not. In order to make a valid comparison, the two groups must be as similar as possible, with respect to age, gender, intelligence, socioeconomic status, and anything else that might affect the acquisition of child abuse prevention skills. We would have to make every effort to form or select equivalent groups, but the groups are sometimes not as equivalent as might be hoped—especially if we are obliged to work with preformed groups, such as classes of students or community groups. If the two groups are different before the intervention was introduced, there is not much point in comparing them at the end.

Accordingly, preformed groups should be avoided whenever possible. If it is not feasible to do this, rigorous pretesting must be done to determine in what ways the groups are (or are not) equivalent, and differences must be compensated for with the use of statistical methods.

Mortality

The seventh threat to internal validity is mortality, which simply means that individual research participants may drop out before the end of the study. Their absence will probably have a significant effect on the study's findings because people who drop out are likely to be different in some ways from the other participants who stay in the study. People who drop out may be less motivated to participate in the intervention than people who stay in, for example.

Since dropouts often have such characteristics in common, it cannot be assumed that the attrition occurred in a random manner. If considerably more people drop out of one group than out of the other, the result will be two groups that are no longer equivalent and cannot be usefully compared. We cannot know at the beginning of the study how many people will drop out, but we can watch to see how many do. Mortality is never problematic if dropout rates are five percent or less *and* if the dropout rates are similar for the various groups.

Reactive Effects of Research Participants

The eighth threat to internal validity is reactive effects. Changes in the behaviors or feelings of research participants may be caused by their reaction to the novelty of the situation or the knowledge that they are participating in a research study. A mother practicing communication skills with her child, for example, may try especially hard when she knows the social worker is watching. We may wrongly believe that such reactive effects are due to the independent variable.

The classic example of reactive effects was found in a series of studies carried out at the Hawthorne plant of the Western Electric Company in Chicago many years ago. Researchers were investigating the relationship between working conditions and productivity. When they increased the level of lighting in one section of the plant, productivity increased; a further increase in the lighting was followed by an additional increase in productivity. When the lighting was then decreased, however, production levels did not fall accordingly but continued to rise. The conclusion was that the workers were increasing their productivity not because of the lighting level but because of the attention they were receiving as research participants in the study.

The term *Hawthorne effect* is still used to describe any situation in which the research participants' behaviors are influenced not by the independent variable but by the knowledge that they are taking part in a research project. (See Box 1.1 for additional details of the Hawthorne experiment.) Another example of such a reactive effect is the placebo or sugar pill given to patients, which produces beneficial results because they believe it is medication.

Reactive effects can be controlled by ensuring that all participants in a research study, in both the experimental and control groups, appear to be treated equally. If one group is to be shown an educational film, for example, the other group should also be shown a film—some film carefully chosen to bear no relationship to the variable being investigated. If the study involves a change in the participants' routine, this in itself may be enough to change behavior, and care must be taken to continue the study until novelty has ceased to be a factor.

Interaction Effects

Interaction among the various threats to internal validity can have an effect of its own. Any of the factors already described as threats may interact with one another, but the most common interactive effect involves differential selection and maturation.

Let us say we are studying two groups of clients who are being treated for depression. The intention was for these groups to be equivalent, in terms of both their motivation for treatment and their levels of depression. It turns out that Group A is more generally depressed than Group B, however. Whereas both groups may grow less motivated over time, it is likely that Group A, whose members were more depressed to begin with, will lose motivation more completely and more quickly than Group B. Inequivalent groups thus grow less equivalent over time as a result of the interaction between differential selection and maturation.

Relations Between Experimental and Control Groups

The final group of threats to internal validity has to do with the effects of the use of experimental and control groups that receive different interventions. These effects include: (1) diffusion of treatments, (2) compensatory equalization, (3) compensatory rivalry, and (4) demoralization.

Diffusion of Treatments   Diffusion, or imitation of treatments, may occur when the experimental and control groups talk to each other about the study. Suppose a study is designed that presents a new relaxation exercise to the experimental group and nothing at all to the control group. There is always the possibility that one of the participants in the experimental group will explain the exercise to a friend who happens to be in the control group. The friend explains it to another friend, and so on. This might be beneficial for the control group, but it invalidates the study's findings.

Compensatory Equalization   Compensatory equalization of treatment occurs when the person doing the study and/or the staff member administering the intervention to the experimental group feels sorry for people in the control group who are not receiving it and attempts to compensate them. A social worker might take a control group member aside and covertly demonstrate the relaxation exercise, for example. On the other hand, if our study has been ethically designed, there should be no need for guilt on the part of the social worker because some people are not being taught to relax. They can be taught to relax when our study is "officially" over.

Compensatory Rivalry   Compensatory rivalry is an effect that occurs when the control group becomes motivated to compete with the experimental group. For example, a control group in a program to encourage parental involvement in school activities might get wind that something is up and make a determined effort to participate too, on the basis that "anything they can do, we can do better." There is no direct communication between groups, as in the diffusion of treatment effect—only rumors and suggestions of rumors. However, rumors are often enough to threaten the internal validity of a study.

Demoralization   In direct contrast with compensatory rivalry, demoralization refers to feelings of deprivation among the control group that may cause them to give up and drop out of the study, in which case this effect would be referred to as mortality. The people in the control group may also get angry.

Threats to External Validity

External validity is the degree to which the results of our research study are generalizable to a larger population or to settings outside the research situation or setting.

Pretest-Treatment Interaction

The first threat to external validity, pretest-treatment interaction, is similar to the testing threat to internal validity. The nature of a pretest can alter the way research participants respond to the experimental treatment, as well as to the posttest. Suppose, for example, that an educational program on racial tolerance is being evaluated. A pretest that measures the level of tolerance could well alert the participants to the fact that they are going to be educated into loving all their neighbors, but many people do not want to be "educated" into anything. They are satisfied with the way they feel and will resist the instruction. This will affect the level of racial tolerance registered on the posttest.

Selection-Treatment Interaction

The second threat to external validity is selection-treatment interaction. This threat commonly occurs when a research design cannot provide for random selection of participants from a population. Suppose we wanted to study the effectiveness of a family service agency staff, for example. If our research proposal was turned down by 50 agencies before it was accepted by the 51st, it is very likely that the accepting agency differs in certain important aspects from the other 50. It may accept the proposal because its social workers are more highly motivated, more secure, more satisfied with their jobs, or more interested in the practical application of the study than the average agency staff member.

As a result, we would be assessing the research participants on the very factors for which they were unwittingly (and by default) selected—motivation, job satisfaction, and so on. The study may be internally valid, but, since it will not be possible to generalize the results to other family service agencies, it would have little external validity.

Specificity of Variables

Specificity of variables has to do with the fact that a research project conducted with a specific group of people at a specific time and in a specific setting may not always be generalizable to other people at a different time and in a different setting. For example, a measuring instrument developed to measure the IQ levels of upper-socioeconomic level, Caucasian, suburban children does not provide an equally accurate measure of IQ when it is applied to lower-socioeconomic level children of racial minorities in the inner city.

Reactive Effects

The fourth threat to external validity is reactive effects which, as with internal validity, occur when the attitudes or behaviors of our research participants are affected to some degree by the very act of taking a pretest. Thus, they are no longer exactly equivalent to the population from which they were randomly selected, and it may not be possible to generalize our study's results to that population. Because pretests affect research participants to some degree, our results may be valid only for those who were pretested.

Multiple-Treatment Interference

The fifth threat to external validity, multiple-treatment interference, occurs if a research participant is given two or more interventions in succession, so that the results of the first intervention may affect the results of the second one. A client attending treatment sessions, for example, may not seem to benefit from one therapeutic technique, so another is tried. In fact, however, the client may have benefitted from the first technique but the benefit does not become apparent until the second technique has been tried. As a result, the effects of both techniques become commingled, or the results may be erroneously ascribed to the second technique alone.

Because of this threat, interventions should be given separately if possible. If our research design does not allow this, sufficient time should be allowed to elapse between the two interventions in an effort to minimize the possibility of multiple-treatment interference.

Researcher Bias

The final threat to external validity is researcher bias. Researchers, like people in general, tend to see what they want to see or expect to see. Unconsciously and without any thought of deceit, they may manipulate a study so that the actual results agree with the anticipated results. A practitioner may favor an intervention so strongly that the research study is structured to support it, or the results are interpreted favorably.

If we know which individuals are in the experimental group and which are in the control group, this knowledge alone might affect the study's results. Students who an instructor believes to be bright, for example, often are given higher grades than their performance warrants, while students believed to be dull are given lower grades. The way to control for such researcher bias is to perform a double-blind experiment in which neither the research participants nor the researcher knows who is in the experimental or control group or who is receiving a specific treatment intervention.

GROUP RESEARCH DESIGNS

While, in a particular case, a group research design may need to be complex to accomplish the purpose of the study, a design that is unnecessarily complex costs more, takes more time, and probably will not serve its purpose nearly as well as a simpler one. In choosing a research design (whether a single case [see

TABLE 11.2   KNOWLEDGE LEVELS AND CORRESPONDING
RESEARCH DESIGNS

Knowledge Levels	Research Designs
1. EXPLORATORY	a: One-group posttest-only b: Multigroup posttest-only c: Longitudinal case study d: Longitudinal survey
2. DESCRIPTIVE	a: Randomized one-group posttest-only b: Randomized cross-sectional and longitudinal survey c: One-group pretest-posttest d: Comparison group posttest-only e: Comparison group pretest-posttest f: Interrupted time-series
3. EXPLANATORY	a: Classical experimental b: Solomon four-group c: Randomized posttest-only control group

next chapter] or group), therefore, the principle of parsimony must be applied: The simplest and most economical route to the objective is the best choice. The three knowledge levels and the group research designs that are usually associated with each are listed in Table 11.2 above.

Exploratory Designs

At the lowest level of the continuum of knowledge that can be derived from research studies are exploratory group research designs. An exploratory study explores a research question about which little is already known, in order to uncover generalizations and develop hypotheses that can be investigated and tested later with more precise and, hence, more complex designs and data-gathering techniques.

The four examples of exploratory designs given in this section do not use pretests; they simply measure the dependent variable only after the independent variable has been introduced. Therefore, they cannot be used to determine whether changes took place in the study's research participants; these designs simply describe the state of the research participants after they had received the independent variable (if any—see Box 11.1).

There does not necessarily have to be an independent variable in a study, however; we may just want to measure some variable in a particular population such as the number of people who receive AFDC benefits over a ten-year period. In this situation, there is no independent or dependent variable.

One-Group Posttest-Only Design

The one-group posttest-only design (Design 1a) is sometimes called the one-shot case study or cross-sectional case study design. It is the simplest of all the group research designs.

Suppose in a particular community, Rome, Wisconsin, there are numerous parents who are physically abusive toward their children. The city decides to hire a school social worker, Antonia, to implement a program that is supposed to reduce the number of parents who physically abuse their children. She conceptualizes a 12-week child abuse prevention program (the intervention) and offers it to parents who have children in her school who wish to participate on a voluntary basis. A simple research study is then conducted to answer the question, "Did the parents who completed the program stop physically abusing their children?" The answer to this question will determine the success of the intervention.

There are many different ways in which this program can be evaluated. For now, and to make matters as simple as possible, we are going to evaluate it by simply counting how many parents stopped physically abusing their children after they attended the program.

At the simplest level, the program could be evaluated with a one-group posttest-only design. The basic elements of this design can be written as follows:

$$X \quad O_1$$

Where:

X = Independent variable (Child Abuse Prevention Program, the intervention) (see Box 11.1)

O_1 = First and only measurement of the dependent variable (number of parents who stopped physically abusing their children, the program's outcome, or program objective)

All that this design provides is a single measure (O_1) of what happens when one group of people is subjected to one treatment or experience (X). The program's participants were not randomly selected from any particular population, and, thus, the results of the findings cannot be generalized to any other group or population.

It is safe to assume that all the members within the program had physically abused their children before they enrolled, since people who do not have this problem would not enroll in such a program. But, even if the value of O_1 indicates that some of the parents did stop being violent with their children after the program, it cannot be determined whether they quit because of the intervention (the program) or because of some other rival hypothesis.

Perhaps a law was passed that made it mandatory for the police to arrest anyone who behaves violently toward his or her child, or perhaps the local television station started to report such incidents on the nightly news, complete with pictures of the abusive parent. These other extraneous variables may have been more important in persuading the parents to cease their abusive behavior toward their children than their voluntary participation in the program. In sum, this design does not control for many of the threats to either internal or external validity. In terms of internal validity, the threats that are applicable and that are not controlled for in this design are history, maturation, differential selection, and mortality.

Cross-Sectional Survey Design   Let us take another example of a one-group posttest-only design that *does not* have an independent or dependent variable. In survey research, this kind of a group research design is called a cross-sectional survey design.

In doing a cross-sectional survey, we survey *only once* a cross-section of some particular population. In addition to Antonia's child abuse prevention program geared for abusive parents, she may also want to start another program geared for all the children in the school (whether they come from abusive families or not)—a child abuse educational program taught to children in the school.

Before Antonia starts the program geared for the children, however, she wants to know what parents think about the idea. She may send out questionnaires to all the parents or she may decide to personally telephone every second parent, or every fifth or tenth, depending on how much time and money she has. The results of her survey constitute a single measurement, or observation, of the parents' opinions of her second proposed program (the one for the children) and may be written as:

$$O_1$$

The symbol O_1 represents the entire cross-sectional survey design since such a design involves making only a single observation, or measurement, at one time period. Note that there is no X, as there is really no independent variable. Antonia only wants to ascertain the parents' attitudes toward her proposed program—nothing more, nothing less.

Multigroup Posttest-Only Design

The multigroup posttest-only design (Design 1b) is an elaboration of the one-group posttest-only design (Design 1a) in which more than one group is used. To check a bit further into the effectiveness of Antonia's program for parents who have been physically abusive toward their children, for example, she might decide to locate several more groups of parents who had completed her program and see how many of them had stopped abusing their children—and so on, with any number of groups. This design can be written in symbols as follows:

$$
\begin{array}{lll}
\text{Experimental Group 1:} & X & O_1 \\
\text{Experimental Group 2:} & X & O_1 \\
\text{Experimental Group 3:} & X & O_1 \\
\text{Experimental Group 4:} & X & O_1 \\
\end{array}
$$

Where:

X = Independent variable (Child Abuse Prevention Program, the intervention) (see Box 11.1)

O_1 = First and only measurement of the dependent variable (number of parents who stopped physically abusing their children, the program's outcome, or program objective)

With the multigroup design it cannot be assumed that all four Xs (the independent variables) are equivalent because the four programs might not be exactly the same; one group might have had a different facilitator, the program might have been presented differently, or the material could have varied in important respects.

In addition, nothing is known about whether any of the research participants would have stopped being violent anyway, even without the program. It certainly cannot be assumed that any of the groups were representative of the larger population. Thus, as in the case of the one group posttest-only design, the same threats to the internal and the external validity of the study might influence the results of the multigroup posttest design.

Longitudinal Case Study Design

The longitudinal case study design (Design 1c) is exactly like the one-group posttest-only design (Design 1a), except that it provides for more measurements of the dependent variable (Os). This design can be written in symbols as follows:

$$X \quad O_1 \quad O_2 \quad O_3 \ldots$$

Where:

X = Independent variable (Child Abuse Prevention Program, the intervention) (see Box 11.1)

O_1 = First measurement of the dependent variable (number of parents who stopped physically abusing their children, the program's outcome, or program objective)

O_2 = Second measurement of the dependent variable (number of parents who stopped physically abusing their children, the program's outcome, or program objective)

O_3 = Third measurement of the dependent variable (number of parents who stopped physically abusing their children, the program's outcome, or program objective)

Suppose that, in our example, Antonia is interested in the long-term effects of the child abuse prevention program. Perhaps the program was effective in helping some people to stop physically abusing their children, but will they continue to refrain from abusing their children? One way to find out is to measure the number of parents who physically abuse their children at intervals— say at the end of the program, the first three months after the program, then the next three months after that, and every three months for the next two years.

Design 1c can be used to monitor the effectiveness of treatment interventions over time and can be applied not just to groups but also to single client systems, as described in Chapters 12 and 23. However, all of the same threats to the internal and external validity that were described in relation to the previous two exploratory designs also apply to this design.

Longitudinal Survey Design

Unlike cross-sectional surveys, where the variable of interest (usually the dependent variable) is measured only once, longitudinal surveys (Design 1d) provide data at various points so that changes can be monitored over time. Longitudinal survey designs can be written as:

$$O_1 \quad O_2 \quad O_3$$

Where:

O_1 = First measurement of some variable
O_2 = Second measurement of some variable
O_3 = Third measurement of some variable

Longitudinal survey designs usually have no independent and dependent variables and can broken down into three types: (1) trend studies, (2) cohort studies, and (3) panel studies.

Trend Studies   A trend study is used to find out how a population, or sample, changes over time. Antonia, the school social worker mentioned previously, may want to know if parents of young children enroled in her school are becoming more receptive to the idea of the school teaching their children child abuse prevention education in the second grade. She may survey all the parents of Grade 2 children this year, all the parents of the new complement of Grade 2 children next year, and so on until she thinks she has sufficient data.

Each year the parents surveyed will be different, but they will all be parents of Grade 2 children. In this way, Antonia will be able to determine whether parents are becoming more receptive to the idea of introducing child abuse prevention material to their children as early as Grade 2. In other words, she will be able to measure any attitudinal trend that is, or is not, occurring. The research design can still be written:

$$O_1 \quad O_2 \quad O_3$$

Where:

O_1 = First measurement of some variable for a sample
O_2 = Second measurement of some variable for a different sample
O_3 = Third measurement of some variable for yet another different sample

Cohort Studies   Cohort studies are used over time to follow a group of people who have shared a similar experience—for example, AIDS survivors, sexual abuse survivors, or parents of grade-school children. Perhaps Antonia is interested in knowing whether parents' attitudes toward the school offering abuse prevention education to second-grade students change as their children grow older. She may survey a sample of the Grade 2 parents who attend a Parent Night this year, and survey a different sample of parents who attend a similar meeting from the same parents next year, when their children are in Grade 3.

The following year, when the children are in Grade 4, she will take another, different sample of those parents who attend Parent Night. Although different parents are being surveyed every year, they all belong to the same population of parents whose children are progressing through the grades together. The selection of the samples was not random, though, because parents who take the time to attend Parent Night may be different from those who stay at home. The research design may be written:

$$O_1 \quad O_2 \quad O_3$$

Where:

O_1 = First measurement of some variable for a sample drawn from some population

O_2 = Second measurement of some variable for a different sample drawn from the same population one year later

O_3 = Third measurement of some variable for a still different sample, drawn from the same population after two years

Panel Studies   In a panel study, the *same individuals* are followed over a period of time. Antonia might select one particular sample of parents, for example, and measure their attitudes toward child abuse prevention education in successive years. Again, the design can be written:

$$O_1 \quad O_2 \quad O_3$$

Where:

O_1 = First measurement of some variable for a sample of individuals

O_2 = Second measurement of some variable for the same sample of individuals one year later

O_3 = Third measurement of some variable for the same sample of individuals after two years

A trend study is interested in broad trends over time, whereas a cohort study provides data about people who have shared similar experiences. In neither case do we know anything about *individual* contributions to the changes that are being measured. A panel study provides data that we can use to look at change over time as experienced by particular individuals.

Descriptive Designs

At the midpoint of the knowledge continuum are descriptive designs, which have some but not all of the requirements of an "ideal" experiment. They usually require specification of the time order of variables, manipulation of the independent variable, and establishment of the relationship between the independent and dependent variables. They may also control for rival hypotheses and use a second group as a comparison (not a control). The requirement that descriptive designs lack most frequently is the random assignment of research participants to two or more groups.

We are seldom in a position to randomly assign research participants to either an experimental or control group. Sometimes the groups to be studied are already in existence; sometimes ethical issues are involved. It would be unethical, for example, to assign clients who need immediate help to two random groups, only one of which is to receive the intervention. Since a lack of random assignment will affect the internal and external validities of the study, the descriptive research design must try to compensate for this.

Randomized One-Group Posttest-Only Design

The distinguishing feature of the randomized one-group posttest-only design (Design 2a) is that members of the group are randomly selected for it. Otherwise, this design is identical to the exploratory one-group posttest-only design (Design 1a). The randomized one-group posttest-only design is written as follows:

$$R \quad X \quad O_1$$

Where:

R = Random selection from a population
X = Independent variable (see Box 11.1)
O_1 = First and only measurement of the dependent variable

In the example of the child abuse prevention program, the difference in this design is that the group does not accidentally assemble itself by including anyone who happened to be interested in volunteering for the program. Instead, group members are randomly selected from a population, say, of all the 400 parents who were reported to child welfare authorities for having physically abused a child and who wish to receive voluntary treatment in Rome, Wisconsin, in 1997. These 400 parents comprise the population of all the physically abusive parents who wish to receive treatment in Rome, Wisconsin.

The sampling frame of 400 people is used to select a simple random sample of 40 physically abusive parents who voluntarily wish to receive treatment. The program (X) is administered to these 40 people, and the number of parents who stopped being abusive toward their children after the program is determined (O_1). The design can be written as:

$$R \quad X \quad O_1$$

Where:

R = Random selection of 40 people from the population of physically abusive parents who voluntarily wish to receive treatment in Rome, Wisconsin

X = Child Abuse Prevention Program (see Box 11.1)

O_1 = Number of parents in the program who stopped being physically abusive to their children

Say that the program fails to have the desired effect, and 39 of the 40 people continue to physically harm their children after participating in the program. Because the program was ineffective for the sample and the sample was randomly selected, it can be concluded that it would be ineffective for the physically abusive parent population of Rome, Wisconsin—the other 360 who did not go through the program. In other words, because a representative random sample was selected, it is possible to generalize the program's results to the population from which the sample was drawn.

Since no change in the dependent variable occurred, it is not sensible to consider the control of rival hypotheses. Antonia need not wonder what might have caused the change—X, her program, or an alternative explanation. If her program had been successful, however, it would not be possible to ascribe her success solely to the program.

Randomized Cross-Sectional and Longitudinal Survey Design

As discussed earlier, a cross-sectional survey obtains data only once from a sample of a particular population. If the sample is a random sample—that is, if it represents the population from which it was drawn—then the data obtained from the sample can be generalized to the entire population. A cross-sectional survey design using a random sample can be written:

$$R \quad O_1$$

Where:

R = Random sample drawn from a population
O_1 = First and only measurement of the dependent variable (see Box 11.1)

Explanatory surveys look for associations between variables. Often, the suspected reason for the relationship is that one variable caused the other. In Antonia's case, she has two studies going on: the child abuse prevention program for parents who have physically abused their children, and her survey of parental attitudes toward the school that is teaching second-grade children child abuse prevention strategies. The success of the child abuse prevention program (her program) may have caused parents to adopt more positive attitudes toward the school in teaching their children child abuse prevention (her survey). In this situation, the two variables, the program and survey, become commingled.

Demonstrating causality is a frustrating business at the best of times because it is so difficult to show that nothing apart from the independent variable could have caused the observed change in the dependent variable. Even supposing that this problem is solved, it is impossible to demonstrate causality unless data are obtained from random samples and are generalizable to entire populations.

One-Group Pretest-Posttest Design

The one-group pretest-posttest design (Design 2c) is also referred to as a before-after design because it includes a pretest of the dependent variable, which can be used as a basis of comparison with the posttest results. It is written as:

$$O_1 \quad X \quad O_2$$

Where:

O_1 = First measurement of the dependent variable
X = Independent variable, the intervention (see Box 11.1)
O_2 = Second measurement of the dependent variable

The one-group pretest-posttest design, in which a pretest precedes the introduction of the independent variable and a posttest follows it, can be used to determine precisely how the independent variable affects a particular group. The design is used often in social work decision making—far too often, in fact, because it does not control for many rival hypotheses. The difference between O_1 and O_2, on which these decisions are based, therefore, could be due to many other factors rather than the independent variable.

Let us take another indicator of how Antonia's child abuse prevention program could be evaluated. Besides counting the number of parents who stopped physically abusing their children as the only indicator of the program's success, she could have a second outcome indicator such as reducing the parents' risk for abusive and neglecting parenting behaviors. This dependent variable could be easily measured by an instrument that measures their attitudes of physical punishment of children.

Let us say that Antonia had the parents complete the instrument *before* the child abuse prevention program (O_1) and *after* it (O_2). In this example, history would be a rival hypothesis or threat to internal validity because all kinds of things could have happened between O_1 and O_2 to affect the participants' behaviors and feelings—such as the television station deciding to publicize the names of parents who are abusive to their children. Testing also could be a problem. Just the experience of taking the pretest could motivate some participants to stop being abusive toward their children. Maturation—in this example, the children becoming more mature with age so that they became less difficult to discipline—would be a further threat.

This design controls for the threat of differential selection, since the participants are the same for both pretest and posttest. Second, mortality would not affect the outcome, because it is the differential drop-out between groups that causes this threat and, in this example, there is only one group.

Comparison Group Posttest-Only Design

The comparison group posttest-only design (Design 2d) improves on the exploratory one-group and multigroup posttest-only designs by introducing a comparison group that does not receive the independent variable, but is subject to the same posttest as those who do (the experimental group).

A group used for purposes of comparison is usually referred to as a comparison group in an exploratory or descriptive design and as a control group in an explanatory design. While a control group is always randomly assigned, a comparison group is not. The basic elements of the comparison group posttest-only design are as follows:

> Experimental Group: X O_1
> Comparison Group: O_1

Where:

X = Independent variable, the intervention
O_1 = First and only measurement of the dependent variable

In Antonia's child abuse prevention program, if the January, April, and August sections are scheduled but the August sessions are canceled for some reason, those who would have been participants in that section could be used as a comparison group. If the values of O_1 on the measuring instrument were similar for the experimental and comparison groups, it could be concluded that the program was of little use, since those who had experienced it (those receiving X) were not much better or worse off than those who had not.

A problem with drawing this conclusion, however, is that there is no evidence that the groups were equivalent to begin with. Selection, mortality, and the interaction of selection and other threats to internal validity are, thus, the major difficulties with this design. The comparison group does, however, control for such threats as history, testing, instrumentation, and statistical regression.

Comparison Group Pretest-Posttest Design

The comparison group pretest-posttest design (Design 2e) elaborates on the one-group pretest-posttest design (Design 2c) by adding a comparison group. This second group receives both the pretest (O_1) and the posttest (O_2) at the same time as the experimental group, but it does not receive the independent variable. This design is written as follows:

> Experimental Group: O_1 X O_2
> Comparison Group: O_1 O_2

Where:

O_1 = First measurement of the dependent variable, the parents' scores on the measuring instrument

X = Independent variable, the intervention

O_2 = Second measurement of the dependent variable, the parents' scores on the measuring instrument

The experimental and comparison groups formed under this design will probably not be equivalent, because members are not randomly assigned to them. The pretest scores, however, will indicate the extent of their differences. If the differences are not statistically significant, but are still large enough to affect the posttest, the statistical technique of analysis of covariance can be used to compensate for this. As long as the groups are equivalent at pretest, then, this design controls for nearly all of the threats to internal validity. But, because random selection and assignment were not used, the external validity threats remain.

Interrupted Time-Series Design

In the interrupted time-series design (Design 2f), a series of pretests and posttests are conducted on a group of research participants over time, both before and after the independent variable is introduced. The basic elements of this design are illustrated as follows:

$$O_1 \quad O_2 \quad O_3 \quad X \quad O_4 \quad O_5 \quad O_6$$

Where:

Os = Measurements of the dependent variable

X = Independent variable (see Box 11.1)

This design takes care of the major weakness in the descriptive one-group pretest-posttest design (Design 2c), which does not control for rival hypotheses. Suppose, for example, that a new policy is to be introduced into an agency whereby all promotions and raises are to be tied to the number of educational credits acquired by social workers. Since there is a strong feeling among some workers that years of experience should count for more than educational credits, the agency's management decides to examine the effect of the new policy on morale.

Because agency morale is affected by many things and varies normally from month to month, it is necessary to ensure that these normal fluctuations are not confused with the results of the new policy. Therefore, a baseline is first established for morale by conducting a number of pretests over, say, a six-month period before the policy is introduced. Then, a similar number of posttests is conducted over the six months following the introduction of the policy. This design would be written as follows:

$$O_1 \quad O_2 \quad O_3 \quad O_4 \quad O_5 \quad O_6 \quad X \quad O_7 \quad O_8 \quad O_9 \quad O_{10} \quad O_{11} \quad O_{12}$$

The same type of time-series design can be used to evaluate the result of a treatment intervention with a client or client system, as in case-level designs described in Chapter 21. Again, without randomization, threats to external validity still could affect the results, but most of the threats to internal validity are addressed.

Explanatory Designs

Explanatory group research designs approach the "ideal" experiment most closely. They are at the highest level of the knowledge continuum, have the most rigid requirements, and are most able to produce results that can be generalized to other people and situations. Explanatory designs, therefore, are most able to provide valid and reliable research results that can serve as additions to our professions' knowledge base.

The purpose of an explanatory design is to establish a causal connection between the independent and dependent variable. The value of the dependent variable could always result from chance rather than from the influence of the independent variable, but there are statistical techniques for calculating the probability that this will occur.

Classical Experimental Design

The classical experimental design (Design 3a) is the basis for all the experimental designs. It involves an experimental group and a control group, both created by a random assignment method (and if possible, random selection from a population). Both groups take a pretest (O_1) at the same time, after which the independent variable (X) is given only to the experimental group, and then both groups take the posttest (O_2). This design is written as follows:

```
Experimental Group:  R   O₁  X  O₂
     Control Group:  R   O₁      O₂
```

Where:

R = Random selection from a population and random assignment to group
O_1 = First measurement of the dependent variable
X = Independent variable, the intervention
O_2 = Second measurement of the dependent variable

Because the experimental and control groups have been randomly assigned, they are equivalent with respect to all important variables. This group equivalence in the design helps control for rival hypotheses, because both groups would be affected by them in the same way.

Solomon Four-Group Design

The Solomon four-group research design (Design 3b) involves four rather than two randomly assigned groups as in Design 3a. There are two experimental groups and two control groups, but the pretest is taken by only one of each of these groups. Experimental Group 1 takes a pretest, receives the independent variable, and then takes a posttest. Experimental Group 2 also receives the independent variable but takes only the posttest. The same is true for the two control groups; Control Group 1 takes both the pretest and posttest, and Control Group 2 takes only the posttest. This design is written in symbols as follows:

```
Experimental Group 1:  R   O₁  X  O₂
     Control Group 1:  R   O₁      O₂
Experimental Group 2:  R       X  O₂
     Control Group 2:  R           O₂
```

Where:

R = Random assignment to group
O_1 = First measurement of the dependent variable
X = Independent variable, the intervention
O_2 = Second measurement of the dependent variable

The advantage of the Solomon four-group research design is that it allows for the control of testing effects, since one of the experimental groups and one of the control groups do not take the pretest. All of the threats to internal validity are addressed when this design is used. It has the disadvantage that twice as many study participants are required, and it is considerably more work to implement than the classical experimental design.

Randomized Posttest-Only Control Group Design

The randomized posttest-only control group research design (Design 3c) is identical to the descriptive comparison group posttest-only design (Design 2d), except that the research participants are randomly assigned to two groups. This design, therefore, has a control group rather than a comparison group.

The randomized posttest-only control group research design usually involves only two groups, one experimental and one control. There are no pretests. The experimental group receives the independent variable and takes the posttest; the control group only takes the posttest. This design can be written as follows:

$$\text{Experimental Group: } R \quad X \quad O_1$$
$$\text{Control Group: } R \qquad\quad O_1$$

Where:

R = Random selection from a population and random assignment to group
X = Independent variable, the intervention
O_1 = First and only measurement of the dependent variable

Suppose we want to test the effects of two different treatment interventions, X_1 and X_2. In this case, Design 3c could be elaborated upon to form three randomly assigned groups, two experimental groups (one for each intervention) and one control group. This design would be written as follows:

$$\text{Experimental Group 1: } R \quad X_1 \quad O_1$$
$$\text{Experimental Group 2: } R \quad X_2 \quad O_1$$
$$\text{Control Group: } R \qquad\quad O_1$$

Where:

R = Random selection from a population and random assignment to group
X_1 = Different independent variable than X_2
X_2 = Different independent variable than X_1
O_1 = First and only measurement of the dependent variable

In addition to measuring change in a group or groups, a pretest also helps to ensure equivalence between the control and experimental groups. As you know, this design does not have a pretest. The groups have been randomly assigned, however, as indicated by R, and this, in itself, is theoretically enough to ensure equivalence without the need for a confirmatory pretest. This design is useful in situations where it is not possible to conduct a pretest or where a pretest would be expected to strongly influence the results of the posttest due to the effects of testing. This design also controls for many of the threats to internal validity.

SUMMARY

Group research designs are conducted with groups of cases rather than on a case-by-case basis. They cover the entire range of research questions and provide designs that can be used to gain knowledge on the exploratory, descriptive, and explanatory levels.

A group research study is said to be internally valid if any changes in the dependent variable, Y, result only from the introduction of an independent variable, X. In order to demonstrate internal validity, we must first document the time order of events. Next, we must identify and eliminate extraneous variables. Finally, we must control for the factors that threaten internal validity. In summary, threats to the internal validity of a research design address the assumption that changes in the dependent variable are solely because of the independent variable. "Ideal" experimental designs account for virtually all threats to internal validity—a rarity in social work research studies.

External validity is the degree to which the results of a research study are generalizable to a larger population or to settings other than the research setting. If a research study is to be externally valid, we must be able to demonstrate conclusively that the sample we selected was representative of the population from which it was drawn. If two or more groups are used in the study, we must be able to show that the two groups were equivalent at the beginning of the study. Most importantly, we must be able to demonstrate that nothing happened during the course of the study, except for the introduction of the independent variable, to change either the representativeness of the sample or the equivalence of the groups.

The degree of control we try to exert over threats to internal and external validity varies according to the research design. Threats to internal and external validity may be more or less problematic depending on what particular research design we select. When we design a study, we must be aware of which threats will turn into real problems and what can be done to prevent or at least to minimize them. When doing an exploratory study, for example, we will not be much concerned about threats to external validity because an exploratory study is not expected to have any external validity anyway. Nor do we attempt to control very rigorously for threats to internal validity.

When we use a descriptive research design, we might be trying to determine whether two or more variables are associated. Often, descriptive designs are employed when we are unable, for practical reasons, to use the more rigorous explanatory designs. We do our best to control for threats to internal validity because, unless we can demonstrate internal validity, we cannot show that the variables are associated.

When using explanatory designs, we are attempting to show causation; that is, we are trying to show that changes in one variable cause changes in another. We try hard to control threats to internal validity because, if the study is not internally valid, we cannot demonstrate causation. We would also like the results of the study to be as generally applicable as possible and, to this end, we do our best to control for threats to external validity.

Exploratory designs are used when little is known about the field of study and data are gathered in an effort to find out "what's out there." These ideas are then used to generate hypotheses that can be verified using more rigorous research designs. Descriptive designs are one step closer to determining causality. Explanatory designs are useful when considerable preexisting knowledge is available about the research question under study and a testable hypothesis can be formulated on the basis of previous work. They have more internal and external validity than exploratory and descriptive designs, so they can help establish a causal connection between two variables.

No one group research design is inherently inferior or superior to the others. Each has advantages and disadvantages in terms of time, cost, and the data that can be obtained. Those of us who are familiar with all three categories of group research designs will be equipped to select the one that is most appropriate to a particular research question. In the following chapter we will turn our attention away from group research designs and concentrate on case study designs.

REFERENCES AND FURTHER READINGS

ANASTAS, J.W., & MACDONALD, M.L. (1994). *Research design for social work and the human services* (pp. 22-32, 53-99, 142-145). New York: Lexington.

BABBIE, E.R. (1995). *The practice of social research* (7th ed., pp. 83-107). Belmont, CA: Wadsworth.

BAILEY, K.D. (1994). *Methods of social research* (4th ed., pp. 36-41, 275-292). New York: Free Press.

CAMPBELL, D.T., & STANLEY, J.C. (1963). *Experimental and quasi-experimental designs for research*. Skokie, IL: Rand McNally.

CRESWELL, J.W. (1994). *Research design: Qualitative & quantitative approaches.* Newbury Park, CA: Sage.

FRANKFORT-NACHMIAS, C., & NACHMIAS, D. (1992). *Research methods in the social sciences* (4th ed., pp. 97-99, 271-290). New York: St. Martin's Press.

GABOR, P.A., & GRINNELL, R.M., JR. (1994). *Evaluation and quality improvement in the human services* (pp. 3-40). Needham Heights, MA: Allyn & Bacon.

GRINNELL, R.M., JR. (1993). Group research designs. In R.M. Grinnell, Jr. (Ed.), *Social work research and evaluation* (4th ed., pp. 118-153). Itasca, IL: F.E. Peacock.

GRINNELL, R.M., JR., & STOTHERS, M. (1988). Research designs. In R.M. Grinnell, Jr. (Ed.), *Social work research and evaluation* (3rd ed., pp. 199-239). Itasca, IL: F.E. Peacock.

GRINNELL, R.M., JR., & WILLIAMS, M. (1990). *Research in social work: A primer* (pp. 138-176). Itasca, IL: F.E. Peacock.

JUDD, C.M., SMITH, E.R., & KIDDER, I.H. (1991). *Research methods in social relations* (6th ed., pp. 27-36, 298-320). Fort Worth, TX: Harcourt Brace.

KRYSIK, J., HOFFART, I., & GRINNELL, R.M., JR. (1993). *Student study guide for the fourth edition of social work research and evaluation* (pp. 3-4). Itasca, IL: F.E. Peacock.

LEEDY, P.D. (1993). *Practical research: Planning and design* (5th ed., pp. 113-128, 137-147). New York: Macmillan.

MARLOW, C. (1993). *Research methods for generalist social work* (pp. 23-27, 66-68, 95-96). Pacific Grove, CA: Brooks/Cole.

MONETTE, D.R., SULLIVAN, T.J., & DEJONG, C.R. (1994). *Applied social research* (3rd ed., pp. 82-92). Fort Worth, TX: Harcourt Brace.

RUBIN, A., & BABBIE, E.R. (1993). *Research methods for social work* (2nd ed., pp. 29-30, 106-112, 357-365). Pacific Grove, CA: Wadsworth.

SINGLETON, R.A., JR., STRAITS, B.C., & MILLER STRAITS, M. (1993). *Approaches to social research* (2nd ed., pp. 67-87, 91-96). New York: Oxford.

TRIPODI, T. (1981). The logic of research design. In R.M. Grinnell, Jr. (Ed.), *Social work research and evaluation* (pp. 198-225). Itasca, IL: F.E. Peacock.

TRIPODI, T. (1985). Research designs. In R.M. Grinnell, Jr. (Ed.), *Social work research and evaluation* (2nd ed., pp. 231-259). Itasca, IL: F.E. Peacock.

TUTTY, L.M., ROTHERY, M.A., & GRINNELL, R.M., JR. (Eds.). (1996). *Qualitative research for social workers*: *Phases, steps, and tasks* (pp. 3-22). Needham Heights, MA: Allyn & Bacon.

WEINBACH, R.W., & GRINNELL, R.M., JR. (1996). *Applying research knowledge: A workbook for social work students* (2nd ed., pp. 33-40). Needham Heights, MA: Allyn & Bacon.

WILLIAMS, M., TUTTY, L.M., & GRINNELL, R.M., JR. (1995). *Research in social work: An introduction* (2nd ed., pp. 195-122). Itasca, IL: F.E. Peacock.

YEGIDIS, B.L., & WEINBACH, R.W. (1996). *Research methods for social workers* (2nd ed., pp. 89-111). Needham Heights, MA: Allyn & Bacon.

C h a p t e r **12**

Case Designs

T
HE PREVIOUS CHAPTER PRESENTED basic content for the understanding of group-level research designs—designs that usually study more than one research participant at a time. As we know, however, group designs can also study a single group of people (or objects or events) such as all four of the exploratory designs (i.e., 1a, b, c, d), and four of the six descriptive designs (i.e., 2a, b, c, f) as illustrated in Table 11.2. This chapter elaborates on the preceding one by describing how any one-group nonrandomized design can be turned into a case study design. Many of the concepts of the previous 11 chapters are utilized in case designs so it may be a good time to review them.

THE CASE

The case is the basic unit of social work practice, whether it be *an* individual, *a* couple, *a* family, *an* agency, *a* community, *a* county, *a* state, or *a* country. Case studies are more useful than traditional group designs when we want to study situations in depth and to understand how our therapeutic processes effect client outcomes. A case study fits naturally with many forms of social work practice, and by definition, it is an intense in-depth study of "one unit." Our profession deals with these "one units," which are always embedded in multiple societal, environmental, financial, and personal contexts.

The "Case" and Social Work Practice

Although case studies have much utility, our profession has had a love-hate relationship with them. Their main shortcoming is that they contain multiple variables that usually are not controllable (either statistically or through the manipulation of variables). We have used case studies for research and teaching for decades, however. The "case" has been the basis for the construction of various theories, such as the theories of human behavior, psychotherapy, family therapy, and cognitive development.

THE CASE STUDY

The recognition of the interaction of the numerous variables within a client system (a unit, or the case) is a defining characteristics of our profession. Thus, a case study considers the multiple variables (e.g., intervening, extraneous, independent) that affect the "unit" of study within its own context. Case study research does not ignore the major contextual variables that affect the course of our treatment—which sometimes happens when doing a group research project that strives to increase its internal and external validity, as illustrated in the preceding chapter.

Characteristics

As we know from the last chapter, there are a variety of ways to do group research designs. So, too, in case study research. They can be constructed using quantitative approaches (Chapter 4) and/or qualitative approaches (Chapter 5). They can be applied or pure; their links to theory can be deductive or inductive, or in some combination.

We can use a wide range of data sources (e.g., individuals, families, groups, organizations, couples) and data-collection methods (e.g., surveys, interviews, participant observation, document analysis—all discussed in Parts V and VI). A case study routinely uses multiple data sources and data-collection methods in order to attain an in-depth understanding of the case being studied. As mentioned, data can be quantitative or qualitative or both. Measurements can be taken at a single time and setting, or over time and multiple settings. Case studies perform many of the tasks that traditional group research designs do and can range from exploratory to explanatory.

Developing Theory and Testing Hypotheses

Case studies are used to develop theory and test hypotheses. These studies can include modified analytic induction, task analysis, and grounded theory (Berlin, Mann, & Grossman, 1991; Bogdan & Biklen, 1992; Gilgun, 1992b, 1995; Glaser & Strauss, 1967). In modified analytic induction and task analysis, our research study begins with a hypothesis that is tested on more than one case. Then, our hypothesis is continuously modified in response to the data generated from case to case (Chapter 5). Case studies can also be used in grounded theory research studies where our main purpose is to develop hypotheses and concepts (Charmaz, 1990; Gilgun, 1994a, 1994c; Glaser & Strauss, 1967; Strauss & Corbin, 1990).

Both modified analytic induction and grounded theory facilitate an in-depth understanding of the phenomena being studied. In addition, they follow many procedures similar to the procedures of direct practice, and we, therefore, already have many of the skills necessary to conduct excellent grounded theory and analytic induction studies (Gilgun, 1992a).

CASE STUDIES AND THE THREE COMPONENTS OF PRACTICE

There are three main types of case studies: (1) case studies that generate knowledge about our clients and their situations [assessment], (2) case studies that evaluate social work intervention, or therapeutic processes [intervention], and (3) case studies that evaluate client outcome [client outcome].

Assessment

Let us take an example of how case study research can contribute to the enhancement of our assessment techniques. In a case study research project, only two research participants (or cases) provided data to demonstrate that preverbal children can store their memories of sexual abuse and retrieve and articulate those memories when they are older (Hewitt, 1994). The author presented rich detail on both cases and provided concrete data that these two children were able to articulate experiences they had when they were too young to talk. These findings can be helpful in our assessment and treatment planning.

In another case study research project, 11 perpetrators of child sexual abuse as avengers, conquerors, playmates, and lovers were interviewed (Gilgun, 1994b). Based on intensive interviews, this project presented in detail the subjective accounts by perpetrators of child sexual abuse of their relationships with child victims. Such data help persons who have been victimized understand how much planning, manipulation, and self-deception are involved in the perpetrators' destructive behaviors. Thus, this project provided data to help us understand client situations and to aid in our assessments and treatment plans with this particular group of individuals.

Assessment-related case studies are particularly helpful in presenting our clients' perspectives. This quality is important, since a guiding principle of social work practice is to "start where the client is." In sum, we must grasp, interpret, and understand the perspectives and experiences of our clients if we are to be effective (Denzin, 1989; Goldstein, 1983).

Evaluating the usefulness of assessment-relevant case studies involves appraising whether they depict the subjective experiences of our clients; how they view their world, how they understand their experiences and relationships with other people, and how they account for their own behaviors and the behaviors of others. An in-depth understanding of our clients' perspectives fosters a unique collaboration between us and our clients, provides a firm basis for treatment planning, and, when sufficiently compelling, can lead to major advances in policy and social service delivery programs.

In general, the following guidelines are utilized when evaluating an assessment-related case study. It:

- Focuses on the perspectives of the study's participants
- Provides new insights into causes of clients' conditions
- Provides new insights into the meaning of a participant's life
- Clarifies confusing aspects of a participant's issue(s)
- Helps social work practitioners make new connections
- Conveys the historical and social conditions under which a participant developed (e.g., provides a thick description of context)

Intervention

As social workers, we are immersed in the intervention process. By examining these processes, we can illuminate the micro-steps that lead to good client outcomes. An excellent example of process research is a study where two social workers interviewed 15 of their colleagues who had experienced psychotherapy (Mackey & Mackey, 1994). They simply wanted to know how therapy affected the social workers' practice. Through a detailed analysis of comprehensive interviews, they demonstrated that a social worker's own therapy can have a profound positive affect on the intervention processes of his or her practice.

Process research and client outcome (to be discussed) are important parts of our profession. Simply put, good client outcomes depend on good interventions. The more we can identify the interventive processes that lead to good client outcomes, the more likely we are to replicate effective practice. In this age of managed physical and mental health care, accountability is taking on new and compelling meanings. Some social service delivery programs, for example, may not be funded when they cannot demonstrate their effectiveness. Process-oriented case studies may prove to be central to effective responses to increased demands for accountability. These types of case studies can be evaluated on the following criteria:

- Illuminate the "black box" of intervention (e.g., describe patterns, linkages, and interactions)
- Advance our understanding of exactly what happened
- Describe how programs and interventions work and what they do
- Reflect the complexity of implementing treatment interventions
- Show the human, subjective, and reflective side of intervention processes
- Provide new insights that affect client outcomes

Client Outcome

As should be evident by now, the ultimate goal of social work practice is to: assess correctly, intervene appropriately, and have good client outcomes. To achieve that, we must have knowledge of our clients and their situations (assessment), we must pay attention to therapeutic processes (intervention), and we must have evidence that our client outcomes were in fact achieved (client outcome).

A study of a woman being treated for obsessive-compulsive disorders is a good example of an outcome-oriented case study (Cooper, 1990). In a single case, the outcome variable was easily measured—a simple count of her obsessive-compulsive behaviors, which were graphed over time. This process indicated whether there was a reduction of these behaviors over the course of treatment.

Some outcome studies are not so quantifiable, however, and a study's results cannot be put on a graph. Sometimes these studies require the qualitative accounts (words) of clients and our qualitative observations. In the case study discussed earlier on school-aged children's ability to recall sexual abuse before they could talk, the outcome variable was simply their ability to recall their sexual abuse that took place when they were pre-verbal. This outcome is not quantifiable, per se, but nevertheless, it is a bona fide client outcome. The researcher simply gave a clear and credible account of the outcome instead of providing numbers, statistics, and graphs. How to evaluate the reliability and validity of such client outcomes depends on the nature of the outcome. Some outcomes are qualitative, some quantitative.

Outcome-oriented case studies can be evaluated on the following criteria:

- *Statistical conclusion validity* (see Chapter 11):
  — Demonstrates that a relationship between two variables exists
  — Conditions under which data are collected are standardized within and across cases

— Sufficient detail is present so that readers can draw independent conclusions about whether our interventions and client outcomes are related
— For studies utilizing quantification:
— Appropriate statistics are used
— Reliable and valid measuring instruments are used
- *Internal validity* (see Chapter 11):
— Rules out alternative hypotheses
— Points out alternative hypotheses that cannot be ruled out
— Uses pretests, baselines, and/or participant recall (if possible)
— Continues measurement after the intervention until trends appear to stabilize (if possible)
— Uses multiple cases (if possible)
- *Construct validity* (see Chapter 7)
- *External validity* (see Chapter 11):
— The context of the intervention is described in detail
— The intervention is described in detail
— Research participants are described in detail
— Findings are discussed as hypotheses to be tested in other situations

CONSIDERATIONS WHEN DOING CASE STUDIES

Case studies are complex and can be difficult to conceptualize, operationalize, execute, and evaluate. Yet, we must try, since they have a great potential to contribute to our knowledge base. In the final analysis, however, the value of case study research is whether their findings will enhance our assessments, interventions, and client outcomes. This section explores some of the general issues we need to address when doing case study research: (1) generalizability, (2) conceptual issues, (3) contextual detail, (4) causation, (5) construct validity, and (6) presentation of findings.

Generalizability

Findings from a case study are not generalizable to the same extent as research findings generated from a group design that utilized a random sample. Nevertheless, they are generalizable to some degree. As we know from Chapter 10, research findings generated with random samples can be generalized to populations from which they were drawn. Applying research findings from a group research design or a case study design to an individual case is identical. We cannot, for example, assume that any research finding, whether derived from a survey, a randomized group design, or a case study, will fit a particular case. In a nutshell, each and every research finding must be tested for its fit with an individual case.

The Case Represents Itself

The individual case is unique and represents only itself. In fact, the root meaning of *ideographic* is the study of a unique case. No single case is likely to be identical to any other case. This is not a hard concept for us to understand, since we are trained to view each case as unique and to individualize a client's situation. We also know that even individual and unique cases often have something in common with other cases. Furthermore, working with cases is facilitated by our level of knowledge in the problem area, amount of practice experience, personal experience, use of research findings, and use of theory. Generalizing from one case to another requires at least three skills:

- The ability to draw practice principles from individual cases
- The ability to test whether practice principles derived from previous cases fit the present case
- The willingness to change even cherished practice principles when data from new cases contradict these principles

The type of generalizability associated with case studies is called *analytic generalization*. This means that their research findings are not assumed to fit another case no matter how apparently similar. Instead, research findings are tested to see if they do in fact fit. As discussed earlier, these processes are no different from how findings from any other kind of research study are used. Furthermore, the findings of case study research are not definitive. That is, they are not true for all persons, settings, and times—as often has been the goal in group studies aiming for probabilistic generalizability. Instead, case study findings are open-ended and are subject to revision as new data are discovered.

Let us go back to our example of the school-aged children's ability to recall sexual abuse before they could talk. This case study can illustrate the above principles. As discussed, the study used two children who articulated sexual abuse that occurred years earlier when they were pre-verbal. This is a practice principle, but it only opens up possibilities. It does not guarantee that all children who have been sexually abused when they were pre-verbal will later be able to articulate such abuse. As a working hypothesis, however, we can test whether this principle illuminates our practice with our clients who have been sexually abused when very young and whether it will hold up in other similar cases. As our clinical experiences accumulate, we may be able to delineate specific conditions under which this principle holds—and conditions under which it does not.

Analytic Generalizations as Working Hypotheses

Those of us who use analytic generalization view practice principles as working hypotheses, subject to revision when new data emerge. In using analytic generalization, we actively seek to contradict our practice principles in an effort to ensure that we truly are individualizing our practice knowledge and are not imposing our *general* preconceived ideas upon an *individual* client. Since using analytic generalization involves modifying our practice principles to fit individual cases, we do not try to mold our clients to fit our preconceived ideas.

Conceptual Issues

Like other forms of research endeavors, conceptual issues also need to be taken into account in case studies. Conceptual frameworks must be clearly delineated by making a direct statement on the study's purpose and presenting its guiding principles—which usually are hypotheses or research questions. In addition, we must share our reasoning that lead to the hypotheses or research questions and meticulously define all relevant concepts. Literature reviews and practice wisdom are the usual sources of conceptual frameworks for case studies. Below are a few criteria for evaluating the conceptual framework for a case study research project:

- Purpose of the study is clearly stated
- Principles guiding the study are clearly stated—either as hypotheses or as research questions
- Reasoning leading to the hypothesis or research question is clearly stated; this should be based on a literature review and on the reasoning of the researcher(s)
- Concepts are carefully defined

Contextual Detail

The unit of analysis in a case study is embedded in its environment, which deeply affects how the unit functions. To provide a basis for the understanding and interpreting of case studies, therefore, we must provide meaningful contextual detail. Notions of multiple, interactive, and contextual systems contained in the ecosystemic conceptual framework are useful in developing contextual detail.

Specific details of how our case study was conducted, with whom, and under what conditions are important to note. We must give enough information about our research participants, research setting, data collection sources and methods, and data analysis so that readers of our report can make a judgment about the adequacy of our research effort. This will also permit someone else to replicate our study.

This discussion demonstrates the importance of contextual detail in evaluating case studies for internal, construct, and external validity. With adequate detail, those who read our case studies (or hear about them at case conferences) will have enough information to evaluate our conclusions. The readers can make their own independent judgments. When sufficient contextual detail is present in case studies, the case study is interpretable. Another social worker with a similar case using similar intervention methods may obtain very different results, however. Divergent therapeutic processes and client outcomes with apparently similar cases are attributable to many factors.

Causation

As we know, our profession is an applied one whose goal is to understand social processes and, when they are problematic, to change them. If we are to understand change, we must be able to identify both the variables that caused the undesirable social conditions in the first place and the variables that can ameliorate them. Causation, then, is at the heart of social work practice—and social work research for that matter. The interventions we devise are meant to bring about positive change in client systems. In the language of research, we are seeking to identify and then implement the independent variables (Xs) that bring about the occurrence of dependent variables (Ys). We want to know: Does X cause Y? In social work practice, we want to know if the interventions that compose X cause outcomes that compose Y. We want to identify causal variables because, when we do, our interventions will be more effective and more efficient.

Deterministic Versus Probabilistic Causation

There is more than one way to think about cause, however. One definition is deterministic: When a particular effect appeared, the associated cause was always there. No other variables influenced the relationship between cause and effect—there is no effect in the absence of the cause. Another definition is probabilistic: When the presumed cause was present, the associated outcome may or may not have been present. Shooting another person in the eye, for example, deterministically will cause a great deal of physical and psychological harm. Other outcomes are not deterministic. Being sexually abused in childhood does not deterministically cause individuals to be sexually abusive people when they are older. There is a probability that these people will become sexually abusive, but not a certainty. Other variables, or factors, influence whether people who have been previously sexually abused when they were young actually become sexually abusive when they grow older.

Intervening and Extraneous Variables

Intervening and extraneous variables can mediate client outcomes. Competent social work practice identifies them and rules them out as competing alternative causes. The case study earlier in this chapter describing a woman who had obsessive-compulsive disorders illustrates these principles. The author attributed the reduction of her client's symptoms to a behaviorally oriented intervention. Yet, other variables may have affected her client's outcome. In the author's in-depth description of her client's history, she reported that her client had several years of psychodynamic therapy before undergoing behavioral treatment. In addition, the woman was married while in treatment. These and other extra-treatment circumstances (intervening and extraneous variables) might have influenced the client's outcome.

In this case, then, the causal agent (the intervention) was not 100 percent clear. Both within-treatment and extra-treatment variables may have been responsible for the outcome. The causal variable, was thus *confounded*. This is a typical kind of client outcome. We often cannot be sure if our treatment intervention was *solely* responsible for our client's outcome when other influences may have facilitated or undermined it.

External conditions are likely to be part of the package of processes leading to client change. Confounding is part and parcel of social work practice because client systems are embedded in many environments that affect their functioning. Interactions between clients and practitioners are sources of other possible confounds. These variables mediate between our interventive efforts and our client outcomes.

Cause, then, rarely is easily identifiable in doing a case study. We, and our clients alike, are contending with too many variables to identify a specific causal variable(s). The best we can do is to rule out plausible rival hypotheses to our original hypothesis. When we cannot rule out plausible alternative hypotheses to client change, then we must delineate all the possible intervening and extraneous variables associated with client change.

Assessing trends in client behaviors or feelings of interest and then noting if the trend changes in response to our intervention can help identify and rule out rival hypotheses. Baselines, pretests, and asking our clients about pertinent issues prior to intervention are all helpful in assessing trends. Graphing trends over the course of treatment also help establish internal validity, although the possibility of rival hypotheses needs to be continually monitored (see Chapter 21).

We can, however, tentatively rule out rival hypotheses and have some confidence that our treatment intervention had a causal relationship to our client outcome. This is done when several cases are conducted at various times, with a number of similar people, with a variety of practitioners, and embedded in variety of settings, and they show similar results (Kazdin, 1981). External conditions vary from one client system to another. Consistency of findings across similar conditions bolsters an argument that a particular form of treatment was the causal variable and is effective for a particular type of client problem.

Thus, replication of causal studies increases their internal validity. To demonstrate the effectiveness of behavioral approaches with persons with obsessive compulsive behaviors, then, Cooper (1990) would have to replicate her study with several other cases—not only one. Then, other practitioners would have to do this as well. Despite this goal of multiple replications, the findings of a single case study can be a rich source for the construction of a working hypothesis.

In addition, replication across persons, settings, and time also bolsters arguments for a general applicability of findings—that is, *external validity*. However, even widely replicated findings must be tested for fit with individual cases.

Construct Validity

Construct validity is explained in detail in Chapter 7. Though concerned with intervening and extraneous variables, as discussed earlier, construct validity has other facets. In general, construct validity directs us to pay careful attention to how and whether we identify and define our treatment interventions and client outcome variables.

Convergence and Divergence

Construct validity is based on the ideas of convergence and divergence, in addition to the idea of multiple data collection methods and data sources. A study of staff/patient communication on a few neonatal units is exemplary in its use of multiple data methods and sources (Bogdan, Brown, & Foster, 1984). The data collection methods included observations (Chapter 13) and interviews (Chapter 14) with a range of informants (data sources) over time at four neonatal units. This approach developed a trustworthy understanding of the multiple facets of staff/patient communication in a typical neonatal unit.

Sometimes the purpose, or feasibility, of a case study puts some limits on using multiple data collection methods and sources, however. If our research goal is to understand only our key informant's perspective, or, if the informant is the only source of knowledge about phenomena—such as experiences of near death—then we only need one informant per study.

On the other hand, if our goal is to understand multiple perspectives within a system, such as a couple, a family, or an agency, then multiple persons need to be interviewed. Testing for the generality of findings requires multiple case studies, although the findings of even these replications have to be assessed for their fit with any individual case.

The rationale for the use of multiple data sources is based on the ideas of convergence and replication. As occurrences of a phenomenon increase, we can place more confidence that a finding is reliable. Replication can be difficult to achieve, however. The concepts that we deal with are often embedded in multiple contexts and are contingent upon time. When this is combined with variations in individual client systems and how we practice, replication can be extremely difficult to achieve. Yet, some findings actually do repeat themselves over people, places, and times.

When these multiple data sources do not overlap, we can assume that the variables we are measuring are not the same. When data from different sources converge, then we can assume that the variables we are measuring are indeed similar. As we know from Chapter 5, the use of multiple data sources is called *triangulation*.

The notion of construct validity also guides us to use multiple measures at pretests, during interventions, and at posttests (outcomes). Rarely does any intervention involve one outcome, and rarely is only one part of a client system relevant in assessment and treatment planning. Therefore, in order to understand and identify the variables that are of an interest to us, we must use multiple measures.

Construct validity is also about operational definitions. When we define our constructs of interest, readers of our case studies can evaluate the adequacy of our assessments, interventions, and evaluations. Adequate definitions inform others of how we thought about what they were doing. Readers can then draw their own conclusions about whether we were dealing with what we thought we were dealing with and whether we were doing what we thought we were doing. Careful operational definitions not only increase our understanding but foster replication of case study findings.

Finally, ideas embedded in the notion of construct validity direct us to account for multiple client outcomes, not simply a dominant outcome. Hewitt (1994), for example, could have added a third case to her research study, a case where a child could not recall documented sexual abuse that occurred while she was preverbal. In that way, Hewitt would have had a stronger argument for the construct validity of her study. She could have argued that she presented the dominant finding and another finding that was not consistent with the dominant one. Thus, case studies are strengthened when dominant patterns and exceptions to dominant patterns are reported.

Presentation of Findings

Presentation of a case study's findings is challenging. Accurate accounts of our study's findings require much thought, excellent analytic skills, and data that fit the analysis. Case studies typically generate a great deal of data, and we must identify themes and concepts that organize them—that become the headings of the final report. The various ways to identify themes and concepts is beyond the scope of this chapter, but excellent guidance can be found in Chapter 22.

In presenting a study's findings, we must persuade our readers that the conclusions we drew were based on the data. The usual mode of presenting findings involves general statements about the findings, supported by data derived from the case. Citing findings not supported by data is a common error that harms the study's credibility. Dominant patterns in our findings as well as exceptions to the dominant patterns are presented. Finally, our findings are linked to previous research studies, theory, and practice wisdom. Below are a few criteria for evaluating the clarity and accuracy of findings presented in a final report:

- *Findings are well organized and communicated clearly:*
  - A general statement is made about each research finding
  - Each general statement is supported by evidence taken from the data
  - Presentation of findings is separate from the categories that organize the findings
  - Multiple dimensions of the findings are clearly presented including:
    - Dominant patterns and exceptions to dominant patterns
    - Descriptions of conditions under which patterns appear
- *Interpretation of the study's findings based on data:*
  - Generalizations are based on the data
  - Findings are clearly interpreted in a pattern-matching way and not in a probabilistic way
  - More than one person interpreted the data
  - Research participants read and comment on the final report
  - Other knowledgeable persons read and comment on the final report
  - Relates findings to previous research studies and theory
  - Discusses clinical and theoretical relevance and programmatic or policy implications

SUMMARY

The findings from case studies can be a rich source of practice knowledge. To develop them effectively, however, we need to pay attention to the guidelines discussed in this chapter. Case studies must be evaluated for what they are. They cannot do what experiments do, but they can be a major factor in the development of practice guidelines. They are particularly useful for obtaining the perspectives of key informants and for tracking the therapeutic processes that lead to client outcomes.

Case studies fit well with social work practice. Not only do they support the three components of practice—assessment, intervention, and evaluation—but they call upon the skills that trained social workers already have.

REFERENCES AND FURTHER READINGS

BENNER, P. (Ed.). (1994). *Interpretive phenomenology.* Newbury Park, CA: Sage.

BERLIN, S.B, MANN, K.B., & GROSSMAN, S.F. (1991). Task analysis of cognitive therapy for depression. *Social Work Research and Abstracts, 27,* 3-11.

BOGDAN, R., & BIKLEN, S.K. (1992). *Qualitative research for education* (2nd ed.). Needham Heights, MA: Allyn & Bacon.

BOGDAN, R., BROWN, M.A., & FOSTER, S.B. (1984). Ecology of the family as a context for human development. *Human Organization, 41,* 6-16.

CAMPBELL, D.T., & STANLEY, J.C. (1966). *Experimental and quasi-experimental designs for research.* Chicago: Rand McNally.

CHARMAZ, K. (1990). "Discovering" chronic illness: Using grounded theory. *Social Science in Medicine, 30,* 1161-1172.

COLEMAN, H., & UNRAU, Y. (1996). Phase three: Analyzing your data. In L.M. Tutty, M.A. Rothery, & R.M. Grinnell, Jr. (Eds.), *Qualitative research for social workers; Phases, steps, and tasks* (pp. 88-119). Needham Heights, MA: Allyn & Bacon.

COOK, T.D., & CAMPBELL, D. (1979). Quasi-experimentation: Design and analysis for field settings. Boston: Houghton Mifflin.

COOPER, M. (1990). Treatment of a client with obsessive-compulsive disorder. *Social Work Research & Abstracts, 26,* 26-35.

CRESWELL, J.W. (1994). *Research design: Qualitative & quantitative approaches.* Newbury Park, CA: Sage.

CRONBACH, L., & MEEHL, P.E. (1955). Construct validity in psychological tests. *Psychological Bulletin, 52,* 281-302.

DENZIN, N.K. (1978). *The research act.* New York: McGraw-Hill.

DENZIN, N.K. (1989). *Interpretative interactionism.* Newbury Park, CA: Sage.

GARMEZY, N. (1982). The case for the single case in research. In A.E. Kazdin & A.H. Tuma (Eds.), *New directions for methodology of social and behavioral sciences* (pp. 517-546). San Francisco, CA: Jossey-Bass.

GILGUN, J.F. (1988). Decision-making in interdisciplinary treatment teams. *Child Abuse and Neglect, 12,* 231-239.

GILGUN, J.F. (1992a). Definitions, methods, and methodologies of qualitative family research. In J.F. Gilgun, K. Daly, & G. Handel (Eds.), *Qualitative methods in family research* (pp. 22-39). Newbury Park, CA: Sage.

GILGUN, J.F. (1992b). Observations in a clinical setting: Team decision-making in family incest treatment. In J.F. Gilgun, K. Daly, & G. Handel (Eds.), *Qualitative methods in family research* (pp. 236-259). Newbury Park, CA: Sage.

GILGUN, J.F. (1994a). A case for case studies in social work research. *Social Work, 39,* 371-380.

GILGUN, J.F. (1994b). Avengers, conquerors, playmates, and lovers: Roles played by child sexual abuse perpetrators. *Families in Society, 75,* 467-480.

GILGUN, J.F. (1994c). Hand into glove: The grounded theory approach and social work practice research. In E. Sherman & W.J. Reid (Eds.), *Qualitative research in social work* (pp. 115-125). New York: Columbia University Press.

GILGUN, J.F. (1995). The moral discourse of incest perpetrators. *Journal of Marriage and the Family, 57,* 265-282.

GILGUN, J.F., DALY, K., & HANDEL, G. (Eds.). (1992). *Qualitative methods in family research.* Newbury Park, CA: Sage.

GLASER, B., & STRAUSS, A.L. (1967). *The discovery of grounded theory.* New York: Aldine.

GOLDSTEIN, H. (1983). Starting where the client is. *Social Casework, 65,* 267-275.

GRINNELL, R.M., JR., & WILLIAMS, M. (1990). *Research in social work: A primer.* Itasca, IL: F.E. Peacock.

HARTMAN, A. (1978). Diagrammatic assessment of family relationships. *Social Casework, 59,* 465-476.

HEWITT, S.K. (1994). Preverbal sexual abuse: What two children report in later years. *Child Abuse and Neglect, 18,* 821-826.

KAZDIN, A.E. (1981). Drawing valid inferences from case studies. *Journal of Consulting and Clinical Psychology, 49,* 183-192.

MACKEY, R.A, & MACKEY, E.F. (1994). Personal psychotherapy and the development of a professional self. *Families in Society, 75,* 490-498.

MARSH, J.C. (1983). Research and innovation in social work practice: Avoiding the headless machine. *Social Service Review, 57,* 584-598.

MARSHALL, C., & ROSSMAN, G.B. (1995). *Designing qualitative research* (2nd ed.). Newbury Park, CA: Sage.

MCCLELLAND, R., & AUSTIN, C.D. (1996). Phase four: Writing your report. In L.M. Tutty, M.A. Rothery, & R.M. Grinnell, Jr. (Eds.), *Qualitative research for social workers; Phases, steps, and tasks* (pp. 120-150). Needham Heights, MA: Allyn & Bacon.

MEYER, C. (1983). *Clinical social work in the eco-systems perspective.* New York: Columbia University Press.

MORSE, J.M., & FIELD, P.A. (1995). *Qualitative research methods for health professionals* (2nd ed.). Newbury Park, CA: Sage.

PATTON, M.Q. (1990). *Qualitative evaluation and research methods* (2nd ed.). Newbury Park, CA: Sage.

REID, W.J. (1990). Change process research: A new paradigm? In L. Videka-Sherman & W.J. Reid (Eds.), *Advances in clinical social work research* (pp. 130-148). Silver Spring, MD: National Association of Social Workers.

ROGERS, G., & BOUEY, E. (1996). Phase two: Collecting your data. In L.M. Tutty, M.A. Rothery, & R.M. Grinnell, Jr. (Eds.), *Qualitative research for social workers: Phases, steps, and tasks* (pp. 50-87). Needham Heights, MA: Allyn & Bacon.

SHERMAN, E. (1994). Discourse analysis in the framework of change process research. In E. Sherman & W.J. Reid (Eds.), *Qualitative research in social work* (pp. 228-241). New York: Columbia University Press.

STAKE, R.E. (1995). *The art of case study research.* Newbury Park, CA: Sage.

STRAUSS, A.L. (1987). *Qualitative analysis for social scientists.* Cambridge: Cambridge University Press.

STRAUS, A.L., & CORBIN, J. (1990). *Basics of qualitative research: Grounded theory procedures and techniques.* Newbury Park, CA: Sage.

STRAUSS, A.L., & HAFEZ, H. (1981). Clinical questions and "real research." *American Journal of Psychiatry, 138,* 1592-1597.

TAYLOR, S.J., & BOGDAN, R. (1984). *Introduction to qualitative research: The search for meanings.* New York: John Wiley & Sons.

TUTTY, L.M., ROTHERY, M.A., & GRINNELL, R.M., JR. (Eds.). (1996). *Qualitative research for social workers: Phases, steps, and tasks.* Needham Heights, MA: Allyn & Bacon.

PART V

OBTRUSIVE DATA COLLECTION METHODS

313

Heather Coleman
Donald Collins
Richard A. Polster

C h a p t e r **13**

Structured Observation

MOST OF THE DATA COLLECTION METHODS described in the preceding chapters (excluding Chapter 12 on case designs) were surveys of some kind or another. As we know, respondents to survey instruments are the persons about whom facts are being gathered or whose attitudes, feelings, or beliefs are being explored. The instruments may be rating scales or questionnaire-type scales, and they may be self-reports or completed by interviewers or others at various times and in various research situations.

The data collection method described in this chapter depends on structured observations in which people are observed in their natural environments. This form of data collection is extremely useful in doing case studies, as outlined in the previous chapter. Observations are made by trained observers in a specified place and over a specified time period, using specified methods and measurement procedures. This data collection method therefore is highly structured—probably the most highly structured of all the ones that are discussed in this text—and rigid procedures must be followed in order to produce reliable data.

In addition, it is the most obtrusive data collection method that can be used in social work research situations. This means that our research participants usually are aware that we are observing them.

USES IN SOCIAL WORK RESEARCH

The term *target problem*, introduced in Chapter 23 in relation to case-level evaluation designs, is used in this chapter to refer to a measurable behavior, feeling, or cognition (idea, belief, or attitude) that is either a problem in itself or symptomatic of some other problem. In the structured-observation method of data collection, the target problem in the research question or hypothesis is operationally defined, a measuring instrument is selected or constructed for recording the data, direct observations are made of the individuals or groups, and data on the observations are recorded and analyzed.

Structured observation can be used in both case-level evaluations to study client target problems (Chapters 12 and 23) and group research designs (Chapter 11) to study research questions or test hypotheses. This method of data collection is generally used when the target problem is not amenable to traditional measurement techniques and survey instruments such as questionnaires, interviews, and self-reports, or when an outside, presumably more objective, assessment seems necessary. Observing participants in their natural environments as well as in clinical or laboratory settings also can provide us with data that are otherwise not obtainable.

In a case-level evaluation, for example, we may directly observe the behavior of clients in order to supplement our assessment of the clients' self-reports. Both the self-report measuring instruments and our direct observations can provide reliable data on the success of treatment interventions.

In a group research design to study the aggressive behavior of small children, an observer might be asked to watch a children's group through a one-way mirror and record acts of aggression according to a prescribed set of instructions. Or a study by a social service agency to identify the intervention techniques commonly employed by its staff might use trained observers to watch videotapes of social workers' interviews and code the types and frequency of techniques they use. In both instances, the observer would use a measuring instrument and an accompanying set of instructions to make the ratings.

OBSERVATIONAL DATA RECORDING

Each of the various methods used to record data from observations of people in their natural environments provides a different type of data. The method chosen must be consistent with the characteristics of the target problem being observed. We must also take into account who will be making the observations and recording the data and the amount of instruction they will need in order to produce valid and reliable data. Figure 13.1 summarizes six methods that we can use in making direct observations and measuring and recording the data needed to examine a research question or test a hypothesis. These methods described in this section are (1) interval recording, (2) frequency recording, (3) duration recording, (4) magnitude recording, (5)spot-check recording, and (6) permanent-product recording.

Interval Recording

Interval recording involves continuous, direct observation of individuals during specified observation periods divided into equal time intervals. The observations recorded following this paragraph show the number of times a target problem was observed for an individual during a one-minute period divided into six-ten-second intervals. An observer recorded instances of the problem at least once during the first, second, third, and sixth intervals.

SIX TIME INTERVALS (IN SECONDS)

0-10	11-20	21-30	31-40	41-50	51-60
✓	✓		✓		✓

Occurrence data are obtained by recording the first occurrence of the target problem in each time interval. Subsequent occurrences during the same interval are not recorded. Nonoccurrence data can be obtained by recording those intervals in which the problem did not occur.

The resulting data will show the number of intervals during which the target problem occurred at least once and the number of intervals during which the target problem did not occur. These data are presented in terms of the percentage of intervals in which the target problem occurred at least once or did not occur. For example, the data directly above indicate that the target problem occurred in four out of six (two-thirds), or 67 percent, of the intervals.

If we want to know the duration of the target problem, data should be recorded only when it occurs throughout the entire interval (ten seconds in this example). In this case, a problem that occurs for only a portion of the interval would not be recorded. This procedure might be used, for example, to record the duration of a worker's on-task performance. Occurrence of the target problem (on-task behavior) would be recorded only if the worker was on task for the entire interval. An interval during which both on-task and off-task behavior were exhibited would be recorded as off-task. The resulting data would indicate the number of intervals during which the worker sustained on-task activity, but it would not indicate the precise amount of time the worker was on task.

A good procedure is to attach a form, containing the time intervals as shown above, to a clipboard with a stopwatch fastened to the top. Audio-recorders with earphones also can be used to play back prerecorded tapes which signal intervals as time passes.

Recording Method	Target Problems (behaviors, feelings, cognitions)	Kinds of Information Gained	Formality of Observer Training	Relative Expense
Interval	Appropriate for measuring problems with high frequencies or highly variable frequencies and multiple behaviors, feelings, or cognitions	Fine-grained (precise) measures; Percent of intervals with occurrence or nonoccurrence of target problem; Patterns of behavior, feelings, or cognitions and relationships among them	Extensive; Formal training necessary	High due to costs for outside observers and observer training
Frequency	Appropriate for high- or low-frequency problems; Interest in how often problem occurs	Gross measures; Total occurrences per observation	Informal if observational code is simple; Formal if code is complex	Low to high, depending on complexity of code and collateral or self-recording vs. trained observers
Duration	Appropriate for problems with measurable duration; Interest in how long occurrence lasts or how long until it appears	Gross measures; Length of time per occurrence	Informal if observational code is simple; Moderate if code is complex	Low to high, depending on complexity of code and collateral or self-recording vs. trained observers
Magnitude	Appropriate for problems that vary in degree performed	Medium-grained measures; Rating on scale per occurrence; Profiles problem by frequency or severity of occurrence	Moderate if observational code is simple; Formal training if code is complex	Low to high, depending on complexity of code and collateral or self-recording vs. trained observer
Spot check	Appropriate for sustained, ongoing problems	Gross measures; Occurrence or nonoccurrence per spot check	Informal if observational code is simple; Moderate if code is complex	Low to moderate, depending on complexity of code and collateral or self-recording vs. trained observers
Permanent product	Appropriate for problems that produce lasting effects on the environment or are recorded as part of ongoing process	Gross- to medium-grained measures; Frequency or duration or magnitude of occurrence	Informal if product code is simple; Moderate if code is complex	Low—requires no direct observation of behavior, feeling, or cognition, only coding of end products

FIGURE 13.1 CHARACTERISTICS OF DATA RECORDING METHODS FOR STRUCTURED OBSERVATION

Occurrence or nonoccurrence of the target problems is noted by placing a check mark in the space corresponding to each time interval. Ideally, environmental conditions that would affect the occurrence of the target problem or the accuracy of the observation should be controlled for (Bloom, Fischer, & Orme, 1995; Fischer & Corcoran, 1995). If possible, the observer should ignore environmental stimuli such as crying children or other activities taking place and should observe from an unobtrusive location.

The data obtained through interval recording are highly detailed and provide a temporal picture (over time) of the target problem, in addition to information about the frequency or duration of the problem. Because small changes in the rate or pattern of behavior can usually be observed in the data, they provide fine-grained, or precise, measures for use in data analysis. Other data collection methods for structured observation provide gross, or broad, measures, at the other extreme, or medium-grained measures, which are neither too precise nor too broad (see Figure 13.1).

Reliability

The reliability of the data collected with interval recording is computed by having at least two independent observers simultaneously record the same target problem or problems. The percentage of agreement in the observations is a measure of the overall reliability of the data. The common formula for computing percentage of agreement in interval recording data is as follows:

$$\text{Percentage of agreement} = \frac{\text{Agreements}}{\text{Disagreements} + \text{Agreements}}$$

Agreements can be calculated by comparing the two recording forms and counting the intervals for which both observers recorded occurrence or nonoccurrence of the target problem. Disagreements occur when one observer records occurrence and the other records nonoccurrence in the same interval.

Applications

We can use the patterns of occurrence of target problems to plan treatment interventions. Since more than one target problem in the same time interval can be recorded, temporal relationships between target problems for an individual can be easily examined. We can determine whether a specific target problem usually follows, precedes, or occurs at the same time as another target problem, for example. Target problems of people interacting in dyadic relationships, such as parent-child, teacher-student, or husband-wife, or in small-group situations also can be studied. The effects of a teacher's use of contingent reinforcement on a student's rate of task completion is one example.

Because interval recording involves continuous, concentrated observation over a relatively short time period, it is more suitable for target problems that occur frequently. Economically, it is not suited to recording problems that occur at low frequencies. The shorter the intervals used, the more precisely can the time at which the target problems occur be determined.

Since this is a complex and time-consuming data recording procedure, observers who record interval data must be highly trained. Before beginning a study, practice recording sessions should be conducted to ensure that observers will be able to produce reliable data. Interval recording is not recommended for use by indigenous observers (those who are part of the environment in which the observations are made) unless the target problem to be recorded is simple and discrete and the intervals are large. Since an observer cannot do anything else while recording data, this procedure cannot be used for self-recording.

Compared to the other data recording methods discussed in this chapter, interval recording is the most rigorous, precise, and expensive. Disregarding cost, the decision to use this method should depend on whether the target problem occurs at a high enough frequency to warrant its use and whether, for practical purposes, the research question requires such detailed data.

Frequency Recording

Like interval recording, frequency recording involves the direct observation of individuals, but the techniques used for recording the data are less complex. Thus, the target problem can be observed over a longer period of time. Frequency recording is appropriate with both high- and low-frequency target problems.

During the specified observation period, each occurrence of a target problem is noted on a data recording form with an *X*. The *X*s are totaled for each period and can be expressed as the number of occurrences per the length of the observation period. An example of frequency recording during a three-hour observation period in which there were five recorded occurrences of the target problem is given below:

Observation period	Number of occurrences
8:00 A.M. to 11:00 A.M.	*X X X X X*

The rate of the target problem, five occurrences in three hours, can be expressed as 5/3, or 1.7 occurrences per hour.

Reliability

As with interval recording, the reliability of the data collected with frequency recording can be determined by having two observers simultaneously and independently record data on the same target problem. Frequency data, however, provide only a gross measure indicating the total number of times the target problem has occurred during a specific time period. Therefore, comparison of the data recorded by the two observers only shows whether they recorded the same number of occurrences of the target problem.

The common formula for computing reliability in frequency recording (with two observers) is based on the percentage of agreement between the observer with the lower frequency and the observer with the higher frequency.

$$\text{Percentage of agreement} = \frac{\text{Lower frequency observed}}{\text{Higher frequency observed}} (100)$$

This reliability computation will not indicate whether the two observers recorded the same occurrences of the target problem. Each observer could miss 25 percent of the occurrences and still arrive at the same number of occurrences. While this method is not highly accurate, it can allow us to conclude that the data are representative of the frequency of the target problem. Confidence in the reliability of the frequency recording can be increased by having both observers record the actual time the target problem occurred, so it is possible to determine if the same problem was recorded by both of them at the same time.

Applications

Frequency recording is appropriate when the number of times the target problem occurs is the relevant measure. An administrator, for example, might use frequency recording to calculate the effect of a new policy to evaluate the work performance of social workers by measuring such tasks as the number of referrals processed or the number of clients served. Community organizers might use frequency recording to evaluate the effectiveness of a community action program by recording the number of requests for social services.

Target problems such as hitting, arguments, temper tantrums, compliance, communication, and physical affection can easily be measured with frequency recording. The frequency rates of the target problem may vary for different activities, particularly in settings such as homes or schools in which the schedule of activities changes often. Therefore, frequency data should be recorded under standardized conditions as much as possible. The number of arguments a couple has between 6:00 P.M. and 10:00 P.M. might vary according to the activities in which they are involved, for example. An evening at the movies or a party may result in few arguments; an evening at home may include many.

Generally, all three types of observers discussed further in a later section of this chapter can be used for frequency recording. These types are trained outside observers; indigenous observers who are naturally part of the research participant's environment, such as relevant others (family members, peers) and collaterals (caseworkers, other staff members); and self-observers, or research participants who make self-reports. The amount of observer training required to record frequency data depends on the number and complexity of the target problem. If fine discriminations must be made or if many target problems are to be recorded, observers may need extensive training and practice. To facilitate the implementation of frequency recording, the target problem should be clearly defined, especially when collaterals or relevant others are recording the data.

Frequency data recording is relatively inexpensive if the data are recorded by collaterals or research participants. If trained observers are used or extensive training is necessary, however, it may be as costly as interval recording.

Duration Recording

Duration data are obtained by directly observing the target problem and recording the length of time taken by each occurrence within the specified observation period. The duration of an occurrence can be measured in seconds or minutes by watching a clock, triggering a stopwatch, or noting the time the target problem begins and ends and calculating the duration later.

In the following simple example of duration recording, the target problem occurred three times in the one-hour observation period, and the observer noted the duration for each occurrence.

Observation period	*Number and duration (in minutes)*
6:00 P.M. to 7:00 P.M.	(1) 3; (2) 25; (3) 5

The first occurrence lasted for 3 minutes, the second for 25 minutes, and the third for 5 minutes.

Reliability and Applications

In calculating the reliability of the data in duration recording, two observers simultaneously and independently use synchronized timepieces to note the time of onset and completion of the problem. Comparison of the two observers' times indicates whether they were recording the same occurrence of the behavior, feeling, or cognition.

One common use of duration data is in case-level evaluation designs, to compare the duration of occurrences of the target problem before and after intervention. It can also be used to determine the cumulative time engaged in the target problem by an individual during the observation period by totaling the duration data for each occurrence. When this sum is divided by the total length of the observation period, the average amount of time engaged in the target problem by the individual is produced.

The duration of each occurrence during the observation period may also be averaged, but this could obscure important variations in the data. For instance, in the example where the occurrences of the target problem lasted from 3 to 25 minutes, with one occurrence of 5 minutes, the average occurrence is 11 minutes. This calculation hides the fact that the longest episode was more than twice as long as the average (Weinbach & Grinnell, 1995).

Duration data can easily be recorded by trained observers, collaterals, or research participants. Unless the target problem is difficult to discriminate, observer training should be minimal. If the problem is highly noticeable and occurs infrequently, other activities can be engaged in until it appears, and there is no need to be preoccupied with waiting for it. If the target problem is subtle at the outset, is of high frequency, or has an extremely long duration, the observer may need to concentrate on recording the data.

Duration recording should be used only when the length of time a target problem persists is the relevant issue. Many target problems can be measured in terms of both their duration and their frequency. The selection of the specific data recording method depends on the target problem to be measured.

Some examples of target problems that can be measured by duration recording are the length of episodes of crying, arguments, work breaks, illness, and time engaged in a task without interruption. It can also be used to measure the length of time between the presentation of a stimulus and the onset of the target problem, such as the elapsed time between a call for emergency services (stimulus) and delivery of the services (target problem), or the time between a parent's request and a child's compliance.

If trained outside observers are used, duration recording will be as expensive as interval recording. However, the training time will most likely be shorter. In many cases, duration data can be recorded by indigenous observers or self-observers at minimum expense.

Magnitude Recording

Magnitude recording involves recording data on the amount, level, or degree of the target problem during each occurrence. A magnitude recording can also be made by rating the target problem at prescribed intervals according to frequency or severity of occurrence. Ratings are made on a scale that shows the most minor level of the problem at one end and the most major level at the other.

The following example is a four-point scale to measure the magnitude of a child's temper tantrums:

1. Child cries and whines—low volume.
2. Child screams and shouts—high volume.
3. Child uses body to hit or throw inanimate objects; stamps feet on floor, kicks furniture, throws objects (but not in the direction of a person), hits furniture with hands.

4. Child uses body to strike other persons or self; throws an object in the direction of, or hits, another person.

These points on the scale should be operationally defined whenever possible, but a simple four-point subjective rating scale could be used by collaterals or relevant others to rate their observations. Research participants can also use this recording method to record their own target problems related to private events such as degree of depression or anxiety.

Reliability

When simultaneous and independent ratings by two observers are used as a reliability check, the data should correspond not only to the number of occurrences but also to the magnitude rating. As in frequency recording, it is not possible to ensure that the observers have recorded and rated the same occurrence of the target problem unless the exact time of occurrence is noted.

An example of a reliability computation for magnitude recording, in which two observers each made three observations, is given below:

Observer 1		Observer 2	
Time	Magnitude	Time	Magnitude
10:02	3	10:02	3
10:57	2	10:57	3
11:17	3	11:17	3

Because the observers achieved 100 percent agreement on the time the target problems occurred, they were able to compare their ratings on each episode. There was agreement on the ratings of two out of three occurrences, for a 67 percent level of agreement on magnitude.

Applications

Magnitude recording is an appropriate measure for target problems that are characterized by a wide range of responses, provided the degree of the response is the relevant issue. Measures of magnitude can provide data about a problem that would not be reflected in a duration or frequency measure. A community organizer, for example, may want to know if the degree to which school board members use community complaints as an input for planning has improved over the past year. The board's responses to each citizen complaint could be rated according to the following five-point scale:

1. Refuses to hear complaint.
2. Gives time for complaint but does not respond.

3. Discusses complaint but does not attempt to solve problem.
4. Devises solution to citizen problem.
5. Devises solution, discusses implication for future planning, and implements plan.

Magnitude recording requires more training than frequency or duration recording because observers need to make judgments about the degree of the target problem, in addition to noting its occurrence. Minor distinctions between the levels of the target problem may necessitate the use of trained outside observers. For most target problems with distinct levels and clear operational definitions, however, one practice session is likely to afford sufficient training.

If outside observers are not used, magnitude recording is a relatively inexpensive method of data recording. Recording the magnitude of target problems requires attention to every detail, so it may be time-consuming if the problem is of long duration.

Spot-Check Recording

Spot-check recording occurs when we observe the target problem at specified intervals. Unlike the four methods discussed above, spot checks involve our intermittent rather than continuous observations. At the specified observation time, we record whether or not the individual being observed is engaged in the target problem at that moment. Spot-check recording produces occurrence-nonoccurrence data on the target problem.

To determine the percentage of spot checks in which the target problem occurred, the number of spot checks in which the target problem was observed is divided by the total number of spot checks conducted. If the problem is spot-checked a number of times each day, the percentages can be compared and the daily data averaged to compare data from day to day. Target problems of groups of individuals can be expressed as the percentage of group members who were engaged in the behavior, feeling, or cognition in the observation period.

Reliability and Applications

The reliability of data in spot-check recording is computed with the same formula used to determine reliability in frequency recording, by comparing the data collected by two independent observers. Because observation periods last only a moment, the two observers must be precisely synchronized to record simultaneously.

Spot-checking is a useful method for assessing the target problems of individuals in a group. For instance, the social behavior of nursing home residents could be measured by counting the number who are alone in their rooms at a specific time. Continued spot checks at prescribed intervals would indicate the level of social activity among the residents, and activity programs designed to affect social behavior could also be evaluated using this measure. This method can be used by observers who spend minimal time in the settings or by indigenous observers such as nurses who have little time to record data.

Generally, spot checks are best suited for measuring target problems that occur at a high frequency or are sustained over a long period, such as social interaction, play, and work. Low-frequency target problems may not be accurately represented by this method.

Spot checks can be conducted by observers who are normally part of the environment or by outside observers. Research participants may react more to outside observers; because the observer is present only intermittently for the spot checks, the stimulus may continue to be novel. Participants can record spot-check data on their own target problems by using a timer to signal the instants when they should record whether or not they are engaged in the target problem. Naturally occurring time intervals such as lunch breaks, coffee breaks, and end of work can also be used as signals to record data.

The amount of observer training needed is minimal unless the target problem to be measured is difficult to distinguish from other target problems. Instructions alone may be sufficient, but a practice session or two are advisable.

Spot checks are typically the least expensive direct-observation method of data collection, since the target problem is observed only intermittently. This also enables collaterals and research participants to record data with minimal interruption of their normal activities.

Permanent-Product Recording

Permanent-product recording does not require direct observation of the occurrences of the target problem. Instead, the occurrence is determined by observing the product of the problem. Examples of permanent-product recording include records of social services provided, teachers' records, and end products of work activity, such as empty wastebaskets and vacuumed carpets for custodial work. Data can be recorded at a convenient time after the occurrence of the target problem but before the product is altered or obliterated by subsequent target problems.

Reliability and Applications

Reliability of the data is determined by comparing the data of two or more independent observers. The reliability measures do not have to be taken simultaneously, however. In most instances, durable records can be stored indefinitely for future reference.

Permanent-product recording is appropriate for measuring target problems that alter the state of the environment or are recorded in a lasting form. Written reports of such matters as school attendance, work completion, and various crimes can be measured by inspecting the records maintained on these problems rather than by observing the problems themselves.

A staff trainer, for example, may want to know if treatment intervention plans improve after staff members take part in a new program that teaches techniques for maintaining clinical records. Frequency of record completion or duration of work on the intervention plans would not reflect an improvement in quality. A frequency count could be made of all intervention plans that meet minimal standards, but those data would indicate only how many intervention plans do or do not meet these standards. Instead, the records could be compared over time according to a standard of "completeness" or quality that was taught in the training session. The permanent product of the case reports then could be used to demonstrate fine-grained changes in the quality of work over time.

Target problems that produce an observable change in the environment can easily be measured by observing and recording the changes rather than observing the target problem as it occurs. A parent, for example, can record data on a child's completion of assigned chores, such as taking the garbage out, by looking to see if the garbage has been removed after the deadline for completion of the chore. Or the effectiveness of a policy on recruiting and hiring members of racial minority groups can be evaluated by recording the number of minority staff actually hired after the policy was introduced.

Permanent-product recording can also be used to measure a target problem that could not be observed otherwise. An individual, for example, could demonstrate mastery of the cognitive process of learning how to perform a mathematical function such as multiplication by consistently producing the correct answers to multiplication problems. The written answers are permanent products that indicate whether or not learning has occurred. Measuring instruments such as questionnaires or tests can also create permanent products.

Permanent-product data can be recorded by trained observers, collaterals, and relevant others, or self-observers. Since the measure relies on ongoing recording of environmental changes, this type of recording can usually be implemented in the absence of the research participants. Therefore, it is the least intrusive method of recording data. Permanent-product recording, however, provides data only on the end result of the target problem, not on the problem itself. Other data recording methods, such as interval recording, must be used to measure the process of the target problem.

THE ROLE OF THE OBSERVER

Regardless of the data recording method used in direct observations, the data obtained will be only as good as the observers or recorders who collect them. With each method, the reliability of the data is determined by comparing the results obtained by two or more independent observers. To ensure that the data collected will be determined reliable, the target problem should be clearly defined so it can be differentiated from other problems, recording procedures should be made as simple as possible, and observers should be carefully trained so they know precisely what to look for, at what time, and how it should be recorded. Reliability checks should be made as often as possible during the study, using the prescribed formulas and methods to determine the percentage of agreement in the data of two or more observers.

Observer reliability is analogous to the test-retest and alternate-forms methods of establishing the reliability of measuring instruments discussed in Chapter 7. It is concerned with the stability of observations made by a single observer at several points in time (intra-observer reliability) or the equivalence of observations made by two or more observers at one point in time (inter-observer reliability).

Inter-observer reliability, which is also referred to as inter-judge, inter-rater, or inter-coder reliability, has been widely used in social work research. In this approach, the reliability of the observations of two or more observers who use the same instrument to measure the same individuals at a certain point in time is assessed by calculating the percentage of agreement between them. Procedures for doing this for the various types of structured observations were explained in the preceding section.

Selection of Observers

Observers who collect and record data by direct observation may be selected from several categories:

- Outside observers, often professionally trained, who are engaged to record data.
- Indigenous observers, including relevant others (such as family members and peers) and collaterals (such as social service staff members), who are naturally a part of the research participants' environment.
- Research participants, who provide self-reports.

A number of factors need to be taken into consideration in deciding which of these sources to use. These include direct costs; time—both the observer's time and the time frame of the research situation; type of data required; and clinical factors such as intrusion into participants' lives.

Outside Observers

Observers brought in for the purpose of recording data are expensive to use and may not always be available. Since they are not a part of the participants' normal environment, they are likely to intrude into their lives in a way that indigenous observers will not. In some situations, the presence of an outside observer can alter the target problem being measured and produce erroneous results.

Most outside observers, however, have had considerable training and experience and know how to use sophisticated procedures to record data on complex target problems. Because of this, and because outside observers have no vested interest in the results of the study, data obtained by them are generally considered to be more reliable than data from other sources.

Indigenous Observers

Indigenous observers are naturally a part of the research participant's environment. They may be members of the individual's family or staff members in an institution, such as a hospital, school, residential facility, or agency. Such collaterals, however, have their own jobs to do, and a major consideration in employing them as observers must be the amount of time required for data collection. Will it interfere with their other work if they are asked to make a frequency recording of a particular person's target problem? Will they resent the extra burden placed on them and fail to cooperate? A spot-check recording would take less time, but would such data be sufficiently accurate to fulfill the research study's requirements?

A compromise in research methods often is necessary when we find ourselves in a position where the gathering of interval or frequency data by outside observers would be too expensive or intrusive, and the use of indigenous observers would be too time-consuming. While the way in which a research question is formulated determines what and how data are to be collected, the practical difficulties in the collection of data also affect the formulation of the question. This is one of the factors to take into account when deciding on a hypothesis to be tested. In this case, we would be obligated to adapt our question to fit the data collection methods that are actually open to us.

The problem of time is not so large when members of the research participant's family are asked to gather data and there is no direct cost. There are other difficulties, however. It is far easier for a staff member in an institution to observe a person unobtrusively than it is for a member of the individual's family to do so in the home.

A person who is aware of being watched might well alter the target problem, even subconsciously. Difficulties might also arise over which family members are selected to record the data; jealousies and frictions normally present within the family system might be aggravated. Observation of one family member by others, even with the best of intentions, may not be advisable.

Since family members usually have no training or experience in recording data, they must be carefully trained. Even so, they may only be able to cope with simple recording procedures and straightforward target problems that can be easily differentiated from other problems. The type and reliability of data obtained from family members are often limited.

Self-Observers

Self-recording may be the only possible alternative when data are needed on an individual's thoughts and feelings, or when the act of observation would change the target problem. Moreover, some target problems occur in situations that preclude the presence of an observer. Cost and the observer's time are seldom considerations when the data are self-recorded. Some recording methods, however, such as interval recording, cannot be used in self-recording because it is difficult for the participant to experience the target problem and record it at the same time.

The most important consideration when data are self-recorded is reliability. Even when the research participant is cooperative and truly wishes to record the problem accurately, it is very difficult to prevent the recording process from interfering with the target problem being recorded. Sometimes self-reports can be verified by other observers. People who report feelings of depression, for example, may exhibit behaviors (or target problems) consistent with depression, such as crying spells or unusual sleeping habits, which can be observed by others.

UNSTRUCTURED OBSERVATION

Not every observational method of data collection uses structured observations—as is done in the types that have been discussed in this chapter. In unstructured or nonsystematic observations, one or more observers provide narrative or qualitative accounts of their observations, without using structured, numerical categories to observe and record target problems. As we will see in Chapter 15, unstructured observation is generally used in the qualitative research approach. Social work practitioners make unstructured observations all the time when working with clients, and these observations can be used to generate clinical or research questions to be tested.

SUMMARY

The six basic methods of data recording—interval, frequency, duration, magnitude, spot-check, and permanent product—draw data from structured observations. The observations are made in a specified place and over a specified time period; the target problem to be observed is operationally defined, and the data are recorded on an instrument designed for the purpose. In each case, reliability is determined by calculating the level of agreement between the observations or ratings of two or more independent observers.

Which method or combination of methods is selected for a particular study will depend on the kind of data required for the study—that is, the formulation of the research question to be investigated and the hypothesis to be tested. The choice is also determined by constraints of time and money and the availability of observers who are willing and able to collect the necessary data. Observers may be outside observers, indigenous observers, or research participants.

As in all research situations, the factors to be considered in formulating a research question or hypothesis and in selecting a data collection procedure are interdependent. The question will determine which data collection method is to be selected, and this, in turn, will determine how the observers are to be selected. The availability and willingness of observers to perform the necessary operations will affect which method is to be used, and this, in turn, will affect the research question. The art of constructing any research hypothesis lies in juggling these factors so that a meaningful hypothesis can be formulated from the research question and data can be collected to test it within the context of the research situation.

The most widely used data collection procedure in social work research is the survey, as noted in Chapter 9. The use of the survey method in face-to-face interviews, self-reports, and telephone surveys is described in the following chapter.

REFERENCES AND FURTHER READINGS

BARLOW, D.H., HAYES, S.C., & NELSON, R.O. (1984). *The scientist-practitioner: Research and accountability in applied settings*. Elmsford, NY: Pergamon.

BARLOW, D.H., & HERSEN, M. (1984). *Single-case experimental designs: Strategies for studying behavior change* (2nd ed.). Elmsford, NY: Pergamon.

BLOOM, M., FISCHER, J., & ORME, J. (1995). *Evaluating practice: Guidelines for the accountable professional* (2nd ed.). Englewood Cliffs, NJ: Prentice-Hall.

BLYTHE, B.J., & TRIPODI, T. (1989). *Measurement in direct practice*. Newbury Park, CA: Sage.

DEPOY, E., & GITLIN, L.N. (1994). *Introduction to research* (pp. 113-114). St. Louis: Mosby.

FISCHER, J., & CORCORAN, K.J. (1995). *Measures for clinical practice* (2 vols., 2nd ed.) New York: Free Press.

GABOR, P.A., & GRINNELL, R.M., JR. (1994). *Evaluation and quality improvement in the human services* (pp. 123-147). Needham Heights, MA: Allyn & Bacon.

GRINNELL, R.M., JR., & WILLIAMS, M. (1990). *Research in social work: A primer* (pp. 232-264). Itasca, IL: F.E. Peacock.

KRYSIK, J., HOFFART, I., & GRINNELL, R.M., JR. (1993). *Student study quide for the fourth edition of social work research and evaluation* (pp. 13-14). Itasca, IL: F.E. Peacock.

MARLOW, C. (1993). *Research methods for generalist social work* (pp. 29, 151-173). Pacific Grove, CA: Brooks/Cole.

MONETTE, D.R., SULLIVAN, T.J., & DEJONG, C.R. (1994). *Applied social research* (3rd ed., pp. 282-311). Fort Worth, TX: Harcourt Brace.

NURIUS, P.S., & HUDSON, W.W. (1993). *Human services: Practice, evaluation, and computers*. Pacific Grove, CA: Brooks/Cole.

POLSTER, R.A., & COLLINS, D. (1993). Structured observation. In R.M. Grinnell, Jr. (Ed.), *Social work research and evaluation* (4th ed., pp. 244-261). Itasca, IL: F.E. Peacock.

ROYSE, D.D. (1995). *Research methods in social work* (2nd ed., pp. 49-72). Chicago: Nelson-Hall.

RUBIN, A., & BABBIE, E.R. (1993). *Research methods for social work* (2nd ed., pp. 292-328). Pacific Grove, CA: Brooks/Cole.

WEINBACH, R.W., & GRINNELL, R.M., JR. (1995). *Statistics for social workers* (3rd ed.). White Plains, NY: Longman.

WEINBACH, R.W., & GRINNELL, R.M., JR. (1996). *Applying research knowledge: A workbook for social work students* (2nd ed., pp. 73-80). Needham Heights, MA: Allyn & Bacon.

WILLIAMS, M., TUTTY, L.M., & GRINNELL, R.M., JR. (1995). *Research in social work: An introduction* (2nd ed., pp. 161-194). Itasca, IL: F.E. Peacock.

Steven L. McMurtry

Chapter **14**

Survey Research

ALMOST EVERYONE has been asked to take part in a survey of some form or another—a curbside interview, an exit poll after voting, a mass-mailed marketing survey, a seemingly random telephone opinion poll. To some extent, every research study that uses a survey as the data collection method can be called "survey research."

These studies can be designed to achieve a variety of ends, but they all seek to collect data from many individuals in order to understand something about them as a whole. It is essential, therefore, that survey research procedures produce data that are accurate, reliable, and representative, so findings can be generalized from a sample to the larger population or to different research situations. Survey research thus is a systematic way of collecting data by obtaining opinions or answers from selected respondents who represent the population of interest, or, occasionally, from an entire population.

The major steps in survey research are outlined on the left side of Figure 14.1, and the tasks to be completed in each step are listed on the right side.

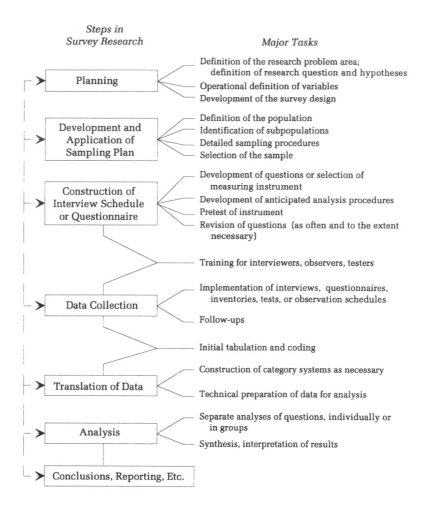

*Steps in
Survey Research*

Major Tasks

Planning
— Definition of the research problem area; definition of research question and hypotheses
— Operational definition of variables
— Development of the survey design

Development and Application of Sampling Plan
— Definition of the population
— Identification of subpopulations
— Detailed sampling procedures
— Selection of the sample

Construction of Interview Schedule or Questionnaire
— Development of questions or selection of measuring instrument
— Development of anticipated analysis procedures
— Pretest of instrument
— Revision of questions (as often and to the extent necessary)

— Training for interviewers, observers, testers

Data Collection
— Implementation of interviews, questionnaires, inventories, tests, or observation schedules
— Follow-ups

— Initial tabulation and coding

Translation of Data
— Construction of category systems as necessary
— Technical preparation of data for analysis

Analysis
— Separate analyses of questions, individually or in groups
— Synthesis, interpretation of results

Conclusions, Reporting, Etc.

FIGURE 14.1   STEPS AND TASKS IN THE SURVEY RESEARCH PROCESS

Development and application of the sampling plan is essential to ensure the representativeness of the data collected (see Chapter 10). In most surveys, random sampling procedures are used to increase the probability that every person in the population has an equal opportunity of being selected for the sample. Probability sampling of this sort makes it possible to calculate the degree to which the sample is representative of the population from which it was drawn.

The steps in the research process that are unique to the survey method of data collection correspond to the measurement process that is at the center of any research effort. These steps include the construction of the interview schedule (for face-to-face and telephone interviews) or questionnaire (for mail surveys), the procedures for data collection, and to some extent, data coding and analysis.

Survey research was introduced in Chapter 9 as an example for the discussion of the design and construction of measuring instruments. Surveys can be used to collect data on facts about individuals separately and in organizations and communities, as well as data on their behaviors and unobservable variables such as attitudes, beliefs, feelings, and ethical standards.

SURVEY RESEARCH DESIGNS

Because survey research studies social phenomena by collecting data on numerous individuals in order to understand the group or population they represent, the research designs used usually follow the principles of group designs discussed in Chapter 11. The design selected for a particular survey research study accordingly depends on the research question and how much knowledge about the problem area is available.

Knowledge Level

As Chapter 11 points out, the knowledge levels at which research studies are conducted are arranged on a three-point continuum from exploratory at the lowest level, to descriptive, to explanatory at the highest level, where "ideal" experiments can be conducted. Data can be collected with surveys at all three levels of design.

In exploratory designs, data are collected in order to form general ideas and tentative theories about the research question. In descriptive designs, the collection of data should result in more specific descriptions of the variables of interest; surveys are used as the data collection method in most descriptive studies to gather data on a sample or population in order to characterize it in terms of the variables under study.

A survey design that serves a descriptive purpose can also be exploratory if the collection of data allows the formulation of hypotheses that can be submitted to further study. One way this can be accomplished is with the use of open-ended questions in the survey instrument; this was the method employed in a study on sources of antiwar sentiment during the Vietnam era (Schuman, 1972).

Explanatory research designs are concerned with developing an understanding of social phenomena on the basis of the relationships among the variables of interest. Surveys are less commonly thought of as tools for explanatory studies, but they can be used effectively in these situations. Consider an executive director in a social work agency who is trying to determine if the agency should adopt a new technique for counseling victims of violent crime. For a number of reasons, it is decided that an experimental study (in which clients would be randomly assigned to the old or new method) is just not feasible. The director, however, reasons that another way to assess the quality of the new counseling approach would be to ask clients how satisfied they were with the outcomes it produced. This is an explanatory research problem, but in this case the only way to address it would be with survey methods such as mailing self-administered questionnaires to former clients of the agency.

The Dimension of Time

The dimension of time also must be taken into account in deciding on a survey research design. Most phenomena are subject to change over time, and many variables that are of interest in social work research, such as attitudes, emotional states, and social service utilization, can change rapidly. The two basic types of survey research designs are defined in terms of whether the variable is to be measured once, with a cross-sectional design, or over time, with a longitudinal design. Examples of these two types of survey designs are discussed in Chapter 11; the randomized cross-sectional survey, and the randomized longitudinal survey.

To find out how satisfied an agency's clients are with the quality of services they have received, for example, the simplest and most direct approach would be to survey a sample of former clients about their attitudes toward services at the time they terminated. Even though a few weeks might be needed to survey enough clients to secure a sample of reasonable size, all data would be collected within a narrow time interval to provide data on clients' attitudes toward services at the time of termination. Cross-sectional designs use a "snapshot" method of data collection to provide data that are specific to a particular point in time.

If only the most satisfied clients actually complete the program, however, and many others who are dissatisfied drop out before completion, surveying only those who completed the program could provide a distorted picture of the true level of client satisfaction with the agency. To control for this threat to internal validity, a sample of clients might be followed from the start of services until they have all either dropped out or completed them. During this time, regular measurements would be taken of the clients' satisfaction with their services, and the variation of these measurements across time would be evaluated. Longitudinal designs use this method of data collection to monitor changes in variables of interest over an extended period of time.

Cross-Sectional Designs

Studies based on cross-sectional designs are usually associated with exploratory and descriptive research designs because they do a good job of providing data on the characteristics of a sample or population. A cross-sectional survey can be used to determine whether a particular problem exists within a group of clients and what the level of the problem is. Needs assessments, used by community development workers to identify neighborhood problems and service gaps, are an example. The principal advantage of this approach to survey research is that the necessary data can be collected quickly and inexpensively.

Cross-sectional studies are also used in explanatory designs to test relationships among characteristics of members of a sample or population. The main problem with these studies is that, because of their one-shot nature, they cannot clearly establish the time order of variables (see Chapter 11).

Longitudinal Designs

In longitudinal studies, data collected to indicate characteristics of a sample or population are repeated over two or more time periods, which allows consideration of how the sample characteristics have changed. The three types of longitudinal studies—trend, cohort, and panel studies—all use this repeated-measures approach to data collection.

Trend Studies   Trend studies utilize data from surveys carried out at periodic intervals on samples drawn from a particular population. The U.S. Department of Labor, under contract with the Census Bureau, for example, conducts the Current Population Survey (CPS) every March. Though a new sample is drawn each year, the population of interest remains the same. The data collected by the CPS are used primarily to gauge annual trends in unemployment and labor-force participation, but they also provide valuable data on other changes in the characteristics of the U.S. population. The accuracy of the assessments of trends revealed by these types of surveys depends on their regular use over a considerable period of time.

Cohort Studies   Cohort studies focus on specific groups of people who share certain characteristics. A cohort can be defined as a set of individuals who undergo a particular experience at a certain time, such as all high school graduates entering college in a certain year. Successive random samples are drawn from this group to monitor how the characteristics of members change over time. The baby boom generation is an example of a birth cohort—in this case, all persons born in the period from approximately 1946 to 1962. Studies of random samples of its members have been used to identify trends in American life, from fashion to family structure to political preferences.

A foster care administrator might use a cohort study to evaluate services to children who entered foster homes during a particular year. In each subsequent year a random sample would be drawn from among members of the cohort who remained in care, and data from these samples could be used to distinguish children who had exited quickly from the program from those who had experienced long or repeated stays in out-of-home care.

Panel Studies   Both trend studies and cohort studies monitor changes in a population through use of a series of random samples of the members of the group, with each sample being comprised of a different group of individuals. In contrast, a panel study is designed to follow the same set of individuals over time and to collect data on a regular basis.

Some of the best-known research studies on the effects of public assistance programs have come from the Panel Study on Income Dynamics (PSID), conducted by researchers at the University of Michigan's Survey Research Center. The project began with 5,000 families in 1968 and included more than 20,000 families some 20 years later. The longitudinal nature of this study has enabled researchers to examine transitions into and out of poverty and to study events associated with these transitions through related studies that have produced important results. Mary Jo Bane (1986), for example, studied episodes of poverty among children in the sample, recognizing that most poor children are not always poor but instead live in families that move into and out of poverty as their circumstances change. Her findings showed that many white children made the transition into poverty as a result of becoming part of a female-headed household, but for African-American children, poverty more often resulted from being born into a poor family.

Social workers have begun to recognize the advantages offered by longitudinal studies over the cross-sectional approach. The opportunity to monitor the service histories of clients or groups over time is often more valuable than simply determining their average condition at a particular point in time. Still, longitudinal designs are more costly, time-consuming, and complex than cross-sectional studies. In addition, the successful use of longitudinal designs requires careful planning and an orientation toward long-term rather than short-term research goals.

APPROACHES TO DATA COLLECTION FOR SURVEYS

The general classes of survey measuring instruments—self-report questionnaires and interview schedules for face-to-face and telephone interviews—were identified in Chapter 9. This chapter distinguishes among these approaches to data collection for surveys on the basis of the assistance offered to respondents from the researcher.

In the face-to-face interview, the interviewer poses questions directly to each member of the study sample and immediately records the responses on an interview schedule. In self-administered surveys, respondents complete the survey instrument without any direct assistance from an interviewer. This type includes group-administered questionnaires and mail surveys; by far the most frequently used form is the mailed questionnaire, which relies on respondents both to fill out the survey instrument and to mail it back. In telephone interviews, the interviewer poses questions and records data provided by respondents, but there is no face-to-face contact.

The three principal approaches to data collection in surveys are listed in Figure 14.2 along with the advantages and disadvantages of each one.

Technique	Advantages	Disadvantages
Face-to-face Interview	◦ Highest response rate ◦ Subjects tend to provide more thoughtful answers ◦ Allows for longer, more open-ended responses ◦ Allows recording of non-verbal information ◦ Can reach disabled or illiterate respondents ◦ Interviewer can clarify questions for respondent ◦ Subjects more willing to answer sensitive questions	◦ Highest cost ◦ Highest chance for introduction of experimenter bias ◦ Respondent may react to personality of interviewer rather than content of the interview ◦ Interviewer may misrecord response
Mail Survey	◦ Lowest cost ◦ Subjects can read and respond to questions at their own pace ◦ Visual arrangement of items on written instrument can facilitate comprehension ◦ Provides greatest sense of anonymity/ confidentiality ◦ Lowest chance of introduction of experimenter bias	◦ Lowest response rate ◦ Feasible only with subjects having relatively good reading skills ◦ No opportunity to clarify confusing items ◦ Difficult to get in-depth or open-ended responses ◦ Cannot ensure that intended respondents are the actual respondents
Telephone Survey	◦ Relatively low cost ◦ Can be completed quickly ◦ Interviewer can clarify questions for respondent ◦ Can reach respondents with poor reading/writing skills ◦ Allows direct computer data entry	◦ Not useful for low-income respondents who do not have a telephone ◦ High initial vocal interaction, misses nonverbal responses ◦ Requires simple questions, unless a copy of the survey instrument is mailed in advance

FIGURE 14.2   ADVANTAGES AND DISADVANTAGES TO THREE PRINCIPAL APPROACHES TO DATA COLLECTION IN SURVEY RESEARCH

FACE-TO-FACE INTERVIEWS

Face-to-face verbal contact is the most basic and most common form of communication among humans. Survey respondents are usually more willing to participate when questions are posed directly by someone in their presence, so response rates for face-to-face interviews are relatively high. Respondents also are less likely to give distracted or ill-considered answers to questions in the presence of a person who directly asks for their views.

Even the simplest questions in an interview schedule may be confusing to some people or in some circumstances, and an interviewer can explain the meaning each question is intended to convey in a way that is impossible with self-administered written survey instruments. Face-to-face interviews also allow inclusion of respondents who have various disabilities, such as a lack of reading and writing skills, language barriers, or visual or physical impairments.

Within limits, the interview setting also avoids some of the rigid structure that must be imposed on the construction of questions and responses in a written instrument. Not only can the interviewer explain the questions in detail, but, particularly if a tape recorder is used, detailed verbal answers that respondents would be unable or unwilling to put in writing can be recorded. Face-to-face interviews thus can incorporate more open-ended questions than is possible with mailed surveys. Moreover, the presence of the interviewer makes it possible to capture nuances of responses that would otherwise be lost.

Somewhat paradoxically, respondents have been found to be more likely to answer sensitive personal questions when they are posed by face-to-face interviewers rather than telephone interviewers (Groves, 1988). One explanation is that face-to-face interviewers are better able to establish legitimacy by sending cover letters, presenting their credentials, and maintaining a professional demeanor.

Limitations

In spite of these advantages, comparatively few surveys employ face-to-face interviews as the principal data collection method. The main reason is the cost of employing and training interviewers; this is often the major expenditure in survey research, and it is extremely high with face-to-face interviewing. In order to satisfy cost constraints, we may have to abandon plans for such interviews or drastically scale down the scope of our study. This is particularly a problem with longitudinal studies and lengthy cross-sectional projects, where substantial time, energy, and expense may be needed to train interviewers to replace those who leave.

The time and cost for interviewers to travel to meet with respondents represent another expense. The Postal Service does the work of delivering mail surveys, and telephone interviewers are connected instantly to respondents, but face-to-face interviewers often must go where the respondents are. Moreover, when respondents are not at home, telephone interviewers can call back later, and mailed questionnaires wait to be retrieved from the mailbox. In studies using face-to-face interviews, respondents who cannot be located or who fail to keep an appointment also add to the expense of follow-up.

While the direct human interaction in face-to-face interviews facilitates respondents' willingness to participate and improves their understanding of the survey instrument, it may also bias their answers in various ways and thus be a source of measurement error. Respondents may answer in a way that they believe will please the interviewer rather than according to their own beliefs, or if they are participating reluctantly or take a dislike to the interviewer, they may deliberately misrepresent their views. Because of their response sets (see Chapter 7), survey participants may give answers that they believe are socially acceptable, agree with statements regardless of their opinion, or try to give unusual or unexpected responses.

Interviewers also can be a source of bias or error. Poorly trained personnel often make clerical errors or are inconsistent in recording data, and even the best-trained interviewers can subtly influence respondents' answers through verbal or nonverbal cues of which they themselves may be unaware.

Preparing for the Interview

When face-to-face interviewing is the data collection method, preparation for the interview is a very lengthy process indeed. Before the interview takes place, we must lay the groundwork by developing the interview schedule, hiring and training interviewers, choosing the sample, obtaining respondents' consent, and making arrangements for the interview.

Developing the Interview Schedule

The interview schedule is the survey instrument used with both face-to-face and telephone interviews. The guidelines presented in Chapter 9 for constructing questionnaires for use as survey instruments are applicable to interview schedules as well. Interview schedules, however, have certain features that distinguish them from other types of questionnaires, particularly those used in mailed surveys.

Figure 14.3 reproduces the opening portion of an interview schedule used with 300 mothers whose children had been placed in foster care (Jenkins & Norman, 1972). The entire interview instrument covered 34 pages and included open- and closed-ended questions, checklists, and scales; the interview lasted about two hours. Figure 14.4 presents the entire interview schedule for a study by Harvey Gochros (1970) on postplacement adoption services, for which he was the sole interviewer. This schedule was used with 114 adoptive parents, and a similar one was used with 18 postplacement social workers. Extensive use of

---

A. MAIN QUESTION: RESPONDENT'S STATEMENT OF PROBLEM

1. First of all, would you tell me in your own words what brought about the placement of _____ away from home in foster care?
   (Probe if not spontaneously answered.)

   1a. Who first had the idea to place _____?
      Did anyone oppose it or disagree with it?
         If yes:
            a. Who?
            b. Why?

   1b. Were any attempts made to make other arrangements for _____ other than placement?
         If yes:
            a. What?
            b. Who did this?
            c. Why didn't it work out?

   1c. Was there anyone whom you usually depend on who couldn't or didn't help out?
         If yes:
            a. Who? (relationship)
            b. Why did the individual not help out?

   1d. Did all your children who were in your home go into placement at that time?
         If no:
            a. Which children were not placed at that time (name, age, gender, father)?
            b. Why weren't they placed?

   1e. Who was caring for _____ just before he/she was placed?
         If other than natural mother:
            a. For how long had he or she been caring for _____?
            b. Why was he or she (rather than the child's mother) caring for the child?

FIGURE 14.3   PORTION OF AN INTERVIEW SCHEDULE ON FOSTER CARE PLACEMENT

abbreviations (AP = adoptive parent, CW = caseworker, SP = supervisory or postplacement period) contributed to the brevity of the instrument.

Interview schedules do not look like familiar questionnaire forms because they are designed to be completed by the interviewer rather than the respondent. With self-administered questionnaires, substantial design efforts are necessary

1. What were you told about the purposes and content of the SP?
2. What did you expect the visits to be like?
3. How were they different from what you expected?
4. Why do you think there is a SP?
5. How many SP visits were there? Average length?
6. How many AP initiated? Why?
7. How many unexpected? Opinion
8. How many were you present:
9. Ever feel left out?
10. What did you talk about?
11. What do you think CW wanted you to bring up or discuss in SP visits?
12. Subsequent contacts.
13. What sort of problems did you run into during the SP?
14. Books recommended? Why? Read? Useful?
15. Did you think of CW more as a friend or caseworker?
16. What did you like most about CW? What did you like least about CW?
17. Did CW create the kind of atmosphere where you felt free to talk over your real feelings about things?
18. Did you ever withhold any information or feelings from CW?
19. How much do you think CW knew about child care and development?
20. What did you think about when you knew a visit was scheduled?
21. What did you think about just after the visit was over?
22. Did your feelings change about the visits during the SP?
23. What did you find most helpful result of the visits?
24. What did you find to be the least and most unpleasant aspect the CW?
25. Any way agency could have been more helpful during the SP?
26. How helpful was the SP to you, overall?
27. Will the visits by helpful to you in the future?
28. How did you feel when the decree was finally granted?
29. Do you think there should be a waiting period?
30. If yes, how long?
31. Should there be CW visits? Why?
32. Compulsory? Why?
33. If they had been voluntary, would you have requested any?
34. If adopt again and if voluntary, would you have requested any?
35. Groups for parents of 5-year-olds, interested?
36. Groups for parents of adolescents, interested?
37. If ran into a problem with a child, contact worker?
38. Second child: planning, applied, placed, not planning?
39. If worker was different from study, was transition difficult?
40. Comments:

FIGURE 14.4   INTERVIEW SCHEDULE USED FOR STUDY ON POSTPLACEMENT ADOPTION SERVICES

to ensure that respondents will be able to understand and complete all questions on the form. Because interview schedules are seen only by the interviewer, design efforts can be directed to maximizing the ease and accuracy of data recording and subsequent coding. Instructions to respondents are also included in interview schedules, but because they are read and, if necessary, explained by the interviewer, they can be more concise.

A particularly useful characteristic of interview schedules is that they can include prompts, reminders, and explanatory notes for interviewers. In a survey of client satisfaction, for example, clients might be asked to identify the one aspect of an agency's services that they thought was most helpful. The schedule could include instructions for the interviewer on how to help clients who offer more than one answer to select the most appropriate one. Clients might be asked to list all the services they had received at the agency as a way of indicating those that they found memorable. Other prompts could be included for use in stimulating clients' memories, but their selective use by interviewers can introduce problems of response bias.

Some studies supplement the interview schedule with written material to be given to respondents. Lengthy questions, those that are based on prior contingencies (e.g., "If yes,"), and those in which the respondent is asked to choose from a long list of possible responses are often enhanced by written aids, for example.

Hiring and Training Interviewers

In the same way that counseling requires greater verbal ability than simple conversation, face-to-face interviewing requires more skill than everyday communication. Careful selection of interviewers and training to develop their skills are crucial in the use of face-to-face interviews. Competent interviewers are more likely to elicit truthful, comprehensive data from respondents and less likely to make mistakes in administering the interview schedule and recording the data.

Hiring interviewers who are appropriate to the task is the first consideration; there must be a good fit between the interviewer and the respondent. Because people generally relate best to those they perceive as similar to themselves, interviewers should, as far as possible, reflect the characteristics of potential respondents in such variables as age, gender, race or ethnicity, and life experiences (Schuman & Converse, 1971; Singer, Frankel, & Glassman, 1983). For studies that focus on a very narrow sample or involve only a small number of interviewers, the goal should be to select interviewers who could put the respondents at ease and overcome their perceptions of differences between themselves and the interviewer.

The traits to look for in interviewers are similar to those that characterize good social workers—warmth, sincerity, appropriate dress and appearance, and good verbal and nonverbal skills. Interviewers must also possess the skills necessary to read and understand the interview schedule, interpret it for respondents, and express their responses in writing.

The process of training interviewers is devoted to enhancing these basic skills, with the goal of reducing bias or other sources of measurement error. Among the most common sources of error in interviewing are instruction and interrogation error (not reading the instructions or questions exactly as they are written on the interview schedule), response option error (failing to give the exact list of possible responses to a question from which the respondent is to choose), and recording error (inaccurately recording the response) (Alreck & Settle, 1985). More difficult to monitor is interviewer bias, which occurs when interviewers give cues concerning the responses they expect or favor, or when they interpret and record respondents' answers in a way that fits their own desires or expectations.

Choosing the Population or Sample

The basic sampling principles presented in Chapter 10 apply to any data collection technique. With face-to-face interviews, however, a specific consideration is the use of the smallest possible sample that will allow for acceptable sampling error, due to the expense associated with interviewing each member of the sample. Somewhat smaller samples may be accepted with this data collection method than with mail or telephone surveys, on the premise that the quality of data gathered by the interview will balance the increased likelihood of incorrectly inferring population characteristics due to the smaller sample size.

Research studies based on face-to-face interviews often make use of a form of cluster sampling known as area probability sampling, in which the sample is selected from persons living in selected geographic areas. This not only ensures the geographic representativeness of the sample, it also facilitates efficient transportation arrangements for interviewers.

These studies also use nonprobability sampling techniques such as convenience or snowball sampling to select respondents. In one study, for example, a researcher conducted in-depth interviews with a sample of 20 individuals who had been divorced after reaching the age of 60 (Weingarten, 1988). Members of the sample were selected on the basis of their association with a support group for people who had experienced late-life divorce. Convenience sampling was the only practical means of identifying members of this unique population, and their special needs were perhaps best served by face-to-face interviews.

Obtaining Consent of Respondents

Before data can be collected from respondents in any research study, their written, informed consent must be obtained (see Chapter 2). Informed consent means that respondents have agreed to participate after having been notified of at least the general purpose of the study, the uses to be made of the data, and the means by which confidentiality is to be maintained.

Though agency-based studies such as those used as examples in this chapter may not be subjected to the formal scrutiny of an institutional review board, they are expected to conform to the ethical standards enforced by such boards. We must ensure that our research participants will not be subjected to any unnecessary risks. For example, one risk is that topics covered in the interview schedule might involve sensitive or stressful issues for some respondents. Another is the risk to the privacy of respondents who are asked to provide information that they might otherwise not want to reveal.

To counter such risks, we can contact potential respondents in advance by mail, telephone, or personal communication to explain the type of information to be sought and the safeguards that are to be taken to ensure their confidentiality. Often this notification takes the form of a cover letter that includes a consent form to be signed by respondents who agree to participate. Examples of cover letters are given in Figures 2.1, 9.1, and 14.5. A checklist for developing cover letters can be found in Figure 14.6.

Informed consent may also be obtained through an organization with which potential respondents are affiliated. In this case, obtaining consent is a two-stage process in which we must gain the sanction of the organization before contacting its members. In any case, our task is to explain the merits of our study in such a way that those contacted will be able to make the decision to participate or decline freely and on a factual basis.

Arranging the Interviews

Once enough respondents for the sample have given their consent to take part in our study, we need to perform the logistical tasks involved in arranging the interviews. Advance planning is necessary; arrangements often must be made at the time the respondent is asked to participate. The characteristics of sample members may dictate that interviews must be conducted in the evening or on weekends, for example, and this would affect the hiring of interviewers. It also would restrict the number of interviews that can be completed in a day or a week, so we might have to hire more interviewers or extend the study.

The location of the interview is another consideration. Because people generally are more comfortable in familiar surroundings, the best location often is in the respondent's home, office, or some similar setting. Other options are the interviewer's office or a meeting place that is neutral for both respondent and interviewer. The preferences of the respondent, the cost of transportation, and safety concerns for both the respondent and the interviewer must be taken into account. Some areas are dangerous for both residents and visitors, especially if the interview must be scheduled late in the day.

The location also must be conducive to the interviewing process. Because clients are often more willing to discuss personal issues at home and professional issues at the office, the subject matter of the interview should be considered in determining the location. Potential problems with a location should be antici-

[University Letterhead]

Dear _____:

As part of my doctoral program in Social Welfare at the University of Washington, I am seeking information about the attitudes and perceptions of mental health agency staff regarding program evaluation and accountability of mental health professionals.

As an employee of one of the mental health agencies in this state, you are being asked to complete two questionnaires regarding the subjects mentioned above. The first questionnaire is attached. The second questionnaire will follow in approximately four months. Each questionnaire will take about 20–30 minutes to complete. Should you complete the first questionnaire, I ask that this be an expression of your intent to complete the second questionnaire, although participation in both cases is entirely voluntary. You are free to withdraw your consent to participate or discontinue participation at any time.

All questionnaires will be kept in a locked file and I am the only person who will have access to this file. All questionnaires will be destroyed 6 months following completion of the study.

I hope you will be willing to help in this project but wish to assure you that your participation is entirely voluntary. You are welcome to ask questions regarding the study and your participation in it. I will be visiting your agency when I distribute the questionnaires or you may contact me at the University. I wish to remind you that your comments will remain strictly confidential. Thank you for your assistance and cooperation.

_____ Investigator   _____ Date
   Joan Avery

I voluntarily agree to complete this questionnaire and have the opportunity to ask questions.

_____ Respondent   _____ Date

FIGURE 14.5   EXAMPLE OF A SIMPLE COVER LETTER

pated; a home, workplace, or neutral site such as a crowded restaurant may be plagued by high noise levels, lack of privacy, and distractions that can interfere with the success of the interview.

Some cancellations and no-shows by respondents are inevitable, but their frequency and the amount of difficulty they create can be minimized. One of the simplest but most effective precautions is to contact respondents ahead of time, usually the day before the interview, to remind them of the appointment and

	YES	NO
1. Does the letter communicate the appeal to respondents?	——	——
2. Does it include a reasonable explanation of the study by anticipating and countering respondents' questions?	——	——
3. Does it set forth the benefits of the study?	——	——
4. Does it describe the importance of the respondent to the study and indicate that no one else can be substituted?	——	——
5. Does it exceed the maximum of one page?	——	——
6. Does it appear under an appropriate letterhead?	——	——
7. Do the individualized name and address and the date appear on the letter?	——	——
8. Is the investigator's individually applied signature included?	——	——
9. Does the letter include a confidentiality statement and explanation of the coding procedures?	——	——
10. Does the attachment to the cover letter include a stamped, self-addressed questionnaire reply envelope?	——	——
11. Does the letter indicate how results will be shared with respondents?	——	——
12. Are there instructions for indicating that a copy of the results is wanted (e.g., placing name and address on back of return envelope)?	——	——
13. Is the letter reproduced on a word processor?	——	——

FIGURE 14.6　　　CHECKLIST FOR DEVELOPING A COVER LETTER

confirm the time and location. Monetary rewards are another strategy that can improve participation. The payment is usually small, from $5 to $50, but offering it can increase respondents' willingness to take part in the study and likelihood of keeping the interview appointment. If scheduled interviews do not take place, we must remain polite and accommodating and try to reschedule.

Interviewing Skills

The basic principles of research interviewing are well established, and a few of the most important skills interviewers should have are identified in this section. These are not traits possessed by certain individuals but abilities that can be learned or improved by any competent person.

Rapport-building involves the interviewer's ability to make personal contacts with respondents beyond just asking them questions. Rapport is the spirit of affinity with respondents communicated by the interviewer, so they know they are recognized and appreciated as real people, not simply as guinea pigs or faceless sources of information. The level of rapport appropriate to a research interview is much lower than in a counseling interaction, because the interviewer is only collecting data, not offering professional assistance. Still, people are more truthful and open with those who they believe are genuinely interested in them. An interviewer who engages in a brief conversation before the interview will often be rewarded with more accurate and informative responses.

The interviewer must also be willing to answer questions from respondents concerning the purpose of the study, the nature of the interview schedule, and other aspects of the study. We can anticipate such questions and incorporate the answers in written instructions to the interviewer or in a set of standardized responses to be learned by the interviewer. Unanticipated questions do arise, however, and we must learn how to respond to them without biasing responses.

Another concern is the overly talkative respondent. Many studies in which face-to-face interviews are used focus on populations that are difficult to reach by other means, so people sampled from these populations may be isolated and lonely and welcome the opportunity to interact with the interviewer. Difficulties arise when this need for interaction interferes with the interviewer's ability to complete the schedule. Conversational digressions can be controlled by gently but consistently bringing the respondent back to the question at hand, but a certain amount of extraneous dialogue must be accommodated. Allowing extra time between interviews is often helpful.

During the actual data collection process, the interviewer must follow the precise wording of instructions and questions on the interview schedule. If there are variations from this script, different respondents will have different understandings of what is being asked, and inconsistencies or inaccuracies can be a source of measurement error.

Variations in the way the interview schedule is presented may also bias the respondent toward giving a particular type of answer. This does not mean that the interviewer should adopt a robotic approach in conducting the interview.

SELF-ADMINISTERED SURVEYS: GROUP-ADMINISTERED QUESTIONNAIRES

The critical barrier to the use of face-to-face interviews is the expense involved in hiring, training, and transporting interviewers. The obvious solution to this problem is to devise means whereby respondents can complete the survey instrument by themselves without the necessity of having an interviewer present. Of the two most common types of self-administered surveys (i.e., group-administered questionnaires and mail surveys), the first is discussed in this section, and the following section is devoted to mail surveys.

Group-administered questionnaires are used in situations where respondents can be brought together for the purpose of completing a survey instrument. The questionnaire is distributed to a group of respondents who complete it individually, though a member of the research team is usually present to assist. A cover letter to explain the project and obtain the respondents' consent should be handed out with the questionnaire (see Figure 14.5). A more detailed discussion of cover letters for use with self-administered questionnaires is given in the section on mail surveys.

To assess client satisfaction with agency services, for example, we might begin by sampling clients by community areas and making arrangements for those living in each area to gather at a central location. The cost of securing a meeting place and transporting clients to and from the site is likely to be much less than the cost of sending interviewers to many locales to meet with individual respondents. The arrangements for group administration are outlined in Figure 14.7. In addition, a checklist for introducing group-administered questionnaires to potential respondents is displayed in Figure 14.8.

Group administration is also used with groups who meet on a regular basis. An agency administrator examining social workers' reactions to revised state guidelines for assistance to low-income clients could use this approach, for example. At a regular meeting of workers for case staffings and training, questionnaires could be distributed to solicit workers' anonymous opinions on the change and their experiences in acquainting clients with the new regulations.

Group administration is less expensive than face-to-face interviews, and it usually yields a much higher response rate than mail surveys. Nevertheless, for numerous other reasons, mailed questionnaires are the type of self-administered survey that is used most frequently.

SELF-ADMINISTERED SURVEYS: MAIL SURVEYS

Until recently, when telephone surveys became commonplace, mail questionnaires were the method of data collection most commonly associated with survey research. In the United States, the most familiar example of a mail survey is the national population census conducted every 10 years by the Bureau of the Census, most recently in March 1990. Though the census still makes some use of face-to-face interviews, most of the data are collected from mail questionnaires.

Indeed, with a survey that attempts to collect data on the entire population of a country with some 260 million people, no other method of data collection currently used would be economically feasible. The U.S. census is unusual because it attempts to cover an entire population rather than a sample of its members, but it demonstrates the importance of mail surveys in allowing us to study a much larger number of respondents than is otherwise possible.

	YES	NO
1. Are there enough questionnaires?	___	___
2. Have plans been developed for persons unable to attend the questionnaire completion session to complete and return the instrument at another time?	___	___
3. Have all staff been notified in writing and verbally at a staff meeting about the date and time of the group administration?	___	___
4. Has the physical environment been checked in advance to make sure there will be sufficient space and adequate lighting for writing?	___	___
5. Have efforts been made to anticipate and eliminate possible sources of noise or distraction during the questionnaire completion session?	___	___
6. Are there plans to read aloud the instructions on the face sheet at the questionnaire completion session?	___	___
7. Will specific instructions be given on how to mark the questionnaire or answer sheet?	___	___
8. Is sufficient time allowed for questions from respondents before beginning to complete the questionnaire?	___	___
9. Will clarification announcements based on respondents' questions about an item on the questionnaire be made slowly, in a clear voice that is loud enough for all to hear?	___	___
10. Are all questionnaires to be collected immediately after completion and checked for completed identification information and consent form signature?	___	___
11. Have all respondents been informed of a sign-up roster to receive copies of the results of the study?	___	___
12. Will each respondent be personally thanked when the questionnaire is returned?	___	___
13. Are follow-up letters to be sent to agency administrators and key staff members who facilitate the implementation of the group-administered questionnaire?	___	___

FIGURE 14.7   CHECKLIST FOR ADMINISTRATION OF GROUP-ADMINISTERED QUESTIONNAIRES

By far the most important advantage of mail surveys is their low unit cost. These savings are possible because recipients themselves complete the questionnaire, so there is no cost for interviewers' time, and the survey instrument is both delivered and returned by mail, which is substantially less expensive than transporting interviewers to and from respondents' locations. Mail surveys also usually are less expensive than telephone interviews, particularly where respondents are widely distributed geographically. The cost of mailing a questionnaire is the same whether it is mailed across town or across the country.

The fact that the questionnaire is self-administered, so no contact with another person is required, can be a disadvantage. Respondents who do not understand a question cannot readily obtain clarification, and more detailed verbal responses cannot be recorded. At the same time, there are no problems with interviewer error or bias, either in asking for data or in recording responses.

Reliance on written instruments can also be a liability. It is virtually impossible to write a questionnaire that does not contain at least a few potentially confusing questions. In the absence of an interviewer who can explain the questions, respondents must interpret each one as best they can, which increases the possibility of error in the data. Moreover, written questionnaires are useful only with respondents who have the reading comprehension, sight, and other physical capacities necessary to complete the forms. Surveys of populations that include illiterate or visually or physically disabled persons cannot make use of these instruments unless personnel are assigned to assist respondents who are unable to complete the questionnaires on their own.

Nevertheless, the ability of mail surveys to present questions in written form can greatly enhance both the clarity of the questions and the types of data that can be gathered. Interview schedules, for example, have a restricted range of response categories for a given question because respondents can keep only a

	YES	NO
1. Does the face sheet of the questionnaire include general information about the purpose of the study?	_____	_____
2. Is there an indication of how much time it should take to complete the questionnaire?	_____	_____
3. Is a separate consent form attached to the questionnaire for the respondent to sign?	_____	_____
4. Does the face sheet include all necessary instructions for completing all items (e.g., "Don't skip around," "Answer all items to the best of your ability.")?	_____	_____

FIGURE 14.8   CHECKLIST FOR INTRODUCING GROUP-ADMINISTERED QUESTIONNAIRES

limited number of options in mind. Written questionnaires can list a wide range of options for review and reference as necessary.

Graphic illustrations of response categories also can be provided to enhance respondents' understanding. One study that focused on children, for example, gave examples of pictorial scales, including one that offered response categories in the form of simple drawings of faces with expressions ranging from happy to sad (Alreck & Settle, 1985). Children who might not comprehend the numerical gradations on a typical rating scale can use this type of visual representation to express variations in their feelings.

Overcoming the Disadvantage of Low Response Rates

The primary disadvantage of a mail survey is its low response rate. A person who receives a questionnaire in the mail usually can opt not to participate by passive means such as setting it aside and forgetting it, deciding not to fill it out, or throwing it away. Choosing not to participate in other types of surveys usually involves a more direct (and therefore more difficult) refusal.

Without careful efforts to increase returns, it is not uncommon for mail surveys to yield response rates of only 10 to 20 percent. Rates this low call into question the external validity of the data, which has its basis in the assumption that those who did return the questionnaire comprise a sample that is representative of the larger population. The measurement validity of a survey design, or the assumption that the survey measures what it is supposed to measure and does so accurately, also can be jeopardized by a low response rate.

To ensure the most accurate count in the 1990 national census of the U.S. population, massive information programs preceded the mailing of official survey forms to residential addresses, follow-ups were sent requesting compliance with instructions to complete the forms, and face-to-face interviews were conducted among the homeless, immigrants, and others who might be missed. Nevertheless, after a follow-up survey, including a random sample of racial, ethnic, and other groups, the Census Bureau reported in June 1991 that the 1990 census had missed 2.1 percent of the U.S. population overall, and 4.8 percent of African Americans and 5.2 percent of Hispanics had been undercounted. By the revised figures, the U.S. population was 253.9 million in 1990, 5.3 million people more than had originally been counted, and the percentages of African Americans and Hispanics missed were more than double the average.

There are no absolute standards for response rates in mail surveys used by social workers, and the question of what constitutes a minimally acceptable response rate can be a difficult one. Earl R. Babbie (1995) offers a rough guide of 50 percent as an "adequate" response rate, 60 percent as a "good" rate, and 70 percent as "very good." This is consistent with the views of most social work researchers, but the question still remains about what to do with studies that yield lower response rates.

This question is gaining greater immediacy as mail survey research becomes harder to carry out effectively. The proliferation of pseudo-surveys, such as sales promotions or political tracts disguised as questionnaires, along with surveys that are poorly designed or executed make the public less willing to participate. Because of this, those of us conducting legitimate, good-quality studies are struggling to obtain adequate response rates.

When initial response rates are low, we must be willing to make a dispassionate and open-minded assessment of whether our study is worth pursuing further. Among the questions to be considered in such an assessment are:

- Have procedures for maximizing response rates been fully employed (see below), and is it clear that further follow-up efforts would not be helpful?
- What are the potential sources of bias in the responses received (e.g., is it likely that certain types of sample members responded while others did not)? What effect might these biases have had, and how substantial is that effect?
- Did the original sample include extra cases (an oversample) in anticipation of survey nonresponse? If so, was the number of extra cases appropriate to the actual number of nonresponses?
- What is the purpose of the study? Will the benefits of providing data on a previously little-studied topic outweigh the risks of reporting results that may be inaccurate due to low response rates? What data will be provided to readers to allow them to make their own judgments about this issue?

As the above questions suggest, determination of what constitutes a satisfactory response rate is more often a matter of reasoned judgment than the application of absolute standards. In general, the best way to deal with the problem is to minimize it through vigorous efforts to reduce nonresponses. The following sections of this chapter offer ways in which response rates can be optimized without sacrificing the cost effectiveness and other advantages of mail surveys.

Use a Good Cover Letter

A straightforward, easy-to-read cover letter may improve return rates and response accuracy more than any other single factor, while a vague or highly technical letter can have the opposite effect. A good cover letter for a mail survey should perform the following functions:

- Give the exact date of the mailing of the questionnaire.
- Identify the researcher and institutional affiliation, preferably on official, printed stationery that is unique to the project or organization.
- Explain the research project sufficiently to allow the respondent to understand its general purpose, but not in such detail as to be confusing or discouraging.
- Explain the significance of the study in terms of its potential benefit to

policy or practice.
- Convey to the respondent the importance of participation in the study.
- Estimate how long the questionnaire will take to complete.
- Explain how the responses are to be used and how confidentiality will be maintained.
- Instruct the respondent how to return the completed form.
- Identify the person to contact with questions or concerns about the survey.

Some cover letters contain basic instructions on how to complete a questionnaire, but detailed directions should usually be reserved for the survey instrument. Some also specify a date by which the questionnaire is to be returned. This gives respondents a greater sense of urgency about the project, but the message must be carefully worded so they do not feel they are being pressured.

Before word processors made it easy to personalize letters, generic cover letters that were not addressed to any particular individual were used, or stick-on labels identical to those used to address the envelopes were added to the letters. Now most word processing and data management software programs for desktop computers can create individual labels and merge the names into the text of the letter. Personalized cover letters, which improve the likelihood of a response, then can be generated quickly and easily. The computerized label file also can produce address labels for the mailing envelopes, or with some computer printers, envelopes can be fed in and addressed directly from the file.

Reduce Mailing Costs

Preparing a survey mailing becomes a balancing act between minimizing mailing costs and maximizing the appearance and readability of the questionnaire and the likelihood that it will be completed and returned. In an era of scarce funding for social programs in general and research projects in particular, the ability to cut costs is a critical factor in the successful completion of a study.

One problem is how to minimize the weight of the questionnaire in order to reduce the cost of both the initial mailing and the return postage. A comparatively easy option is to use both sides of the paper when printing the instrument, but this does not work when single sheets are stapled together.

The cover letter may appear on the front page of the booklet, with the questionnaire beginning on the first inside or first right-hand page. Using double-sided printing can cut as much as half the weight of the questionnaire. With lengthy instruments, it also reduces bulkiness, making them appear less formidable to respondents.

Other savings can be obtained in mailing survey instruments by using bulk mail rates or special discounts for nonprofit organizations. Bulk mail rates are based on volume—the larger the number of mailings, the cheaper the rate. The discount is higher still for nonprofit agencies.

Using bulk mail rates does have certain drawbacks. One is that the U.S.

Postal Service requires all such mailings to be sorted by zip code before being delivered to the post office. This regulation can involve substantial expense in studies with a large number of mailings, and it has prompted many researchers to organize lists of survey recipients in zip-code order rather than alphabetical order. Another drawback is that bulk mail receives the lowest priority for handling, and slow delivery can cause problems if a timely response is needed. Moreover, letters sent by bulk mail to incorrect or nonexistent addresses are usually discarded by the Postal Service rather than returned to the sender, and this makes the survey's nonresponse rate seem higher than it actually is. A comparatively new drawback of bulk mailings is their effect on recipients as mass mailings have proliferated. Many recipients have become skilled in spotting "junk" mail, usually by looking for the bulk mail classification on the postage stamp or meter mark, and envelopes bearing such marks are often discarded without being opened.

For any of these reasons, when a high return rate is important, we may choose to bear the added expense of first-class (or sometimes even special delivery) mail rates in order to improve the chances that the mail will be delivered on time, opened, and examined.

Enclose Suitable Return Envelopes

Another consideration in preparing mailings is to make it easy for respondents to return the completed questionnaire. Usually a return envelope is enclosed in the initial mailing, in most cases with return postage attached. The return envelope must fit easily inside the outgoing envelope but be large enough to accommodate the completed questionnaire.

Too little postage on the return envelope will cause the questionnaire to be sent back to the respondent, so the questionnaire should be weighed with the return envelope to determine the exact amount of postage needed. In the United States, an alternative is to use business reply envelopes. We are billed only for questionnaires that are returned, but business reply mail is billed at a higher rate than regular postage, so it might not be cost effective when high return rates are expected. Because bulk mail rates cannot be used on return envelopes, it is not unusual for the cost of returns to exceed that of outgoing mailings. A checklist for survey mailing procedures can be found in Figure 14.9.

Assure the Confidentiality of Respondents

Including some sort of identification of respondents on survey instruments is helpful in keeping track of those who have completed and returned them, so the number of follow-ups necessary is reduced. However, the use of any type of identifier (such as a number) can jeopardize the principle of confidentiality of participants. One way to deal with this is to inform respondents that identifying

	YES	NO
1. Is the envelope an unusual size, shape, or color to attract attention, along with embellishments such as "Immediate reply requested"?	____	____
2. Has the size of the questionnaire and envelope been determined in relationship to using first-class postage and minimizing the appearance of bulky contents?	____	____
3. Has a mailing list been developed which includes the number of the questionnaire beside the name of the respondent?	____	____
4. Are the envelope contents folded together when inserted so that respondents will find all relevant materials on opening the envelope?	____	____
5. Is the mailing planned for early in the week in anticipation of time needed to forward mail to new addresses?	____	____
6. Will the mailing avoid a holiday period when respondents are likely to be away from home, and will it avoid December and the crush of holiday mail?	____	____

FIGURE 14.9   CHECKLIST FOR SURVEY MAILING PROCEDURES

information included on the questionnaires in the form of a numerical code can only be interpreted from a master list retained by those administering the survey. Respondents also should be apprised of the measures that will be taken to maintain the security of this list and assured that it will be destroyed once the study has been completed.

Instead of identifying information on the questionnaire, each initial mailing could include a self-addressed, stamped postcard with coded information identifying the respondent. When respondents return these postcards separately at the same time they put the completed questionnaires in the mail, we can identify those who have returned the survey without being able to link them to a particular completed form. Follow-ups then need to be sent only to those who did not return the postcards and the completed questionnaires.

Follow Up on the Mailing

Procedures for following an initial mailing with subsequent reminders are often crucial to attaining a satisfactory return rate. The two major considerations in planning follow-ups are timing, or the intervals at which follow-ups should be sent, and format, or the types of follow-ups to be sent. Generally, for any survey there should be at least two follow-ups at roughly three-week intervals. These intervals can be reduced if initial returns are slow, but postponing follow-ups for more than three weeks risks losing the impact of the mailings. More than two follow-ups also may be appropriate, particularly if each is successful in bringing in a new wave of returns.

A variety of formats may be used for follow-ups, including postcards, letters, additional copies of the questionnaire, telephone calls, and face-to-face contacts. Donald A. Dillman (1978) argues for the use of a variety of these methods, with certain types of follow-ups occurring at specific intervals after the initial mailing. A postcard reminder is sent one week after the initial mailing; a follow-up letter, with an additional copy of the questionnaire and return envelope, two weeks later; and a final letter and another questionnaire copy and return envelope by certified mail on the seventh week following the initial mailing.

Some of us have added telephone contacts to this sequence. These can be extremely effective, because they convey our desire to obtain a response much more personally and directly than is possible in a letter, and they can produce immediate responses. A checklist for survey follow-up procedures is found in Figure 14.10.

TELEPHONE SURVEYS

Use of the telephone as a tool for conducting surveys has developed only within the past 25 years or so. Prior to this time, the proportion of households having telephones was too small to justify their use in data collection. As recently as 1960, only 78.5 percent of households in the United States had telephone service; excluding those who did not, those who tended to live in certain areas, or those who had certain other characteristics would lead to systematic bias in a study's findings (Lavrakas, 1987). In 1987, however, 92.5 percent of households had service, so the telephone became more viable as a research tool (U.S. Bureau of the Census, 1987).

Indeed, telephone surveys have become something of a modern phenomenon, assuming a place in the mind of the public that was once occupied by person-on-the-street interviewers or door-to-door census takers. These developments have been both favorable and unfavorable for surveys, as will be shown in this section.

One reason for the growth of telephone surveys is that they offer many of the merits of face-to-face interviews and mail survey techniques, without some of their drawbacks. Telephone interviews are relatively inexpensive, particularly compared to face-to-face interviews, because there are no transportation costs for either the interviewers or respondents. Moreover, local telephone calls are often cheaper than first-class postage, and even if long-distance calls are necessary, WATS lines and other discounts for high-volume calling can keep unit costs comparatively low. Printing expenses also are generally lower for telephone

	YES	NO
1. Is there a preprinted follow-up postcard for mailing one week after mailing of cover letter?	_____	_____
2. Does the postcard include the respondent's name and address and the investigator's signature?	_____	_____
3. Does it thank the respondent if the questionnaire has already been returned?	_____	_____
4. Is a second follow-up letter ready for sending three weeks after mailing of the cover letter, with a replacement questionnaire and return envelope?	_____	_____
5. Is a third follow-up letter ready for certified mailing to remaining nonrespondents seven weeks after original mailing, with a replacement questionnaire and return envelope?	_____	_____

FIGURE 14.10   CHECKLIST FOR SURVEY FOLLOW-UP PROCEDURES

surveys because interviewers need only one copy of an interview schedule. Nevertheless, telephone surveys are more expensive than mailings, falling about midway between mail surveys and face-to-face interviews.

Another reason telephone interviews are popular is that studies employing this technique can be completed much faster than those using other methods. Survey findings based on a representative sample of the U.S. population can be obtained by telephone interviewers in less than 24 hours, provided that a large and well-trained staff of interviewers, ample access to direct-dial long-distance telephone lines, and a prepared and tested interview schedule are all available.

Political pollsters and other public opinion research firms now employ telephone methods almost exclusively, for example. Opinion poll results and survey ratings of winners and losers in political debates can be announced quickly, because interviewers can enter responses directly into a computer file that can be analyzed immediately once the data collection has been completed.

As with face-to-face interviews, in telephone interviews an interviewer is present to offer assistance to respondents who need it. Thus it is possible to directly explain instructions, clarify questions, and deal with any other concern a respondent may have.

Limitations

The interaction of an interviewer with respondents is not always an advantage in telephone surveys. It can be a drawback, because it introduces opportunities for interviewer bias in data collection and coding. This source of error must be controlled for through the careful selection and training of the interviewers. At the same time, because telephone interviews do not allow visual contact between the interviewer and respondent, establishing rapport with respondents and gaining their trust and cooperation is more difficult. In addition, there is no opportunity to observe or record nonverbal communication.

Because the time respondents are willing to talk with an interviewer is usually much shorter on the telephone than in person, both the length of the survey instrument and the scope of respondents' answers are restricted. Telephone interview schedules also must be kept simple and direct because respondents cannot refer to written versions of the questions. To allow more latitude, a cover letter and questionnaire may be sent by mail in advance for respondents to use as a reference during the telephone interview. Of course, this appreciably increases costs.

Telephone surveys usually are not prearranged, however, and a common problem is an inability to reach intended respondents. The contact rate for telephone surveys in the United States (operationally defined as reaching a viable respondent on the first call) was about 56 percent in 1989. Thus for almost half of all respondents, at least two calls were required to reach them. Moreover, just 53 percent of individuals contacted in 1989 agreed to complete a telephone survey. Like the proliferation of junk mail, the rapid growth of telephone sales, solicitations, and pseudo-surveys has saturated homes with unwanted calls, increasing the likelihood that people will decline to participate in legitimate research efforts presented by phone. Data indicate that only 30 percent of prospective respondents to a telephone survey can be expected to be reached on the first call and to agree to participate in the study. If contact and cooperation rates continue to drop, the traditional advantages of telephone surveys over mail surveys with respect to ease of use and high response rates can be expected to diminish.

Despite the fact that the great majority of households now have telephones, a disproportionate number of poor people are among those who do not. This is important for social work researchers because low-income families comprise a sizable share of social service clients, and underrepresentation of these individuals can lead to measurement error in survey results. Studies of the distribution of U.S. households having telephones show that in regions such as the South, which has a high rate of rural poverty, more than 20 percent of households still lack telephone service (Groves, 1988). Accordingly, telephone surveys are inappropriate for use with rural populations or in geographic areas that are known to have a large number of low-income residents.

Sampling Approaches for Telephone Surveys

Most sampling approaches used with face-to-face interviews or mail surveys can also be used in telephone surveys. It can be more difficult to obtain telephone numbers than addresses of potential respondents, however. Even if most people have telephones, some will have unlisted numbers, which are not available to researchers. In 1989, over 31 percent of all telephone customers in the United States had unlisted numbers, up from 22 percent in 1984 (Survey Sampling, 1990). In some parts of the country (California, for example), the proportion of households with unlisted numbers is almost one-half. Since such households may differ in some systematic way from those with listed numbers, a sample that excludes them can threaten the external validity of the data for making inferences about the population of interest.

One way to address this problem is with random-digit dialing (RDD), in which numbers that have been generated at random are dialed. In fact, RDD is not entirely random, since most research projects are targeted toward a particular geographic location, and telephone companies generally assign seven-digit numbers with different three-digit prefixes for various localities. Thus a researcher interested in households in a particular neighborhood who knows they all have telephone numbers beginning with 256, 257, 292, and 294 can restrict the selection of random numbers to the range of possible telephone numbers beginning with these four prefixes.

As a rule, the best use of RDD is for studies in which results from a sample will be generalized to the entire population of interest. The selection of potential sample members cannot be narrowed by any other criteria than three-digit prefixes or area codes that encompass an entire city or metropolitan area. In public opinion polls or practice applications such as needs assessments, this is not a major drawback. RDD, however, would clearly be inappropriate in cases such as an agency study to evaluate former clients' satisfaction with services. A telephone survey could be used, but it would be necessary to work from a list of former clients in order to identify the sample of potential respondents. If the list has a high percentage of missing, incorrect, or unlisted telephone numbers, the likelihood of obtaining a representative sample of former clients would be small.

A new type of telephone poll, promoted by newspapers, television stations, and special-interest groups, asks people to call a particular number to record their opinion about some topic or issue. Often a 900 area-code number is used and a charge is added to the caller's phone bill. Such polls do not constitute telephone survey research, because the sampling techniques do not produce generalizable data. The people who call in to register their opinions have strong feelings on the subject (especially if they are willing to pay the fee), and those who do not feel so strongly are not represented in the survey. As a consequence, the results of such surveys cannot be generalized to any larger population.

Telephone Interviewing Skills

The skills and attributes necessary for effective telephone interviewers vary in some respects from those required for face-to-face interviewers. The need to match characteristics of interviewers and respondents is not so great in telephone surveys, because personal differences are less apparent over the telephone. Other considerations such as voice quality, telephone manner, and ability to cope with the sometimes tedious aspects of telephone interviewing have a greater priority.

Of greatest importance in telephone surveys are the interviewer's verbal skills and familiarity with telephone etiquette—the conventions for considerate, polite behavior in telephone communications. A courteous attitude must be maintained, even if telephone customers decline to participate in ways that are not socially acceptable. Some may agree to complete the survey but change their minds or become uncooperative midway through the interview. In such situations, the interviewer must be able to avoid losing composure, be able to reassure respondents and encourage them to continue, and know when and how to end a session.

Since telephone interviews are rarely preceded by cover letters, interviewers must be able to establish their own legitimacy and that of the study to the satisfaction of the respondent. An interviewer's legitimacy can be undermined by unclear speech, a flippant or disinterested attitude, exaggerated mannerisms, or poor grammar. Sometimes it is best for the interviewer to strictly follow the text of the interview schedule, though this can create other problems, such as reading in a dull or halting manner.

Interviewers must also know how to mediate between the goals of the study and the needs of the respondent. While some contacts refuse to participate, others provide far more data than the interviewer can handle or indulge in conversation that has nothing to do with the study. The interviewer must be able to weigh the benefits of completing such an interview against the costs of taking too long to do so. If respondents are reticent, the interviewer must know how to probe for additional information without seeming to be too inquisitive or aggressive. If respondents have difficulty understanding or keeping track of questions, the interviewer must be prepared to repeat or clarify.

Perhaps the best way to develop the skills needed by telephone interviewers is through techniques such as role-playing, in which prospective interviewers take the roles of interviewers and respondents in hypothetical telephone surveys in a controlled setting. By participating in problematic situations, they learn how to deal with them and can practice appropriate responses until they become confident. Another training technique is to allow prospective interviewers to listen in on a second phone to interviews conducted by more experienced staff. Or the researcher or a supervisor might listen in on an interviewer's first few calls to prospective respondents and offer feedback on the exchange and suggestions for improvement. Calls also can be monitored throughout the data collection to ensure that the interviews are being conducted properly.

COMPUTERIZED DATA COLLECTION IN SURVEYS

Computers have become a basic tool in surveys, particularly for recording and analyzing data. In many cases, however, the process of translating data from respondents onto a form that can be read by a computer (called coding) still requires a number of laborious steps. In self-administered surveys, for example, responses to a questionnaire are usually reviewed and translated into numerical codes by a reader who writes them out in rows of numbers on a coding form. Data from these forms are then transferred by entering them into a computer file, using a keyboard and video display screen. Some of us have begun coding data from survey instruments onto optical scanning forms similar to those used with standardized tests. These forms can be read by a scanner which then transfers the data to a computer, thus saving a step in the coding process.

The greater the number of steps between getting an answer from a respondent and recording it in a computer, the greater the number of coding errors the data are likely to contain. With telephone surveys, interviewers can enter data on responses directly into a computer. This process is known by the acronym CATI, for computer-assisted telephone interviewing. It is not possible with self-administered questionnaires, except in rare cases where skilled respondents can sit at a computer to answer questions. It also has not been feasible in face-to-face interviews, though the growing use of laptop computers is creating new possibilities.

CATI allows the elimination not only of coding forms but also of written interview schedules. Questions to be asked of respondents are displayed on the computer screen, along with prompts for recording the answer, gathering supplementary data, or proceeding to another part of the instrument.

Figure 14.11 provides an example of a computerized interview schedule in the form of a series of computer screens developed for a telephone interview. An interviewer sitting in front of the computer would see only one screen at a time. As each question is read and the required data are entered, the program automatically proceeds to the next screen. In cases where one type of response would lead to a certain question and a different response would lead to another, the program automatically takes the interviewer to the appropriate screen. In Screen 1, for example, when the interviewer enters a 9, indicating that the respondent has refused to participate, the program skips to a screen that provides a message for the interviewer to read, expressing regrets that the person has chosen not to participate. If the respondent agrees to complete the survey, the program skips to Screen 2, where the interviewer is instructed to enter the person's identifier, and so on.

With this approach, the interviewer is unlikely to lose the place or skip questions. The computer can be programmed to signal when invalid values are entered, thus reducing coding errors. Data entered on each screen are automatically entered in the computer in a form that can be directly extracted and analyzed.

CATI systems require a personal computer for each interviewer or a network of keyboards and display screens linked to a single computer. Some types of telephones are better than others; a headset with earphones and microphone that fits into a standard-sized jack can be purchased or rented for moderate cost. Using a headset frees up the interviewer's hands to dial the telephone and record

---

_____ SCREEN 1 _____
question 0a   column(s) —

  The ASU Center for Business Research is sponsoring a survey about when and why people move into and out of Arizona. This information is important for the economy of the state.

  In order for men and women to have an equal chance of being interviewed, I need to talk to the head of the household or the spouse of the head of the household. Which one had the most recent birthday?

   1. *GIVES NAME* — type in at next question
   9. *REFUSED* (skip to q 998c)

_____ SCREEN 2 _____
question 0b   column(s) — 1–3
[Type in RESPONDENT'S NAME OR IDENTIFIER — husband, wife, son, father, etc.]

   (If informant is respondent, Type in ID)

_____ SCREEN 3 _____
question 0c   column(s) —
[REPEAT intro if necessary]

  (The ASU Center for Business Research is sponsoring a survey about when and why people move into and out of Arizona. This information is important for the economy of the state.)

  Before I start, I would like to assure you that this interview is completely confidential, voluntary, and will only take five minutes.

   (Press RETURN to continue)

_____ SCREEN 4 _____
question 1a   column(s) — 5

  I am going to begin with some questions about how long you have been in Arizona and how much time you spend here.

  Do you usually spend more than thirty days in a row per year outside of Arizona?

   1. *YES*
   2. *NO* (skip to q 5)
   9. *DON'T KNOW* (skip to q 5)

_____ SCREEN 5 _____
question 2   column(s) — 6–7

  How many months per year do you spend outside of Arizona?
   (Type in NUMBER)

FIGURE 14.11   EXAMPLE OF A COMPUTERIZED TELEPHONE
INTERVIEW SCHEDULE

data. With personal computers, the interviewer's headset can be connected to a telephone modem in the computer, and the machine will automatically dial each number.

Beyond a basic knowledge of the use of personal computers, special expertise is not required to create and use computerized interview schedules. With commercial software packages, users can devise their own CATI and other computer systems for recording and analyzing survey data.

EMERGING DATA COLLECTION APPROACHES

Approaches to data collection in survey research are tied to the means by which information may be exchanged, thus new modes of communication bring about fresh possibilities for conducting surveys. Face-to-face communication, for example, is as old as the human race, but reliable mail service has been around for a few hundred years at best, and the telephone came into wide use only in this century. Now, the breakneck pace of advancement in modern technology may soon bring about a variety of new methods of conducting surveys.

One example is electronic mail, in which people communicate through computers hooked to telephone lines, satellite relays, and other transmission media. This remains a very new technology, and the 13 percent of Americans who report having been "online" (Fineman, 1995) is about the same percentage as households in the U.S. that had telephones in 1910 (Fischer, 1992).

Roughly one-third of American households now have at least one computer, however, and the presence of both computers and online capabilities continues to grow rapidly. Also, virtually all American households have television sets, and the technology of interactive cable television is another source of two-way communication that will gradually become widespread. In fact, the mainstay of the coming "Information Superhighway" is likely to be a single, high-capacity, fiber optic cable carrying television, telephone, and other forms of communication to most households.

Still, many barriers need to be overcome before these technologies become broadly useful for survey research in social work. One problem is that computers, modems, and interactive cable links are expensive, thus there is a wide disparity in access to them between wealthy and poor families. Almost three-fourths of families with annual incomes greater than $75,000 own computers, but this is true of a mere fraction of poor families. Ownership is also distributed unequally across ethnic and racial groups, with three times as many white families owning computers as black or Hispanic families (Snyder, 1994).

Finally, as noted earlier in the chapter, the proliferation of junk mail, telephone solicitations, and sales pitches disguised as surveys has made legitimate survey research much harder to conduct. The same is likely to be true of surveys using newer technologies, the difficulty increasing almost simultaneously with the growth of new communication technologies.

SUMMARY

As one of the most common forms of data collection methods, survey research is often chosen as the means for studying groups and social phenomena by collecting data on individuals, organizations, and communities. As with other types of data collection methods, the genesis of survey research is in the formulation of the research question; only by clearly defining what it is we wish to know can the means for obtaining an answer be selected.

If our research question can be addressed by survey methods, the choice is between cross-sectional designs, which gather data on a particular population at a given moment in time, and longitudinal designs, which examine changes in the population over time. The three main methods of data collection in surveys are face-to-face and telephone interviews, in which interviewers are present to explain and interpret questions, and self-administered surveys, which rely on self-reports to group questionnaires and mail survey instruments.

The following chapter continues our discussion of data collection by describing secondary analysis. Unlike surveys, which collect original data to address research questions, secondary analyses draw on data that already exist.

REFERENCES AND FURTHER READINGS

ALRECK, P.L., & SETTLE, R.B. (1985). *The survey research handbook*. Homewood, IL: Irwin.

BABBIE, E.R. (1995). *The practice of social research* (7th ed., pp. 256-277). Belmont, CA: Wadsworth.

BAILEY, K.D. (1994). *Methods of social research* (4th ed., pp. 148-172, 196-208). New York: Free Press.

BANE, M.J. (1986). Household composition and poverty. In S.H. Danziger & D.H. Weinberg (Eds.), *Fighting poverty: What works and what doesn't* (pp. 209-231). Cambridge, MA: Harvard University Press.

DePOY, E., & GITLIN, L.N. (1994). *Introduction to research* (p. 117). St. Louis: Mosby.

DILLMAN, D.A. (1978). *Mail and telephone surveys: The total design method*. New York: Wiley.

FINEMAN, H. (1995, February 27). The brave new world of cybertribes. *Newsweek, 125,* 30-33.

FISCHER, C.S. (1992). *America calling: A social history of the telephone to 1940*. Berkeley, CA: University of California Press.

FRANKFORT-NACHMIAS, C., & NACHMIAS, D. (1992). *Research methods in the social sciences* (4th ed., pp. 215-237). New York: St. Martin's Press.

GABOR, P.A., & GRINNELL, R.M., JR. (1994). *Evaluation and quality improvement in the human services* (pp. 148-189). Needham Heights, MA: Allyn & Bacon.

GRINNELL, R.M., JR., & WILLIAMS, M. (1990). *Research in social work: A primer* (pp. 204-231). Itasca, IL: F.E. Peacock.

GOCHROS, H.L. (1970). The caseworker-adoptive parent relationships in post-placement services. In A. Kadushin (Ed.), *Child welfare services*. New York: Macmillan.

GROVES, R.M. (1988). *Telephone survey methodology*. New York: Wiley.

JENKINS, S., & NORMAN, E. (1972). *Filial deprivation and foster care.* New York: Columbia University Press.

JUDD, C.M., SMITH, E.R., & KIDDER, L.H. (1991). *Research methods in social relations* (6th ed., pp. 100-127, 213-227). Fort Worth, TX: Harcourt Brace Jovanovich.

KRYSIK, J., HOFFART, I., & GRINNELL, R.M., JR. (1993). *Student study guide for the fourth edition of social work research and evaluation* (pp. 14-15). Itasca, IL: F.E. Peacock.

LAVRAKAS, P.J. (1987). *Telephone survey methods: Sampling, selection, and supervision.* Newbury Park, CA: Sage.

LEEDY, P.D. (1993). *Practical research* (5th ed., pp. 185-195, 213-216). New York: Macmillan.

MARLOW, C. (1993). *Research methods for generalist social work* (pp. 65-77). Pacific Grove, CA: Brooks/Cole.

MONETTE, D.R., SULLIVAN, T.J., & DEJONG, C.R. (1994). *Applied social research* (3rd ed., pp. 153-186). Fort Worth, TX: Harcourt Brace.

NEUMAN, W.L. (1994). *Social research methods* (2nd ed., pp. 221-258). Needham Heights, MA: Allyn & Bacon.

RUBIN, A., & BABBIE, E. (1993). *Research methods for social work* (2nd ed., pp. 332-356). Pacific Grove, CA: Brooks/Cole.

SCHUMAN, H. (1972). Two sources of antiwar sentiment in America. *American Journal of Sociology, 78,* 513-536.

SCHUMAN, H., & Converse, J.M. (1971). The effects of black and white interviewers on black responses. *Public Opinion Quarterly, 35,* 44-68.

SINGER, E., FRANKEL, M.R., & GLASSMAN, M.B. (1983). The effect of interviewer characteristics and expectations on response. *Public Opinion Quarterly, 47,* 68-83.

SINGLETON, R.A., JR., STRAITS, B.C., & MILLER STRAITS, M. (1993). *Approaches to social research* (2nd ed., pp. 246-279). New York: Oxford.

SNYDER, T.D. (1994). *Digest of education statistics.* (NCES Publication No. 94-115). Washington, DC: US Department of Education, Office of Education Research and Improvement.

SURVEY SAMPLING, INC. (1990). *A survey researcher's view of the U.S.* Fairfield, CN: Author.

U.S. BUREAU OF THE CENSUS (1987). *Statistical abstract of the United States, 1988.* Washington, DC: Author.

WEINBACH, R.W., & GRINNELL, R.M., JR. (1996). *Applying research knowledge: A workbook for social work students* (2nd ed., pp. 49-56). Needham Heights, MA: Allyn & Bacon.

WEINGARTEN, H.R. (1988). Late life divorce and the life review. *Journal of Gerontological Social Work, 12,* 83-97.

WILLIAMS, M., TUTTY, L.M., & GRINNELL, R.M., JR. (1995). *Research in social work: An introduction* (2nd ed., pp. 239-260). Itasca, IL: F.E. Peacock.

Gayla Rogers
Elaine Bouey

C h a p t e r **15**

Participant Observation

L IKE SURVEY RESEARCH presented in the last chapter, participant observation is both an obtrusive data collection method and a research approach. Like all the other data collection methods presented in this book, its appropriateness for any particular research study is directly related to the study's research question. This chapter provides a definition and description of participant observation and discusses its practical application to social work research. We both describe various roles that a participant observer, the researcher, can take and present a step-by-step overview of how to do a participant observation study.

DEFINITION

It is difficult to provide an exact definition of participant observation, since there are many different ways of defining it depending on the discipline of the definer and how it has been applied to research situations over the past eighty years. Participant observation as a data collection method began with early anthropological ethnomethodology studies in the 1920s. Since then, it has undergone a radical transformation in an effort to look for new ways to obtain useful, reliable, and valid data from research participants. Currently, participant observation is viewed as more of a mind-set (or an orientation) toward research rather than as a set of specific, applied data collection techniques (Neuman, 1994). Further, the terms *field research, ethnographic research,* and *ethnography* are often used interchangeably with *participant observation.*

Distinguishing Features

What main feature distinguishes participant observation as an obtrusive data collection method from the other two obtrusive methods presented in the previous two chapters, structured observation (Chapter 13), and survey research (Chapter 14)? The answer is simple—it requires the one doing the study, the participant observer, to undertake roles that involve establishing and maintaining ongoing relationships with research participants who are often in field settings.

The passage of time is also an integral part of participant observation. We need to consider, for example, the sequences of events (and monitor processes) over time so the relationships and meanings of what our research participants are experiencing can be discovered. We gather data primarily through direct observation, supplemented with other data-gathering methods such as, interviewing, using existing documents (Chapters 16–19), and using our own personal experiences.

Participant observation is an excellent way to gather data for understanding how other people see or interpret their experiences (Spradley, 1980). It represents a unique opportunity to see the world from *other* points of view, often at the sites where the activities or phenomena occur. It is also compatible with the "reflective practitioner" model of social work practice, as a part of the process involves examining our personal insights, feelings, and perspectives in order to understand the situations we are studying (Papell & Skolnik, 1992; Schön, 1983).

A key factor of participant observation is its emphasis on *less structured* data gathering methods, such as observing everyday events in natural settings in an effort to understand how other people see or interpret their experiences, then stepping outside that perspective to add a "more objective" viewpoint (Neuman, 1994). In practice, however, it is often a back and forth (or recursive) process. Through observations and interactions with research participants over time (e.g., weeks, months, years) a great deal can be learned about them—their histories, habits, and hopes; and their cultures, values, and idiosyncrasies as well. These observations and interactions can be fascinating and fun as well as time-consuming, costly, and emotionally draining.

As we know, data derived from a participant observation study can easily be augmented with survey research data. In addition it can be used with both research approaches—quantitative or qualitative. Using different data gathering methods, such as participant observation and survey research, in addition to using different data sources such as existing documents, as well as observing people in different roles, create the potential for a fuller understanding of the phenomena being studied.

Participant observation is an excellent data collection method for exploring a wide variety of social settings, subcultures, and most aspects of social life. It is valuable, for example, in studying deviant behavior (e.g., prostitution, drug use), unusual or traumatic circumstances (e.g., spinal cord injury, rape), and important life events (e.g., birth, divorce, death). It can be used to study entire communities in a range of settings, or relatively small groups who interact with each other on a regular basis in a fixed setting. Some examples include studies of women's emergency shelters, the workings of social service agencies from the perspective of the members in those settings, or an immigrant group living in a particular neighborhood. Participant observation can also be used to study social experiences that are not fixed in a place but where in-depth interviewing and direct observation are the only ways to gain access to the experience—for example, the feelings of women who have left violent relationships.

Researchers participating in these settings can also occupy other roles including: social worker, volunteer, English as a Second Language tutor, program aide, or administrative assistant. The more roles we assume, the better our understanding of the situation because of different points of view.

When to Use Participant Observation

Participant observation as a data collection method is well suited to situations where we wish to better understand how people see their own experiences, as well as when we want to gain an in-depth perspective on people within the contexts and environments in which these events occur. It is exceptionally useful when it is applied to the study of processes, interrelationships among people and their situations, and events that happen over time and the patterns that have developed, as well as the social and cultural contexts in which human experiences occurred (Jorgensen, 1989).

Participant observation allows for the collection of data about phenomena that are not commonly obvious from the viewpoint of the nonparticipant. It provides an opportunity for a comprehensiveness of understanding of human situations, and richly textured perspectives. Furthermore, when conducted in natural settings, it has the potential to elucidate certain nuances of attitude, or behaviors that may not be included when data are gathered using other data collection methods.

Participant observation is often helpful in identifying problem areas that can be the topics for subsequent studies that use other data collection methodologies. We can then *triangulate*, or compare and contrast, the data gathered via these different methods in order to enhance our study's credibility. We may initially select a role as a volunteer in a women's emergency shelter, for example, find that we would like to learn more about the conditions that led women to the shelter, and subsequently gain permission to review intake records plus conduct structured interviews with a sample of women who enter the shelter. Participant observation is especially appropriate for scholarly problems in the following circumstances (Jorgensen, 1989):

- Little is known about a situation or event (e.g., job satisfaction among workers at a women's emergency shelter).
- There are important differences between the views of one group and another (e.g., perspectives on domestic violence as held by police and medical service professionals versus perspectives of social workers inside a women's emergency shelter).
- The phenomenon is obscured in some way from those outside a setting (e.g., spouse battering within a community of immigrants who do not commonly interact with social service agencies, and who do not speak English).
- The phenomenon is hidden from society in general (e.g., drug abuse treatment of those in higher socioeconomic statuses).

While participant observation is appropriate for gathering data for almost any aspect of human existence, it is, however, not suited to every scholarly research enquiry involving humans and their interactions with one another. It is particularly applicable to exploratory and descriptive studies out of which theoretical interpretations and hypotheses emerge. Its primary contribution allows for the creation of in-depth understandings of situations in an effort to support the development of different theoretical view points.

Minimal Conditions for Participant Observation

In using participant observation as a data collection method, there are minimal conditions that must be present (Jorgensen, 1989):

- The research question is concerned with human meanings and interactions viewed from the insider's perspective.
- The phenomenon is observable within an everyday life setting or situation.
- Gaining access to an appropriate setting is not a problem.
- The phenomenon is sufficiently limited in size and location to be studied as a case (Chapter 12).
- The research question is appropriate for a case study (Chapter 3).
- The research question can be addressed by qualitative data gathered by direct observation and other means pertinent to the field setting (Chapters 5, 6, and 12).

Getting Involved and Observing

Participant observation involves a dual purpose: *getting involved* in activities appropriate to the situation, and *observing* people, the physical site, and the events happening in a particular context or setting. While a regular member experiences events in a direct and personal manner, the participant observer experiences being both an insider (with a "subjective" view point) and an outsider (with a more "objective" view point). Thus, it requires personal preparation and ongoing mindfulness to maintain an objective perspective at the same time as being involved in a field setting as a participant. It means being explicitly aware of our values and assumptions while holding our judgments in abeyance. This is often challenging and proves to be a very intensive experience for the participant observer.

There is little question that the participant observer's involvement in a setting can have an emotional impact of varying degrees. As Neuman (1994) notes:

> Field research can be fun and exciting, but it can also disrupt one's personal life, physical security, or mental well being. More than other types of social research, it reshapes friendships, family life, self identity, or personal values. (p. 335)

Since we are the primary instruments through which our data are gathered and interpreted, we may have a potential influence on our study. This is why it is crucial to prepare ourselves as much as possible in advance for this experience, maintain a separate log of personal notes and reflections, as well as make arrangements for regular advisory and debriefing sessions.

It is also important to note that some of us may be very well suited to use participant observation as a data collection method, while others may be advised to use other data collection methodologies. Thus, a team approach is often appropriate, with one person doing participant observation, and another conducting structured interviews and examining existing documentation, for example.

ROLES

This section provides an overview of the various roles for those involved in a participant observation study and describes the tasks associated with each role. Being a *participant observer* in a field setting is quite different from being a *regular participant* in a field setting.

Researchers using participant observation as a data collection method often assume a variety of roles. These roles can be placed on a continuum and are classified into four categories as presented in Figure 15.1: (1) complete participant, (2) observer-participant, (3) participant-observer, and (4) complete observer.

We can sit in on staff meetings, for example, and view other operational activities as a *complete observer* to gather data on how social agency staff function in an office setting; or with varying degrees of involvement as a *participant observer* or *observer participant*, we can be volunteers who come in to help with some aspect of the program's operation on a regular basis to gather data on how a particular program works; or as a *complete participant* we can, at the other end of the continuum, be one of the permanent staff in an agency who also happens to be doing a research study on the day-to-day activities within the program.

Balancing the Roles

In assuming any one of the four roles in doing a participant observation study, we need to be acutely aware of the need to maintain a balance between our participation and our ability to be objective. There may be many temptations to become so totally involved that we can easily lose this balanced perspective. This is often a particular challenge when we are *complete participants* as compared to *complete observers*. Some aids to maintaining this balance include reflective journal writing and regular debriefing sessions with other professionals who are not familiar with our field setting.

When we take on different roles, however, these roles can be overtly revealed, or in some cases they can be undertaken on a covert basis and not revealed. We strongly recommend, whenever possible, that any role played be on an overt or openly explained basis. This helps us with ethical considerations as well as in keeping with the way in which participant observation has evolved and its application to social work settings.

If we are going to be studying a women's emergency shelter with all the appropriate advance clearances for access to that setting, for example, and if we assume a role as a children's playroom assistant so that we can observe the interaction of the children with their mothers and with the shelter's staff, it is absolutely mandatory that we let the parents, the shelter's staff, and the children know why we are there (our dual role) and what we will be doing with the data collected. These need not be lengthy explanations initially, but they set the stage for trust and acceptance. We should be ready to answer questions as they surface. On the other hand, sharing of the initial analyses of our raw observational data, or our personal recorded reflections, is not appropriate. Yet, it is quite reasonable to provide a summary (or full copy) of our final research report to interested participants.

In assuming roles in a field setting, we should be aware that the social and physical locations are very important influences on the type of data we will be

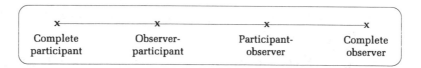

| Complete participant | Observer-participant | Participant-observer | Complete observer |

FIGURE 15.1   CONTINUUM OF PARTICIPANT OBSERVATION

able to collect. As we note *what* occurs at different points in time and space, we may begin to recognize that *when* something occurs is often important. In a women's emergency shelter, for example, the physical locations at which we observe could include the children's playroom, the outside playground, and the dining room. The different roles we could take—such as a social worker or a children's playroom aide—would affect our interactions with those at the shelter and, in turn, would provide us with a rich variety of different perspectives. In some cases it might be difficult to operate in these different roles in one field setting, so we could choose to select one or two roles at one women's shelter, and others at another shelter.

NEEDED STRATEGIES AND SKILLS

As previously mentioned, the participant observation experience is intense and demanding. It is both an art and a science, calling on many aspects of our capabilities. In order to deal with the many situations that come up in a field setting, there are a few strategies we can use to both minimize difficulties and stresses for all those involved, as well as to ensure that a high-quality research study takes place.

- We need to practice observing and making notes that are as detail rich as possible, based on our recall of events (e.g., we could observe people interacting in a busy city recreation center).
- We need to keep a daily personal journal that includes our reflections on events that are occurring in our life; this will help with both the discipline of writing field notes, and with enhancing our self-knowledge.
- We need to get help from a knowledgeable advisor in designing, planning, and implementing our research study, as well as setting up a regular schedule of debriefing and advisory sessions throughout the study.
- We need to tap into supporting systems and services regarding our physical, emotional, and spiritual well-being.
- We need to develop a working knowledge of our topic area by reading the literature and talking with people who have done research studies in our particular research area.
- We need to identify, record, and, if possible, let go of our assumptions or preconceptions that might influence the study.

The specific skills needed for using participant observation as a data collection method are:

- The skills of careful looking and listening—paying attention to all possible details.
- The skills of remembering things—including verbatim comments, nonverbal cues, and "climatic" conditions.

- The skills of disciplined, regular writing—describing events and exchanges as well as personal reactions and reflections.
- The skills of tuning into oneself—knowing our vulnerabilities, values, and views; owning our thoughts and feelings, assumptions, and biases.

STEPS IN DOING PARTICIPANT OBSERVATION

Our direct participation in, and observation of, events as they occur in their natural field settings is the cornerstone of using participant observation as a data collection method. Thus, it is essential that we be well organized and prepared, but also flexible and adaptable enough to change with the circumstances. The specific steps of using participant observation as a data collection method cannot be entirely predetermined, however they can serve as a guide to the overall process. We need to recognize and seize opportunities and rapidly adjust to these new situations as they occur in the field. In the beginning of our study, we can expect to have little control over our data and not much focus. Once we are socialized into our field setting, however, we can focus our inquiry and gain some control over the data we finally end up gathering.

Notwithstanding that participant observation is characterized by a back and forth, nonlinear process, there are six fundamental steps that serve as a guide. These steps are: (1) Gaining access and entry to a study site, (2) engaging and forming relationships, (3) gathering the data, (4) recording the data, (5) making sense of the data, and (6) reporting the findings.

Step 1: Gaining Access and Entry to a Study Site

A site is the context in which our study occurs and it need not be a fixed geographic location. A particular group of research participants, for example, may interact across several sites. In addition, our own characteristics may limit access to a site. A white single male, for example, may have a difficult time gaining access to a group of single-parent women of color. Physical access can also be an issue, in that we may find that we are not allowed on a site(s) or there are legal or political barriers to access, such as in public schools, hospitals, and prisons. Access to such settings depends on *gatekeepers*—those with formal or informal authority to control access to sites. Permission is usually required from a gatekeeper and involves bargaining and negotiating. In some cases, permission from gatekeepers may inhibit the cooperation of people whom we want to study. Juvenile offenders, for example, may not want to participate in a study if they know that the Director of Secure Treatment has authorized us to be there. Gaining access and entering a site depends on our personal attributes, prior connections, and social skills.

Entry and access is more analogous to peeling away the layers of an onion than it is to opening a door. We begin at the outermost layer where access is easy.

At this stage, as outsiders, we are most likely looking for data more or less in the public domain. The next layer requires an increased degree of access as we become more of a passive unquestioning observer of events occurring in the field setting. Over time, and as trust develops, we peel off another layer and observe more sensitive interactions or activities and ask for clarification of our personal observations. At yet a deeper layer, we can shape or influence the interaction so that particular data or certain behaviors are revealed. This layer is also necessary in order to access highly sensitive material that requires a deep level of trust.

Step 2: Engaging and Forming Relationships

The process of engaging and developing relationships with our research participants requires sensitivity and well-developed communication and inter-personal skills. We must be prepared to explain what we are doing and why, repeatedly with each research participant. We should be ready to deal with a degree of hostility, rejection, and resistance. There will be more or less of this depending on who we are and the population we are studying. Gaining entry and access to women with breast cancer, for example, may pose fewer obstacles if the researcher is a woman who has had breast cancer, than if she is trying to enter a poor Hispanic neighborhood and is seen as part of the "white establishment."

The participant observer must establish rapport and build relationships. This is not always easy, as field settings can be very uncomfortable and individuals in these settings can behave in frightening ways. Building trust is a complex matter: It develops over time, and requires continual reaffirmation. We need to learn the language and the meanings constructed by the research participants we are studying—how to think and act from the perspective of the *insiders*. In short, we need to empathize and understand their experiences. Thus, it is crucial to monitor how our actions and appearances affect the members so that the data we gather are as rich and reflective as possible. This requires a degree of sharing and disclosure on our part; we cannot remain neutral or distant and expect to be a participant observer.

Our relationships must be characterized by dialogue and partnership, mutual interest and reciprocity, trust and cooperation, while we are still working within the parameters of professional ethics. This means we must be alert to the dimensions of cultural, ethnic, and other differences while being sensitive to the dynamics of power and privilege in the relationships we are building. The longer (or more often) we are in a field setting, the more we will be regarded as non-threatening and our presence taken for granted.

As our relationships evolve and deepen over time, we must be careful about not slipping over into roles that may be an aside to being a researcher, which would breach the agreement we made with our research participants. In some circumstances it may be easier to become a therapist, change agent, advocate, or active member (full participant), than it is to remain a participant observer. Should we undertake such roles, however, we will change the nature of our relationships, which will impact and likely thwart the original purpose of our research study.

Some of the first questions that research participants ask are, "Why should I cooperate with your research study?" "What's in it for me/us?" "What's in it for you?" Our direct and candid answers to these questions are important. Research participants need to know that we seek to understand and describe their reality from their point-of-view, and that ultimately there is value in having their stories told. But they also need to know that we expect to gain such things as publications, expertise, or an academic degree from the study. The data collected will hopefully contribute to existing knowledge and may lead to solutions to their problems. They also need to know, however, that there are no absolute guarantees; nor is it the intent that our study will change their lives in any meaningful way.

Engaging and forming relationships that are sustained over time with insiders in a field setting is imperative to gathering meaningful, valid, and reliable data. Building these relationships is like being socialized into a way of life. We need to "be there," to "hang out," to "watch, listen, and learn the norms, language, and patterns of interaction." The same skills used to make friends are used to connect with the insiders, our research participants, in a field setting so that we have the ability to gather meaningful data that will be used to answer our research question.

Step 3: Gathering the Data

Participant observation data are usually gathered in four nonmutually exclusive ways: (1) observing, (2) interviewing, (3) using existing documents and other materials, and (4) reflecting upon our personal experiences.

Observing

Good observers need to use all of their senses to notice what they saw, heard, touched, smelled, and tasted. Start with the physical surroundings of the settings, for example, and pay particular attention to the details that influence human behavior such as lighting, temperature, colors, odors, and available space.

The next level is observing people and their actions. Begin by noting observable physical characteristics of individuals and the composition of the group in such areas as gender, ethnicity, age, shape/size, and appearance. Notice what people do in relation to each other, such as who talks, who listens, and who sits or stands next to whom. As our observations become more focused, we pay more attention to such issues as the nature of the gathering and discern if this is typical or unusual. At this stage, however, our observations serve the purpose of familiarizing ourselves with the field setting, getting a "feel for the people and the place." These observations allow the widest possible field of vision. We are, however, limited to learning by looking and listening and will soon need to more sharply focus our attention and move away from passive observation to being a more active participant by asking questions through interviewing.

Interviewing

The data collected at the beginning of a participant observation study is in the form of words, including direct quotes and thick descriptions of particular events. There are general guidelines for asking good questions, but the type and style depends on the purpose and nature of the specific research study. Figure 5.1 provides four types of questions that can be asked during an interview with a research participant.

Questions that ask *what, when, where,* and *how* provide good descriptive data. Questions that ask *why* pressure people, put them on the defensive, and should therefore be selectively used. *Compare and contrast* questions illustrate another type of inquiry. By asking how things are similar to and different from one another, we can discern what is included or excluded, what is part of or outside of the phenomena, and start to grasp the multiple meanings and layers involved in understanding the phenomena we are studying.

Data gathered by engaging in dialogue and asking questions may be undertaken in a variety of situations ranging from casual conversations through formal interviews. Data gathered by a structured interview schedule through formal interviews, where specific questions are asked in exactly the same way with different research participants, have the advantage of producing a uniform set of data.

On the other hand, as we know from the previous chapter, unstructured interviews have the advantage of producing richly qualitative data at a more in-depth level of disclosure. Both structured and unstructured interviewing contributes useful and meaningful data. Gayla Rogers and Elaine Bouey (1996) present a clear description of how to collect interview data in qualitatively oriented research studies. Figure 15.2 provides a summary of the main differences between survey and participant observation interviewing (Neuman, 1994).

Using Existing Documents and Other Materials

In the course of a participant observation study, it is not unusual to come across existing documents, such as files, records, articles, pamphlets, and other materials, such as objects, artwork, videos, clothing, which provide different sources of data. These data are extremely useful in providing support for the findings we derived from our observing and interviewing. They also provide a background, in addition to alternative points-of-view or explanations. The use of existing documents are unobtrusive data collection methods and are discussed in detail in Chapters 16 to 19.

Survey Interview	Participant Observation Interview
1. It has a clear beginning and conclusion.	1. The beginning and end are not clearly defined. The interview can be picked up later.
2. The same standard questions are asked of all research participants in the same order.	2. The questions and the order in which they are asked are tailored to certain people and situations.
3. The interviewer remains neutral at all times.	3. The interviewer shows interest in responses, encourages elaboration.
4. The interviewer asks questions, and the interviewee answers.	4. It is like a friendly conversational exchange, but with more interview-like questions.
5. It is almost always with a single research participant.	5. It can occur in group setting or with others in area, but varies.
6. Professional tone and businesslike focus. Diversions are ignored.	6. It is interspersed with jokes, asides, stories, diversions, and anecdotes, which are recorded.
7. Closed-ended questions are common, with rare probes.	7. Open-ended questions are common, and probes are frequent.
8. The interviewer alone controls the speed and direction of the interview.	8. The interviewer and insider jointly influence the pace and direction of the interview.
9. The social context in which the interview takes place is not considered and is assumed to make little difference.	9. The social context of the interview is noted and seen as essential for interpreting the meaning of responses.
10. The interviewer attempts to shape the communication pattern into a standard framework.	10. The interviewer adjusts to the insider's norms and language usage, following his or her lead.

FIGURE 15.2   SURVEY RESEARCH INTERVIEWS VERSUS PARTICIPANT OBSERVATION INTERVIEWS

Reflecting Upon Our Personal Experiences

Our feelings, insights, and perceptions are other sources of data and should be treated as just that—duly documented and reported, however. By participating in the world of those we are studying, we generate the experiences of an insider.

Reflecting upon our personal experiences in our field setting gives us access to the standpoint of the insider. It provides us with insights and new understandings of particular ways of life. These data can be used as a source of further questions to be asked of our research participants in order to check out our inner responses, hypotheses, and assumptions.

Through these various methods, high-quality data are gathered. This means our data are richly varied, detailed descriptions that emerge from our observations and experiences. Given the sheer volume of data, considerable attention needs to paid to how the data will be managed and analyzed—the topic of Chapter 22.

Step 4: Recording the Data

Regardless of the type of data collected, their purpose is lost if we fail to adequately record our observations, impressions, and actual words. In addition to our notes, tapes, and transcriptions, we can use visual aids, such as diagrams, flow charts, eco-maps and genograms, and photographs. Their type, form, and content depend on a number of factors: the field setting, the available and suitable technologies, the purpose of our study, and our personal preferences.

There is a great temptation to postpone systematically recording the gathered data. This is a mistake, as data that are not carefully organized and stored after they have been recorded create many challenges in the data analysis stage (Chapter 22). Developing a habit of regularly recording what is seen, heard, and experienced is strongly encouraged.

There are many ways to record data when using participant observation as a data collection method. Three of the more common ones are: (1) using field notes, (2) using taping devices, and (3) using visual aids.

Using Field Notes

The majority of gathered data are in the form of field notes. Writing field notes requires self-discipline and a time allocation for the task. We will save a lot of backtracking (not to mention aggravation) if we organize our notes into categories at the outset of the study. Visualize creating separate containers to hold different types of notes. Factual observations, for example, are noted separately from personal feelings, impressions, or speculations; notes about our reactions to an interview or extraneous factors affecting the interview are kept separate from transcriptions or direct quotes from an interview. It may be hard to decide, particularly during the initial stages, what constitutes something worth noting. It may also worry us at later stages, that having made all these notes, we have so much data that it seems impossible to decipher any of them. These concerns can be addressed by following the recommendations noted below for making field notes (Neuman, 1994):

- Make notes as soon as possible after each period in the field.
- Begin a record of each field visit with a new page, and the date and time noted.
- Use jotted notes only as a temporary memory aid—with key words or terms, or the first and last things said.
- Use wide margins and double-space everything to make it easy to add to notes at any time. Add to the notes if you remember something later.
- Type notes and store on disk in separate files so it will be easy to go back to them later.
- Record events in the order in which they occur, and note how long they last (e.g., a 15-minute wait, a one-hour ride).
- Make notes as concrete, specific, complete, and comprehensible as possible.
- Use frequent paragraphs and quotation marks. Exact recall of phrases is best, with double quotes; use single quotes for paraphrasing.
- Record small talk or routines that do not appear to be significant at the time; they may become important later.
- "Let your feelings flow" and write quickly without worrying about spelling or "wild ideas." Assume that no one else will see the notes, but use pseudonyms as a precaution to maintain confidentiality.
- Never substitute tape recordings completely for field notes.
- Include diagrams or maps of the setting, and note your own movements and those of others during the period of observation.
- Include your own words and behavior in the notes. Also record emotional feelings and private thoughts in a separate section.
- Avoid evaluative summarizing words. Use nonjudgmental, descriptive words. Instead of "The sink looked disgusting," say, "The sink was rust-stained and looked as if it had not been cleaned in a long time. Pieces of food and dirty dishes that looked several days old were piled into it."
- Reread notes periodically and record ideas triggered by the rereading.
- Organize materials neatly into types, or methods of data collected so they can be easily accessed.
- Always make one or more backup copies, keep them in a locked location, and store the copies in different places in case of fire.

There are many different types of field notes. We have chosen to describe four that represent different levels of data: (1) using direct observation notes, (2) using interpretive notes, (3) using thematic notes, and (4) using personal journal notes.

Using Direct Observation Notes   The first level of field notes, *direct observation notes*, are usually organized chronologically and contain a detailed description of what was seen and heard. At this level the notes report the facts— such as, who, what, when, and where—and include verbatim statements, paraphrases, and nonverbal communications. These also include summary notes made after an interview.

Using Interpretive Notes   The next level of field notes are *interpretive notes*. Our interpretations of events are kept separate from the record of the facts noted as direct observations, but need to be located in an adjacent column to the direct observations. These notes include our interpretation of the meanings inferred by the words and gestures we observed. We can speculate about the social relationships, the emotions, and the influence of culture and context on what actually took place. By keeping our interpretations separate, we leave room for multiple interpretations (or different interpretations) to arise as our knowledge and experience increase. If we are not vigilant, however, it is quite easy to combine the facts with our interpretation of them, and we run the risk later on of viewing our interpretations as fact, which in turn might narrow our ability to see other versions or meanings emerge.

Using Thematic Notes   The third level of field notes is *thematic notes.* They provide a place to record our emerging ideas, hypotheses, theories, and conjectures. This is the place to speculate and identify themes, make linkages between ideas and events, and articulate our thoughts as they emerge while we are still in the field setting. In these notes, we might expand on some of the ideas that have occurred, and develop our theories as we go, or as we reread our direct observation notes and interpretive notes. This is the place to describe the thoughts that emerge in the "middle of the night" or to elaborate on any "Aha!" connections. Thus, it is critical to have a separate container for these thoughts at this level, even if they are speculative and in early stages of development, because we might lose an important seed for later analysis if it is not recorded.

Using Personal Journal Notes   Keeping a journal of *personal notes* provides an outlet for recording our feelings and emotional reactions, as well as the personal experiences of being the researcher or the participant observer. These are a rich source of data. They give voice to our journey over time and provide a place to consider such things as what is going on at any given time during our involvement in the field. A running record of personal life events, feelings, physical well-being, and our moods, particularly as they relate to events in the field, will facilitate our data analysis. In this way we can capture any particular intrapersonal or interpersonal experiences that might affect the way we make sense of the data. The process has an effect upon the quality of the content gathered, our interpretation of the content, and what next steps we decide to take. Identifying these effects as they are revealed also facilitates our interpretation and reporting of them later.

The four different levels of field notes are shown below using an example of recording a period of observation in a field setting with a woman named Kay (Neuman, 1994):

- **Direct Observation**   Sunday, October 4, 1997: Kay's Cafe 3:00 P.M. Large white male in mid 40s, overweight, enters. He wears worn brown suit. He is alone sits at booth #2. Kay comes by asks, "what'll it be?" Man says, "Coffee, black for now." She leaves and he lights cigarette and reads menu. 3:15 P.M. Kay turns on radio.
- **Interpretive**   Kay seems friendly today, humming. She becomes solemn and watchful. I think she puts on the radio when nervous.

- **Thematic** Women are afraid of men who come in alone since the robbery.
- **Personal Journal** It is raining. I am feeling comfortable with Kay but am distracted today by a headache.

Using Taping Devices

As we participate more actively and purposefully in the field setting and as our interactions with our research participants become less casual and more planned, we conduct interviews that are recorded and later transcribed. There are three typical approaches to recording the data gathered in qualitative research interviews: (1) taping the interview (either audio or video); (2) taking notes during the interview; and (3) recording immediately following the interview.

Taping the Interview   There are both advantages and disadvantages to *tape-recording* interviews. The presence of a recorder can be intrusive and a barrier to full disclosure, however it may be the only way to capture the richness and subtleties of speech. In the case of video recording, it is the only way to capture the nonverbal language used by our research participants, or to accurately identify each speaker in a group situation. Recording devices may also be a means of self-monitoring and an improvement for the interviewer. The tape recorder may provide us with confidence to focus all our attention on the person being interviewed, knowing we do not have to worry about remembering all of the details or writing notes. At the same time, however, knowing the tape will record everything that is said, we might be tempted to let our minds wander.

Ultimately, the decision about whether to tape depends on what we want to do with the data gathered. If we want to include many direct quotes, for example, then it is useful to have the verbatim account, which can be transcribed and subjected to editing at a later date. If capturing the exact phrasing of all interview responses is not critical to the study, then note-taking may suffice. If time and money are not an issue, it is clearly best to fully transcribe all interviews from the tape. On the other hand, if time and money are limited, we might listen to the tape and use our notes to help decide what parts to transcribe and paraphrase.

Taking Notes During the Interview   Many interviewers advocate *taking notes during the interview* as well as tape-recording them. The notes serve as a backup or safeguard against mechanical difficulties. They also serve as guides to the tape in helping decide what to transcribe and what to leave out. In some cases, where tape-recording is not possible, brief notes may be the only way of recording the data. In this case we would try to write down some exact quotations and brief comments, supplemented by notes after the interview.

Recording Immediately Following the Interview   The third approach to recording interview data is to *make a record of the interview soon after it occurs*. This can be done in a variety of ways but it is important to allow sufficient time for this. One hour of interviewing may require four hours to develop the notes afterwards, particularly if this is the only record of the interview. Writing a process recording of the interview as soon as possible after the interview helps. The same four levels used in making field notes can be used in writing up research interviews—that is, to use a four-column format. In the first column we write as close to a verbatim account of the interview as we can recall. This would include our questions, probes and statements as well as the interviewee's responses.

Use the next column to note our interpretations of the meanings, emotions, and relationships inferred from the words and gestures. In the third column, any insights or themes that occur are noted. The fourth column is to reflect on what we were thinking or feeling at the time and to note other things that were occurring that may have caused interference (e.g., room was too warm or too noisy, other distractions).

Using Visual Aids

Data are recorded using a variety of visual aids to supplement and support our field notes and tapes. Diagrams show how ideas are related, and flow charts outline sequences, processes, and events. Eco-maps and genograms present relationships and their various dimensions. Photographs capture the field setting or environment. All of these visual aids contain a great deal of data and depict our specific field setting and the people within it, in a manner that written words simply cannot convey as effectively or as economically. Visual aids add an additional dimension in combination with other data collection methods.

Step 5: Making Sense of the Data

Analyzing qualitative data is presented in depth in Chapter 22. It is important to keep in mind at this point, however, that we need to make some sense of our experiences as participant observers. This involves analyzing the data collected. At some point, notwithstanding some initial prior reviews of the data as they are being gathered and organized, there comes a time when a full-scale intensive analysis occurs as the next step in the research process.

Step 5 is marked by a critical shift in how we have been working so far, and it requires the use of a different set of skills and abilities. It is also a time when we are quite overwhelmed with the prospect of wading through masses of data and making sense of them. It may be a particular challenge to move into this step, particularly if our forte has been the developing of social relationships, taking on various participant observer roles, and being flexible and resourcefully adaptable in our field setting in an effort to ensure that we have good data to analyze.

We do not present a discussion of how to analyze qualitative data, as this is presented in Chapter 22. The analysis step allows our data to be coded, sifted, sorted, and categorized so that themes, theories, and generalizations can be constructed and generated. In this way, meaning can be made of our research endeavor, and our results can be reported.

Step 6: Reporting the Findings

As should be evident by now, participant observation studies allow for the creation of a rich source of data about a situation or phenomenon involving people. The raw data include such items as our written observation notes and correspondence, audiotapes, videotapes, personal journals with reflections, as well as notes made after debriefing and consultation sessions with research advisors. A final report of our study includes an overview of our research question and the methods and techniques used in the study, detailed descriptions of the people and related phenomena, themes or hypotheses emerging from all the different data sources, information about our personal process, biases, and assumptions, and recommendations based upon our findings.

Normally, once the data are gathered and analyzed, they are written up as a case study using quite detailed descriptions about the events or situation being studied. The final report includes themes and theoretical interpretations (or hypotheses) emerging from the data. It includes recommendations for further study or action.

The intended audience of the report impacts what and how it is written. The general public requires a different level of explanation than does an academic audience. The use of jargon is avoided unless the audience is comprised of others working in a similar or related area. Other possible audiences include other researchers or professional practitioners and government departments or agencies. Given the newly emerging view of research participants as having a vital partnership role in the research process, all those having a part in our study should have access to, or otherwise be provided with, a summary or a full copy of the final report.

Writing is facilitated by having blocks of uninterrupted time and perseverance. It involves drafting and editing, and often includes showing early drafts to some or all of the insiders and consulting with research advisors. Eventually, a unique document is produced that is appropriate for the study undertaken and its intended audience.

Robert McClelland and Carol D. Austin (1996) present a very clear description of exactly how to write up a qualitatively oriented final report.

ETHICAL CONSIDERATIONS

Ethical considerations must be taken into account for any research situation. There are additional ethical issues that must be addressed in doing participant observation because of the close and sustained relationships with research participants and the fact that the balance of research activities occurs in a field setting where many other influences may surface and need to be dealt with as the study proceeds. Thus, through proper sponsorship and approvals, plus informed consent of all those involved, it is crucial to attend to what is required to prevent adverse consequences.

Beyond this, there is the issue of the level of information we provide our research participants in reference to the roles we assumed during the study, and the degree to which we disclosed personal information. While there are different views on this, we advise that, wherever possible, our research participants should be included as co-partners in our research study in as open and as equal a way as possible. We have to decide how much to reveal about ourselves and the research project itself.

Disclosure ranges on a continuum from fully covert (no one in the field setting is aware of the study) to fully disclosed (everyone knows the specifics of the study). It is unlikely, however, that a social work research project would get approval from an ethics board either in an academic or in a social-work–related setting, unless it was near the fully disclosed end of the spectrum, where our research participants give their informed consent and know how our data will be stored and used. Covert research studies are simply not ethical.

SUMMARY

This chapter presented an overview of participant observation as an obtrusive data collection method. It described its unique characteristics, such as issues of gaining access and entry into a field setting, forming and sustaining relationships (which includes the continuum of roles adopted by the researcher), and data gathering involving the use of less structured data gathering approaches.

We included strategies for recording the data and have attempted to create an awareness of the fine and delicate balance that exists between the participant-observer and the research participants, and of how crucial it is for us to be both attuned to this, as well as to make the necessary adjustments as our study unfolds to assure that the perspective of our research participants comes through clearly, accurately, and in considerable detail.

This is the final chapter on the use of obtrusive data collection methods. We now turn our attention to unobtrusive methods—those methods that do not require the researcher to obtain data directly from individuals. As we know from Part V, obtrusive data collection methods consist of structured observation (Chapter 13), surveys (Chapter 14), and participant observation (this chapter). Part VI presents unobtrusive methods of data collection, which indirectly obtain data from research participants through such methods as secondary analysis of existing data (Chapter 16), utilizing existing statistics (Chapter 17), content analysis (Chapter 18), and historical research (Chapter 19).

REFERENCES AND FURTHER READINGS

DENZIN, N., & LINCOLN, Y.S. (Eds.). (1994). *Handbook of qualitative research.* Newbury Park, CA: Sage.

JORGENSEN, D.L. (1989). *Participant observation: A methodology for human studies.* Newbury Park, CA: Sage.

McCLELLAND, R.W., & AUSTIN, C.D. (1996). Part four: Writing your report. In L.M. Tutty, M.A. Rothery, & R.M. Grinnell, Jr. (Eds.), *Qualitative research for social workers: Phases, steps, and tasks* (pp. 120-150). Needham Heights, MA: Allyn & Bacon.

NEUMAN, W.L. (1994). *Social research methods* (2nd ed.). Needham Heights, MA: Allyn & Bacon.

PAPELL, C.P., & SKOLNIK, L. (1992). The reflective practitioner: A contemporary paradigm's relevance for social work education. *Journal of Social Work Education, 28,* 18-26.

PATTON, M.Q. (1990). *Qualitative evaluation and research methods* (2nd ed.). Newbury Park, CA: Sage.

ROGERS, G., & BOUEY, E. (1996). Part two: Collecting your data. In L.M. Tutty, M.A. Rothery, & R.M. Grinnell, Jr. (Eds.), *Qualitative research for social workers: Phases, steps, and tasks* (pp. 50-87). Needham Heights, MA: Allyn & Bacon.

ROTHERY, M.A., TUTTY, L.M., & GRINNELL, R.M., JR. (1996). Part one: Planning your study. In L.M. Tutty, M.A. Rothery, & R.M. Grinnell, Jr. (Eds.), *Qualitative research for social workers: Phases, steps, and tasks* (pp. 24-49). Needham Heights, MA: Allyn & Bacon.

SCHÖN, D.A. (1983). *The reflective practitioner: How professionals think in action.* New York: Basic Books.

SPRADLEY, J.P. (1980). *Participant observation.* New York: Holt, Rinehart, & Winston.

TUTTY, L.M., ROTHERY, M.A., & GRINNELL, R.M., JR. (Eds.). (1996). *Qualitative research for social workers: Phases, steps, and tasks.* Needham Heights, MA: Allyn & Bacon.

UNOBTRUSIVE DATA COLLECTION METHODS

Judy Krysik

C h a p t e r **16**

Secondary Analysis

T HE PRACTICE OF ANALYZING an existing data set for a purpose other than the purpose for which it was originally collected is referred to as a *secondary analysis*—an unobtrusive data collection method. Thus, secondary analysis is any further analysis of an existing data set that presents interpretations, conclusions, or knowledge additional to, or different from, those presented in prior analyses of the data.

SECONDARY ANALYSIS: PAST AND PRESENT

Although gaining in popularity, the use of secondary data sets is not new. One of the earliest examples of a secondary analysis of existing data sets is Emile Durkheim's 1897 study on suicide. Durkheim and his associates collected data from existing hospital death records to understand the social factors associated with suicide (Pope, 1976). Thus, Durkheim used existing data for a purpose not intended by those who originally collected them. As should be very evident by now, analyzing existing data sets is an unobtrusive data collection strategy in that it does not collect original data from research participants. Thus, we do not intrude into our research participants' lives to collect data.

Advanced computer technology and the widespread implementation of management information systems (MIS) have made the task of accessing and analyzing secondary data sets much easier than in Durkheim's era. In fact, a plethora of data sets are available on individuals, families, organizations, communities, and countries. The current state of secondary analyses was perhaps best captured by Hyman (1987) who stated, "Now, late in the twentieth century, social scientists can also be described as standing atop of a giant mountain of data, from which they might see farther back into the past, away into remoter regions of the world, and over a larger vista of problems than ever before."

Upon identifying a research problem area appropriate for a secondary analysis, we need to choose from a variety of data sets. Most of these secondary data sets can be accessed in a matter of a week or two, in computer readable form, ready for analysis. Along with the data set we can expect to receive information on: (1) the name and affiliation of the data collector, (2) the data collection period, (3) the type of sampling method used, (4) the size of the sample, (5) the data collection method, including the survey instrument or interview schedule, (6) the data source, (7) notes on data coding procedures, and (8) suggestions for analyses. Most data sets are available at a fraction of what they cost to produce.

TYPES OF SECONDARY DATA

There are three principal types of secondary data that are available. They are (1) micro-level data, (2) aggregate-level data, and (3) qualitative-level data.

Micro-Level Data

The term *micro-level data* is used to describe data derived from individual units of analysis, whether these data sources are persons, households, or organizations. Number of children, for example, is a micro-level variable. For the past two centuries, the federal government has been the most important source of micro-level data by providing large national surveys of households through means such as the population census (Oyen, 1990).

Aggregate-Level Data

Aggregate-level data consists of statistics and/or tables derived from quantitative micro-level data, in which the characteristics of individual units of analysis are no longer identifiable. Unemployment rate, for example, is an aggregate-level variable. The calculation of an unemployment rate requires a number of individuals to respond to a question asking whether or not they are gainfully employed. The micro-level data from individual respondents are then aggregated to produce an aggregate measure of unemployment. Chapter 17 describes in detail how to use aggregate-level data to answer research questions or test hypotheses.

Qualitative-Level Data

Qualitative-level data are any kind of nonquantitative data. Secondary data sets that are qualitative in nature include descriptive narratives and records of personal communication such as diaries and letters. Understanding soldiers' experiences of war by examining letters they sent home would be an example of a secondary analysis using qualitative-level data. Chapters 5, 6, 12, 15, and 22, present in-depth discussions of how qualitative-level secondary data can be useful in social work research studies.

Combining Types of Data for a Particular Analysis

As stressed throughout this book, most research problems are best understood and answered through the use of both qualitative-level data and quantitative data. Secondary analyses provides a means to this end by blending both research approaches. While many studies using secondary data are based on only one type of data (i.e., micro-, aggregate-, or qualitative-level), some studies combine all three types.

LOCATING SECONDARY DATA SETS

A major challenge in collecting primary data for a given research study is to locate and secure the participation of research participants. In contrast, for the secondary analyst, the challenge is to locate an appropriate existing data set. Thus we need to be aware of the many published guides, directories, and other resources available for identifying existing data sets. However, while books and articles that list existing data sets are available, such resources can become quickly obsolete (e.g., Dale, Arber, & Proctor, 1988; Kiecolt & Nathan, 1985).

Increased computer technology has prompted the development of numerous data archives throughout Europe and North America. They primarily hold micro-level data and have become an important source in secondary data analyses. The largest data archive in the world is the Inter-University Consortium for Political and Social Research (ICPSR). Currently, the ICPSR has more than 17,000 files of computer-readable data that span two centuries and more than 130 countries. The ICPSR, as do many data archives, has university member affiliates that entitles faculty and students to use the data sets at a minimal cost (if any). Most data archives publish catalogues on an annual basis to inform the public of their holdings. Other less formal sources of micro-level data exist, however, such as government departments, social service agencies, private foundations, charitable organizations, and private industry, and usually require more effort to locate.

Aggregate data are available in standardized and unstandardized formats. The Congressional Information Services (CIS) publishes an index to the statistical publications of international, intergovernmental organizations on an annual basis. It is not the intent of CIS, however, to present data in a standardized format. As an alternative, the Organization for European Cooperation and Development (OECD), the International Labor Office (ILO), and the Euromonitor are three sources that publish data using standardized operational definitions of certain variables.

Data from publications that attempt standardization of variables are superior for secondary analyses. For instance, in Durkheim's era, official suicide rates varied by region according to whether secular or religious officials were responsible for recording the cause of death. We could argue, therefore, that the lack of a standardized operational definition of suicide was a limitation in Durkheim's study.

Secondary data sets are not always in the form of surveys and official records, however. Qualitative-level data may be gathered from a variety of sources such as books, unpublished manuscripts, articles, monographs, personal communication, and even audio and video tape recordings. Locating the best source (or sources) of data for a particular research study is often a trial-and-error process. Contacting a reference librarian at a university library for assistance is an excellent way to start.

EXAMPLE: THE WELFARE STATE AND WOMEN'S EMPLOYMENT

To demonstrate how a secondary analysis is done, an example is used throughout this chapter that involves the use of several existing data sets archived in the Luxembourg Income Study (LIS). The LIS is an international data cooperative that has available family and household micro-level data for over 21 countries from the late 1960s to early 1990s. The data sets for LIS are national income surveys administered by each member country. The U.S. Current Population Survey and the Canadian Survey of Consumer Finances are included in the LIS database.

Even though women in North America have entered the labor force in large numbers, they remain disadvantaged. This disadvantage has multiple forms—for instance, low employment participation rates, low pay, a predominance of part-time labor, and occupational segregation. For women, full integration into paid labor has implications that extend far beyond economic well-being. Employment may impact women's physical and emotional well-being, for example, as well as their participation in cultural, political, and social life.

Although women are increasingly involved in employment, they still carry the majority of responsibility for family care. The interface between employment and family creates significant tensions that may present barriers to women's participation in paid labor. Women's opportunities to enhance their employment careers rest on their access to income-generating work and on support for domestic responsibilities. For many women, such access may be reflected in welfare state policies and programs that address issues such as employment equity, parental leave, and child care.

Thus, to the extent that the modern welfare state intervenes to address tensions between employment and family and thereby attempts to influence gender equity, it would be expected that the welfare state would be more or less successful in decreasing women's labor force disadvantage. Examining the relationship between the welfare state and women's employment falls clearly in the domain of our profession.

STEPS IN SECONDARY ANALYSES

At a basic level, a secondary analysis follows seven steps. They are: (1) selecting a problem area, (2) formulating a research question or hypothesis, (3) formulating a research design, (4) evaluating the data set, (5) constructing operational definitions, (6) analyzing the data, and (7) writing the research report.

Step 1: Selecting a Problem Area

The first task in conducting any research study is to decide on a problem area. It is important that we devote as much time and effort defining the research problem in a secondary analysis as we would in conducting a primary research study that requires original data. As can be expected, there is some temptation with a secondary analysis to formulate the research problem based on whatever data are available. This approach, however, will seldom lead to worthwhile results.

With regard to our example, a review of the literature indicated that the welfare state has been a major contributor in reducing poverty among demographic groups such as the elderly and the disabled. When observed cross-nationally, however, a great deal of variation in the redistributive capacities of various welfare states has been noted. In Scandinavian countries, for example, the redistributive effects of the welfare state are substantial, whereas the United States is often characterized as a welfare state laggard. This variation in welfare state performance has been explained in a typology of welfare state regimes (Esping-Andersen, 1990).

The research problem in our example is, "How might Esping-Andersen's typology of welfare state regimes apply to women's employment outcomes?" If three different types of welfare state regimes do exist, then it could be expected that women's employment outcomes would differ across countries according to the type of welfare state regime it had. Thus, if policy makers could identify countries based on their achievement of positive outcomes, then they could consider the transferability of the welfare state strategies employed in these countries.

Step 2: Formulating a Research Question or Hypothesis

In order for a problem area to be researched it must be formulated into more manageable questions or hypotheses. A review of the literature on women's employment suggested that inequities resulting from macroeconomic conditions such as unemployment, as well as social differences such as marital status, education, and number of children, could be reduced by policies and programs introduced by the welfare state.

Based on Esping-Andersen's typology of welfare state regimes we were able to hypothesize what employment outcomes each type of welfare state regime would produce. For instance, countries with social democratic welfare state regimes, because of their commitment to full employment and gender equity, should be characterized by high levels of female participation in employment, a predominance of full-time labor at relatively high wages, and low gender segregation within occupations.

The conservative welfare state regime, in contrast, supports the traditional roles of wife and mother. Women's employment participation in the conservative welfare state regime was therefore predicted to be low and characterized by part-time status in female-dominated occupations. Because the state monetarily supports nonemployment, the demand for labor in the conservative welfare state regime would be low.

Given that some participation in paid labor among women is necessary to meet the demands of capitalism, wages must be high enough to make women's employment worthwhile, and low enough to keep demand and supply in equilibrium, resulting in moderate wage rates. In the liberal welfare state, the inability to earn income outside of the market system will force women to accept whatever labor is available. Because women need paid labor to survive, the supply of female laborers will exceed the demand for labor, increasing competition and forcing wages downward. A lack of support for family responsibilities will constrain women's availability, leading to moderate rates of labor force participation and a predominance of part-time, gender-segregated labor.

Finally, if women's employment is systematically influenced by the welfare state, employment outcomes should be different across the various regime types and similar within each regime. Without a thorough understanding of the problem area, we might not have considered the multifaceted nature of employment inequity. For instance, we may have dealt only with women's employment participation, ignoring hours employed, pay, and occupational segregation.

Two research questions (derived from the research problem) were formulated to represent our study's general problem area: (1) What are the differences in women's labor force participation outcomes across western industrialized countries? and (2) Are differences in women's labor force participation outcomes related to the nature of the welfare state? At times, the only way to answer a certain research question is through secondary analysis. Imagine, for a moment, that we were interested in women's employment and attempted to collect nationally representative, original data from several countries. The scope of the data required and cost would be prohibitive, not to mention language barriers and time.

Step 3: Formulating a Research Design

Secondary analysis is extremely versatile in the sense that it can be used to examine the present or the past, understand change over time, examine phenomena comparatively, and replicate or expand on prior research studies. Each of these uses requires a different research design, developed according to the requirements of the research question or hypothesis. Three of the most common research designs that are easily facilitated through a secondary analysis are (1) comparative research designs, (2) temporal research designs, and (3) cross-sectional research designs.

Comparative Research Designs

The study of more than one group, event, or society in order to isolate factors that explain patterns is called *comparative research*. Designs that facilitate comparative studies can be divided into two basic strategies: (1) the study of elements that differ in many ways but that have some major factor in common, or (2) the study of elements that are highly similar but that differ in some important respect (Vogt, 1993).

Following the first strategy, if we were interested in gender we could examine the distribution of unpaid labor and educational attainment across many countries to explain the universal nature of women's disadvantaged economic status. To ascertain the impact of the welfare state on women's employment, however, we choose to study only western industrialized countries.

Holding constant key variables that could influence employment, such as democratic political institutions, market economies, and cultural and religious traditions was important to do in order to isolate their effects on the welfare state.

Temporal Research Designs

All temporal research designs include time as a major variable. Their purpose is to investigate change in the distribution of a variable (or in relationships among variables) for entire populations or subgroups. As discussed in Chapters

11 and 14, there are three types of temporal research designs: cohort, panel, and trend.

Cohort studies investigate characteristics of groups that have experienced some major life event, such as entry into the labor force at a particular interval. A temporal cohort study, for example, might compare the employment profiles of women born in three different decades: pre-World War II, baby boomers, and Generation X.

Panel studies utilize data to study the same persons or entities over time. We could, for example, analyze data to understand how employment careers change before, during, and after childbearing years. Cohort studies require data from only one point in time, whereas panel studies require data to be collected more than once from the same individuals.

Trend studies also look at change, but they do not require data from the same persons or entities. A trend study, for example, might look at attitudes toward women's employment over three different time periods, such as the 1930s, the 1970s, and the 1990s.

Cross-Sectional Research Designs

Cross-sectional designs examine a phenomenon at one point in time and can be used to address a wide range of research questions. Our study on women's employment, for example, was interested in only one period of data collection. We chose data from the mid 1980s because this period was characterized by slow economic growth, high unemployment rates, and rising deficits in social service budgets among all western nations. Thus, the period was considered appropriate for assessing welfare state performance under adverse economic conditions.

Step 4: Evaluating the Data Set

Not all secondary data sets are equally valid or reliable. We need to answer four questions prior to engaging in analyzing an existing data set.

Question 1: What Was the Original Purpose of the Data Set?

Data are not collected without a purpose. At times, they may be collected to support a particular point of view or to test a particular research hypothesis. If this is the case, the data set may be limited in scope and may not lend itself to testing an alternative explanatory model.

The degree of precision in data collection, the variable categories used, and the method of data collection are all influenced by the primary researcher's intent. Understanding the original purpose of the study, therefore, is mandatory.

Question 2: How Credible Are the Data Source and Data Set?

Credibility refers not only to potential biases the original researcher might have had, but to his or her knowledge of research methodology and level of access to physical and financial resources. Official surveys tend to have greater financial sponsorship, which generally results in larger samples and higher response rates than those obtained by nonofficial surveys. Sample size and representation have implications for those of us who are interested in studying small subgroups within a population.

Another advantage of using data from official sources is that the limitations of standard operational definitions are well documented by both the provider of the data set and by others who have used it. This provides some preliminary guidance for those of us who are embarking on a statistical analysis of the data.

Question 3: Are the Data Representative of the Population?

Knowledge of the sampling frame used provides an indication of the extent to which the study's sample is likely to correspond to the true population from which it was drawn. For instance, our interpretation of a finding that 80 percent of survey respondents did not support affirmative action might be very different if we were to learn that the sample was drawn from a list of Republicans in California. Knowledge of the sampling frame, rates of nonresponse, and the amount of missing data are important points to consider if generalizations from the data set's sample to the population are to be supported. If rates of nonresponse and/or missing data are high, we may want to obtain additional information from other sources and data sets to evaluate the extent of misrepresentation. The sampling method used also has implications for the kinds of statistical analyses that are appropriate.

Question 4: Are Weighting Procedures Needed?

When subgroups in the data set are over- or underrepresented, in comparison to their actual distribution within the population, we may need to employ a weighting procedure. Adjusting data to reflect differences in the number of population units that each case represents is referred to as weighting.

Some data sets, the LIS data in particular, provide the option of using weighted or nonweighted data. It is also possible to pool data from two or more data sets to create a larger data set that will facilitate the examination of underrepresented groups. This procedure is particularly helpful for studying ethnic minorities and never-married mothers, for example.

Step 5: Constructing Operational Definitions

As we know, operationalization is the process of defining variables so they can be measured. In primary research studies, a considerable amount of effort is invested in operationalizing variables before the data are actually collected. On the other hand, in secondary analysis, we create operational definitions after the data are in hand, making the most of whatever is available within the data set. A distinctive feature of a secondary analysis, therefore, is the derivation of new variables by combining a number of variables or by recoding existing ones.

In our study, for example, the LIS data sets did not include a variable to indicate whether or not women were employed. The absence of a variable to indicate employment participation prompted us to construct a new operational definition. In our new operational definition, women were considered to be employed if their income from annual wages (or salaries) was greater than zero. If income from annual wages or salary was equal to zero, a woman was classified as nonemployed. We made a decision to exclude "self-employed income" from the calculation of income because the LIS data sets did not differentiate between income from labor and income from capital, such as rental property. This process of redefining one variable, such as income, into a second variable, such as employment participation, is known as recoding.

At times we may want to create an index as an alternative to using a single indicator variable. An index is nothing more than a composite measure of a general concept that is constructed from multiple variables to produce a single variable (Vogt, 1993). Jodi Jacobson (1992), for instance, developed a single index of "human development" that included three variables: (1) the degree to which people have the option to lead a long and healthy life, (2) the degree to which people have the option to be become knowledgeable, and (3) the degree to which people have the option to find access to the assets, employment, and income needed for a decent standard of living.

It is our task when doing a secondary analysis to create operational definitions that are meaningful, valid, and reliable. If this is not possible given the existing data set, an alternative data set may have to be accessed or the objectives of our research study revised. If a secondary analysis will not permit us to adequately measure the variables required, it may not be the appropriate data collection method to use.

Step 6: Analyzing the Data

The statistical methods used to analyze secondary data sets are the same as those used to analyze original data sets. A common characteristic of secondary data sets, however, is the generally large number of cases and variables they contain. Thus, the statistical techniques employed often require advanced knowledge of statistical methods and competency in computer use. There is no single computerized statistical software program that is most appropriate for statistical analyses. Many are available, and the final choice is dictated by the requirements of the analysis, availability, familiarity, and personal preference.

The data sets used in our example present an anomaly. Whereas most secondary analysts access data sets from a computer-readable data tape that can be copied onto a personal or mainframe computer, direct access to our LIS data sets was not permitted. Researchers access the LIS data sets by electronic mail. Computerized statistical programs were developed in SPSS *(Statistical Package for the Social Sciences)* language and were sent to the Government of Luxembourg mainframe computer where the data sets are stored. Statistical results were returned by electronic mail. The rationale for limiting access to the LIS data sets is to protect the privacy and confidentiality of survey respondents.

We should always begin the statistical analysis of secondary data by investing time in becoming familiar with the data set. This means generating basic descriptive statistics for key variables and comparing them with existing sources to check for compatibility. When the data are congruent across multiple independent sources, we can have more confidence in our analysis.

When disagreement results, it may be necessary to identify potential reasons for such differences and to determine which data source is the more credible. When differences occur, however, we should be skeptical of the data. Some data sources provide basic descriptive statistics on key variables to facilitate comparison. Besides basic descriptive statistics, those people judged to be specialists in a particular area can assist in evaluating the validity of the results.

Step 7: Writing the Research Report

Research reports based on the analysis of a secondary data set are not readily distinguishable from those based on an original data set. The author may refer the reader to the original research report for details of the methodology used. Moreover, it is contingent upon the author to document the limitations of the data set being used. In addition, some suppliers of data sets have certain requirements regarding their use. The source for the LIS data sets, for example, requires that any paper published using the LIS data sets must be included in the *Luxembourg Income Study Working Paper Series.*

ADVANTAGES AND DISADVANTAGES

Weighing the advantages of secondary analysis against its limitations can help decide when to use a secondary data set versus gathering original data.

Advantages

Five of the most salient advantages of secondary data analyses are: (1) maximizing resources, (2) increasing accessibility, (3) avoiding intrusiveness, (4) developing knowledge, and (5) facilitating replication.

Maximizing Resources

One of the most important ways to maximize limited resources is to build on the work already done by others. The cost of conducting original research studies includes the development of survey instruments and interview schedules, and the hiring and training of data collectors, data coders, and data-entry personnel. By using secondary data, savings are incurred in money, time, and personnel. Often it is the only feasible means of obtaining representative data. Conducting a secondary data analysis is not, however, cost free. The cost of conducting a secondary analysis can vary depending on the cost of the data set(s) and the requirements of its use. Some data archives offer workshops to those interested in secondary analysis. With research dollars becoming increasingly scarce, it is important that resources be saved by using secondary data wherever possible so that money can be diverted to studies requiring original data.

Increasing Accessibility

The current state of secondary analyses means that the opportunity of conducting research studies is no longer in the hands of a privileged few. Affordable computer technology has made secondary data sets broadly accessible to the point that even a social work student can conduct a large-scale research project. The development of numerous data archives has both increased the likelihood that data will be discovered and facilitated their use.

Avoiding Intrusiveness

As we know from Chapter 14, recent studies have shown that survey response rates are declining in general (Groves & Cialdini, 1992). This decrease has been attributed in part to the large number of surveys that are now being conducted. The use of secondary data sets limits the reporting burden placed on the public. Also, there are occasions when the introduction of a survey would create tensions or intensify negative emotions. In these circumstances, secondary data can be particularly beneficial.

Developing Knowledge

Secondary data analyses are used to create knowledge at all three levels. At the exploratory level, secondary data are used to generate relevant research questions and tentative hypotheses. They are used at the descriptive level by describing a phenomenon or the characteristics of a population. Many descriptive demographic research studies are based on the analysis of secondary data. Secondary analysis is also useful in explanatory studies. By comparing Esping-

Andersen's three theoretical welfare state regimes to actual situations, for example, knowledge development moves from comparative descriptions to explanatory statements.

Facilitating Replication

Because secondary data sets exist in the public domain, further research studies are easily replicable. Replication is a powerful tool for making research findings less vulnerable to error, as well as protecting them from the transient circumstances of respondents. In addition, the same data set can be analyzed from different perspectives and theoretical frameworks, producing a more holistic understanding of the phenomena under study (Dale, Arber, & Procter, 1988).

Disadvantages

As secondary data analysis is not without limitations, before embarking on a secondary analysis we should avoid potential difficulties by becoming aware of the more common ones. Four of these are: (1) lack of standardization, (2) omission of relevant variables, (3) overabundance of data, and (4) complicated statistical analyses.

Lack of Standardization

Secondary data sets are commonly confronted with a lack of standardized operational definitions of their variables. In the LIS data sets used in our example, the education variable was coded as "years of schooling" in the United States and as "education level" in Canada, Australia, Germany, and the Netherlands. This required recoding of the education variable into the two dichotomous categories of high and low, where "high" represented some post-secondary education, and "low" represented no post-secondary education. The process of dichotomizing the variable was necessary to include "education" in the statistical analysis of more than one country, but resulted in decreased measurement precision. The lack of fit between concepts and the variables they contain is always a problem in analyzing secondary data sets.

Despite recoding, some variables are not sufficiently comparable to allow for their inclusion in a data analysis. In the LIS data, for example, the categories for the ethnicity variable were not comparable across country data sets. The United States differentiated ethnicity by the categories: White, Black, Spanish origin, and other races. In Australia, ethnicity was defined by country of birth and included Australia, the United Kingdom, Italy, Other Europe, Asia, North/South America, Africa, and Oceania. In Canada, ethnicity was defined as Canadian born or immigrant. In Germany, ethnicity was recorded as German, Turkish, Yugoslav, Greek, Italian, Spanish, or other nationality.

The data set for The Netherlands did not contain any information on ethnicity, and, surprisingly, aboriginal status was not recognized in any of the U.S., Australian, and Canadian data sets. Because of the variability in definition and the lack of validity in variable categories, ethnicity is not a valid variable to include in cross-national research studies using the LIS data sets. In our study on women's employment, the inability to include ethnicity may have masked important differences in employment participation and pay across all countries included in our study.

Omission of Relevant Variables

The omission of relevant variables in secondary data sets can also be a problem. Studies focusing on gender may be particularly difficult because many national census and surveys have not included social indicators meaningful to the experiences of women (Norris, 1987). Data on unpaid domestic labor, for instance, are not collected despite its impact on paid labor. In our example on women's employment, social characteristics such as the number of children, age of the youngest child, and marital status were used as proxies for domestic responsibility. A proxy is an indirect measure of a variable.

The use of proxies to represent domestic responsibility is somewhat problematic in that domestic responsibility associated with marriage and children is likely to be inversely related to class status. Households with higher overall income, for example, are more apt to purchase domestic services such as ready-made foods, child care, laundry, and cleaning, than are low income households. The extent that women and men conform to traditional gender roles will also influence women's domestic responsibilities. The lack of a better measure of domestic responsibility contained in the LIS data sets represents a threat to the validity of our study's findings and implications.

Overabundance of Data

For many secondary data sets, the abundance of variables is so great that it sometimes gets difficult to decide which variables to include and which to exclude from any given data analysis. The decision on which variables to include is made easier when our study is guided by a thorough literature review. Without such advance preparation, we can be adrift in a sea of computer printouts, searching aimlessly for statistically significant results that will invariably occur but which are unlikely to have any substantive meaning. An overabundance of data is best confronted by having a thorough understanding of the research problem, and a well-designed and well-documented plan of data analysis.

Complicated Statistical Analyses

The degree of difficulty involved in analyzing secondary data sets depends to a large extent on the number of data sources required for a particular analysis. In general, the greater the number of sources, the more complex the data analysis. This is especially true if different units of analysis, (e.g., individual, family, community) must be considered. In the example we have been using on women's employment, one of the research questions we were interested in answering was: Are differences in women's employment participation rates affected by the welfare state, controlling for macroeconomic and social factors? Ideally, to answer this question, we should have included in our statistical analysis variables from each of the welfare states, macroeconomic, and social subsets.

Examining a small number of countries, however, limits the ways in which aggregate-level and micro-level data can be combined. Five countries are too few to represent sufficient variation on aggregate-level variables such as unemployment rate. When aggregate-level data are merged with micro-level data, each case in a specific country is assigned the category, or value, for unemployment rate. Unemployment rates for the five countries included in our study on women's employment ranged from a low of 6.9 percent to a high of 9.6 percent, a mere 2.7 percentage points difference. A lack of variability in the range of responses on this variable severely limited its utility to our research study.

SUMMARY

Secondary analyses in social work research are increasing. Much of this increase can be easily attributed to advanced computer technology that has made the analysis of secondary data sets more accessible and affordable. There are many data archives available, and the search for the most appropriate one is a process of trial and error.

There are many benefits in analyzing secondary data sets. They include savings in time, money, and personnel; increased access to research opportunities; decreased intrusiveness, and ease of replication. Certain limitations are also present, however. Data available through secondary sources are often not exactly what is desired. The lack of standardized operational definitions among variables and the omission of relevant variables within various existing data sets are common problems. We must be prepared to do the best we can with what is available. This may mean recoding variable values, using proxy variables, and developing indexes. If the data are not sufficient to represent the study's important concepts, using more than one data set may be necessary.

It is particularly important that we become fully aware of the nature of the data set to be used, its method of collection, and any limitations that this imposes on our study's findings and implications. Prerequisite skills that the secondary analyst should have are a good knowledge of research designs, statistical techniques, and facility with computers.

REFERENCES AND FURTHER READINGS

BABBIE, E.R. (1995). *The practice of social research* (7th ed., pp. 274-276, 321-335). Belmont, CA: Wadsworth.

BAILEY, K.D. (1994). *Methods of social research* (4th ed., pp. 294-319, 410-412). New York: Free Press.

DALE, A., ARBER, S., & PROCTOR, M. (1988). *Doing secondary analysis.* Boston: Unwin Hyman.

ESPING-ANDERSEN, G. (1990).Three post-industrial employment regimes. In J. E. Kolberg (Ed.), *The Welfare State as Employer* (pp. 148-188). Armonk, NY: M.E. Sharpe.

FRANKFORT-NACHMIAS, C., & NACHMIAS, D. (1992). *Research methods in the social sciences* (4th ed., pp. 291-318). New York: St. Martin's Press.

GROVES, R.M., & CIALDINI, R.B. (1992). Understanding the decision to participate in a survey. *Public Opinion Quarterly, 56,* 475-496.

HAKIM, C. (1982). *Secondary analysis in social research: A guide to data sources and methods with examples.* London: Allen & Unwin.

HYMAN, H.H. (1987). *Secondary analysis of sample surveys: With a new introduction.* New York: Harper & Row.

JACOBSON, J.L. (1992). *Gender bias: Roadblock to sustainable development.* ISBN 1-87071-10-6. Paper 110. Washington, DC: Worldwatch Institute.

KIECOLT, K.J., & NATHAN, L.E. (1985). *Secondary analysis of survey data.* Newbury Park, CA: Sage.

MONETTE, D.R., SULLIVAN, T.J., & DEJONG, C.R. (1994). *Applied social research* (3rd ed., pp. 187-212). Fort Worth, TX: Harcourt Brace.

NORRIS, P. (1987). *Politics and sexual equality: The comparative position of women in western democracies.* Boulder, CO: Lynne Rienner.

OYEN, E. (1990). *Comparative methodology: Theory and practice in international social research.* Newbury Park, CA: Sage.

POPE, W. (1976). *Durkheim's suicide: A classic analyzed.* Chicago: University of Chicago Press.

RUBIN, A. (1993). Secondary analysis. In R.M. Grinnell, Jr. (Ed.), *Social work research and evaluation* (4th ed., pp. 290-303). Itasca, IL: F.E. Peacock.

RUBIN, A., & BABBIE, E. (1993). *Research methods for social work* (2nd ed., pp. 404-431, 449-501). Pacific Grove, CA: Brooks/Cole.

VOGT, W.P. (1993). *Dictionary of statistics and methodology: A nontechnical guide for the social sciences.* Newbury Park, CA: Sage.

WILLIAMS, M., TUTTY, L.M., & GRINNELL, R.M., JR. (1995). *Research in social work: An Introduction* (2nd ed., pp. 261-276). Itasca, IL: F.E. Peacock.

Jackie D. Sieppert
Steven L. McMurtry
Robert W. McClelland

Chapter **17**

Utilizing Existing Statistics

T HE PREVIOUS CHAPTER PRESENTED how secondary data are used as an unobtrusive data collection method—a method that uses existing micro-level, aggregate-level, and qualitative-level data. This chapter continues our discussion of using existing data by concentrating on the use of aggregate-level data within a secondary analysis. In a nutshell, analyzing existing statistics is nothing more than performing a secondary analysis of aggregate-level data.

This unobtrusive data collection method requires that we *utilize existing statistics*, the title of this chapter. Like the chapter before (and after) this one, this unobtrusive data collection method does not collect primary, or firsthand data. Rather, we turn to existing statistical records as our data sources.

As explained in Chapter 16, an unobtrusive data collection method uses existing data sources located within government, private, and collaborative international organizations. It is technically correct to assume, however, that the "real data sources" are not those organizations that have the existing data, but are the individual units of analyses on which the statistics are based.

As we know from the three chapters in Part V, obtrusive data collection methods (i.e., structured observation, surveys, participant observation) collect firsthand data directly, in one way or another, from the research participants themselves (individual units of analyses). When using these obtrusive data collection methods, we are totally responsible for our study's internal and external validities, from selecting our research question to disseminating our results. This is not true when using existing statistics as a data collection method because we have no control over how the statistics were derived; they have been computed by other researchers.

Thus, research studies that use existing statistical records focus not on reexamining the *data* collected by others, but rather on examining the *data analyses* previously generated by others. Aggregated summaries and reports, not micro-level data, are the fuel that drive research studies using existing statistical records. This point represents a subtle but important difference that makes research studies using existing aggregated statistics sufficiently unique to warrant a closer examination. We will now turn our attention to locating these existing aggregated statistics.

LOCATING SOURCES OF EXISTING STATISTICS

The range of research topics that can be studied using existing statistical data is matched by the wide variety of organizations and groups that collect such data. Aggregated statistics are reported on almost all aspects of our personal and professional lives—by governments, by employers, by private marketing firms, by professional associations, and so on. For this reason, finding the right source of existing statistics to answer a particular research question can be a huge task.

The single most important piece of advice that can be given to a person using existing statistics as a data collection method is to seek help from information specialists found in local college and university libraries. These people are often very familiar with major sources of existing statistical data and are knowledgeable about the types of data (unit of analysis) contained in each source. If they do not know of a particular existing source appropriate to answer a specific research question, they have the knowledge and skills to track down sources that otherwise might never be discovered. Thus, we usually begin a search for an existing statistical data source at the local college or university library.

As we have said, sources of statistical data are generally classified into three broad categories: (1) government and other public agencies; (2) private, or proprietary organizations; and (3) collaborative, international organizations. Each offers aggregated-level data, in the from of statistics, suitable for answering different types of research questions. Thus, with relevant research questions and variables in mind, we can locate an appropriate source(s) of statistical data and then examine it in order to answer our research question. Let us now turn our attention to the first source of existing statistics—government and other public agencies.

Government and Other Public Agencies

Federal, state, and municipal governments are the most available and largest sources of existing statistics. Departments and agencies at most levels produce numerous books, reports, and computerized compilations of data acquired through various sources. The U.S. Bureau of the Census annually publishes a book called the *Statistical Abstract of the United States*, for example, which is a collection of statistics gathered from over 200 government and private agencies. Presented in a wide variety of statistical lists, charts, figures, and tables, the *Statistical Abstract of the United States* contains data about many of the topics relevant to our profession. It contains, for example, statistics about death rates within states, the percentage of families with children who live in poverty, spending on law enforcement and rehabilitation, changes in divorce rates, number of physicians by region of the country, trends in the population of elderly Americans, and hundreds of other social work–relevant topics.

In fact, the only way to grasp the scope and magnitude of the *Statistical Abstract* is to obtain a copy and explore its contents. Best of all, the book is available free of charge at most public libraries. Computerized versions are being developed for easy access through large-scale data networks like the Internet. Also, most university and college libraries and larger municipal libraries, have separate sections for government documents such as the *Statistical Abstract*.

Many other forms of federal, state, and municipal statistics also exist. Answers to research questions can be found in existing statistics published by public agencies such as the National Center for Health Statistics, the Department of Labor, and the Federal Bureau of Investigation. State agencies (such as each state's department of social services) provide statistics about social workers' caseloads in public social service agencies, changes in reporting of alleged child sexual abuse cases, recidivism rates among young offenders, patterns of physical and mental health care usage, and so on.

Municipal departments are obviously more limited in scope and resources, but they too compile statistics relevant to our profession. We must never overlook any of these public departments and organizations, as they are often a good starting point for any piece of social work research that uses existing statistics as a data collection method. Government agencies can be found in local telephone books (many of which have a "blue pages" section for governmental listings). We need to look through these listings and make note of those agencies that appear to be related to our research question. We can then call these agencies to find out whether they publish annual reports on our topic.

Private, or Proprietary Organizations

A second source of existing statistical data is the myriad of nonprofit or proprietary agencies and organizations. Statistics collected and/or reported by private sources are often harder to locate than those provided by governmental sources. They may be more expensive to access as well. However, such sources provide statistical data that may be unavailable in any other form. If we wanted to conduct a research study on attitudes about abortion in a particular state, for example, the best source of data might be existing statistics that were generated by a commercial polling firm in the region. Or, to find data about changes in housing availability and construction in a particular geographical area, we might turn to the local Chamber of Commerce.

Even private social service agencies increasingly collect and report statistical data as part of their emphasis on accountability. Finally, "watchdog" organizations and various advocacy groups make disseminating statistics a particular part of their work. Together these can provide data to examine an agency's effectiveness and efficiency, for example.

There are other nongovernmental organizations that can also provide useful statistics. Two private sources of existing statistical data most relevant to our profession are the National Association of Social Workers (NASW) and the Council on Social Work Education (CSWE). Like other professional accrediting organizations, they keep records regarding the characteristics and activities of their members. Both organizations produce numerous statistical reports about issues of interest to their members. We could turn to the NASW for data about the number of Americans with no or inadequate health insurance coverage, for example. The CSWE regularly publishes statistics on faculty and students within all accredited undergraduate and graduate schools and departments of social work in the United States.

What about organizations that focus on specific substantive issues? In child welfare, for example, there are organizations such as the Child Welfare League of America, the American Association for Protecting Children, the American Public Welfare Association, and the Children's Defense Fund. Other professional fields have similar organizations and serve the same purpose as those in social work.

Collaborative International Organizations

The third, and final, source of existing statistical data is collaborative international organizations. These organizations operate on a cooperative basis to collect and distribute statistical data that allow for cross-cultural comparisons on issues of direct relevance to social policy. The United Nations, for example, publishes the *Demographic Yearbook* and the *United Nations Statistical Yearbook*. These two publications supply data from many countries regarding birth rates, death rates, literacy rates, the proportion of people living in urban areas, and numerous other variables.

With the rapid evolution of computers, and thus information technology, international compilations of existing statistics are increasing in both their scope and quality. Statistical databases are becoming more comprehensive, more timely, and more easily accessed. A good illustration of this is the *Luxembourg*

Income Study (LIS), mentioned in Chapter 16. The *LIS* is a financially independent division of the Center for the Study of Population, Poverty, and Public Policy/International Networks for Studies in Technology, Environment, Alternatives, & Development (CEPS/INSTEAD).

This lengthy acronym just means that the Luxembourg Government has created an independent organization whose mandate is to foster international comparative research on income and well-being. The organization maintains over 40 data sets that contain comprehensive measures of income and well-being for over 17 modern industrialized welfare states. Each country contributes a wide range of statistical data, such as population demographics, family structure, levels of income, and changes in industrial or agricultural output. Use of these statistical summaries is restricted to social science research purposes, however, and no private or commercial use is permitted. *LIS* is one example of a source for comparative and policy research in applied economics, sociology, and public policy. Existing statistical data sets on other topics are increasingly becoming available through improved computer technology.

Whether we turn to governmental agencies, private and proprietary channels, or international organizations, it is clear that existing statistical data *are* available to answer many research questions. Once we know what we want to study, and go to the library to talk with an information specialist, we will soon be immersed in statistical data that we might never have dreamed existed.

Let us take a simple example to illustrate how the above three data sources can be used to examine a simple research problem—the overrepresentation of ethnic minorities in foster care services. How might the above organizations, the data sources, be helpful in studying this issue? The example in Box 17.1 shows how we could turn to private and governmental child welfare organizations as a way of gathering data on this issue.

ADVANTAGES AND DISADVANTAGES

Like all data collection methods, analyzing existing statistics has its advantages and disadvantages.

Advantages

Analyzing existing statistics has many benefits. Among these are that existing statistics: (1) provide historical and conceptual contexts to a research study that uses primary, or firsthand, data (2) can be the only data collection method available; (3) save time, money, and labor; (4) facilitate the development and refinement of the research question; and (5) facilitate theory development.

BOX 17.1

USING GOVERNMENTAL AND PRIVATE-AGENCY STATISTICS

Fran is clinical director of a private, nonprofit agency that provides foster care, group-home care, and residential treatment for children in a small city in Arizona. She has noticed that there is a higher number of ethnic minority children in her agency's caseload than would be expected based on the proportion of ethnic minority children in the general population. She decides to do a study of this issue using existing statistics already gathered by various sources as her data collection method.

Fran first talks with the information specialist at the local library, asking for help to conduct a computer search through the library's existing data bases. The search reveals a series of reports, titled *Characteristics of Children in Substitute and Adoptive Care,* that were sponsored by the American Public Welfare Association and that provide several years of data reported by states on their populations of children in various kinds of foster and adoptive care. She also locates an annual publication produced by the Children's Defense Fund, and this provides a variety of background data on the well-being of children in the United States. Next, Fran checks in the library's government documents section. She locates recent census data on the distribution of persons under the age of 18 across different ethnic groups in her county.

Fran now turns to state-level resources, where a quick check of government listings in the telephone book reveals two agencies that appear likely to have relevant data. One is the Foster Care Review Board, which is comprised of citizen volunteers who assist juvenile courts by reviewing the progress of children in foster care statewide.

A quick call to the Board reveals that they produce an annual report which lists a variety of statistics. These include the number of foster children in the state, where they are placed, and how long they have been in care, and descriptive data such as their ethnicity, race, gender, age and so on.

Fran also learns that the Board's annual reports from previous years contain similar data, thus a visit to the Board's office provides her with the historical data needed to identify trends in the statistics she is using. Finally, she discovers that two years earlier the Board produced a special issue of its annual report that was dedicated to the topic of ethnic minority children in foster care, and this issue offers additional statistics not normally recorded in most annual reports.

Another state agency is the Administration for Children, Youth, and Families, a division of the state's social services department. A call to the division connects her with a staff member who informs her that a special review of foster children was conducted by the agency only a few months before. Data from this review confirm her perception that minority children are overrepresented in foster care in the state, and it provides a range of other data that may be helpful in determining the causes of this problem.

From these sources Fran now has the data she needs to paint a detailed picture of minority foster children at the national and state levels. She also has the ability to examine the problem in terms of both point-in-time circumstances and longitudinal trends, and the latter suggest that the problem of over-representation has grown worse. There is also evidence to indicate that the problem is more severe in her state than nationally. Finally, corollary data on related variables, together with the more intensive work done in the special studies by the Foster Care Review Board and the Administration for Children, Youth, and Families, give Fran a basis for beginning to understand the causes of the problem and the type of research study that must be done to investigate solutions.

Provides Historical and Conceptual Contexts

Utilizing existing statistics provides a historical or conceptual context to a research study that uses primary, or firsthand, data. If we wanted to study the effects of poverty among single parent families, for example, we might first want to determine the nature of poverty in our society. Existing statistics are ideal for this purpose. Through official governmental reports we could determine overall poverty rates, poverty rates for different types of families, long-term changes in family incomes, and so on. We might even be able to tell what percentage of families live under the poverty line in a particular geographical region, and how many of these are single-parent families. These data alone would allow us to do a better job in conceptualizing and operationalizing our study.

Can Be the Only Data Collection Method Available

Existing statistical records are extremely useful in situations where our research questions are unanswerable by other data collection methods. Take, for example, the concepts of crime rates, health indicators, prevalence of child abuse, death rates, affirmative action, immigration trends, changes in unemployment, and so on. We cannot directly observe these concepts, and primary, firsthand, obtrusive data collection methods such as surveys, for example, are usually far beyond the resources available. However, the data (the statistics) we need may already exist, we just have to find them and make them work for us to answer our research question.

Much of what we know about our past, the current structures in society, and societal change is a direct product of analyzing existing statistics gathered by others. It is best, therefore, not to view the use of existing statistics as a limited, rarely employed data collection method. Instead, our ability to answer many important research questions may be limited only by our own research skills and the quality of available statistical data sources.

Saves Time, Money, and Labor

On a practical level, we can save a considerable investment in time, money, and labor by using existing statistics (Singleton, Straits, and Miller Straits, 1993). These savings are realized because the cost of developing data collection instruments and the effort of actually collecting the data have already been borne by others. We do not have to find resources to design questionnaires or interview schedules, train interviewers, devise sampling strategies, place telephone calls to research participants, and so on.

Similarly, the process of collecting, aggregating, and reporting the statistics has been done for us. This obviously saves time and money. Even when a fee is charged for using an existing statistical data set, the true cost of conducting the original study is almost always substantially higher than the fee. In a nutshell, using existing statistical data often allows us to answer research questions that we could not possibly answer on our own limited research budgets.

Facilitates the Development and Refinement of the Research Question

In addition to making a large-scale research study more feasible, existing statistics also facilitate the development and refinement of our research question. By first exploring statistical records, for example, we can often test the potential of future research efforts. This is usually accomplished by testing our preliminary hypothesis using existing statistics. If our hypothesis is not supported we can rethink the theoretical foundations underlying the hypothesis, reshape the conceptual and operational definitions of the concepts within it, or consider alternative measurement instruments.

Facilitates Theory Development

Using existing statistical records as a data collection method contributes to theory development. Most social work research studies, for example, are based on small sample sizes and often lack longitudinal time frames. This obviously limits their generalizability and thus their contributions to our profession's knowledge base. Statistical data are often compiled (via aggregation) from large randomly selected samples. The statistics provided by the U.S. Census Bureau, for example, are based on a wide range of data collection methods and data sources. They incorporate data about diverse respondents and social problems.

The unique nature of statistical data contributes to theory development in one more way. Many organizations that distribute statistical data have been collecting the same data for decades. This enables us to compare statistical data across different time periods in an attempt to understand social and cultural change. We can use statistics from the U.S. Census Bureau, for example, to trace changes in family structures in America, the aging of our population, the impact of Generation X on the labor force, and so on. The contribution of existing statistical records to this type of theory development cannot be overemphasized. Research studies using existing statistics as a data collection method is one of the few ways we can effectively conduct long-term longitudinal studies.

Disadvantages

Existing statistical records are usually intended to serve administrative and public policy uses. This creates a number of methodological concerns when they are employed for research purposes. In general, there are four broad concerns that apply to any given statistical record. They include: (1) the "ecological fallacy" issue, (2) reliability, (3) validity, and (4) missing data.

The "Ecological Fallacy"

We frequently want to learn something about single individuals (units of analysis). What do we know about individuals who live below the poverty line in a particular city or town, for example? What is their life like, and what problems do they face in trying to make a living? Existing statistics often cannot provide data that easily answer these questions. As we know, existing statistics are published in the form of aggregate-level data. They summarize and describe the characteristics of larger groups, but tell us nothing about individuals, or micro-level data. This represents a critical distinction in terms of our unit of analysis.

Published statistics provide estimates of how many people live below the poverty line in the whole nation, or in a particular state, for example. They may even provide the sources of income the poor rely on, what their average income is, or how that income is spent. All of these aggregated statistical estimates, though, tell us only about "groups" of the poor. We cannot make any inferences about the characteristics or experiences of any individual person from the aggregated statistics. To do so would be to commit an *ecological fallacy*, which is a serious threat in research studies using existing statistical records. An ecological fallacy occurs when the characteristics or properties of a group are used to draw conclusions about an individual.

Using our example, we might be tempted to make inferences about the poor who rely on a local food bank for assistance. Based on *group* data, or aggregated-level data, it would be all too easy to conclude that these people are mother-only families, work in unpaid or low-wage jobs, or have limited educational attainment. In reality, though, some individuals who visit the food bank may be very different than the aggregated-level data suggest. Some people may be comparatively well educated and members of intact family units that were unexpectedly caught in the decline of a vital local industry.

The lesson to be drawn from these examples is that when using existing statistical records for any research study, we must first identify our unit of analysis. It is then necessary to examine our data source to ensure that the data relate to the unit we wish to describe.

Assessing Reliability

From Chapter 7 we know that reliability is essentially a matter of consistency. The reliability of existing statistical records refers to the same thing. That is, do the records reliably report the variables they claim to report? There are two common reliability problems that appear when using existing statistical records: changes, over time, in how variables are conceptually and operationally defined; and alternate definitions of those variables across multiple data sources.

Changes in Conceptual and Operational Definitions   The first reliability issue—changes in conceptual and operational definitions over time—is one that affects most existing statistical records. Changes occur in the official definitions of many variables targeted by social work researchers. The operational definitions of variables measuring poverty, unemployment, types of crime, child abuse, and so on often change as our own perspectives about the problem change. Child abuse is a good example. Thirty or forty years ago, views about what constitutes child abuse were very different than those now espoused by our society. A slight spanking was considered by many to be a routine part of parenting. Now, this once-sanctioned act might often be considered a form of child abuse. Thus, the findings from a longitudinal study on the rates of child abuse, using existing statistics, may be inconsistent and thus not reliable. The operational definition of the variable being measured has simply changed over time.

Temporal changes affect more than operational definitions, however. They also have subsequent impacts on the way the data are collected. Let us look again at child abuse as an illustration of this point. Twenty years ago all recording of alleged child abuse perpetrators was done on paper files. Today, most of our child welfare agencies rely on computerized management information systems. These changes allow for more timely and accurate record keeping regarding alleged perpetrators. In other words, computerized management information systems may have indirectly helped to increase the apparent rates of child abuse. Also, public awareness of child abuse may have made it much more likely to be reported, though the actual incidence may not have changed.

Alternate Operational Definitions of Variables   The second issue surrounding reliability of existing statistics relates to the equivalence of the statistics across multiple data sources. There is always more than one way to measure any variable, and many are open to a variety of operational definitions. A good example of this can be found in crime statistics.

Most police departments maintain records about the incidence of domestic violence in their particular communities. Keeping statistics about domestic violence would appear to be a relatively routine and straightforward matter. The operational definition of domestic violence, however, more often than not differs from one department to another. In reports of domestic violence, some departments might include incidents of verbal abuse, or cases where official charges were not filed against the alleged offender.

On the other hand, other departments might record only those incidents in which official criminal charges were filed or some severe form of violence occurred. This makes discrepancies between police department records not only possible, but very likely. Reported incidence of domestic violence, therefore, may often be very different than the *actual* incidence of domestic violence in any particular geographical area. It would be high if a department chose to have a very loose and global operational definition of domestic violence, and it would be low if a department chose to have a narrow and strict operational definition of domestic violence.

The reliability of existing domestic violence statistics depends on more than operational definitions alone, however. Let us say that police statistics report the incidence of domestic violence to be much higher in California than in other states. Even if we have ruled out differences in operational definitions, there are other factors that could produce this result. The state's apparently higher incidence of domestic violence might simply reflect the results of a crackdown on domestic violence, which served to increases domestic violence arrest rates. The results might also reflect a broader societal awareness of domestic violence, or increased media coverage of the problem (remember the O.J. Simpson trial in California?). In any case, the reliability of these data would have to be examined closely.

Another reliability problem is that changes occur over time in both *how* statistics are reported and *which* statistics get reported. Suppose, for example, we are tracking physical and mental health records that report the incidence of alcoholism by age groups. For several years, data may be reported on age groups 15 to 25, 25 to 35, 35 to 45, and over 45. Suddenly, however, the age groups change to 10 to 20, 20 to 30, 30 to 40, and so on. Comparisons of alcoholism in age groups across time would thus be difficult to analyze because of the inconsistency in the way age groups were aggregated.

Changes in which statistics are reported are also problematic. We may be interested in tracking trends in binge drinking as one particular form of alcoholism, for example. Current statistical reports available from one key source may provide these data, breaking down alcoholism into statistics on binge drinking and other forms. We may find, however, that earlier reports from the same source do not separate various types of alcoholism in this way. Thus, we could be thwarted in our efforts to make comparisons over time, because we would have no reliable way of determining how many alcoholics were binge drinkers at the earlier date.

Assessing Validity

Some of the major benefits offered by existing statistical records can also lead to validity problems. As we know from Chapter 7, validity has to do with whether the variable we are measuring is being measured accurately. Problems can occur because we trade savings in time, money, and labor for our direct control over the entire research study. Such control is always maintained by the organization that originally collected and aggregated the data. This means that our research question, conceptual and operational definitions, research methods and procedures, and statistical reports were all previously chosen by the organization supplying the statistics. Any errors in these areas represent errors in measurement, and hence validity problems.

There are a few methods we can use to ensure that conceptual or data collection errors have been avoided in any given existing statistical data source. Most important of these is that we must carefully and critically examine how the data were collected in the first place, with an eye toward the study's "scientific rigor." Were understandable questions asked, and could they in fact be answered? Were respondents selected using appropriate random sampling techniques? Were data collection procedures rigorous, and were they closely followed? Were the variables measured correctly? Answering such questions provides a solid foundation from which to judge the validity of an existing statistical data record.

Deductive Versus Inductive Reasoning   Even if a critical review of the statistical data is positive, however, problems of validity still arise. One of the most common validity problems revolves around the issue of using existing data in an inductive research study (Monette, Sullivan, & DeJong, 1990). A research study using existing statistics as a data collection method can indeed be an deductive one, however. That is, a deductive study starts with a theoretical framework and has a hypothesis derived from the framework. The hypothesis is operationally defined, research measuring instruments are selected, and data collection is implemented. The data are analyzed, and based upon the data analysis, the hypothesis is rejected or accepted. Our study is conducted in a deductive manner, progressing from an abstract way of thinking to a concrete way of thinking.

As noted above, however, research studies using existing statistics as a data collection method do not have to rely on a deductive process. Instead, they can also use inductive processes where we move from a concrete way of thinking to an abstract way of thinking. Our inquiry begins not with a well-defined theoretical framework, as in deductive studies, but with micro-level data aggregated in a statistical report(s). These inductive studies start out by examining the existing statistics in relation to the general research questions. From this point, we focus on detecting patterns within the statistics themselves. Are there, for instance, employment, educational, and family characteristics that are typical of poor families in a particular state? If such patterns are found, our next step is to develop hypotheses and theories that might explain the findings. Over time these hypotheses might be supported by detecting the same patterns in other existing statistical records, thereby building upon or altering an existing theory.

There are two major ways that the inductive research process generates validity problems: (1) the lack of an original theoretical framework for collecting the data, and (2) the need to construct indirect measures of variables.

1. *Lack of an original theoretical framework*   The theoretical framework used to guide the original data collection strategy is often not made clear in subsequent statistical reports. This means that the rationale underlying such steps as the selection of and the operationalization of variables is unknown. Just as frequently, our own conceptualizations can differ from those of the persons who collected the original data. In either case, a common theoretical framework is lacking, meaning that the variables found in the existing statistical records may not be a valid measure of the concept we are trying to assess in our study.

Consider the work that women do in our society as an example. In studying the contributions made by women to the workforce, official government agencies tend to define women's labor only in terms of paid employment, and they tend to ignore work that does not earn cash for the family (Jacobsen, 1992). When studying the same topic, using the statistics provided by those same government agencies, we would likely want to expand our operational definition of "work."

Along with paid labor, our new operational definition of work might include meal preparation, child care, and general housework. This new operational definition would not be measured by official statistics, however. It might be argued that our definition of "work" is more valid than that used in the government statistics. The problem is that by expanding our operational definition of work we might begin to address an entirely different concept than the one measured by "the official statistics." By relying on existing statistical records, therefore, we are constrained by the initial measures used in compiling the statistics, and our own study may be limited by the degree of validity of those initial measurements.

2. *Indirect measurement of variables*   The second validity issue directly relates to the first. It occurs when the variables of interest are not measured directly within the existing statistical records. This situation is common in social science research. Even though social service programs collect statistics on many aspects of their operations, few directly measure the achievement of their objectives, client change, or worker effectiveness. In such situations, we are forced to construct proxy variables from the available statistics. In other words, we need to create an indirect measure of the concept we are studying. Unfortunately, the validity of this indirect measure or proxy variable is hard to establish.

A good example of constructing indirect measures is found in assessments of physical and mental health in the elderly. The U.S. Census Bureau might ask elderly citizens a series of questions about their physical and mental health. These questions might ask them to compare how "healthy" they are relative to others their age, whether they are physically active, whether they have had a major physical or mental problem over the last year, whether they received medical assistance over the last year, and whether they suffered an accidental injury over the last year.

Now, suppose we want to use these existing statistics to conduct a study of the elderly, and we need a measure of their *current* physical and mental health status. None of these variables directly measure what we want. However, we could construct a proxy variable—an index that uses all of these variables—to identify those seniors who are most likely to enjoy good health right now. If the seniors are physically active, feel healthy, and have been both accident and illness free for the last year, we could conclude that they are probably healthy right now. There are, however, no guarantees that such responses to these questions ensure current good health. Our proxy variable, physical and mental health, would have an unknown degree of error, or uncertain measurement validity.

Assessing the Extent of Missing Data

We all know some people who refuse to answer certain questions on any survey. It might be a question about their income, their age, or any other topic they might consider sensitive. Whenever an individual refuses to answer such questions, it creates gaps in the subsequent data set and any statistics computed from it. Such refusals are common in most studies. We are rarely able to ensure that all respondents answer every question asked of them. This means that missing data are inevitably an issue in any research study using existing statistical records.

Missing data cannot be blamed on respondents alone, however. Many other factors play a role in contributing to missing data. The original research team, for example, may have inadvertently neglected to interview all respondents from a preselected neighborhood. Or perhaps social workers delegated to collect data on particular variables found it very difficult to do so and thus did not provide data on those variables for many of their cases. One example is data on household income which, for a variety of reasons, is often very difficult to collect accurately.

Still other reasons for missing data include failure by the administrator, or researcher, to provide clear instructions on how line-level staff should record the data. A common example is written forms or computerized information systems that are sometimes so difficult to understand that data are frequently omitted. Finally, we may find that data are missing from statistical records simply because those who originally collected the data did not share our ideas about what was important and thus did not gather data on one or more variables we see as being critical.

Next to respondent refusals, the most common reason for missing data in existing statistical data sets is probably societal change itself. As society changes, questions that are deemed important also change. Statistics regarding liquor prohibition do not mean much in today's society, for example. Nor were questions about the growth of HIV/AIDS even known in past decades. As a reflection of these changes, organizations that collect data regularly start or stop gathering certain types of data. This practice inevitably generates missing data in statistical records.

Random and Systematic Errors   Regardless of the reason for missing data, it is a very serious issue. The occurrence of missing data introduces error into the statistics. As we know from Chapters 7 and 10, this error has two forms, random error and systematic error. Random error occurs when, for no particular reason, data are lacking on some cases in the data set from which the statistics were compiled. Because there is no pattern as to which cases are missing data and which cases are not, it is also unlikely that the presence of random error will bias the statistics in any particular direction.

Of greater concern is systematic error. This occurs when data are missing on specific types of cases from which statistics were compiled. For example, suppose statistics were gathered on employment in a particular region, but the people on which the statistics were based included only those with known residences. This would mean that homeless people would not be among those included in the statistics. Because homeless people have a much higher rate of joblessness, the effect of their omission would be to cause the statistics to underestimate the level of joblessness in the region, and this, in turn, would drastically limit the overall value of the data.

The only solution is to exercise caution when using statistical records. Before we commit to conducting a research study using a particular statistical record, we need to ensure that the data set is not missing an inordinate amount of data. In addition, we need to spend some time exploring the statistics provided. Not only should the data be generally complete, but the people who collected the original data should have reported the steps that were taken to minimize missing data.

STEPS IN ANALYZING EXISTING STATISTICS

We recently completed a study that utilized existing statistical records as a data collection method. We will use it as an example here because of our familiarity with how the study was conducted and because it addresses an issue of interest to social work students—faculty/student ratios within graduate schools of social work (McMurtry & McClelland, 1995). This section address four basic steps when using existing statistics as a data collection method: (1) formulating the research question, (2) finding existing statistical records, (3) assessing validity and reliability, and (4) analyzing the data.

Step 1: Formulating the Research Question

Our study began with personal experiences suggesting that the number of undergraduate and graduate social work students was increasing, but few corresponding increases were occurring in the number of social work faculty available to teach them. This raised a concern that there may be too few qualified faculty to meet the needs of social work students. From this assumption, two research questions were generated: (1) what are the trends in social work student enrollments, staffing patterns, and faculty/student ratios in schools and departments of social work in recent years? and (2) how do these trends compare to those in related disciplines?

Step 2: Finding Existing Statistical Records

As mentioned earlier, after developing the initial research questions, our next step in using existing statistical records as a data collection method was to identify an appropriate data source. In our case, we were aware that the accrediting body for social work programs in the United States, CSWE, publishes an annual report on accredited schools and departments. This report is titled *Statistics on Social Work Education in the United States*. Its primary unit of analysis is the social work programs themselves. These data are collected via cross-sectional surveys mailed to each social work program each year.

Schools and departments are asked to provide data on their students, their faculty, and other aspects of their program as of November 1 of the year being studied. Five standardized, self-administered survey instruments are used to collect data on: faculty, bachelors programs, masters programs, doctoral programs, and programs in candidacy. Each school or department receives only the instrument(s) that apply to its specific programs.

Our study's original intent was to examine faculty/student ratios in social work programs at all three degree levels. Standards recommended by the CSWE are for a 1:12 ratio of faculty to students at the Masters level and a 1:25 ratio at the bachelors level (no specific standard is suggested for doctoral programs). As can be all too common when doing a research study using statistical records, we found we had to narrow our study's focus because of the lack of data in the CSWE's published statistics.

Specifically, the CSWE annual statistics did not record data on faculty/student ratios at the bachelors level, and it was impossible to compute these ratios retroactively from the data available. General data on faculty/student ratios were available for doctoral programs, but other data (such as the number of faculty specifically assigned to doctoral education in each school or department) were not present, so our study had to be narrowed to masters programs alone, where a full range of necessary data was readily available.

Step 3: Assessing Validity and Reliability

Our next consideration was the validity and reliability of the statistics in the CSWE annual reports, our data sources. Copies of these reports were obtained for the years 1977 to 1993, which allowed us to review trends over the 17-year period. To do this reliably, however, data on key variables such as student enrollment and faculty numbers would have to have been collected in a consistent way over that entire 17-year period. Fortunately, we found that in gathering data from member schools and departments, the CSWE has used the same operational definition over time for each variable used in computing faculty/ student ratios in schools and departments of social work. All part-time students, for example, are assigned a value of one-half, and full-time students a value of one.

Faculty numbers are differentiated by whether they hold tenured or non-tenured positions and by the amount of time they spend teaching at the BSW, MSW, and doctoral levels. Also, data in the annual report show that response rates for the survey have remained high over the years. For masters programs, nonresponse rates averaged between one and three percent per year, meaning that missing data were not sufficiently frequent to cast doubt on the consistency of the data over time.

While these factors suggest that the CSWE data were reliable, determining validity is an equally important but often more difficult task. Low reliability is often a sign that validity is also low, but high reliability is not a guarantee of high validity. This is because the measure in question may be reliably measuring the wrong variable. In our study, for example, the reliability of the CSWE data appeared to be high, so our task in assessing the validity of these data was to examine whether ambiguity existed in the operational definitions of the variables that could lead to their being misunderstood and thus mismeasured. Fortunately, the CSWE data had four important strengths that, when combined, suggested that the validity of the statistics they presented was high. First, the variables being measured—student enrollments and faculty numbers—are relatively straightforward and unambiguous variables.

Second, these variables (and others such as, full-time-equivalency of faculty and students, distinctions between degree-seeking and nondegree-seeking students, etc.) are based on established measurement practices in higher education and are thus familiar to most respondents. Third, these variables were clearly explained and operationalized in the data collection instruments.

Finally, the instruments used in the CSWE's data collection process remained similar and predictable over time, and response rates remained high over the 17-year period assessed in our study.

One issue regarding validity did arise, however. Despite ongoing high response rates to the CSWE surveys, there was usually some missing data. In a few cases all the data for a particular variable were missing; in others cases some but not all of the data for a variable were provided. No patterns in the missing data were evident, and the amount of missing data was small (seldom exceeding one to two percent of all cases). Still, as in other research studies using existing statistics as a data collection method, the issue of missing data should be considered a caution against overgeneralizing a study's findings.

To discover how trends in social work education compared with those in related disciplines, we then had to find the accrediting organization for each of those disciplines and determine whether the organization published data similar to that in the CSWE annual statistics.

An information specialist at our university library helped us find a publication titled *Accredited Institutions of Post Secondary Education*, which is published by the American Council on Education. This book lists all the accredited programs in various disciplines at U.S. universities and colleges, and it also lists the name, address, and telephone number of each accrediting organization. From this list, we identified 13 related disciplines with which social work might appropriately be compared.

Each organization was contacted by phone, given a description of the CSWE annual statistics, and asked whether it published a similar report. Unfortunately, only four disciplines—communication sciences and disorders, law, public affairs and administration, and psychology—were found to publish comparable statistics. Copies of relevant reports were obtained either directly from the accrediting bodies for these disciplines or, when available, in our university library. Data from these reports became the basis for comparing these fields with social work.

Step 4: Analyzing the Data

This brings us to the question of what our study found. After producing numerous statistics and graphs, we found that faculty/student ratios have risen steadily, from a median of 1 faculty member to 9.9 students in 1981 to a median of 1 faculty member to 13.4 students in 1993. Remembering the 1 to 12 ratio recommended by CSWE, it is evident that faculty/student ratios have been higher than desirable since 1988, with the current ratio now being almost 12 percent above the maximum ratio set by the CSWE.

In 1981, for example, most schools had a faculty/student ratio in the range of eight to nine students per faculty member, and only about 10 percent of them reported faculty/student ratios over 1 to 14. In contrast, by 1993 the most frequently occurring level of faculty/student ratios was over 15 students per faculty member. Almost 40 percent of the schools and departments had faculty/student ratios at or above the level of 1 to 14.

The CSWE statistics were also used to examine other aspects of the issue of faculty/student ratios. We looked at trends in MSW student enrollment, for example. Results showed that MSW enrollment has grown markedly in recent years. Though the number of full-time MSW students declined during the early and middle 1980s, since 1986 enrollments have increased by 50 percent. As of late 1993, more than 21,000 full-time MSW students were enrolled in accredited U.S. schools and departments of social work, a higher number than ever before.

Growth has also occurred in the number of part-time MSW students. The CSWE statistics show that enrollment of part-time MSW students has increased steadily, almost tripling since 1977 to a total of more than 11,000. Together, part-time and full-time MSW students numbered more than 32,000 in late 1993.

We also found that the number of full-time, tenure-track faculty members in the CSWE-accredited schools and departments was about the same in 1993 as in 1977, with the 1993 number actually being slightly lower. This contrasts sharply with the high growth in student (undergraduate and graduate) enrollment of more than 50 percent over that same period. Clearly, schools and departments of social work in the United States have taken in many additional students without commensurately increasing tenure-track faculty.

With regard to whether similar trends have occurred in related disciplines, we were able to obtain suitable comparative data from the four fields noted earlier (communication sciences and disorders; law; public affairs and administration; psychology). In the process, though, we also encountered one of the major difficulties of using existing statistical records. This is, the CSWE statistics and those of the other four accrediting organizations were collected at different times, for different periods, and in different ways. Thus, we had to report separately the data gathered from each discipline, and it also made the process of comparing across disciplines more difficult.

Our research study could not have been done without the use of statistical records. With them, however, we were able to show some important changes that have affected how graduate social work education is provided. These changes are meaningful for social work graduate students, since they imply that each student now has a one-third smaller share of any faculty members' time than 11 years ago. Moreover, the faculty members whose time students now seek are more likely to be part-time instructors and other nontenure-track faculty than they are to be full-time faculty. Since part-time faculty usually do not remain on site, students are probably even more isolated from faculty than the overall faculty/student ratios suggest.

Of course many part-time and nontenure-track faculty are very capable instructors, and some are better than many tenure-track faculty. Still, data from the CSWE statistics show that as of 1993, full-time tenure-track faculty were four times more likely to have a doctoral degree than full-time nontenure-track faculty or part-time faculty. Assuming that doctoral-level training has value for social work educators, there are clearly qualitative issues raised by these trends.

One implication is that graduate social work education may be making a *de facto* return to a kind of apprentice model, where experienced practitioners (part-time faculty hired from field settings) teach those in the next generation. Meanwhile, workloads for full-time faculty may continue to increase as their numbers relative to part-time faculty drop and student enrollments rise. It should be no surprise to learn that full-time faculty report feeling less productive, while graduate students struggle with gaining access to their professors.

SUMMARY

The process of using existing statistical records as a data collection method is relatively straightforward and quite simple. We begin with a general research question or a specific hypothesis. A statistical data record(s) that might answer our question or hypothesis is then identified, often with the assistance of an information specialist located at a local library. Existing statistics are obtained and their quality is assessed by examining factors such as the conceptual framework used to shape the data collection process, the scientific rigor of data collection procedures, and the appropriateness of measures used to collect the data. If the reported statistics indeed seem to be empirically sound, we then conduct a quantitative data analysis of the statistics to answer our research question or to test our hypothesis.

As we know, using existing statistics as a form of data collection is unobtrusive, that is, we do not intrude into our research participants' lives in any way. The following chapter continues our discussion of unobtrusive data collection methods by presenting how a social work research study can use another unobtrusive data collection method, known as content analysis, for doing a research study.

REFERENCES AND FURTHER READINGS

JACOBSEN, J.L. (1992). *Gender bias: Roadblock to sustainable development*. Washington, DC: Worldwatch Institute.

MCMURTRY, S.L., & MCCLELLAND, R.W. (1995, March). *Alarming trends in faculty/student ratios in MSW programs*. Paper presented at the meeting of the Council on Social Work Education, San Diego, CA.

MONETTE, D., SULLIVAN, T., & DEJONG, C. (1990). *Applied social research: Tools for the human services.* (2nd ed.). Fort Worth, TX: Holt, Rinehart, Winston.

NEUMAN, W. (1991). *Social research methods: Qualitative and quantitative approaches.* Needham Heights, MA: Allyn & Bacon.

RUBIN, A. (1993). Secondary analysis. In R.M. Grinnell, Jr. (Ed), *Social work research and evaluation* (4th ed., pp. 290-303). Itasca, IL.: F.E. Peacock.

RUBIN, A., & BABBIE. E. (1989). *Research methods for social work* (2nd ed.). Belmont, CA: Wadsworth.

SINGLETON, R.A, JR., STRAITS, B.C., & MILLER STRAITS, M. (1993). *Approaches to social research* (2nd ed.). New York: Oxford.

Craig W. LeCroy
Gary Solomon

C h a p t e r **18**

Content Analysis

CONTENT ANALYSIS is similar to secondary analysis, discussed in the preceding two chapters, in that both use existing data sets. In content analysis, however, the data are generated by quantifying units of analysis in the content of recorded communications so they can be counted. Because content analysis allows us to investigate research questions without needing to collect original data, we can formulate research questions about anything that has taken place and been recorded. Our research question may involve content describing some historical situation or something that occurred a moment ago. In either case, the content is defined, coded, and tallied to generate new data that may be analyzed immediately or at some future date.

If our research question can be stated in terms that meet the criteria of specificity, relevancy, researchability, feasibility, and ethical acceptability (see Chapter 3), and if recorded communications on the question exist, a content analysis could well be the best method of collecting data to investigate it. Content analyses are well suited to the study of communications because they address the questions of who says what to whom, why, how, and with what effect. The "what" of a research study, or the defining aspect, is found in the content of the text to be studied.

CHARACTERISTICS OF CONTENT ANALYSES

In content analyses, communications are examined in a systematic, objective, and quantitative manner (Holsti, 1969). To be systematic, a content analysis must follow specified procedures. If we want to compare the lyrics in the songs of three different rock groups, for example, we must systematically use the same procedures in examining the content for each group. As we know from Chapter 7, if the same measuring procedures are not used, our results will not be considered reliable; it could be argued that the difference in the way the criteria were applied to the groups is a source of bias or error in our results. This occurs when we structure our data collection procedures to confirm our own predictions or support our own theoretical positions.

Objectivity is another characteristic of content analyses that helps ensure validity and avoid bias. This characteristic is concerned with making the criteria or rules used to categorize the contents of the text impartial and objective. Clearly defining the criteria to be applied and making explicit the rules to be used in classifying the content of a communication help control any special interest or ideology that might influence our research study (Williamson et al., 1982).

In our study of rock lyrics, for example, the rules to be used in categorizing the lyrics must be specified. Otherwise a conclusion that rock lyrics consist of sexual and violent content, or a conclusion that they are harmless, could be considered invalid. While people interested in the results of our research study might not agree with the categories that we devised, the standards for deciding how to categorize the data and code them for recording would be clear, so others could evaluate how our conclusions had been reached. Objective procedures also allow others to replicate our study; even if they have different biases, if they follow the same rules for categorizing the content, the results should be the same.

A Quantitative Research Approach

Content analyses are ordinarily used in quantitative research approaches because they focus on the operational definitions and quantifications of the dependent variables (and sometimes the independent variables) in research questions or hypotheses. Before the content of any communication can be analyzed it must be possible to quantify it in some manner. In a study to examine the way women are portrayed in children's books, for example, the number of times women are portrayed as mothers and as workers outside the home could be counted. The unit of analysis is women. Each time a unit occurs in a particular category (mother or worker), it is "counted" and recorded in that category.

A common use of content analyses is recording the frequency with which certain symbols or themes appear in a communication. Dodd, Foerch, and Anderson (1988), for example, did a content analysis of women and racial and ethnic minorities as subjects of newsmagazine covers, an indication of their coverage in the content of a particular issue. The covers of *Time* and *Newsweek* from 1953 through 1987 were studied, and each appearance of a woman or minority member was counted. The researchers then could determine whether these variables were represented in relation to their proportions in the U.S. population and whether there had been changes in the subjects of the covers and cover stories over time.

When quantification is used in this manner, the results are usually presented in terms of simple proportions or percentages. A content analysis of a diary, for example, may reveal that the term "love" made up 5 percent of the total words used or that it appeared on 61 percent of the pages. Also, it could show an increase in use of the term between certain dates.

Quantification is not always that easy, however. We must often attempt to examine not just the frequency of a variable but also its intensity or deeper meaning. To compare how liberal two congressional candidates are, a content analysis of their speeches could be done. In addition to counting the number of "liberal" statements each one made, according to some specified criteria, there might be an attempt to evaluate how liberal each statement is. The task of devising adequate categories then would become much more complicated. Perhaps each statement could be rated as extremely liberal, moderately liberal, or minimally liberal. Because the concept of liberalism is becoming increasingly difficult to define in terms of political parties or ideologies, there would be limits to the possible options in using such a content analysis.

STEPS IN DOING A CONTENT ANALYSIS

To illustrate the process of conducting a content analysis, we will use an example involving a problem area of great social concern to social workers: suicide. While the steps in this process closely follow those in the quantitative research process described in Chapter 4, they are collapsed in this section to four distinctive steps that emphasize the nature and characteristics of content analyses: (1) developing a research question, (2) selecting a sample, (3) selecting the unit of analysis, and (4) coding, tallying, and analyzing the data.

Step 1: Developing a Research Question

As in all research studies, content analyses begin with a researcher's interest in a problem area and the development of a specific research question or hypothesis. In our example, we are interested in the problem area of suicide, and the purpose of our study is to contribute to an understanding of why people commit suicide. From this general perspective, a group of research questions could be advanced:

- Are there predictable patterns of behavior in people who commit suicide?
- Are the reasons for suicide different now than they were 20 years ago?
- Can we predict the act of suicide by examining the themes in suicide notes?
- Do people who leave suicide notes use similar words or describe common experiences and feelings?
- Do the suicide notes written by women and men differ?

For this example, our study will focus on the last two questions. The method will be a content analysis of suicide notes written in recent years.

Step 2: Selecting a Sample

Choosing the appropriate sampling strategy in a content analysis can be tedious. Suppose, for example, we are interested in how men and women are portrayed in children's books. Our population is all available children's books, and it is necessary to decide which parameters should be used to limit the sample. A sample from the population of writers might be selected, or the books published in a certain year might be chosen instead. Our sample could be limited to schoolbooks used for second- and third-graders, and if this universe is still too large, the books used by all elementary schools in a specific city might be sampled. Such options must be considered in an attempt to gather a representative sample. The sample selection process also can redefine the specific problem area.

The decisions that must be made in selecting a sample for a research study are discussed in Chapter 10. For our suicide note example, the sampling plan is relatively straightforward. The universe (or population) from which our sample is to be extracted is identified as the suicide notes in the files of the Suicide Prevention Center, which collects and records suicide notes written in various U.S. cities that agree to participate. Although the content analysis for this example will be limited to what is available at the Center, that universe is still large, and sampling considerations are necessary.

The Center has been in existence for over 20 years and has collected over 15,500 suicide notes. For our study, therefore, our universe is further limited to suicide notes written in a two-year period, and only the suicide notes of adult men and women (21 years of age and older) are included. Within these parameters, a total of 1,327 suicide notes is available. From this population, a random sample of 100 suicide notes is selected.

Random sampling thus is chosen as the sampling strategy, but other techniques could also be used. With stratified sampling, for example, the suicide notes would be grouped according to strata such as year written, age category, or gender. After grouping, equal-sized samples of notes would be generated for each stratum and sampled separately, using simple or systematic random sampling techniques.

The limitation of the population parameters to determine the composition of our sample often follows a three-part process: sampling of sources (which suicide notes), sampling of dates (suicide notes from what years), and sampling of units (which aspects of the notes are to be analyzed). When sampling according to units analyzed, our decisions are often based on what characterizes the content best for purposes of our study.

Step 3: Selecting the Unit of Analysis

In all content analyses, the specific unit of analysis, that is, what is to be counted, must be specified. This step is dependent on the quantification, or operational definition, of the dependent variable(s) in our research question. Units of analysis vary considerably, depending on the complexity of the research question and the universe of communications to be sampled. In many studies, recording the unit of analysis is simple, such as counting the number of certain words; in others, recording involves the establishment of complex categorical systems and coding rules and procedures.

In our suicide note example, the word content of suicide notes is chosen as the unit to be counted. To begin, the choice of a single concept, death, as a unit of analysis keeps our coding simple and reliable. We do not have to struggle to make judgments about whether a particular unit fits in the category—all the units do. We simply count the number of words that refer to the variable, death. But because many different words refer to death, there must be coding rules to clarify what to code in the category of death. In our example, any reference to death—words such as dying, dead, ending, or terminating—is to be used as the unit of analysis and counted.

Step 4: Coding, Tallying, and Analyzing the Data

The coding of data has to do with the categories of the unit of analysis. With a single concept such as death, there is only one category, but the different words that refer to death are defined as belonging in that category. With a concept such as gender there are two obvious categories, male and female. Thus, coding data is dependent on the way the categories are operationally defined; they should reflect the concepts (the dependent and independent variables) represented in the research question.

To aid in the data collection process, a coding or tally sheet is developed. Figure 18.1 is an example of a coding sheet used to record the data we want to extract from the suicide notes sampled. Three references to death were counted in Note 1, written by a male, and five references to death in Note 2, written by a female. The coder continues to count and tally until all 100 randomly selected suicide notes have been tallied. Then the individual tallies are totaled and the frequencies of the tallies for men and women are compared.

If different units of analysis, other than the concepts of death and gender, were used, additional concepts and categories would be included in the tally sheet. For instance, the age of the writer, the city of residence, any reference to a friend, parent, spouse, or relevant other, or a mention of a plan for the suicide might be operationally defined, coded, and tallied.

Categorizing Latent Content

In our example, coding is limited to the tabulation of gender and the frequency of occurrence of words relating to death. This type of information is referred to as manifest content—the obvious, clearly evident, viable aspects of the communication. Examples of coding manifest content are counting certain types of words, coding whether men or women appear on the cover of a magazine, and counting the number of times violence occurs in a television program.

Beyond the manifest content of communications, we often are interested in their latent content—content that is present but not evident or active. Latent content is an indicator of the underlying meaning of what is communicated. We may, for example, want to assess the political orientation of a newspaper editorial or the intensity of the violence portrayed on certain television shows. Manifest content is specific, is easy to code, and produces reliable data. Latent content is less specific and more difficult to code because it represents the meaning, depth, and intensity of a communication.

In our example, we may want to understand what people considering suicide think and feel. Because it could be difficult to get these impressions via simple word counts, we attempt to characterize the meanings expressed in the suicide notes, which requires more judgment and interpretation.

Suicide Notes	Death Concept Tally	Gender of Writer	
		Male	Female
Note 1	3	✔	
Note 2	5		✔
Note 3			
Note 4			
Note 5			
Note 6			

FIGURE 18.1   RECORDING SHEET FOR TWO
CATEGORIES IN SUICIDE NOTES

As we study the various suicide notes in the sample, we recognize several recurrent themes. We may decide, for example, to code the notes according to four themes identified in suicide notes (Schneidman, 1985): unendurable psychological pain, searching for solutions, helplessness and hopelessness, and constriction of options. Obviously, these themes are difficult to code, but operational definitions could be formulated from types of statements found in the notes. For the first two concepts, for example, *unendurable psychological pain* could be coded from the statements: "I feel so desperate" and "This will all be over soon"; *searching for solutions* could be coded from the statements: "I can't face life, there's only one thing to do" and "I've done everything I can, there are no more options for me."

By uncovering such themes, we may develop an interest in discovering in what ways the themes differ in notes written by men and women, or we may want to examine the degree of intensity in each theme. Using such latent content results in a complex coding task because the themes must be identified in the content and then coded or placed in an assigned category, to indicate the intensity with which the theme is being expressed. Once the theme of helplessness and hopelessness has been defined in terms of certain types of statements found in suicide notes, for example, three ordinal categories might be set up to indicate the intensity of particular statements:

1 = Great feelings of helplessness and hopelessness
2 = Average feelings of helplessness and hopelessness
3 = Minimal feelings of helplessness and hopelessness

The coder must identify each statement according to theme and determine in which of the three categories of intensity it belongs.

When such judgments must be made in the coding of data, the reliability of the data produced by the coding system must be established. This is done in terms of interrater reliability, using a process whereby two or more independent coders or judges agree on how a unit of analysis should be categorized. While it is not necessary for them to agree completely on the categorization of every statement, if they can reach no agreement, the study's results will lack reliability and will seriously jeopardize the findings.

Coders, or judges, should agree on their coding results about 80 percent of the time. To achieve good reliability, coders often go through a training program to teach them how to compare and discuss their decisions about the coding and categorization of data. Code books are often developed with operational definitions and rules for how the data should be coded.

Content analysis thus can go beyond simple word counts and manifest content to examine communications more intensively. For some research questions, studies that have great specificity and reliability are required; for others, it is necessary to attempt to grapple with the meaning of the content in depth. When the research study uses latent content to elicit depth and meaning, several considerations emerge: the number of categories increases, the time required to do the coding increases, and the reliability of the coding decreases, because more interpretation by coders is necessary. Nevertheless, the research questions asked often determine the necessity of searching for depth and meaning in order to explore answers for them.

USES IN SOCIAL WORK RESEARCH

Despite the structured process of content analyses, they can be put to a variety of uses in social work research. They serve several distinct purposes and can be used in combination with other data gathering methods. Developments in methodology, such as the use of computers to analyze communications with both quantitative and qualitative content and the acceptance of less structured forms such as ethnographic analyses, are increasing the range of uses to which content analyses can be put.

Classification of Content Analyses by Purpose

Content analyses can be classified into four broad categories according to the purpose of the analysis: (1) to make inferences to the source of communications, (2) to make inferences to populations, (3) to evaluate the effects of communications, or (4) to make structured observations (Williamson et al., 1982).

Inferences to the Source of Communications

An example of how content analyses are used to make inferences about the source of communications is analysis of the content of messages in an effort to understand the motives, values, or intentions of those who wrote them. Content analyses also may be done in order to understand something about people or institutions through their symbolic communications, which can reveal attitudes or beliefs. To do this, such documents as diaries, speeches, newspapers, or transcriptions of interviews might be examined.

Diaries or personal documents were used in some of the first examples of content analyses. An example is an early study of the psychology of adolescence, for which a collection of over 100 diaries of adolescent girls was established at the Psychological Institute at the University of Vienna. This made possible a comparison of adolescents at two different time periods, 1873 and 1910, which would have been difficult with other methods of data collection. The results indicated that despite the significant cultural changes that took place between these years, many basic developmental issues such as the need for intimate personal relationships remained the same. Changes were observed, however, in such factors as the girls' relationships with their parents. Analysis of the diaries, particularly the girls' descriptions of rare or significant events, produced unique knowledge and provided a perspective on the inner aspects of life for adolescents in those times.

A much more recent content analysis was done to examine the experience of loneliness, using the accounts of people who were asked to describe in writing their loneliest experience (Rokach, 1988). Analysis of these descriptions enabled the researcher to build a conceptual model to help explain the phenomenon of loneliness.

Other content analyses attempt to build understanding of how political or social issues are reflected in the content of communications such as professional journals, laws, and existing policies (Williamson et al., 1982). To evaluate how social work practice had changed from 1960 to the 1980s, for example, one such study involved a content analysis of social work practice position vacancy descriptions (Billups & Julia, 1987). Job advertisements in the *Journal of Social Casework* and the *NASW News* were randomly sampled to determine how job titles and fields of practice had changed over three consecutive 10-year periods, the 1960s, 1970s, and 1980s. This study helped answer such research questions as: Have there been changes in the way social work practice is conceptualized? What jobs are being advertised most frequently?

In a similar manner, a content analysis of course outlines of social work practice courses was done to discover the extent to which the teaching of these courses reflected current theoretical and ideological issues in social work (LeCroy & Goodwin, 1988). Course units, required textbooks, required outside readings, and types of assignments were used as categories of practice courses (the unit of analysis), and the researchers attempted to make inferences about how these courses were being conceptualized. This study sought to answer such questions as: Is there any commonality among the course units? Do the courses include content on women and ethnic minorities? What textbooks are used most often? The results were used as a basis for characterizing the content and teaching methods currently being used in social work practice courses.

Inferences to Populations

By making inferences to populations, content analyses can be used to ascertain the values of the audiences that are reached by various communications. A well-known content analysis, for example, examined the relationship between economic development and the value a society places on achievement. David C. McClelland (1961) operationalized the definition of achievement as the presence of achievement themes in over 1000 children's stories from almost every country in the world and the definition of a society's economic development in terms of such factors as coal and electricity consumption. The results of this study indicated that countries with high achievement values were more likely to have higher rates of economic growth than countries with lower achievement values.

Other content analyses have attempted to make inferences about social change and cultural values. The portrayal of women and men in the content of television commercials (Bretl & Cantor, 1988) and the portrayal of violence on prime-time television (Cumberbatch, Jones, & Lee, 1988) have been analyzed, for example. Such studies must be understood in terms of the assumption that the content being analyzed represents society's values.

In the content analysis of the covers of two major newsmagazines described earlier in this chapter (Dodd, Foerch, & Anderson, 1988), it was concluded that society did not see women and minorities as more newsworthy in the 1980s than in the preceding decades, and values about how women and minorities are perceived had not changed. But would it be accurate to say that the covers of two magazines represent how society perceives women and minorities? Such conclusions point to the need for replications of the study using different printed media to see if similar conclusions are reached.

Evaluating the Effects of Communications

In addition to studying themes discerned in communications, content analyses can focus on the effects of items of analysis recorded in communications. One of the earliest uses of content analysis in social work research was in an attempt to measure the effectiveness of social work interventions, using clients' records. John Dollard and O. H. Mowrer (1947), for example, hypothesized that the effectiveness of social work intervention would be revealed in reduced tension in the clients. They evaluated the variable of tension according to a change in the relative proportions of verbal expressions of discomfort (or distress) and expressions of relief from distress recorded in the clients' case records. They then developed a complex coding system to classify emotional tone as a unit of analysis according to categories of distress clauses, relief clauses, or neither.

They also devised a distress quotient, the number of distress clauses divided by the sum of distress and relief clauses, to be used in measurement. Unfortunately, this complex method was found to have little relationship to client change. Later research studies in which similar methods were used to analyze client case records did establish the effectiveness of short-term interventions, however (Reid & Shyne, 1969).

A more recent application of an outcome-oriented content analysis was a single-case study with an emotionally disturbed child. The goal of this study was simply to evaluate the effects of the social worker's behavior (the intervention) on the client's acting-out behavior (Broxmeyer, 1979). Recorded and transcribed interviews were analyzed, and two behaviors the social worker used in working with the child—empathy and limit setting—were coded. These behaviors were then correlated with the child's acting-out behavior.

The results of the content analysis revealed that the social worker had responded to acting out with empathic responses eight times, and on six of those occasions the child stopped; therefore there was a 75 percent reduction in the behavior. When the social worker used limit setting, the child discontinued the behavior 45 percent of the time. When the worker displayed no response, there was only a 25 percent reduction in the child's acting out.

In these examples the focus of the research studies was to determine whether communications can indicate the cause of certain behaviors. Studies that make such inferences are experimental in nature, and measurement of the dependent and independent variables must be carefully controlled. If this is done, analysis of the relationships between variables indicated in recorded communications can contribute to the knowledge base of social work as much as other experimental studies can.

Making Structured Observations

Content analysis can also be used with other data collection methods, such as structured observation (see Chapter 13). A content analysis of observational data can specify clearly what is being observed and what measurements are to be used. Typically, the frequency, duration, intensity, and effects of various verbal and nonverbal behaviors are coded in the analysis.

Robert F. Bales (1950) conducted numerous research studies on small-group behavior by developing a coding scheme for group behaviors. He divided small-group interactions into three classes:

1. Positive interactions in the social-emotional area
2. Negative interactions in the social-emotional area
3. Neutral interactions in the task area

Under each category the observational unit could represent various behaviors such as agrees, disagrees, gives suggestions, and asks for opinions. Observers also gathered qualitative data by taking notes on events not covered by the three categories. Much of what is known about small-group behavior is a result of these types of research studies.

By coding various units of verbal and nonverbal behavior observed in marital interactions, John Gottman (1979) developed an elaborate Couples Interaction Scoring System. The system involved transcribing videotaped interactions and breaking them down into thought units for analysis. Each thought unit received a verbal content code and a nonverbal content code. The verbal content code included categories such as agreement, disagreement, mind reading, summarizing self, and feelings about a problem.

In the nonverbal content code were such categories as positive, neutral, or negative ratings, based on nonverbal cues from face, voice, and body movements. It took approximately 28 hours to transcribe and code each hour of videotape—a time-consuming process. But the process made it possible to examine the effects of different interactions; for example, one partner who is mind reading is most likely to cause the other partner to disagree.

Developments in Procedures

A large part of a content analysis involves the tedious process of coding the data. Computers are proving invaluable in counting and synthesizing masses of data, not only from communications such as books and records in which the units of analysis can be easily defined in quantitative terms, but from communications such as speeches and interviews with extensive qualitative content. As we have seen in Chapter 5, a less formal form of analysis that deals with qualitative data sources is ethnographic content analysis, another development that some researchers have found useful.

Computerized Content Analysis

Computer programs are increasingly being used in content analysis (Weber, 1984; Weitzman & Miles, 1995). Analyzing a large body of text very quickly is facilitated by computerized text coding, which requires unambiguous coding rules and classifications. Computerized content analyses are limited to the study of manifest content and typically are used for data reduction and analyses in which words or phrases are the units of analysis.

Two widely used computer software programs in content analyses are the *General Inquirer* and *Textpack*. These programs code the text according to word groupings, using electronic dictionaries in which specific words have been tagged. The computer is programmed to identify these tag words and put them in previously defined categories. The computerized analysis produces data such as a list of tag words, the frequency of tag words, the proportion of sentences in the text containing certain tag words, and so forth.

There are limitations to the use of electronic data processing in content analysis. Complex or abstract notions cannot be reduced to word groupings, and the communication as a whole may have to be considered. The meaning of a communication comes from sentences, phrases, and paragraphs—not single words. Therefore, computers cannot be used for content analysis when there is an interest in the abstract or thematic meaning of a communication (Weitzman & Miles, 1995). To understand such latent content, interpretive judgments about the meaning of the content must be made before assigning a unit of analysis to a category.

Ethnographic Content Analyses

As we know from Chapter 5, ethnographic content analysis, a form developed in the qualitative research approach, is used to document the communication of meaning as well as to verify theoretical relationships. Its distinctive characteristic is the highly reflexive and interactive nature of the relationships between the researcher and the study's concepts, data collection, and analysis.

In an ethnographic content analysis, the researcher is a central figure in evaluating the meaning of the content. It is less rigid in its research approach, compared to traditional content analyses. Categories and variables guide the study; however, as is the practice in the qualitative research approach, ethnographic content analysis allows for the emergence of new categories and variables during the study.

ADVANTAGES AND DISADVANTAGES

Like all the data collection and utilization methods considered in Parts V and VI of this text, content analyses have advantages and disadvantages. Perhaps the greatest advantage is its unobtrusive nature. Observations, interviews, self-report surveys, and other data collection methods used in social work research intrude into the research situation and may produce reactive effects that change or disturb the concepts under study in some way. Content analyses do not fall into this trap because what is being studied has already taken place. The measuring instrument is applied to an undisturbed system, allowing content analyses to uncover data without influencing the data collection process.

If we want to find out which candy is most popular at the state fair, for example, we could approach customers and ask, "What is your favorite candy?" We could stand by the candy counter and record the purchases. In either case, our presence may affect the outcome, and it may be difficult to approach each customer or to observe clearly what candy is being purchased in a crowd. So we could go to the trash cans, collect the wrappers, divide them into piles and draw conclusions from the findings. Or we could get the records of suppliers and determine how many boxes of each kind of candy were ordered and how many were unsold or returned at the end of the fair. These unobtrusive options are examples of content analyses.

These unobtrusive options also would be the least expensive and time-consuming, because observers and interviewers would not have to be trained and paid to be present for a specified period. For many research studies, a content analysis may be the most economical and time-efficient data collection method.

As presented in Chapter 19, another advantage is that a content analysis can be used in a historical research study to answer questions about the past that cannot be examined with other research methods (Woodrum, 1984). Communications from any time period can be used, as long as historical documents are available for study. A content analysis therefore allows for the examination of trends in both recent times and the distant past. An example was our study described earlier in this chapter which used the diaries of adolescent females written in 1873 and 1910 to examine how relationships with parents had changed between these periods. Thus, we can use content analyses to bridge the gap in time that separates us from our research participants or respondents.

Content analysis is not without disadvantages, however. By definition, the method is confined to the exploration and examination of previously recorded data. If the data are not part of a permanent record, they cannot be content-analyzed.

A distinct disadvantage is the questionable validity of the data provided by some content analyses. Whether what is being measured is really a valid measure of the unit of analysis must be determined, particularly when inferences about populations are to be made. Accurate operational definitions of the units and their categories are essential to ensure validity. The effects of reducing data to categories, as a result of which the true meaning of the data may be lost, must also be taken into account.

The quantification of the data that characterize content analyses can be both an advantage and a disadvantage. It allows for a systematic and objective approach to social work research studies, but the cost may be in terms of limits to the depth of understanding that the analysis can provide. Over time, social work researchers have increasingly become interested in studying the latent content of data in order to get at the underlying meaning.

SUMMARY

A content analysis is a versatile data collection method in which communications are examined in a systematic, objective, and quantitative manner. It can be applied to different types of content, including personal documents such as diaries and suicide notes; mass communications such as magazine covers and television programs; and interviews such as counseling sessions. It is often used to discover themes present in a communication—for example, themes that represent the inner aspects of an individual's life, the values of a society, or the effects of a communication.

The process of conducting a content analysis is straightforward, consisting of four steps. From a problem area, we formulate a research question, which leads to a consideration of how to sample the content of interest. The unit of analysis is operationally defined and categories are developed for the coding of the data. Findings and conclusions are then drawn from the data gathered.

Content analysis is an unobtrusive data collection method. As long as we develop reliable coding procedures and valid categories for the classification of the data, content analyses will be able to build new knowledge for social work practice.

REFERENCES AND FURTHER READINGS

ALTHEIDE, D. (1987). Ethnographic content analysis. *Qualitative Sociology, 10,* 62-77.

BALES, R.F. (1950). *Interaction process analysis.* Reading, MA: Addison-Wesley.

BILLUPS, J.O., & JULIA, M.C. (1987). Changing profile of social work practice: A content analysis. *Social Work Research and Abstracts, 23,* 17-22.

BRETL, D., & CANTOR, J. (1988). The portrayal of men and women in U.S. television commercials: A recent content analysis and trends over 15 years. *Sex Roles, 18,* 595-609.

BROXMEYER, N. (1979). Practitioner-researcher in treating a borderline child. *Social Work Research and Abstracts, 14,* 5-10.

CUMBERBATCH, G., JONES, I., & LEE, M. (1988). Measuring violence on television. *Current Psychological Research and Review, 7,* 10-25.

DODD, D.K., FOERCH, B.J., & ANDERSON, H.T. (1988). Content analysis of women and racial minorities as newsmagazine cover persons. *Journal of Social Behavior and Personality, 3,* 231-236.

DOLLARD, J., & MOWRER, O.H. (1947). A method of measuring tension in written documents. *Journal of Abnormal and Social Psychology, 42,* 3-22.

GABOR, P.A., & GRINNELL, R.M., JR. (1994). *Evaluation and quality improvement in the human services* (pp. 98-120). Needham Heights, MA: Allyn & Bacon.

GOTTMAN, J.M. (1979). *Marital interaction.* New York: Academic Press.

GRINNELL, R.M., JR., & WILLIAMS, M. (1990). *Research in social work: A primer* (pp. 204-231). Itasca, IL: F.E. Peacock.

HOLSTI, O. (1969). *Content analysis for the social sciences and humanities.* Reading, MA: Addison-Wesley.

LECROY, C.W., & GOODWIN, C. (1988). New directions in teaching social work methods: A content analysis of course outlines. *Journal of Social Work Education, 19,* 43-49.

LECROY, C.W., & SOLOMON, G. (1993). Content analysis. In R.M. Grinnell, Jr. (Ed.), *Social work research and evaluation* (4th ed., pp. 304-316). Itasca, IL: F.E. Peacock.

MCCLELLAND, D.C. (1961). *The achieving society.* New York: Free Press.

REID, W.J., & SHYNE, A. (1969). *Brief and extended casework.* New York: Columbia University Press.

ROKACH, A. (1988). The experience of loneliness: A tri-level model. *Journal of Psychology, 122,* 531-544.

SCHNEIDMAN, E. (1985). At the point of no return. *Psychology Today, 19,* 55-58.

WEBER, R.P. (1984). Computer-aided content analysis: A short primer. *Qualitative Sociology, 7,* 126-147.

WEINBACH, R.W., & GRINNELL, R.M., JR. (1996). *Applying research knowledge: A workbook for social work students* (2nd ed., pp. 65-66). Needham Heights, MA: Allyn & Bacon.

WEITZMAN, E.A., & MILES, M.B. (1995). *Computer programs for qualitative data analysis: A software sourcebook.* Newbury Park, CA: Sage.

WILLIAMSON, J.B., KARP, D.A., DALPHIN, J.R., & GRAY, P.S. (1982). *The research craft.* Boston, MA: Little Brown.

WOODRUM, E. (1984). Mainstreaming content analysis in social science: Methodological advantages, obstacles, and solutions. *Social Science Research, 13,* 1-19.

Paul H. Stuart

C h a p t e r **19**

Historical Research

THE WORD *HISTORY* has three distinguishable meanings. In everyday speech, it refers to events that have occurred in the past, a living reality that is not accessible in the present. Second, it refers to the writings that attempt to describe and explain that past reality—history as a written product. Finally, there is "doing history," the process by which written history is produced, as we construct a report from the evidence left from the past (Hexter, 1971).

This chapter focuses on historical research in our profession in the third sense: the process by which we study the past. It is the fourth and last unobtrusive data collection method that is presented in this book. It should be noted, however, that a historical research study can indeed become an obtrusive data collection method if people are interviewed as data sources. As with the six data collection methods described earlier, historical research can also be viewed as a research approach.

PURPOSE OF HISTORY

There are potentially as many reasons for doing a historical research study as there are people. Some of us simply find the past interesting, sometimes because we are disaffected with the present and wish to return to a presumably simpler time. On the other hand, others may find past-time heroes and heroines whose exemplary behavior provides a model for the present. Some historians view history as a story of progress: They seek the origins of modern practices and institutions in the past. Others see history as a story of decline; they look for the seeds of decay (Fischer, 1970).

Ideally, we should always attempt to understand the past on its own terms. Real historical understanding is not achieved by the subordination of the past to the present, but rather by making the past our present and attempting to see life with the eyes of another century than our own (Butterfield, 1931). Such a goal implies that we attempt to achieve objectivity in our description of a past empirical reality.

A *biography* tells the story of one individual's life, often suggesting what the person's importance was for social, political, or intellectual developments of the times. Much historical writing in social work is biographical. There are book-length biographies that focus on prominent individuals as well as collections of brief biographical sketches of important social workers and social reformers (e.g., Trattner, 1987; Seidl, 1995).

Collective biographies are studies of the characteristics of groups of people who lived during a past period and who had a common trait. These biographies make it possible to concentrate on ordinary individuals. A study of people who worked for the Philadelphia Society for Organizing Charity in 1880, for example, provides a useful check on generalizations derived from biographies of individuals who were prominent in the charity organization movement (Rauch, 1975). An examination of early settlement house leaders enabled a person to explore the forces that led to a long-term commitment to activism (Kalberg, 1975).

Much historical research in our profession is generated by general theoretical questions. Studies of the development of social work, for example, may be informed by general theories about how professions develop. In addition, theories of organizational change have led to studies of agency development. Many of the hypotheses derived from social science theory can be investigated only by using historical research methodology. The nature of the ideas underlying social work at various points in time has stimulated many historical research studies. Often, a historical report on a specialized topic suggests new research areas.

What these efforts have in common is that they attempt to describe a past reality. Since the past is inaccessible to direct observation, historical research methods rely on analyzing existing documents, physical remains, and memories left over from the past. Social workers doing a historical research study are seldom present at the events they are studying; thus they must rely on unobtrusive measures that yield data not obtained directly by personal interviews or survey questionnaires.

We frequently use in our historical studies the *findings* from past personal interviews and surveys, however. Unobtrusive measures have the advantage of being nonreactive; that is, the people being studied are not aware that they are being observed. Thus, they do not alter their "normal" responses for the benefit of the researcher. We have the additional advantage of knowing the outcomes of the events—a knowledge that was obviously denied to the participants.

Explaining the Past

Written history is based on an analysis of the remains left over from the past. These remains are both abundant and incomplete, and we must assess them for accuracy and significance before we can synthesize them into written history. Such remains are generally documents produced by people with a personal stake in the events being studied. Thus, it is important for us to understand these people and the social contexts in which they lived. It is this appreciation of the context of events that provides the greatest utility of historical research, since it requires us to enter into the life of another era. We must have empathy as well as an objective understanding of the social forces that influenced the past events.

There is a large range of material that we must take into account when doing a historical research study. Some have argued that we need to make more use of social science concepts and methods. Each topic presented in this book is potentially useful to those of us who wish to carry out a historical research study. As we know, the research question we are trying to answer determines which data collection method(s) and analysis(es) are used in any given research study.

STEPS IN DOING HISTORICAL RESEARCH

Social workers who are doing a historical research study attempt to explain the past based on surviving remains. These remains can be documents, artifacts, and sometimes people's memories, if the participants in the events we are studying are still alive or if their recollections have been preserved in interviews or recorded by some other means. As we have previously mentioned, our temporal distance from the events we are studying makes direct observation impossible, but in another way a temporal distance might be to our advantage. We may be able to be more objective and to take a "broader view."

The difficulties we face when doing a historical research study have to do with focusing on a specific researchable topic, assembling the sources of data necessary to provide objective data, arriving at an understanding of the topic, and constructing a narrative that describes and explains what happened.

We can list these four steps as follows: (1) choosing a research question, (2) gathering evidence that bears on the research questions, (3) determining what the evidence means (synthesis), and (4) writing the report. Together, these four steps provide us with a framework for doing a historical research study.

Step 1: Choosing a Research Question

In choosing a research question, the most important consideration is the extent of our personal interest in the topic, although we must also know something about the period we choose. We may be interested in a specialization within the field of social work, such as school social work; in an early use of a particular social work method, such as behavior modification; in services to a racial or ethnic group, such as day care services; or in the development of an agency or organization, such as the United Way.

The ideas about poverty and deviance that people had in the past might also be of interest to us. As in every other kind of research endeavor, it is important to know what others have written on our topic.

It has been said that historians write for today, for their own times. The history we write is influenced by the times in which we live. New times yield new ideas and thus new ways of understanding our past. Also, new problems in the present may cause us to search the past for analogs. Thus, publications on the major topics in American history appear every generation, offering different explanations and interpretations of the past.

Presentism

There is a danger in selecting research questions solely on the basis of their importance for the present. We may emphasize "modern" elements that occurred in the past to the extent that certain other important elements having no analog in the present are excluded from our study. This error is called *presentism*. Some social workers in the 1920s, for example, were interested in psychoanalytic thought. Later, social work historians who were conscious of the significance of psychoanalysis for casework practice in their own times, wrote about a "psychiatric deluge" as characterizing the period (Borenzweig, 1971). These writers implied that most social workers became Freudians after World War I.

A reexamination of the casework literature of the period, however, produced little evidence for this interpretation (Alexander, 1972). A subsequent investigation of casework practice in one Illinois social work agency led to the conclusion that psychoanalytic theory had very little impact on actual casework practice in that agency until after World War II (Field, 1980). Since most social workers doing historical research are highly aware of today's social problems, presentism is a problem to which they are unusually prone. This underscores the importance of choosing the best evidence (or data) and assessing it carefully.

Antiquarianism

The reverse of presentism is *antiquarianism*, which is an interest in past events without reference to their importance or significance. A fascination with the past (as the past) may lead us to distort our understanding of it by focusing only on those elements that made the past different from the present. It is analogous to the fascination with the exotic that characterizes some students of other cultures, who emphasize differences between groups and ignore commonalties.

Antiquarianism is perhaps rare in social work history. It is most likely to be a problem characteristic of those of us who detest the present or those who seek too rigidly to avoid presentism. These people may be tempted to cut themselves off from the present but, in doing so, they may also cut themselves off from new methods of understanding the past. In short, we need a *balance* between present-mindedness and total isolation from the present when we do a historical research study.

Step 2: Gathering Evidence

Once we have selected a specific research question, our next task is to locate sufficient data to describe and explain what happened. Our goal is to write a report about the past—a report that is accurate and relatively complete, which provides an explanation for past events and which will be meaningful for today's practitioners. In order to write such a report, it is necessary to rely on the work of other historians and the best data available from the past.

The primary materials that we use are the documents and other remains left over from the past. More often than not, we find that these materials are, paradoxically, both abundant and scarce. An imposing amount of material remains, although materials that bear on our research question may be incomplete and fragmentary. We must be skilled in selecting particular materials from the many that are available. We must be skilled, too, in dealing with fragmentary and incomplete sources.

Types of Source Materials

We can utilize virtually any surviving document, artifact, or person's memory in doing a historical research study. Often these materials, particularly those that have been published, can be found in libraries. Many libraries have interlibrary loan services to exchange scarce materials.

Unpublished materials, such as letters, reports, and memoranda, are held by specialized libraries and archives. The most important archive for social workers is the Social Welfare History Archives Center at the University of Minnesota, at Minneapolis. D.J. Klaassen (1995) discusses the holdings of the Center, as well as major holdings in other depositories. Individuals associated with many important social welfare activities may still be alive and may respond to requests for interviews or correspondence. Some social welfare leaders have consented to be interviewed for oral history collections. F.P. Prucha (1994, Chapter 12) describes the major aids that help us to locate oral history materials.

Social service agencies also produce a variety of printed and nonprinted materials, including annual reports, manuals of procedures, employee and client records, and interoffice memoranda. Some of these materials have been placed in libraries or archives; others may be held by the originating agency. P. Romanofsky (1978) provides essays on the major national voluntary social agencies, together with a discussion of the secondary literature and information on the location of the records of each agency. Foundations were important funders of social work, particularly in the decades before the Great Depression; H.M. Keele and J.C. Kiger (1984) provide similar essays on the major foundations.

Newspapers provide a record of social and political developments, including the activities of social service agencies. Files of back issues are held by newspapers and libraries; their availability is improved if they have been microfilmed. Many newspapers, as well as transcripts of some oral history interviews, have been microfilmed by the Microfilming Corporation of America, P.O. Box 10, Sanford, North Carolina 27330.

Locating these printed and unprinted documents is made easier by the finding aids available in college and university libraries. F.P. Prucha (1994) provides a guide to these finding aids as well as other reference works found in academic libraries. General and specialized bibliographies are a good place for us to start in the search for secondary sources. F. Freidel (1974) provides a useful general bibliography of American history, subdivided by topical, chronological, and geographical categories. It also lists the major archives and serials. W.I. Trattner and W.A. Achenbaum (1983) is the best available published bibliography of social welfare history. It may be supplemented by Chambers (1995), which provides annotations of writings published between 1982 and 1990. *The Newsletter of the Social Welfare History Group* (1956–present) provides an annual bibliography of writings in social welfare history.

Printed documents issued by state and federal governments are primary sources for many topics. Government documents include reports of legislative committee hearings and investigations, studies commissioned by legislative commissions and executive agencies, statistical compilations such as the census, the regular and special reports of executive agencies, and much more. Major federal agencies are described in Whitnah (1983). The laws of the state and federal governments form a specialized group of government documents. M.R. Lewis (1976) provides a useful guide to compilations of state and federal laws and other legal documents.

Most academic libraries have librarians who specialize in government publications or reference. They can help users locate needed government publications. Because of the large volume of United States government documents, specialized finding aids have been published to help us in the identification of the documents important to our research question. L.E. Schmeckebier and R.B. Eastin (1969) provide a good introduction to government documents. It may be supplemented by Prucha (1994, Chapter 13). U.S. government documents are available in depository libraries. These libraries have agreed to receive selected government publications and make them available to the public.

Many academic libraries are depository libraries for U.S. government documents. Most urban areas have several depository libraries. State documents may be found in state libraries and archives and sometimes in academic and large public libraries. The availability of many specific documents and records can be established only by inquiry.

Unpublished records of federal, state, and local governments provide a rich primary source for social welfare history. Agencies that are part of local, state, or federal government are governed by general policies regarding the disposition, accessibility, and retention of records. Many governments have archives that preserve the more important records of their agencies. Federal records are held by the National Archives and Records Service. This agency maintains central facilities in Washington, D.C., and College Park, Maryland, twelve Regional Archives, and ten presidential libraries. Some of the unprinted documents in the National Archives have been microfilmed and are available for purchase; they are also available through interlibrary loan services.

Selection of Sources

Once we have identified a group of sources like those mentioned above, our next question is which source(s) to use. In general, our guiding criteria involve the closeness of the source to the event described. If we are going to use a document as a source, for example, we must first determine if the writer was present when the event took place. If not, we must find out how the writer learned of the event. If, the writer read of the event in a newspaper, for example, the newspaper account would be a better source to use since it is "closer" to the event that was described.

The best historical research study, therefore, is based on the exploration of primary sources. A *primary* source provides the words of the witnesses or first recorders of an event. *Secondary sources* are accounts, including books and articles, that are based on the analyses of primary sources. While secondary sources are important for framing questions and getting a context for an investigation, historical reports based only on secondary sources, with few exceptions, add little that is new to our knowledge of the past. In addition, using secondary sources exclusively may perpetuate the errors made by earlier writers.

Primary sources include a broad range of materials: diaries, letters, and other documents produced by the participants in an event; laws, regulations, and records produced by organizations; and many others. Obviously, these are not of equal value for any given study. We must always assess the value of the primary sources before we decide which ones to use. Primary sources may be assessed by asking whether the author of the document had the opportunity to observe what was recorded; whether he or she was an objective witness, and whether the author was honest and unbiased. In addition, when the document was written may be important. Was it completed soon enough after the event described so that problems of faulty memory need not be of concern?

Some historians have emphasized that those doing historical research should assess the sources' internal and external validity. Internal validity involves asking whether the document is internally consistent. External validity is a measure of the degree to which information in the document is consistent with what is already known about the period or event in question.

The transcripts of oral history interviews, as well as autobiographies, present additional problems. If a central person or an autobiography can be located, we must ask how much time has elapsed between the event being described and the person's recollection of the event. In general, the shorter the time between observation and recording, the better the evidence may be. A second question involves the bias of the source. The production of most documentary evidence is subjective: the author may have an interest in the event that biases the account. That is, people may recall or record events in such a way as to magnify their role in them or to make them conform to their own ideological beliefs. Such a problem may be particularly acute in oral history interviews where the individuals know that they are "speaking for the record."

Few sources are completely acceptable on all counts, however. If the authors of primary sources were able to observe the events they described, they probably had a vested interest in them. We must also recognize the fact that the observers may have been limited in their ability to observe because of their preconceptions or ignorance. Consequently, it is important to use as many relevant sources as possible in writing a historical report. We must always know our sources well. Did the writers have a vested interest in the outcome of an event? Were their beliefs involved in the event? In what ways do their accounts of the event differ from those of other participants?

Special Problems with Sources   We may find that particular sources present special problems. Some sources may be systematically selective in the information they provide. Newspapers that slanted the news in accordance with a particular political point of view provide a familiar example. We can attempt to neutralize such selectivity by using a second source that corrects for the bias of the first one. Other sources that we find may be "unslanted" but may provide us with a very incomplete picture of what happened.

The laws passed by a legislature, for example, tell us little about how, or whether, the laws were enforced. One historical researcher dismissed a series of books on colonial public welfare programs written in the 1930s because they often provided "a sterile and unimaginative survey of the laws, without attention to colonial society" (Rothman, 1971). We should never neglect an available source that may bear on our research question. If we rely on a single source alone, our account may lack vitality because of the restricted information on which the narrative rests.

A recent novel makes this point well. The narrator described an account of a riot in an African country in the 1930s. Although many of the participants in the riot must still have been alive, the author of the account chose to rely on local newspapers alone. The newspapers of colonial Africa, however, printed only a portion of the truth. The resulting account was obviously biased. It reduced a complex human event to a recitation of dry half-truths, all properly footnoted (Naipaul, 1979).

Those of us who use existing statistical data, such as census reports, agency reports of caseloads and expenditures, and enrollment figures for schools of social work, face an analogous problem (see Chapter 18). Data are only as good as the procedures used to gather them. Quite frequently, the data collection methods have been less than desirable. A notorious example is the reporting of American Indian reservation populations by American Indian agents in the late 19th century. Some agents reported more American Indians than were actually present as a means of increasing the supplies allocated to the reservations by the United States Office of Indian Affairs. Consequently, the population figures for tribes reported by the Indian Office can be accepted only with caution.

It must not be assumed that only 19th century data are questionable. Reports of local governments on how they spent federal revenue-sharing funds in the 1970s were often inaccurate, to say the least (Magill, 1977). For some widely used statistical data, such as the United States decennial census reports, the problems of accuracy have been well-documented. For less frequently used data, we must evaluate the accuracy of the data for ourselves. An understanding of the accepted techniques of survey research as presented in Chapter 14 can help to assess the strengths and weaknesses of statistical data.

Agency and other organizational records can provide information regarding how these data were collected. The completed questionnaires, interview schedules, or forms, if they are available, may suggest how much care was taken in compiling the data. Our knowledge of agency interests may provide us with clues for investigating probable data collection problems. As we have seen in Chapter 16, we can reanalyze the data if the questionnaires and unanalyzed responses are available.

An excellent example of a reevaluation of a source on which many earlier historians had relied involved an 1834 British government report. The report, which was based on a questionnaire distributed to English poor-law officials, resulted in the enactment of the restrictive Poor Law Amendment Act of 1834. Over 100 years later, an investigation of the original questionnaires revealed examples of faulty data analysis. Reanalysis of the data supported the conclusion that the providing of relief to large families was the result of low wages in the agricultural parishes of England, not the cause, as the Poor Law Commission had concluded (Blaug, 1963, 1964).

Fragmentary Evidence

Gaps usually remain even when we have assembled all of the sources bearing on our research problem. Remains from the past are subject to attrition for a variety of reasons. Documents may be destroyed or lost, memories may be faulty, and individuals may not have had access to paper and pencil until long after the event. Since the research questions that interest us may not have interested the participants in a past event, the sources may not speak to the questions we wish to study. For this reason, many of our historical research studies involve filling in the gaps in the historical record. For some of us, the gaps alone are the primary reasons for conducting a historical research study. The fact that the record is always incomplete is what makes history possible.

Gaps in the documentation may be welcomed as providing the incentive to do a historical research study. The "leaps" we make when writing our report, however, must always be consistent with the known facts. Our "leaps" must also be plausible, given our understanding of the period. We need to understand individual psychology, culture, and social systems theory in order to avoid making implausible connections across the gaps. Social science theory may provide useful hypotheses to bridge the gaps.

Gaps in statistical data present a special problem. Most standard computer packages have subroutines for handling missing observations, based on the assumption that the missing observations are randomly distributed. This assumption is untenable for many of the statistical data with which we work. Limiting the analysis to the surviving complete observations may be worse than assuming that individual missing observations are distributed randomly, since the sample may be severely biased as a result.

In some cases, it may be possible to estimate the values of the missing observations using statistical techniques. In other cases, we may simply present our fragmentary data with a full account of their shortcomings. Often, in historical research, we either use incomplete data and learn something, however inadequate, or reject such data and learn nothing.

Step 3: Determining What the Evidence Means (Synthesis)

After we have selected our research question and have extracted as much data as possible that bear on the research question, our real work begins. We will seldom find that the evidence "speaks for itself." The heart of a historical research study involves asking certain questions about the data we have gathered. It is somewhat artificial, therefore, to discuss synthesis in isolation from the selection of the research question and data gathering. The search for meaning in our sources is an activity to be engaged in at every step of the research process. The manner in which we write a historical research report must reflect this process.

In framing the research question, we are usually guided by a theoretical framework, or a set of statements about how the world works, which guides our research study. Sometimes this is left unstated, as an implicit theoretical framework, but it is always better to make the framework explicit. Specifying our theoretical framework and assumptions clarifies our written report since our assumptions determine the way in which our evidence is used and identify what evidence we consider to be important (Fogel, 1970).

Social workers doing a historical research study enjoy an interactive relationship with their sources. The work consists of presenting a number of hypotheses to the sources that they have found. A hypothesis that can be ruled out may advance the progress of a piece of historical research as much as a hypothesis that can be confirmed. Usually, in asking questions, we will be led to search for other sources of information. It is helpful to use an explicit organizing framework to guide the investigator in the acceptance or rejection of the hypotheses. The research methods should always be appropriate for the research question being studied (Stuart, 1981).

Synthesis involves determining how the facts established from the evidence fit together. Written history fills in the gaps in our understanding of the past by providing an interpretation that is plausible and consistent with available evidence. Most historical writing can be distinguished from writings in other social sciences by its primary purpose, which is to describe a past reality rather than to search for general laws of human behavior (Berkhofer, 1969).

In attempting to describe a past reality, we strive to present an interpretation of a whole—whether the unit is a person, a group, a social service agency, a social welfare system, or a society. This understanding is based on an implicit or explicit set of propositions about human behavior that provide a way for us to structure the facts derived from our evidence. The propositions we use should be made explicit, since these are an essential part of the historical research process. In many recent historical research studies, the propositions were derived from the social sciences.

As an example, consider the synthesis presented in an administrative history of the United States Office of Indian Affairs between 1865 and 1900 (Stuart, 1979). The major "facts" that were derived from the evidence included the following: during the late 19th century, the Indian Office changed the way in which it selected employees, the way in which it monitored the behavior of employees, the number of employees in various categories, and the purposes for which it spent money. The tendencies increasingly were for the employees to be appointed by the Commissioner of Indian Affairs, for their behavior to be circumscribed by rules and monitored by inspectors rather than supervisors, and for staff and funds to be channeled into the organization's educational subdivisions.

Without a theoretical framework, these might seem to be a set of unrelated facts, of little interest in themselves except to antiquarians interested in western lore. But when viewed in the light of institutionalization, a shorthand term for a set of propositions about organizational behavior, these isolated "facts" seem to take on new meaning. Organizations that institutionalize tend to become more centralized; to become better bounded; to develop automatic, objective criteria for making decisions; and to develop clearer goals and objectives (Selznick, 1957). Changes in personnel selection and the monitoring of employee behavior in the Indian Office increased centralization and boundedness.

The proliferation of rules further increased centralization and made the criteria for decision making explicit. The increasing emphasis on education in the organization's budget and deployment of staff reflected the development of a set of goals for American Indians that guided organizational effort. The Indian Office thus became an institution in the late 19th century, and the concept of institutionalization tells us something more about the organization than we had known previously.

The task of synthesis, then, is to determine what the facts derived from the evidence mean when they are put together. In putting the facts together, we are always guided by implicit or explicit propositions about individual or collective behavior. As stated previously, these propositions must be made explicit, since they are an essential part of the historical research process. The underlying propositions, the steps in gathering the evidence, the assessment of the quality of the evidence, and the facts and syntheses derived from the evidence must be clearly stated in written history that is produced.

Step 4: Writing the Report

The purpose of writing a historical research report is twofold—to describe a past reality and to describe the methods we used to investigate it. Consequently, the organization of our report must reflect our methods of investigation, as well as the answer to our research question. In addition, our writing should be clear and simple, without jargon or cliches. As we know, the purpose of any report is to communicate, not to impress or overwhelm the reader.

It is helpful to begin our report with a statement of our research question. As suggested above, if our topic can be put in the form of a question, the specific steps to take to answer the research question become more clear, and the reader can better understand where our report is going. We may also state our research question in the form of a hypothesis, which is derived from existing theory and specifies the conditions under which it can be confirmed.

The introduction of our report discusses the assumptions and propositions that guided the entire research study. In addition, the secondary sources (other histories) that speak to our research question are discussed in the introduction. Primary sources that presented unusual or special problems are also discussed. Technical discussions regarding evidence is presented in an appendix.

Our introduction may be a few paragraphs in a short report or one or more chapters in a longer one. Its purpose is to introduce the reader to our research question, the various data sources we used, and our assumptions and guiding propositions that informed the entire research process. Consequently, its form and content will be determined by the topic being investigated.

Just as an introduction is needed, so is a conclusion. The introduction tells the readers where they are going; the conclusion reviews where they have been. The major conclusions may be summarized, and directions for further study may also be suggested. The importance of the synthesis presented must be made clear. The book on the late 19th century Indian Office, discussed above, ends with a chapter that pulls together the evidence for institutionalization presented in earlier chapters. It also relates this synthesis to developments in other parts of the federal government in the late 19th century and suggests how the institutional-ization of the Indian Office may help to explain what happened to the organiza-tion in the 20th century (Stuart, 1979).

Between the introduction and the conclusion lies the body of the report. It can be organized in a variety of ways, always keeping in mind the question being studied and the techniques employed in answering it. Some historical research reports are organized chronologically, others topically, and still others by a combination of the two methods. A rigid adherence to chronology may distort the reader's understanding of important events. The occurrence and magnitude of change should be built into the structure of the report (Berkhofer, 1969).

Most reports are organized on principles somewhere between strictly chrono-logical and strictly thematic. The specific organization used depends on the topic and the nature of the research question being examined.

THE PROMISE OF HISTORICAL RESEARCH

Although many social workers like to describe our profession as a young one, it nevertheless has had a long history. It was founded at the turn of the century, and its roots go back a century or more. Social welfare (organized social provision for human needs) has an even longer history. There is little that is new in social work. Most of the problems our profession faces today have analogs in the past, and continuity, rather than revolutionary change, characterizes much of our profession's development. Social workers study the past for many reasons: to learn how our profession faced problems similar to those it faces today, to understand the origins of modern social policies and social problems, or to add to knowledge of how organizations grow and change, among many others.

Recent historical writing has examined the social work profession's "aban-donment of the poor" (Specht & Courtney, 1994), the failure of the settlement house movement to address the problems of African Americans (Lasch-Quinn, 1993), the functions of orphanages in early twentieth century Baltimore (Zmora, 1994), the changing treatment of unmarried mothers (Kunzel, 1993), the origins of AFDC (Gordon, 1994), and the evolution of the American social security system (Berkowitz, 1991). These problems are important to social work today; studying how people addressed them in the past may help us to better under-stand present-day social problems and the social service programs created to address them. We may also gain a better idea about where we have been as a profession and where we are going.

The value of historical research for our profession depends on how well it is conducted. Some of the past historical writings are of limited value because secondary sources were used to the exclusion of primary ones; questions and assumptions that underlay the research question were not stated explicitly; or the reports were written in too rigid a chronological format. Better history will tell us where we have been. These writings may also help us to understand where we are now and suggest hypotheses regarding the future of our profession.

SUMMARY

Social workers study the past for many reasons: to learn how our profession faced problems similar to those it faces today; to understand the origins of modern social policies and social problems; or to add to the knowledge of how organizations grow and change, among others. What these efforts have in common is that they all attempt to describe a past reality. Since the past is inaccessible to direct observation, we must rely on secondary analyses of existing documents, physical remains, and memories left over from the past. As in any research study, we must inquire into the validity and reliability—that is, the accuracy and significance—of the sources utilized before we attempt to synthesize them into a written history.

No research study can be attempted without a theoretical framework or paradigm. A general framework for doing a historical research study includes choosing a research problem, gathering evidence that bears on the research problem, determining what the evidence means, and writing the report. Discussing these steps in isolation from one another is somewhat artificial. To a certain extent, as with any problem-solving paradigm, all the steps are conducted simultaneously.

To choose a topic intelligently, we must know the previously published literature and how it relates to the research problem we are trying to study. This knowledge enhances our understanding of the gaps that demand historical explanation and the questions about which historians disagree. It is also helpful for us to know something of the primary sources that bear on the research problem. Thus, the first requirement in doing a historical research study is to read widely, paying careful attention to the footnotes. What sources did the authors use? Do the same sources lead different people to different conclusions?

The library is the place to begin a historical research study. General histories of social work and social welfare provide the broad outlines of development. Collections of documents make it possible to follow these developments as they were described by contemporaries. More narrow topics in the history of social work and social welfare are explored in monographs and journals.

Reading secondary sources may lead to questions about the authors' contentions or curiosity about some area that is not treated fully. This curiosity and questioning are often the source of the ideas that guide a study. Once the primary sources that bear on the area under investigation have been located—in archives, libraries, or in the possession of individuals or social agencies—we can be well on the way to producing our own history.

REFERENCES AND FURTHER READINGS

ALEXANDER, L.B. (1972). Social work's Freudian deluge: Myth or reality? *Social Service Review, 46,* 517-538.

BERKHOFER, R.F., JR. (1969). *A behavioral approach to historical analysis.* New York: Free Press.

BERKOWITZ, E.D. (1991). *America's welfare state: From Roosevelt to Reagan*. Baltimore, MD: Johns Hopkins University Press.

BLAUG, M. (1963). The myth of the old poor law and the making of the new. *Journal of Economic History, 23*, 151-184.

BLAUG, M. (1964). The Poor Law Report reexamined. *Journal of Economic History, 24*, 229-245.

BORENZWEIG, H. (1971). Social work and psychoanalytic theory: A historical analysis. *Social Work, 16*, 7-16.

BUTTERFIELD, H. (1931). *The Whig interpretation of history*. London: Bell.

CHAMBERS, C.A. (1995). *History of Social Work Bibliography: Writings, 1982-1990*. Minneapolis, MN: Social Welfare History Archives, University of Minnesota-Twin Cities.

FIELD, M.H. (1980). Social casework practice during the "psychiatric deluge." *Social Service Review, 54*, 482-507.

FISCHER, D.H. (1970). *Historians' fallacies: Toward a logic of historical thought*. New York: Harper & Row.

FOGEL, R.W. (1970). Historiography and retrospective economics. *History and Theory, 9*, 245-264.

FREIDEL, F. (Ed.). (1974). *Harvard guide to American history* (2 vols., rev. ed.). Cambridge, MA: Harvard University Press.

GORDON, L. (1994). *Pitied but not entitled: Single mothers and the history of welfare, 1890-1935*. New York: Free Press.

HEXTER, J.H. (1971). *Doing history*. Bloomington, IN: Indiana University Press.

KALBERG, S. (1975). The commitment to career reform: The settlement movement leaders. *Social Service Review, 49*, 608-628.

KEELE, H.M., & KIGER, J.C. (Eds.). (1984). *Foundations*. Westport, CN: Greenwood.

KLAASSEN, D.J. (1995). Archives of social welfare. In *Encyclopedia of Social Work, 19th edition* (Vol. 1, pp. 225-231.). Washington, DC: NASW Press.

KUNZEL, R.G. (1993). *Fallen women, problem girls: Unmarried mothers and the professionalization of social work, 1890-1945*. New Haven, CN: Yale University Press.

LASCH-QUINN, E. (1993). *Black neighbors: Race and the limits of reform in the American settlement house movement, 1890-1945*. Chapel Hill, NC: University of North Carolina Press.

LEWIS, M.R. (1976). Social policy research: A guide to legal and government documents. *Social Service Review, 50*, 647-654.

MAGILL, R.S. (1977). Who decides revenue sharing allocations? *Social Work, 22*, 297-300.

NAIPAUL, V.S. (1979). *A bend in the river*. New York: Knopf.

PRUCHA, F.P. (1994). *Handbook for Research in American History: A Guide to Bibliographies and Other Reference Works* (2nd ed.). Lincoln, NE: University of Nebraska Press.

PUMPHREY, R.E., & PUMPHREY, M.W. (1961). *The heritage of American social work: Readings in its philosophical and institutional development*. New York: Columbia University Press.

RAUCH, J.B. (1975). Women in social work: Friendly visitors in Philadelphia, 1880. *Social Service Review, 49*, 241-259.

ROMANOFSKY, P. (Ed.). (1978). *Social service organizations*. Westport, CT: Greenwood.

ROTHMAN, D. (1971). *The discovery of the asylum: Social order and disorder in the new republic*. Boston: Little, Brown.

SCHMECKEBIER, L., & EASTIN, R.B. (1969). *Government publications and their use* (2nd ed.). Washington, DC: Brookings Institution.

SEIDL, F. (Ed.). (1995). Biographies. In *Encyclopedia of Social Work* (19th ed., Vol. 3, pp. 2569-2621). Washington, DC: NASW Press.

SELZNICK, P. (1957). *Leadership in administration.* New York: Harper & Row.

SPECHT, H., & COURTNEY, M.E. (1994). *Unfaithful angels: How social work has abandoned its mission.* New York: Free Press.

STUART, P. (1979). *The Indian Office: Growth and development of an American institution, 1865-1900.* Ann Arbor, MI: UMI Research Press.

STUART, P. (1981). Historical research. In R.M. Grinnell, Jr. (Ed.), *Social work research and evaluation* (pp. 316-332). Itasca, IL: F.E. Peacock.

STUART, P. (1985). Administrative reform in Indian affairs. *Western Historical Quarterly, 16,* 133-146.

TRATTNER, W.I. (Ed.). (1987). *Biographical dictionary of social welfare in America.* Westport, CN: Greenwood Press.

TRATTNER, W.I. (1994). *From poor law to welfare state: A history of social welfare in America.* (5th ed.). New York: Free Press.

TRATTNER, W., & ACHENBAUM, W.A. (1983). *Social Welfare in America: An Annotated Bibliography.* Westport, CN: Greenwood Press.

WHITNAH, D. (Ed.). (1983). *Government agencies.* Westport, CN: Greenwood.

WOODROOFE, K. (1962). *From charity to social work in England and the United States.* Toronto: University of Toronto Press.

ZMORA, N. (1994). *Orphanages reconsidered: Child care institutions in progressive-era Baltimore.* Philadelphia, PA: Temple University Press.

Yvonne A. Unrau

Chapter **20**

Selecting a Data Collection Method and Data Source

D ATA COLLECTION IS THE HEARTBEAT of a research project. The goal is to have a steady flow of data collected systematically and with the least amount of bias. When the flow of data becomes erratic or stops prematurely, a research study is in grave danger. When data collection goes well it is characterized by an even pulse and is rather uneventful. This chapter examines the data collection process from the vantage point of choosing the most appropriate data collection method and data source for any given research study.

DATA COLLECTION METHODS AND DATA SOURCES

There is a critical distinction between a data collection method and a data source that must be clearly understood before developing a viable data collection plan. A data collection method consists of a detailed plan of procedures that aims to gather data for a specific purpose; that is, to answer a research question or to test a hypothesis. As we know, the previous seven chapters in this book presented seven different data collection methods. Each one can be used with a variety of data sources, which are defined by who (or what) supplies the data. Data can be provided by a multitude of sources such as people, existing records, and existing databases.

When data are collected directly from people, data may be first- or second-hand. Firsthand data are obtained from people who are closest to the problem we are studying. Male inmates participating in an anger management group, for example, can provide firsthand data about their satisfaction with the program's treatment approach. Secondhand data may come from other people who are indirectly connected to our primary problem area. The anger management group facilitator or the prison social work director, for example, may be asked for a personal opinion about how satisfied inmates are with treatment. In other instances, secondhand data can be gained from existing reports written about inmates or inmate records that monitor their behavior or other important events.

DATA COLLECTION AND THE RESEARCH PROCESS

Data collection is a critical step in the research process because it is the link between theory and practice. Our research study always begins with an idea that is molded by a conceptual framework, which uses preexisting knowledge about our study's problem area. Once our research problem and question have been refined to a researchable level, data are sought from a selected source and gathered using a systematic collection method. The data collected are then used to support or supplant our original study's conceptions about our research problem under investigation. The role of data collection in connecting theory and practice is understood when looking at the entire research process.

As we have seen in Chapters 4 and 5, choosing a data collection method and data source follows the selection of a problem area, selecting a research question, and developing a sampling plan. It comes before the data analysis phase and writing the research report phase. Although data collection is presented in this text as a distinct phase of the research process, it cannot be tackled separately or in isolation. All phases of the research process must be considered if we hope to come up with the best strategy to gather the most relevant, reliable, and valid data to answer a research question or to test a hypothesis. This section discusses the role of data collection in relation to four steps of the research process: (1) selecting a problem area and research question, (2) formulating a research design, (3) analyzing data, and (4) writing the research report.

Selecting a Problem Area and Research Question

The specific research question identifies the general problem area and the population to be studied. It tells us what we want to collect data about and alerts us to potential data sources. It does not necessarily specify the exact manner in which our data will be gathered, however. Suppose, for example, a school social worker proposes the following research question: How effective is our Students Against Violence Program (SAVP) within the Forest Lawn High School? One of the many objectives of our program is "To increase student's feelings of safety at school." This simple evaluative research question identifies our problem area of interest (school violence) and our population of focus (students). It does not state how the question will be answered.

Despite the apparent clarity of our research question, it could in fact be answered in numerous ways. One factor that affects how this question is answered depends upon how its variables are conceptualized and operationalized. Students' feelings of safety, for example, could be measured in a variety of ways. Another factor that affects how a research question is answered (or a hypothesis is tested) is the source of data; that is, who or what is providing them. If we want to get firsthand data about the student's school safety, for example, we could target the students as a potential data source.

If such firsthand data sources were not a viable option, secondhand data sources could be sought. Students' parents, for example, can be asked to speculate on whether their children feel safe at school. In other instances, secondhand data can be gained from existing reports written about students (or student records) that monitor any critical danger or safety incidents.

By listing all possible data collection methods and data sources that could provide sound data to answer a research question, we develop a fuller understanding of our initial research problem. It also encourages us to think about our research problem from different perspectives, via the data sources. Because social work problems are complex, data collection is strengthened when two or more data sources are used. If the students, teachers, and parents rate students' feelings of safety as similar, then we can be more confident that the data (from all these sources) accurately reflect the problem being investigated. Reliability of data can be assessed, or estimated, when collected from multiple sources.

The exercise of generating a list of possible data collection methods and sources can be overwhelming. With reasonably little effort, however, we can develop a long list of possibilities. We may also end up seeing the problem in a different light than what we had thought of previously. By considering parents as a source of secondhand data, for example, we open up a new dimension of the problem being studied. All of a sudden, family support factors may seem critical to how safe students feel at school.

We may then want to collect data about the family. This possibility should be considered within the context of our study's conceptual framework. Once we have exhausted all the different ways to collect data for any given study, we need to revisit our original research question. In doing so, we can refocus it by remembering the original purpose of the study.

Formulating a Research Design

As we know, the research design flows from the research question, which flows from the problem area. A research design organizes our research question into a framework that sets the parameters and conditions of the study. As mentioned, the research question directs *what* data are collected and *who* data could be collected from. The research design refines the *what* question by operationalizing variables and the *who* question by developing a sampling strategy. In addition, the research design also dictates *when, where,* and *how* data will be collected.

The research design states how many data collection points our study will have and specifies the data sources. Each discrete data gathering activity constitutes a data collection point and defines *when* data are to be collected. Thus, using an exploratory one-group, posttest-only design, we will collect data only once from a single group of research participants. On the other hand, if a classical experimental design is used, data will be collected at two separate times with two different groups of research participants—for a total of four discrete data collection points.

The number of times a research participant must be available for data collection is an important consideration when choosing a data collection method. The gathering of useful, valid, and reliable data is enhanced when the data collection activities do not occur too frequently, and are straightforward and brief. Consider the high school students targeted by our SAVP. Already, many of the students live with the fears of avoiding confrontations with hostile peers and *if* they should tell someone about being threatened or harmed. Asking students about their feelings of safety too often may inadvertently make them feel less safe, or alternatively they may tire of the whole process of inquiry and refuse to participate in our study.

Where the data are collected is also important to consider. If our research question is too narrow and begs for a broader issue that encompasses individuals living in various geographic locations, then mailed surveys would be more feasible than interviews. If our research question focuses on a specific population where all research participants live in the same geographic location, however, it may be possible to use direct observations or individual or group interviews.

Because most social work studies are applied, the setting of our study usually involves clients' in their natural environments where there is little control over extraneous variables. If we want to measure the students' feelings toward school safety, for example, do we observe students as they walk the school halls, observe how they interact with their peer groups, or have them complete a survey form of some kind? In short, we must always consider which method of data collection will lead to the most valid and reliable data to answer a specific research question or to test a specific hypothesis.

The combination of potential data collection methods and potential data sources is another important consideration. A research study can have one data collection source and still use multiple data collection methods. High school students (one data source) in our study, for example, can fill out a standardized questionnaire that measures their feelings of safety (first data collection method) in addition to participating in face-to-face interviews (second data collection method).

In the same vein, another study can have multiple data sources and one data collection method. In this case, we can collect data about how safe a student feels through observation recordings by the students' parents, teachers, or social workers. The combination of data collection methods should not be too taxing on any research participant or any system, such as the school itself. That is, data collection should try not to interfere with the day-to-day activities of the persons providing (or responsible for collecting) the data.

In some studies, there is no research design *per se*. Instead we can use existing data to answer the research question. Such is the case when a secondary analysis is used. Content analysis may also be used on existing data, as when we gather data from existing client records. When the data already exist, we must then organize them using the best-case scenario given the data at hand and the details of how they were originally gathered and recorded. In these situations, we give more consideration to the analysis of data.

Analyzing Data

Collecting data is a resource intensive endeavor that can be expensive and time consuming. The truth of this statement is realized in the data analysis phase of our research study. Without a great deal of forethought about what data to collect, data can be thrown out because they cannot be organized or analyzed in any meaningful way. In short, data analyses should always be considered when choosing a data collection method and data source because the analysis phase must summarize, synthesize, and ultimately organize the data in an effort to have as clear-cut an answer as possible to our research question. When too much (or too little) data have been collected, we can easily become bogged down or stalled by difficult decisions that could have been avoided with a little forethought.

After we have thought through our research problem and research question and have arrived at a few possible data collection methods and data sources, it is worthwhile to list out the details of how the dependent and independent variables will be measured by each data collection method and each data source. We must think about how they will be used in our data analysis. This exercise provides a clearer idea of the type of results we can expect.

One of the dependent variables in our example is the students' feelings of safety. Suppose the school social worker decides to collect data about this variable by giving students (data source) a brief standardized questionnaire (data collection method) about their feelings of safety. Many standardized questionnaires contain several subscales that, when combined, give a quantitative measure of a larger concept. A questionnaire measuring the concept of feelings of safety, for example, might include three subscales: problem awareness, assertiveness, and self-confidence. We need to decide if each subscale will be defined as three separate subvariables, or if only the total combined scale score will be used.

Alternatively, if data about feelings of safety were to be collected using two different data sources such as parent (Source 1) and teacher (Source 2) observations, we must think about how the two data types "fit" together. That is, will data from the two sources be treated as two separate variables? If so, will one variable be weighted more heavily in our analysis than the other? Thinking about how the data will be summarized helps us to expose any frivolous data—that is, data that are not suitable to answer our research question.

It is also important to be clear on how our independent variable(s) will be measured and what data collection method would be most appropriate. In our example, we want to know whether our SAVP is effective for helping students feel more safe in the school environment. Because a social service program is being evaluated, it is essential to know what specific intervention approach(es), procedures, and techniques are used within the program. What specific intervention activities are used? Is student participation in our SAVP voluntary? How often do our SAVP's intervention activities occur in the school? Anticipating the type of data analysis that will be used helps to determine which data collection method and data source provide the most meaningful and accurate data to gather.

Besides collecting data about the independent and dependent variables, we must also develop a strategy to collect demographic data about the people who participated in our study. Typical demographic variables include: age, gender, education level, and family income. These data are not necessarily used in the analysis of the research question. Rather, they provide a descriptive context for our study. Some data collection methods, such as standardized questionnaires, include these types of data. Often, however, we are responsible for obtaining them as part of the data collection process.

Writing the Research Report

It is useful to think about our final research report when choosing a data collection method and data source as it forces us to visualize how our study's findings will ultimately be presented. It identifies both who the audience of the study will be and the people interested in our findings. Knowing who will read our research report and how it will be disseminated helps us to take more of an objective stance toward our study.

In short, we can take a third-person look at what our study will finally look like. Such objectivity helps us to think about our data collection method and data source with a critical eye. Will consumers of our research study agree that the students in fact were the best data collection source? Were the data collection method and analysis sound? These are some of the practical questions that bring scrutiny to the data collection process.

CRITERIA FOR SELECTING A DATA COLLECTION METHOD

Thinking through the research process, from the vantage point of collecting data, permits us to refine the conceptualization of our study and the place of data collection within it. It also sets the context within which our data will be gathered. At this point, we should have a sense of what the ideal data collection method and data source would be. Clearly, there are many viable data collection methods and data sources that can be used to answer any research question. Nevertheless, there are many practical criteria that ultimately refine the final data collection method (and sources) to fit the conditions of any given research study. These criteria are: (1) size, (2) scope, (3) program participation, (4) worker cooperation, (5) intrusion into the lives of research participants, (6) resources, (7) time, and (8) previous research findings. They all interact with one another, but for the sake of clarity each one is presented separately.

Size

The size of our study reflects just how many people, places, or systems are represented in it. As with any planning activity, the more people involved, the more complicated the process and the more difficult it is to arrive at a mutual agreement. Decisions about which data collection method and which data source to use can be stalled when several people, levels, or systems are consulted. This is simply because individuals have different interests and opinions. Administrators, for example, may address issues such as accountability more than do line-level social workers.

Imagine if the effectiveness of our SAVP were examined on a larger scale such that all high schools in the city were included. Our study's complexity is dramatically increased because of such factors as the increased number of students, parents, school principals, teachers, and social workers involved. Individual biases will make it much more difficult to agree upon the best data collection method and data source for our study.

Our study's sample size is also a consideration. The goal of any research study is to have a meaningful sample of the population of interest. With respect to sample size, this means that we should strive for a reasonable representation of the sampling frame. When small-scale studies are conducted, such as a program evaluation in one school, the total sampling frame may be in the hundreds or fewer. Thus, dealing with the random selection of clients poses no particular problem.

On the other hand, when large-scale studies are conducted, such as when the federal government chooses to examine a social service program that involves hundreds of thousands of people, dealing with a percentage is more problematic. If our sample is in the hundreds, it is unlikely that we would be able to successfully observe all participants in a particular setting. Rather, a more efficient manner of data collection—say a survey—may be more appropriate.

Scope

The scope of our research study is another matter to consider. Scope refers to how much of our problem area will be covered. If in our SAVP, for example, we are interested in gathering data about students' academic standings, family supports, and peer relations, then three different aspects of our problem area will be covered. In short, we need to consider whether one method of data collection and one data source can be used to collect all the data. It could be that school records (Chapters 16–19), for example, are used to collect data about students' academic achievements, interviews with students (Chapter 14) are conducted to collect data about students' family supports, and observation methods (Chapters 13 and 15) are used to gather data about students' peer relationships.

Program Participation

Many social work research efforts are conducted in actual real-life program settings. Thus, it is essential that we gain the support of program personnel to conduct our study. Program factors that can impact the choice of our data collection methods and data sources include variables such as the program's clarity in its mandate to serve clients, its philosophical stance toward clients, and its flexibility in client record keeping.

First, if a program is not able to clearly articulate a client service delivery plan, it will be difficult to separate out clinical activity from research activity, or to determine when the two overlap.

Second, agencies tend to base themselves on strong beliefs about a client population, which affect who can have access to their clients and in what manner. A child sexual abuse investigation program, for example, may be designed specifically to avoid the problem of using multiple interviewers and multiple interviews of children in the investigation of an allegation of sexual abuse. As a result, the program would be hesitant for us to conduct interviews with the children to gather data for "research purposes."

Third, to save time and energy there is often considerable overlap between program client records and research data collection. The degree of willingness of a program to change or adapt to new record-keeping techniques will affect how we might go about collecting certain types of data.

Worker Cooperation

On a general level, programs have few resources and an overabundance of clients. Such conditions naturally lead their administrators and social workers to place clinical activity as a top priority. When our research study requires social workers to collect data as a part of their day-to-day client service delivery, it is highly likely that they will view it as additional work. In short, they may not be likely to view these new data collection activities as a means to expedite their work, at least not in the short term.

Getting cooperation of social workers within a program is a priority in any research study that relies directly or indirectly on their meaningful participation. They will be affected by our study whether they are involved in the data collection process or not. Workers may be asked to schedule additional interviews with families or adjust their intervention plans to ensure that data collection occurs at the optimal time. Given the fiscal constraints faced by programs, the workers themselves often participate as data collectors. They may end up using new client recording forms or administer questionnaires. Whatever the level of their participation, it is important for us to strive to achieve a maximum level of their cooperation.

There are three factors to consider when trying to achieve maximum cooperation from workers. First, we should make every effort to work effectively and efficiently with the program's staff. Cooperation is more likely to be achieved when they participate in the development of our study plan from the beginning. Thus, it is worthwhile to take time to explain the purpose of our study and its intended outcomes at an early stage in the study. Furthermore, administrators and front-line workers can provide valuable information about what data collection method(s) may work best.

Second, we must be sensitive to the workloads of the program's staff. Data collection methods and sources should be designed to enhance the work of professionals. Client recording forms, for example, can be designed to provide focus for supervision meetings, as well as summarize facts and worker impressions about a case.

Third, a mechanism should be set up by which workers receive feedback based on the data they have collected. When data are reported back to the program's staff before the completion of our study, we must ensure that the data will not bias later measurements (if any).

Intrusion Into the Lives of Research Participants

When clients are used as a data source, client self-determination takes precedence over research activity. As we know, clients have every right to refuse participation in a research study and cannot be denied services because they are unwilling to participate. It is unethical, for example, when a member of a group-based treatment intervention has not consented to participate in the study, but participant observation (Chapter 15) is used as the data collection method. This is unethical because the group member ends up being observed as part of the group dynamic in the data collection process. The data collection method(s) we finally select must be flexible enough to allow our study to continue, even with the possibility that some clients will not participate.

Cultural consideration must also be given to the type of data collection method used. One-to-one interviewing with Cambodian refugees, for example, may be extremely terrifying for them, given the interrogation they may have experienced in their own country. As presented in the appendix, if direct observational strategies (e.g., Chapters 13 and 15) are used in studies in which we are from a different cultural background than our research participants, it is important to ensure that interpretation of their behaviors, events, or expressions is accurate from their perspectives.

We must also recognize the cultural biases of standardized measuring instruments, since most are based on testing with Caucasian groups. The problems here are twofold. First, we cannot be sure if the concept that the instrument is measuring is expressed the same way in different cultures. For instance, a standardized self-report instrument that measures family functioning may include an item such as, "We have flexible rules in our household that account for individual differences," which would likely be viewed positively by North American cultures, but negatively by many Asian cultures. Second, because standardized measuring instruments are written in English, research participants must have a good grasp of English to ensure that the data collected from them are valid and reliable.

Another consideration comes into play when particular populations have been the subject of a considerable amount of research studies already. Many aboriginal people living on reserves, for example, have been subjected to government surveys, task force inquiries, independent research projects, and perhaps even to the curiosities of social work students learning in a practicum setting. When a population has been extensively researched, it is even more important that we consider how the data collection method will affect those people participating in the study. Has the data collection method been used previously? If so, what was the nature of the data collected? Could the data be collected in other ways, using less intrusive measures?

Resources

There are various costs associated with collecting data in any given research study. Materials and supplies, equipment rental, transportation costs, and training for data collectors are just a few things to consider when choosing a data collection method. In addition, once the data are collected, additional expenses can arise when they need to be entered into a computer or transcribed.

An effective and efficient data collection method is one that collects the most valid and reliable data to answer a research question or test a hypothesis while requiring the least amount of time and money. In our example, to ask students about their feelings of safety via an open-ended interview may offer rich data, but we take the risk that students will not fully answer our questions in the time allotted for the interview. On the other hand, having them complete a self-report questionnaire on feelings of safety is a quicker and less costly way to collect data, but it gives little sense about how well the students understood the questions being asked of them or whether the data obtained reflect their true feelings.

Time

Time is a consideration when our study has a fixed completion date. Time constraints may be self- or externally imposed. Self-imposed time constraints are personal matters we need to consider. Is our research project a part of a thesis or dissertation? What are our personal time commitments?

Externally imposed time restrictions are set by someone other than the one doing the study. For instance, our SAVP study is limited by the school year. Other external pressures may be political, such as an administrator who wants research results for a funding proposal or annual report.

Previous Research

Having reviewed the professional literature on our problem, we need to be well aware of other data collection methods that have been used in similar studies. We can evaluate earlier studies for the strengths and weaknesses of their data collection methods and thereby make a more informed decision as to the best data collection strategy to use in our specific situation. Further, we need to look for diversity when evaluating other data collection approaches. That is, we can triangulate results from separate studies that used different data collection methods and data sources to answer a research question or test a hypothesis.

SELECTION OF A DATA COLLECTION METHOD

As should be evident by now, choosing a data collection method and data source for a research study is not a simple task. There are numerous conceptual and practical factors that must be thought through if we hope to arrive at the best possible approach to gathering data. How do we appraise all the factors to be considered in picking the best one? The previous seven chapters in this book present seven different non–mutually exclusive data collection methods. Theoretically, all of them could be used to evaluate the effectiveness of our SAVP. Each one would offer a different perspective to our research question and would consider different data sources.

Table 20.1 is an example of a grid that can be used to assist us in making an informed decision about which data collection method is best. The grid includes both general and specific considerations for our study question. The first section of the grid highlights the eight criteria for selecting a data collection method discussed earlier. The bottom section of the grid identifies five additional considerations that are specific to our SAVP.

The grid can be used as a decision-making tool by subjectively rating how well each data collection method measures up to the criteria listed in the left-hand column of Table 20.1. We mark a "+" if the data collection method has a favorable rating an a "–" if it has an unfavorable one. When a particular criterion

TABLE 20.1   DECISION-MAKING GRID FOR
CHOOSING A DATA COLLECTION METHOD

	Data Collection Methods						
	Structured Observation	Survey Research	Participant Observation	Secondary Analysis	Content Analysis	Existing Statistics	Historical Research
General Criteria							
1. Size	0	+	0	+	+	+	+
2. Scope	−	+	−	−	−	−	−
3. Program participation	0	+	0	+	+	+	+
4. Worker cooperation	−	+	−	+	+	+	+
5. Intrusion to clients	−	−	−	+	+	+	+
6. Resources	−	+	−	+	+	+	+
7. Time	−	+	−	+	+	+	+
8. Previous research	0	+	0	−	−	−	−
Specific Criteria							
1. Student availability	+	+	+	0	0	0	0
2. Student reading level	0	+	0	0	0	0	0
3. School preference	−	+	−	−	−	−	−
4. School year end	−	−	−	+	+	+	+
5. Access to existing records	0	0	0	+	+	+	+
Totals...	−6	8	−6	5	5	5	5

is neutral, in which case it has no positive or negative effect, then a zero is indicated.

Once each data collection method has been assessed on all eight criteria, we can simply add the number of +'s and −'s to arrive at a plus or minus total for each method. This information can be used to help us make an informed decision about the best data collection method, given all the issues raised. Based on Table 20.1, the survey research method of data collection is most appealing for our study if a single method of data collection is used.

TRYING OUT THE SELECTED DATA COLLECTION METHOD

Data collection is a particularly vulnerable time for a research study because it is the point where "talk" turns to "action." So far, all the considerations that have been weighed in the selection of a data collection method have been in theory. All people involved in our research endeavor have cast their suggestions and doubts on the entire process. Once general agreement has been reached about which data collection method and data source to use, it is time to test the waters.

Trying out a data collection method can occur informally by simply testing it out with available willing research participants or, at the very least, with anyone who has not been involved with the planning of the study. The purpose of this trial run is to ensure that those who are going to provide data understand the questions and procedures in the way that they were intended. Data collection methods might also be tested more formally, such as when a pilot study is conducted.

As we know from Chapter 9, a pilot study involves carrying out all aspects of the data collection plan on a mini-scale. That is, a small portion of our study's actual sample is selected and run through all steps of the data collection process. In a pilot study, we are interested in the process of the data collection as well as the content. In short, we what to know whether our chosen data collection method produces the expected data. Are there any unanticipated barriers to gathering the desired data? How do research participants (data source) respond to our data collection procedures? Is there enough variability in research participants' responses?

IMPLEMENTATION AND EVALUATION

The data collection phase of a research study can go smoothly if we act proactively. That is, we should guide and monitor the entire data collection process according to the procedures and steps that were set out in the planning stage of our study and were tested in the pilot study.

Implementation

The main guiding principle to implementing the selected data collection method is that a systematic approach to data collection must be used. This means that the steps to gathering data should be methodically detailed so that there is no question about the tasks of the person(s) collecting the data—the data collector(s). This is true whether using a quantitative or qualitative research approach. As we know from Chapters 4–6, the difference between these two research approaches is that the structure of the data collection process within a qualitative research study is often documented as the study progresses. On the other hand, in a quantitative research study, the data collection process is decided at the study's outset and provides much less flexibility after the study is under way.

It must be very clear from the beginning who is responsible for collecting the data. When we take on the task, there is reasonable assurance that the data collection will remain objective and be guided by our research interests. Data collection left to only one person may be a formidable task. We must determine the amount of resources available to decide what data collection method is most realistic. Regardless of the study size, we must attempt to establish clear roles and boundaries with those involved in the data collection process.

The clearer our research study is articulated, the less difficulty there will be in moving through all the phases of the study. In particular, it is critical to identify who will and will not be involved in the data collection process. To further avoid mix-up and complications, specific tasks must be spelled out for all persons involved in our study. Where will the data collection forms be stored? Who will administer them? How will their completion be monitored?

In many social work research studies, front-line social workers are involved in data collection activities as part of their day-to-day activities. They typically gather intake and referral data, write assessment notes, and even use standardized questionnaires as part of their assessments. Data collection in programs can easily be designed to serve the dual purposes of research *and* clinical inquiry. Thus, it is important to establish data collection protocols to avoid problems of biased data. As mentioned, everyone in a research study must agree *when* data will be collected, *where*, and in *what* manner. Agreement is more likely to occur when we have fully informed and involved everyone participating in our study.

Evaluation

The process of selecting a chosen data collection method is not complete without evaluating it. Evaluation occurs at two levels. First, the strengths and weakness of a data collection method and data source are evaluated, given the research context in which our study takes place. If, for example, data are gathered about clients' presenting problems by a referring social worker, it must be acknowledged that the obtained data offer a limited (or restricted) point of view about the clients' problems. The strength of this approach may be that it was the only means for collecting the data. Such strengths and weakness are summarized in the decision-making grid presented in Table 20.1.

A second level of evaluation is monitoring the implementation of the data collection process itself. When data are gathered using several methods (or from several sources), it is beneficial to develop a checklist of what data have been collected for each research participant. Developing a strategy for monitoring the data collection process is especially important when the data must be collected in a timely fashion. If pretest data are needed before a client enters a treatment program, for example, the data collection must be complete before admission occurs. Once the client has entered the program, opportunity to collect pretest data is lost forever.

Another strategy for monitoring evaluation is to keep a journal of the data collection process. The journal records any questions or queries that arise in the data gathering phase. We may find, for example, that several research participants completing a questionnaire have difficulty understanding one particular question. In addition, sometimes research participants have poor reading skills and require assistance with completion of some self-report standardized questionnaires. Documenting these idiosyncratic incidents accumulates important information by which to comment on our data's validity and reliability.

SUMMARY

There are many possible data collection methods and data sources that can be used in any given research situation. We must weigh the pros and cons of both within the context of a particular research study to arrive at the best data collection method and data source. This process involves both conceptual and practical considerations. On a conceptual level, we review the phases of the research process through a "data collection and data source lens." We think about how various data collection methods and data sources fit with each phase of the research process. At the same time, considering the different data collection methods and data sources helps us to gain a fuller understanding of our problem area and research question.

On a practical level, there are many considerations that need to be addressed when deciding upon the best data collection method(s) and data source(s) for a particular study. Factors such as worker cooperation, available resources, and consequences for the clients all influence our final choices. We can map out such decision-making criteria by using a grid system, by which all criteria to be considered are listed and evaluated for each potential data collection method and data source.

REFERENCES AND FURTHER READINGS

SIMON, J. (1969). *Basic research methods in social science*. New York: Random House.

THOMAS, E.J. (1975). Uses of research methods in interpersonal practice. In N.A. Polansky (Ed.), *Social work research: Methods for the helping professionals* (rev. ed., pp. 254-283). Chicago: University of Chicago Press.

TOSELAND, R.W. (1993). Choosing a data collection method. In R.M. Grinnell, Jr. (Ed.), *Social work research and evaluation* (4th ed., pp. 317-328). Itasca, IL: F.E. Peacock.

DATA ANALYSIS

Leslie M. Tutty
Richard M. Grinnell, Jr.
Margaret Williams

Chapter **21**

Quantitative Data Analysis

A FTER QUANTITATIVE DATA ARE COLLECTED they need to be analyzed—the topic of this chapter. To be honest, a thorough understanding of quantitative statistical methods is far beyond the scope of this book. Such comprehension necessitates more in-depth study, through taking one or more statistics courses. Instead, we briefly describe a select group of basic statistical analytical methods that are used frequently in many quantitative *and* qualitative social work research studies. Our emphasis is not on providing and calculating formulas, but rather on helping the reader to understand the underlying rationale for their use.

We present two basic groups of statistical procedures. The first group is called *descriptive statistics*, which simply describe and summarize one or more variables for a sample or population. They provide information about only the group included in the study. The second group of statistical procedures is called *inferential statistics*, which determine if we can generalize findings derived from a sample to the population from which the sample was drawn. In other words, knowing what we know about a particular sample, can we infer that the rest of the population is similar to the sample that we have studied? Before we can answer this question, however, we need to know the level of measurement for each variable being analyzed. Let us now turn to a brief discussion of the four different levels of measurement that a variable can take.

LEVELS OF MEASUREMENT

The specific statistic(s) used to analyze the data collected is dependent on the type of data that are gathered. The characteristics or qualities that describe a variable are known as its *attributes*. The variable *gender*, for example, has only two characteristics or attributes—*male* and *female*—since gender in humans is limited to male and female, and there are no other possible categories or ways of describing gender. The variable *ethnicity* has a number of possible categories: *African American, Native American, Asian, Hispanic American,* and *Caucasian* are just five examples of the many attributes of the variable ethnicity. A point to note here is that the attributes of gender differ in kind from one another—male is different from female—and, in the same way, the attributes of ethnicity are also different from one another.

Now consider the variable *income*. Income can only be described in terms of amounts of money: $15,000 per year, $288.46 per week, and so forth. In whatever terms a person's income is actually described, it still comes down to a number. Since every number has its own category, as we mentioned before, the variable income can generate as many categories as there are numbers, up to the number covering the research participant who earns the most. These numbers are all attributes of income and they are all different, but they are not different in *kind*, as male and female are, or Native American and Hispanic; they are only different in *quantity*.

In other words, the attributes of income differ in that they represent more or less of the same thing, whereas the attributes of gender differ in that they represent different kinds of things. Income will, therefore, be measured in a different way from gender. When we come to measure income, we will be looking for categories that are lower or higher than each other; when we come to measure gender, we will be looking for categories that are different in kind from each other.

Mathematically, there is not much we can do with categories that are different in kind. We cannot subtract Hispanics from Caucasians, for example, whereas we can quite easily subtract one person's annual income from another and come up with a meaningful difference. As far as mathematical computations are concerned, we are obliged to work at a lower level of complexity when we measure variables like ethnicity than when we measure variables like income. Depending on the nature of their attributes, all variables can be measured at one (or more) of four measurement levels: (1) nominal, (2) ordinal, (3) interval, or (4) ratio.

Nominal Measurement

Nominal measurement is the lowest level of measurement and is used to measure variables whose attributes are different in kind. As we have seen, gender is one variable measured at a nominal level, and ethnicity is another. *Place of birth* is a third, since "born in California," for example, is different from "born in Chicago," and we cannot add "born in California" to "born in Chicago," or subtract them or divide them, or do anything statistically interesting with them at all.

Ordinal Measurement

Ordinal measurement is a higher level of measurement than nominal and is used to measure those variables whose attributes can be rank ordered: for example, socioeconomic status, sexism, racism, client satisfaction, and the like. If we intend to measure *client satisfaction*, we must first develop a list of all the possible attributes of client satisfaction: that is, we must think of all the possible categories into which answers about client satisfaction might be placed. Some clients will be *very satisfied*—one category, at the high end of the satisfaction continuum; some will be *not at all satisfied*—a separate category, at the low end of the continuum; and others will be *generally satisfied, moderately satisfied*, or *somewhat satisfied*—three more categories, at differing points on the continuum, as illustrated in Figure 21.1.

Figure 21.1 is a five-point scale, anchored at all five points with a brief description of the degree of satisfaction represented by the point. Of course, we may choose to express the anchors in different words, substituting *extremely satisfied* for *very satisfied*, or *fairly satisfied* for *generally satisfied*. We may select a three-point scale instead, limiting the choices to *very satisfied, moderately satisfied,* and *not at all satisfied*; or we may even use a ten-point scale if we believe that our respondents will be able to rate their satisfaction with that degree of accuracy.

Whichever particular method is selected, some sort of scale is the only measurement option available because there is no other way to categorize client satisfaction except in terms of more satisfaction or less satisfaction. As we did with nominal measurement, we might assign numbers to each of the points on the scale. If we used the five-point scale in Figure 21.1, we might assign a 5 to

| Very satisfied | Generally satisfied | Moderately satisfied | Somewhat satisfied | Not at all satisfied |

FIGURE 21.1   SCALE TO MEASURE CLIENT SATISFACTION

very satisfied, a 4 to *generally satisfied*, a 3 to *moderately satisfied*, a 2 to *somewhat satisfied*, and a 1 to *not at all satisfied*.

Here, the numbers do have some mathematical meaning. Five (*very satisfied*) is in fact better than 4 (*generally satisfied*), 4 is better than 3, 3 is better than 2, and 2 is better than 1. The numbers, however, say nothing about *how much better* any category is than any other. We cannot assume that the difference in satisfaction between *very* and *generally* is the same as the difference between *generally* and *moderately*. In short, we cannot assume that the intervals between the anchored points on the scale are all the same length. Most definitely, we cannot assume that a client who rates a service at 4 (*generally satisfied*) is twice as satisfied as a client who rates the service at 2 (*somewhat satisfied*).

In fact, we cannot attempt any mathematical manipulation at all. We cannot add the numbers 1, 2, 3, 4, and 5, nor can we subtract, multiply, or divide them. As its name might suggest, all we can know from ordinal measurement is the order of the categories.

Interval Measurement

Some variables, such as client satisfaction, have attributes that can be rank-ordered—from *very satisfied* to *not at all satisfied*, as we have just discussed. As we saw, however, these attributes cannot be assumed to be the same distance apart if they are placed on a scale; and, in any case, the distance they are apart has no real meaning. No one can measure the distance between *very satisfied* and *moderately satisfied*; we only know that the one is better than the other.

Conversely, for some variables, the distance, or interval, separating their attributes *does* have meaning, and these variables can be measured at the interval level. An example in physical science would is the Fahrenheit or Celsius temperature scales. The difference between 80 degrees and 90 degrees is the same as the difference between 40 and 50 degrees. Eighty degrees is not twice as hot as 40 degrees; nor does zero degrees mean no heat at all.

In social work, interval measures are most commonly used in connection with standardized measuring instruments, as presented in Chapter 8. When we look at a standardized intelligence test, for example, we can say that the difference between IQ scores of 100 and 110 is the same as the difference between IQ scores of 95 and 105, based on the scores obtained by the many thousands of people who have taken the test over the years. As with the temperature scales mentioned above, a person with an IQ score of 120 is not twice as intelligent as a person with a score of 60: nor does a score of 0 mean no intelligence at all.

Ratio Measurement

The highest level of measurement, ratio measurement, is used to measure variables whose attributes are based on a true zero point. It may not be possible to have zero intelligence, but it is certainly possible to have zero children or zero money. Whenever a question about a particular variable might elicit the answer "none" or "never," that variable can be measured at the ratio level. The question, "How many times have you seen your social worker?" might be answered, "Never." Other variables commonly measured at the ratio level include length of residence in a given place, age, number of times married, number of organizations belonged to, number of antisocial behaviors, number of case reviews, number of training sessions, number of supervisory meetings, and so forth.

With a ratio level of measurement we can meaningfully interpret the comparison between two scores. A person who is 40 years of age, for example, is twice as old as a person who is 20 and half as old as a person who is 80. Children aged 2 and 5, respectively, are the same distance apart as children aged 6 and 9. Data resulting from ratio measurement can be added, subtracted, multiplied, and divided. Averages can be calculated and other statistical analyses can be performed.

It is useful to note that, while some variables *can* be measured at a higher level, they may not need to be. The variable *income*, for example, can be measured at a ratio level because it is possible to have a zero income but, for the purposes of a particular study, we may not need to know the actual incomes of our research participants, only the range within which their incomes fall. A person who is asked how much he or she earns may be reluctant to give a figure ("mind your own business" is a perfectly legitimate response) but may not object to checking one of a number of income categories, choosing, for example, between:

1. less than $5,000 per year
2. $5,001 to $15,000 per year
3. $15,001 to $25,000 per year
4. $25,001 to $35,000 per year
5. more than $35,000 per year

Categorizing income in this way reduces the measurement from the ratio level to the ordinal level. It will now be possible to know only that a person checking Category 1 earns less than a person checking Category 2, and so on. While we will not know *how much* less or more one person earns than another and we will not be able to perform statistical tasks such as calculating average incomes, we will be able to say, for example, that 50 percent of our sample falls into Category 1, 30 percent into Category 2, 15 percent into Category 3, and 5 percent into Category 4. If we are conducting a study to see how many people fall in each income range, this may be all we need to know.

In the same way, we might not want to know the actual ages of our sample, only the range in which they fall. For some studies, it might be enough to measure age at a nominal level—to inquire, for example, whether people were born during the depression, or whether they were born before or after 1990. In short, when studying variables that can be measured at any level, the measurement level chosen depends on what kind of data are needed, and this in turn is determined by why the data are needed, which in turn is determined by our research question.

COMPUTER APPLICATIONS

The use of computers has revolutionized the analysis of quantitative and qualitative data. Where previous generations of researchers had to rely on hand-cranked adding machines to calculate every small step in a data analysis, today we can enter raw scores into a personal computer, and, with few complications, direct the computer program to execute just about any statistical test imaginable. Seconds later, the results are available. While the process is truly miraculous, the risk is that, even though we have conducted the correct statistical analysis, we may not understand what the results mean, a factor that will almost certainly affect how we interpret the data.

We can code data from all four levels of measurement into a computer for any given data analysis. The coding of nominal data is perhaps the most complex, because we have to create categories that correspond with certain possible responses for a variable. One type of nominal level data that is often gathered from research participants is *place of birth*. If, for the purposes of our study, we are interested in whether our research participants were born in either the United States or Canada, we would assign only three categories to *place of birth*:

1. United States
2. Canada
9. Other

The *other* category appears routinely at the end of lists of categories and acts as a catch-all, to cover any category that may have been omitted.

When entering nominal level data into a computer, because we do not want to enter *Canada* every time the response on the questionnaire is Canada, we may assign it the code number 1, so that all we have to enter is 1. Similarly, the United States may be assigned the number 2, and "other" may be assigned the number 9. These numbers have no mathematical meaning: We are not saying that Canada is better than the United States because it comes first, or that the United States is twice as good as Canada because the number assigned to it is twice as high. We are merely using numbers as a shorthand device to record *qualitative* differences: differences in *kind*, not in amount.

Most coding for ordinal, interval, and ratio level data is simply a matter of entering the final score, or number, from the measuring instrument that was used to measure the variable directly into the computer. If a person scored a 45 on a standardized measuring instrument, for example, the number 45 would be entered into the computer.

Although almost all data entered into computers are in the form of numbers, we need to know at what level of measurement the data exist, so that we can choose the appropriate statistic(s) to describe and compare the variables. Now that we know how to measure variables at four different measurement levels, let us turn to the first group of statistics that can be helpful for the analyses of data—descriptive statistics.

DESCRIPTIVE STATISTICS

Descriptive statistics are commonly used in most quantitative and qualitative research studies. They describe and summarize a variable(s) of interest and portray how that particular variable is distributed in the sample, or population. Before looking at descriptive statistics, however, let us examine a social work research example that will be used throughout this chapter.

Thea Black is a social worker who works in a treatment foster care program. Her program focuses on children who have behavioral problems who are placed with "treatment" foster care parents. These parents are supposed to have parenting skills that will help them provide the children with the special needs they present. Thus, Thea's program also teaches parenting skills to these treatment foster care parents. She assumes that newly recruited foster parents are not likely to know much about parenting children who have behavioral problems. Therefore, she believes that they would benefit from a training program that teaches these skills in order to help them to deal effectively with the special needs of these children who will soon be living with them.

Thea hopes that her parenting skills training program will increase the knowledge about parental management skills for the parents who attend. She assumes that, with such training, the foster parents would be in a better position to support and provide clear limits for their foster children.

After offering the training program for several months, Thea became curious about whether the foster care providers who attended the program were, indeed, lacking in knowledge of parental management skills as she first believed (her tentative hypothesis). She was fortunate to find a valid and reliable standardized instrument that measures the knowledge of such parenting skills, the Parenting Skills Scale (*PSS*). Thea decided to find out for herself how much the newly recruited parents knew about parenting skills—clearly a descriptive research question.

At the beginning of one of her training sessions (before they were exposed to her skills training program), she handed out the *PSS*, asking the 20 individuals in attendance to complete it and also to include data about their gender, years of education, and whether they had ever participated in a parenting skills training program before. All of these three variables could be potentially extraneous ones that might influence the level of knowledge of parenting skills of the 20 participants.

For each foster care parent, Thea calculated the *PSS* score, called a *raw score* because it has not been sorted or analyzed in any way. The total score possible

TABLE 21.1 DATA COLLECTED FOR FOUR VARIABLES FROM FOSTER CARE PROVIDERS

Number	PSS Score	Gender	Previous Training	Years of Education
01	95	male	no	12
02	93	female	yes	15
03	93	male	no	08
04	93	female	no	12
05	90	male	yes	12
06	90	female	no	12
07	84	male	no	14
08	84	female	no	18
09	82	male	no	10
10	82	female	no	12
11	80	male	no	12
12	80	female	no	11
13	79	male	no	12
14	79	female	yes	12
15	79	female	no	16
16	79	male	no	12
17	79	female	no	11
18	72	female	no	14
19	71	male	no	15
20	55	female	yes	12

on the *PSS* is 100, with higher scores indicating greater knowledge of parenting skills. The scores for the *PSS* scale, as well as the other data collected from the 20 parents, are listed in Table 21.1.

At this point, Thea stopped to consider how she could best utilize the data that she had collected. She had data at three different levels of measurement. At the nominal level, Thea had collected data on gender (3rd column), and whether the parents had any previous parenting skills training (4th column). Each of these variables can be categorized into two responses.

The scores on the *PSS* (2nd column) are ordinal because, although the data are sequenced from highest to lowest, the differences between units cannot be placed on an equally spaced continuum. Nevertheless, many measures in the social sciences are treated as if they are at an interval level, even though equal distances between scale points cannot be proved. This assumption is important because it allows for the use of inferential statistics on such data

Finally, the data on years of formal education (5th column) that were collected by Thea are clearly at the ratio level of measurement, because there are equally distributed points and the scale has an absolute zero.

TABLE 21.2   FREQUENCY
DISTRIBUTION

PSS Score	Absolute Frequency
95	1
93	3
90	2
84	2
82	2
80	2
79	5
72	1
71	1
55	1

In sum, it seemed to Thea that the data could be used in at least two ways. First, the data collected about each variable could be described to provide a picture of the characteristics of the group of foster care parents. This would call for descriptive statistics. Secondly, she might look for relationships between some of the variables about which she had collected data, procedures that would utilize inferential statistics. For now let us begin by looking at how the first type of descriptive statistic can be utilized with Thea's data set.

Frequency Distributions

One of the simplest procedures that Thea can employ is to develop a frequency distribution of her data. Constructing a frequency distribution involves counting the occurrences of each value, or category, of the variable and ordering them in some fashion. This *absolute* or *simple frequency distribution* allows us to see quickly how certain values of a variable are distributed in our sample or population.

The *mode*, or the most commonly occurring score, can be easily spotted in a simple frequency distribution (see Table 21.2). In this example, the mode is 79, a score obtained by five parents on the *PSS* scale. The highest and the lowest score are also quickly identifiable. The top score was 95, while the foster care parent who performed the least well on the *PSS* scored 55.

There are several other ways to present frequency data. A commonly used method that can be easily integrated into a simple frequency distribution table is the *cumulative frequency distribution*, shown in Table 21.3.

In Thea's data set, the highest *PSS* score, 95, was obtained by only one individual. The group of individuals who scored 93 or above on the *PSS* measure includes four foster care parents. If we want to know how many scored 80 or

TABLE 21.3   CUMULATIVE FREQUENCY AND
PERCENTAGE DISTRIBUTIONS OF
PARENTAL SKILL SCORES

PSS Score	Absolute Frequency	Cumulative Frequency	Percentage Distribution
95	1	1	5
93	3	4	15
90	2	6	10
84	2	8	10
82	2	10	10
80	2	12	10
79	5	17	25
72	1	18	5
71	1	19	5
55	1	20	5
Totals...	20		100

above, if we look at the number across from 80 in the cumulative frequency column, we can quickly see that 12 of the parents scored 80 or better.

Other tables utilize percentages rather than frequencies, sometimes referred to as *percentage distributions*, shown in the right-hand column in Table 21.3. Each of these numbers represents the percentage of participants who obtained each *PSS* value. Five individuals, for example, scored 79 on the *PSS*. Since there was a total of 20 foster care parents, 5 out of the 20, or one-quarter of the total, obtained a score of 79. This corresponds to 25 percent of the participants.

Finally, *grouped frequency distributions* are used to simplify a table by grouping the variable into equal-sized ranges, as is shown in Table 21.4. Both absolute and cumulative frequencies and percentages can also be displayed using this format. Each is calculated in the same way that was previously described for nongrouped data, and the interpretation is identical.

Looking at the absolute frequency column, for example, we can quickly identify the fact that seven of the foster care parents scored in the 70–79 range on the *PSS*. By looking at the cumulative frequency column, we can see that 12 of 20 parents scored 80 or better on the *PSS*. Further, from the absolute percentage column, it is clear that 30 percent of the foster parents scored in the 80–89 range on the knowledge of parenting skills scale. Only one parent, or 5 percent of the group, had significant problems with the *PSS*, scoring in the 50–59 range.

Note that each of the other variables in Thea's data set could also be displayed in frequency distributions. Displaying years of education in a frequency distribution, for example, would provide a snapshot of how this variable is distributed in Thea's sample of foster care parents. With two category nominal variables, such as gender (male, female) and previous parent skills training (yes,

TABLE 21.4 GROUPED FREQUENCY DISTRIBUTION OF PARENTAL SKILL SCORES

PSS Scores	Absolute Frequency	Cumulative Frequency	Absolute Percentage
90 – 100	6	6	30
80 – 89	6	12	30
70 – 79	7	19	35
60 – 69	0	19	0
50 – 59	1	20	5

no), however, cumulative frequencies become less meaningful and the data are better described as percentages. Thea noted that 55 percent of the foster care parents who attended the training workshop were women (obviously the other 45 percent were men) and that 20 percent of the parents had already received some form of parenting skills training (while a further 80 percent had not been trained).

Measures of Central Tendency

We can also display the values obtained on the *PSS* in the form of a graph. A *frequency polygon* is one of the simplest ways of charting frequencies. The graph in Figure 21.2 displays the data that we had previously put in Table 21.2. The *PSS* score is plotted in terms of how many of the foster care parents obtained each score.

As can be seen from Figure 21.2, most of the scores fall between 79 and 93. The one extremely low score of 55 is also quickly noticeable in such a graph, because it is so far removed from the rest of the values.

A frequency polygon allows us to make a quick analysis of how closely the distribution fits the shape of a normal curve. A *normal curve*, also known as a *bell-shaped distribution* or a *normal distribution*, is a frequency polygon in which the greatest number of responses fall in the middle of the distribution and fewer scores appear at the extremes of either very high or very low scores (see Figure 21.3).

Many variables in the social sciences are assumed to be distributed in the shape of a normal curve. Low intelligence, for example, is thought to be relatively rare as compared to the number of individuals with average intelligence. On the other end of the continuum, extremely gifted individuals are also relatively uncommon.

Of course, not all variables are distributed in the shape of a normal curve.

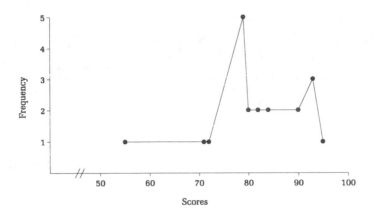

FIGURE 21.2   FREQUENCY POLYGON OF
                   PARENTAL SKILL SCORES (FROM
                   TABLE 21.2)

Some are such that a large number of people do very well (as Thea found in her sample of foster care parents and their parenting skill levels). Other variables, such as juggling ability, for example, would be charted showing a fairly substantial number of people performing poorly. Frequency distributions of still other variables would show that some people do well, and some people do poorly, but not many fall in between. What is important to remember about distributions is that, although all different sorts are possible, most statistical procedures assume that there is a normal distribution of the variable in question in the population.

When looking at how variables are distributed in samples and populations it is common to use measures of *central tendency*, such as the mode, median, and mean, which help us to identify where the typical or the average score can be found. These measures are utilized so often because, not only do they provide a useful summary of the data, they also provide a common denominator for comparing groups to each other.

Mode

As mentioned earlier, the mode is the score, or value, that occurs the most often—the value with the highest frequency. In Thea's data set of parental skills scores the mode is 79, with five foster care parents obtaining this value. The mode is particularly useful for nominal level data. Knowing what score occurred the most often, however, provides little information about the other scores and how they are distributed in the sample or population. Because the mode is the least precise of all the measures of central tendency, the median and the mean

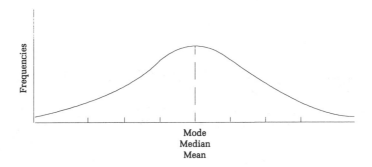

FIGURE 21.3   THE NORMAL DISTRIBUTION

are better descriptors of ordinal level data and above. We now turn our attention to the second measure of central tendency, the median.

Median

The median is the score that divides a distribution into two equal parts or portions. In order to do this, we must rank-order the scores, so at least an ordinal level of measurement is required. In Thea's sample of 20 *PSS* scores, the median would be the score above which the top ten scores lie and below which the bottom ten fall. As can be seen in Table 21.2, the top ten scores finish at 82, and the bottom ten scores start at 80. In this example, the median is 81, since it falls between 82 and 80.

Mean

The mean is the most sophisticated measure of central tendency and is useful for interval or ratio levels of measurement. It is also one of the most commonly utilized statistics. A mean is calculated by summing the individual values and dividing by the total number of values. The mean of Thea's sample is 95 + 93 + 93 + 93 + 90 + 90 + ... 72 + 71 + 55/20 = 81.95. In this example, the obtained mean of 82 (we rounded off for the sake of clarity) is larger than the mode of 79 or the median of 81.

The mean is one of the previously mentioned statistical procedures that assumes that a variable will be distributed normally throughout a population. If this is not an accurate assumption, then the median might be a better descriptor.

The mean is also best used with relatively large sample sizes where extreme scores (such as the lowest score of 55 in Thea's sample) have less influence.

Measures of Variability

While measures of central tendency provide valuable information about a set of scores, we are also interested in knowing how the scores scatter themselves around the center. A mean does not give a sense of how widely distributed the scores may be: This is provided by measures of variability such as the range and the standard deviation.

Range

The range is simply the distance between the minimum and the maximum score. The larger the range, the greater the amount of variation of scores in the distribution. The range is calculated by subtracting the lowest score from the highest. In Thea's sample, the range is 40 (95 – 55).

The range assumes equal intervals and so should be used only with interval or ratio level data. It is, like the mean, sensitive to deviant values, because it depends on only the two extreme scores. We could have a group of four scores ranging from 10 to 20: 10, 14, 19, and 20, for example. The range of this sample would be 10 (20 – 10). If one additional score that was substantially different from the first set of four scores was included, this would change the range dramatically. In this example, if a fifth score of 45 was added, the range of the sample would become 35 (45 – 10), a number that would suggest quite a different picture of the variability of the scores.

Standard Deviation

The standard deviation is the most well-used indicator of dispersion. It provides a picture of how the scores distribute themselves around the mean. Used in combination with the mean, the standard deviation provides a great deal of information about the sample or population, without our ever needing to see the raw scores. In a normal distribution of scores, described previously, there are six standard deviations: three below the mean and three above, as is shown in Figure 21.4.

In this perfect model we always know that 34.13 percent of the scores of the sample fall within one standard deviation above the mean, and another 34.13 percent fall within one standard deviation below the mean. Thus, a total of 68.26 percent, or about two-thirds of the scores, is between +1 standard deviation and –1 standard deviation from the mean. This leaves almost one-third of the scores to fall farther away from the mean, with 15.87 percent (50% – 34.13%) above +1

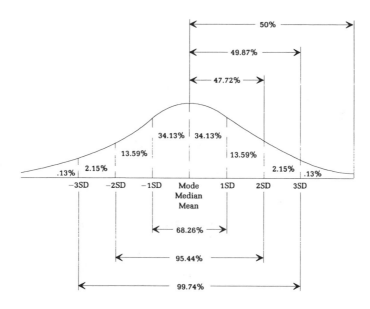

FIGURE 21.4   PROPORTIONS OF THE
NORMAL CURVE

standard deviation, and 15.87 percent (50% – 34.13%) below –1 standard deviation. In total, when looking at the proportion of scores that fall between +2 and –2 standard deviations, 95.44 percent of scores can be expected to be found within these parameters. Furthermore, 99.74 percent of the scores fall between +3 standard deviations and –3 standard deviations about the mean. Thus, finding scores that fall beyond 3 standard deviations above and below the mean should be a rare occurrence.

The standard deviation has the advantage, like the mean, of taking all values into consideration in its computation. Also similar to the mean, it is utilized with interval or ratio levels of measurement and assumes a normal distribution of scores.

Several different samples of scores could have the same mean, but the variation around the mean, as provided by the standard deviation, could be quite different, as is shown in Figure 21.5a. Two different distributions could have unequal means and equal standard deviations, as in Figure 21.5b, or unequal means and unequal standard deviations, as in Figure 21.5c.

The standard deviation of the scores of Thea's foster care parents was calculated to be 10. Again, assuming that the variable of knowledge about parenting skills is normally distributed in the population of foster care parents, the results of the *PSS* scores from the sample of parents about whom we are making inferences can be shown in a distribution like Figure 21.6.

As can also be seen in Figure 21.6, the score that would include 2 standard

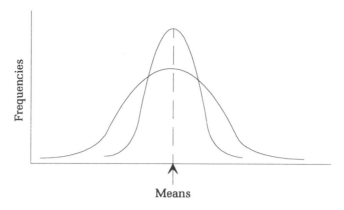

(*a*)   Equal means, unequal standard deviations

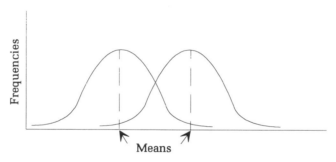

(*b*)   Unequal means, equal standard deviations

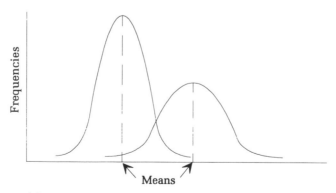

(*c*)   Unequal means, unequal standard deviations

FIGURE 21.5   VARIATIONS IN NORMAL
                       DISTRIBUTIONS

deviations, 102, is beyond the total possible score of 100 on the test. This is because the distribution of the scores in Thea's sample of parents does not entirely fit a normal distribution. The one extremely low score of 55 (see Table 21.1) obtained by one foster care parent would have affected the mean, as well as the standard deviation.

INFERENTIAL STATISTICS

The goal of inferential statistical tests is to rule out chance as the explanation for finding either associations between variables or differences between variables in our samples. Since we are rarely able to study an entire population, we are almost always dealing with samples drawn from that population. The danger is that we might make conclusions about a particular population based on a sample that is uncharacteristic of the population it is supposed to represent.

For example, perhaps the group of foster parents in Thea's training session happened to have an unusually high level of knowledge of parenting skills. If she assumed that all the rest of the foster parents that she might train in the future were as knowledgeable, she would be overestimating their knowledge, a factor that could have a negative impact on the way she conducts her training program.

To counteract the possibility that the sample is uncharacteristic of the general population, statistical tests take a conservative position as to whether or not we can conclude that there are relationships between the variables within our sample. The guidelines to indicate the likelihood that we have, indeed, found a relationship or difference that fits the population of interest are called *probability levels*.

The convention in most social science research is that variables are significantly associated or groups are significantly different if we are relatively certain that in 19 samples out of 20 (or 95 times out of 100) from a particular population, we would find the same relationship. This corresponds to a probability level of

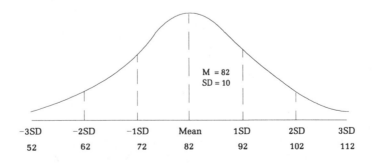

-3SD	-2SD	-1SD	Mean	1SD	2SD	3SD
52	62	72	82	92	102	112

M = 82
SD = 10

FIGURE 21.6   DISTRIBUTION OF PARENTAL SKILL SCORES

.05, written as (p < .05). Probability levels are usually provided along with the results of the statistical test to demonstrate how confident we are that the results actually indicate statistically significant differences. If a probability level is greater than .05 (e.g., .06, .10), this indicates that we did not find a statistically significant difference.

Statistics That Determine Associations

There are many statistics that can determine if there is an association between two variables. We will briefly discuss two: chi-square and correlation.

Chi-Square

The *chi-square test* requires measurements of variables at only the nominal or ordinal level. Thus, it is very useful since much data in social work are gathered at these two levels of measurement. In general, the chi-square test looks at whether specific values of one variable tend to be associated with specific values of another. In short, we use it to determine if two variables are related. It cannot be used to determine if one variable *caused* another, however.

In thinking about the foster care parents who were in her training program, Thea was aware that women are more typically responsible for caring for their own children than men. Even if they are not mothers themselves, they are often in professions such as teaching and social work where they are caretakers. Thus, she wondered whether there might be a relationship between having had previous training in parenting skills and gender, such that women were less likely to have taken such training since they already felt confident in their knowledge of parenting skills. As a result, her one-tailed hypothesis was that fewer women than men would have previously taken parenting skills training courses. Thea could examine this possibility with her 20 foster care parents using a chi-square test.

In terms of gender, Thea had data from the nine (45%) men and 11 (55%) women. Of the total group, four (20%) had previous training in foster care training, while 16 (80%) had not. As shown in Table 21.5, the first task was for Thea to count the number of men and women who had previous training and the number of men and women who did not have previous training. She put these data in one of the four categories in Table 21.5. The actual numbers are called *observed frequencies*. It is helpful to transform these raw data into percentages, making comparisons between categories much easier.

We can, however, still not tell simply by looking at the observed frequencies whether there is a statistically significant relationship between gender (male or female) and previous training (yes or no). To do this, the next step is to look at how much the observed frequencies differ from what we would expect to see if, in fact, if there was no relationship. These are called *expected frequencies*.

TABLE 21.5 Frequencies (and Percentages) of Gender by Previous Training (from Table 21.1)

| | Previous Training | | |
Gender	Yes	No	Totals
Male	1 (11)	8 (89)	9
Female	3 (27)	8 (73)	11
Totals	4 (20)	16 (80)	20

Without going through all the calculations, the chi-square table would now look like Table 21.6 for Thea's data set.

Since the probability level of the obtained chi-square value in Table 21.6 is greater than .05, Thea did not find any statistical relationship between gender and previous training in parenting skills. Thus, statistically speaking, men were no more likely than women to have received previous training in parenting skills; her research hypothesis was not supported by the data.

Correlation

Tests of correlation investigate the strength of the relationship between two variables. As with the chi-square test, correlation cannot be used to imply causation, only association. Correlation is applicable to data at the interval and ratio levels of measurement. Correlational values are always decimalized numbers, never exceeding ±1.00.

The size of the obtained correlation value indicates the strength of the association, or relationship, between the two variables. The closer a correlation is to zero, the less likely it is that a relationship exists between the two variables. The plus and minus signs indicate the direction of the relationship. Both high positive (close to +1.00) or high negative numbers (close to –1.00) signify strong relationships.

In positive correlations, though, the scores vary similarly, either increasing or decreasing. Thus, as parenting skills increase, so does self-esteem, for examle. A negative correlation, in contrast, simply means that as one variable increases the other decreases. An example would be that, as parenting skills increase, the stresses experienced by foster parents decrease.

Thea may wonder whether there is a relationship between the foster parents' years of education and score on the *PSS* knowledge test. She might reason that the more years of education completed, the more likely the parents would have greater knowledge about parenting skills. To investigate the one-tailed hypothesis that years of education is positively related to knowledge of parenting skills,

TABLE 21.6   CHI-SQUARE TABLE FOR GENDER BY PREVIOUS TRAINING (FROM TABLE 21.5)

Gender	Previous Training	No Previous Training
Male	$O = 1$ $E = 1.8$	$O = 8$ $E = 7.2$
Female	$O = 3$ $E = 2.2$	$O = 8$ $E = 8.8$

$\chi^2 = .8$, $df = 1$, $p > .05$
O = observed frequencies (from Table 21.5)
E = expected frequencies

Thea can correlate the *PSS* scores with each person's number of years of formal education using one of the most common correlational tests, Pearson's *r*.

The obtained correlation between *PSS* score and years of education in this example is $r = -.10$ ($p > .05$). It was in the opposite direction of what she predicted. This negative correlation is close to zero, and its probability level is greater than .05. Thus, in Thea's sample, the parents' *PSS* scores are not related to their educational levels. If the resulting correlation coefficient (*r*) had been positive and statistically significant ($p < .05$), it would have indicated that as the knowledge levels of the parents increased so would their years of formal education. If the correlation coefficient had been statistically significant but negative, this would be interpreted as showing that as years of formal education increased, knowledge scores decreased.

If a correlational analysis is misinterpreted, it is likely to be the case that the researcher implied causation rather than simply identifying an association between the two variables. If Thea were to have found a statistically significant positive correlation between knowledge and education levels and had explained this to mean than the high knowledge scores were a result of higher education levels, she would have interpreted the statistic incorrectly.

Statistics That Determine Differences

Two commonly used statistical procedures, *t*-tests and analysis of variance (ANOVA), examine the means and variances of two or more separate groups of scores to determine if they are statistically different from one another. *T*-tests are used with only two groups of scores, whereas ANOVA is used when there are more than two groups. Both are characterized by having a dependent variable at the interval or ratio level of measurement, and an independent, or grouping, variable at either the nominal or ordinal level of measurement. Several assumptions underlie the use of both *t*-tests and ANOVA.

First, it is assumed that the dependent variable is normally distributed in the population from which the samples were drawn. Second, it is assumed that the variance of the scores of the dependent variable in the different groups is roughly the same. This assumption is called *homogeneity of variance*. Third, it is assumed that the samples are randomly drawn from the population.

Nevertheless, as mentioned in Chapter 11 on group research designs, it is a common occurrence in social work that we can neither randomly select nor randomly assign individuals to either the experimental or the control group. In many cases this is because we are dealing with already preformed groups, such as Thea's foster care parents.

Breaking the assumption of randomization, however, presents a serious drawback to the interpretation of the research findings that must be noted in the limitations and the interpretations section of the final research report. One possible difficulty that might result from nonrandomization is that the sample may be uncharacteristic of the larger population in some manner. It is important, therefore, that the results not be used inferentially; that is, the findings must not be generalized to the general population. The design of the research study is, thus, reduced to an exploratory or descriptive level, being relevant to only those individuals included in the sample.

Dependent T-*Tests*

Dependent *t*-tests are used to compare two groups of scores from the same individuals. The most frequent example in social work research is looking at how a group of individuals change from before they receive a social work intervention (pre) to afterwards (post). Thea may have decided that, while knowing the knowledge levels of the foster care parents before receiving training was interesting, it did not give her any idea whether her program helped the parents to improve their skill levels. In other words her research question became: "After being involved in the program, did parents know more about parenting skills than before they started?" Her hypothesis was that knowledge of parenting skills would improve after participation in her training program.

Thea managed to contact all of the foster care parents in the original group (Group A) one week after they had graduated from the program and asked them to fill out the *PSS* knowledge questionnaire once again. Since it was the same group of people who were responding twice to the same questionnaire, the dependent *t*-test was appropriate. The research design is as follows:

$$O_1 \quad X \quad O_2$$

Where:

O_1 = First administration of the *PSS*, the dependent variable
X = The skills training program, the independent variable
O_2 = Second administration of the *PSS*, the dependent variable

Using the same set of scores collected by Thea previously as the pretest, the mean *PSS* was 82, with a standard deviation of 10. The mean score of the foster care parents after they completed the program was calculated as 86, with a standard deviation of 8.

A *t*-value of 3.9 was obtained, significant at the .05 level, indicating that the levels of parenting skills significantly increased after the foster care parents participated in the skill training program.

The results suggest that the average parenting skills of this particular group of foster care parents significantly improved (from 82 to 86) after they had participated in Thea's program.

Independent T-Tests

Independent *t*-tests are used for two groups of scores that have no relationship to each other. If Thea had *PSS* scores from one group of foster care parents and then collected more *PSS* scores from a second group of foster care parents, for example, these two groups would be considered independent, and the independent *t*-test would be the appropriate statistical analysis to determine if there was a statistically significant difference between the means of the two groups' *PSS* scores. This design could be written as:

Mean of Group A: O_1
Mean of Group B: O_1

Where:

O_1 = Mean score on the *PSS* before they went through the skills training program

Thea decided to compare the average *PSS* score for the first group of foster care parents (Group A) to the average *PSS* score of parents in her next training program (Group B). This would allow her to see if the first group (Group A) had been unusually talented, or conversely, were less well-versed in parenting skills than the second group (Group B). Her hypothesis was that there would be no differences in the levels of knowledge of parenting skills between the two groups.

Since Thea had *PSS* scores from two different groups of participants (Groups A & B), the correct statistical test to identify if there are any statistical differences between the means of the two groups is the independent *t*-test. Let us use the same set of numbers that we previously used in the example of the dependent *t*-test in this analysis, this time considering the posttest *PSS* scores as the scores of the second group of foster care parents. As can be seen from Figure 21.7, the mean *PSS* of Group A was 82 and the standard deviation was 10. Group B scored an average of 86 on the *PSS*, with a standard deviation of 8. Although the means of the two groups are four points apart, the standard deviations in the distribution of each are fairly large, so that there is considerable overlap between the two groups. This would suggest that statistically significant differences will not be found.

The obtained *t*-value to establish whether this four-point difference (86 – 82) between the means for two groups was statistically significant was calculated to be $t = 1.6$ with a $p > .05$. The two groups were, thus, not statistically different from one another and Thea's hypothesis was supported. Note, however, that Thea's foster care parents were not randomly assigned to each group, thus breaking one of the assumptions of the *t*-test. As discussed earlier, this is a serious limitation to the interpretation of the study's results. We must be especially careful not to generalize the findings beyond the groups included in the study.

Note that in the previous example, when using the same set of numbers but

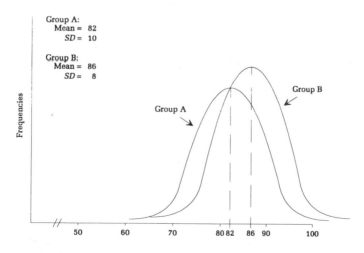

FIGURE 21.7   FREQUENCY DISTRIBUTIONS OF *PSS* SCORES FROM TWO GROUPS OF FOSTER CARE PROVIDERS

a dependent *t*-test, we found a statistically significant difference. This is because the dependent *t*-test analysis is more robust than the independent *t*-test, since having the same participant fill out the questionnaire twice, under two different conditions, controls for many extraneous variables, such as individual differences, that could negatively influence an analysis of independent samples.

One-Way Analysis of Variance

A one-way ANOVA is the extension of an independent *t*-test that uses three or more groups. Each set of scores is from a different group of participants. For example, Thea might use the scores on the *PSS* test from the first group of foster care parents from whom she collected data before they participated in her program, but she might also collect data from a second and a third group of parents before they received the training. The test for significance of an ANOVA is called an *F*-test. We could actually use an ANOVA procedure on only two groups and the result would be identical to the *t*-test. Unlike the *t*-test, however, obtaining a significant *F*-value in a one-way ANOVA does not complete the analysis. Because ANOVA looks at differences between three or more groups, a significant *F*-value only tells us that there is a statistically significant difference among the groups: It does not tell us between which ones.

To identify this, we need to do a *post-hoc* test. A variety are available, such as Duncan's multiple range, Tukey's Honestly Significant Difference test, and Newman-Keuls, and are provided automatically by most computer statistical programs. But one caution applies: A post-hoc test should be used *only after finding a significant F-value*, because some of the post-hoc tests are more sensitive than the *F* test and so might find significance when the *F*-test does not. Generally, we should use the most conservative test first, in this case the *F*-test.

In the example of Thea's program, let us say that she collected data on a total of three different groups of foster care parents. The research design could be written as follows:

> Group A: O_1
> Group B: O_1
> Group C: O_1

There is no *X* in the design, since the measures were taken before the training (the *X*) was provided. The first group of foster care parents scored an average of 82 on the *PSS* (standard deviation 10). The second group scored an average of 86 (standard deviation 8), while the mean score of the third group was 88 with a standard deviation of 7.

The obtained F-value for the one-way ANOVA is 2.63, with a $p > .05$. Thus, we must conclude that there are no statistically significant differences between the means of the groups (i.e., 82, 86, 88). Since the F-value was not significant, we would not conduct any post-hoc tests. This finding would be interesting to Thea, since it suggests that all three groups of foster care parents started out with approximately the same knowledge levels, on the average, before receiving training.

SUMMARY

This chapter provided a beginning look at the rationale behind some of the most commonly used statistical procedures, both those that describe samples and those that analyze data from a sample in order to make inferences about the larger population.

The level of measurement of the data is key to the kind of statistical procedures that can be utilized. Descriptive statistics are utilized with data from all levels of measurement. The mode is the most appropriate measure of central tendency for measurements of this level. It is only when we have data from interval and ratio levels that we can utilize inferential statistics—those that extend the statistical conclusions made about a sample by applying them to the larger population.

Descriptive measures of central tendency, such as the mode, median, and mean of a sample or population, all provide different kinds of information, each of which is applicable only to some levels of measurement. In addition to knowing the middle or average of a distribution of scores as provided by measures of central tendency, it is useful to know the value of the standard deviation that shows us how far away from the mean the scores are distributed. It is assumed that many variables studied in social work can be found in a normal distribution in the total population. Consequently many descriptive and inferential statistics assume such a distribution for their tests to be valid.

Chi-square and correlation are both statistical tests that determine whether variables are associated, although they do not show causation. In contrast, t-tests and analysis of variance (ANOVA) are statistical procedures for determining whether the mean and variance in one group (often a treatment group) is significantly different from those in another (often a comparison or control group).

REFERENCES AND FURTHER READINGS

ANASTAS, J.W., & MACDONALD, M.L. (1994). *Research design for social work and the human services* (pp. 411-476). New York: Lexington.

BABBIE, E.R. (1995). *The practice of social research* (7th ed., pp. 367-384). Belmont, CA: Wadsworth.

BAILEY, K.D. (1994). *Methods of social research* (4th ed., pp. 337-345, 378-389). New York: Free Press.

DePOY, E., & GITLIN, L.N. (1994). *Introduction to research* (pp. 229-236, 237-252). St. Louis: Mosby.

FRANKFORT-NACHMIAS, C., & NACHMIAS, D. (1992). *Research methods in the social sciences* (4th ed., pp. 339-367). New York: St. Martin's Press.

JUDD, C.M., SMITH, E.R., & KIDDER, L.H. (1991). *Research methods in social relations* (6th ed., pp. 351-372). Fort Worth, TX: Harcourt Brace.

LEEDY, P.D. (1993). *Practical research* (5th ed., pp. 42-45, 243-273). New York: Macmillan.

MARLOW, C. (1993). *Research methods for generalist social work* (pp. 189-210). Pacific Grove, CA: Brooks/Cole.

MONETTE, D.R., SULLIVAN, T.J., & DeJONG, C.R. (1994). *Applied social research* (3rd ed., pp. 364-373). Fort Worth, TX: Harcourt Brace.

NEUMAN, W.L. (1994). *Social research methods* (2nd ed., pp. 282-294). Needham, Heights, MA: Allyn & Bacon.

ROYSE, D.D. (1995). *Research methods in social work* (2nd ed., pp. 239-244). Chicago: Nelson-Hall.

RUBIN, A., & BABBIE, E.R. (1993). *Research methods for social work* (2nd ed., pp. 449-475). Pacific Grove, CA: Brooks/Cole.

SINGLETON, R.A., JR., STRAITS, B.C., & MILLER STRAITS, M. (1993). *Approaches to social research* (2nd ed., pp. 425-434). New York: Oxford.

WEINBACH, R.W., & GRINNELL, R.M., JR. (1995). *Statistics for Social Workers* (3rd ed.). White Plains, NY: Longman.

WILLIAMS, M., TUTTY, L.M., & GRINNELL, R.M., JR. (1995). *Research in social work: An introduction* (2nd ed., pp. 283-293). Itasca, IL: F.E. Peacock.

YEGIDIS, B.L., & WEINBACH, R.W. (1996). *Research methods for social workers* (2nd ed., pp. 195-203). Needham Heights, MA: Allyn & Bacon.

Yvonne A. Unrau
Heather Coleman

C h a p t e r **22**

Qualitative Data Analysis

F OLLOWING THE LAST CHAPTER on analysis of quantitative data, this chapter continues our discussion of data analysis by focusing on how to analyze qualitative data. As we know from the preceding chapters in this book, unlike quantitative data that are in the form of numbers, qualitative data are typically in the form of words. Words contain both rich descriptions of situations and an understanding of their underlying meaning (Miles & Huberman, 1994). Words are "fatter" than numbers and have multiple meanings, making the analysis of qualitative data quite a challenge.

As throughout this book, we present analyzing qualitative data in a straightforward, simplified, step-by-step process. As we know, this simplicity does not hold up in the real world of qualitative research, however. In contrast to quantitative studies, where data are collected and then analyzed using an appropriate statistical procedure, in qualitative studies it is not uncommon to conduct further and/or new interviews after the data have been analyzed from previous research participants. Furthermore, the data analysis is a multi-step process that involves considering the fit of each piece of data in relationship to all the other pieces. Thus, we must continually move back and forth between initial and later interviews, identifying units of meaning, coding, and interpreting the data as we go along. Such a blending of data collection and data analysis permits us to continue interviewing people for as long as is necessary until we truly grasp the meaning of our study's findings.

There are several ways to approach the task of analyzing interview data. One way is to look for the major themes and patterns in the data, and then to break these down into subthemes and categories as such distinctions become important. In essence, we start out with a broad look at the data and then break them into smaller units.

This chapter, in contrast, suggests we start our data analysis by first looking at the smaller units. Later, we will identify similarities and differences between these, to formulate how they fit together as themes and patterns. With this approach, then, we begin with the smaller pieces but ultimately identify the broad themes.

Both approaches to data analysis are appropriate, and the two can converge to yield a similar interpretation of the data. We decided to present a systematic analysis of small units in this chapter for one reason only: We believe that this approach is more likely to allow our results to emerge from the data. The process of systematically comparing and contrasting the small segments of interviews keeps us thinking about what each individual is saying. There is a greater risk when we start with the broad perspective that, once having identified important themes, we will apply these to segments with less attention to what is actually being said.

Nevertheless, we have the capacity to consider both broad themes and small meaning units almost simultaneously. Experiment with the best data analysis method, and do not be disconcerted by the existence of different data analysis approaches.

The social work example we used in Box 6.1 (women not returning to live with their physically abusive partners after leaving a women's emergency shelter), is used throughout this chapter. Thus, it may be a good time to review Chapter 6 so the contents of this chapter are more readily grasped.

THE PURPOSE OF DATA ANALYSIS

The central purpose of qualitative data analysis is to sift, sort, and organize the masses of data acquired during the data collection phase in such a way that the themes and interpretations that emerge from the process address the original research question(s). The strength of the conclusions drawn from a qualitative research study ultimately rests with the plan for *data analysis*. If we develop a research project without a systematic plan to guide our data analysis we are likely to produce biased results. Nevertheless, as with the use of an unstructured interview where our research questions unfold throughout the process instead of being fixed at the outset, a data analysis will develop differently from study to study, depending on what the research participants reveal.

Rather than present a set of concrete rules and procedures about how to analyze qualitative data, we describe the general process of such an analysis. The interaction between data collection and analysis allows greater flexibility in interpreting the data and permits greater adaptability when conclusions are drawn from the data.

There are assumptions underlying the qualitative research approach that are directly relevant to the analysis phase. These assumptions are:

- The goal of our research study (and thus of our analysis) is to understand the personal realities of our research participants in depth, including aspects of their experience that may be quite unique to them.
- We should strive to understand human experience in as much complexity as possible. This means aiming for a deep understanding of both the experience and the meanings attached to it, as well as of the context within which the experience is reported. The context includes the research study itself—for example, our relationship with our research participants is part of what needs to be understood when our findings are analyzed.
- Given the complexity of social behavior, there are many topics in social work that are difficult to measure in the way that we would in a quantitative study. In the example that was used in Box 6.1 (women not returning to live with their physically abusive partners after leaving a women's emergency shelter), one woman was beaten to the point of needing medical treatment and another's life was threatened regularly with a gun. It would be a questionable goal to attempt to establish which woman experienced more fear. With such research topics, quantification reduces the data to trivial levels. In contrast, in a qualitative study we could describe the experience of each woman in a meaningful way. In the data analysis phase we should organize the data in such a manner that the words, thoughts, and experiences of our research participants can be clearly communicated.
- The extent to which previous research studies and theory should influence our study is a contentious issue, and we need to exercise our own best judgment. The arguments for and against familiarity with the literature do not need repetition here, but we do need to note that the issues remain relevant. We may find that a literature search is relevant in the middle of our data analysis, for example. As we are analyzing our transcripts, the concepts and relationships between the concepts that we identified may suggest more reading to discover whether others have thought of similar ideas.

    In our study, the extent to which the women expressed difficulties about going to court over custody, access to children, and divorce issues prompted us to search for literature identifying this as a problem. Similarly, when we approach the end of our data analysis, a literature search comparing our conclusions with the findings of other studies is often advisable.

ESTABLISHING AN INITIAL FRAMEWORK

There are two major steps involved in establishing an initial framework for any given qualitative data analysis. First, the data must be prepared in transcript form (Step 1), and second, a preliminary plan for proceeding with the data analysis needs to be developed (Step 2).

Step 1: Preparing Data in Transcript Form

A transcript is the written record of interviews and any other written material that may have been gathered. As the core of our data analysis, it will consist of more than merely the words spoken by each person during the interview. In addition, comments are included that reflect nonverbal interactions such as pauses, laughing, and crying.

Preparing data in transcript form involves five basic substeps: (1) choosing a method of analysis, (2) determining who should transcribe the data, (3) considering ethical implications in the data analysis, (4) transcribing raw data, and (5) formatting the transcript for analysis.

Step 1a: Choosing a Method of Analysis

As mentioned previously, the qualitative research process usually results in masses of data. A tape-recorded interview lasting an hour may result in a typed transcript of 20 to 50 pages. Interview data can be collected using a variety of aids, such as tape recordings, videotapes, and field notes. Additional data can also be gathered unobtrusively from existing documents (Chapters 16–19), such as newspaper clippings, abstracts, diaries, and letters. Throughout the data collection phase of a qualitative research study, we must actively examine any relevant written materials and take copious notes on our reactions and ideas.

Word processing programs have made the task of transcribing large amounts of data much simpler. Besides presenting the data in a uniform way, such programs allow us to make changes to the interviews quickly and easily, producing a clean copy of the data to analyze. Nevertheless, it is important to remember that, after the data have been transcribed, the original sources of data must be safely stored away in case we wish to use these sources again.

Part of the reason that a qualitative analysis is considered to be a massive responsibility is that we ultimately end up comparing and sorting multiple segments from the large amount of data that have been collected. Several methods of data analyses are possible, and this choice affects the manner in which the data are transcribed. The first option is to analyze our data using the traditional "cut-and-paste" method, whereby we use scissors to cut the typed transcript into the categories we have decided on, and to sort these into relevant groupings. Some qualitative researchers still prefer this method, remaining skeptical about the use of computers.

A second option is to use a regular word processing program. Even with limited knowledge of word processing, we are likely to be familiar with enough commands to sort our data into the appropriate groupings for our analysis.

The third option is to use a computer program that has been developed specifically to assist in the analysis of qualitative data. Programs such as *The Ethnograph* and *AskSam* are only two of the more familiar names. The software market changes so quickly that we must consult with other qualitative researchers or computer companies about what programs they recommend. While no one has yet found a way to replace the thinking that is the critical determinant of whether an analysis truly reflects the data gathered, qualitative data analyses have become simpler with the introduction of computer programs that are able to sort and organize segments of the text with ease. Computers also assist in mechanical tasks, such as recording, editing, and formatting. They do not do the "analytical work," however.

Most computer programs that aid in the analysis of qualitative data require the interview data to be entered into a word processor. There are dozens of word processing software packages available on the market. It is necessary to select a package that can download the text into an ASCII format, however, because a number of the qualitative data analysis programs require that the data be in ASCII.

One rationale for using computers in a qualitative data analysis is to free up time so we can concentrate on interpreting the meaning of the data. It is doubtful that any computer program will ever replace our role in an analysis, however, since we need to be intensely involved in the reading of the data in order to understand them. Please note that the analysis of qualitative data consequently draws heavily on *our own* personal skills and resources.

Step 1b: Determining Who Should Transcribe the Data

The scope of a qualitative research study determines the number of resources needed to complete each step and substep. In smaller studies, we are likely to have the sole responsibility for all steps and substeps from beginning to end. Although the data analysis phase may sound like a lot of work, there is a considerable benefit to transcribing the interviews ourselves. Simply put, we become more thoroughly acquainted with the content of the interviews—a critical aspect for the process of data analysis—and transcribing provides an additional opportunity to "review and connect" with the data.

In large studies, we may have secretarial support or a research assistant to help with data transcribing. When we are fortunate enough to have the assistance of others, it is essential that all persons working on the research study operate according to the same principles and procedures. We need to provide some form of systematic training for them so that all data are treated according to the same decision-making rules.

In this case, we might personally transcribe some of the interviews our self at the beginning, so we can be clear with our assistants about what we want. Also, all transcribers should be informed about the importance of including nonverbal communication, such as laughs or pauses in conversation, in the data text. Despite the advantages of having additional assistance in transcribing, many qualitative researchers prefer to transcribe their own data if at all possible.

Step 1c: Considering Ethical Issues

As discussed throughout this book, ethics is a critical consideration throughout the research process. In the data analysis phase, confidentiality is a central ethical issue, especially when tapes and transcripts are given to research assistants or to secretaries. To safeguard the interviewee's confidentiality, no identifying data should be included on this material. Instead, a code name or number is assigned to identify the research participant at the beginning of the tape and then only first names are used throughout the transcript.

No recognizable information such as birth date, social security number, or address in our code names is used. In addition, we must make adequate provision to protect the privacy of our research participants by ensuring that details that might identify them are concealed. If we include excerpts of interviews in our final report, for example, a reader could potentially identify a person on the basis of his or her professional status, the names, ages, and gender of children, and the details of the unique experience. Such recognizable data must be masked in any examples used in the final report.

In our study, we had to be particularly careful to disguise identifying features because of the intensely personal nature of the situations that the women were describing. In one case, a woman's husband was being investigated as a suspect in the sexual abuse and abduction of her ten-year-old daughter. With the widespread newspaper coverage of the event, we were extremely cautious—not only did we transcribe the tape ourselves, but no details of the family's situation were typed into the transcript or our final report.

Step 1d: Transcribing Raw Data

Transcribing data from audio- or videotapes is a long and arduous process, requiring careful attention and precise transcription. In most cases, transcripts should be produced *verbatim* to allow the context of the conversation to provide as much meaning as possible. Editing and censoring during transcription can easily wipe out the context of the data and, in the process, conceal the meaning of the text.

In the example of an interview segment presented below, we can see how the context of the conversation gives flavor and texture to the data. Most importantly, it allows us to become completely involved in the data and to view it holistically. It is, therefore, critical that we record nonverbal interview events such as pauses, laughs, nervous moments, and excitement. We may also choose to insert notes based on our impressions or guesses about the context of the verbal comments, such as "seems reluctant to talk about what her parents thought about her going to a shelter." Below is part of the interview that includes the interviewer's notes about nonverbal communication in parentheses:

> **Interviewer**   Now that we've got the ethics forms completed, I'd like to tell you how much I appreciate you taking this time to talk about our experience after leaving Transition House.

> **Joy**   (enthusiastically) I have only good things to say about that place. It was so peaceful being there, you know, you don't have to worry, you don't have to be concerned. You know our children are safe and everything (pause) and you're safe. The counselors were really helpful, too. No, I really liked that place. That was my second time there (pause). Silly me (in an embarrassed tone, shifting in seat, sounds uncomfortable) I've got involved in the same relationship twice. (Sounding more solid) I decided to give it another chance because of the baby. Yeah, no ... I liked that place a lot, it was just excellent.

Step 1e: Formatting the Transcript for Analysis

The format of the transcripts should facilitate very easy reading and allow sufficient space for writing comments. We recommend using standard-size paper and leaving the right margin as wide as two inches. In this way, the transcripts are structured so that we can easily write notes, codes, and line numbering alongside the corresponding text.

Numbering each line of the transcripts helps to organize data; some word processing or computer programs that assist in the qualitative data analysis process, such as *The Ethnograph*, will do this automatically. With such numbering we can easily identify specific segments of data and determine where a particular word, sentence, or paragraph begins and ends, as illustrated below:

> **01.**   **Joy**   (sadly) The booze was just too much. He destroyed our house
> **02.**   and two apartments—things broken everywhere, holes in the wall,
> **03.**   doors torn off hinges, all kinds of stuff. (pause) Yeah,
> **04.**   after the last time at Transition House my initial thought
> **05.**   was to leave him and not go back, pregnant or not. And then we
> **06.**   got talking. (sighs) I didn't phone him for a long time
> **07.**   but he kept phoning me at work, trying to see me at work, you

08. know, saying, "I want to work this through." That was great,

09. I believed him, I trusted him, and then when I finally said,

10. "Okay, I'll come back," (pause) he kept to it for a little while.

11. And then he just started breaking his promises again.

12. And then he started sneaking drinks. It kept on increasing ...

13. problems, fights kept on intensifying and that was all I could take.

14. The final blow was down at the fairgrounds because he wanted a

15. gun, a little carved gun that shoots elastics ...

16.

17. **Interviewer** You're kidding!

18.

Step 2: Establishing a Plan for Data Analysis

Having spent a great deal of time in planning our qualitative study and collecting the data, we may now be feeling anxious to get the data analysis out of the way quickly. Unfortunately, given the many steps and substeps and the complex thinking involved in a qualitative data analysis, we can expect to expend considerably more time and patience in processing all of the data collected.

One advantage of a qualitative data analysis is that it is not subject to the same methodological rigor as a quantitative analysis. We have more freedom to consider the unique qualities of the data set, rather than being limited to how people do "on the average." This does not mean, however, that a qualitative data analysis is not a systematic effort. It is essential that we document the rules and procedures used in our analysis in enough detail that the analytic procedures used can be repeated and applied to each step in the analysis.

While qualitative analysis is both purposeful and systematic, in the initial stages it is guided only by *general* rules. We develop these rules to guide us in deciding what pieces of data fit together in a meaningful way and how these should be coded (to be presented shortly). In subsequent stages of the analysis, we clarify and refine the rules through reflection on and critical analysis of the situations in which each should be applied. By the end of the study, we must consistently apply the rules to all units of data.

Developing a preliminary plan for data analysis involves two general substeps: (1) previewing the data, and (2) planning what to record in our journal.

Step 2a: Previewing the Data

Although, in some cases, we transcribe and analyze our interviews as we collect them, in others we start our data analysis only after we have completed interviewing. Before we launch into the steps and substeps of coding and interpreting our data, it is important to become familiar with the entire data set by reading all of the available interviews. At this point, it is important not to impose, or force, a framework on the data. As mentioned previously, when we first become familiar with our qualitative data, we may be tempted to begin classifying it into a preconceived framework from our first glance.

We might also apply theories with which we are familiar, or create a few hypotheses. Doing so, however, creates a funnel effect by which we screen out important data that are recorded in the latter parts of the data set. The meaning of the data in a qualitative analysis should emerge from the data. Thus, if ideas are prematurely imposed, the interpretation of data could be colored by preconceived notions or our own particular viewpoints.

There are several strategies that help avoid becoming focused too quickly. First, if our transcripts are extensive, we do not attempt to read them all at once. When our mind starts to wander or we become impatient or start feeling uninterested, it is time to pause. Remember that a qualitative data analysis takes time. If we want to produce a quality product, we must respect the process—which to a large extent, cannot be forced.

Second, refrain from always reading notes and transcripts from the beginning of a document. When we begin reading, we are usually in peak form. If we always confine this energy to the first section of our data, we are more likely to exclude or overlook valuable data from later sections. Reading the last third of the interview before the first portion is one technique that may help shed new light on each interview.

Step 2b: Using a Journal During Data Analysis

As noted in Chapters 4, 5, 6, and 15, we use a journal to record the process of our qualitative research study and our reactions to the emerging issues in our analysis. Yvonna Lincoln and Egon Guba (1985) suggest that a qualitative journal should include two key components: (1) notes on the method used in our study, and (2) notes on issues of credibility and audit trail notes (to be described later). Each component should include a section on what decisions were made during the analysis and the rationale for these.

The schemes that we develop are critical segments of the methodology section of our journal. When we unitize and initially categorize (code) our data, we come up with numerous questions and ideas about the data. Making notes in our journal about these questions or comments with respect to identifying meaning units and categories (to be discussed shortly) is referred to as writing "analytical memos." It is a useful strategy for organizing our thoughts.

Although the format used for analytical memos tends to reflect the individual style of the researcher, Anselm Straus and Juliet Corbin (1990) offer some hints about how to make useful analytical memos:

- Record the date of the memo.
- Include any references or important sources.
- Label memos with headings that describe the primary category or concept being earmarked.
- Identify the particular code(s) to which the theoretical note pertains.
- Use diagrams in memos to explain ideas.
- Keep multiple copies of all memos.
- Do not restrict the content of memos; allow for a flow of ideas.
- Note when you think that a category has been sufficiently defined.
- Keep analytical memos about our own thinking process to assist you in moving the analysis from description to interpretation.

The process of writing analytical memos is what some authors refer to as leaving an "audit trail." An audit trail is used when an outside person is called in to review what we have done, to ensure that there were no serious flaws in the conduct of our study. This individual may retrace our steps starting from collection of the raw data, carefully examining every decision we have made in the study. Since the work we do should be open to scrutiny by others, precise journal notes about our methodology are crucial.

Our journal also helps to ensure that the rules guiding the definition of categories and the assignment of units of data to those categories become universal and are consistently applied. Keeping notes about the coding process ensures greater consistency of coding to protect rules from any whims or impulsive decisions. We also record the code acronym (the shortened version of the category name) that is assigned to each category, as well as the characteristics of the meaning unit that qualify it to be categorized in that particular way.

Later, we may want to revise the categorization scheme, a point at which we again clearly record the reasons for our decision and how the characteristics of the data have changed. This process, then, will track the developmental history of our data analysis.

We also use a journal to record our notes about what transpired in our interviews and how we obtained our research participants. We take special note of our honest reactions to the people that we interviewed, since these comments eventually will be used to assess the credibility of the research participants in our study. If, for example, we have overrelied on one informant or developed a bias against one subset of interviewees, then our conclusions will be one-sided. Such biases will, hopefully, become more evident as we read our journal entries.

It is also essential to record other attempts at establishing the credibility of our study, such as asking others to unitize and categorize our data to provide evidence that our categorization scheme is useful and appropriate. (This process, called "triangulation of analysts," is described in more detail later.) Finally, our journal should contain a section that covers our personal reactions to our study, not unlike a personal diary.

Following is an example of a comment from the journal in our study. The example shows an analytical memo that speaks to issues of both credibility and reactions to the study as a whole:

May 16, 1997 I can't help but feel that the interview with Joy went extremely well. She was surprisingly open about her story and seemed very concerned that other women who might be living with men such as her ex-partner know what options they have. She is really quite remarkable to have set up a new home with two small children, and with so little income. I think her narrative really adds to the interviews we've conducted so far because she is doing so well under difficult circumstances.

FIRST- AND SECOND-LEVEL CODING

The previous two steps deal with establishing an initial framework for doing a qualitative data analysis. Steps 3 and 4 deal with first- and second-level coding.

Step 3: First-Level Coding

Once we have transcribed our data, and reviewed it in a preliminary way, we can launch into first-level coding: a combination of identifying meaning units, fitting them into categories, and assigning codes to the categories. This section presents each of these substeps individually, but, once again, in practice, they overlap. We may be thinking about how to categorize certain meaning units as we are identifying them in the transcripts (and will use analytical memos to make sure that we do not forget these initial ideas), for example.

Coding begins at the point when we first notice similarities and differences between data segments or meaning units. We may also see patterns in the data that we will mentally label. As we read new data and reread old data, we conceptually connect similar meaning units together as categories. We use a procedure called the constant comparison method: Meaning units of data with the same characteristics are considered to fit within the same category and are given the same code; meaning units that are different in important ways are put into different categories and given other codes.

Coding proceeds in stages, and there are several substeps involved in coding at various stages of the analysis. First-level coding is predominantly concrete, and involves identifying properties of data that are clearly evident in the text. Such content is found without combing the data for underlying meaning. Second-level coding (Step 4) is more abstract and involves interpreting the meaning underlying the more obvious ideas portrayed within the data.

By the end of our analysis, we will have worked with both concrete and abstract content. We start with concrete coding at the beginning of the analysis, but work toward understanding the deeper, abstract content in the final stages of the analysis. Remember, qualitative research is more than description—it takes a natural interest in the meaning underlying the words.

In summary, the primary task of coding is to identify and label relevant categories of data, first concretely (in first-level coding) and then abstractly (in second-level coding). First-level coding is a lengthy and detailed process that involves eight substeps: (1) identifying meaning units, (2) identifying categories, (3) constant comparison, (4) creating categories, (5) reassessment, (6) assigning codes to categories, (7) refining and reorganizing coding, and (8) deciding when to stop. Once again, the substeps overlap one another and they should be viewed as absolutely essential in the first-level coding process.

Step 3a: Identifying Meaning Units

Once the data have been previewed, they need to be organized into a manageable format. To do this, we first identify the important experiences or ideas in our data. This is the process of classifying and collapsing the data into "meaning units." We make decisions about what pieces of data fit together; ultimately, these are the segments that are categorized, coded, and sorted, and then form the patterns that are used to summarize our interpretation of the data.

Units are the segments (or chunks) of data that are the building blocks of a categorization scheme. A unit can consist of a single word, a partial or complete sentence, a paragraph, or more. It is a piece of the transcript that we consider to be meaningful by itself. At this point we are not analyzing what the data mean, we are simply identifying the important bits of what the research participants are saying.

Of course, what constitutes a clear meaning unit to us may not be clear to outside readers. The developers of *The Ethnograph* computer program studied how a group of students analyzed an identical data file. While some students identified very small meaning units of 5 to 50 lines of transcript, others identified larger units, analyzing segments of between 50 and 200 lines. Further, the category labels (codes) that the students attached to the meaning units varied considerably. Some students labeled categories in a concrete and detailed manner, while others were more impressionistic and abstract. Some students identified categories similar to those of other students, but still others identified categories that were unique.

This example simply illustrates the fact that different individuals identify and label the same meaning units differently within the same data set. The lesson is that there is no inherent "right" or "wrong" way to organize qualitative data. How a single person chooses to reduce data into a manageable form is an individual endeavor.

In the segment of the data set previously presented from our research study, we identified the following meaning units (the first underlined, the next in italics) early in our first-level coding process:

01. **Joy** (sadly) <u>The booze was just too much</u>. *He destroyed our house*
02. *and two apartments—things broken everywhere, holes in the wall,*
03. *doors torn off hinges, all kinds of stuff.* (pause) <u>Yeah,</u>
04. <u>after the last time at Transition House my initial thought</u>
05. <u>was to leave him and not go back</u>, <u>pregnant or not</u>. <u>And then we</u>

06. got talking. (sighs) <u>I didn't phone him for a long time</u>
07. <u>but he kept phoning me at work</u>, <u>trying to see me at work</u>, <u>you</u>
08. <u>know</u>, <u>saying "I want to work this through</u>." That was great,
09. <u>I believed him</u>, <u>I trusted him</u>, <u>and then when I finally said</u>,
10. "<u>Okay</u>, <u>I'll come back</u>," (pause) <u>he kept to it for a little while</u>.
11. *And then he just started breaking his promises again.*
12. *And then he started sneaking drinks. It kept on increasing ...*
13. *problems, fights kept on intensifying and that was all I could take.*
14. *The final blow was down at the fairgrounds because he wanted a*
15. *gun, a little carved gun that shoots elastics ...*
16.
17. Interviewer   You're kidding!

In our journal, for example, we recorded that the first meaning unit relates to her ex-partner's drinking (line 1), and the second is about his past destructive behavior (lines 1–3).

The third meaning unit (lines 3–10) is rather long and may need to be broken down further later on. It describes the process of reuniting with a partner after a previous shelter stay. The final meaning unit (lines 11–15) documents the experience that prompted the final shelter stay. The topics in the meaning units may become categories if the content is repeated later on in this interview or if other interviewees identify similar issues.

The first run-through to identify meaning units will always be somewhat tentative and subject to change. If we are not sure whether to break a large meaning unit into smaller ones, it may be preferable to leave it as a whole. We can always break down meaning units more finely later on in our analysis. This process is somewhat easier than combining units later, especially once second-level coding (Step 4) begins.

Step 3b: Identifying Categories

Once we have identified the meaning units in the transcripts, our next task is to consider which of them fit together into categories. Especially in first-level coding, the categories identified should logically and simply relate to the data they represent. The categories may emerge from the questions asked, or they may simply reflect the critical events that were identified in our research participants' stories.

As mentioned previously, though, while the rationale behind the categories does not have to be explained at the beginning, we must clearly explain our grounds as the data analysis proceeds and becomes more complex. The categories and their respective codes must all be defined by the end of the study.

Step 3c: Constant Comparison

Earlier, we introduced the method of constant comparison, which is the major technique guiding the categorization process. Constant comparison begins after the complete set of data has been examined and meaning units have been identified. Each unit is classified as either similar or different from the others. If the first two meaning units possess somewhat similar qualities, they are tentatively placed in the same category and classified by the same code created for that category.

We must remember to make notes about the characteristics of the meaning units that make them similar, and record these observations in our journal. If the first two meaning units are not similar in these identified qualities, a separate category and a new code are produced for the second one. Again, the data about what defines the second category should be recorded, since the process will solidify the rules governing when to include specific meaning units in that category.

We simply repeat these steps to examine the remaining meaning units. The third meaning unit is examined for similarities and differences with the first and the second category, for example. If it differs, a third category and code are created. Constant comparison continues until all meaning units are classified into either previously described or new categories.

Step 3d: Creating Categories

To illustrate how to create categories from meaning units, we will use the previous excerpt from our study. The first meaning unit identified, "the booze was just too much" (line 1), fit with a number of Joy's other comments, as well as comments from other research participants relating to their ex-partner's abuse of substances. The category was hence labeled "Partner's Substance Abuse." The rule was that past and present substance abuse issues of the ex-partner would be included under this category.

Issues related to any substance abuse by the interviewee herself, however, were placed in a different category: "Research Participant's Substance Abuse." Thus, each meaning unit is considered in comparison to other similar meaning units, and the category is a way of identifying important similarities within and across individuals.

The number of categories expands every time we identify meaning units that are dissimilar in important ways from those we have already categorized. We also need to attempt to keep the number of categories within manageable limits, however. At the beginning of constant comparison, new categories are created quickly, and then more slowly after we have analyzed between four and five dozen meaning units.

Sometimes, meaning units cannot be clearly placed into any of the categories developed in the analysis and fall into the category of "miscellaneous." These misfits should be set aside in a separate "pile" with other units that are difficult to classify. We must make special note of why they do not fit. At some point, such unclassifiable meaning units may begin to resemble one another and are placed in a category of their own. After reviewing all the categories, we simply inspect the miscellaneous pile to decide what units might fit together in a new category or a new set of categories.

If we find that we are throwing data into the miscellaneous pile too often, fatigue may be a factor. This would be a good time to pause and return to the analysis when refreshed. The use of a miscellaneous pile prevents us from throwing out what seem to be irrelevant meaning units. Such tossing is a risky move, because in some situations we may decide that our categorization scheme needs massive revision and that we must start the whole process again from scratch. On the other hand, miscellaneous units should make up less than ten percent of the total data set. More than that suggests that there is a problem with the original categorization scheme.

Step 3e: Reassessment

Occasionally, we will need to stop and reaffirm the rules that qualify the meaning units to be placed within each category. These decisions need to be justified, a factor that later serves as the basis for tests of whether others who utilize our rules identify similar meaning units and categories.

The categories for any qualitative study develop and change over time. It is natural for some categories to change or to become irrelevant (decay) in the later stages of a data analysis, however. In such instances, new categories are created and old categories are either revised, merged with others, or eliminated completely.

The number of categories in a study depends upon the breadth and the depth we seek in the analysis of the data. Some topics require very detailed and precise analyses, with nearly every line of the transcript coded into different categories. For less detailed work, it is possible to code larger segments, for example, every 50 or even every 200 lines.

The complexity of the categorization also needs to be considered. One meaning unit may, in fact, fit into more than one category. It is also possible to code meaning units that overlap with one another. In another case called a nested code, smaller categories fit within larger, more inclusive ones. Furthermore, there can also be a combination of multiple and overlapping categories.

In the interview with Joy, for example, the large meaning unit talking about the couple's reconciliation (lines 3–10) could also be considered as two smaller categories, one labeled "Partner's Past Reconciliation Attempts" (lines 5–10) and another called "Reasons for Past Breakdown of Reconciliation" (lines 11–13). These may overlap with the category "Partner's Substance Abuse" (lines 1 & 12), so that substance abuse issues are sometimes coded into the category of "Reasons for Past Breakdown of Reconciliation."

The categories must be clear enough to simplify the data and prevent unnecessary backtracking and recoding. The category labels (codes) must also reflect the substance of the meaning units. In our study, many women reported having low self-esteem, which they found interfered in their ability to feel successful or to live independently from their abusive partner. In the first round of categorization, meaning units reflecting the self-esteem issue were categorized as "Self-concept: Valueless." These words did not adequately reflect the meaning of the segments in the interviews, since not one interviewee reported that she was valueless, but many noted that they had low self-esteem. The relabelled category "Low Self-esteem" more accurately reflected what the data meant.

Step 3f: Assigning Codes to Categories

As we know from Chapters 5 and 12, codes are simply a form of the category name that becomes a shorthand method of identifying the categories. Codes typically take the form of strings of letters and/or symbols. The form of the code used in *The Ethnograph*, for example, assumes up to ten letters and can also include symbols. Codes are usually displayed in the margins (often the right margin) of the transcribed text.

As we can see from our example, we have already made some distinctions that should be included in part of the code. One obvious issue is that some comments are about the woman herself, some about her partner, and some about her children. Thus we used *W* as the first letter of the code name if related to the woman, *P* if related to her partner, and *C* if related to her children. A second important distinction was whether issues were past (*P*), current (*C*), or anticipated in the future (*F*).

Finally, in a list of categories about the problems encountered, the substance abuse category was labeled *SA*. Thus, the code that we wrote in the margin next to the meaning unit "The booze was just too much" was *P-P-SA*, standing for the partner's past substance abuse. As the analysis becomes more complex, the codes become longer. When we get to the initial stages of second-level coding, the codes in the margins are used to collect all the meaning units from all of the interviews that fit within a particular category.

Step 3g: Refining and Reorganizing Coding

Before moving on from first-level coding, we need to make a final sweep through the data to ensure that our analysis reflects what our research participants have said. We need to pause and reflect upon our analysis thus far, considering the logic of the ideas that form the basis of the rules for each category. Rather than discovering at the end of our analysis that we have made an error in judgment, now is the most appropriate time to reexamine our thinking.

We may, for example, be confused about why we created some categories, or feel uncertain about the rules of categorization for others. We may find that some categories are too complex and may be effectively split into several new categories. This is the time to clarify and confirm what qualifies each meaning unit to fit within a particular category.

We need to review all the categories to see how the units "fit" with each. We can now tighten our rules to ensure that there is no vagueness about how any meaning unit is categorized. If we have conceptualized the meaning units accurately, the categories will "hang together" internally and be easily distinguished from other categories.

We might find that some categories are not completely developed or are only partially defined. Similarly, we might discover that categories that we had originally thought would emerge from the data are completely missing. We are most likely to discover missing categories while we are thinking about the underlying logic of our categorization scheme. In such a case, we simply make a note of the missing categories, as well as of incomplete or otherwise unsatisfactory categories. We may, in fact, wish to conduct additional interviews to address any of these gaps.

This would be a good time to ask a colleague to analyze one or two of our interviews using the rules that we have devised. This process is a check to ensure that the categories and the rules that define them make sense. If our colleague organizes meaning units in a significantly different way, our categorization scheme may need to be substantially revised.

Step 3h: Deciding When to Stop

What are the indicators that signal an appropriate time to stop first-level coding? The most common indicator is that when we interview new research participants the meaning units fit easily into our current categorization scheme and no new categories emerge. This process is called "category saturation." In essence, the data become repetitive, and further analyses only confirms the ground that we have already covered. This is a good point to perform one final review of all the categories to ensure the thoroughness of our analysis. We will now turn our attention away from first-level coding and address the next major step in the data analysis process—second-level coding.

Step 4: Second-Level Coding

When completed thoroughly, the substeps of initial coding (Step 3) produce a solid foundation from which to further refine the data analysis process. By this point, our data have been reduced and transformed in several ways. Sections from the transcribed interviews have been selected and identified as meaning units. The units have been subsequently classified as fitting into categories, with an identifying code attached. We have read through our entire set of transcripts, coding the appropriate meaning units with the category code name. As a part of this process we have also reviewed the rules that we have developed to ensure that we can clearly explain what types of data are included in each category.

As noted earlier, second-level coding is more abstract, and involves interpreting what the first-level categories mean. Reporting on abstract content demands that we produce detailed examples of the transcript to back up each interpretation. Bruce L. Berg (1995) suggests we need at least three independent examples to support each of these interpretations. In second-level coding, we will pull together or "retrieve" the meaning units that fit within each category, either by computer or by cutting and pasting.

This process allows us to examine the units in the categories away from any association with the person who originally stated the idea. The focus of the analysis thus shifts from the context of the interviewee to the context of the categories. Through this process, the analysis has become one level more abstract, because it is one step further removed from the original interviews.

The major task in second-level coding is to identify similarities and differences between the categories in an attempt to detect relationships. In sum, the next step of coding involves two substeps: (1) retrieving meaning units into categories, and (2) comparing categories.

Step 4a: Retrieving Meaning Units into Categories

Earlier we identified distinct units of data and grouped and coded these based on similarities and differences. During second-level coding, we retrieve the coded units of each category, either by cutting and pasting the typed manuscript or by using a computer program. Via this process, all the meaning units that fit within the first category are grouped together, as are the units that fit within category two, and so on. We must always remember that our meaning units have been collected from a number of different interviewees.

Thus, this process pulls each unit away from the context of an individual's story. A drawback of the process, then, is that we might lose or misinterpret a meaning unit once it is separated from the context of each research participant's experience. The advantage is that we can consider the data in each category in a different way, across individuals. We can thus see how important it is that our rules for placing a meaning unit into a particular category were clarified during the initial coding process (Step 3g).

Step 4b: Comparing Categories

Whereas previously we looked for similarities and differences between meaning units to separate them into distinct categories, the next step is to compare and contrast the categories themselves in order to discover the relationships between them. At this point in the analysis, our goal is to integrate the categories into themes and subthemes based on their properties. Finding themes involves locating patterns that repeatedly appear among our categories. Once a theme is identified, we develop a code for it in the same manner as we coded categories. The themes will, in most cases, form the basis of the major conclusions emerging from our analysis.

What possible types of relationships among categories might we find?

- There might be a temporal relationship, so that one category always precedes another. In cases such as this we may be able to identify a process that has some importance to the issue at hand. In our study, for example, we found that although children often initially react positively to living away from their abusive father, later they are likely to push for a reconciliation.
- There may be a causal relationship, so that one category is the cause of another. We found that the women who had no further contact with their assaultive partners after leaving the shelter, for example, seemed generally able to function better. Note, though, that it is risky to assume that one category caused another when, in fact, the opposite may be true. In this example, perhaps it is the fact that the women were functioning well that led them to cease contact with their ex-partners.
- One category may be contained within another category or may be another type of the first category. In our study, we originally saw the category wherein the men beseeched and even bribed the women to return to the relationship as different from the category of threatening the women with, for example, further abuse or no support payments if they did not return. In this phase of analysis, however, we shifted to seeing the "loving" pleas as related to the threats. The new theme combining these was called "Partner's Strategies to Reunite."

Obviously, we may find other types of relationships between categories, but the previous examples are commonly found. Some categories may contain enough data to be considered themes in and of themselves.

As another example of combining categories into themes, consider the possibility that the three categories of "Custody Issues Regarding Children," "Separation or Divorce Proceedings," and "Obtaining Restraining Orders" all involve relationships with various aspects of the legal system, including the police, lawyers, and judges. The substance of the three categories is similar in that the women were more likely than not to have had difficulty in adequately dealing with these systems. Furthermore, the experience was likely to reignite marital issues, putting the women at risk of further abuse. The theme "Difficulties with the Legal System" was, therefore, created by combining the three categories.

LOOKING FOR MEANING AND RELATIONSHIPS

In addition to organizing the data, the first- and second-level codes we develop also bring meaning to the data being examined. Once we move to the "formal" step of interpreting the data, however, coding at both levels is considered complete. Two important steps are involved in looking for meaning and relationships in our data. First, we develop an interpretation of our data. Interpretations are sometimes descriptive, but may also speculate about causal explanations of important events. Second, the research process and the conclusions must be assessed for credibility and dependability.

Step 5: Interpreting Data and Theory Building

Drawing meaning from our data is perhaps the most rewarding step of a qualitative data analysis. It involves two important substeps: (1) developing conceptual classifications systems, and (2) presenting themes or theory.

Step 5a: Developing Conceptual Classification Systems

The ultimate goal of a qualitative research study is to identify any relationships between the major themes that emerge from the data set. To do this we must develop logical interpretations of the themes that remain consistent with our earlier categorization schemes and meaning units. One idea that may help us to get a sense of the relationships between the themes and the overall nature of the data is to visually display themes and categories in a diagram. The visual representation of our themes may help us to organize the write-up of our conclusions. It may also help to clearly identify the interconnections between themes and categories or to identify missing categories among the data set. Matthew B. Miles and Michael A. Huberman (1994) suggest several strategies for extracting meaning from a data set:

- **Draw a Cluster Diagram** This form of diagram helps us to think about how themes and categories may or may not be related to each other. Draw and label circles for each theme and arrange them in relation to each other. Some of the circles will overlap, others will stand alone. The circles of the themes of more importance will be larger, in comparison to themes and categories that are not as relevant to our conclusions. The process of thinking about what weight to give the themes, how they interact, and how important they will be in our final scheme will be valuable in helping us to think about the meaning of our research study.
- **Make a Matrix** Matrix displays may be helpful for noting relations between categories or themes. Designing a matrix involves writing a list of categories along the left side of a piece of paper and then another list of categories or themes across the top. In each cell we will document how the two categories fit or do not fit together. Using our study, for example, along the side we could write categories

that reflect the theme "Partner's Strategies to Reunite." Across the top we could write categories from the theme of "Women's Beliefs About Leaving Their Abusive Partner." Where two categories intersect on the matrix we could note with a plus sign (+) those beliefs that fit with the ex-partner's desire to live together once more, and mark with a minus sign (–) those at odds with each other. Such a matrix gives us a sense between the balance of the push to leave the abusive relationship and the pull to return.

- **Count the Number of Times a Meaning Unit or Category Appears** Although numbers are typically associated with quantitative studies, it is acceptable to use numbers in qualitative ones to document how many of the participants expressed a particular theme. We might, for example, be interested in finding out how many of our interviewees experienced different problems after separating from their abusive partners. We would write the code names for the women down the left side of a piece of paper and the list of problems across the top. To fill in the chart, we would simply place a check mark beside each woman's name if she experienced that particular problem.

  Numbers will help protect our analysis against bias that occurs when particularly poignant but rare examples of themes are presented. In our study, for example, one woman described the death of her daughter at the hands of her ex-partner, an event that immediately preceded their separation. Although an emotionally laden event, it was certainly not typical of the experience of most of the other women. A majority of the women, however, did express concerns about past abuse of their children by their ex-partners. Although we do not discount the experience of the woman whose daughter died, that event could be better discussed in the context of the range of severity of abuse of the children.

- **Create a Metaphor** Developing metaphors that convey the essence of our findings is another mechanism for extracting meaning. In her qualitative study of battered women who remain with their partners, Lenore Walker (1979), for example, identified a cycle that commonly occurs whereby tension builds between a couple until the husband beats his wife. This abusive incident is followed by a calm, loving phase until the tension starts to build once again. Walker's name for this process, "the cycle of violence," is an example of a metaphor that so effectively describes this pattern that the metaphor has been extensively adopted.

- **Look for Missing Links** If two categories or themes seem to be related, but not directly so, it may be that a third variable connects the two.

- **Note Contradictory Evidence** Remember that contradictory evidence must be accounted for. The chain of evidence must be thorough, so that any connections between categories and themes are accounted for. While we traditionally focus on looking for evidence to support our ideas, we must also identify themes and categories that raise questions about our conclusions. Such evidence can ultimately be very useful in providing exceptions to the process that we have described.

Step 5b: Presenting Themes or Theory

Although many qualitative researchers conclude their studies by presenting descriptions of the major themes that emerged from their data, others utilize the themes and their interpretations to create hypotheses or theory. In our study on abused women we simply presented the major themes that emerged from the data without any attempt to formulate these into a theory. Even so, the themes could have been reworded as questions that could then become hypotheses in future research efforts. One core theme, for example, was that the ex-partner's access to children created a situation wherein women were placed at risk of continued abuse. As a hypothesis, this could be reworded as, "Women whose abusive partners visit with their children after a marital separation are more likely to experience continued abuse than women who do not see their partner under such circumstances."

In contrast, theories answer questions such as "Why does a phenomenon occur?" or "How are these two concepts related?" If theory does develop from the study, it will not be apparent at the beginning, but will grow out of the process of analysis. This is most likely to occur during the stage of classifying the categories into themes and looking for relationships between those themes.

An example of a theory that emerged from a different qualitative study of battered women is Lenore Walker's (1979) "cycle of violence," mentioned previously as an example of a metaphor. The development of theories such as Walker's involves a shift from looking at specific instances to examining general patterns. With each step of a qualitative data analysis, our thinking becomes more abstract; in other words, we become further removed from the concrete examples on the original transcript. By using the constant comparison method, we arrive at an understanding of basic patterns or ideas that connect the categories and themes developed earlier.

Step 6: Assessing the Trustworthiness of the Results

Although developing interpretations and theory can be an exciting step in a qualitative data analysis, throughout the research process we must act responsibly to ensure the trustworthiness of the conclusions that we finally draw. Qualitative researchers have identified a number of issues for consideration to enhance the believability of a study's findings. Approaches and emphases vary (as does the depth of detail in discussions of techniques that can be employed). At this point, we discuss the challenges that are important to address during a qualitative analysis. The three substeps include: (1) establishing our own credibility, (2) documenting what we have done to ensure consistency, and (3) documenting what we have done to control biases and preconceptions.

Step 6a: Establishing Our Own Credibility

Since a qualitative study depends so much on our human judgment, it is necessary to indicate why we should be believed. This is partly a matter of indicating our relevant training and experience and partly a matter of recording, in our journal, the procedures we followed, the decisions we made (with the rationale for them), and the thought processes that led us to our conclusions. Meticulous records of this sort do much to convince those who must assess our work that they can believe in it.

Step 6b: Document What We Have Done to Ensure Consistency

Consistency (which is sometimes called dependability) is another key to establishing the believability of our study. While qualitative work is influenced by the unique events and relationships that unfold in the course of the study, a reasonable degree of consistency is still desirable. Hopefully, we have been rigorous in our interviewing and in developing the rules for coding, and have written detailed records of our decision making. If this is the case, another researcher should be able to follow our process and arrive at similar decisions. Also, if we, ourselves, redo parts of the analysis at a later date, the outcome should be closely similar to that produced in our original analysis. Specific issues that we may need to address to ensure consistency include:

- **The Context of the Interviews** Some data collection circumstances yield more credible data than others, and we may thus choose to weight our interviews accordingly. Some authors, for example, claim that data collected later in the study may be more relevant than those gathered in the beginning, likely because our interviewing style will be more relaxed and less intrusive. In addition, data obtained firsthand we considered stronger than those reported by a third person. Data provided voluntarily can be assumed to be more trustworthy, as are data collected when we are alone with the research participant.
- **Triangulation** This is a common method to establish the trustworthiness of qualitative data. There are several different kinds of triangulation, but the essence of the term is that multiple perspectives are compared. This might involve having a colleague use our data collection rules to see if he or she makes the same decisions about meaning units, categories, and themes; or it may consist of collecting multiple sources of data in addition to our interviews. The hope is that the different perspectives will confirm each other, adding weight to the credibility of our analysis.
- **Member Checking** Obtaining feedback from our research participants is an essential credibility technique that is unique to qualitative methods. While feedback from research participants should be part of the ongoing process of the qualitative research study, it is particularly useful when our analysis and interpretations have been made and conclusions drawn. In other words, we go back to our research participants, asking them to confirm or refute our interpretations.

Research participants may not always agree with the data, with each other, or with our interpretations. In such cases we need to decide whether to exclude the data to which the research participants object, or to record the dissenting opinion in some way and indicate our position in relation to it.

Step 6c: Document What We Have Done to Control Biases and Preconceptions

When our findings are reported, it is useful to include a careful inventory of our biases and preconceptions. Cataloguing these reminds us to keep checking to ensure that our conclusions are dictated by the data rather than by our established beliefs. A list of this sort is also useful to readers, who want to assess how successful we have been in keeping our biases under control during data collection and analysis phases.

Our journal, recording analytical memos and a record of our decision-making process, will also be valuable for this purpose. Someone who wishes to scrutinize our work especially closely will be interested in the evidence these offer regarding our attempts to be open to what our research participants had to say. Below are a few threats to the credibility of qualitative research studies that are relevant to the question of bias, and which we may wish to think about:

- Our personal bias and life views may affect our interpretation of the data. Bias is a natural human quality, and as we move from the particular to the general there is a tendency to manipulate data to fit with what we already believe.
- We may draw conclusions before the data are analyzed or before we have decided about the trustworthiness of the data collected.
- We might censor, ignore, or dismiss data as irrelevant. This may occur as a result of data overload or because the data contradict an already established mainstream way of thinking.
- We may make unwarranted or unsupported causal statements based on our impressions rather than founding them on solid analysis.
- We may be too opinionated and reduce our conclusions to a limited number of choices or alternatives.

Michael A. Huberman and Matthew B. Miles (1994) have suggested strategies to deal with the above risks:

- Member checking has already been described in the above step, but is noted again here for its utility as a way of guarding against our own biases dictating our conclusions.
- In our analysis, it is easy to unthinkingly give certain events and people more credibility than others. This prevents us, however, from making accurate interpretations of our data, because the people and the events selected are not sufficiently representative. We may come to the conclusion that we relied upon information that was too easily accessible, or that we weighted our results toward people we liked. To compensate for such possibilities, we can deliberately search for events and people that differ markedly from those we have already interviewed, to help

balance the perspective of the data that we have collected. If we detect such a bias, we can interview more people, looking especially for atypical research participants and events.

- Another source of bias is the effect that we may have upon our interviewees as well as the effect that they may have on us: We should assess our interaction with the research participants. The effects of these interactions are particularly powerful in qualitative methods, where data collection may involve our spending long periods of time with our interviewees. It is not uncommon for the interviewer to become personally responsive to interviewees, especially when they are revealing intimate details of their experience. While we are not suggesting that we remain aloof, if we are too responsive our interviewees may become misleading in an effort to please us.
- Looking for negative evidence resembles constant comparison, looking for outliers, and using extreme cases. Negative evidence should be actively sought when preliminary conclusions are made, to see if any data contradict or are inconsistent with our conclusion. We must actively hunt for contradictory data in case it counters the preliminary conclusion and what the researcher believes.

SUMMARY

This chapter presented a systematic and purposeful approach to data analysis in a qualitative research study. The predominant steps of a data analysis include transcript preparation (Step 1), establishing a preliminary plan for data analysis (Step 2), first-level coding (Step 3), second-level coding (Step 4), data interpretation and theory building (Step 5), and assessing the trustworthiness of our results (Step 6). Although these steps are presented in a linear fashion, the data analysis process is not that simple. We must be flexible and move back and forth between and among the steps and substeps to produce rich and meaningful findings.

REFERENCES AND FURTHER READINGS

ALTHEIDE, D., & JOHNSON, J. (1991). Criteria for assessing interpretive validity in qualitative research. In N.K. Denzin & Y. Lincoln (Eds.), *Handbook of qualitative research* (pp. 485-499). Newbury Park, CA: Sage.

BERG, B.L. (1995). *Qualitative research methods for the social sciences* (2nd ed.). Needham Heights, MA: Allyn & Bacon.

CHARMAZ, K. (1983). The grounded theory methods: An explication and interpretation. In R. Emerson (Ed.), *Contemporary field research* (pp. 109-126). Boston: Little, Brown.

COLEMAN, H., & UNRAU, Y.A. (1996). Phase three: Analyzing your data. In L.M. Tutty, M.A. Rothery, & R.M. Grinnell, Jr. (Eds.). *Qualitative research for social workers: Phases, steps, and tasks* (pp. 88-119). Needham Heights, MA: Allyn & Bacon.

DENZIN, N.K. (1994). The art and politics of interpretation. In N.K. Denzin & Y. Lincoln (Eds.), *Handbook of qualitative research* (pp. 500-515). Newbury Park, CA: Sage.

ELY, M., ANZUL, M., FRIEDMAN, T., GARNER, D., & McCORMACK-STEINMETZ, A. (1991). *Doing qualitative research: Circles within circles.* New York: Falmer Press.

ERLANDSON, D., HARRIS, E., SKIPPER, B., & ALLEN, S. (1993). *Doing naturalistic inquiry: A guide to methods.* Newbury Park, CA: Sage.

FIELDING, N.G., & FIELDING, J.L. (1986). *Linking data: Qualitative research methods series No. 4.* Newbury Park, CA: Sage.

FIELDING, N.G., & LEE, R. (Eds.). (1992). *Using computers in qualitative research.* Newbury Park, CA: Sage.

GLASER, B., & STRAUS, A. (1967). *The discovery of grounded theory: Strategics for qualitative research.* New York: Aldine de Gruyter.

GLESENE, C., & PESHKIN, A. (1992). *Becoming qualitative researchers: An introduction.* White Plains, NY: Longman.

HUBERMAN, M.A., & MILES, M. (1994). Data management and analysis methods. In N.K. Denzin & Y. Lincoln (Eds.), *Handbook of qualitative research* (pp. 428-444). Newbury Park, CA: Sage.

KIRK, J., & MILLER, M. (1986). *Reliability and validity in qualitative research.* Newbury Park, CA: Sage.

KREFTING, L. (1991). Rigor in qualitative research: The assessment of trustworthiness. *The American Journal of Occupational Therapy, 45,* 214-222.

LINCOLN, Y., & GUBA, E. (1985). *Naturalistic inquiry.* Newbury Park, CA: Sage.

MILES, M., & HUBERMAN, M.A. (1994). *Qualitative data analysis: A sourcebook of new methods* (2nd ed.). Newbury Park, CA: Sage.

PATTON, M.Q. (1990). *Qualitative evaluation and research methods.* Newbury Park, CA: Sage.

PFAFFENBERGER, B. (1988). *Microcomputer applications in qualitative research.* Newbury Park, CA: Sage.

RICHARDS, L., & RICHARDS, T. (1991). Computing in qualitative analysis: A healthy development? *Qualitative Health Research, 1,* 234-262.

SCHATZMAN, L., & STRAUSS, A. (1973). *Field research: Strategies for a natural sociology.* Englewood Cliffs, NJ: Prentice-Hall.

SEIDEL, J., KJOLSETH, R., & SEYMOUR, E. (1988). *The Ethnograph* (Version 3.0). Corvallis, OR: Qualis Research Associates.

SEIDMAN, I. (1991). *Interviewing as qualitative research: A guide for researchers in education and the social sciences.* New York: Teachers College Press.

SILVERMAN, D. (1993). *Interpreting qualitative data: Methods for analyzing talk, text, and interaction.* Newbury Park, CA: Sage.

STRAUS, A., & CORBIN, J. (1990). *Basics of qualitative research.* Newbury Park, CA: Sage.

TESCH, R. (1990). *Qualitative research: Analysis types and software tools.* New York: Falmer Press.

WALKER, L. (1979). *The battered woman.* New York: Harper & Row.

WOLCOTT, H. (1994). *Transforming qualitative data: Description, analysis, and interpretation.* Newbury Park, CA: Sage.

EVALUATION IN ACTION

Richard M. Grinnell, Jr.
Margaret Williams
Leslie M. Tutty

C h a p t e r **23**

Case-Level Evaluation

I N THE PREVIOUS seven parts of this book, we have covered the place of research in social work (Part I) and presented the process of going from research problems to questions to hypotheses (Part II). In addition, we now know how to conceptualize and operationalize variables (Part III) and have learned what constitutes an "ideal" experiment, given the various threats to internal and external validity (Part IV). We also know about the various data collection methods and data sources we can use within research studies (Parts V and VI). And we have considered both quantitative and qualitative data analysis (Part VII). We will apply this knowledge to the concept of evaluation, starting with the simplest type of evaluation—the single-case evaluation, or case-level evaluation.

On a very general level, case-level evaluation designs are more "practice orientated" than "research orientated." That is, they are used more by social work "practitioners" than by social work "researchers." Nevertheless, they can also be used in research situations when group research designs that use two or more groups of research participants cannot be used.

PURPOSE OF CASE-LEVEL EVALUATION DESIGNS

Research studies conducted to evaluate treatment interventions with social work clients are called case-level evaluation designs. They are also called *single-subject designs, single-case experimentations*, or *idiographic research*. Single-case research designs are used to fulfil the major purpose of social work practice: to improve the situation of a client system—*an* individual client, *a* couple, *a* family, *a* group, *an* organization, or *a* community. Any of these client configurations can be studied with a case-level evaluation design. In short, they are used to study *one* individual or *one* group intensively, as opposed to studies that use two or more groups of research participants.

Case-level evaluation designs can provide information about how well a treatment intervention is working, so that alternative or complementary interventive strategies can be adopted if necessary. They can also indicate when a client's problem has been resolved. Single-case studies can be used to monitor client progress up to, and sometimes beyond, the point of termination.

They can also be used to evaluate the effectiveness of a social work program as a whole by aggregating or compiling the results obtained by numerous social workers serving their individual clients within the program. A family therapy program might be evaluated, for example, by combining family outcomes on a number of families that have been seen by different social workers.

REQUIREMENTS

In order to carry out a single-case research study, the client's problem must be identified, the desired objective to be achieved must be decided upon, the intervention that is most likely to eliminate the client's problem must be selected, the intervention must be implemented, and the client's progress must be continually monitored to see if the client's problem has been resolved, or at least reduced. If practitioners are careful to organize, measure, and record what they do, single-case studies will naturally take shape in the clients' files, and the results can be used to guide future interventive efforts.

Only three things are required when doing a single-case study: (1) setting client objectives that are measurable, (2) selecting valid and reliable outcome measures, and (3) graphically displaying the results of the outcome measures.

Setting Measurable Objectives

One of the first tasks a worker does when initially seeing a client is to establish the purpose of why they are together. Why has the client approached the worker? Or, in many nonvoluntary situations, such as in probation and parole or child abuse situations, why has the worker approached the client? The two need to formulate objectives for their mutual working relationship. A specific, measurable, client desired outcome objective is known as a *client target problem*. Client target problems are feelings, knowledge levels, or behaviors that need to be changed.

Many times clients do not have just one target problem, they have many. They sometimes have a number of interrelated problems and, even if there is only one that is more important than the rest, they may not know what it is. Nevertheless, they may be quite clear about the desired outcome of their involvement with social work services. They may want to "fix" their lives so that, "Johnny listens when I ask him to do something," or "My partner pays more attention to me," or "I feel better about myself at work." Unfortunately, many clients express their desired target problems in vague, ambiguous terms, possibly because they do not know themselves exactly what they want to change; they only know that something should be different. If a worker can establish (with the guidance of the client) what should be changed, why it should be changed, how it should be changed, and to what degree it should be changed, the solution to the problem will not be far away.

Consider Heather, for example, who wants her partner, Ben, to pay more attention to her. Heather may mean sexual attention, in which case the couple's sexual relations may be the target problem. On the other hand, Heather may mean that she and Ben do not socialize enough with friends, or that Ben brings work home from the office too often, or has hobbies she does not share, or any of a host of things.

Establishing clearly what the desired change would look like is the first step in developing the target problem. Without this, the worker and client could wander around forever through the problem maze, never knowing what, if anything, needs to be solved. Desired change cannot occur if no one knows what change is desired. It is, therefore, very important that the target problem to be solved be precisely stated as early as possible in the client–social worker relationship.

Continuing with the above example of Heather and Ben, and after a great deal of exploration, the worker agrees that Heather and Ben have many target problems to work on, such as improving their child discipline strategies, improving their budgeting skills, improving their communication skills, and many other issues that, when dealt with, can lead to a successful marriage. For now, however, they agree to work on one target problem of increasing the amount of time they spend together with friends. To do this, the worker, Heather, and Ben must conceptualize and operationalize the term "increasing the amount of time they spend together with friends." As we saw from Chapters 5–7, a variable is conceptualized by defining it in a way that is relevant to the situation and operationalized in such a way that its indicators can be measured.

Heather may say that she wishes she and Ben could visit friends together more often. The target problem has now become a little more specific: It has narrowed from "increasing the amount of time they spend together with friends" to "Heather and Ben visiting friends more often.""Visiting friends more often with Ben," however, is still an ambiguous term. It may mean once a month or every night, and the achievement of the target problem's solution cannot be known until the meaning of "more often" has been clarified.

If Heather agrees that she would be happy to visit friends with Ben once a week, the ambiguous objective may be restated as a specific, measurable objective—"to visit friends with Ben once a week." The social worker may discover later that "friends" is also an ambiguous term. Heather may have meant "her friends," while Ben may have meant "his friends," and the social worker may have imagined that "the friends" were mutual.

The disagreement about who is to be regarded as a friend may not become evident until the worker has monitored their progress for a month or so and found that no improvement was occurring. In some cases, poor progress may be due to the selection of an inappropriate interventive strategy. In other cases, it may mean that the target problem itself is not as specific, complete, and clear as it should be. Before deciding that the interventive strategy needs to be changed, it is always necessary to clarify with the client exactly what it is that specifically needs to be achieved.

Selecting Outcome Measures

A target problem cannot really be said to be measurable until it is decided how it will be operationalized, or measured. Can Heather and Ben, who wanted to visit friends more often, be trusted to report truthfully on whether the friends were visited? Suppose she says they were not visited and he says they were? Social workers must always be very conscious of what measurement methods are both available and feasible when formulating a target problem with a client. It may be quite possible for the social worker to telephone the friends and ask if they were visited; but, if the worker is not prepared to get involved with Heather's and Ben's friends, this measurement method will not be feasible. If this is the case, and if Heather and/or Ben cannot be trusted to report accurately and truthfully, there is little point in setting the target problem.

Heather's and Ben's target problem can be easily observed and measured. However, quite often, a client's target problem involves feelings, attitudes, knowledge levels, or events that are known only to the client and cannot be easily observed and/or measured.

Consider Bob, a client who comes to a social worker because he is depressed. The worker's efforts may be simply to lessen his target problem, depression, but how will the worker and/or Bob know when his depression has been alleviated or reduced? Perhaps he will say that he feels better, or his partner may say that Bob cries less, or the worker may note that he spends less time in therapy staring at his feet. All these are indicators that his depression is lessening, but they are not very valid and reliable indicators.

What is needed is a more "scientific method" of measuring depression. Fortunately, a number of paper-and-pencil standardized measuring instruments have been developed that can be filled out by the client in a relatively short period of time, can be easily scored, and can provide a fairly accurate picture of the client's condition. One such widely used instrument that measures depression is the General Contentment Scale (*GCS*). Since higher scores indicate higher levels of depression, and lower scores indicate lower levels of depression, the target problem in Bob's case would be to reduce his score on the *GCS* to a level at which he can adequately function (which is usually a score of 30 or less).

People who are not depressed will still not score zero on the *GCS*. Everyone occasionally feels blue (Item 2) or downhearted (Item 10). There is a clinical cutting score that differentiates a clinically significant problem level from a nonclinically significant problem level, and it will often be this score that the client aims to achieve. If the target problem is, "to reduce Bob's score on the *GCS* to or below the clinical cutting score of 30," the worker will know not only what the target problem is, but precisely how Bob's success is to be measured.

Usually, client success, sometimes referred to as client outcome, can be measured in a variety of ways. Bob's partner, Maria, for example, may be asked to record the frequency of his crying spells, and the target problem here may be to reduce the frequency of these spells to once a week or less. Again, it would be important to further operationalize the term "crying spell" so that Maria knows exactly what it was she has to measure. Perhaps "crying spell" would be operationally defined as ten minutes or more of continuous crying, and a gap of at least ten minutes without crying would define the difference between one "spell" and another.

There are now two independent and complementary indicators of Bob's level of depression: the *GCS* as rated by Bob, and the number of his ten-minute crying spells per day as rated by Maria. If future scores on both indicators display improvement (that is, they both go down), the worker can be reasonably certain that Bob's depression is lessening and the intervention is effective.

If the two indicators do not agree, the worker will need to find out why. Perhaps Bob wishes to appear more depressed than he really is, and this is an area that needs to be explored. Or perhaps Maria is not sufficiently concerned to keep an accurate recording of the number of Bob's ten-minute crying spells per day; and it may be Maria's attitude that has caused Bob's crying in the first place. Accurate measurements made over time can do more than reveal the degree of a client's improvement. They can cast light on the problem itself and suggest new avenues to be explored, possibly resulting in the utilization of different interventive strategies.

Be that as it may, a client's target problem cannot be dealt with until it has been expressed in specific measurable indicators. These indicators cannot be said to be measurable until it has been decided how they will be measured. Specification of the target problem will, therefore, often include mention of an instrument that will be used to measure it. It will also include who is to do the measuring, and under what circumstances. It may be decided, for example, that Bob will rate himself on the *GCS* daily after dinner, or once a week on Saturday morning, or that Maria will make a daily record of all crying spells that occurred in the late afternoon after he returned home from work. The physical record itself is very important, both as an aid to memory and to track Bob's progress. In a single-case study, progress is always monitored by displaying the measurements made in the form of graphs.

Graphically Displaying Data

As we know from Chapter 7, the word *measurement* can be simply defined as the process of assigning a number or value to a variable. If the variable, or target problem, being considered is depression as rated by the *GCS*, and if Bob scores, say 72, then 72 is the number assigned to Bob's initial level of depression. The worker will try to reduce his initial score of 72 to at least 30—the minimum desired score. The worker can then select and implement an intervention and ask Bob to complete the *GCS* again, say once a week, until the score of 30 has been reached. Bob's depression levels can be plotted (over a 12-week period) on a graph, such as the one shown in Figure 23.1.

In the graph, Bob's depression level for each week is plotted on the *y*-axis, while time, in weeks, is plotted on the *x*-axis. There is a reason for this. Obviously, the social worker is hoping that the selected intervention will result in lowering Bob's level of depression, over time, as measured by the *GCS*. In other words, the worker is hypothesizing that: If Intervention *A* is implemented, Bob's depression will decrease. In research terminology, the independent variable in this hypothesis is the intervention (*X*) and the dependent variable (*Y*) is Bob's depression level. The frequency of Bob's ten-minute crying spells per day, as recorded by Maria, could also be graphed.

EXPLORATORY CASE-LEVEL EVALUATION DESIGNS

As discussed in previous chapters, exploratory, descriptive, and explanatory research studies fall on a knowledge-level continuum, as presented in Figure 3.1. To review briefly, exploratory studies begin with little knowledge in the problem area and produce only uncertain knowledge. Descriptive studies provide further descriptive facts, while explanatory studies attempt to explain the facts already gathered and produce the most certain level of knowledge.

Single-case studies are categorized as exploratory, descriptive, or explanatory, depending on the level of certainty they provide regarding the effectiveness of the intervention in resolving the client's target problem. Inevitably, the least complex research designs, at the exploratory level, provide the least certainty about whether the intervention was effective in bringing about the desired change.

We will briefly discuss three kinds of exploratory case-level evaluation designs: (1) the *B* design, (2) the *BC* design, and (3) the *BCD* design.

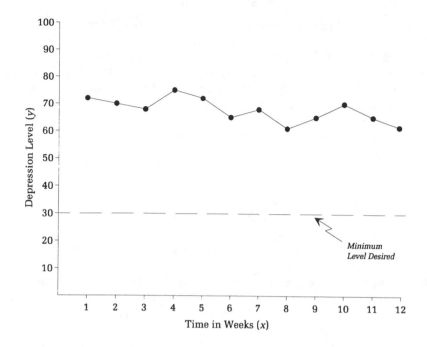

FIGURE 23.1   BOB'S DEPRESSION LEVEL OVER TIME

The *B* Design

The first type of exploratory case-level evaluation design is the *B* design, which is the simplest of all case-level evaluation designs. The italicized letter *B* refers to the fact that an intervention of some kind has been introduced. Let us take a simple example of how a *B* design works.

A couple, David and Donna, have had a long history of interrupting one another while the other is talking. They have tried to stop the pattern of this destructive behavior, to no avail. They have finally decided to do something about this and have sought out the services of a social worker. After some exploration, it becomes apparent that the couple need to concentrate on their interruptive behaviors. In short, the worker wishes to reduce the frequency with which David and Donna interrupt each other while conversing. This could be observed and measured by having them talk to each other while in weekly, one-hour sessions.

The worker teaches basic communication skills (the intervention) to the couple and has them practice these skills during each weekly session while other marital relationship issues are being addressed. Each week during therapy, while the couple is engaged in conversation, the worker makes a record of how many times each partner interrupts the other. Thus, in this situation, the worker is trying to reduce the number of interruptions—the target problem. For now, suppose that the data for David and Donna over a 12-week period look like those displayed in Figure 23.2.

Figure 23.2 shows that the number of times interruptions occurred decreased gradually over the 12-week period until it reached zero in the twelfth week—that is, until the goal of therapy had been achieved. Even so, the worker could continue to record the level of the target problem for a longer period of time to ensure that success was being maintained.

In this case, the worker hypothesized that if the intervention—teaching communication skills—were implemented, then the number of times the couple interrupted each other while conversing during therapy sessions would be reduced. Figure 23.2 shows that the target problem was achieved for both partners, but it does not show that the worker's hypothesis was in fact correct. Perhaps teaching communication skills had nothing to do with reducing the couple's interruptions. The interruptions may have been reduced because of something else the worker did (besides the communication skills training), or something the couple did, or something a friend did. There is even the possibility that their interruptions would have ceased if no one had done anything at all. Be that as it may, extraneous variables have not been controlled for. Thus, we cannot know how effective this particular intervention is in solving this particular target problem for this particular couple.

If we use the same interventive strategy with a second couple experiencing the same target problem and achieve the same results, it becomes more likely that the intervention produced the results. If the same results follow the same intervention with a third similar couple, it becomes more likely still. Thus, we can become more certain that an intervention causes a result the more times the intervention is successfully used with similar target problems.

However, if an intervention is used only once, as is the case with the exploratory *B* design, no evidence for causation can be inferred. All that can be gleaned from Figure 23.2 is that, for whatever reason, David's and Donna's target problem was reduced: or, if a graph such as Figure 23.3 is obtained instead, this indicates that the problem has not been resolved, or has been only partly resolved. If David and Donna continued to interrupt each other, week after week, a graph like the one shown in Figure 23.3 would be produced.

The data from graphs, such as the data presented in Figures 23.2 and 23.3, are extremely useful since a worker will be better able to judge whether the intervention should be continued, modified, or abandoned in favor of a different interventive strategy. In the simplest of terms, the *B* design only monitors the effectiveness of an intervention over time and indicates when the desired level of the target problem has been reached.

The *BC* and *BCD* Designs

The second and third types of exploratory case-level evaluation designs are the *BC* and *BCD* designs. In the *B* design previously described, the italicized

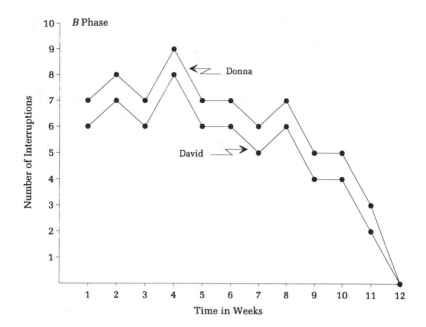

FIGURE 23.2   *B* DESIGN: FREQUENCY OF
INTERRUPTIONS FOR A COUPLE DURING
ONE INTERVENTION INDICATING AN
IMPROVEMENT

letter *B* represents a single interventive strategy. Suppose now that a *B* intervention, such as communication skills training, is implemented with David and Donna, and a graph like the one shown in Figure 23.4 is obtained. The left side of the graph shows that the problem is not being resolved with the implementation of the *B* intervention, and the social worker may feel that it is time to change the intervention, so a *C* intervention is tried starting the fifth week. Four weeks, for example, may have been as long as the worker was prepared to wait for the hoped-for change to occur for the *B* intervention to work.

As can be seen in Figure 23.4, the worker implemented a second different intervention, *C*, starting the fifth week and measured the target problem in the same way as before, by making weekly recordings of the number of times that each partner interrupts the other during the course of therapy sessions. These measurements are graphed as before, plotting the level of the client's target problem along the *y*-axis and the time in weeks along the *x*-axis. The data are shown in the *C* phase of Figure 23.4.

Figure 23.4 shows that no change occurred in the target problem after Intervention *B* was implemented, but the target problem was resolved following the implementation of Intervention *C*. As before, extraneous variables have not been

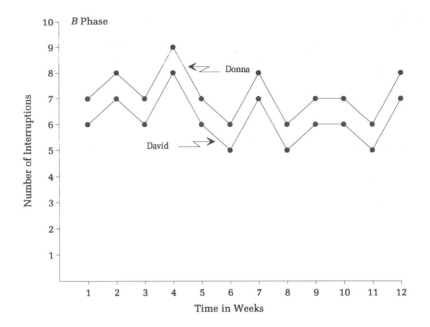

FIGURE 23.3   *B* DESIGN: FREQUENCY OF
INTERRUPTIONS FOR A COUPLE DURING
ONE INTERVENTION INDICATING NO
IMPROVEMENT

considered, and Figure 23.4 does not show that Intervention *C* caused the problem to be resolved: It shows only that success occurred during Intervention *C* but not during Intervention *B*.

In order to demonstrate causation, the worker would have to obtain successful results with Intervention *C* on a number of occasions with different couples experiencing the exact same target problem. Similarly, the inherent uselessness of Intervention *B* could be shown only if it was implemented unsuccessfully with other couples—an unlikely event since the most hopeful intervention surely would be implemented first.

If Intervention *C* does not work either, the worker will have to try yet another intervention (Intervention *D*). Combined graphs may be produced, as in Figure 23.5, illustrating the results of the entire *BCD* case-level evaluation design.

Since the *BC* and *BCD* designs involve successive, different interventions, they are sometimes known as successive interventions designs. It is conceivable that an *E* intervention might be necessary, forming a *BCDE* design, and even an *F*, forming a *BCDEF* design. Multiple-treatment interference, discussed in Chapter 11, is a major threat to the external validity of successive intervention designs. Let us now turn our attention to descriptive case-level evaluation designs.

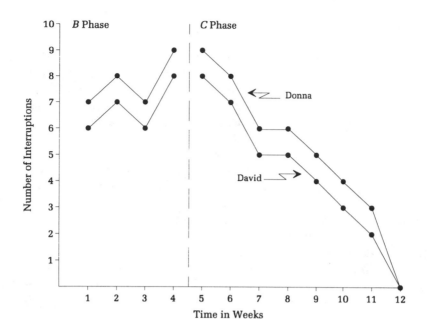

FIGURE 23.4   *BC* DESIGN: FREQUENCY OF
INTERRUPTIONS FOR A COUPLE AFTER
TWO INTERVENTIONS INDICATING AN
IMPROVEMENT WITH THE SECOND
INTERVENTION

DESCRIPTIVE CASE-LEVEL EVALUATION DESIGNS

One of the difficulties with the three exploratory case-level evaluation designs previously discussed (*B*, *BC*, and *BCD* designs) is that they provide no data about the level of the client's target problem *before* the intervention was introduced. Bob, for example, might show himself to be severely depressed according to his initial score of 72 (Figure 23.1) on the *GCS*. Perhaps the cause of his depression, however, is the recent death of his 20-year-old cat, Teddy; and the problem will resolve itself naturally as he recovers from Teddy's loss.

Or perhaps he was more depressed on the day that he approached the worker than he usually is. Thus, it would have been useful if we had had an accurate measure of Bob's depression levels over time *before* he received social work services. Descriptive case-level evaluation designs provide such a procedure. We will briefly discuss two types of descriptive case-level evaluation designs: (1) the *AB* design, and (2) the *ABC* design. We will now turn our attention to the *AB* design.

The *AB* Design

An *AB* design is useful when a worker can afford to monitor a client's target problem for a short time *before* implementing an intervention. Suppose a social worker is seeing Juan, who experiences a great deal of anxiety in social situations, for example. He is nervous when he speaks to his teacher or boss or when he meets people for the first time, and the prospect of speaking in public appalls him.

The worker could decide that progress for Juan's target problem might be measured in two ways: first, he will complete the Interaction and Audience Anxiousness Scale (*IAAS*) that measures social anxiety. For the first four weeks, the worker will not intervene at all. The purpose of the worker's contact, in these weeks, will be merely to gather data on the initial level of Juan's anxiety—that is, to gather baseline data.

The period in which initial data are being gathered is known as the *A* phase of the study. The italicized letter *A* symbolizes no intervention—in the same way as the letters *B, C,* and *D* symbolize the first, second, and third interventive strategies, respectively. Suppose, now, that Juan scores 60 on the *IAAS* the first

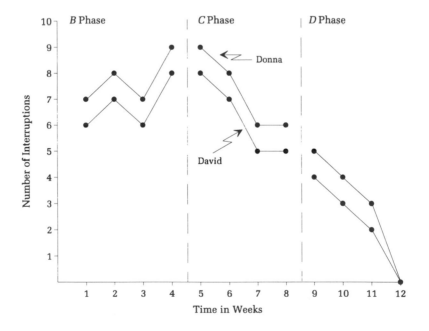

| **FIGURE 23.5** | *BCD* Design: Frequency of Interruptions for a Couple After Three Interventions Indicating the Best Improvement with the Third Intervention |

week he is assessed, 55 the second week, 62 the third, and 58 on the fourth. Juan's anxiety scores for this four-week period before an intervention was introduced can be graphed as shown in Figure 23.6.

Taken together, the four scores in Figure 23.6 show that Juan's anxiety level is reasonably stable at about an average of 59. Since it has remained relatively stable over a four-week period, the likelihood is that it will continue to remain at the same level if a social worker does not intervene: That is, Juan's problem will not solve itself. The worker would be even more justified to intervene immediately if Juan achieved anxiety scores as illustrated in Figure 23.7. Here, Juan's anxiety level is rising: his anxiety problem is growing worse.

Conversely, if he achieved the four scores shown in Figure 23.8, the worker might be reluctant to intervene, because Juan's anxiety level is decreasing anyway. If the worker did intervene, however, and his anxiety level continued to decrease, we would never know if the worker's intervention had a positive effect or if the same result would have been achieved without it.

The four scores shown in Figure 23.9 vary to such an extent that it is not possible to tell how anxious Juan really is. Again, we would be reluctant to intervene because there would be no way of knowing whether Juan was making progress or not, and whether the intervention was helpful or not. In order to conduct an *AB* single-case research study—and in order to be helpful to a client—the level of the target problem must be stable (e.g., Figure 23.6), or getting worse (e.g., Figure 23.7) in the *A* phase.

Suppose that it has been established that Juan's target problem level is stable, as illustrated in Figure 23.6. An objective may then be set: to reduce Juan's social anxiety level to 40. Forty has been selected because people who suffer from social anxiety at a clinically significant level tend to score *above* 40 on the *IAAS*, while people whose social anxiety is not clinically significant score *below* 40. It will not really matter whether the objective is precisely met. If Juan becomes more confident in social situations, feels more ready to meet people, and only reaches a score of 45, this may be good enough to warrant termination of services.

Having produced a baseline graph and established a target problem, the worker can now implement an intervention package that could include such activities as role-playing through anxiety-producing situations and coping strategies. Whatever the intervention package, it is important that a record of its process is made so that another worker will know, in the future, exactly what the specific intervention was.

Once the baseline, or *A* phase, has been established, the *B* phase will proceed as in the three exploratory *B* designs previously discussed. Juan will complete the *IAAS* weekly, or every two weeks, or however often is appropriate, and the scores will be graphed. Figure 23.10 shows a relatively stable *A* phase over the first four weeks (from Figure 23.6), and a decreasing anxiety level over the next eight weeks, while the intervention is being implemented. The dashed vertical line on the graph indicates the time at which the intervention was begun.

The worker could continue to monitor the level of Juan's target problem after it has been achieved in order to ensure that progress is being maintained. We

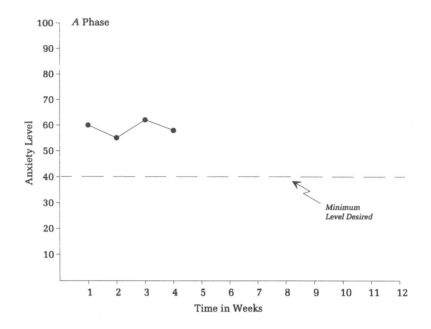

FIGURE 23.6   MAGNITUDE OF JUAN'S ANXIETY LEVEL
BEFORE AN INTERVENTION INDICATING
A STABLE BASELINE

cannot adequately judge the usefulness of an intervention until it is known not only that it works, but that it continues to work when it is no longer the focus of our attention. It is, therefore, essential to make follow-up measurements whenever possible, perhaps a month, six months, and a year after the client's target problem appears to have been resolved. The actual number and frequency of follow-up measurements will depend on the type of problem and the client's situation.

The *ABC* Design

The second type of descriptive case-level evaluation design is the *ABC* design. Figure 23.11 shows the same *A* phase as in Figure 23.10, but now the *B* phase indicates that Juan's problem is not being satisfactorily resolved. In this case, his worker will probably want to change the *B* intervention, initiating a *C* intervention. Juan's problem level will be continually measured over time and may progress to the level set in the objective. On the other hand, if there is still no improvement, or an insufficient improvement, a *D* intervention may need to be implemented.

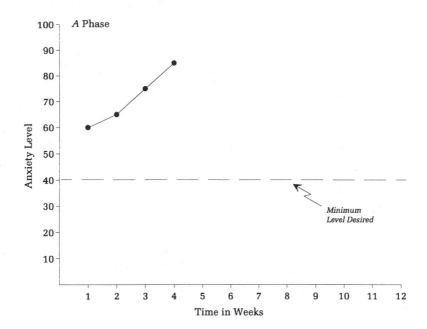

FIGURE 23.7   MAGNITUDE OF JUAN'S ANXIETY LEVEL
BEFORE AN INTERVENTION INDICATING
A DETERIORATING BASELINE

As with the exploratory *BC* and *BCD* designs presented earlier, descriptive *ABC* and *ABCD* case-level evaluation designs involve trying successive interventions until the target problem level is reached, or almost reached. However, exploratory designs only enable workers to compare the progress made in each new phase with progress in the previous phase or phases. Look at Phase *B* in Figure 23.11. Juan's *B*-phase scores are slightly lower than his *A*-phase scores. Some improvement has occurred, although a worker may not have been able to judge that from the *B*-phase if baseline scores were not established. When the results are not clear-cut, it is the *A* phase that enables us to see whether there has been a little progress from the initial problem level, no progress at all, or perhaps even a regression.

When a new intervention is initiated in the *C* phase, the social worker is not really starting again from the beginning. The worker is starting from where the problem level was at the end of the *B* phase. If the *C* intervention is successful in resolving the problem, it is impossible to tell, without further studies, whether the *C* intervention would have worked alone or whether it was the combination of *B* and *C* that did the trick. If a *D* intervention is employed as well, the various effects of *B*, *C*, and *D* grow even more intertwined, so that we cannot know which intervention had what effect—even supposing that a given intervention had any

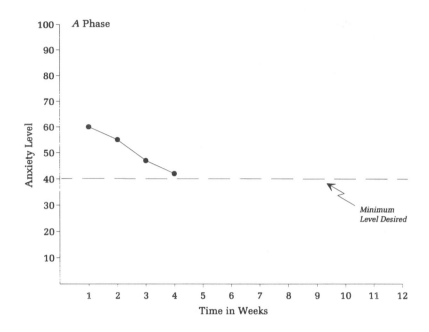

FIGURE 23.8   MAGNITUDE OF JUAN'S ANXIETY LEVEL
BEFORE AN INTERVENTION INDICATING
AN IMPROVING BASELINE

effect whatsoever. We will now turn our attention to explanatory case-level evaluation designs.

EXPLANATORY CASE-LEVEL EVALUATION DESIGNS

Explanatory case-level evaluation designs attempt to come to grips with the problem of cause and effect. If a worker wants to know whether a particular intervention is effective in a particular problem area, the following question needs to be answered: Did intervention X cause result Y? At an explanatory level, the worker needs to be sure that nothing other than the intervention caused the result.

As we know from Chapter 11, a research study in which changes in the dependent variable result only from changes in the independent variable is said to be internally valid. Explanatory case-level evaluation designs attempt to control for the threats to internal validity.

In order to conduct an internally valid study, three factors need to be taken into account. First, we must show that the independent variable occurred before the dependent variable. Second, the inevitable cohort of extraneous variables

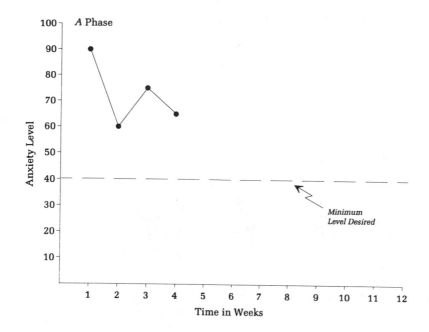

FIGURE 23.9   MAGNITUDE OF JUAN'S ANXIETY LEVEL
BEFORE AN INTERVENTION INDICATING
A FLUCTUATING BASELINE

must be identified and dealt with. Third, a worker will need to consider other general factors that may pose a threat to internal validity. An improvement in a client's level of self-esteem, for example, may occur not only from the interventive efforts. The improvement may be due to changes in another aspect of the client's life, such as getting a new job, or an intervention by another practitioner such as being placed on medication. Alternatively, things may improve spontaneously.

Explanatory case-level evaluation designs attempt to control for such other occurrences by showing that there were two or more times in which improvement was noted in the client after a given intervention. If such is the case, then the likelihood of the improvement being related to other rival hypotheses is decreased. We will briefly discuss three types of explanatory case-level evaluation designs: (1) the *ABAB* design, (2) the *BAB* design, and (3) the *BCBC* design.

The *ABAB* Design

As the name might imply, an *ABAB* case-level evaluation design is simply two descriptive *AB* designs strung together. This design is most appropriate with

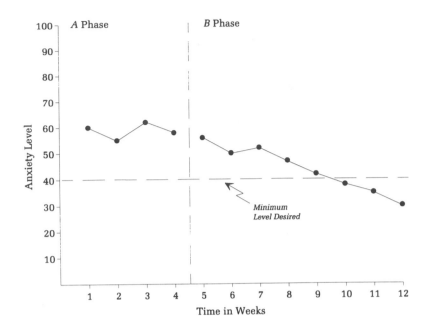

FIGURE 23.10   *AB* Design: Magnitude of Juan's Anxiety Level Before and After an Intervention Indicating an Improvement

interventions that produce temporary or easily removable effects, or when an intervention is withdrawn but measurements on the client's target problem continue to be made.

Referring back to Juan, whose target problem is social anxiety, Figure 23.10 illustrates a descriptive *AB* design as previously described. It shows a stable *A* or baseline phase, followed by a successful *B* phase, where his social anxiety level is gradually reduced to below 40 during the 10th week. It cannot be certain, however, that the intervention caused the reduction in anxiety until the same intervention has been tried again and has achieved the same result. The more times the same intervention is followed by the same result, the more certain it will become that the intervention caused the result.

Suppose, now, that Juan successfully reached his objective score of 40 during the first *B* phase (6th week) as illustrated in Figure 23.12. After services are withdrawn, Juan then experiences some social reversals as his anxiety mounts once more as indicated in the second *A* Phase in Figure 23.12. The worker provides services for the second time and has Juan complete the same *IAAS* during the second *B* phase.

The worker goes through the same process as was done the first time, estab-

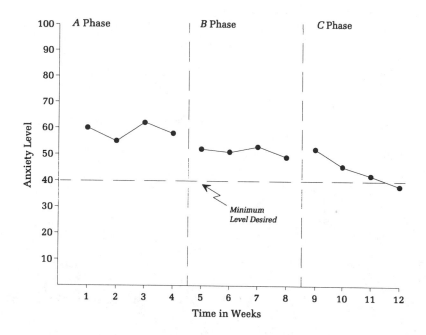

FIGURE 23.11   *ABC* DESIGN: MAGNITUDE OF JUAN'S
ANXIETY LEVEL BEFORE AND AFTER
TWO INTERVENTIONS INDICATING AN
IMPROVEMENT WITH THE *C*
INTERVENTION

lishing a baseline score, or *A* phase, in the first few weeks before the introduction
of an intervention. The same intervention is implemented, and measurements of
Juan's progress are obtained through the *B* phase, producing almost the same
result.

We can now be more certain that the intervention caused the result since the
same intervention was followed by the same result on two separate occasions. In
this example, Juan's social anxiety level returned to the original baseline
level—the level established in the first *A* phase. From a research perspective, this
is an ideal state of affairs, since the first *AB* study can now be duplicated almost
exactly. From a practice perspective, however, it is worrisome as we would like
to think that a client will continue to benefit from an intervention after it has
been withdrawn.

In fact, many clients do continue to benefit. Juan may have learned and
remembered techniques for reducing his anxiety, and it would be unusual for his
problem to return to its exact original level. Figure 23.13 illustrates a scenario in
which Juan's anxiety problem did not return to its original level.

In a case such as that shown in Figure 23.13, it is still quite possible to

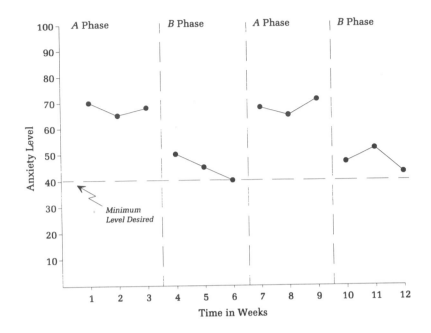

FIGURE 23.12   *ABAB* Design: Magnitude of Juan's Anxiety Level Before and After an Intervention Indicating High Deterioration in the Second A Phase

conduct an *ABAB* study. The baseline scores in the second *A* phase are relatively stable, even though they show an improvement over the first *A* phase; and the second *B* phase shows once again that the intervention has been followed by a reduction in Juan's social anxiety level.

Sometimes it is important to continue to measure the target problem even after it appears to have been resolved and the intervention has been withdrawn. Those workers who continue to measure a client's target problem, perhaps while working on a different issue, are essentially constructing another baseline. This can be used as an additional *A* phase if the client suffers a regression and needs the intervention to be repeated.

An *ABAB* design in which the target problem, once resolved, reverts to its original level, is known as a reversal design. Such a design may be implemented accidentally. We never intend that the client's target problem should reoccur. If an *ABAB* design is to be conducted purposefully, in order to attain more certainty about the effectiveness of an intervention, then another way to proceed is to use a multiple-baseline design.

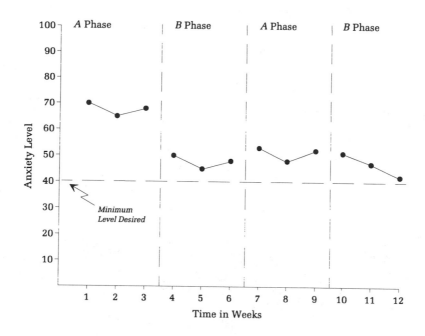

FIGURE 23.13   *ABAB* DESIGN: MAGNITUDE OF JUAN'S
ANXIETY LEVEL BEFORE AND AFTER
AN INTERVENTION INDICATING LOW
DETERIORATION IN THE SECOND *A*
PHASE

Multiple-Baseline Designs

In multiple-baseline designs, the *AB* phase is duplicated not with the same client and the same target problem but with two or more different clients (e.g., Figure 23.14), across two or more different settings (e.g., Figure 23.15), or across two or more different problems (e.g., Figure 23.16).

Two or More Clients   Suppose a worker has not just one client with a social anxiety problem but two or more. He or she could establish a baseline with each client, implement an identical intervention with each one, and compare several *AB* designs with one another. If the *B* phases show similar results, the worker has grounds to speculate that the intervention caused the result.

As always, we must take care that the effect ascribed to the intervention did not result, instead, from extraneous variables. If the worker's socially anxious clients all happened to be residents of the same nursing home, for example, some event in the nursing home could have contributed to the reduction in their anxiety: perhaps a newly instituted communal activity. This possibility can be

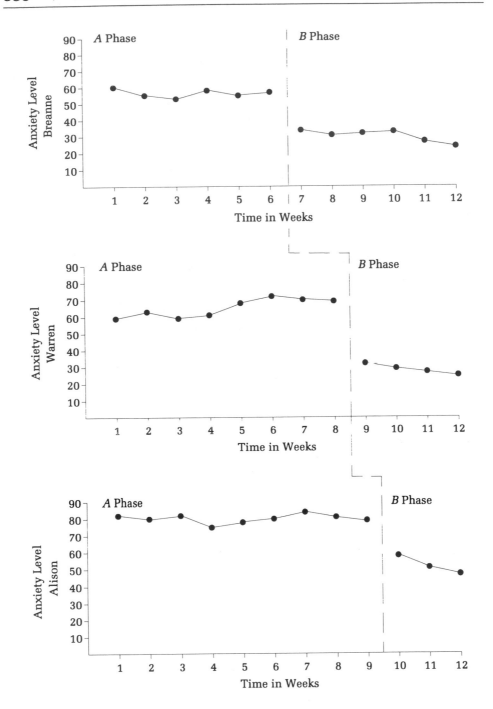

FIGURE 23.14   Multiple-Baseline Design Across Clients:
Magnitude of Anxiety Levels for Three
Clients Indicating an Improvement

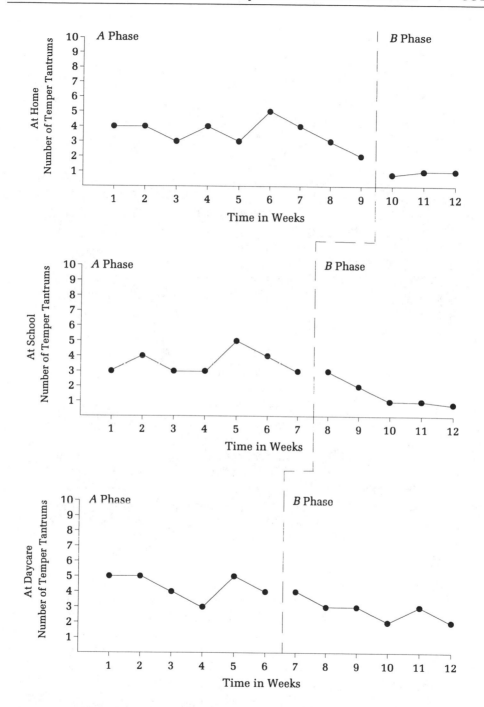

FIGURE 23.15   MULTIPLE-BASELINE DESIGN ACROSS SETTINGS:
NUMBER OF TEMPER TANTRUMS FOR ONE CLIENT
IN THREE SETTINGS INDICATING AN IMPROVEMENT

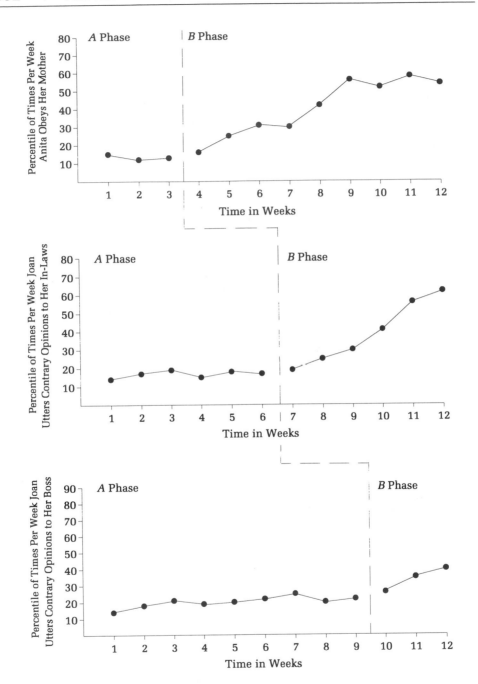

FIGURE 23.16   MULTIPLE-BASELINE DESIGN ACROSS CLIENT TARGET PROBLEMS: MAGNITUDE OF THREE CLIENT TARGET PROBLEM AREAS FOR ONE CLIENT INDICATING AN IMPROVEMENT

controlled for—that is, we can ensure that extraneous variables have not occurred—by introducing the same intervention with each client at different times. Figure 23.14 illustrates an example of a multiple-baseline design across three clients who are being seen by a social worker for anxiety problems.

Had an extraneous variable been responsible for the reduced anxiety demonstrated by Breanne, the other two clients, Warren and Alison, would also have demonstrated reduced anxiety, even though the worker was not intervening on their behalf. The fact that the baseline scores of the second two clients remained stable until the introduction of the intervention is a good indication that no extraneous variables were present, and that the intervention is a probable cause of the result.

While a multiple-baseline design requires more effort than a simple *AB* design, it is often clinically feasible. A multiple-baseline study across clients can sometimes be carried out by several workers at the same time.

Two or More Settings   Another way to conduct a multiple-baseline study is to use not separate clients, but two or more separate settings. Suppose that an objective is to reduce the number of a child's temper tantrums. Three parallel single-case research studies could be conducted: one at home, one at school, and one at the day-care center where the child goes after school. At home, a parent might count the number of temper tantrums per day, both before and during the intervention. A teacher might do the same thing at school, as would a staff member at the day-care center. Again, extraneous variables can be controlled for by beginning the *B* phase at different times, as illustrated in Figure 23.15.

Two or More Problems   A third way to conduct a multiple-baseline study is to use the same intervention to tackle different target problems. Suppose that Joan is having trouble with her daughter, Anita.

In addition, Joan is having trouble with her in-laws and with her boss at work. After exploration, a worker may believe that all these troubles stem from her lack of assertiveness. Thus, the intervention would be assertiveness training.

Progress with Anita might be measured by the number of times each day she is flagrantly disobedient. Progress can be measured with Joan's in-laws by the number of times she is able to utter a contrary opinion, and so on. Since the number of occasions on which Joan has an opportunity to be assertive will vary, these figures might best be expressed in percentiles. Figure 23.16 illustrates an example of a multiple-baseline design that was used to assess the effectiveness of Joan's assertiveness training in three problem areas.

Whether it is a reversal design or a multiple-baseline design, an *ABAB* explanatory design involves establishing a baseline level for the client's target problem. This will not be possible if the need for intervention is acute, and sometimes the very thought of an *A*-type design will have to be abandoned. It is sometimes possible, however, to construct a retrospective baseline—that is, to determine with a reasonable degree of accuracy what the level of the target problem was *before* an intervention is implemented.

The best retrospective baselines are those that do not depend on the client's memory. If the target problem occurs rarely, memories may be accurate. For example, Tai, a teenager, and his family may remember quite well how many times he ran away from home during the past month. They may not remember nearly so well if the family members were asked how often he behaved defiantly. Depending on the target problem, it may be possible to construct a baseline from archival data: that is, from written records, such as school attendance sheets, probation orders, employment interview forms, and so forth.

Although establishing a baseline usually involves making at least three measurements before implementing an intervention, it is also acceptable to establish a baseline of zero, or no occurrences of a desired event. A target problem, for example, might focus upon the client's reluctance to enter a drug treatment program. The baseline measurement would then be that the client did not go (zero occurrences) and the desired change would be that the client did go (one occurrence). A social worker who has successfully used the same tactics to persuade a number of clients to enter a drug treatment program has conducted a multiple-baseline design across clients.

As previously discussed, a usable baseline should show either that the client's problem level is stable (e.g., Figure 23.6) or that it is growing worse (e.g., Figure 23.7). Sometimes an *A*-type design can be used even though the baseline indicates a slight improvement in the target problem (e.g., Figure 23.8). The justification must be that the intervention is expected to lead to an improvement that will exceed the anticipated improvement if the baseline trend continues.

Perhaps a child's temper tantrums are decreasing by one or two a week, for example, but the total number per week is still 18 to 20. If a worker thought the tantrums could be reduced to four or five a week, or they could be stopped altogether, the worker would be justified in implementing an intervention even though the client's target problem was improving slowly by itself.

In a similar way, a worker may be able to implement an *A*-type design if the client's baseline is unstable, provided that the intervention is expected to exceed the largest of the baseline fluctuations. Perhaps the child's temper tantrums are fluctuating between 12 and 20 per week in the baseline period and it is hoped to bring them down to less than 10 per week.

Nevertheless, there are some occasions when a baseline cannot be established or is not usable, such as when a client's behaviors involve self-injurious ones. Also, sometimes the establishment of a baseline is totally inappropriate.

The *BAB* Design

As the name suggests, a *BAB* design is an *ABAB* design without the first *A* phase. Many times a social worker may decide that immediate intervention is needed and that there is not time to collect baseline data. The client's progress can be monitored, as is done in a *B* design, and the intervention can be withdrawn later when the problem appears to be resolved. Previous experience has indicated that sometimes even the best-resolved client problems tend to reoccur, however, and the worker therefore, continues to measure the target problem level, constructing an *A* phase almost incidentally. When the client's target problem does reoccur, the worker still has a good record of what happened to the problem level after the intervention was withdrawn. Figure 23.17 illustrates an example of a *BAB* design.

Since there is no initial baseline data, we cannot know whether the resolution of the client's target problem on the first occasion had anything to do with the intervention. The problem may have resolved itself, or some external event may have resolved it. Nor can we know the degree to which the problem level changed during the intervention, since there was no baseline data with which to compare the final result. An indication of the amount of change can be obtained by comparing the first and last measurements in the *B* phase, but the first measurement may have been an unreliable measure of the client's target problem level. The client may have felt more or less anxious that day than usual; and a baseline is necessary to compensate for such fluctuations.

Since the effectiveness of the intervention on the first occasion is unknown, there can be no way of knowing whether the intervention was just as effective the second time it was implemented, or less or more effective. All we know is that the problem level improved twice, following the same intervention; and this is probably enough to warrant using the intervention again with another client.

The *BCBC* Design

In the same way that an *ABAB* design comprises two *AB* designs, a *BCBC* design is simply two *BC* designs strung together. In order to conduct a *BC* design, we can implement an intervention without collecting baseline data, and subsequently introduce a second intervention, both of which may be potentially useful. Although the social worker does not have baseline data, and thus has no record of how serious the problem was initially, the worker is able to use this design to compare the efficacy of the two or more different interventions.

ADVANTAGES AND DISADVANTAGES

This section explores some of the more common advantages and disadvantages in using case-level evaluation designs.

Advantages

Single-case research studies can benefit clients in a number of ways, both directly and indirectly. A social worker is obliged to think through the client's target problem more carefully than might otherwise have been done, since the

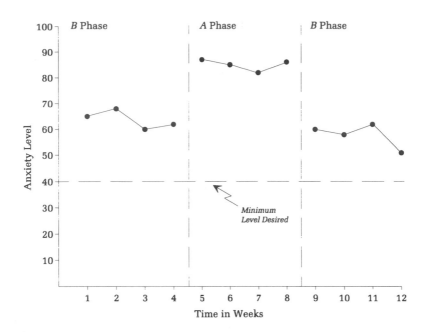

FIGURE 23.17   *BAB* DESIGN: MAGNITUDE OF JUAN'S ANXIETY LEVEL DURING AND AFTER AN INTERVENTION IN THE *A* PHASE

client's problem must be operationally defined in a way that will allow it to be measured. Desired change must be specified in the form of a client target problem so that we know when the objective has been achieved. In other words, a worker must know precisely what the client's problem is and what it is that the client wants to change.

A case-level evaluation design also requires that a careful, visual record be kept of whatever change occurs in the client's target problem. When graphs are produced, everyone concerned can see what changes have really occurred and what changes they only think are occurring. Possibly, the study will not be very successful. There might be fluctuations in the baseline data, for example, that make it impossible to carry out an intended *AB* study. However, these very fluctuations may throw light upon the problem. A client named Darcy, for example, may discover that she is more depressed on days when she visits her sister in the nursing home. Her worker may then be able to trace Darcy's depression to an unadmitted fear of dependency and death.

As findings from single-case research studies are duplicated, they offer increasing guidance as to what specific interventions work with what specific kinds of clients in what specific circumstances. They can also generate more precise hypotheses for testing in the increasingly complex group research designs discussed in Chapter 11. The most important advantage of single-case studies, however, is that they can be undertaken by line-level social workers seeing clients on a day-to-day basis. They are consistent with case needs in everyday practice situations, and they are neither expensive to implement nor time-consuming.

Case-level evaluation designs have additional advantages. First, they do not limit a worker to any particular theoretical or practice approach. The worker can intervene in any way desired, as long as he or she knows exactly what was done, and in what sequence. Second, the graphed results build up a repertoire of successful intervention strategies. If client records are adequate, a worker can look back at a specific target problem he or she may have encountered a year ago. This process would help remind the worker about what worked and what did not, and how former clients progressed.

Disadvantages

The first and most obvious limitation of a single-case research study is that it may not work. The client may have a problem that cannot be changed in the 4-to-12-week period that is normal for an *AB* study. Or the selected intervention, and the next one, and the one after that may be unsuccessful in bringing about the desired change. Of course, a study can continue for longer than twelve weeks—it can continue for as long as necessary—but often clients, and social workers too, tire of making measurements after the first three months, and the study will die a natural death if it is not brought to a planned conclusion.

Second, simply because an intervention worked with one client does not necessarily mean that it will be as effective with a similar client. The issue of generalizability to other cases, or the external validity, is described in Chapters 11 and 12. Suffice it to say that in case-level evaluation designs we sacrifice concerns about generalizability and focus on how well an intervention works for one client system. Generalizability is essentially impossible to establish in single-case studies; we would have to be able to demonstrate that the clients to whom the intervention is given are representative of a larger group of clients to whom the intervention might be applied.

Then, there may be problems with operational definitions and with measurements. A mother who is asked to keep count of her daughter's temper tantrums may exaggerate in order to impress the worker with the severity of her daughter's problem. Or she may forget to count and invent a figure in order to save herself embarrassment. Or she may merely be unsure of just what constitutes "a temper tantrum." Does shouted defiance count, or improper language, or a covert kick at her little brother, or must it be a prolonged assault on furniture or persons? However minutely we try to define these, there is often a period of confusion at the beginning of the study, when the hoped-for baseline data never actually seem to be collected.

The usual problems with measurement also apply. Measuring instruments may not be reliable or valid, measurements may not be taken regularly, or the act of measuring may influence the target problem being measured.

Finally, case-level evaluation designs work best for interventions that are specific to certain problem areas, rather than to general methods of problem solving. Thus, for example, teaching behavioral skills to become more assertive, or relaxation-training to help overcome phobias, fits with case-level evaluation designs nicely, since the intervention can be easily withdrawn by not providing the intervention in a particular session. If a social worker is using generic counseling methods, though, these may not be as easily withdrawn without a concern for the client.

SUMMARY

Single-case studies are undertaken for the purpose of monitoring client progress up to, and sometimes beyond, the point of termination. Data gained in this way help to judge whether our intervention should be changed, modified, or terminated, and whether it is good enough to use with another client. The three requirements for a single-case study are: setting measurable objectives, selecting outcome measures, and graphically displaying data.

An objective is a specific, measurable, desired outcome and is referred to as a client target problem. Before it can be said to be measurable, each concept in it must be conceptualized and operationalized—that is completely and specifically defined—and the measuring instrument to be used must be specified.

In a single-case study, change in the target problem is always monitored by displaying the measurements made in the form of graphs such as the 17 figures displayed in this chapter. Single-case studies can be categorized as exploratory, descriptive, or explanatory, depending on the level of certainty they provide regarding the effectiveness of the intervention in resolving the target problem. The least complex research designs, at the exploratory level, provide the least certainty about whether the intervention was effective in bringing about the desired change. Exploratory case-level evaluation designs include *B*, *BC*, and *BCD* designs, where the italicized letters *B*, *C*, and *D* represent the first, second, and third interventive strategies, respectively.

Descriptive case-level evaluation designs include *AB* and *ABC* designs, where the italicized letter *A* represents a period of no intervention, during which baseline data are collected. Baseline data provide data about the initial problem level, allowing us to judge whether an intervention is necessary, or might be harmful, and whether a gentle or vigorous intervention is most appropriate. Measurement of the initial problem level over time also lets us judge the effectiveness of the intervention since we can see the degree of change that has occurred.

Exploratory and descriptive designs provide no evidence for causation if they are used only once. Conversely, explanatory case-level evaluation designs attempt to come to grips with the problem of cause and effect. They do so by ensuring that the intervention preceded the result, and by controlling for extraneous variables. The fact that interventions are provided, withdrawn, and provided once again, deals with many of the potential threats to internal validity that were discussed in detail in the previous chapter.

Explanatory case-level evaluation designs include *ABAB, BAB,* and *BCBC* designs. An *ABAB* design in which the target problem, once resolved, reverts back to its original level is known as a reversal design. A multiple-baseline design is one in which the *AB* phase is duplicated not with the same client and the same problem but with two or more different clients, two or more different settings, or across two or more different problems.

The following chapter expands upon this one by presenting how social work programs are evaluated.

REFERENCES AND FURTHER READINGS

BARLOW, D.H., HAYES, S.C., & NELSON, R.O. (1984). *The scientist-practitioner: Research and accountability in applied settings.* Elmsford, NY: Pergamon.

BARLOW, D.H., & HERSEN, M. (1984). *Single-case experimental designs: Strategies for studying behavior change* (2nd ed.). Elmsford, NY: Pergamon.

BLOOM, M., FISCHER, J., & ORME, J. (1995). *Evaluating practice: Guidelines for the accountable professional* (2nd ed.). Englewood Cliffs, NJ: Prentice-Hall.

GABOR, P.A., & GRINNELL, R.M., JR. (1994). *Evaluation and quality improvement in the human services* (pp. 123-147). Needham Heights, MA: Allyn & Bacon.

GRINNELL, R.M., JR., & WILLIAMS, M. (1990). *Research in social work: A primer* (pp. 232-264). Itasca, IL: F.E. Peacock.

KRYSIK, J., HOFFART, I., & GRINNELL, R.M., JR. (1993). *Student study guide for the fourth edition of social work research and evaluation* (pp. 6-8). Itasca, IL: F.E. Peacock.

NURIUS, P.S., & HUDSON, W.W. (1993). *Human services: Practice, evaluation, and computers.* Pacific Grove, CA: Brooks/Cole.

POLSTER, R.A., & LYNCH, M.A. (1985). Single-subject designs. In R.M. Grinnell, Jr. (Ed.), *Social work research and evaluation* (2nd ed., pp. 381-431). Itasca, IL: F.E. Peacock.

RUBIN, A., & BABBIE, E.R. (1993). *Research methods for social work* (2nd ed., pp. 292-328). Pacific Grove, CA: Brooks/Cole.

THYER, B.A. (1993). Single-system designs. In R.M. Grinnell, Jr. (Ed.), *Social work research and evaluation* (4th ed., pp. 94-117). Itasca, IL: F.E. Peacock.

THYER, B.A., & CURTIS, G.C. (1983). The repeated pretest-posttest single-subject experiment: A new design for empirical clinical practice. *Journal of Behavior Therapy and Experimental Psychiatry, 14,* 311-315.

WEINBACH, R.W., & GRINNELL, R.M., JR. (1996). *Applying research knowledge: A workbook for social work students* (2nd ed., pp. 73-80). Needham Heights, MA: Allyn & Bacon.

WILLIAMS, M., TUTTY, L.M., & GRINNELL, R.M., JR. (1995). *Research in social work: An introduction* (2nd ed., pp. 161-194). Itasca, IL: F.E. Peacock.

Allen Rubin
Earl R. Babbie

Chapter **24**

Program-Level Evaluation

I N RECENT YEARS a form of applied research has developed that is sensitive to the political and social contexts in which it takes place. This applied research is known as *evaluation research*, or *program evaluation*. It refers to the purpose of our research efforts rather than to any specific research design (Part IV) or data collection method (Parts V and VI). Its purpose is simply to assess and improve the conceptualization, design, planning, administration, implementation, effectiveness, efficiency, and utility of social work interventions (Rossi & Freeman, 1989).

Toward that end, program evaluation systematically applies many research designs and data collection methods, such as experiments (Chapter 11), case studies (Chapters 12 and 21), structured observations (Chapter 13), surveys (Chapter 14), participant observation (Chapter 15), secondary analyses (Chapter 16), utilizing existing statistics (Chapter 17), content analysis (Chapter 18), historical research (Chapter 19), and so forth.

In short, the previous chapter detailed how we can evaluate our effectiveness with individual client systems (case-level evaluation). We will continue our discussion of evaluation by presenting how we evaluate social service delivery programs (program-level evaluation).

At the start of this text we distinguished social work research from basic social scientific research by its purpose, citing the former's focus on practical knowledge that we need to solve the problems we confront in our practice and that social service programs need to guide their efforts to alleviate human suffering and promote social welfare.

In light of that focus, program evaluation—when applied to social work settings and issues—is conceptually very similar to social work research, and many of the research studies we conduct have a program evaluation purpose. Because program evaluation has more to do with the purposes of our research effort than with specific research designs and data collection methods, we focus more on the implications of those purposes for carrying out research than on particular research designs and data collection methodologies. Although we examine some methodological content, it is important to recognize that throughout this book we have been discussing research designs and data collection methods that can be applied in both case- and program-level evaluation purposes.

HISTORICAL OVERVIEW

Although the growth of program evaluation is a fairly recent phenomenon, planned social evaluation is quite old. Some authors have dated it back to 2200 B.C. in China, and connected it with personnel selection (Shadish et al., 1991). Whenever people have instituted a social reform for a specific purpose, they have paid attention to its actual consequences, even if they have not always done so in a conscious, deliberate, or systematic fashion or called what they were doing program evaluation. In the mid-nineteenth century, for example, the reform movement for more humane care of the mentally challenged succeeded in getting states to build more public state psychiatric hospitals. Some of the hospitals' superintendents contributed to their growth by citing data that proved the hospitals' success in "curing" mental illness (Grob, 1973).

Those superintendents were discharging 90 percent or more of their patients and claiming this meant they were achieving 90 percent to 100 percent cure rates! At the time, notions of rehospitalization, relapse, and chronicity were not in vogue, and the superintendents therefore temporarily got away with using "discharge from the state psychiatric hospital" as the operational definition of recovery from mental illness, although they did not use the term "operational definition." (Here we begin to see the importance of the political context of program evaluation, a theme that runs throughout this book.)

More systematic approaches to program evaluation can be traced back to the beginning of the twentieth century. Early efforts evaluated schools that used different teaching approaches and compared educational outcomes by examining student scores on standardized tests. Several decades later, experimental program evaluation studies examined the impact of worker morale on industrial productivity and the impact of public health education programs on hygienic practices.

In the 1940s, after New Deal social welfare programs were implemented, studies examined the effects of work relief versus direct relief, the effects of public housing, and the effects of treatment programs on juvenile delinquency. Program evaluation received additional impetus during World War II, with studies such as Samuel Stouffer's (1949-1950) research on soldier morale and the impact of personnel and propaganda policies on morale. After the war, large public expenditures were committed to social service programs that attempted to improve housing, public health, attitudes toward minorities, and international problems in health, family planning, and community development. As expenditures grew, so did interest in "objective data" on the results of these programs.

Program evaluation became widespread by the late 1950s as efforts increased to alleviate or prevent social problems such as juvenile delinquency and to test out treatment innovations in psychotherapy and new psychopharmacological discoveries. By the late 1960s textbooks, professional journals, national conferences, and a professional association on evaluation research emerged. This explosion of interest in program evaluation continued during the 1970s, as the public increasingly demanded evidence regarding the return on its investment in various programs to combat poverty, child abuse, substance abuse, crime and delinquency, mental illness, and so on.

But by the late 1970s, after public funding for these programs waned, declines began in the funding of studies to evaluate them. This trend toward reduced funding of program evaluation accelerated during the 1980s, as federal evaluation offices were hit hard by the budget cuts of the Reagan administration (Shadish, Cook, & Leviton, 1991).

Although the government today provides less funding for program evaluation than it did before the 1980s, we still live in an "age of accountability," as liberals and conservatives alike demand that social service programs be more accountable to the public regarding whether they are really delivering what they promise to deliver. In fact, the need to evaluate them may be greater when their funding is scarce than when it is abundant, since the scarcity of funds intensifies concerns that we not waste what little funds we have on ineffectual programs.

In this connection, it is a mistake to assume that only fiscal conservatives, those reluctant to spend money on social service programs, are the ones expressing skepticism about what "bang the public is getting for its buck." Individuals of all political persuasions have this interest, including human service professionals who fiercely support increased social welfare spending but who are dedicated to finding better ways to help people and do not want to see scarce welfare resources squandered on programs that do not really help their intended target populations. In fact, a major group that has historically been a force in favor of greater accountability consists of consumer rights advocates concerned about whether the consumers of our services are being served properly.

As a result of these forces, and despite recent funding cuts, program evaluation today has become ubiquitous in the planning and administration of social welfare policies and programs. In fact, instead of having a program evaluator position, a social service program might assign responsibility for program evaluation activities to personnel called "planners or program analysts" (Posavac & Carey, 1994). Funding sources still require both a program evaluation component as a prerequisite for approving grant applications and supportive evaluative data as a basis for renewing funding. This requirement has been a mixed blessing, however. On one hand, the requirement that programs evaluate their efforts induces program personnel to support more applied research that could help them improve their policies and programs and find better ways to help people. On the other hand, this requirement means that agency personnel and others have vested interests in the study's findings.

THE POLITICS OF PROGRAM EVALUATION

Because the findings of a program evaluation study can provide ammunition to the supporters or opponents of the program, intense political pressure is introduced into the entire program evaluation process. Vested interests can impede the atmosphere for free, scientific inquiry. Instead of pursuing truth as scientifically as possible in order to improve human well-being, program evaluation efforts may be implemented in ways that fit perceived program maintenance needs. Sometimes this means that there will be intense pressure to design a program evaluation study (or to interpret its findings) in ways that are likely to make the program look good.

Other times it may simply mean that a program evaluation is conducted in the least expensive, most convenient way possible, guided by the belief that funding sources do not pay much attention to the quality of the study's methodology and just want to be able to say that the programs they fund have been evaluated. Consequently, it is naive to suppose that when administrators hire someone to be responsible for program evaluation activities (or to conduct a specific program evaluation), they will pick the person most qualified from a scientific, research methodology standpoint.

Political considerations—that the evaluation will be done to favor vested interests—may be a much higher priority. Indeed, it probably is not overly cynical to suppose that commitment to conducting the most scientific program evaluation study possible will threaten administrators and be perceived as a problem. They are unlikely to admit as much; rather, they may call individuals with a devotion to methodological rigor "too ivory towerish and out of touch with the real world." (And sometimes they are correct—if zeal for methodological rigor blinds us and makes us insensitive to realistic feasibility constraints that make some methodological compromises appropriate and unavoidable.)

Consequently, it is not unusual to see programs fill program evaluation positions with people who lack any special proficiency in or dedication to research design, but who instead are good computer jocks—high-tech bureaucrats who massage the computer in order to grind out evaluative data that will put the program in a favorable light and who will not make waves about academic issues like the internal or external validity of the evaluative effort.

When program evaluators are employed by the program being evaluated, they are called in-house evaluators. Program evaluators also work for external agencies (called external evaluators) such as governmental or regulating agencies and private research consultation firms (which often bid for government grants to evaluate programs receiving public funds). University faculty members also secure research grants to evaluate programs or simply wish to conduct applied research studies as part of their scholarly duties.

In-house evaluators have certain advantages over external evaluators. They have greater access to program data and personnel, more knowledge about program processes that bears upon the design of an evaluation or the meaning of findings, and more sensitivity to the research needs of the program and to the realistic obstacles to the feasibility of certain research designs or data collection methods. They are also more likely to be trusted by program personnel and consequently to receive better cooperation and feedback from them. But the flip side of the coin is that their commitment to their program, to their superiors, or to the advancement of their own careers may make them less objective and independent than external evaluators.

But it would be naive to suppose that external evaluators are never subjected to the same kinds of political considerations as are in-house evaluators. External evaluators may have very strong incentives to get and stay in the good graces of the personnel of the program being evaluated. If they alienate those personnel, the quality of their evaluation may be imperiled by the lack of cooperation with the evaluation agenda. In fact, one criterion for choosing the recipient of a program evaluation grant might be the quality of the relationship the evaluator has with the social service program and the potential of that relationship for securing cooperation from the program's participants (clients).

Also, it is incorrect to assume that external sponsors of a program evaluation are always more objective than in-house personnel. Perhaps the sponsors of the evaluation want to stop funding the program and need negative evaluation results to justify the cessation of funding to their own constituents. On the other hand, the sponsors might fret that negative results would make them (the sponsors) look bad and in turn threaten their own fund-raising efforts. We once worked on an evaluation research project that illustrates this point.

Example: Community Mental Health Curriculum Evaluation

During the mid-1970s the Council on Social Work Education (CSWE) was awarded a research grant by the social work training unit of the National Institute of Mental Health (NIMH) to evaluate the community mental health curriculum component within graduate schools of social work. A prime purpose of this evaluation was to describe the different ways in which the schools were implementing their NIMH training grants. At that time almost every Masters degree program in social work was receiving thousands of dollars annually in order to prepare students for practice in the field of community mental health, and our evaluation project sought to identify community mental health curriculum innovations fostered by the NIMH grants.

We were able to identify innovative community mental health curricula in some graduate schools of social work. But based on the data we gathered over a two-year period during multiple site visits to participating schools, we concluded that most graduate schools of social work had initiated no curriculum innovations associated specifically with community mental health. Instead, their NIMH grant funds enabled them to expand their traditional curriculum, and they justified that practice on the grounds that everything that has always been taught in a graduate school of social work is related to community mental health.

We might anticipate that faculty members and administrators in these schools would be upset with the preceding conclusion, which was included in the final evaluation report. We believed that school personnel might fear that it would threaten the continuation of their NIMH funding (Rubin, 1979). At the same time, we also anticipated that the NIMH social work training staff would appreciate the candor of our report, thinking that they then could use the report to distinguish those schools making appropriate use of the NIMH funding from those that were not and to influence the latter schools to be more accountable to them. But as it turned out, according to the CSWE administrators, the NIMH staff expressed more consternation about the findings than did anyone else.

Their fear was that bureaucrats in other units of the NIMH—units that were in competition with social work for federal funds—could use the report as ammunition in their efforts to secure a bigger slice of the funding pie for their units at the expense of social work training. If that were to happen, not only would graduate schools of social work receive less funding, but the staff of the social work training unit would lose status in the bureaucracy and see their own budget reduced.

Thus, the web of politics in program evaluation can be widespread, and sometimes the external groups sponsoring an evaluation are not as independent and objective as we might suppose. In the foregoing example, the NIMH social work training staff were quite eager to get a report that would portray graduate schools of social work as doing wonderfully innovative things with their NIMH funds, a report that they could then use to justify their own performance in allocating funds and monitoring their usage and in order to argue for more funding for their unit.

And in choosing the CSWE to conduct the evaluation, it is reasonable to suppose that they fully expected that a glowing report would be forthcoming because the CSWE is funded and governed by representatives of graduate schools of social work and because one of the main goals of the CSWE is to lobby for greater funding for social work education. In fact, the CSWE's administrative staff expressed displeasure with our report and tried to influence us to modify our interpretations of the findings in order to depict more favorably the benefits of the NIMH funding for graduate schools of social work.

Utilization of Program Evaluation Findings

As the preceding discussion illustrates, the findings derived from program evaluation studies affect jobs, programs, and investments. Beliefs and values are at stake as well. Consequently, political and ideological forces influence whether and how findings from a particular program study are utilized.

Let us take an example to illustrate this point. As president, Richard Nixon appointed a blue-ribbon national commission to study the consequences of pornography. After a diligent, multifaceted evaluation, the commission reported that pornography did not appear to have any of the negative social consequences often attributed to it. Exposure to pornographic materials, for example, did not increase the likelihood of sex crimes. We might have expected liberalized legislation to follow from the research findings. Instead, the president said the commission was wrong.

Less dramatic examples of the failure to follow the implications of evaluation research could be listed almost endlessly. Undoubtedly all evaluation researchers can point to studies they conducted—studies providing clear research results and obvious policy implications—that were just simply ignored. There are three important reasons why the implications of evaluation research results are not always put into practice:

- The study's final report is presented in such a way that is meaningless to "nonresearchers."
- Evaluation results sometimes contradict deeply held beliefs. That was certainly the case with the pornography commission just mentioned. If everybody *knows* that pornography is bad, that it causes all manner of sexual deviance, then it is likely that research results to the contrary will have little immediate impact.
- Evaluation results sometimes become commingled with vested interests. Suppose, for example, a group of practitioners in a family service agency, after receiving extensive training (and indoctrination) in a new model of family therapy, succeed in convincing their colleagues and superiors within the agency to let them form a new unit specializing in service delivery based on that model of family therapy. They are convinced that their services will be effective, and forming the new unit has significantly enhanced their prestige and autonomy within the agency. What are they going to do when an evaluation suggests that their model does not work? It is highly unlikely that they will fold up their tents, apologize for misleading people, and return willingly to their old routines. It is more likely, however, that they will point out inescapable methodological and statistical limitations in the evaluation study, call it misleading or worthless, and

begin intense lobbying with colleagues and superiors to have their model of family therapy continue.

Logistical Problems

The social context of program evaluation affects not only the utilization of the outcomes of evaluative studies but also the logistics involved in their implementation. *Logistics* refers to getting research participants to do what they are supposed to do, getting research instruments distributed and returned, and other seemingly unchallenging tasks.

Motivating Sailors

When Kent Crawford and his colleagues (1980) set out to find a way to motivate "low performers" in the U.S. Navy, they found out just how many problems can occur. The purpose of their evaluation study was to test a three-pronged program for motivating sailors who were chronically poor performers and who were often in trouble aboard ship.

First, a workshop was to be held for supervisory personnel, training them in effective leadership of low performers.

Second, a few supervisors would be selected and trained as special counselors and role models—people the low performers could turn to for advice or just as sounding boards.

Finally, the low performers themselves would participate in workshops aimed at training them to be more motivated and effective in their work and in their lives. The project was conducted aboard a particular ship, with a control group selected from sailors on four other ships.

To begin, the researchers reported that the supervisory personnel were not exactly thrilled with the program (Crawford, et al., 1980):

> Not surprisingly, there was considerable resistance on the part of some supervisors toward dealing with these issues. In fact, their reluctance to assume ownership of the problem was reflected by "blaming" any of several factors that can contribute to their personnel problem. The recruiting system, recruit training, parents, and society at large were named as influencing low performance—factors that were well beyond the control of the supervisors. (p. 488)

Eventually, the reluctant supervisors came around and this initial reluctance gave way to guarded optimism and later to enthusiasm. The low performers themselves were even more of a problem, however. Their research design called for pretesting and posttesting of the sailors' attitudes and personalities, so that their attitude and personality changes, brought about by the program, could be evaluated. As Crawford and his colleagues note (1980):

Unfortunately, all of the LPs (Low Performers) were strongly opposed to taking these so-called personality tests and it was therefore concluded that the data collected under these circumstances would be of questionable validity. Ethical concerns also dictated that we not force "testing" on the LPs. (p. 490)

As a consequence, they had to rely on interviews with the low performers and on the judgments of supervisors for their measures of attitude change. The research participants continued to present problems, however.

Initially, the ship's command ordered 15 low performers to participate in the study. Of the 15 people, however, one went into the hospital, another was assigned duties that prevented his participation, and a third went over the hill (absent without leave). Thus, the study began with 12 people. But before it was completed, three more people completed their enlistments and left the Navy, and another was thrown out for disciplinary reasons. The study concluded, then, with eight research participants. Although the evaluation pointed to positive results, the very small number of remaining research participants warrants caution in any generalizations derived from the study.

The special, logistical problems of evaluation research grow out of the fact that it occurs within the context of uncontrollable daily life.

Administrative Control

As suggested in the previous example, the logistical details of an evaluation project are often under the control of program administrators. Let us suppose we are evaluating whether conjugal visits improve morale among prison inmates (our program). On the fourth day of our program, for example, a male prisoner knocks out his wife, dresses up in her clothes, and escapes. Although we might be tempted to assume that his morale was greatly improved by escaping, this turn of events would complicate our study's research design in many ways. Perhaps the warden will terminate our program altogether, and where is our evaluation then? Or, the warden may review the files of all those prisoners we selected randomly for our experimental group and veto the "bad risks."

There goes the comparability of our experimental and control groups. As an alternative, stricter security measures may be introduced to prevent further escapes, and the security measures may have a dampening effect on the inmates' morale. So the experimental stimulus has changed in the middle of our research project. Some of the data will reflect the original stimulus, other data will reflect the modification. Although we will probably be able to sort it all out later, our carefully designed evaluation study has become a snakepit.

Let us say we have been engaged to evaluate the effect of race relations lectures on prejudice in the Army. We have randomly assigned some soldiers to attend the lectures and others to stay away. The rosters have been circulated weeks in advance, and at the appointed day and hour, the lectures begin. Everything seems to be going smoothly until we begin processing the files: The names do not match. Checking around, we discover that military field exercises, KP

duty, and a variety of emergencies required some of the experimental participants to be elsewhere at the time of the lectures.

That is bad enough, but then we learn that helpful commanding officers sent
others to fill in for the missing soldiers. And whom do you suppose they picked
to fill in? Soldiers who did not have anything else to do or who could not be
trusted to do anything important. We might learn this bit of information a week
or so before the deadline for submitting our final report on the impact of the race
relations lectures.

These are examples of only a few of the logistical problems we can face. We
need to be familiar with them and understand why some research procedures
may not measure up to the classical experimental design. As we read reports of
evaluation research, however, we will find that—all our earlier comments
notwithstanding—it is possible to carry out controlled social work research
studies in real-life practice situations.

Let us now look at some of the steps that we can take to prevent or minimize
logistical problems and to promote the utility and ultimate use of our evaluation
findings.

Planning an Evaluation and Fostering Its Utilization

Emil Posavac and Raymond Carey (1994) propose a number of steps that help
us anticipate and deal with potential logistical problems and potential resistance
to an evaluation and its ultimate utilization. There are basically two ways we can
deal with these issues: (1) involving a program's stakeholders, and (2) writing a
useful final report.

Involving Stakeholders

We need to learn as much as possible about the program's *stakeholders*—those with vested interests in our evaluation whose beliefs, income,
status or careers, and workload might be affected by the evaluation's results. In
order to promote their identification with the evaluation and their support of it
during the data collection phase, it is essential that they be involved in a meaningful way in planning the evaluation. Service recipients (clients) are also stakeholders and therefore should be included in the planning process.

It also is important at the outset to find out who wants the evaluation, why
they want it, and who does not want it. If, for example, program sponsors want
the evaluation but program personnel either do not know about it or do not want
it, then we should try to make the program personnel more comfortable with the
evaluation in order to foster their cooperation in collecting and interpreting the
data.

One way to do this, of course, is by involving them as stakeholders, and by
sharing mutual incremental feedback throughout all phases of the evaluation

process. Then, involvement should begin early in the planning of the evaluation, not just after the research design is ready to be implemented. In addition to fostering cooperation with the evaluation, involving personnel in the planning is thought to improve the chances for identifying those daily organizational realities that might pose logistical obstacles to alternative research designs or data collection methodologies.

As a final step in engaging program personnel in planning our evaluation, we need to obtain their feedback regarding a written proposal that reflects their input. The purpose of presenting them with the proposal is to make certain that they agree with us about the components of the evaluation and the nature of the program being evaluated. In addition, by reconsidering everything in a final, written package, they might see problems not apparent in earlier discussions.

Planning an evaluation is a two-way street. We not only need to consider potential problems posed by the program's stakeholders, but we also must consider the potential problems stemming from mistakes we might make in designing the study. Involving decision makers who are likely to utilize our study's findings, for example, helps ensure that we will address questions relevant to their decision-making needs rather than questions that are trivial or of interest only to audiences who are not in a position to act upon the study's findings. Also, without input from a program's personnel, we might choose or develop the wrong data collection instruments, such as standardized self-reports that clients might not understand or be willing to complete.

Conceivably the attainment of a program's objectives might need to be measured idiosyncratically for each client because each client has unique needs and target problems. If so, we need to assess clients' goal attainment through an aggregation of single-case designs rather than through a group experiment that assesses all clients with the same outcome measures (see Chapter 23). We also might not understand the unrealistic burden that our data collection procedures might place on practitioners who already are strained trying to meet heavy paperwork requirements without sacrificing the quality of service they are providing to their clients.

The cooperation of a program's personnel can be fostered further by assuring them that they will get to see and respond to a confidential draft of our evaluation report before it is finalized and disseminated to other stakeholders. While they should not be made to feel that they will be able to censor our report, they should be assured that their suggestions will be taken very seriously. By meeting with key personnel to discuss the report, we can point out and clarify implications of the study's findings that personnel might find particularly useful for improving the program.

Writing a Useful Final Report

Finally, we can foster the utilization of our evaluation report by tailoring its form and style to the needs and preferences of those in a position to utilize it.

Clear, succinct, and cohesive composition always helps, as does careful typing and a neat, uncluttered layout. The briefer and neater the report, the more likely busy administrators and practitioners are to read it carefully. When adapting the report to an audience of program personnel, every peripheral finding is not mentioned. In addition, negative findings are never bluntly and tactlessly presented. If program objectives are not being attained, findings are couched in language that recognizes the good efforts and skills of program personnel and that does not portray them as inadequate.

We must try not to convey a message of success or failure, but rather provide suggestions for developing new programs or improving existing ones. We need to alert program personnel in the planning stage that all reports bring some good news and some bad news and that our focus will be less on judging the value of the program than on identifying feasible ways to improve it. Sufficient attention must also be given to the practical implications of our study's findings.

PURPOSES OF PROGRAM EVALUATION

So far, we have been discussing the politics of program evaluation primarily in connection with assessing the effectiveness of programs in attaining their formal written goals. Asking whether a program is achieving a successful outcome is perhaps the most significant evaluative question that could be asked, and it probably is the question that immediately comes to mind when we think about program evaluation. It may also be the most politically charged question because it bears directly on key vested interests, such as those associated with the program's funding.

But, as noted at the beginning of this chapter, program evaluation can have other purposes than evaluating whether a program is effective or not. It can also focus on a program's conceptualization, design, planning, administration, and implementation of its interventions.

At this point, then, we are going to look at the different purposes of program evaluation. This is done paying particular attention to methodological issues, but, nevertheless, political considerations keep popping up as we compare these alternative purposes of program evaluations. On a general level, there are four broad purposes of program evaluation research: (1) evaluating a program's outcome, (2) evaluating a program's efficiency, (3) evaluating the implementation of a program, and (4) evaluating if a program is needed.

Before we elaborate on each of these purposes, however, two terms need to be introduced that have been commonly used to classify these alternative purposes: *summative evaluations* and *formative evaluations*. *Summative evaluations* are concerned with the first two purposes, involving the ultimate success of a program and decisions about whether it should be continued or chosen in the first place from among alternative options. The results of a summative evaluation convey a sense of finality. Depending on whether the results imply that the program succeeded, the program may or may not survive.

Formative evaluations, on the other hand, are not concerned with testing the success of a program. They focus instead on obtaining data that are helpful in planning the program and in improving its implementation and performance (Posavac & Carey, 1994). These types or purposes of program evaluation are not mutually exclusive, however. Rather, they complement one another, and some evaluations cover more than one of these purposes, such as when an evaluation finds that a program failed to attain its formal written goals because it was never properly implemented in the first place.

Evaluating a Program's Outcome

Evaluations of program outcome assess whether the program is effectively attaining its formal written goals, whether it has any unintended harmful effects, whether its success (if any) is being achieved at a reasonable cost, and how the ratio of its benefits to its cost compares with the benefits and costs of other programs with similar goals.

This approach to evaluation refers to the formal written goals and mission of a program—whether it is achieving what its founders or the general public want it to achieve. Typically, in designing these evaluations, the program's formal written goals are specified as dependent variables and operationally defined in terms of measurable indicators of the program success. The focus is on maximizing the *internal validity* of the evaluation design to rule out bias and other plausible rival explanations of outcome and to be able to determine whether the particular outcomes observed were really *caused* by the program.

Thus, these evaluations strive to use the most internally valid experimental designs possible and to use rigorous, objective, quantitative measures. Ideally, program participants, such as service recipients, will make up the experimental group, and their counterparts who do not participate, or who receive an alternate program, will make up the control or comparison group. Alternatively, quasi-experimental designs that do not require a control group, can be used. In short, this approach to program evaluation primarily applies the principles discussed in Part IV of this book in order to infer causal connections between program efforts and indicators of program outcome.

When people do not like a message they receive, they often blame the messenger. In the same vein, when they do not like the findings of an outcome evaluation, they often blame the evaluation's methodology. It is commonly perceived, that over the years, evaluations of program outcomes have had far more negative findings, indicating program failure, than positive findings. It is also widely believed that studies with negative findings tend not to be utilized because of the vested interests at stake. And expectations that rigorous, experimental outcome studies tend to produce negative findings have made administrators wary of such studies and reluctant to authorize them. One common complaint is that all that these studies do is tell us that we are failing; they do not show us how to do things better.

One important criticism of the traditional approach to evaluating a program's outcome correctly points out that the determination of a program's goal and the measurable indicators of obtaining its goal can be hazardous at the best of times. Sometimes the mission, or goal, of a social service program is stated in such grandiose terms that no one really take it seriously—terms that were articulated for political reasons or to convince legislators or others that a program should be funded. Consequently, it is argued that finding negative outcomes in evaluations of the attainment of a program's goal is a foregone conclusion—that evaluators are doomed to keep coming up with negative findings if they keep taking formally stated goals seriously.

In addition to their grandiosity, formal goals are often stated so vaguely that different evaluators may find it impossible to agree on what they really mean in terms of specific, measurable indicators of success. The Head Start program in the War On Poverty is often cited as a case in point. Its formal mission was to offset the effects of poverty in order to enhance the opportunities of children. That indeed is a noble mission, but what are its operational indicators?

Evaluative researchers have disagreed over whether the focus of the outcome measures should be on indicators of learning readiness, academic achievement, emotional development and self-esteem, classroom conduct, delinquency later in life, physical health and nutrition, or something else. The possibilities seem endless, and often a program's personnel themselves cannot agree on what specific indicators of success are implied by their program's mission statement.

Consequently, when evaluators choose a few operational indicators of success, they risk missing areas in which the program really is succeeding. If so, then their negative findings may be misleading and may endanger the continuation of programs that are succeeding in other, equally important ways. In light of these problems, some argue that the evaluation of outcome ought to be abandoned altogether and replaced by evaluations of program processes. Others argue that, even with these problems, outcome studies at least tell us some things about what is and is not being attained, which is better than having no data at all about program outcomes, particularly if appropriate caution is exercised in acting upon the study's findings.

Evaluating a Program's Efficiency

No matter how rigorous the assessment of a program's outcome, an evaluation may be deemed incomplete unless it also assesses the costs of obtaining the outcome. In other words, how *efficient* is the program in achieving its outcome? Suppose, for example, that an evaluation of a case management program to prevent rehospitalization of the chronically mentally challenged concludes that the program successfully reduces the number of days patients are hospitalized. Suppose further that the total number of days hospitalized for 50 case-managed patients during the course of the evaluation is 400 days, as compared to 500 days for 50 control group patients.

In other words, the case management program made a difference of 100 fewer hospitalized days. So far, so good. But suppose the extra cost of providing the case management services during the study period was $50,000. Thus, each day of hospitalization saved by providing case management was costing $500 (which we get by dividing $50,000 by 100). If the cost of hospital care was less than $500 per day per patient, then some might conclude that, despite the program's effectiveness, it was not an efficient way to care for the mentally challenged.

Such questions of efficiency tend to be purely economic and may not take into account important value judgments, such as those dealing with the worth of humanistic benefits reaped by service recipients. The costs of the preceding hypothetical program to the public at large may seem high, but some might believe that those costs are justified by the improved quality of life experienced by patients when they reside in the community. Thus, once again we see the social and political context of program evaluation. Different stakeholders might disagree about whether a particular benefit of a program is worth the extra cost, depending on which stakeholder is bearing the cost and which is reaping the benefit. And many client-related benefits, such as improved health or an individual's self-esteem, cannot be valued in dollars.

But it is nevertheless useful to assess a program's efficiency. Even if humanistic considerations lead us to believe that a less efficient program is still the most desirable option, at least we could make that decision in light of the ratio of costs to benefits. And sometimes assessing efficiency helps us to determine which alternative program provides more humanistic benefits.

Suppose, for example, that an alternative type of case management program that costs $25,000 for 50 cases results in 425 hospitalized days for the same study period as the case management program that resulted in 400 hospitalized days. Although the $25,000 program had a slightly worse outcome, its costs were only half that of the $50,000 program. That means that an allocation of $50,000 would enable us to provide the less expensive program to twice as many cases as the more expensive program. Therefore, assuming that a finite level of funding does not permit us to provide the more expensive program to most of the target population, the slightly less effective—but much more efficient—program might yield greater humanistic benefits.

Cost-Effectiveness and Cost-Benefit Analyses

The two major approaches to assessing the efficiency of a program are called *cost-effectiveness analysis* and *cost-benefit analysis*. In *cost-effectiveness analysis*, the only monetary considerations are the costs of the program itself, the monetary benefits of the program's effects are not assessed. In *cost-benefit analysis*, in addition to monetizing program costs, an effort is made to monetize the program's outcome.

In the foregoing case management example, we would be conducting a cost-effectiveness analysis if we limited our focus to the program-cost-per-day of hospitalization prevented. Thus, if we report that one program costs $500 per hospitalized day prevented, and another program costs $300 per hospitalized day prevented, we have reported the findings of a cost-effectiveness analysis. If, on the other hand, we had attempted to monetize outcome by assessing the societal benefits of the program in terms such as the increased economic productivity of the individuals receiving case management, then we would have been conducting a cost-benefit analysis.

Borrowing from Karl White (1988), we can illustrate the difference between cost-benefit and cost-effectiveness analyses with the following example. Suppose two alternative school social work interventions are evaluated, each of which aims to reduce the dropout rate of youths at inner city high schools. Existing data, reported prior to our study, have shown that the graduation rate in the targeted high schools is only 50 percent. Intervention A costs $50,000, is utilized by 100 students, and 75 of the 100 graduate from high school. Intervention B costs $40,000, is utilized by 100 students, and 60 of them graduate from high school. Based on the previously established 50 percent graduation rate, we would expect 50 of every 100 students to graduate.

Since 75 of 100 (75%) participating in Intervention A graduated, a cost effectiveness analysis would find that Intervention A had the effect of adding 25 graduates at a cost of $50,000, or $2,000 per additional graduate. Intervention B was $10,000 cheaper to implement ($40,000 is $10,000 less than the $50,000 cost of Intervention A), but had the effect of adding only ten graduates for the $40,000, which comes to $4,000 per additional graduate. Thus, Intervention A is more cost-effective, because $2,000 per additional graduate is a better cost-effectiveness ratio than $4,000 per additional graduate.

Notice that so far we have not estimated the monetary value of graduating from high school, an estimate that would be required if we were conducting a cost-benefit analysis. Suppose we did conduct such an analysis and found that the projected increased career earnings of the high school graduates was $50,000 per graduate and that the government would have to spend $10,000 less on social services and welfare benefits to each high school graduate, as compared to each dropout.

Adding those two figures together, we could estimate that the monetary benefit per additional graduate is $60,000. Since Intervention B had the effect of adding ten graduates, we could conclude that its monetized outcome was ten times $60,000, or $600,000. That figure would be far in excess of the intervention's $40,000 cost, so we could argue that the intervention is worth funding—that it is cost-beneficial because the dollar value of benefits resulting from the intervention exceed the dollar value costs of providing the intervention.

Note that we could draw this conclusion without ever comparing Intervention B to Intervention A. Of course, were we to estimate the cost benefit of Intervention A, we would find that Intervention A's monetized outcome would be even more cost-beneficial (with benefits equaling 25 times $60,000, or $1,500,000) than Intervention B's. A cost-benefit analysis need not ask whether one program's benefits-to-costs ratio is better than another program's. It may just look at one program and ask whether its monetized benefits exceed its monetary costs.

Assessing the costs of a social service program is highly complex. It requires technical expertise in cost accounting and deals with such accounting concepts as: variable costs, fixed costs, incremental costs, sunk costs, recurring costs, nonrecurring costs, hidden costs, obvious costs, direct costs, indirect costs, future costs, opportunity costs, and so forth (Posavac & Carey, 1994). Because program evaluators often lack that expertise, they often do not include cost-effectiveness or cost-benefit analyses as part of their evaluations. The cost accounting concepts just mentioned go beyond the scope of this chapter.

Because a cost-effectiveness analysis attempts to monetize only program costs and not program outcomes, it involves fewer cost accounting complexities and fewer questionable monetizing assumptions than does cost-benefit analysis. When we attempt to monetize the outcome of health and welfare programs, we get into difficult value issues, such as attaching a dollar figure to the value of human lives. Karl White (1988) offers the example of neonatal intensive care units to illustrate this point.

Although intensive care units for very low birth weight babies are not cost-beneficial, every major hospital in this country spends hundreds of thousands of dollars providing them. The same point applies to the frail elderly. No matter what the costs are for nursing homes or other programs of care for the frail elderly, the monetized benefits of those programs—such as through increased earning capacity—are not going to exceed the program costs. We do not put a dollar value on the quality of life benefits that we seek to provide the frail elderly.

Likewise, when hospice programs attempt to alleviate the pain and suffering of the terminally ill, they cannot monetize that benefit in terms of dollars that the outcome of their care generates through increased earning capacity. Because of the values problem in attempting to reduce benefits to monetary terms, as well as the difficulty in foreseeing and monetizing all the costs and benefits that might be attributable to a program's outcome, cost-effectiveness analyses are generally considered less controversial and more doable than are cost-benefit analyses. Still, excellent cost-benefit analyses can be found in the literature.

Evaluating the Implementation of a Program

As has been noted, some social work programs have unsuccessful outcomes simply because they are not being implemented properly. Suppose, for example, an AIDS prevention program develops a high school education leaflet and decides to evaluate its effectiveness in a particular high school. Suppose further that the program's personnel deliver the leaflets to the vice principal of the school, who agrees to disseminate them to all students. Suppose that for some reason—unanticipated opposition by the principal or the PTA, mere oversight, or whatever—the leaflets never get disseminated. Or perhaps they get disseminated in an undesirable way. Maybe, instead of handing them out to every student in a school assembly, the vice principal merely deposits them in each teacher's mailbox with a vague message encouraging them to distribute the leaflets to their students. Maybe some teachers distribute the leaflets but most do not.

Suppose further that the program's personnel never learn that the leaflets were not disseminated as intended. The implications of this turn of events would be quite serious. Because few or no students would have received the leaflet in the first place, the intervention (the program) was never implemented as planned and the program had no chance to succeed. No matter what indicators of outcome were chosen, the leaflet dissemination effort would be doomed to fail. But it would fail not because it was a bad idea or an ineffectual leaflet but because it was never really tried. If we had merely conducted an outcome study and had not assessed whether and how the program got implemented, we would be in danger of abandoning a public education intervention that, if only implemented properly, might effectively prevent the spread of AIDS.

This simple example illustrates the fact that no matter how well an outcome evaluation is designed, if it is not supplemented by an evaluation of a program's implementation, then we run the risk of not identifying or misinterpreting the meaning of negative results. In turn, no matter how highly we value a specific outcome study, there is a clear need to evaluate the program's implementation on which the outcome study was based.

Even when we can be sure that we have properly identified the written official formal goal of a social service program (and its operational indicators), we cannot assume that this goal is the real priority of the program's personnel who are responsible for attaining it. Program personnel at all levels tend over time, to become preoccupied with their daily routines and with their own agendas—that is, with unofficial program goals pertaining to organizational maintenance, personal prestige and career advancement, bureaucratic rules and procedures, and the like. As these unofficial goals displace the program's written official formal goal, they may result in activities that are either irrelevant to or at odds with the attainment of the program's official goal.

Thus, for example, administrators of family service agencies may secure federal poverty funds not because they are devoted to fighting poverty, but because those funds will help balance their budgets and enhance their performances. Suppose the administrators propose to use the funds so they can reach out to more poverty-stricken individuals and thus try to engage them in receiving the agencies' direct services. Once they have received the funds, however, there is no guarantee that the agencies will try to reach poor clients as diligently as they promised in their initial grant applications. Even if the administrators sincerely sought to do so, they might run into unanticipated resistance by direct-service practitioners who think that such efforts would be an unrewarding and improper use of their therapeutic talents and who prefer to continue serving the kind of clientele with whom they are familiar and comfortable.

Consider the implications for a program evaluation using the foregoing hypothetical example. Suppose a nationwide program evaluation outcome study was done to see if the federal funding of direct social service programs resulted in a reduction in poverty or a reduction in various psychosocial problems among the poor. If the family service agencies, due to their own internally directed objectives, never really tried very hard to serve poor clients, then the outcome would in all likelihood be negative. But it would be wrong to conclude from such results that the provision of direct services to the poor is an ineffective way to help them deal with the problems of poverty, because the services never reached enough poor people in the first place.

For the same reasons, we can see from this example the importance of evaluating program implementation even without any evaluation of program outcome. If we found that the agencies never implemented the program as planned—that poor people were not being served—then who needs an outcome evaluation? And those results would be quite useful. Instead of just depicting the program as a success or failure, we would identify what went wrong and could help policymakers consider ways to improve the program's implementation. In addition, simply monitoring a program's implementation helps keep the program accountable to its funders. Ultimately, of course, they would want to know the outcome of the program. But, in the meantime, just knowing how the program is being implemented is invaluable.

Evaluations of program implementation are not necessarily concerned only with the question of whether a program is being implemented as planned. There are many other possible questions that examine how best to implement, as well as maintain, a program. Below are a few of the important questions that can be studied without getting into questions of a program's outcome:

- Which fund-raising strategy yields the most funds?
- What proportion of our target population is being served?
- What types of individuals are we *not* reaching?
- Why are so many of our targeted individuals refusing our services?
- What outreach clinic locations are reaching the most clients?
- What types of our practitioners seem to have the best attitudes about working with certain underserved target populations?
- Do practitioners in our specialized units have better attitudes toward their clients than those in multipurpose units?
- How skillful are the various types of our practitioners in their clinical interventions?
- In what areas do our clients seem least prepared and in need of continuing education?
- Are our clients satisfied with our services? Why or why not?
- Why do so many of our clients drop out of treatment prematurely?

All of the methodologies covered in the foregoing chapters of this book can be applied to evaluate a program's implementation. The most appropriate methodology to use depends on the nature of the evaluation question asked.

Surveys utilizing standardized questionnaires might be used to assess staff, client, or community attitudes that affect program implementation decisions (Chapter 14). Participant observation might be used to assess how staff relate to clients or to one another (Chapter 15). In some studies, evaluators have posed as clients and observed how staff members behaved and the ways in which their behavior affected clients (Chapters 13 and 15).

Available records might be analyzed to assess whether the attributes of clients being served matched program priorities regarding the intended target population (Chapters 16–19). Experimental or quasi-experimental designs might be used to assess the effectiveness of alternative fund-raising strategies, to measure the impact of different organizational arrangements on staff attitudes, to determine which outreach strategies are most successful in engaging hard-to-reach prospective clients in treatment (Chapters 11–12), and so on.

Evaluating If a Program Is Needed

Thus far we lave been discussing the evaluation of programs that have already been implemented. But the term *program evaluation* also connotes diagnostic evaluation. Just as clinical practitioners evaluate client problems and needs during a preintervention assessment period in order to develop the best treatment plan, program evaluators can assess a program's target population in order to enhance its program planning. They might assess the extent and location of the social problems the program seeks to ameliorate, as well as the target population's characteristics, problems, expressed needs, and desires. These data are then used to guide a program's planning and development concerning such issues as what services to offer, how to maximize service utilization by targeted subgroups, and where to locate services.

For example, suppose we are planning a new statewide program to help the homeless. What would we need to know to guide our planning effort? We might want to find out how many homeless people there are in the state. How many are there in specific locations in the state? What are the reasons for each individual's homelessness, and how many people are there for each reason? How many choose to be homeless? How many seem to be homeless because of mental illness or substance abuse? How many are homeless because they lost their jobs and cannot find work? How long have they been homeless? How many of the homeless are in different ethnic groups, and how many are recent immigrants or do not speak English? What proportion of the homeless consists of children and entire family units? What special problems do the children experience in such matters as education, health, nutrition, self-esteem, and so on? What special problems and needs are expressed by the adult homeless, those with emotional disorders, and others? These are just a few of the diagnostic questions we might ask; the resultant answers will help us suggest what interventions to develop, where to locate them, how to staff them, and so on.

The process of systematically researching diagnostic questions like the ones just mentioned is called *needs assessment*. The term *needs assessment* is widely used to cover all sorts of techniques for collecting data for program planning purposes.

Normative Versus Demand Needs

What are needs, however? This questions is best answered on whether needs are defined in normative terms or in terms of demand. If needs are defined normatively, then our needs assessment would focus on comparing the objective living conditions of our target population with what society, or at least that segment of society concerned with helping the target population, deems acceptable or desirable from a humanitarian standpoint. Normatively defining the needs of the homeless, for example, might lead us to conclude that certain housing or shelter programs need to be developed for individuals living in deplorable conditions on the streets, even if those individuals do not express any dissatisfaction with their current homelessness.

If needs are defined in terms of demand, however, then only those individuals who indicate that they feel or perceive the need themselves would be considered to be in need of a particular program or intervention. Thus, in this homelessness example, individuals who prefer to be homeless might not be counted as in need of a community-based shelter program. Defining needs in terms of demand can be tricky in the best of times. Perhaps individuals expressed no need for the shelter because they did not understand how it would help them. In addition, they may have come to expect that every time a social service program is provided to them it is stigmatizing or unacceptable to them in some other way.

Thus, in assessing whether the homeless need a new shelter program, many homeless individuals might express no need for the program and might even disdain the idea because they have no reason to believe that the new program really will be more acceptable to them than the filthy, crowded, dangerous shelters they already refuse to use.

The need for undergraduate social work education programs provides another example of the complexities involved regarding normative needs and felt needs. Many argue that the number of social work programs and social work majors that our society needs should be gauged by social welfare labor force needs. That is, the need for social work education would be defined in terms of the job market demand to hire social work majors to fill social worker positions. If the number of graduates with social work majors exceeds labor force demands for social workers, those defining need in terms of demand would see this situation as a problem and argue that we ought to reduce social work enrollments.

But those who define needs normatively might disagree, arguing that even if social work majors do not get social work jobs, even if there is no demand for their services, our society is still improved by having more social work majors. The rationale would be that social work education, even if it does not lead to a job, helps prepare better citizens who are more understanding of social welfare problems and needs and who will be more likely to contribute to societal efforts to alleviate social welfare problems. In other words, they would argue that our society needs more social work majors even if it does not recognize that need and is not prepared to utilize them.

How we define needs affects the choice of specific techniques to assess them. For example, if we define needs normatively, then we might be able to establish the need for a particular social service program by analyzing existing statistics (Chapters 16–18). Thus, if census data showed a relatively high number of unmarried teenage mothers in a particular geographical area, then we might be predisposed to conclude that more family planning or child-rearing education services are needed in that area. But if we take demand into account, then we might want to supplement the census data by conducting a survey of teenage mothers to determine the conditions, if any, under which they would actually utilize the particular services that we are contemplating (Chapter 14).

PROGRAM EVALUATION MODELS

William Shadish and his colleagues (1991) have conceptualized a typology of three models of program evaluation practice—a typology that addresses many of the issues that have been covered in this chapter. These three models are: (1) the manipulation solution model, (2) the generalizable explanation model, and (3) the stakeholder service model.

The Manipulable Solution Model

The manipulable solution model of program evaluation closely resembles an outcome evaluation discussed earlier. It states that the greatest priority in a program evaluation is to serve the public interest, not the interests of its stakeholders who have vested interests in the program being evaluated. Advocates of this model believe that summative evaluations, which test out whether programs really work—whether they are effective in delivering the public benefits they promise—are more important than finding out how and why they work.

In this connection, proponents of this model ideally would like to see a sort of "experimenting society" in which multiple alternative solutions to the social problems the public seeks to ameliorate are tested for their effectiveness. Multiple solutions are tested (instead of just one program) in order to increase the chances of finding one that works and in order to see which solution works best. In short, maximizing internal validity in order to reduce uncertainty about a program's effects is preferred over flexible (perhaps qualitative) research methods geared to discovering how to improve an existing program.

The Generalizable Explanation Model

In contrast to the manipulable solution model is the generalizable explanation model of evaluation practice. Those who advocate this model believe that many solutions will be effective and that their effects will differ under different conditions. A social service program may be effective under certain conditions, however, but may have opposite effects under different conditions. Outcomes associated with case management vary from study to study, for example. Thus, it could be hypothesized that this variation may be influenced by the way case management is operationally defined and the service delivery conditions under which it is implemented (Rubin, 1992).

Case managers who have light caseloads and work in well-endowed social service delivery systems, for example, may be much more effective than those with heavier caseloads and more fragmented service delivery systems. In addition, simply finding that a specific case management program is effective with a specific client population at a specific time does not mean that a similar case management program will be "the solution" for a similar client population at a different time. In a nutshell, the, generalizable explanation model is less concerned with internal validity than with external validity, seeking more to identify multiple variables that bear on differential program outcomes in different settings than to test program effects in one carefully controlled randomized study. This model also emphasizes problems in the implementation of identified solutions.

The Stakeholder Service Model

Proponents of the stakeholder service model of evaluation practice argue that program evaluations will be more likely to be utilized, and thus have a greater impact on social problems, when they are tailored to the stakeholder's data needs. Some proponents of this model focus on program managers as the stakeholders to whom evaluations are geared, since the managers have more control over social service programs than do other stakeholders. Other proponents of this model emphasize a broader focus that includes stakeholders such as the intended clients, service providers, and board members of a program.

Proponents of this model agree that the purpose of a program evaluation is not to generalize findings to other sites, but rather to restrict the evaluation effort to a particular program. They also agree that stakeholders (not the evaluators) should play the key role in making decisions as to the design and purpose of the program evaluation (in light of the evaluator's informed input). They criticize proponents of the other two models as being too concerned with theory and methodology at the expense of the practical data needs of real people with real problems that require immediate action. Although it is not inconceivable that some stakeholders might desire a summative evaluation, formative evaluations tend to be associated with this model.

Critics of the stakeholder model contend that stakeholders may seek data that are not relevant to ameliorating social problems—asking questions that are uninformed, lack general value, and are geared to the stakeholder's own vested interests. They further contend that political and economic priorities compromise the integrity of the evaluation, and that sacrificing methodological principles in order to be more responsive to the need for immediate answers geared to the concerns of stakeholders may result in producing inaccurate, and possibly misleading, data.

These three models of program evaluation practice are not mutually exclusive. The manipulable solution model, for example, blends into the generalizable explanation model when its adherents implement simultaneous replications of experiments in different settings, or when we conduct meta-analyses. Likewise, some stakeholders, such as congressional committees, may have social problem solving as their chief priority. As is the case with social work practitioners choosing among models of direct social work practice, it is perhaps best not to adhere dogmatically to just one model of program evaluation practice.

We might be better advised to apply certain aspects of each model selectively, depending upon the unique situation. If we work as in-house evaluators for a social service agency, for example, it may be extremely unwise to ignore some of the advantages of the stakeholder model. If, on the other hand, we are external evaluators concerned primarily with testing a proposed solution (the program) to a social problem, it may not make sense to sacrifice that priority in pursuit of the immediate data needs of program managers. At the same time, however, we may be well advised to engage stakeholders in the evaluation planning process (in line with some of the principles discussed earlier in this chapter) and to recognize the potential contextual issues that may limit the generalizability of our study's results.

A QUALITATIVE APPROACH TO PROGRAM EVALUATION

In numerous places throughout this text we have reiterated the view that quantitative and qualitative approaches to research and evaluation are equally important. We can use both research approaches when doing a program evaluation, each one has its advantages and disadvantages.

An example of a qualitative program evaluation is a study done by Robert Bogdan and Steve Taylor (1990). They evaluated the effects of institutionalization and deinstitutionalization of people with developmental disabilities. They questioned the policy of institutionalization and became strong advocates for deinstitutionalization and the integration of people with disabilities into their local communities. Their review of qualitative studies that documented the plight of disabled people who have been transferred from dehumanized institutions to dehumanized conditions in the community, however, raised questions about how to improve the integration of this target population into their local communities.

The researchers believed that many quantitatively oriented outcome evaluations on the effects of deinstitutionalization have asked the wrong question, which they call, the "Does it work?" question. In their apparent orientation to the stakeholder service model of evaluation, they note that community-based practitioners, like human service practitioners in general, believe in their work. They are not skeptical about what they do and therefore find no value in evaluative studies that merely tell whether a particular social service program was or was not effective. When "Does it work?" studies produce pessimistic results, they attribute the findings to the unfortunate prevalence of poorly funded, poor quality, community-based programs.

Moreover, Bogdan and Taylor tended to see community integration as a moral question. Rather than study whether community integration works, they asked, "What does integration mean?" (notice the qualitative orientation to meanings) and, "How can it be accomplished?" They saw these questions as more optimistic than asking whether community integration works. They also saw these questions as more responsive to practitioner/stakeholder needs, not only because practitioners are optimistic about what they do, but because they are more interested in formative data about how better to accomplish their aims than they are in summative outcome conclusions.

Their focus on discovering insights about what community integration means and how better to achieve it led them to eschew probability sampling and to use instead qualitative strategies that employed aspects of snowball sampling, extreme case sampling, and critical incidents sampling (all of which were discussed in Chapters 5 and 10). Bogdan and Taylor were not interested in studying typical, or average, social service programs. Neither were they interested in representativeness. Instead, they sought to identify exemplary social service programs that were reputed to be doing well in achieving community integration.

Their sampling efforts toward identifying exemplary programs employed a variety of techniques, including announcements in professional newsletters, national mailings, and reviews of the professional literature. They also contacted a number of key informants who could tell them which programs they felt were doing a good job and who could also identify other key informants who might know of additional exemplary programs. The key informants included disability rights activists, university-based researchers, and leaders of parent and professional groups.

Bogdan and Taylor conducted in-depth, open-ended phone interviews with officials in each program who were identified in their snowball sample. The purpose of these interviews was to obtain data to help them whittle the sample down to eight social service programs that promised to yield the most comprehensive understanding of what community integration means and how best to achieve it. Their interview questions attempted to probe into what the programs were doing, how well they seemed to be doing it, and how sincere they seemed to be in their efforts. These questions, as well as some routine questions about a program's characteristics, enabled them to select a sample of programs that all seemed exemplary, but which varied in geographic location, services offered, and administrative arrangements.

The reason for the small sample size was that each program in the sample was studied intensively, including a series of on-sight visits over a three-year period. To gain entry into a program, and to foster the program staff's cooperation with the study, Bogdan and Taylor honestly told them that their program had been nominated as innovative or exemplary. This not only flattered administrators but helped them realize that their participation provided an opportunity to gain national visibility as a "model program." Bogdan and Taylor reported that, ironically, this seemed to lead many officials and staff to talk more openly about their problems than they otherwise might have done.

Each program site visit lasted several days, during which the two employed a grounded theory approach involving triangulated qualitative data collection methods such as direct observation (Chapters 4, 6, 12, 13, 14, and 15), intensive interviewing (Chapters 14 and 15), and document analysis (Chapters 16–19). The interviews were conducted with staff, clients and their family members, and representatives of other programs in the vicinity. The site visits yielded thousands of pages of field notes and interview transcripts.

Bogdan and Taylor's prime approach to data presentation was through case studies (Chapter 12). The case studies were prepared after each program visit. They provided a program overview, described the innovative program policies that seemed to be fostering community integration, and provided illustrative case examples of how program innovations were perceived to be impacting on people's lives. When applicable, they also reported program problems and dilemmas. The case study "stories" of the programs were then disseminated to the field as a whole through short stories in relevant newsletters and journal articles that focused on the positive aspects of the visited programs. The articles attempted to disseminate state-of-the-art descriptions to provide readers with new ideas that they may have been able to adapt in their efforts to improve community integration in their own programs.

With this positive, "optimistic," qualitative approach that focused on process, Bogdan and Taylor believed they were producing research findings that would have greater utility to the field, and ultimately do more to improve the well-being of individuals who were disabled, than they would if they were producing quantitative studies of program outcome. Although many may disagree as to whether their particular research approach is more valuable than others, we think few will fail to appreciate the value of their approach as one of a variety of useful ways to use research in our efforts to improve practice, alleviate human suffering, and promote social welfare.

As we end our discussion of program evaluation, it should be obvious that program evaluations inescapably involve trade-offs. There is no one perfect way to do social work research and evaluation, and no study is ever immune to potential error. No matter how sophisticated a study's research design or data analyses procedures may be, no study ever "proves" anything. We simply do the best we can, within the feasibility constraints we face, to add something to our profession's knowledge base. We will always need to replicate studies and conduct new ones. Using the research method in social work—or in any other discipline—means that what we think we know is always open to question. If we really care about helping people, we will keep an open mind and attempt to improve our knowledge base.

Social work research and evaluation, like social work practice itself, is a problem-solving process. In attempting to provide our practitioners with the knowledge they need to solve the social problems they encounter, social work research and evaluation can be seen as inescapably connected to social work practice. Ultimately, the success of our profession, and the welfare of our clients, will be affected by the degree to which social work practitioners take an objective outlook and support the social work research and evaluation enterprise.

SUMMARY

Program evaluation applies various research approaches and data collection methods in order to assess and improve the conceptualization, design, planning, administration, implementation, effectiveness, efficiency, and utility of social service programs. Although people have always evaluated, in some way, the reforms they have instituted, systematic and scientific approaches to program evaluation are a recent phenomenon as increased social welfare spending has spawned an "age of accountability."

The importance of program evaluation in funding decisions creates a highly political atmosphere in which stakeholders with vested interests can impede scientific inquiry. Political considerations not only affect in-house evaluators, but also bias external evaluators who seem to be more independent. Even funding sources and other external sponsors of an evaluation have a stake in its outcome and may try to influence it for political reasons.

Political and ideological forces influence not only the methodology and interpretation of evaluative research, but also whether and how its findings get utilized. It cannot be assumed that an evaluation's implications will necessarily be put into practice, especially if they conflict with official interests or points of view. The social context of program evaluation studies also affects the logistics involved in implementing them.

A number of steps have been proposed to help alleviate potential problems in the logistics of evaluation studies, as well as to alleviate resistance to them and to their utilization. These steps involve learning as much as possible about the stakeholders and their vested interests in the evaluation effort, involving them in meaningful ways in all phases of planning and performing the evaluation, maintaining ongoing mutual feedback between them and the evaluators, and tailoring the evaluation and its reportage to their needs and preferences as much as possible without sacrificing objectivity.

Although the evaluation of program outcome is one of the first things that come to mind when people think of program evaluation, other important foci of evaluation research address research questions concerned with planning new programs and monitoring their implementation.

REFERENCES AND FURTHER READINGS

BABBIE, E.R. (1995). *The practice of social research* (7th ed., pp. 338-358). Belmont, CA: Wadsworth.

BAILEY, K.D. (1994). *Methods of social research* (4th ed., pp. 486-490). New York: Free Press.

BOGDAN, R., & TAYLOR (1990). Looking at the bright side: A positive approach to qualitative policy and evaluation research. *Qualitative Sociology, 13,* 183-192.

CRAWFORD, K., THOMAS, E.D., & FINK, J.J. (1980). Pygmalion at sea: Improving the work effectiveness of low performers. *The Journal of Applied Behavioral Science, 23,* 482-505.

GABOR, P.A., & GRINNELL, R.M., JR. (1994). *Evaluation and quality improvement in the human services.* Needham Heights, MA: Allyn & Bacon.

GRINNELL, R.M., JR., & WILLIAMS, M. (1990). *Research in social work: A primer* (pp. 58-85). Itasca, IL: F.E. Peacock.

GROB, G.N. (1973). *Mental institutions in America.* New York: Free Press.

POSAVAC, E.J., & CAREY, R.G. (1994). *Program evaluation: Methods and case studies* (3rd ed.). Englewood Cliffs, NJ: Prentice-Hall.

ROSSI, P.H., & FREEMAN, H.E. (1989). *Evaluation: A systematic approach* (4th ed.). Newbury Park, CA: Sage.

RUBIN, A. (1979). *Community mental health in the social work curriculum.* New York: Council on Social Work Education.

RUBIN, A. (1992). Is case management effective for people with serious mental illness? A research review. *Health and Social Work, 17,* 138-180.

RUBIN, A., & BABBIE, E.R. (1993). *Research methods for social work* (2nd ed., pp. 536-568). Pacific Grove, CA: Brooks/ Cole.

SHADISH, W.R., COOK, T.D., & LEVITON, L.C. (1991). *Foundations of program evaluation.* Newbury Park, CA: Sage.

STOUFFER, S., ET AL. (1949-1950). *The American soldier* (3 vols.). Princeton, NJ: Princeton University Press.

WEINBACH, R.W., & GRINNELL, R.M., JR. (1996). *Applying research knowledge: A workbook for social work students* (2nd ed., pp. 81-88). Needham Heights, MA: Allyn & Bacon.

WHITE, K. (1988). Cost analyses in family support programs. In H.B. Weiss & F.H. Jacobs (Eds.), *Evaluating family programs* (pp. 429-443). New York: Aldine de Gruyter.

Yvonne A. Unrau
Peter A. Gabor

Chapter **25**

Implementing Evaluations

THIS CHAPTER FOCUSES on the implementation of the two complimentary evaluation approaches, case level and program, presented in the two preceding chapters. Our emphasis is on creating case- and program-level data systems that are integrated within a typical social service delivery system. These systems provide data on which to base decisions about individual client cases and specific social service programs.

As we know, numerous evaluation methods exist that evaluate social work practice at both the case and program levels. Although evaluation principles are applied, the evaluation process is not the same as the process of conducting a pure research study or an individual assessment (Posavac & Carey, 1994). Because evaluations are carried out in the context of ongoing service delivery, it is difficult to apply single-case or group designs with the same level of rigor expected in "pure" research studies.

Random assignment is usually not possible, some variables are not controllable, withdrawal designs may be precluded by ethical considerations, and the overall evaluation process is affected by the unique context of the setting in which it takes place. Evaluations are usually less rigorous then would be desirable from a purely research perspective. Thus, some people who misunderstand the evaluation process tend to dismiss its findings. In reality, truly air-tight methodological designs are rare even in "pure" research studies; in evaluation research, however, they are almost never seen. Nevertheless, well-designed and well-implemented evaluations provide valuable data upon which to base practice and program decisions.

PRINCIPLES UNDERLYING THE DESIGN OF EVALUATIONS

Three important principles affect the design and implementation of evaluations: (1) feedback, (2) development, and (3) integration.

Feedback

Feedback is the major purpose of an evaluation, whether at the case or program level; that is, feedback generates data upon which further practice and program decisions are based. All social systems are feedback directed and function better when data are available about the degree to which they are moving toward (or away) from their formally stated objectives. This is similar to a child, named Ben, who is playing the game of "blind person's bluff." As long as Ben is receiving accurate data about whether he is getting "warmer" or "colder" he will find the object fairly quickly. In the absence of these meaningful feedback cues, however, Ben's search may be lengthy and unsuccessful. Likewise, feedback is indispensable to the achievement of practice and program objectives.

Expanding on the content above, the more frequent the feedback, the more efficient the achievement of objectives. Returning to our example, if Ben receives continuous data about how warm or cold he is getting, he will find the hidden object much more quickly than if he received infrequent or occasional feedback. Therefore, in the absence of continuous feedback, numerous wrong turns and directions can be taken. Thus, practice and program evaluations provide continuous on-going feedback and make the achievement of their objectives much more efficient by reducing the amount of time spent "off task."

Development

A second principle underlying evaluations is that they are conducted primarily for developmental purposes. In other words, feedback obtained from the data is most helpful when the feedback is used to guide continued practice and program development. This concept is more applicable to a program-level evaluation than a case-level evaluation, however. In this approach, sometimes referred to as *formative* evaluation, various aspects of a program's performance are continually monitored and the resulting data are used to make incremental changes to the program's services. On the other hand, a *summative* evaluation is used for the purpose of making judgments about a program's performance. Summative evaluations lead to major decisions about a program's expansion, replication, downsizing, or termination.

It goes without saying that formative evaluations are more likely than summative evaluations to create less stress and anxiety within a program. They are likely to be seen as a constructive means for improving the program's services rather than judging them. When an evaluation's purpose is developmental, methodological rigor becomes less critical; the key issue is to generate the best possible data upon which to base further developmental decisions.

Integration

The third principle underlying evaluations relates to the integration of evaluation activities with normal day-to-day practice activities. In social service agencies, evaluations are too often conceived of as something separate from service provision as they utilize a different set of activities. In such situations, many staff members may view data collection as additional chores that yield little immediate relevant utility. A more constructive approach, however, is one that fits with the concepts of continuous feedback, program development, and integration of evaluative activities with normal day-to-day service delivery. Using this approach, "practice" data that also can be used for "evaluation" data are collected at each step of service delivery .

STAKEHOLDERS

The starting point in designing any evaluation is to know the stakeholder groups for whom it is intended. Each stakeholder group has a different set of questions regarding the program's overall operations and subsequent outcomes. Thus, in designing a built-in evaluation system in any social service organization, it is important to be clear about each stakeholder's data needs. On a general level, there are five nonmutually exclusive groups of stakeholders for any given program: (1) clients, (2) social work practitioners, (3) policy makers and funders, (4) managers and administrators, and (5) the general public.

- *Clients* are obviously concerned with their personal and immediate problems. Prior to entering a social service program as consumers, they want to know if a particular program is the best one to address their specific problems. Sometimes they even want to know how the program operates. Whom does it serve? What types of services does it provide?

What treatment interventions are used? Does it consider ethnic and religious differences? Do clients have input into treatment interventions?

Once receiving services, clients become primarily interested in data that relate to their overall progress. It is useful to provide clients with objective feedback related to how their identified needs and problems are changing, and at the rate at which they are changing. This provides both the workers and the clients additional data to decide whether they are going to reach their practice objectives that were established at the beginning of the intervention.

- *Social work practitioners* are also interested in questions that relate to their clients' needs and their day-to-day practice problems. A summative evaluation of an entire social service program (or part of the program), however, does not answer questions about individual clients. We can carry out formative case-level evaluations to determine the degree to which our clients' practice objectives are being met. Is a particular treatment intervention with this particular client working? What mix of treatment activities best facilitates a client's progress?

- *Policy makers and funders* focus their interests on expenditures. In other words: Is the money they provide being spent wisely? Is a program cost-efficient and cost-effective? How many clients are being served given the amount of funds? What proportion of funds is allotted to client services versus administrative costs? How could money be put to better use? Are services being responsibly managed? How should money be allocated among competing similar programs?

  Policy makers and funders are concerned with very broad issues. They often want data in relation to a program's effectiveness and efficiency. They are interested in knowing: Is the program fulfilling its formal mandate? Does the program's goal reflect the needs of the clients it purports to serve? Is the program achieving desirable client outcomes? How does a specific program compare to similar programs? If one type of program is more effective than another but also costs more, are the higher costs justified? Should certain types of programs be modified, expanded, or abandoned?

- *Managers and administrators* are aware of accountability questions that are often asked by the policy makers and funders mentioned above. As well, they focus on questions specific to client needs, program operations, and client outcomes. Managers need to know: What is the typical client profile? Are the program's objectives being met? What interventions are most efficient and effective? What staffing is needed? Are clients satisfied with the services they received?

- The *general public* is a lay citizen group and their evaluation questions reflect the concerns raised by political leaders and the media. What is being done about a specific social problem? How much money is being spent and where is it being spent?

CASE AND PROGRAM DECISION MAKING

Given the various stakeholder groups briefly mentioned above, and the many types of evaluation questions that can be asked of any social service program, the purpose for which an evaluation is designed can vary tremendously. An evaluation can yield important data about client needs, program operations, service outcomes, cost-benefits, and cost-effectiveness. The common thread among these different functions, however, is the type and kind of data that are collected which in turn are used for decision making.

The result of an evaluation is the analysis of the collected data. The data should help us better understand some aspect of delivering services within a program. In turn, this understanding helps us to assess the results of our previous decisions and to provide a sound base for making further decisions. In general, decision making occurs at two nonmutually exclusive levels: (1) at the case level, in relation to individual clients, or groups of clients; and (2) at the program level, in relation to the program as a whole and the relationship between the program and the local community, including policymakers, funders, and the general public. We will now turn our attention to case-level decision making.

Case-Level Decision Making

Evaluation activities provide important data that can enhance our decision making at all phases of intervention, from intake to follow-up. As we know, these decisions must be made on useful, valid, and reliable data. Often, these decisions are made quickly, and it is important that we always have at hand current and accurate data about a client's situation.

Data collected at regular intervals (or at predetermined times) provide information on which to base client-related decisions. Each decision in turn leads to the collection of more data that, once properly analyzed and synthesized, yield further data to form the basis of future client-related decisions. Data gained in this way are never a substitute for our professional judgment, but they can guide our client-related decisions and provide a method whereby decisions, once made, can be evaluated.

The use of data for case-level decision making also serves to empower our clients because the clients can take an active role in the measurement process, particularly when standardized self-administered measuring instruments are used. Being actively involved in data collection, clients are likely to develop a better understanding of their own needs and progress. They can then take a more active role in interpreting evaluation data to make informed decisions about the amount of time, energy, effort, and money going into specific interventions.

In summary, the benefits of using evaluation data to make case-level decisions are: (1) it yields current, comprehensive, and accurate data to guide decision making; (2) it allows us to retrace our steps and evaluate our client-related decisions in a timely fashion so that our interventions can be continued, discontinued, or changed where indicated; (3) it permits us to continually evaluate the effectiveness of our own practices; and (4) measurement results can be readily shared with our clients enabling them to see their progress (if any).

Program-Level Decision Making

A social service program is a coordinated set of objectives that seeks to fulfil its formal goal. Decisions made at the program level focus on the program's functioning so that it can be further developed and improved. "Functioning" includes all aspects of the program: how well the program is meeting community needs; whom it is serving; how well the program's activities are designed and implemented; how well it is managed; and, how effectively and efficiently it is achieving its objectives. Access to data can help in choosing between various interventive options and also provides the means of monitoring how the chosen alternative works out. In short, an evaluation allows links to be established between community needs, program process, and program results (or client outcomes) so that all facets of the program can be considered as a whole.

Administrators often are faced with problems of restructuring or reorganizing their program's services. In times of economic cutbacks, the "do more with less" scenario is now an administrative motto. What should be changed, both administratively and programmatically, and how? In other situations, administrators want to know which programs are most effective. Based on evaluations results, decisions can be taken to increase funding for successful programs and to reduce or terminate funding for less effective ones. It is more likely, however, that administrators will make incremental changes to programs in an effort to improve existing social services. In this way, program decisions are based, at least partly, on evaluation results.

Policy makers and funders, who have little direct contact with a program, are often provided an annual report that presents the program's results. Program successes are highlighted to justify current funding or proposed expansion. In instances where a program's results do not show great promise, data are used to identify areas for its further development. This allows policy makers to ensure that funds are spent on effective services.

Program results are also used to build public support for a social service program. Data help to educate the community about social needs that exist as well as about the efforts undertaken by the program to meet these needs. In addition, program outcomes are used to educate other helping professionals about a program's intervention options and their effectiveness.

THE MONITORING APPROACH TO EVALUATION

Approaches to evaluation are continually changing. The traditional, "project" approach, usually associated with summative evaluations, is slowly giving way to the monitoring approach, usually associated with formative evaluations. The monitoring approach is more congruent with the principles of feedback, development, and integration than the project approach. This approach uses data that are continuously collected, synthesized, and analyzed to provide solid data on which practice and program decisions are based.

The monitoring approach to evaluation provides ongoing feedback so that a program can be improved as it continues to operate. It differs from the project approach in which a program (or some component of a program) is assessed on a one-shot basis, a summative method of evaluation. The monitoring approach is integrated into the program's operations where evaluation and clinical activity are jointly designed. It provides data about the extent to which a program is reaching its intended population, how well its services measure up to what were intended to be delivered, and the extent to which it is meeting its program objectives. In addition, this approach provides immediate and continuous feedback on client progress. There are several benefits to using a monitoring approach to evaluation:

- This type of evaluation is internally driven by program staff. Evaluation methods are put into place and used by practitioners for their own benefit (and their clients' as well) without the request from any outside source.
- When evaluation is a process instead of an event, practitioners generally are more cooperative because it is an accepted part of the daily routine of delivering high-quality services to clients.
- Because evaluation methods are routinely used to improve services to clients, they do not interfere with the task at hand because they are an integral part of that task.
- Data are made available to all social workers for ongoing feedback.
- A monitoring approach allows workers themselves to identify practice and program problems and suggest tentative solutions. It avoids problems of top-down solution strategies, in which practitioners are not consulted about the changes or cannot see that they solve any specific problem.
- A monitoring approach gives rise to continual minor adjustments instead of the larger, more traumatic changes that may result from a project evaluation. When changes occur regularly as a result of an ongoing monitoring process, they tend to be small. In short, the monitoring approach engages a program in its continuous pursuit of quality improvement.

ETHICAL CONSIDERATIONS

Data obtained through an evaluation are a powerful means for improving a program's services. The evaluation process and its results, like any powerful tool, can be misused and abused, however. Potential misuses include justifying decisions already made, using results for public relations or performance appraisal purposes, and fulfilling funding requirements. The two most appropriate uses of an evaluation are for decision making and for meeting accountability demands. Thus, evaluations must not be misused but must be conducted in accordance with ethical and professional standards.

Ethical Standards

In general, all research-related ethical guidelines (Chapter 2) are applicable to evaluations. The most important ones are discussed in this section.

As in any ethical research project, informed consent is obtained from all those involved. This means that clients understand the purpose of the evaluation, know what is going to happen in the course of it, understand its possible consequences, and have voluntarily agreed to participate. Needless to say, clients are informed that they can decline to participate or may withdraw from the evaluation process at any time, without penalty.

When evaluation activities are integrated as a normal part of service provision, the process of informing a client about an evaluation is part and parcel of explaining the program. Clients usually do not object to an evaluation when they understand that it is used to ensure that they receive the best possible service. We should never presume that our clients are not willing to participate in an evaluation or that it will have negative effects on them. The principle of self-determinism applies to all aspects of the helping relationship, including evaluation activities. Thus, clients ought to be informed about the evaluation process in the same way as they are told about other aspects of service delivery.

Confidentiality issues apply in the same way as they do in normal service delivery. Those conducting evaluation activities are responsible for ensuring that only authorized persons have access to data and that individual clients cannot be identified or connected to any data presented in written program evaluation reports.

The selection of an evaluation design also involves ethical considerations. At both the case and program levels, the use of inferentially powerful designs is likely to create ethical problems. In the case of withdrawal designs, for example, such as the *ABAB* design, it is not ethical to withdraw a successful intervention simply to build an explanatory single-case design. In the case of group explanatory designs, withholding service to randomly selected clients for the purpose of creating a control group is similarly unethical if withholding of the targeted service will, in any way, be harmful to clients. Given the many ethical issues that can arise, the use of any explanatory design must be justifiable on practice grounds. Such clearance is usually provided by an independent ethics review board.

Finally, evaluations should be conducted in an atmosphere of openness and honesty. This should characterize all evaluation phases, from initial conceptualization and operationalization to report writing. Initially, the purpose of an evaluation should be spelled out with clarity and frankness. Those who are asked to participate in any aspect of an evaluation, as well as those who may be affected by its results, have a right to know what the true purpose of the evaluation is and what decisions are likely to be based on its results.

Hidden agendas regarding its purpose serve to deceive clients, staff members, and others involved and are, therefore, incompatible with social work ethics. In the same vein, early and wide dissemination of an evaluation's results should be the normal practice. Withholding or delaying results is an inequality of power between those who have the results and those who do not and creates the possibility that its results will be used in a manipulative manner.

Professional Standards

In addition to carrying out evaluations in an ethical manner, it is important that they be competently conducted in accordance with accepted professional standards. The Joint Committee on Standards for Educational Evaluation has identified several general guidelines, three of which will be briefly discussed.

First, if the evaluation results of an evaluation are to be relied on, it is obviously important that they be based on valid, reliable, and accurate data. Second, in addition to accuracy, the results are affected by such methodological choices as the definition of the population or sample, the timing of data collection, and the selection of data that is reported. Competing interests can influence the people conducting the evaluation. The requirement of fairness implies that a well-balanced, representative, accurate picture of the program is presented.

Finally, evaluations are more practical than theoretical; they have practical utility to those who are responsible for decision making. Obviously, their results are presented in a clear and understandable manner. Moreover, evaluators establish links between evaluation results and the decisions to be based on those results; all recommendations must be feasible in the circumstances of a specific program.

EVALUATION IN ACTION

Although there is no single strategy for designing and implementing case- and program-level evaluations, it is advisable to base an evaluation design on the principles of feedback, development, and integration. As well, knowing the intended audience for an evaluation effort helps to frame relevant questions. Beyond these general guidelines, however, every evaluation situation is unique; if an evaluation is to be successful, it must be planned to meet the specific needs and fit into the specific context of the given situation.

In the remaining part of this chapter, the evaluation process is discussed using an example. We focus on the question of whether or not a Teen Parenting Program (TPP) is effective in attaining one of its many program objectives—to increase positive physical contact between teen parents and their infants.

Operationalizing Service Delivery

The first step in implementing an evaluation is to clearly operationalize the program. This step must never be underestimated. Operationalizing a program means that its goal, objectives, and activities are articulated so that all staff have a common understanding of the general nature of the services it provides, as well as of the specific operations involved in client service delivery. The program's goal is a statement that flows logically from its mandate and announces the expected general outcomes dealing with the social problem that it is attempting to prevent, eradicate, or ameliorate.

Our TPP's goal is: *to build healthy parent-child relationships by developing a home environment that is nurturing and safe.* The stated goal is broad, and thus, is not directly evaluated. Rather, the program's objectives are articulated, which gives the flavor of its service delivery structure. Program objectives are statements that clearly and exactly specify the expected change, or intended result, for clients receiving its services. Three objectives of our TPP are:

- To increase positive physical contact between teen parents and their infants
- To increase teen parents' abilities to cope with stressful situations
- To increase teen parents' knowledge levels about infant and child development

Meaningful evaluation questions cannot be developed without clear program objectives. The first objective stated above acts as a guide to developing case-level questions (e.g., What interventions will increase teen parents' positive physical contact with their infants? Do different parents respond better or worse to different interventions?), and program-level questions (e.g., What proportion of parents increase the amount of positive physical contact given to their infants at program completion? What alternative parenting skills are taught to parents in the program?).

Design Selection at the Case Level

Given the problem-solving nature of our profession, we engage in a constant process of evaluation. In our TPP, for example, we can assess client needs, estimate levels of client problems, appraise client strengths, and gauge client progress. As such, we can participate in informal processes of evaluation through supervisory meetings, case consultation, and case conferences. We can then generate tentative hypotheses about client concerns. In most cases, such data provides us with a starting place when working with clients.

The primary purpose of case-level evaluation designs is to objectively examine client strengths, client problems, and client needs. Data obtained in the assessment phase are examined to confirm any clinical hunches. Ideally, an explanatory case level is used to evaluate a treatment intervention for each client. Like life itself, however, evaluation designs need to be flexible. The contextual variables of the client situation often dictate the most viable evaluation design. We have the choice to initiate, remove, or reinstate observation or intervention periods within a case-level design; however, the contextual variables of a client's situation greatly influence the nature of such choice. In planned interventions, we may have more opportunity to select a design, but in crisis interventions, the evaluation or practice design is established by the circumstances of the client's unique situation.

Planned Interventions

Social workers in our TPP can use case-level designs as a method of monitoring clients' individualized treatment objectives. Factors that influence the choice of design and measurement tools include the clients' abilities to measure their own progresses, their involvement with other family members, and the opportunity to manipulate a single intervention. Furthermore, we must orient our client to the terminology and procedures of evaluative practice. By stating our first program objective—to increase positive physical contact between teen parents and their infants—we help our clients to understand that the services they receive are specifically intended to help them learn new ways to nurture and show physical affection toward their infants.

We simply explain to teen parents how important it is that they understand our intervention process and participate in monitoring their own results. The data collected from this evaluation procedure are presented at case conferences at the end of the intervention, where the social worker, the program's administrator, Sharon, and the teen parent assess progress and the need, if any, for further services.

The complex nature of problems faced by teen parents compels us to initiate several different intervention strategies concurrently. We could, for example, address problems related to the teen parents' lack of supports, as well as work with teens to develop plans to improve their parenting abilities. Given that several important clinical activities can be occurring at once, it is even more important that we be clear about the specific interventions used. In most cases, we rely on a simple *AB* design, in which Phase *A* reflects the initial assessment and observation period of family members and Phase *B* launches the intervention process. The *B* phase, however is more typically a package of interventions rather than a discrete intervention technique.

Consider Brandy, a 17-year old mother, who is referred to our TPP one month after giving birth to her daughter, Angie. Brandy, who understandably is anxious about her new parenting role, wants to be a good parent for Angie; but rather than express this desire in terms such as, "I want to build a healthy relationship with my child" (i.e., our program's goal), Brandy is more likely to say, "I want to give my daughter the love I never got from my parents."

Further conversation reveals that Brandy views her own childhood negatively. She explains that her parents argued all the time, they did not pay her much attention, and when they did she was usually being yelled at or hit. Brandy's admits that her parents were poor role models and that she is uncertain of how to deal with Angie, especially when Angie cries. Often, Brandy is afraid to hold Angie because of Angie's small size. As Brandy explains her situation, we can reflect on several of our program's objectives as an anchor in determining how to tackle her most pressing problem(s). We decide together to formulate a treatment plan that targets one of Brandy's parenting abilities— her worries about what to do when Angie cries. This plan fits nicely with our first program objective to increase positive physical contact between teen parents and their infants.

To help Brandy achieve our first program objective, for example, it is necessary to determine the various types of positive physical contact possible and to work with Brandy to ensure she fully understands them. Together with Brandy, we operationalize "positive physical contact" when Brandy:

- Lightly strokes Angie's cheek with her finger
- Gently holds Angie in her arms when she is crying
- Carries Angie in a "baby knapsack" when going on an outing
- Lays Angie on her lap while supporting her head

Once we have outlined clear-cut examples of positive physical contact, Brandy can easily count and record the number of times each positive physical contact occurs each day.

The limitation of using an *AB* design is that we cannot determine what factors directly contribute to the change in Brandy's behaviors. Such data could be obtained if we used a more methodical approach to the onset of intervention techniques. After the initial baseline period, for example, we could use a teaching approach where we provide Brandy with basic reading materials about the importance of positive physical contact between parents and their infants. If the amount of positive physical contact between Brandy and Angie, as measured by a simple counting form, shows no change, then we can introduce a second intervention phase, such as actively showing Brandy, by example and coaching, a variety of ways in which she can give positive physical contact to Angie. By delaying the onset of the second intervention, we have effectively developed an *ABC* design. No matter what design is used, however, we have developed a structure for continuous feedback that contributes to our client's understanding of the situation and our decisions about treatment.

Crisis Interventions

When a client's situation involves a crisis, we need to intervene immediately, thus forming a *B* design. Such a design, exploratory in nature, generates data about whether or not our client shows change over time, but it does not tell us whether the change was caused by our intervention, due to the fact that no initial measurements occurred.

Suppose that on the same day that Brandy was referred to our TPP, for example, she has a hostile argument with her parents, who have reluctantly agreed to let Brandy and Angie continue living with them. When we arrive at her parent's home, we witness an argument where Brandy's parents threaten to kick her out of their house. As we enter the home, Brandy's parents leave the house with Brandy crying and screaming after them. Angie is left unattended and crying out from another room.

Clearly, it is neither appropriate to begin recording any baseline data (*A*) of positive physical contact between parent and child, nor appropriate to launch into a full explanation of our TPP's goal and objectives. We immediately shift to a plan to get Brandy into a state of security and stabilization. First, we need to calm Brandy and make sure Angie is attended to so that we can assess the seriousness of her living situation. Without a plan for her immediate problem, Brandy is not able to concentrate on her parenting role with Angie.

Once a satisfactory plan for the immediate problem is developed (e.g., we have identified some steps to take with Brandy's living situation), we are then in a position to explain the services of our TPP. At this point, the time for collecting pretest measures or establishing a true baseline phase (*A*) has past. By necessity, our initial contact with the Brandy has been primarily reactive. That is, we have relied on previous practice experience, in addition to general practice knowledge and intuition to help Brandy through her brief period of crisis.

Although formal measuring instruments (e.g., planned observation or standardized self-report measuring instruments) were not used, this initial period of contact gave us a chance to assess contextual variables, such as Brandy's willingness to accept help and patterns of interaction between her and Angie under stressful circumstances. Because we have already intervened in the situation, any baseline measures are contaminated by our previous interactions. Consequently, work with the Brandy and Angie begins with an intervention phase (*B*).

Throughout the crisis period, we informally collect observational data by which to generate tentative hypotheses about how Brandy and Angie function together and with Brandy's parents. After the crisis period, we can gather other relevant data using more formal assessment approaches. A period of baseline data could be collected, and then an intervention such as the one discussed in the planned situation could be implemented, thus forming a *BAB* design.

Design Selection at the Program Level

Whereas case-level evaluations produce data that are largely used to direct treatment planning, program-level data are concerned more with the overall effectiveness of a program's services. Data obtained from program-level evaluations make a more generalizable contribution to our knowledge base as they offer measurements on a group of clients rather than on a single client.

Nevertheless, the options for selecting a design at either the case or program level are similar. A program evaluation may begin with an exploratory design and later move to descriptive or explanatory design. In our TPP, for example, we can apply: (1) aggregated case-level evaluation designs, and (2) group evaluation designs.

Aggregated Case-Level Evaluation Designs

A number of single-case evaluations with clients who have common treatment objectives can be aggregated, or combined, to examine treatment outcome across a group of clients. Suppose, for example that Sharon, our TPP's administrator, observes that in the past several months 10 teen parents referred to our program had problems with being afraid to physically handle their babies. Furthermore, all of them used a recording form that counted the number of times they gave positive physical contact to their infants. In reviewing client files, Sharon notes that in all 10 cases, workers primarily used teaching and counseling techniques as interventive activities. By grouping individual client outcome scores, she can assess the general change across the 10 clients.

The results are presented in Table 25.1, which shows a self-rating score for the first and last week of intervention. The data show that there was a general trend toward improvement for nine clients and no improvement for one client (i.e., #133). Sharon can also get a sense of the overall improvement for the clients by computing an average score.

By comparing the average score for the first week with the average score for the last week, she can get a sense of how much clients improved after receiving

TABLE 25.1 AGGREGATED CASE-LEVEL DATA: FREQUENCY OF POSITIVE PHYSICAL CONTACT

Client #	First Week	Last Week	Difference
121	12	20	08
122	11	19	08
124	13	14	01
126	13	25	12
127	13	16	03
129	14	24	10
130	12	22	10
131	13	17	04
133	11	10	−01
134	12	25	13
Mean	12.4	19.2	6.8

services. A quick glance at the actual measurements used by clients will tell her the clinical significance of the observed change.

Aggregated case-level designs provide only a rough estimate as to how a similar group of clients are progressing within a program. Because measurements are developed according to the idiosyncratic needs of each client (they are not standardized instruments), they provide a crude measure of change. Nevertheless, the aggregated data offer valuable feedback for Sharon and her co-workers to consider. First, workers can assess whether the reported changes are clinically significant. Are the items contained within the measurement too easy or too difficult to attain? Second, by comparing the client scores in the last week, the program can develop a profile that reflects the level of parenting skill that clients have achieved when exiting the program. Third, attention may be given to the client who did not show improvement (i.e., #133). Were the client's circumstances unique? Are there reasons as to why the client did not improve? If so, what are they?

Questions that arise from aggregated case-level evaluations are relevant, as they can be introduced at case review sessions to help stimulate ideas for program development. The feedback gained from the evaluation process helps all of us to more fully understand the problems faced by our clients.

Group Evaluation Designs

Group evaluations differ from aggregated case-level evaluations in that they are pre-planned and are directly aimed to answer a specific evaluation question, such as, "Is the program effective?" To measure a program's effectiveness, for example, pretest and posttest scores on the program's objectives can be gathered using an appropriate valid and reliable measuring instrument(s).

To examine trends that appear to arise from the grouped case-level data, descriptive group designs (see Chapter 11) can be employed. Suppose, for example, Sharon learns from her co-workers that they favor a particular intervention, a self-help support group. In reviewing files of the past six months, she notices that about one third of the clients participated in the program's self-help support group. Further, single-case evaluations suggest that clients who participated in weekly support group meetings displayed higher rates of improvement, than those who did not. Sharon has a hunch that participation in the support group is related to improvement but she would like to support the hunch by using an explanatory-level group design known as the classical experimental design.

This design can be implemented by randomly assigning start dates to clients. Random assignment is possible because there happen to be 16 clients eligible for support group services but the group only has eight spots. Because the support group is not considered a critical service, Sharon chooses to randomly assign half of the teen parents to the next round of support group sessions (the experimental group). The remaining eight teen parents are placed on a waiting list for the support group. They receive all other program services, however. Clients with delayed starting dates form the control group, as they do not receive support group treatment for a six-week period. After six weeks, pretest and posttest scores of the two groups are compared to determine if there are clinically or statistically significant differences in client outcome. If clients who participate in the support group consistently show improvement on a specified program objective over those who do not, then more confidence can be placed in the support group intervention.

Group evaluations incorporate many more research principles, such as sampling, manipulation of an independent variable, and careful measuring of the dependent variable. As such, the data generated by group-level evaluations are more valid and reliable, as compared to aggregate case-level evaluations. The results are useful because we can assess client change using data from standardized measuring instruments. These data not only give us a measure of client change, but they also give us a sense as to how an individual client's score compares to the scores of other clients with similar problems. The results of a grouped evaluation also provide data that are useful to our profession. Program data can be summarized and carefully compared with results from other similar programs. Are outcome results comparable for programs with similar client profiles? Are there unique features of one program that appear to have a great impact on client change?

SUMMARY

The focus of this chapter has been on integrating evaluation activity with client service delivery. The primary purpose of implementing a monitoring evaluation system is to provide ongoing, accurate, and useful feedback. These data are then used to fine-tune the service delivery of a social service program. The specific nature of evaluation activities is influenced by the targeted evaluation consumers. Policymakers and funders are interested in program data that are more general, while program administrators and workers are interested in data that offer a richer understanding of a program's service delivery structure and client outcomes.

There are several steps to take prior to implementing evaluations. Most important are ethical considerations. By adapting ethical and professional standards to evaluation activity within a program, clients are ensured a quality service and we can account for our actions.

As with pure research studies, applied research studies (i.e., evaluations), are always easier to read about then they are to implement. This chapter provided examples of evaluation in action using a single program. A Teen Parenting Program was used to demonstrate how evaluation is implemented to assist with case-level and program-level decision making. At the case-level evaluation, efforts can be used in planned or crisis situations. Using an evaluation framework helps a worker structure and direct the course of client interventions. At the program level, program administrators can gain important evaluation data using aggregate or group designs. The implementation of evaluation is a critical aspect of service provision that can enhance decision making and ensure that all clients have a rich understanding of the services a program offers.

REFERENCES AND FURTHER READINGS

BABBIE, E.R. (1995). *The practice of social research* (7th ed., pp. 338-358). Belmont, CA: Wadsworth.

BAILEY, K.D. (1994). *Methods of social research* (4th ed., pp. 486-490). New York: Free Press.

GABOR, P.A., & GRINNELL, R.M., JR. (1994). *Evaluation and quality improvement in the human services*. Needham Heights, MA: Allyn & Bacon.

GRINNELL, R.M., JR., & WILLIAMS, M. (1990). *Research in social work: A primer* (pp. 58-85). Itasca, IL: F.E. Peacock.

POSAVAC, E.J., & CAREY, R.G. (1994). *Program evaluation: Methods and case studies* (3rd ed.). Englewood Cliffs, NJ: Prentice-Hall.

ROSSI, P.H., & FREEMAN, H.E. (1982). *Evaluation: A systematic approach*. Newbury Park, CA: Sage.

RUBIN, A., & BABBIE, E.R. (1993). *Research methods for social work* (2nd ed., pp. 536-568). Pacific Grove, CA: Brooks/Cole.

SHADISH, W.R., COOK, T.D., & LEVITON, L.C. (1991). *Foundations of program evaluation*. Newbury Park, CA: Sage.

WEINBACH, R.W., & GRINNELL, R.M., JR. (1996). *Applying research knowledge: A workbook for social work students* (2nd ed., pp. 81-88). Needham Heights, MA: Allyn & Bacon.

William K. Wilkinson
Keith McNeil

Appendix

Cultural Factors Related to Research

B OTH THE CULTURAL DIVERSITY of North America and the ethical guidelines developed by the National Association of Social Workers require social work practitioners to recognize that differences with respect to age, sex, socioeconomic status (SES), and ethnic background can affect the professional relationships between social work practitioners and their clients. Thus, we all need to be aware of issues that may surface when we conduct or evaluate cross-cultural research studies, and as potential social workers we need to know about various strategies for dealing with these issues.

DEFINING AND IDENTIFYING CULTURAL GROUPS

To conduct any cross-cultural research study, we need to develop a strategy for identifying cultural groups. In this section, we discuss these strategies and the potential difficulties in employing them. North America is a culturally diverse continent, so government agencies, social work researchers, and members of other helping professions may be accustomed to using cultural categories or labels—generic labels that facilitate the description and classification of people into distinct groups. However, it may be erroneous to assume that the people being classified are familiar and comfortable with, or accepting of, the labels that are assigned to them. People who immigrate from less culturally diverse countries may not have given much thought to racial, ethnic, or cultural labels, particularly the ones employed by social scientists in North America.

Thus, asking such people to categorize themselves may be a novel and confusing experience for them. For example, an international student from the Middle East was once asked to identify his race when registering at a southwestern university in the United States. Since he had never been asked to do this, he expressed some confusion. The registration clerk finally advised him that he must be "Caucasian" because he was neither "Negroid" nor "Mongoloid."

Social work researchers often use variables such as race, nationality, ethnic culture, and religion to establish a group's identity. Confusion can arise, however, when these terms are used incorrectly. "Race" is sometimes confused with "ethnicity," "nationality," or "religion"; in fact, the variable race is based on physical attributes and can be subdivided into the "Caucasoid," "Negroid," and "Mongoloid" races. "Nationality" refers to country of origin. "Ethnicity" implies a common ancestry and cultural heritage and encompasses customs, values, beliefs, and behaviors (Kumabe, Nishida, & Hepworth, 1985). However, at times people are asked to respond to a question (a variable) about their race using national, ethnic, or religious variable-label categories. For example, the terms "Mexican," "Hispanic," and "Jewish" are sometimes mistakenly used to describe a person's race.

Generic labels can be used to classify groups of people who share certain characteristics. While these labels are convenient, they have inherent disadvantages, including confusion about who does and does not fall under the rubric of the preassigned label. Also, disagreements about labels, about the population for whom the label is intended, and about the clustering of heterogeneous groups into a single homogeneous one are commonly found within social work research studies.

The generic term "Hispanic" was developed by a federal agency—the Office of Management and Budget (OMB)—in 1978 to describe people who are perceived to have a similar ethnic background (*Federal Register*, 1978, p. 19269). The OMB defined a Hispanic person as "a person of Mexican, Puerto Rican, Cuban, Central or South American or other Spanish culture or origin, regardless of race." While the OMB's definition may be generally satisfactory, it also poses some problems. For example, while Brazil is a South American country, Brazilians are excluded from the OMB's definition of Hispanic because they are not of Spanish origin and descent. Indigenous tribes in Mexico and Central and South America speak their own native languages and are not of Spanish descent either. On the other hand, the Spanish did have a significant cultural impact on Filipinos—who are not considered Hispanic.

While we may be satisfied with a certain generic label, there may be disagreement among us about it. Further, those people who are labeled may not concur with the label's generic term; in fact, they may dislike being categorized as belonging to such a group (Marin & Marin, 1991). For example, the term "Hispanic American" may be preferred in some regions of the country, while "Latino" may be the term of choice in other areas.

Hayes-Bautista and Chapa (1987) and Perez-Stable (1987) have argued that "Latino" is more appropriate than "Hispanic American" because it makes explicit the Latin American origins of the people it describes. However, the problems identified with the term "Hispanic American" also apply to "Latino." Other terms such as "Raza," "Chicano," and "Mexican American" have been used when conducting research with Hispanic Americans of Mexican ancestry, but they are not appropriate when studying other Hispanic American groups.

Research participants' identification and comfort with the label employed by the researcher can affect their willingness to participate in a research study as well as their response style (Marin, 1984). For example, if participants are accustomed to describing themselves as "Mexican" or "Honduran," they may resent a researcher who categorizes them as "Hispanic American" or "Latino." They may have a different perception of what the term implies or may feel that their nationality is more important than their ethnicity. Marin and Marin (1991) interviewed Hispanic Americans in San Francisco and found differences in preference for the "Latino" and "Hispanic American" labels as a function of acculturation. More acculturated individuals preferred the term "Hispanic American." Only three percent of the respondents interviewed by these two researchers assigned "no importance" to the label employed to describe them.

The problems discussed so far are not exclusive to Hispanic Americans; similar issues may be encountered when studying other cultural groups. For example, in a course on family ethnicity and diversity, students were asked their opinions about labels. Some students objected to being classified as "Anglo" and expressed a preference for a term that denoted nationality, such as "Irish," "Italian," or "Polish." There was also a debate on the appropriateness of terms such as "black," "African American," "black American," and "Negro." Some students were surprised to discover that persons from the Middle East are from Asia, because they thought the terms "Asian" and "Asian American" referred primarily to persons of Chinese or Japanese descent. One Asian student, for instance, was only familiar with the term "Oriental."

Using surnames to determine cultural or ethnic classification can have advantages as well as disadvantages. If we want to target a specific cultural group, for example, the use of last names can be an initial step in the process. It is highly likely, however, that a high proportion of participants will identify themselves as belonging to that group. We cannot rely completely on surnames to determine ethnic culture. A person with a Spanish last name may be a "Hispanic American," "Native American," "Portuguese," "Italian," or "Filipino."

Simply asking research participants to identify their own cultural group may also lead to misclassification. In addition to the problems with labeling already discussed, it is possible that some participants' "self-identities" may differ from their "social identies." For example, highly acculturated individuals may consider themselves to be "Americans" and not identify with an ethnic or cultural group, even though society may perceive that they are so identified.

Another problem inherent in the use of generic labels has to do with the generalizability of research findings when research participants are culturally diverse. The terms "Hispanic American" and "Asian American," for example, describe groups of people who share commonalities but who may be diverse with respect to language, nationality, immigration history, SES, acculturation, and religion—all of which affect their values, attitudes, and behaviors. Thus, research participants' responses to the research process would consequently be affected. Cross-cultural researchers need to provide information about the cultural subgroups they study and discuss the generalizability of their findings to similar groups of people.

Given the difficulties previously discussed, we can see how important it is to familiarize ourselves with the various labels used to describe the specific group we plan to study. It may also help to find out whether or not the group of interest has shown a preference for a particular cultural label. For example, if we are conducting an investigation in an area in which the term "Latino" is more prevalent than "Hispanic American," we may consider using the former rather than the latter term.

Additionally, Marin and Marin (1991) recommend that we ask research participants to indicate national origin or ancestry in order to make a more accurate identification. If generic labels are used initially, research participants can then be asked to elaborate further and provide information about their nationality or ancestry. This will allow us to describe the cultural group more accurately and better to address the generalizability of any findings.

A MULTICULTURAL APPROACH TO RESEARCH

In this section, we discuss the importance of cross-cultural research and the methodological factors that have limited its use, and we will provide recommendations for enhancing the meaning of this type of research.

Many research studies use college students or middle-class Caucasians as their research participants. While this practice provides valuable data and implications for social work practice, it does not add significantly to the understanding of cultural diversity (Atkinson, 1987, Ponterotto, 1988). In short, placing an overemphasis on one subpopulation contributes to the development of theories and implications that lack cultural relativity (Pedersen, 1987).

Members of the helping professions acknowledge the influence of cultural diversity on human behavior and the need for multicultural research that can enhance the understanding of diversity as it relates to their professions (Pedersen, 1991; Sue, Arredondo, & McDavis, 1992). In recent decades, graduate training programs have taken a proactive stance and have made changes in their programs to facilitate the development of culturally skilled professionals (Sue et al., 1992). Research is a powerful force in the development and testing of theories that facilitate the understanding of human behavior and the development of helping strategies (Borg & Gall, 1989). In a call specific to the helping professions, Sue et al. (1992) issued the following statement:

> Research and counseling may become a proactive means of correcting many of the inadequacies and problems that have plagued us for years... Research would become a powerful means of combating stereotypes and correcting studies. Studies would begin to focus on the positive attributes and characteristics of minorities as well as biculturalism. (p. 480)

However, if multicultural research is to enhance the understanding and appreciation of diversity, we must take certain steps to avoid the pitfalls that reduced the effectiveness of prior research studies and promoted stereotypes that added to the confusion and misperceptions.

A number of factors have limited the efficacy of cross-cultural research studies. Among these are: (1) cultural encapsulation—or assuming that differences between groups represent some deficit or pathology, (2) overemphasis on between-group differences without sufficient attention to between-group similarities as well as within-group differences, and (3) failure to take important socioeconomic variables into account.

Cultural Encapsulation

Cultural encapsulation occurs when people depend entirely on their own values and assumptions and define reality through those cultural assumptions and stereotypes (Pedersen, 1988; Wrenn, 1962). Pedersen (1987, 1988) identified ten assumptions that can contribute to cultural encapsulation and reduce effective relationships in the helping professions. He also discussed reasonable opposites that can enhance effective resource delivery by helping professionals. Several of these assumptions, as well as their reasonable opposites, have relevance for multicultural research.

Some assumptions that can lead to cultural encapsulation are: (1) everyone shares a single view of what constitutes normal behavior, (2) individuals are the basic building blocks of society, (3) abstract words and concepts are used that everyone understands in the same way, and (4) we assume that we are culturally aware and that we already know what all of our assumptions are. If any one of these assumptions is incorrect, the research process can be adversely affected.

Defining Normal Behavior

The first of these culturally biased assumptions is related to determining what constitutes normal behavior. If we fail to examine our own values and assumptions and to examine how they affect the conceptualization of normal behavior and thus the constructs employed in our research study, there is a danger that between-group differences (such as those between African Americans and Anglo-Americans) can be perceived as pathological because they deviate from our idea of "normalcy."

Bias Toward Individualism

Individualistic societies emphasize the independence and autonomy of individuals, whereas collectivistic societies stress interdependence that ensures the welfare and survival of the group rather than of the individual (Gibbons, Stiles, & Shkodriani, 1991). Normal behavior is naturally defined differently in each of these societies. While some standardized psychological tests define and measure normal behavior and identify deviations from this norm as pathological, using this strategy in cross-cultural research is dangerous because cultural differences do not necessarily constitute deviations.

For example, imagine that we are examining family functioning within a culturally diverse group of research participants. If our beliefs are consistent with those found in an individualistic society, we may conceptualize healthy, normal functioning as the fostering of independent, autonomous behaviors among the children, and we may then proceed to measure this construct by noting the degree and intensity of physical contact between grown children and their parents.

But if we examine family functioning in a group that stresses interdependence rather than independence, we may erroneously interpret "too much" closeness, for example, as a deviation. The (interdependence) cultural group may simply espouse a worldview that emphasizes group welfare rather than individual welfare, and close contact between grown children and their parents may represent their use of a natural support system rather than enmeshment or pathological dependence. Again, if we make certain assumptions regarding what constitutes normal behavior, and if these assumptions have limited cultural relevance with the population of interest, then the validity of our study's results is questionable.

Assuming That Constructs Are Universally Understood

Another kind of mistake can occur when we are familiar with and accustomed to using certain constructs or abstractions and assume they are understood by others (Pedersen, 1987, 1988). It the cultural group we are studying is not familiar with the constructs or interprets them in a different way, however, the research study may not be valid (Marin & Marin, 1991).

Decision making for example, has often been examined using a definition of the construct that is derived in one culture—and considered the norm—and then used with groups that are culturally quite different. The results of theses studies have added confusion rather than understanding of cultural diversity and have fostered stereotypes that have negatively affected the helping professions.

Ponterotto (1988) identified the lack of a conceptual framework to guide cross-cultural research as a limiting factor. When assumptions of what constitutes normal behavior and constructs and abstractions are applied universally to culturally diverse groups, we may unwittingly be approaching cross-cultural research from a social deficit (Atkinson, 1987; Cromwell & Ruiz, 1979; Sue et al., 1992).

Pedersen (1991) proposed multiculturalism as a generic approach to counseling research in the helping professions. Multiculturalism is currently considered by some to be the potential "fourth force" in the helping professions; its impact may equal that exerted by the first three forces: psychodynamics, behaviorism, and humanism. In a nutshell, the underlying philosophy of multiculturalism is an acceptance and appreciation of diversity. From a multicultural perspective, diversity is perceived as an attribute rather that a symptom of pathology.

Assuming That We Are Culturally Aware

Pedersen (1988) discussed another assumption that can interfere with the effective provision of social services, namely, that we already know what all of our assumptions are. He proposed that we: (1) engage in self-exploration, (2) gain awareness of our own values and beliefs and the relevance these may have in helping others, and (3) challenge our assumptions by considering alternative ones. Thus, the exploration of our assumptions is facilitated by our understanding cultural relativity.

Cultural Relativity Cultural relativity refers to the idea that peoples' behaviors must be understood within the context of the culture in which they occur (Axelson, 1985; Hall, 1976). In other words, we should attempt to understand behavior from the viewpoint of the cultural group we are studying rather than from our own cultural perspective. Taking this approach will reduce the danger associated with encapsulation. Mistaken assumptions about what constitutes normal behavior can be avoided, thus facilitating the development of a multiculturalistic approach to social work research that sees diversity as a strength rather than a limitation or a sign of pathology.

Marin and Marin (1991) offer additional recommendations for facilitating cultural relativity and avoiding some of the pitfalls discussed in this section. If feasible, we can profitably immerse ourselves in the ethnic culture of the group we are interested in studying. This experience can help us develop a better understanding of what is considered normal behavior in the culture, as well as the relevance of constructs and abstractions that we plan to use. The benefit of the experience can be enhanced if we also learn to consider alternative worldviews.

Marin and Marin (1991) and Ponterotto (1988) encourage social scientists to seek information directly from cultural minorities and not rely too heavily on majority values and perceptions of "normal behavior." Insight into another culture can be gained through collaboration with key informants who are members of the cultural group of interest prior to doing a research study. This type of collaboration can provide valuable data that can increase the validity of the research project and help us anticipate and deal with potential difficulties. Through a collaborative effort, we may obtain data regarding the relevance and appropriateness of constructs, abstractions, measuring instruments, and research design.

Overemphasizing Between-Group Differences

Another factor that has limited the usefulness of cross-cultural research has been the overemphasis on between-group differences—differences between two culturally diverse groups—without sufficient attention to between-group similarities or within-group differences (Lloyd, 1987; Ponterotto, 1988). There is a danger of neglecting the overlap in distribution when comparing two groups. Let us take an example of what this means. Assume that a trait has been measured in two groups of people and each person now has a score on that trait. Let us say there clearly is a difference in the means (average scores) of the two groups, which indicates a between-group difference; but there are also within-group differences—the variability within each of the distributions (e.g., Figure 21.7). In other words, not all people in Group B are alike. The two distributions overlap; some people in Group A have higher scores than those at the Group B mean. Indeed, some people in Group A are closer to the Group B mean than are some members of Group B.

Lloyd (1987) also questioned the value of focusing only on differences and reports from his own experience that doing so has limited his ability to work with culturally diverse groups. Axelson (1985) defines cultural universals as fundamental similarities or universal themes that underlie diverse cultural patterns. The expression of those themes may vary in different cultures, but certain underlying commonalities remain. For example, human beings have basic physiological, emotional, and spiritual needs, but how they go about meeting those needs may vary across cultures. Axelson (1985) notes that overemphasis on the differences to the exclusion of the commonalities will increase the potential for bias and prejudice. Cross-cultural research that is biased does not enhance our understanding and appreciation of diversity but rather contributes to misperceptions and confusion.

Within-group differences are the variations within a cultural group, which may be found with respect to such variables as nationality, religion, language, SES, immigration history, and acculturation level (Axelson, 1985; Lee & Richardson, 1991). All of these factors can influence how research participants respond to a research study; consequently, the external validity of the research findings is affected. Axelson (1985) describes three groups of black Americans with different immigration experiences and historical backgrounds. The experiences of the free blacks differed from those of the freed slaves, who, in turn, differed from West Indian immigrants and Haitian Americans. The experiences of each group of black Americans affected their perceptions of themselves and their perceptions of the world, and consequently, their values, beliefs, behaviors, and goals.

Within-group differences can be found even within a specific group. For example, the early Cuban immigrants, known as the "Golden Exiles" differed from the "Marielitos" who immigrated later. These differences, which were related to income level, race, and degree of acceptance into the United States, affected their worldview (Suarez, 1993). Differences like these may influence how research participants respond to research studies.

Neglecting Socioeconomic Variables

The neglect of important socioeconomic variables such as power, prestige, and money can also confound research findings because we may mistakenly attribute between-group differences to ethnic culture rather than to SES. Axelson (1985) differentiates SES from culture by explaining that socioeconomic variables affect perceptions of locus of control and, therefore, people's beliefs regarding the attainability of goals. People with similarly high aspirations may differ in their expectations of being able to realize their goals as a function of SES.

Frustration with the inability to achieve desired goals can contribute to the development of what Axelson calls a stretched value system, which is accompanied by a low degree of commitment to those values. While the expression of values may vary between groups as a function of socioeconomic factors, these between-group differences are environmentally influenced rather than culturally rooted. As income, power, and prestige change, so may the expression of values.

Failure to account for socioeconomic variables can compromise the validity of cross-cultural research. For example, suppose that we compare family roles, family functioning, and psychological well-being between a group of middle-income Anglo-Americans and a group of low-income African Americans. Any differences found between these two groups may be related to cultural diversity, or they may be associated with other socioeconomic factors. Bowman (1993) shows that employment and income have a significant effect on the way African Americans perceive fulfillment and satisfaction with family roles and family functioning.

Therefore, any observed differences between these groups may disappear when the socioeconomic variable is controlled for in the research design, that is, when middle-income Anglo-Americans are compared with middle-income African Americans. (In this case, SES is used as a selection factor—only middle-income people are selected). We could, on the other hand, use SES as a blocking variable, resulting in six groups: lower-income Anglo-Americans, middle-income

Anglo-Americans, upper-income Anglo-Americans, lower-income African Americans, middle-income African Americans, and upper-income African Americans.

There is a need for well-designed, cross-cultural research studies that can facilitate the understanding and appreciation of diversity, particularly given the cultural composition of North America. Poorly designed cross-cultural research studies can contribute to confusion, misperceptions, and stereotypes.

CULTURAL VARIABLES

Although common variables such as affiliation, communication, and self-esteem needs may transcend culture, the way those needs are met may vary as a function of culture. Cross-cultural differences may be found in the expressions and in the behaviors used to satisfy needs. Theories that help explain and predict behaviors, and ultimately facilitate change when necessary, should take the effect of diversity into account. Cross-cultural researchers also need to be aware of the impact that diversity in values, attitudes, and behaviors can have on the way research participants respond to the research process.

There are only a few studies that have used culturally diverse populations, but the data these studies have provided are valuable. In this section, we examine some variables found among culturally diverse groups and show how they contrast with the mainstream culture. We also discuss how these variables can affect the research process. The variables discussed in this section have been found to be particularly relevant for certain culture groups, but because of within-group differences, individual research participants may vary in their adherence to cultural values. These variables may also be found to a lesser extent among individuals belonging to the mainstream culture.

Collectivism Versus Individualism

We previously discussed the impact of collectivism and individualism on the conceptualization of normal behavior, on the constructs employed in cross-cultural research studies, and on the conclusions that can be drawn from research findings. Collectivism and individualism also influence the way people relate to each other, the manner in which they respond to research studies, and the way research data are gathered.

Again, a collectivistic culture emphasizes the welfare of the group over that of the individual and is associated with interdependence, readiness to be influenced by others, preference for conformity, and cooperation in relationships. On the other hand, an individualistic culture stresses independence, personal rather than group objectives, competition, and power in relationships; this type of culture measures achievement through individual success.

Because cooperation in interpersonal interactions is emphasized in collective cultures, individuals who adhere to these values may respond more favorably to research procedures and techniques that include personal rather than impersonal approaches. In other words, personal invitations to participate, face-to-face interviews, and case studies would be preferred over mailed invitations to participate or standardized questionnaires to complete.

Personal contact with research participants may increase the rate of their participation with collectivistic groups. However, the emphasis placed on cooperation may pose a threat to the internal validity of the study's findings. Participants might provide socially acceptable responses in order to avoid interpersonal conflict—a more likely response than with those who espouse individualistic values (Marin & Marin, 1991).

Deference for both authority and older people are emphasized in collectivistic cultures. Researchers may be regarded with respect because of their social position and educational attainment and viewed as authority figures. Consequently, research participants from collectivistic cultures may be more inclined to show respect for researchers by providing socially acceptable responses. Marin and Marin (1991) suggest that a researcher's respect for participants—acknowledging their expertise, for example—may reduce the power differential between the researcher and the participant and facilitate the entire research process.

Communication Style

Communication appears to be an important factor in people's lives, regardless of cultural differences. Communication styles, however, may vary across cultures; styles may be derived from collectivistic or individualistic values. In individualistic societies, the preferred communication style may be verbal, open, direct, and confrontational if necessary. The assertive expression of ideas and affect is encouraged; people say what they mean and mean what they say.

In collectivistic cultures, the preferred communication style may be nonverbal and indirect, and confrontation is avoided whenever possible because it can disturb relationships and lead to the loss of face. The direct expression of ideas and affect is discouraged, and the establishment of rapport and the development of trust are prerequisites for the discussion of such taboo topics (in that culture) as sex, illness, and death (Attneave, 1982).

Shon and Ja (1982) for example, note that the rules of communication within most Asian cultures are determined by factors such as age, sex, occupation, education, social status, family background, marital status, and parenthood. A researcher interested in examining the grieving process or sexual functioning, for example, among a traditional Asian group must consider a research design that would take into account the cultural variables that affect self-disclosure in that group. The procedure for obtaining data from the Asian group may be different from one that would be used if the group of interest were middle-income Anglo-Americans. Whereas a mailed questionnaire using direct questions may be effective ways to obtain data from the Anglo-American group, the Asian group may require the use of personal face-to-face contact with a highly skilled interviewer who can inspire trust and be alert and responsive to nonverbal cues.

Time Orientation

Time orientation is another important cultural factor to consider when conducting cross-cultural research studies. The ordering of time into past, present, and future varies as a function of culture. Middle-income Anglo-Americans are described as being future-oriented, and time is conceived in this group as future > present > past (Spiegel, 1982). Punctuality, organization, and planning are emphasized because they facilitate the accomplishment of future goals. Time may be broken down into orderly blocks or schedules.

Among several other cultural groups, the ordering of time is present > past > future. This latter time orientation may be found in Hispanic Americans, African Americans, Native Americans, and Asians (Marin & Marin, 1991; McGoldrick, Pearce, & Giordano, 1982). It can also be found in some white ethnic groups: Italian Americans and Irish Americans (Spiegel, 1982) and Appalachian Americans (Axelson, 1985). Individuals who are present-oriented may not be as preoccupied with punctuality and may organize their time according to day-by-day needs rather than a prescribed agenda.

Cross-cultural researchers who develop a time line for their studies need to be aware of differences in time orientation among different groups and exhibit some flexibility in order to accommodate those differences. For example, a researcher who is future-oriented and emphasizes punctuality may be discouraged when research participants do not respond in a timely manner. Participants who are present-oriented may arrive late for an interview, or may not show up at all if something they see as more important arises. The researcher may find participants' lateness or lax attitude toward time offensive or interpret it as an indication of their reluctance to participate in the research study. However, these perceptions may not necessarily be accurate and may merely indicate differences with respect to time orientation. Thus, we should be aware of these differences and be prepared to make modifications in our research time lines or schedules as necessary.

MEASUREMENT IN MULTICULTURAL RESEARCH

The efficacy of cross-cultural research can be facilitated through the use of measuring instruments that are written in the primary language of the research participants. The nonequivalence of measuring instruments, however, can limit the internal validity of cross-cultural research studies. In this section, we discuss some problems with translation as well as strategies that can enhance the equivalence of standardized measuring instruments.

Translating standardized measuring instruments into another language is a difficult process. The constructs, and the instruments used to assess those constructs, must be culturally relevant. The instruments must include content and concepts that ask the same questions as the original instrument and are interpreted in the same manner by research participants from a different culture. Cultural bias, misinterpretation of items, and nonequivalence of measuring instruments may pose difficulties that limit the utility of the research findings (Fouad, Cudeck, & Hansen, 1984; Mayberry, 1984; Scheuneman, 1979).

Before attempting a translation, we should be aware of our own values and how these affect our research interests and our conceptualization of behaviors, feelings, and constructs. As stated previously, the false assumption that others define normal behavior and constructs in the same way as the researcher may lead to the development of encapsulated instruments and biased studies. A researcher can consult with members of the group of interest and see whether the constructs of interest are culturally relevant or not and whether the measuring instruments can accurately assess or measure those constructs.

For example, suppose that a researcher wants to examine egalitarianism between spouses. The researcher conceptualizes egalitarianism as equality in the relationship between the wife and the husband and decides to assess the degree of egalitarianism by using a standardized task-sharing measuring instrument. Influencing that decision is the researcher's assumption that the person with less power takes more responsibility for household chores.

The definition of the construct and the method of assessing it may be relevant with some groups, such as couples who both work but who do not employ housekeepers, but the assessment method may be of limited value with another group. Examples would be working couples who employ housekeepers or couples who do not associate household chores with power in relationships. While direct questions may be useful in one instance, observation of a process may be required in another. How the researcher defines and measures constructs can affect the findings obtained and the conclusions drawn from those findings.

The researcher must take into account any cultural factors that may affect the assessment of the constructs and see to it that the instruments used are culturally equivalent. Even an accurate translation of an instrument may still be biased if cultural variables are ignored. For example, Valencia and Rankin (1985) discuss problems with the assessment of auditory short-term memory and attention among Mexican American children using a translated Spanish version of the McCarthy Scales of Children's Abilities. These researchers note that Mexican American children scored lower than their Anglo-American counterparts on subtests that measured auditory short-term memory and attention through word recall. A language analysis of the English and Spanish versions of the scale revealed important differences between the two languages that affected the construct being measured: With few exceptions, Spanish words contain more syllables than their English counterparts.

The researchers reported that the number of syllables on the Memory I subtest items was 66 percent higher on the Spanish version than on the English version. The Numerical Memory I subtest contained 71 percent more syllables on the Spanish version than on the English version. Therefore, even though both versions of the scale require that children recall essentially the same words or numerals, children who took the Spanish version were required to remember more syllables (and therefore more information) than children who completed the English version. The effect of word length as a function of language differences contributed to bias in the way the construct was measured. Thus, even though the original and translated versions of an instrument appear to be the same, they may not be culturally equivalent.

Conventional translation methods typically consist of three steps: (1) translation, (2) back-translation to the original language, and (3) establishing equivalence of the two forms using bilingual samples (Fouad et al., 1984; Hansen, 1987; Harrington, 1989; Mayberry, 1984). Each step, however, can have problems that can threaten the equivalence or usefulness of the instrument with certain populations.

Translation of Instruments

The first step—translation from the first to the second language—is usually done by skilled, bilingually fluent translators working individually, sequentially, or as a team (Hansen, 1987; Harrington, 1989; Mayberry, 1984). One person translates the instrument and gives the translated version to a second person, who makes revisions and gives it to a third person, who continues this process (Hansen, 1987). The team approach involves either joint translation through a committee or independent translations that are then merged after translators meet and reach a consensus.

The problem with this process is that skilled translators may produce a translation that is accurate but inappropriate for the population of interest. Translators often fail to take relevant socioeconomic and cultural factors of the target population into account, or they use words and phrases that may not be easily understood by the target population. Translators may be from a higher socioeconomic level and may translate the word "x" into the Spanish "y." Although this could be an appropriate translation for a person of a higher SES, a person of a lower SES might interpret the Spanish "y" as the Spanish "z."

Back-Translation of Instruments

Back-translation is done by skilled, bilingual translators. The back-translation is then compared to the original version and assessed for accuracy as well as for potential difficulties in comprehension. A problem at this stage is that the back-translation can have reasonable conceptual similarity to the original, but the original translation may be of poor quality (Mayberry, 1984). Even skilled translators can infer mistaken concepts from poor translations.

Establishing Equivalence of Instruments

The translated instrument is field-tested using bilingual people in order to establish equivalence. Correlation coefficients are examined between parallel forms or between the original and translated forms (Hansen, 1987). A problem here is that using bilingual people in field-testing the translated version assumes that these people represent the monolingual target population—an assumption that is not always correct (Mayberry, 1984). As an example, Diaz (1988) points out that differences exist between the Spanish spoken in the United States and Spanish spoken in Latin American countries; Spanish spoken by bilingual people residing in the United States is often interspersed with Anglicisms (English words given a Spanish sound) that are not used by monolingual Hispanics. This problem is not unique to the Spanish language and can be particularly difficult with research studies that use international samples of research participants.

Problems in Developing a Multicultural Instrument

Gross and Scott (1989) identify a problem with overreliance on bilingual research participants in the translation process—the overestimation of bilingual fluency. These researchers translated a professional certification test to another language and used a small bilingual sample in the field-test. One of these people obtained the highest score on the original version and the lowest score on the translated version—a discrepancy attributed to the person's lack of fluency in the second language.

Another problem with translation occurs when the original instrument is developed with a sample that is not representative of the target population, especially with respect to SES. Thus, the translation may be adequate, but the relevance of the instrument may be questionable with people whose socioeconomic background differs from that of the original population (Hansen, 1987). Finally, verification of the effectiveness of the translation with the population of interest is usually not done until the translated instrument is administered to members of the target population.

Because the relevance of translated instruments is reduced when socioeconomic and cultural factors are ignored or when testing of the translated version is performed with people who are different from the original monolingual population, we should consult with our research participants throughout the translation process in order to enhance instrument equivalence and relevance.

Serial Translation Process

We have listed potential problems that can occur during each step of the translation process. Herrera, DelCampo, and Ames (1993) discuss a serial translation process that may address these difficulties and facilitate the development of an equivalent, culturally sensitive measuring instrument. These steps are listed in Box A-1. While the steps listed do not guarantee cultural equivalence, they can facilitate the process by helping us obtain data from members of our target population throughout the translation process. They can thus take into account cultural and socioeconomic factors that are relevant with our target population.

GATHERING DATA

The researcher who has consulted with members of the target population or with persons who have experience with and knowledge of the culture of the population of interest may obtain data throughout the process regarding strategies that can enhance their participation rate.

Personal Versus Impersonal Approach

Personal contact with members of some groups may be a more effective way of obtaining data than an impersonal strategy such as mailing them a request to participate. The personal approach may involve direct contact to explain the nature of the research study. Data may be obtained through face-to-face interviews or personal delivery and collection of research instruments.

Three factors—collectivism, time orientation, and lack of experience as research participants—may make personal contact a more effective way of obtaining data (Marin & Marin, 1991). Research participants who come from collectivistic cultures may respond more positively if contacted in person, whereas they may fail to respond to a mailed invitation to participate. Participants who are present-oriented may delay responding to an invitation to participate in a research study and may eventually forget about it.

College students—a population that is often used in many research studies—may be accustomed to requests to participate in a research study, but other groups may not understand what is being asked of them, or they may have negative expectations based on previous experience. In some instances, participants may need more extensive instructions and assistance in order to respond to the research instrument.

It is also true that personal communication with research participants may place more demands on the researcher's time. The researcher can employ assistants or a research team that can help in the data collection process. On the other hand, while assistance with data gathering can have certain benefits, it can also pose some potential problems with respect to instrumentation, interrater reliability, and researcher bias.

BOX A-1

A SERIAL STEP-BY-STEP APPROACH TO THE TRANSLATION PROCESS

STEP 1: TRANSLATION

1a. Have two or more translators experienced with the target population produce separate translations, taking the socioeconomic factors of the population of interest into account.

1b. Have translators review and merge the translated versions to arrive at a product they feel will be most appropriate for the target population.

1c. Have the translated version further reviewed for grammar.

STEP 2: ASSESSMENT OF CLARITY AND EQUIVALENCE

2a. Assess reading comprehension with research participants who are representative of the target population. Have them read the translated instrument and identify words or phrases that are difficult to understand.

2b. Administer each item orally to monolingual participants representative of the target population and ask each participant, "What does this question mean to you?" and "What are the instructions asking you to do?"

2c. Record and compare the impressions of the research participants with the items and instructions as they are worded in the original language.

2d. Make changes as necessary and repeat the process until the intent of the items and instructions in the translated version are accurately conveyed.

STEP 3: BACK-TRANSLATION

3a. Audiotape the back-translations of bilingual persons of varying educational levels.

3b. Have a skilled translator listen to the tapes and make changes as necessary in the translated version of the measuring instrument.

STEP 4: FIELD-TESTING THE MEASURING INSTRUMENT

4a. Pretest and posttest with a group using the instrument in the original language to establish a baseline reliability index.

4b. Pretest and posttest using the translated version of the instrument with monolingual representatives of the target population to determine the reliability of the translated instrument with the target population.

4c. Pretest and posttest with two bilingual groups and control for administration order effects.

STEP 5: ASSESSING RELIABILITY

5a. Determine the amount of error due to the reliability of the instrument. If the baseline reliability is low, the instrument itself may not be reliable.

5b. Consider the amount of error that can be attributed to translation problems. Compare the baseline reliability index to the test-retest correlations obtained in the monolingual and bilingual groups. If the baseline reliability index is high and the other correlation indices are low, this usually indicates translation problems.

5c. Examine the translated instrument for reliability using the target population. This is accomplished by comparing the test-retest correlation index of the monolingual group (Group 2) with the baseline reliability index (attained from Group 1) and the test-retest correlations of the bilingual groups. If the reliability index of the monolingual group is low and the others are high, the translation may be accurate but nevertheless inappropriate and unreliable with the target population.

STEP 6: INTERPRETATION

6a. Determine extraneous factors that affected each reliability index by interviewing members of the bilingual and monolingual groups.

6b. Discriminate between extraneous factors and translation problems.

Using Culturally Similar Data Collectors

Marin and Marin (1991) note that there are benefits associated with the use of data collectors who are of the same ethnicity as the target populoation. The similarity of backgrounds between data collectors and research participants can facilitate the development of rapport, trust, and effective communication. Rapport is particularly important with individuals from collectivistic cultures. Trust may be of special significance when the researcher is interested in obtaining data on subjects that may be taboo (sex, family problems, death) with the group of interest.

Trust is also essential when the group of interest has any reason to doubt the purpose of the research study, for example, if people have any concerns regarding the effect of research participation on their legal status in the country. Marin and Marin (1991) also note that some immigrants who come from politically troubled countries may have had negative experiences that can lead to distrust and reluctance to participate in any type of study in which personal data are disclosed or documented.

Speaking the Language of the Research Participant

Communication with culturally diverse research participants can be enhanced if the researcher and/or data collector speaks the person's language—that is, communicates in their native or primary language. However, speaking the same language implies much more than the use of a common language. It also involves knowing both verbal and nonverbal forms of communication. The data collector should be aware of differences in dialects or cultural variations in the meanings assigned to the same words. Variations within the same language were exemplified in a television commercial that showed three Hispanic youths from three different parts of Latin America joking about the different terminology each of them used for "bus" (*camion, gua-gua,* and *bus*) and for "soda" (*gaseosa, refresco,* and *soda*).

Speaking the same language also implies taking into account socioeconomic variables that can affect the communication process. The data collector may need to employ different terminology depending on the participant's level of education. Failure to do so may contribute to confusion or resentment and ultimately to noncompliance.

Knowing the Culture of the Research Participants

Knowledge of a group's culture may also make it easier to understand and process nonverbal communication. As we said earlier, some cultural groups do not emphasize direct communication but depend more on intuition and sensitivity to nonverbal cues. Valuable data may be lost when the data collector is not attuned to these nonverbal messages. Nonverbal cues may also signal a participant's readiness to disclose personal data.

Compensation in the form of a monetary reward, services (e.g., medical or social services), or a gift that can benefit either the participant or the community may increase participation with some cultural groups and convey both respect and appreciation for their willingness to be in a research study. Marin and Marin (1991) indicate that compensating research participants for their participation does not appear to increase selection bias, and it does serve as an incentive for participation. Once again, consultation with persons who know the culture of the target group can help the researcher determine the propriety of compensation, the type of compensation to employ, and the amount that is appropriate. This reduces the potential for the compensation to be perceived as offensive or as a bribe.

BECOMING A CULTURALLY SKILLED RESEARCHER

Members of the helping professions can take steps to facilitate their development into culturally skilled researchers. Since research studies contribute to the understanding of human behavior and the factors that promote well-being, the development of culturally skilled researchers seems paramount. Three process models for the development of cultural awareness are as follows.

Bennet's Model for the Development of Cultural Sensitivity

Henderson, Sampselle, Mayes, and Oakley (1992) discuss Bennet's (1986) developmental model for promoting cultural sensitivity—a model similar to the white racial and minority identity development models discussed in the counseling literature (Atkinson, Morten, & Sue, 1983; Helms, 1984; Ponterotto, 1988; Sabnani, Ponterotto, & Borodovsky, 1991). The process described in these models is associated with the development of awareness, understanding, and appreciation of self and of others. Therefore, these models have relevance for cross-cultural researchers as well.

Bennet's (1986) model for the development of cultural sensitivity (as cited in Henderson et al., 1992) involves six stages: (1) denial, (2) defense, (3) minimization, (4) acceptance, (5) adaptation, and (6) integration. We will integrate aspects of Bennet's model with information presented by Pedersen (1987, 1988).

According to Bennet's model, the individual moves from ethnocentricity to multiculturalism (Pedersen, 1991). In the first stage (denial) the person makes assumptions about normal behavior that are based on his or her own cultural framework without taking cultural relativity into account. In the second stage, cultural differences are conceptualized as pathological because they deviate from the person's definition of normal. In the third stage, there is a recognition of cultural differences and a beginning awareness that the person's own assumptions may have limited relevance in different cultures. However, despite this awareness, there is a continued reliance on encapsulated measuring instruments and methods. Individuals in the fourth stage begin to challenge their assumptions and consider alternate constructs. In the fifth stage, the person can validate cultural differences and perceive the world from a different cultural perspective. In the final stage, the individual can recognize between- and within-group differences and similarities and can understand and appreciate diversity.

White Racial Identity Model

The white racial identity model (Atkinson et al., 1983; Helms, 1984; Ponterotto, 1988) focuses on awareness, understanding, acceptance, and appreciation of self and others; the paradigm involves movement through five stages. In the first stage (preexposure or precontact), a person lacks self-awareness as a racial being, denies his or her own ethnicity, and lacks awareness of the impact of culture on the research process. The danger at this stage is that cultural differences are seen as pathological and that the procedures used in a study will have little or no relevance to culturally diverse groups. Hence, the findings obtained by researchers at this stage may have little or no validity at best and contribute to negative stereotypes at worst.

In the second (conflict) and third (prominority or antiracism) stages, the person examines his or her own cultural values. However, this recognition contributes to cognitive dissonance, rejection of self, and a paternalistic attitude toward persons of diverse cultures. Individuals at this stage may have good intentions, but their depreciating attitudes toward their own culture and paternalistic attitude toward the culturally diverse may contribute to bias in the research process.

In the fourth stage (retreat into white culture), the individual may retreat from multicultural issues, including from multicultural research. This stance does little to further the development of multiculturalism and, given the cultural composition of North America, can limit the development of the social worker.

In the final stage (redefinition and integration), the individual develops an appreciation and respect for diversity (both in self and in others) that may permit the recognition of the impact of culture on the research process. The individual at this stage is able to consult and collaborate with culturally diverse persons and is flexible enough to adapt research methods and procedures in order to make them more culturally relevant. The individual at this stage also recognizes the effect of research findings on potential clients, social work practitioners, and on the social work profession as a whole.

Minority Identity Development Model

The minority identity development model describes a process that members of the nondominant group may experience. Specifically, the stages here deal with how minority members perceive (appreciate or depreciate) themselves, members of their own group, members of other culturally diverse groups, and members of the dominant group. Regardless of the researcher's cultural background, the researcher's level of awareness and attitude toward diversity can have an overt or covert effect on the research process from the topic that is chosen to the conclusions that are drawn from the study. This process, as described by Atkinson et al. (1983), also involves five stages: (1) conformity, (2) dissonance, (3) resistance and immersion, (4) introspection, and (5) synergetic articulation and awareness.

BECOMING CULTURALLY SENSITIVE

Sabnani et al. (1991) describe several tasks that may facilitate movement through the stages of the white racial identity model. These tasks have relevance for multicultural researchers of diverse backgrounds since they foster the awareness and appreciation of diversity. The tasks associated with stage one (preexposure or precontact) include participation in cultural experiences such as ethnic dinners, intercultural sharing, case studies, ethnic literature reviews, and value statements exercises. These tasks can increase understanding of one's own and others' cultural heritage and how this heritage affects values, beliefs, behaviors, and goals.

BOX A-2

Six Basic Steps to Consider When Conducting a Cross-Cultural Research Study

STEP 1: DEFINING THE SAMPLE OR POPULATION OF RESEARCH PARTICIPANTS

1a. Use labels such as race, nationality, ethnicity, religion correctly.

1b. Be familiar with the cultural labels used to describe the group of interest.

1c. Determine whether the group of interest has shown a preference for or resentment of any particular label.

1d. Ask research participants to indicate national origin or ancestry.

STEP 2: ENHANCING THE EFFICACY OF CROSS-CULTURAL RESEARCH AND AVOIDING PREVIOUS PITFALLS

2a. Consider multiculturalism versus social deficit or pathology framework to guide cross-cultural research.

2b. Review Pedersen's (1987, 1988) ten assumptions that can contribute to cultural encapsulation.

2c. Explore reasonable opposites to biased assumptions.

2d. Use cultural relativity to conceptualize behavior.

2e. Use constructs and concepts that are culturally relevant with the group of interest.

2f. If feasible, become immersed in the target group's culture.

2g. Procure cultural data through consultation or collaboration with the group of interest.

2h. Attend to between- and within-group differences and similarities such as race, gender, class, nationality, historical background, language, and acculturation.

2i. Factor in socioeconomic variables to reduce confusion about whether differences are cultural or socioeconomic.

STEP 3: DETERMINING THE EFFECTS OF CULTURAL VARIABLES

3a. *Collectivism Versus Individualism.* If the group of interest demonstrates collectivistic tendencies, consider a personal rather than impersonal approach. For example, send a personal invitation to participate, conduct interviews, do case studies.

3b. *Communication Styles.* If the group of interest uses a nonverbal and indirect communication style, consider personal contact, development of rapport and trust with research participants, mutual respect, and the use of culturally similar research aides.

3c. *Time Orientation.* If the group of interest is present-oriented, understand and accept differences in time orientation and be flexible with respect to time lines and scheduling.

STEP 4: USING VALID AND RELIABLE MEASURING INSTRUMENTS

4a. Ensure the cultural relevance of constructs and concepts.

4b. Use a measuring instrument that employs the same language, that is, one that takes into account language, dialect, fluency, and socioeconomic variables, of the group of interest.

4c. Use a translation process that includes minority cultural information gained through consultation or collaboration and testing.

STEP 5: GATHERING DATA

5a. Find out about the culture of interest through consultation or collaboration.

5b. Use the personal rather than the impersonal approach to gather data.

5c. Use research assistants who are culturally similar to the subject group.

5d. Engender trust.

5e. Speak the language of the research participant.

5f. Know the culture of the research participant.

STEP 6: BECOMING A CULTURALLY SKILLED RESEARCHER

6a. Become familiar with cultural sensitivity and white racial and minority identity development models.

6b. Assess your own developmental stage.

6c. Participate in activities that can promote movement toward the integration stage in which diversity is recognized, valued, and respected.

Tasks associated with stage two (conflict) include exploring one's own stereotypes and prejudices and seeing how these can affect the research process. Examining the roots of racism and the effect of discrimination on race relations are also part of stage two. At stage three (prominority or antiracism), individuals are encouraged to participate in cross-cultural encounter groups, cultural immersion, and consultation with members of culturally diverse groups in order to further increase awareness of the effect of paternalistic attitudes on the research process.

Individuals at stage four (retreat into white culture) are encouraged to participate in cross-cultural encounter groups and develop an understanding of minority and white identity development. Tasks associated with stage five (redefinition and integration) include participation in feedback-related exercises and cross-cultural practices in order to facilitate the development of a cultural identity that allows the individual to value cultural richness and diversity.

Box A-2 provides a summary of the essential steps needed when doing a cross-cultural research study.

SUMMARY

The contents of this chapter describe a process of growth. Culturally sensitive researchers continually challenge their beliefs and assumptions and make adaptations in order to promote the validity and relevant of cross-cultural studies. Culturally sensitive research can create enrichment opportunities for the researcher, the cultural group, and the social work profession. If a researcher is unsure of a situation (whether for cultural reasons or other reasons), an intensive case study might be appropriate. Such an intensive study allows the development of understanding that might not occur in the types of research that are described in the previous chapters of this book.

The entire range of values (for example, from collectivism to individualism) is possible within groups because of between-group similarities and within-group differences. We need to be aware of these cultural variables and make an assessment regarding how well the specific group of interest adheres to them. For example, we may need to employ different procedures for data gathering when studying the behaviors of highly acculturated, Mexican American college students than when doing so with lower-income Mexican nationals or when comparing upper-income Anglo-Americans with lower-income Appalachian Americans or middle-income Italian Americans.

REFERENCES AND FURTHER READINGS

ATKINSON, J. (1987). Gender roles in marriage and the family: A critique and some proposals. *Journal of Family Issues, 8,* 5-41.

ATKINSON, D.R., MORTEN, G., & SUE, D.W. (1983). *Counseling American minorities: A cross-cultural perspective.* Dubuque, IA: Brown.

ATTNEAVE, C. (1982). American Indians and Alaska Native families: Emigrants in their own homeland. In M. McGoldrick, J.K. Pearce, & J. Giordano (Eds.), *Ethnicity and family therapy* (pp. 55-83). New York: Guilford Press.

AXELSON, J.A. (1985). *Counseling and development in a multicultural society.* Belmont, CA: Wadsworth.

BENNET, M.J. (1986). A developmental approach to training for intercultural sensitivity. *International Journal of Intercultural Relations, 10,* 179-196.

BORG, W.R., & GALL, M.D. (1989). *Educational research.* White Plains, NY: Longman.

BOWMAN, P.J. (1993). The impact of economic marginality among African American husbands and fathers. In H.P. McAdoo (Ed.), *Family ethnicity: Strength in diversity* (pp. 120-140). Newbury Park, CA: Sage.

CROMWELL, R.E., & RUIZ, R.A. (1979). The myth of macho dominance in decision making within Mexican and Chicano families. *Hispanic Journal of Behavioral Sciences, 1,* 355-373.

DIAZ, J.O.P. (1988). Assessment of Puerto Rican children in bilingual education programs in the United States: A critique of Lloyd M. Dunn's monograph. *Hispanic Journal of Behavioral Sciences, 10,* 237-252.

FEDERAL REGISTER (1978, May 4). Washington, DC: Government Printing Office.

FOUAD, N.A., CUDECK, R., & HANSEN, J.C. (1984). Convergent validity of the Spanish and English forms of the Strong-Campbell Interest Inventory for bilingual Hispanic high school students. *Journal of Counseling Psychology, 31*, 339-348

GIBBONS, J.L., STILES, D.A., & SHKODRIANI, G.M. (1991). Adolescents' attitudes toward family and gender roles: An international comparison. *Sex Roles, 25*, 625-643.

GROSS, L.J., & SCOTT, J.W. (1989). Translating a health professional certification test to another language. *Evaluations and the Health Professions, 12*, 61-72.

HALL, E.T. (1976). *Beyond culture.* Garden City, NY: Doubleday.

HANSEN, J.C. (1987). Cross-cultural research on vocational interests. *Measurement and Evaluation in Counseling and Development, 19*, 163-176.

HARRINGTON, T.F. (1989). *Adapting instruments for use in other cultures.* (ERIC Document Reproduction Service, No. ED 317 613).

HAYES-BAUTISTA, D.E., & CHAPA, J. (1987). Latino terminology: Conceptual bases for standardized terminology. *American Journal of Public Health, 77*, 61-68.

HELMS, J.E. (1984). Toward a theoretical model of the effects of race on counseling: A black and white model. *The Counseling Psychologist, 12*, 153-165.

HENDERSON, D.J., SAMPSELLE, C., MAYES, F., & OAKLEY, D. (1992). Toward culturally sensitive research in a multicultural society. *Health Care for Women International, 13*, 339-350.

HERRERA, R.S., DELCAMPO, R.L., & AMES, M. (1993). A serial approach for translating family science instrumentation. *Family Relations, 42*, 357-360.

KUMABE, K.T., NISHIDA, C., & HEPWORTH, D.H. (1985). *Bridging ethnocultural diversity in social work and health.* Honolulu: University of Hawaii, School of Social Work.

LEE, C.C., & RICHARDSON, B.L. (1991). Multicultural issues in counseling: New approaches to diversity. Alexandria, VA: American Association for Counseling and Development.

LLOYD, A.P. (1987). Multicultural counseling: Does it belong in a counselor education program? *Counselor Education and Supervision, 26*, 164-167.

MARIN, G. (1984). Stereotyping Hispanics: The differential effect of research method, label and degree of contact. *International Journal of Intercultural Relations, 8*, 17-27.

MARIN, G., & MARIN, B.V. (1991). *Research with Hispanic populations.* Newbury Park, CA: Sage.

MAYBERRY, P.W. (1984). *Analysis of cross-cultural attitudinal scale translation using maximum likelihood factor analysis.* (ERIC Document Reproduction Service, NO. ED 234 947).

McGOLDRICK, M., PEARCE, J.K., & GIORDANO, J. (Eds.). (1982). *Ethnicity and family therapy.* New York: Guilford Press.

PEDERSEN, P. (1987). Ten frequent assumptions of cultural bias in counseling. *Journal of Multicultural Counseling and Development, 15*, 16-24.

PEDERSEN, P. (1988). *A handbook for developing multicultural awareness.* Alexandria, VA: American Association for Counseling and Development.

PEDERSEN, P. (1991). Multiculturalism as a generic approach to counseling. *Journal of Counseling and Development, 19*, 6-12.

PEREZ-STABLE, E.J. (1987). Issues in Latino health care. *Western Journal of Medicine, 146*, 213-218.

PONTEROTTO, J.G. (1988). Racial/ethnic minority research in the *Journal of Counseling Psychology*: A content analysis and methodological critique. *Journal of Counseling Psychology, 35*, 410-418.

SABNANI, H.D., PONTEROTTO, J.G., & BORODOVSKY, L.G. (1991). White racial identity development and cross-cultural counselor training: A stage model. *The Counseling Psychologist, 19*, 76-102.

SCHEUNEMAN, J. (1979). A method of assessing bias in test items. *Journal of Educational Measurement, 16*, 143-152.

SHON, S.P., & JA, D.Y. (1982). Asian families. In M. McGoldrick, J.K. Pearce, & J. Giordano (Eds.), *Ethnicity and family therapy* (pp. 55-83). New York: Guilford Press.

SPIEGEL, J. (1982). An ecological model of ethnic families. In M. McGoldrick, J.K. Pearce, & J. Giordano (Eds.), *Ethnicity and family therapy* (pp. 55-83). New York: Guilford Press.

STAGNER, R. (1988). *A history of psychological theories.* New York: Macmillan.

SUAREZ. Z.E. (1993). Cuban Americans: From golden exiles to social undesirables. In H.P. McAdoo (Ed.), *Family ethnicity: Strength in diversity* (pp. 164-176). Newbury Park, CA: Sage.

SUE, D.W., ARREDONDO, P., & MCDAVIS, R.J. (1992). Multicultural counseling competencies and standards: A call to the profession. *Journal of Counseling and Development, 20*, 477-483.

VALENCIA, R.R., & RANKIN, R.J. (1985). Evidence of content bias on the McCarthy Scales with Mexican American children: Implications for test translation and nonbiased assessment. *Journal of Educational Psychology, 77*, 197-207.

WRENN, C.G. (1962). The culturally encapsulated counselor. *Harvard Educational Review, 32*, 444-449.

Index

SOCIAL WORK RESEARCH AND EVALUATION:
QUANTITATIVE AND QUALITATIVE APPROACHES
Fifth Edition
Edited by John Beasley
Production supervision by Kim Vander Steen
Cover design by Lesiak/Crampton Design, Inc., Park Ridge, Illinois
Internal design and composition by Grinnell, Inc., Dallas, Texas
Printed and bound by Quebecor Printing, Fairfield, Pennsylvania